ITALIAN NEOREALIST CINEMA:
AN AESTHETIC APPROACH

The end of the Second World War saw the emergence in Italy of the neo-realism movement, which produced a number of films characterized by stories set among the poor and working class, often shot on location using non-professional actors. In this study Christopher Wagstaff provides an in-depth analysis of neorealist film, focusing on three films that have had a major impact on filmmakers and audiences around the world: Roberto Rossellini's *Roma città aperta* and *Paisà* and Vittorio De Sica's *Ladri di biciclette*. Indeed, these films are still, more than half a century after they were made, among the most highly regarded works in the history of cinema. In this ambitious, carefully researched study, Wagstaff takes an innovative alternative approach to the analysis of these films, treating them primarily as aesthetic artefacts rather than as accurate representations of historical reality.

The author begins by situating neorealist cinema in its historical, industrial, commercial, and cultural context. He goes on to provide a theoretical discussion of realism and the merits of neorealist films, individually and collectively, as aesthetic artefacts. The core of the book is devoted to a detailed analysis of the three films, concentrating on technical and production aspects as well as on the broader significance of the films as cinematic works of art.

While providing a wealth of information and analysis previously unavailable to an English-speaking audience, *Italian Neorealist Cinema* offers a radically new perspective on neorealist cinema and the Italian art cinema that followed it.

(Toronto Italian Studies)

CHRISTOPHER WAGSTAFF is Senior Lecturer in Italian Studies at the University of Reading.

University of Edinburgh

30150   025115129

CHRISTOPHER WAGSTAFF

Italian Neorealist Cinema

An Aesthetic Approach

UNIVERSITY OF TORONTO PRESS
Toronto Buffalo London

© University of Toronto Press Incorporated 2007
Toronto Buffalo London
Printed in Canada

ISBN 978-0-8020-9761-3 (cloth)
ISBN 978-0-8020-9520-6 (paper)

Printed on acid-free paper

Toronto Italian Studies

Library and Archives Canada Cataloguing in Publication

Wagstaff, Christopher, 1946–
   Italian neorealist cinema : an aesthetic approach / Christopher
Wagstaff.

   (Toronto Italian studies)
   Includes bibliographical references and index.
   ISBN 978-0-8020-9761-3 (bound). – ISBN 978-0-8020-9520-6 (pbk.)

   1. Motion pictures – Italy – Aesthetics.   2. Rosellini, Roberto,
1906–1977 – Criticism and interpretation.   3. De Sica, Vittorio,
1901–1974 – Criticism and interpretation.   4. Motion pictures – Italy –
History.   I. Title.   II. Series.

   PN1993.5.I88W34 2007   791.430945   C2007-904288-0

Publication of this book was made possible by grants from The Leverhulme
Trust, the Arts and Humanities Research Board, and the Department of
Italian Studies of the University of Reading.

University of Toronto Press acknowledges the financial assistance to its
publishing program of the Canada Council for the Arts and the Ontario
Arts Council.

University of Toronto Press acknowledges the financial support for its
publishing activities of the overnment of Canada through the Book
Publishing Industry Development Program (BPIDP).

In loving memory of
Gabriella Verrucchi

Contents

Plates 1–33, stills from *Ladri di biciclette*, follow page 348.

Acknowledgments

This book is dedicated to the enchanting memory of Gabriella Verrucchi. It owes a very great deal to two others who also died while I was writing it, Alberto Farassino and Lino Miccichè. Not only did their writings stimulate it, but their hospitality at retrospectives and debates prompted it and made it possible, as did the hospitality of Gian Piero Brunetta, Pierre Sorlin, Francesco Casetti, Gianluca Farinelli, Gianfranco Casadio, and Vito Zagarrio. Gian Piero has been particularly patient and constant in his support and advice. Vittorio Martinelli's knowledge and love of cinema and his friendship have been an inspiration. Others to whom I am indebted are too numerous to mention here, but include Geoffrey Nowell-Smith, Sam Rohdie, Giorgio De Vincentis, Antonio Costa, Stephen Gundle, Aldo Bernardini, Lorenzo Quaglietti, Alessandro Ferraù, and ANICA. I am enormously grateful to those who read all or parts of the manuscript for their help: David Forgacs, Pierre Sorlin, Alex Marlow-Mann, Severin Schroeder, Christopher Duggan, Thomas and Toby Wagstaff, Giuliana Adamo, and other readers whose identities are unknown to me.

I warmly thank the Leverhulme Trust for a Grant to an Institution for research towards the book, the Arts and Humanities Research Board for a Research Leave grant, the University of Reading for matching the AHRB's grant, and its Department of Italian Studies, as well as each of my colleagues in the department, for constant help and support.

This book owes a great deal to the team at the University of Toronto Press. I can only thank personally those with whom I came into contact. Ron Schoeffel's encouragement and help was invaluable, while John St James's fine copy-editing transformed the manuscript.

ITALIAN NEOREALIST CINEMA:
AN AESTHETIC APPROACH

Introduction

I am going to push an argument about as far as it will go. Any argument finds itself in dialogue with alternative, counter arguments, and it is with this awareness of entering into a dialogue with alternative approaches that I expound an aesthetic approach to neorealist cinema in this book.

There is no single clear reason why an English or North American viewer pays close attention to an Italian neorealist film. In schools and universities such attention is usually justified in terms of the various essentially non-filmic things about which the study of a neorealist film might give knowledge. The film is a historical document, giving knowledge about Italian history through its representation of material and social life in Italy at a particular time; it is a discourse inviting interpretation; it is a moment and an event in an hypothesized history of the cinema as an institution and as a language.

However, paying close attention to a film gives one knowledge, first and foremost, about that film. Any knowledge about the society and culture which produced that artefact, any knowledge of the discourse recoverable from the artefact, and any sense of the film as one moment in the process of filmmaking and film viewing have all to derive from an apprehension of that artefact. To make that apprehension itself derive from one of the other, secondary, kinds of knowledge hypothetically retrievable from the artefact is to put the cart before the horse.

The very name given to the movement in which *Roma città aperta*, *Paisà*, and *Ladri di biciclette*, the films studied here, have been placed, 'neorealism,' draws the viewer's and the critic's attention to the films' *representation* of a material and historical 'reality,' inviting an *interpretation* of that representation (what the films 'say' about that reality, their 'discourse') and an *evaluation* of it (the usefulness of the representation for anything we might want to 'do' about that reality, such as change it). This book aims to *isolate* an approach to certain films as *artefacts* from the question of their representation of 'reality,' and from the interpretation and evaluation of that representation – in other words, to draw attention to the films themselves rather than to something external to them which they represent or depict. The way I intend to do this is by examining how each artefact has been assembled. This requires the exposition of a great deal of 'data,' much of it amounting to a re-viewing of the films through the pages of this book. Far more important than anything I, the critic, might have to say about the films is the body of 'data' itself, which, it is hoped, will enable the reader to come to his or her own conclusions.

Perhaps I can best prepare the reader for what is to follow by making an unexpected comparison. On the desk at which I am writing these words, over to one side, is a pile of fairly recent books heralding and analysing the digital 'revolution' in cinema, resounding with propositions like: 'The fact that the synthetic icon no longer depends for its existence on a pre-existing concrete reality accentuates its affinity with the pictorial image, emphasizing its basic independence from traditional notions such as *original* and *copy*. Digital cinema's new image, no longer regarded as the reproduction of an objectively existing reality, becomes an autonomous creation.'[1] An aesthetic approach to Italian neorealist cinema is rather like an invitation to the reader of this book to view the films themselves in the same way – as autonomous (aesthetic) creations (assemblies) rather than as copies (reproductions) of an original (historical reality) – or to view them in this way *as well as* in other ways. Interpretative, historical, cultural, ideological, and psychoanalytical approaches (as well as many others) to the films analysed in the following chapters are rich, valid, and rewarding, and the reader has a wide critical bibliography to choose from. This book would like to add to, rather than negate, that critical bibliography.

In the overview chapter 1 I will briefly place the films in a commercial and cultural context. Appendices 1 and 2 offer the reader who is new to the field brief summaries of the necessary background. In chapter 2 'Realism' I will lay the basis for paying attention to the films defined as aesthetic artefacts. In the analysis of three films I will describe the films.

The chapter on each film analyses the way the film is assembled, and is inevitably justified or not by the accuracy of its description. The structure of the book as a whole may require a word of justification. If chapters 3, 4, and 5 take an aesthetic approach to the detailed analysis of three films, chapter 2 investigates what it might mean to take an aesthetic approach, and what are the issues raised by such an approach to artefacts generally regarded as being 'realist,' and therefore as drawing their value from considerations other than aesthetic. However, since films are not fashioned in the frugal privacy of a poet's chamber, but rather are the products of multiple public determining factors, chapter 1 briefly examines some of these factors in a specific time and place, paying particular attention to the money that is involved in making films and that, at some point, has to be recovered from the viewing public.

Finally, a word of explanation for the choice of films for analysis (*Roma città aperta*, *Paisà*, and *Ladri di biciclette*). There are three because there is quite simply no room for more in a volume of this type.

The student of film is bombarded with books on 'how to study film.' The aim of this book is to demonstrate one particular approach by example, rather than by precept. I chose the very *last* films one would select for analysis as autonomous aesthetic constructs: films generally regarded as privileging the direct representation of a historical reality over formal and stylistic ambitions. I wanted to see whether canonical neorealist films would bear this type of analysis, and whether it would change our way of looking at them. I must add that I consider it neither the *only* approach appropriate to these films, nor even a *superior* approach to the many others that can be deployed on them. It is one of the available approaches, and it stands and falls on the results which it furnishes.

Chapter 1 hypothesizes a 'hiatus' in the control and domination by producers of Italian film production between the years 1945 and 1949. The three films are chosen from that period as being more plausibly products of their artistic progenitors and less conditioned by other, conventional factors than films deriving from other contexts. I wanted to embrace what I call in the first chapter 'high' neorealism, and to draw readers' attention to aspects of Rossellini's and De Sica's art that have received only occasional attention. Fully to embrace 'high' neorealism would require analysis of films (such as Visconti's *La terra trema*) that raise and illustrate different issues, and would unconscionably extend the length of the volume.

The choice of films, therefore, was determined by expediency, by historical and critical judgment, and by the very nature of the critical challenge posed by those particular films (and by *Ladri di biciclette* in particular). This book does not propose a poetics to cover all films conventionally embraced by the qualification 'neorealist,' but rather proposes that each artefact constitutes its own justification.

1 Overview

The Italian Cinema Industry

Films are very public objects, both in their reception and consumption and in their manufacture. However much I might want to focus attention on them as aesthetic artefacts in subsequent chapters, I must first acknowledge the industrial, commercial, political, ideological, and institutional factors that affect their fashioning and reception. To do otherwise would be to misrepresent their identity and genesis. Neorealist films are seen as products of a particular historical moment, and are frequently evaluated in terms of that historical moment. While not denying that this is entirely appropriate, I should like to steer attention to the extent to which neorealist films participated in a continuity with the rest of Italian cinema, both that which preceded and followed neorealism in time and that which surrounded it during its heyday. Neorealism was both in tension and in continuity with the cinema around it, and this chapter briefly offers indications of how this was the case. Readers unfamiliar with Italian neorealist cinema and with the relevant history of the period are invited to consult appendices 1 ('A standard introduction to neorealism') and 2 ('Historical background for neorealism').

It is instructive to look at Italian films from the perspective of London's cinema-goers. In the period 1910 to 1914 Italian films not only held a strong place in British cinemas (in 1910 15 per cent of the market and growing fast), they were regarded by critics and the discerning public as epitomizing the artistic potential of the new medium, transforming it from a cheap entertainment into a culturally dignified art form.

This was not to last. By February 1935 the London representative of the major Italian production and distribution company Pittaluga was writing to Luigi Freddi (the Italian government official responsible for the cinema industry):

All the films I have offered to the various buyers have invariably been turned down for the same reasons: the weakness and the poor audience-appeal of the story, and technical standards that are mediocre and certainly not up to those of other producing countries ... In the present situation I see no possibility of imposing our production on the British market through exchanges. Nor do I see any practical gain to be got from legislative measures. The problems faced over here by our film industry can therefore only be resolved through an improvement in our production, which will only be arrived at by encouraging various private producers to choose interesting stories, improve their techniques, and take account of the tastes of the English public.[1]

And yet, in March 1950 five of the ten West End London art cinemas were showing Italian films. Over the previous two years, in journals and newspaper reviews, critics had been holding up Italian films as artistic models for British filmmakers, just as they had done before the First World War.

What had happened was that the First World War had disrupted the European cinema industry and its markets at the very same time that the Americans had begun vertically integrating their film industry and increasing both the quantity and quality of its output. The Italian industry collapsed into bankruptcy in the 1920s, and was only gradually resuscitated by state intervention. At the end of the Second World War, however, a group of Italian filmmakers, collectively referred to as the 'neorealists,' captured the attention of a worldwide audience.

At the very end of the 1920s, with government help, Stefano Pittaluga's company, SASP, vertically integrated a bankrupt Italian cinema industry, and the fascist state slowly began to support it and protect it from foreign competition. For a while, Emilio Cecchi at Cines vigorously promoted artistic quality and experimentation. However, Pittaluga died, the shares of SASP ended up in the hands of a state holding company, and Mussolini appointed Luigi Freddi to take charge of the state's responsibilities for the cinema.

The cinema is both an industry and a cultural institution, and the attitude of the state towards it may depend on whether it is regarded as an area belonging to industrial policy or as one belonging to cultural policy. The particular case of the Italian cinema industry between 1922 and 1945 is further complicated by secondary alternatives within and alongside the industrial-cultural one. Fascist industrial policy evolved from merely supporting and protecting private enterprise to, in the second half of the 1930s, exploiting the control sometimes almost fortuitously dropped in the regime's lap by the fact that industries came under state ownership via holding companies (notably IRI, the Institute for Industrial Reconstruction). As for cultural policy, one can say with a certain confidence that fascism never really had one, clear, coherent cultural policy. The regime tried to act as a mediator, reconciling a number of different attitudes towards culture. Where the cinema was concerned, one attitude was that it was a medium offering pure diversion, and that there was only risk (both ideological and financial risk) in trying to make it serve any other purpose. Another attitude was that since the cinema was an industry as well as a cultural institution, the financial well-being of the industry would be best defended by raising as much as possible the 'artistic' quality of the films produced ('artistic' covering everything from the aesthetic and moral content of films to a down-to-earth comparison with the technical skill and narrative competence of Hollywood filmmakers). Yet another attitude was that the cinema offered one of the most effective means for forging the fascist 'nation,' for developing the sense of an Italian identity, and for enshrining the ideals of Italian history (from Rome to the Renaissance, and from the Risorgimento to the glories of Fascist colonialism). This attitude did not simply see propaganda potential in the cinema, but rather would have Italy make films that spoke of and expressed the concerns and aspirations of Italians, and not ape the conventions of foreign cultural institutions. The perceived model for such a cinema was, explicitly and repeatedly, Soviet cinema.

In attempting, therefore, to make sense of the fascist government's treatment of the cinema industry – and notably the gradually increasing role the state played both in financing the industry and in creating institutions designed to promote the quality of the product – one is offered more than one single explanation. Certainly, from 1934 to 1939 Luigi Freddi promoted a policy in which, to survive and prosper, the Italian cinema industry needed to be centrally organized and vertically integrated, with state intervention both to subsidize the industry and to reduce to a minimum destructive competition within the industry itself. He believed that the cinema should be the expression of the fascist nation, with all that this implied, but also that the cinema was an entertainment whose profits depended on recognizing and meeting the needs and tastes of the public. In 1936, at a time when some fascist officials were pointing to Germany as an example of efficient, centralized state control, Freddi wrote a damning report on the German film industry, saying that it had been destroyed by crass nazification and by the expulsion of Jews from the industry, and arguing that the cinema was a delicate organism requiring a multitude of contributions. The verbs he used for the state's role in the industry were *frame, aid, reward, supervise, encourage.* So the position of Freddi is a complex one, and the health of the Italian cinema ever since his time may owe something to his ability to accept the complexities of the institution in his care. (Fascist critics complained that Italian producers would not make propaganda films for fear of boring the public – a complaint that, if taken seriously, would have caused havoc with any serious industrial policy; whereas big producers were trying to oust Freddi for supporting and subsidizing films that competed with the cosy conveyor-belt reproduction of hackneyed formula-films.) In the course of time, the large, established companies won the day, and the emphasis moved from the control to which Freddi aspired and more towards government handouts, with a new law on the cinema passed in 1938, which instituted a wholesale subsidy of the largest entrepreneurs. Meanwhile, paradoxically, the lasting achievement of the institutions founded and controlled by the regime was the creation of a dedicatedly anti-fascist cinema, that of neorealism.

Freddi had brought about a rebirth of Italian production, but his activities caused resentment among private entrepreneurs seeking secure and easy profits who managed to win the support of officials in the Ministry of Popular Culture, among them the minister, Dino Alfieri. The law promulgated in 1938, called the Legge Alfieri, marked the end of Freddi's hegemony. The Legge Alfieri provided for prizes to go to Italian films on a sliding scale based on box-office receipts: the bigger the receipts, the bigger the prize (from 12% of receipts to a maximum of 25%). With a measure like this, the regime relinquished its power to reward high-quality innovative films and to control incentives, and left this kind of discrimination to the marketplace.

Most Fascist laws concerning the cinema, including those that protected it against foreign competition, were abrogated in 1945. The war had devastated the physical plant (equipment and studios), and to this some historians have attributed aspects of the cinematographic *style* of neorealism (lighting, location, shooting, etc.). The laws passed by the government in 1947 and 1949 (the latter dubbed the Legge Andreotti after Giulio Andreotti, cabinet secretary responsible for the cinema) reinstated the conditions created by the Legge Alfieri, giving lavish state subsidies to films on the basis of a percentage of their box-office receipts. This meant that the more a film needed subsidizing, the less it got. Coming at a time when neorealist films, despite the enormous respect they were earning abroad, were struggling to cover their production costs in domestic cinemas, Andreotti's laws clearly had an ideological, as well as an industrial-commercial, purpose: to discourage producers from making such films by seducing them with much larger profits from making conventional, popular genre-vehicles.

It is helpful to draw a simple distinction between two approaches to marketing films, and between the two approaches to subsidizing them. The notion of 'supply push' sees each film put on the market as a unique product, a prototype. It hypothesizes that the higher the quality, and the greater the innovation, of each film marketed, the better will be the health and vigour of the production sector of the cinema industry and, in time, the larger the market share it will command. The notion also contains the implication that the cinema has a significant role to play in the cultural life of the nation. Not surprisingly, this notion was widespread in the post-war neorealist period among writers, directors, actors, and technical staff working in the industry and among certain producers, and was more or less universally held by film critics. Selective subsidy directed towards the 'supply push' model is called 'cultural' subsidy. 'Cultural' subsidy is designed to cushion innovative and artistic films against market forces, raising the quality of filmmaking and eventually its competitiveness. It is criticized as promoting the production of films that cannot find a market, and so consigning the film audience to the American competitor.

The notion of 'demand pull' sees the job of the production sector of the film industry as serving the needs of the exhibition sector (the cinemas) to meet an existing demand in the public for a familiar product. At the broad base of the cinema industry lie the cinemas that stay open from lunchtime to midnight every day and require a constant supply of merchandizable product to bring in a regular flow of customers. A cinema cannot wait for a good film to come along to open its doors and sell tickets, because its overhead costs never take a holiday. Hence, cinemas require a constant flow of 'reliable' product (not necessarily of high quality), which they can be reasonably sure will regularly appeal to their customers. The easiest way to ensure that a film is likely to appeal to customers in the future is for that film to be very similar to films that have appealed to customers in the past, either in terms of the story, or the emotion it provokes in the viewer, or in terms of the stars performing in it – elements that endow a film with what we can call, from a commercial point of view, 'reliable' quality, as opposed to 'high' quality. The public may very well respond positively to a film of high quality, but it will not know that the film is of high quality until it has seen it. The cinema exhibitor has to be able to advertise a product that the public will *predict* will be satisfactory on the basis of past experience. Audience surveys in the 1940s and 1950s indicate that cinema-goers knew in advance on what day of the week they would be going to the cinema, and to which cinema, but not which film they intended to see. Hence, repetition is not just a characteristic that individual films themselves display, but lies at the very basis of the day-to-day functioning of the cinema industry. The high-quality prototypes of the 'supply push' model are far harder to market than the 'reliable'-quality stereotypes of the 'demand pull' model. Non-selective subsidies directed towards the 'demand pull' model, called 'economic' subsidies, target profitable filmmaking and promote continuity of production, wresting exhibition space from the foreign competitor. The Legge Alfieri's subsidies in 1938 were ferociously 'economic.' The laws designed by Giulio Andreotti in 1947 and 1949 *theoretically* combined both 'cultural' and 'economic' subsidies, but producers saw to it that they were applied as 'economic' subsidies.

There is one further factor to put into the equation, so crucial as almost to eclipse all others. At the end of the war, in 1945, Italian moviegoers had experienced a drought of American films. MGM, Twentieth Century Fox, Paramount, and Warner Bros. had all withdrawn from the Italian film market in 1938 in retaliation against the imposition of a state monopoly over the distribution of films imported into Italy. In 1945 it was not difficult for the United States, with the political and economic power the war had conferred upon it, to transform Italy into a totally open market, which it could use to supplement its own falling domestic box-office receipts. Italian distributors and exhibitors were only too eager to promote everything the United States exported, especially since the public responded so positively to this strategy.

In the immediate post-war years, whatever kind of film an Italian producer made, its potential receipts would be limited by the stranglehold Hollywood had over the Italian box office (between 70 and 80 per cent). Protection from Hollywood, and the Legge Alfieri's subsidies in the period 1938–42, had led to the overproduction of poor-quality Italian films (together with a growing sprinkling of innovative, high-quality films). The return in 1945 of Hollywood films en masse, combined with the disarray of Italian production facilities as a result of the war and military occupation and the abrogation of the protectionist measures enacted by the fascist regime, weakened the competitive potential of Italian films, and discouraged entrepreneurs from investing in production. Neorealist filmmakers made a virtue out of necessity, often became their own producers, and developed cheap production methods, concentrating on authentic content rather than on 'production values' such as stars and spectacle. This endowed their films with a freshness and individuality that rapidly gained them a commercially modest but culturally prestigious export market. Hence their post-war presence in London's West End.

Neorealism, therefore, can be seen as occupying an area of artistic freedom and commercial disarray created by the *hiatus* between the abrogation of the Legge Alfieri (1945) and the implementation of the Legge Andreotti (1949, following an initial provision promulgated in 1947), both of which held out to entrepreneurs strong incentives to take a 'demand pull' approach to production.[2] In this hiatus the industry debated two questions. Would the health of Italian cinema benefit from specializing in quality artistic films that could conquer for themselves an export market to help cover the costs of production (the position of writers, directors, actors, and the producer De Laurentiis, for example)? Or would this bankrupt the industry, which really needed an efficient and profitable marketing of film genres for the domestic market (the position of distributors and exhibitors, for example, but also of figures in the ruling Christian Democrat party)? In particular, exhibitors maintained that the lack of stars and the poor genre identity of neorealist films guaranteed their failure at the box office, and gave Hollywood a monopoly. As an industrial policy, the strategy of Giulio Andreotti, the government official responsible for the cinema industry, was to reward sound and profitable investment, as well as shoring up Italian production against American competition, and to ensure that state funds were not propping up unmarketable production. As a cultural policy, it paid lip service to quality in the *letter* of the law, as we shall see, but in its *implementation* deliberately failed to distinguished between mediocre 'reliable' films and challenging 'high quality' films. The largest production company in Italy (the *only* large one at the time), Lux Film, successfully steered a middle course between the two alternatives, dividing its activity more or less equally between films of artistic quality which it vigorously promoted both at home and abroad, and popular genre-vehicles and the occasional 'spectacular' for the domestic market. (See appendix 8, 'Established film production companies in Italy, 1945–1953.')

The three films examined in detail in this book were all products of the 'hiatus' in conventional production that I have described. In each case their financing was an improvised and one-off affair. *Roma città aperta* was very cheaply made; *Paisà* was quite lavishly financed; *Ladri di biciclette* was a quality production that used money-saving procedures to control its costs. All three covered their costs to the producers at the box office: *Paisà* barely (its domestic receipts were high, but not in relation to its high costs; it was successfully sold abroad); *Ladri di biciclette* very satisfactorily (it paid for the losses incurred on De Sica's *Sciuscià*, and benefited both from a carefully planned distribution at home – after a shaky start – and huge publicity deriving from international accolades); *Roma città aperta* only just (and this because the producers sold it for its cost price outright to distributors, who were the ones who profited from the film's considerable box-office success). (See appendix 13, 'Table of production arrangements and costs for five core neorealist films.')

The reception of neorealist films has to be seen from two entirely separate perspectives: one is that of immediate reception, quite another that of long-term reception. But even that does not give us the full picture.

What matters to the producer of a film is how much it takes in at the box office in the first few years of its release. Films are made on credit, which accrues interest, and long-standing debts count as losses. Hence, the fact that De Sica's *Umberto D.* (made in 1951) was watched on television by sixteen million Italians in a single night on 30 April 1975 does not count as part of its commercial reception. Its receipts at the box office in the years after it was made (107 million lire) did not even begin to cover its costs (140 million lire). Visconti's *La terra trema* cost 121 million lire to make and took in 36 million gross at the box office, of which only 5.36 million made its way back to the producers.

However, huge box-office successes were enjoyed by genre-vehicles made in the same year as *Umberto D.* that are still regarded with respect, issued in video, and shown on television: *Anna* (Alberto Lattuada), *I figli di nessuno* (Rafaello Matarazzo), and *Guardie e ladri* (Mario Monicelli and Steno). While most might agree that the genre-vehicles do not, and never did, approach the stature of De Sica's film, it cannot be said that the melodramas and comedy have failed the test of time that the neorealist film has withstood.

Raw box-office receipts require interpretation, and do not tell us enough about the *relative* popularity of individual films with the public. For a start, inflation rose rapidly each year, so it is hard to compare a film made one year with one made another year, and there can be a large rise in inflation between making a film at a certain cost and getting in all the receipts four of five years later (the 'cycle' of exploitation of a film was generally taken to be five years). Then there is the fact that cinema attendances in Italy rose steadily from around 400 million in 1945 to 819 million in 1955. Finally, the *proportion* of ticket sales going to Italian (as opposed to Hollywood) films rose enormously between 1945 and 1955. Perhaps the most useful comparative statistic one can supply for the *relative* popularity of a film (in terms of how many people went to see it during its release) is an approximate calculation of the percentage of total tickets sold in a given year attributable to that particular film.

The *commercial* success of a film is a measure of its receipts relative to its costs. It is hard to find out the production costs of films in this period, for a number of reasons. For this chapter, I have used a wide variety of sources, often anecdotal. Box-office receipts tell us only the gross returns from ticket sales. Using approximate figures, we can look at the situation of a film made under the laws introduced by Giulio Andreotti, the first in 1947, giving subsidies of 16 per cent of gross receipts to producers of 'Italian' films, and the second, in 1949, raising the level to 18 per cent. Various taxes are levied on gross box-office receipts at, let us say, 25 per cent (at times they had been as high as 34%). After tax, the exhibitor takes his 50%. What remains is divided, 40% to the distributor and 60% to the producer. This is the point at which state subsidies to the producer enter the picture, at the rate of 16–18% of gross box-office receipts. It is worth pointing out, incidentally, that the entity that always made the most money from the cinema was the state, through taxes on cinema tickets.

The association of producers and the government maintained that the 'subsidies' were no more than a reimbursement of taxes levied on tickets, given to films of Italian nationality to help them compete with American imports (10% of gross receipts – an 'economic' subsidy), and prizes for Italian films of high artistic quality (the further 6–8% – a 'cultural' subsidy). Producers made sure that *all* films got *both* portions, whatever their quality. But strictly speaking, it is the filmgoer who is taxed, not the producer. Moreover, the whole point of tax revenue is that it is to be spent for socially useful purposes. Reimbursing it in proportion to gross receipts means that most of it goes to increase the profits for producers of films that are already profitable. We could compare two films. *Umberto D.* cost in total 140 million lire and had gross receipts of 107 million. *Before* subsidy, the return to the producer would have been 24 million. *After* subsidy (at 18%) it was about 43 million – still a catastrophic loss. A perfectly respectable, industrially co-produced (70% Italian, 30% French) film qualifying for the subsidy, made and released at the same time as *Umberto D.*, *Anna*, directed by Alberto Lattuada, was hugely successful at the box office, taking in 1006 million lire. The film's budget was for 165 million (its actual costs, which are not available, may have been a little higher), and the producers would have received 225 million *without* subsidy, giving a profit of 60 million (a 36% return on investment). *With* subsidy, total receipts to the producers were 405 million, increasing profits to 240 million. The subsidy *alone* (180 million) would have more than paid for *Umberto D.*

The neorealists viewed the 'economic' system of subsidy from a 'cultural' perspective, and drew the conclusion that the system of subsidy was designed to suppress films like *Umberto D.* Their perspective was not paranoid, as can be seen from a famous open letter published in the press by Giulio Andreotti, the architect of the system, begging De Sica to desist from making films like *Ladri di biciclette* and *Umberto D.*[3]

Credit for making a conventional film came from 'guarantees' issued by distributors, who in turn extracted 'guarantees' from exhibitors – all based on estimates of the proposed film's yield at the box office. Innovative films did not stand a chance of getting this kind of credit, and so could not benefit from cross-subsidy in conventional producer-distributor agreements (that is to say, covering losses with the highly subsidized profits of a very successful film). Cross-subsidy did, in fact, take place, but it was more often a result of laundering otherwise 'blocked' funds (see the next paragraph) than the result of the state's system of subsidy.

Raising the subsidy, in 1949, from 16 to 18 per cent significantly increased the profitability of mainstream commercial films, therefore, without noticeably promoting the production of 'high quality' innovative films, which struggled to cover their costs at the box office. Only a crusading producer would resist the temptation to take the easy money.

But there is more. In order to reduce the flow of hard currency out of the country, the Italian government 'blocked' the profits of imported American films distributed in Italy: those profits could not be taken out of the country. The American distributors set up 'Italian' production companies, investing their 'blocked' profits in 'Italian' films, which were then eligible for Italian state subsidies. Subsequent profits, deriving now from 'Italian' films, together with the subsidies, could then be exported to the United States. Artistically speaking, this was not all bad, because neorealist films like Zavattini's project *Siamo donne*, Antonioni's *I vinti*, and Zampa's *Processo alla città* for example, were made with Twentieth Century Fox's 'blocked' funds – which constituted a form of cross-subsidy.

Andreotti's laws 'permitted' the submission of scripts to the government department responsible for the cinema for 'advice' on how best to secure production credit from the state film financing fund (a special section of the state Banca Nazionale del Lavoro), and on how to be sure of securing the 6 or 8 per cent prize for 'artistic quality' (by avoiding criticism of the status quo) – even though it was in actual fact automatically granted. Government officials erred on the side of caution. These sources of funding were important to producers, who readily accepted the 'advice.'

Without even taking into account the matter of censorship, the hostility of the government and of the Catholic Church, and the cultural strategies of the cold war, the odds were stacked against neorealist films. What is remarkable is that, in these circumstances and notwithstanding the considerable risk of financial loss, a mainstream production company (Peppino Amato and Angelo Rizzoli) put up 140 million lire for De Sica to make *Umberto D.* (a film about an elderly man, played by a linguistics professor from the University of Florence, who catches a cold and goes to bed), and that Salvo D'Angelo (of the Vatican-backed Universalia production company, also supported by major southern banks) stepped in to enable Visconti to complete *La terra trema*.

Both at the time, and ever since, it has generally been asserted that, with notable exceptions, neorealist films did badly at the box office. There are two ways of testing this assertion. One is to check the box-office receipts of each individual film, which leads to the conclusion that some fared very well, some moderately well, and some very badly indeed, considering their quality. (However, when one brings into the equation the type of experience – and sometimes the difficulty of comprehension – that some of the failures presented to the general viewer, their performance is not surprising.) (See appendix 15, 'Fifty-five neorealist films.') Another test is to see how neorealist films fared *as a group*, in comparison with other *groups* of films – in this instance, generic groupings such as comedy, melodrama, and adventure. By this measure, neorealist films fared no worse than any other group, and better than most (See appendix 14, 'Italian public's reception of different categories of Italian films [1945–56]'). Hence, the poor performance asserted for neorealist films *in general* is not supported by the data. We are forced to conclude that two considerations have led to the reigning orthodoxy: first, the poor performance of outstanding films like *La terra trema*, *Umberto D.*, *Germania anno zero*, *Viaggio in Italia*, and *Francesco giullare di Dio*, especially when compared with their worldwide critical reception, is given special weight; second, the *general* performance of neorealist films has been compared with the *most successful* genre films (such as melodramas), rather than with genre films *in general*. It is easy to receive a false impression of the performance of neorealist films relative to that of melodramas and comedies, because with far more of the latter being made and released in a given year, a handful of each group's best performers totally outnumbers the entire output of neorealist films.

It has been asserted that neorealist films were boycotted by exhibitors and received truncated runs in minor cinemas, and certainly there is anecdotal evidence to support this claim in some cases. In comparison with Hollywood films, Italian films *in general* were poorly treated, at least until the 1950s, by the Italian exhibition sector. But this has been a feature of film exhibition in Italy throughout the post-war period, and continues to be the case. Once again, if we look at neorealist films *as a group*, we find that they were given quite respectable, sometimes unusually long, runs in prestigious central cinemas in metropolitan areas. Moreover, they were often 'reprised' in first-run cinemas, rather than moving straightaway and definitively into the second- and third-run circuits (where tickets were cheaper). (See appendix 6, 'Length (in days) of opening runs.') Because of their artistic and cultural quality, they benefited far more than 'mainstream' Italian films in general from prestigious gala launches and previews, and from highly publicized presentations (and awards) at film festivals at home and abroad.

A more serious exhibitors' boycott resulted from the Catholic Church's hostility to neorealist films (for their moral and political content). The Catholic Centre for Cinema (CCC) applied a 'certification' to films, and gave restrictive ratings to *all* neorealist films (except *Cielo sulla palude*). Andreotti's laws gave the minister (a Christian Democrat, and hence Catholic) control over the opening of new cinemas. The Church, with Andreotti's support, opened three thousand *sale parrocchiali* (parish cinemas), which in small towns and rural areas were often the only local cinema; all were obliged to honour the certification of the CCC, and none, therefore, ever showed a neorealist film. This strategy was designed partly to put 'economic' pressure on producers and distributors to desist from making such films. In terms of raw box-office receipts, this strategy was not significant (see appendix 4, 'Categories of cinemas in Italy in 1953'), but its cultural effect was to deny certain sections of the population (particularly in smaller communities and rural areas) access to neorealist films.

Neorealism's critical reception abroad is legendary. The films had a respectable commercial reception too, but generally only in 'art' cinemas in metropolitan areas. *Roma città aperta* ran at the World Theater (admittedly, a 300-seater) in New York for a year and a half; *Ladri di biciclette* got a two-month opening run in Paris; *Paisà* ran at the Academy Cinema in London's West End for five months over the winter of 1948–9. Indeed, success abroad led to cases in which a film would open overseas before it opened in Italy (Parisians saw *Riso amaro* two months before Romans did). To cite just one example of a phenomenon inconceivable before neorealism: in the week of 8–15 November 1948, three Italian films were in first runs in Stockholm (two of them neorealist, one 'sub'-neorealist). It is difficult to know what were the financial returns from foreign success, because production companies have never agreed to release the figures, and often films were sold outright to foreign buyers. The respect that neorealist films earned for the Italian cinema in world markets led to the export of a far wider range of Italian films, which penetrated more commercial exhibition circuits abroad. Neorealism *created* an export market for Italian films where virtually none had existed since 1915, and set in motion a process that led, by the mid-1960s, to the Italian cinema industry getting 60 per cent of its revenue from export.

No 'story' I can tell in this brief introduction to the Italian cinema industry is simple. For the neorealists, Andreotti was the enemy. For mainstream producers, the Americans were the enemy. But Andreotti's strengthening of the industry as a whole led to the great 'art' cinema of the 1960s, born out of neorealism and a strong domestic production sector, and when the Americans withdrew their investment in Italian cinema as a result of the Vietnam war and the rise in the price of oil, the Italian industry collapsed like a punctured tire.

The Cultural Context

During the period of 'high' neorealism (1945–8), cultural considerations played a large part in the making of a number of films, partly as a result of the 'hiatus' in producers' hegemony (artists themselves often arranged the financing of their films). As the industry reorganized, particularly along the lines promoted by the Legge Andreotti of 1949, commercial and industrial considerations took ever greater precedence, and the relative number of films determined by cultural criteria dwindled.

In the late 1930s and early 1940s, the institutions founded under the fascist government (the Centro Sperimentale di Cinematografia and its journal *Bianco e nero*, the Film Sections of the Fascist University Youth, and the cultural journals run by prominent fascist figures, such as *Cinema* and *Primato*) had played a major role in criticizing the cinema of the Legge Alfieri, and in agitating for something very similar to what the neorealists would later produce. Hence, it is possible to say that neorealism was, logically, the product of fascist institutional thinking about the cinema, and that the war swept away Fascism just at the moment (1943–5) at which its projects were bearing fruit. But then Andreotti, in his turn (1949), swept away neorealism.

During the early years of the reconstruction of Italy as a putatively 'anti-fascist' democracy, Fascist cinema was so negatively defined (as escapist, conformist, petit-bourgeois, consolatory, repetitive, uninspired) that to call neorealism a 'break' with it was more or less a tautology. Gradually, as Italian cinema of the 1930s has come to be re-examined, this orthodoxy has increasingly been challenged, and neorealism has come to be recognized as both a product of that cinema and a critique of it. The issue has now become not so much *whether* there was continuity or a break, as *to what extent* was there continuity and precisely *in what ways* did neorealism break with the past. The seeds of neorealism's critique of 1930s Italian cinema (no longer defined as 'fascist') have increasingly come to be seen as having germinated *inside* the Fascist institutions of cinema themselves. If the Fascist regime could be said to have had a cultural policy regarding cinema, at least one ingredient of it consisted in looking at Soviet cinema as a model for a 'national' cinema, from the point of view of a centrally organized industry, from a 'cultural' point of view, and from the point of view of cinema's function in society.

Philosophical concerns figure prominently in this institutional context. Aesthetics in Italy had been – and still was – dominated by Benedetto Croce, who assigned to art an *autonomy* from the practical matters of life, and from science and philosophy. His lucidly articulated aesthetic theories championed an expressive lyricism as the characteristic of 'art,' and this is detectable in Rossellini's defence of the 'essential' fragment, and in De Sica's goal of 'lyricism', as we shall see in later chapters. Croce's aesthetics was accused of encouraging irresponsible 'art for art's sake' and of neglecting the cultural, educational function of art. The aesthetic movements that had most illustrated this danger had been Futurism and d'Annunzianism, both anti-democratic and heavily implicated in the rhetorical excesses and militarism of Fascism. Hence, any cultural project for a new and morally responsible art was deeply suspicious of 'aesthetics.' The official philosopher of Fascism, and especially of its education system, was Giovanni Gentile, for whom reality was the spirit embracing all man's activities: scientific, philosophical, moral, and aesthetic – all ultimately finding their incorporation in the State. While it is easy to mount an argument explaining how far from the idealism of Croce and Gentile neorealism moved, in fact important theorists of Italian cinematic realism, such as Luigi Chiarini (director of the Centro Sperimentale and both friend and protector of the socialist Umberto Barbaro, who taught at the school), were soaked in the aesthetic theories of both philosophers. The inter-war philosophy of idealism generally defined 'realism' in terms of moral and social values, and 'art' in terms of 'realism.' This matter is discussed in the section on 'idealism' in the following chapter. The significant point to note is how much the neorealists inherited from this tradition in their notions of 'realism.'

The counter to Croceanism articulated by the left-wing reconstruction of an anti-fascist democracy was a 'cultural' model of aesthetics: knowledge and ethics, accuracy and inclusiveness of representation, and the 'correctness' of historical vision (as opposed to beauty and pleasure, for example), values that priviled precisely the practical considerations that Crocean aesthetics excluded: films were seen as either confrontational and directed towards progressive social action (culturally positive) or consolatory and supportive of the status quo (negatively escapist). Giving pleasure to the viewer directly through the use of engaging plots, beautiful performers, and formal aspects of cinematography (the stock-in-trade of cinema), as well as any self-expression that did not conform to an ideological orthodoxy, was viewed as an evasion of the primary and urgent 'cultural' project.

A consequence of this struggle in defence of a cultural project and against 'escapism' was to identify neorealism as, *by definition*, the only artistic activity in the cinema worthy of respect, and everything else as corrupting and regressive. While being understandable in the circumstances of a political struggle, this approach bordered on idolatry, and hampered balanced critical assessment of films like Fellini's *Lo sceicco bianco*, Rossellini's *Stromboli*, and De Sica's *Miracolo a Milano*, as well as, of course, of commercial genre cinema.

In the literary world, movements like *Strapaese*, literary neorealism, and the translation, before and during the war, of American narrative (much of it written in response to the Great Depression, in rather the same way that neorealism responded to Fascism and the war) were a further spur to neorealist theorizing. Great weight has been given in historical accounts of neorealism (whether correctly or not is another matter) to the adoption in the early 1940s, by the movement around the journal *Cinema* and by the artistic team involved in Visconti's *Ossessione*, of the late-nineteenth-century realist novelist Giovanni Verga as a model for a realist narrative cinema that was specifically Italian and a bridge between documentary and fiction. By 1954, however, the movement around the journal *Cinema nuovo* was advocating the adoption of a Lukacsian model of realism with, as literary models, Balzac and Tolstoy. By contrast, a director such as Giuseppe De Santis stands out as a figure incorporating popular cultural forms into his neorealist films – peasant culture, popular song, consumerism, comic-book literature, and Hollywood narrative genres – but all in the service of a left-wing ideological orthodoxy.

The *cinematic* 'context' that produced neorealism has been the subject of innumerable books and essays, and there is no need to do more here than list a few of the 'models' that we know, or believe, inspired postwar Italian filmmakers. The German *Neue Sachlichkeit* movement in the cinema, and a film like Piel Jutzi's 1929 *Mutter Krausens Fahrt ins Glück* (*Mother Krausen Goes to Heaven*), with connections to the Soviet school, must have been influential, though references to them are hard to find. Of the Americans, Chaplin and King Vidor were repeatedly referred to, and both Rossellini and De Sica owe debts to the latter. Robert Flaherty was championed by the Venice Film Festival, and references to his films, as well as to those of Pare Lorentz, are frequent in pre-war writings. At the beginning of the war, Giuseppe De Robertis, sometimes in collaboration with Rossellini, made films for the Italian navy that owe an undeniable debt to films of the British Documentary Movement.

Most Italians had had little enthusiasm for the war, and so it is not surprising to find the theme of 'pacifism' running through neorealism's challenge to the recent past. Although Renoir's *La Grande illusion* was banned by the Italian government, it was widely seen, was awarded a prize at the Venice International Festival of Cinematographic Art, and was hugely influential. Its influence on Rossellini is pervasive, starting with his 'patriotic' war story, scripted by Mussolini's son Vittorio, *Un pilota ritorna*, released in 1942, which included in its production team figures who form a link between Rossellini and the group of young left-wing critics around the journal *Cinema* (of which Vittorio Mussolini was director) in the early 1940s. Renoir himself came to work in Rome in the early 1940s, made friends with Italian filmmakers, and was revered as an artistic giant. The French and the Italians have always had a fraternal cinematic relationship, and the films of Clair, Renoir, Carné, and Duvivier were followed with close interest in Italy, just as it was a French critic and admirer of Renoir, André Bazin, who most magisterially championed the films of Rossellini and De Sica.

The presentation of a handful of Soviet films at the 1932 Venice Film Festival generated writing and reflection throughout the 1930s in Italy. The films whose titles recur most frequently are Pudovkin's 1927 *The End of St Petersburg* and Nicolai Ekk's 1931 *The Road to Life*. Both generated Italian imitations (some amateur) in the 1930s. Ekk's film (about the redemption of young abandoned delinquent boys, and its sabotaging) had a particular impact on the influential director Alessandro Blasetti, who was still talking about it in the 1970s, and its story and treatment bring to mind De Sica's post-war films, though I have encountered no mention of it by De Sica himself. Throughout Fascist thinking about the cultural role of cinema and the meaning to be given to 'realism,' the Soviet model is the most constant thread, and already in the 1920s the term *neorealismo* was being used in connection with Russian prose narrative and cinema. At the Centro Sperimentale di Cinematografia (the state film school) Umberto Barbaro drilled his students in analysis of Soviet films, and after the war continued to apply the model to the new Italian movement, as well as translating Pudovkin's writings into Italian. He also directed his pupils' attention to a Neapolitan 'realist' movement before the First World War and to the legendary, but no longer extant, *Sperduti nel buio* of 1914, by Nino Martoglio, linking it to a 'thread' of 'realism' that he claimed permeated the history of Italian cinema. This 'thread' has been picked up by many more recent historians, pointing to *Assunta Spina* (1914), *Sole* and *Rotaie* (both 1929), and in the 1930s *La tavola dei poveri, Vecchia guardia, 1860, Treno popolare,* and *Acciaio*. It is generally agreed there was a 'preneo-realist' period in the early 1940s, as Fascist hegemony collapsed, containing Visconti's *Ossessione*, De Sica's *I bambini ci guardano*, Blasetti's *Quattro passi tra le nuvole*, De Robertis's *Uomini sul fondo*, and Franciolini's *Fari nella nebbia*. Everything points to continuity within a tradition, rather than a violent break with the past, as was the view held at the height of neorealism's struggle for survival.

One area of continuity that has been little explored is the stylistic and narrative continuity between neorealism and the comedy tradition of the 1930s and 1940s. Rossellini baldly asserts it (as we shall see in the chapter on *Roma città aperta*), and De Sica's film career began in comedy. The orthodox historical line has always been that neorealism was an abrupt turning away from the comedy tradition, too easily caricatured as that of the *telefoni bianchi* ('white telephones') films of the 1930s. This is because of a concern with the ideological function of the films, rather than with their narrative function and stylistic procedures. In ensuing chapters we shall only be able to hint at the implications of identifying in neorealist films procedures and functions deriving from that comedy tradition.

It has generally been held that contemporary history was the area in which the referents of neorealist films were (and therefore should be) primarily determined: the films were *about* the war, the Resistance, poverty, social injustice, democracy, and the creation of a humanist society; 'neorealism' meant precisely having these things as referents. Post-war Italian cinema did not give much 'visibility' to Fascism, because the 'memory' would enflame conflict and retard reconstruction. Prominent politicians objected to the referents of De Sica's films because they portrayed Italy to the world in a negative light (though the real objection was to the political implications underlying that portrayal).[4] On the other side, left-wing and democratic forces objected to a rice-worker in *Riso amaro* dancing the boogie-woogie (in other words, partaking in individualistic capitalist culture instead of traditional rural dances), and had quite prescriptive demands about what should be the referents of dignified films, with a distinct suspicion of eroticism. Many on the Left deemed as harmful to the community the films that the Italian public was, in the vast majority, viewing (Raffaello Matarazzo's 'tear-jerkers,' of which *Catene* is an example), precisely because of the ideological implications of the films' referents (family, honour, social conformity), even though their 'style' was close to that of neorealism and they shared with many neorealist films the narrative archetype of 'melodrama.' The fear that the public might prefer these films to the neorealist canon led intellectuals to a great deal of soul-searching: did neorealism come from a progressive 'people' (was it a democratic art form) or from the bourgeois intelligentsia (an elite avant-garde, which the 'people' rejected)?

These intellectuals were responsible for criticism and analysis of Italian cinema and therefore also of neorealism, and were hampered by the limited technical and cultural resources at their disposal. The tools deployed for media analysis were inadequate and out of date: there existed no sophisticated notion either of popular culture or of mass culture, and cinema was viewed through the limited prism of the notion of a conflict between industry and art. Textual analysis of films was almost non-existent, and the Marxist ideological bias against formalism led to a neglect of aesthetic considerations. Narrative and pleasure (eroticism, for example) were condemned as escapist, rather than analysed. Hence, the cultural potential of much of neorealist cinema was ignored or discarded by the movement's own supporters, partly because they were methodologically ill equipped to recognize it. If the artists were ahead of their public, they were also ahead of their critics.

The figures who stood out from this trend were directors such as Giuseppe De Santis, Michelangelo Antonioni, and Federico Fellini and the novelist Italo Calvino, all of whom showed an acute awareness of the new role of the media in society and of the need for the 'people' to derive aesthetic pleasure and self-expression from them. The Communist Party, by contrast held a traditional notion of 'high' culture. It saw its job as that of 'educating' the masses, and often failed to exploit the new media, such as comic books, weekly illustrated magazines, the cinema, the radio, and, later, television, leaving their exploitation to the far cannier free-marketeers and even the Catholic Church. The Communists were suspicious of anything American, whereas De Santis and Pietro Germi grasped the populist essence of Hollywood and used it for their own ends.

The Left made 'mistakes,' but its shortcomings must be seen in the light of a heroic struggle against crushing institutional persecution. The fight for neorealism was a real political battle. The level and quality of the intellectual debate promoted by the Left contributed enormously to the high quality of Italian cinema in the period from the 1940s to the 1970s.

In the immediate post-war period, the freedom of expression and inquiry that neorealist cinema exploited was seen as embodying the spirit required for the rejection and burial of the Fascist mentality, and as the prerequisite for the construction of a truly anti-fascist and democratic nation. This project for the reconstruction of Italy (upon the ravaged landscape of the summer of 1943) faced such innumerable and insuperable obstacles that the project was never fully realized. The obstacles were the following: (a) the determination of the Allies to avoid a repetition of the Greek and Yugoslav wartime experiences, to prevent Italy turning to socialism, and to impose a liberal free-market capitalist regime on the country – indeed, one not very different from that which had reigned under Fascism; (b) the ruthless and single-minded anti-communism of the Catholic Church, and its power and influence over Italian society; (c) the decision of the Italian Communist Party to shore up a pluralist democracy rather than to push ruthlessly for social justice; (d) the failure to implement fully the post-war democratic constitution; and (e) two other forces that, in the struggle between the Right and the Left to modernize Italy, prevailed by default: on the one hand, the bureaucratic institutions inherited from Fascism and, on the other, consumer capitalism, promoted by Italian industry and finance and by the United States in its aid plan. The modernization of Italy proceeded with blithe disregard for the intense soul-searching of the intellectuals.

In the following chapters of this book I shall not be addressing political, cultural, and mediological questions, but rather a certain reticence in the aesthetic treatment of neorealist films as *films*, and the tendency to treat them instead as discourses to be interpreted and analysed. Rather than criticize this tendency, I would be inclined to see it in a positive light as a passionate engagement with the neorealist project, and as an irresistible urge to 'participate' intellectually in a civic endeavour. Nevertheless, a recurrent theme that will emerge from the aesthetic analysis of *Roma città aperta*, *Paisà*, and *Ladri di biciclette* is precisely this helpless grappling with the implications of 'modernization.'

Films

If you look at the organization of filmmaking, the film director appears a rather minor, technical contributor to the overall product. All the major decisions appear to rest with the script writers and the producer, whose instructions the director executes – admittedly, in his own inimitable way.

Production

A thoroughly sound, non-authorial approach to Italian neorealist cinema already exists in the collected volume *Neorealismo Cinema italiano*, and particularly in the introductory essay by its editor, Alberto Farassino, 'Neorealismo, storia e geografia.'[5] A crucial component of the historical explanation of the phenomenon of neorealism is the reduced role of producers in the genesis of the films analysed. This is a widely recognized and easily documented issue, and one to which Farassino himself attributes great importance. In this book it is dealt with in part by means of data in a table in appendix 8, on Italian production companies, which show that 54 per cent of neorealist films involved at least some participation in financing from established production companies; that 34 per cent were made with no established production backing; and that 25 per cent of the large production company Lux Film's output were neorealist films. *La terra trema* began as a Communist Party–funded documentary to help in the 1948 general election. Two films were funded by associations of ex-partisans: *Caccia tragica* and *Il sole sorge ancora*. Carlo Lizzani's *Achtung! Banditi!* was funded by a Genoese cooperative of filmgoers.

Screenwriting

Film narratives are part of a phenomenon of a general explosion of narrative at the end of the war. Narrative often manifested itself in first-person accounts, a simple recounting of experiences, and was produced at every literary level, from the most artistic to the most domestic (a number of periodicals sprang up just to publish it). This suggests that narrative was meeting a need at this historical moment, among all social classes, and that this narrative was closely linked to historical experience. Hence, even if the narratives themselves were not always entirely 'realist,' they gave 'expression' to concerns with practical, concrete matters that existed outside the realm of the aesthetic, in contemporary reality. Critics and historians have tended to interpret this 'function' of narrative in terms of forging a 'new culture,' and as an essentially *ethical* strategy directed towards the *future*, rather than as a *cognitive* strategy for coping with the *past* and the *present*. This is because the dominant philosophical position at the time (historicism) held that 'knowledge' came *from*, and was *about*, history, seen as a teleological process (that is to say, as progressing towards a goal, or as having, if you like, its own 'project').

A less ideologically determined critical approach that has been widely applied to the stories of neorealist films can be subsumed under the notion of the *'film balade'* – punning on the French *se balader* 'to stroll around.' Critics have noticed a looseness to the narrative structure of neorealist films, and indeed the neorealist scriptwriter Cesare Zavattini openly challenged the need for 'stories' in general. Neither *Ladri di biciclette* nor *Umberto D.* have 'endings' in the conventional sense: they both simply stop at a certain point, resolving none of the problems raised in the stories – indeed, the films generally end when all possible solutions have been exhausted. Often, the narratives have a circular structure, returning to a starting point (or describing a repeated series of circles – *La strada* is the most notable example), such that the viewer has the experience of being on a journey (an impression deliberately reinforced by the *titles* of many of the films – not just *'viaggio'* ('voyage'), *'cammino'* ('journey'), or *'strada'* ('road'), but also the plural of *'ladri'* ('thieves'), in *Ladri di biciclette*, for example, which starts and ends with a theft). This structure has led French critics to apply metaphors like *flânerie* ('wandering') to neorealist films. The most appropriate contemporary parallel is the 'road movie.'

The French theorist Gilles Deleuze discusses at length what he sees as a fundamental change in cinematic narrative and representation ushered in by the neorealists: the abandonment of an essentially antagonistic narrative and a tendency to a 'wandering' approach. In his view the films, rather than being constructed around dramatic conflicts, privilege the representation of time and space as it is perceived and experienced both in real life and in the viewing experience.[6] Luigi Comencini explained the unpopularity of neorealism with the public by suggesting that the public wants films that 'tell a story,' while neorealist films 'illustrate a situation' instead. All these observations converge on neorealism's attempt to bring art and life closer together, and to distance itself from the conventionality of genre. Deleuze's and, earlier, André Bazin's acute sensitivity to the special nature of neorealist narrative may, however, owe something to their closeness to the philosophy of phenomenology, which privileges 'experience.'[7] Neorealist films do, indeed, give a higher priority to recreating the 'experience' of their protagonists than to furnishing the viewer with material 'facts' about their situation (you almost never find out exactly how much anyone is paid in a neorealist narrative, but you always know what it feels like to be poor). Seen in this light, neorealism is a special kind of 'realism,' and has not deserved the criticism, often laid at its door, of being 'naturalist' (in the sense of material, economic, and hereditary determinism, as found in Émile Zola's novels, for example). Neorealism's greatest contribution to the cinema may, in fact, be these innovations in the approach towards narrative.

An important issue historically was censorship at the 'story' and script stage. Andreotti's 1947–9 laws invited (they did not oblige) producers to submit scripts for approval. A great many neorealist scripts never became films, and this raises issues concerning what should be included in the artistic manifestation of 'neorealism' – just films in the form in which they were released, films before they were cut, or also 'treatments' and scripts that never got to be filmed. The latter would have only the writers as their 'authors.'

While authorship is an 'issue' in itself, much discussed in film studies, this book will have nothing to say about *theories* of authorship. Data about writers in Italian cinema of the neorealist period is given in a table in appendix 11 ('Writers of neorealist films'.) Three films will be looked at in detail. All three of them had, for a while at least, Sergio Amidei on the writing team. In discussing the films, I treat him as joint author of *Roma città aperta*, while noting how something in his approach led to his being ejected from *Paisà* and *Ladri di biciclette*. Federico Fellini was scriptwriter on one-sixth of neorealist films, his contribution to *Roma città aperta* was important, and he will be treated as something like a subordinate joint author of *Paisà* (which slightly changes the focus of the debate over whether Fellini was a neorealist or not). Cesare Zavattini was the most important writer of *Ladri di biciclette*. I treat him as its co-author. However, since authorship really is an issue with this film, it is touched upon in the chapter devoted to the film. Zavattini was every bit as influential in Italian cinema, and particularly in the 'movement' of neorealism, as any single director, and a section of chapter 2 is devoted to his theories.

A quarter of neorealist films had their origins in artistic literary works. Zavattini himself was a literary man. Hence, whatever else was at work in neorealism, one element was continuity with traditional middle-class literary culture. Nevertheless, neorealism also set itself the goal of tapping into the reservoir of popular narrative that was based on recent historical experiences. Advertisements were placed in periodicals calling for readers to send in stories; competitions were held. Some films (*Sciuscià* and *Roma ore 11*, for example) are famously based on newspaper stories. Zavattini promoted the most radical project, for a regular cinematic 'magazine' recounting true stories and using the real protagonists as performers (*Amore in città* derives from this experiment). The thrust of some of these experiments was to give a democratic cast to the cinema, in the form of an element of audience input.

The credits of a neorealist film tend to list a number of writers. At the time, there existed a body of writers who, as well as working for the cinema, worked on comic magazines (such as the satirical *Marc'Aurelio*), on radio comedy shows, on sketches for the variety theatre, and for the *avanspettacolo* (the live comedy shows that accompanied film showings). (See appendix 11.) They worked together in cafés and small restaurants, in a mobile community, and their creative sessions frequently embraced the directors and producers at the café or restaurant table. At neighbouring tables, ever-changing groups might be throwing together ideas for a neorealist denunciation of poverty, a comedy vehicle for Totò, a nineteenth-century heroic adventure tale, a tear-jerking melodrama, or a satirical radio show. Zavattini emblematically remarked that once producers and directors stopped riding the buses, the Italian cinema ran out of ideas. All of this clearly suggests that neorealist films had part of their origins in a creative activity that did not necessarily separate out neorealist films from other forms of popular and mass culture, and also that to attribute the films to their directors does not always accurately reflect their origins. It is a further reason for examining the continuity between the comedy tradition and neorealist filmmaking.

The entry of dialect into the cinema (it had made some appearances even during the fascist period, but only rarely) was partly the result of the efforts and beliefs of the writers, and is one of the characteristic elements of films of the period, not only neorealist films but also comedies. The use of dialect was also connected with the choice of performers 'taken from the streets' (see below).

The Profilmic

Performances

This area raises, first of all, straightforward questions of 'realism.' Performances are iconic. (A brief explanation of terms is in order here, though they are discussed in more detail in the 'Reference' section of the next chapter. The 'referent' of a sign is the 'thing' in the real world to which it refers. An 'icon' is a sign that imitates its referent, while an 'index' is a sign that is caused by its referent.)

Much has been made, in writing about neorealism, of the significance of the selection of performers 'taken from the streets' (I am translating the Italian *presi dalla strada*), rather than from among professional film actors. This does not, however, change the referent in any way. The fact that Lamberto Maggiorani (Antonio in *Ladri di biciclette*) was a steelworker, or that all the performers in *La terra trema* were inhabitants of the real village of Aci Trezza, does not change the referent of their performances. That is to say, a performance is not more *about* reality simply because the performer is not a professional actor. However, it does narrow the distance between the icon and its referent and, since viewers were told about the performers in promotional material, a form of 'proximity' to the referent was used to suggest greater 'authenticity.'

The use of non-professional performers had been a feature of Soviet cinema in the 1920s, and of dramatized and staged 'documentaries' in the United States and the United Kingdom in the 1930s, and had occasionally entered Italian cinema in the 1930s and early 1940s. While the practice cannot be called a neorealist innovation, feature films of the movement from the production hiatus of 1945–9 made a more systematic use of actors 'taken from the streets' than was common anywhere else at the time. Even so, to take *Ladri di biciclette* as an example, only the three leading roles in a very large cast were performed by non-professionals (the matter is discussed at greater length in that film's chapter).

However, there is another way one could look at the question. Pudovkin's theoretical writings were translated and tirelessly promoted by Umberto Barbaro, a prominent critic, theorist, and teacher at the Centro Sperimentale di Cinematografia (the Italian state film school). These theories emphasized the physical characteristics and personal qualities of performers over their professionalism. The director should choose the right 'person' (rather than the right 'actor') for the part, exploit the free self-expression of that person, but subject it to tight directorial control for the expressive and representational purposes of the film. *Paisà, Francesco giullare di Dio, La terra trema, Ladri di biciclette,* and *Umberto D.* could be said to put these theories into practice (though not necessarily with Pudovkin as their source), leading to a number of implications.

First, choosing a 'visual' type rather than a professional actor emphasizes the visual, pictorial nature of cinematography over the theatrical element of dramaturgy. Second, choosing, from 'reality,' a 'person' to 'be' the part is a movement *away* from 'iconic' reference (imitation) towards 'indexical' reference, in which you put into your film *part* of the reality you want to represent (the same principle applies to location shooting): it is a bringing together (in a theoretically questionable way perhaps) of fiction with documentary (Visconti, in *La terra trema*, sometimes relied on his performers to tell *him* how they would behave and speak in given situations). Furthermore, the less the performer is 'professional,' the greater the directorial control over the performance, provided the right 'person' has been cast. For example, the director never finds himself in conflict with the career goals of the actor or actress, who has to depend on the director's instructions for a successful performance. De Sica is renowned for inspiring this trust in his performers.

The director's freedom and control also increased thanks to the low costs of using non-professional actors (of necessity, a significant proportion of *Roma città aperta*'s budget went to the fees of Anna Magnani and Aldo Fabrizi). Hence, the choice of performers enhanced directorial authorship over the conditioning commercial and industrial elements of the institution of cinema, emphasizing the artefact itself, rather than a 'process' of production for a market. At the same time, it *seemed* to be blurring the boundaries between fiction and reality (even though, in actual fact, it generally did not).

The 'content' of neorealist films, their narratives, involved a 'lowering' of the rhetorical register, as we shall see in the next chapter. One of the reasons why performers could be chosen 'from the streets' for their visual appearance rather than for their professional skills as actors was because neorealist narratives did not *need* theatrical, dramatic professional actors.

There was much hilarity when, at a famous public rally 'in defence of Italian cinema' held in the middle of Rome, the highly paid actress Anna Magnani beseeched the impoverished crowd to 'Help us!' The bond that ties the public to stars is precisely the fact that each actor constructs for himself or herself a *type* that is then merchandized as an inexhaustible series of *tokens* in his or her various roles (the *type* never changes, whatever happens to the *tokens* in the stories of the films, and is endlessly repeatable – Pina dies in *Roma città aperta*, but Anna Magnani lives to repeat her performance in subsequent films). This is the principle behind De Sica's refusal to accept the backing for *Ladri di biciclette* offered by the American producer David O. Selznick, which was conditional upon Cary Grant playing the part of Antonio; it also lay behind De Sica's insistence that Lamberto Maggiorani not act in another film after he had made *Ladri* (Maggiorani kept to the agreement until, later, he lost his job with the engineering firm for which he worked). The use of non-professionals ensured that the *type* chosen by the director was far less susceptible to reproducing *tokens*. The use of actors 'taken from the streets' is a *positive* movement *towards* 'proximity' and 'indexicality,' and a *negative* movement *away* from conventionality and artificiality; it is an important component of neorealism's dependence less on theoretical notions of 'realism' and more on pragmatic notions of 'authenticity.' However, even where performers were taken from the streets, their own voices were not necessarily used for the dialogue soundtrack, which was generally post-dubbed by professionals.

We need an anecdote, however, to reinsert all these idealistic notions into the reality of making fiction films. De Sica needed Enzo Staiola (the boy Bruno in *Ladri di biclette*) to cry, and was having trouble getting this out of the sunny Staiola. Prompted by the production secretary, De Sica surreptitiously put some cigarette butts into Staiola's jacket pocket, and then proceeded to 'discover' them, and scold Staiola for hoarding butts to smoke in secrecy, whereupon the little boy burst into tears. They were *real* tears, but not over the humiliation of his 'father.' The matter does not end here, because in the film *C'eravamo tanto amati* (Ettore Scola, 1974, a film dedicated to De Sica), the writers Age and Scarpelli have one of the protagonists, Nicola, compete in the TV quiz show *Lascia o raddoppia?* on the subject of De Sica's films. In reply to the question 'Name the actor who played Antonio's son in the film, and give the reason why he cries at the end,' Nicola answers: 'Enzo Staiola, and because De Sica put cigarette butts in his pocket.' Nicola loses all his winnings because the organizers of the quiz show say that the correct answer to the second part of the question is, 'Because his father has been caught stealing a bicycle.' Nicola is outraged, maintaining that their answer gives the reason why *Bruno* cries, not why *Staiola* cries. Age and Scarpelli are satirizing the mystifications of the media.

As Michelangelo Antonioni once said, reality is like an onion: peel off one layer and you reveal another beneath it. If you peel off the edifying anecdote I have just recounted, you uncover another layer where De Sica got Staiola to cry by shouting at him and smacking him.[8]

There are some generalizations that can be cautiously made about performers in the neorealist period (who, naturally, spent most of their time acting in non-neorealist films). A viewers' popularity poll in 1945 gave Fosco Giacchetti a massive lead over the competition. Amedeo Nazzari was, over the period, far and away the major male heroic lead, and, in the history of Italian cinema, nearly the last of the 'dramatic' male leads (both in adventure and melodrama). Neither Giacchetti nor Nazzari were widely used in neorealist films. Instead, Massimo Girotti (a personal friend from school days of De Santis) was the most important dramatic male lead taken over by neorealism from Fascist cinema, and it is not coincidental that he was characterized by a lack of self-confidence (he was mostly self-trained).

It has been asserted that the use of non-professionals and the neglect of stars held up the development of male star actors who could provide box-office pull (Raf Vallone and Rossano Brazzi were the only real successes). As a result, from the 1950s onwards male dramatic leads were recruited from Hollywood (these stars also increased the export potential of Italian films, and the crisis in Hollywood made them cheaply available). However, the issue of male leads cannot be separated from the thematic content of neorealist films: oppression, hardship, search, uncertainty, and vulnerability, in which the stereotype is the disempowered male. The negation of the hero offers no position for the viewer and his identification; instead, it offers 'knowledge.' It is honest, but not commercial, if we bear in mind the role that narrative plays in people's lives.

The innovations that neorealism brought to the recruitment of certain female performers (from beauty contests) were of benefit to the industry. This area too is closely related to the thematic content of neorealism. (I will overgeneralize here for brevity's sake.) Anna Magnani represents one end of the spectrum, while the 'natural woman' represents the other; somewhere in the middle is the prostitute. The weak male role resulting from neorealism's rejection of Fascism's rhetorical gender stereotypes leads to the strong female personified by Anna Magnani. Her performances did not prominently raise issues of sexuality, but rather ones connected with the 'organic' human community (for example, the family) of the 'melodramatic narrative matrix,' which will be discussed in the next chapter. The other two archetypes did indeed raise questions of sexuality (and the openness with which they did contributed significantly to neorealism's success in offering an alternative to bland Hollywood fare). The young 'natural woman,' the beauty queen, can be seen as having her roots in the cult of fertility, rurality, creativity, and the life force, expressed in terms of an exhuberant, carefree sexuality (Silvana Mangano, Gina Lollobrigida, Sophia Loren,

Lucia Bosé). In addition, this cult supplies part of the ideology carried by De Santis's films (as well as contributing to a populist ideology based on notions of 'natural' goodness). The prostitute, by contrast, is more closely related to the oppressed figure of the male, to which we have referred. Ever since Petrarch, Italy occupied by foreign powers has been portrayed as a fallen woman, perhaps because, for Italians, the only concrete social entity with ultimate ontological force is the family (with which not even 'the individual' can compete). Furthermore, prostitution is the nodal point at which economic survival and sexuality meet, and was a resource Italians were forced to exploit in the period of post-war scarcity. Not only was prostitution a recurring melodramatic theme in Italian cinema overall in the neorealist period, but it features prominently in Rossellini's portrayal of the post-war world (in the performances of Maria Michi in *Roma città aperta* and *Paisà* for a start), and is a theme in several other neorealist films. Indeed, the problematizing of the relationship between love, sex, and money may be the one theme that most unites quality films from *Ossessione* in 1942 to Antonioni's trilogy in the 1960s (though this might not be asserting very much, given that narrative in general is predominantly about sex, death, and money).

Locations and Sound

Neorealist films are often spoken of as having been filmed in 'real' external locations. The critic Lindsay Anderson (later a film director) wrote in his 1947 review of *Paisà*:

> The film was shot, we are told – and we need no persuading – in every case on the actual location of whatever events are represented; and in every case, whether it is a brothel-cum-night club in Rome, a tart's bedroom, a street of Florence under fire, a monastery, or a sandbank in the Northern marshes, we know that this is exactly what it is like, and that we are really there.[9]

He could not have been more wrong (see the chapter on *Paisà*). *Roma città aperta* uses some 'real' locations, but the film was mostly shot in a studio. *Ladri di biciclette* was mostly shot in the 'real' Roman locations of the story, but not always. *La terra trema*, which started out to be a documentary and uses 'real' locations, is something of a special case. Otherwise, for the neorealists, as for any filmmaker, the task was that of *disguising* the true nature of the 'location' in which they were shooting so that it would 'look like' the place where the events are supposed to have taken place. Nevertheless, the wartime devastation of studio facilities did, indeed, entice neorealist filmmakers out of the studio in the first few years.

Location shooting in sound film presented the same problems to the neorealists as it had to the British Documentary Movement of the 1930s, as one of the latter's cameramen, John Gray explains:

> Most films were now made in the studio: whilst the silent camera had begun to go outside the studio, the sound camera was pretty well confined to the studio. The sound camera was big and heavy, and had to be on a stand of some sort, and heavily blimped to avoid the microphones picking up camera noise. Synchronisation of picture camera and sound recording camera was through three-phase Selsyn motors. Huge cables joined one with the other, the sound camera operator calling 'up to speed' when the cameras locked ... The sound gear was in a three and a half ton truck, and the sound camera could not be more that 300 metres from the truck and linked by cable. There was relatively little synch shooting outside the studio. A close examination of films such as *Night Mail* and *North Sea* (1938) show[s] how dialogue shots were rarely photographed straight on, so that the sound track could be recorded and synced afterwards, often with a voice other than that of the apparent speaker. This is one of the reasons why there is so much commentary. For all these reasons, the documentary films of the time put an emphasis on realism rather than reality. If you could not shoot on the spot, you recreated it.[10]

La terra trema was, once again, a special case, with the performers being recorded in direct sound as they acted. To save money, *Roma città aperta* and *Ladri di biciclette* were filmed without any sound being recorded at all during the filming (not even a 'guide' track to aid in the later dubbing), the whole soundtrack being synthesized at the editing stage (for more on this topic, see chapter 3). *Paisà*, being an expensive production, used a mixture of direct and post-dubbed sound.

The conclusion this is all leading to is that neorealist films, from the point of view of the filming, were made in much the same way as any other film of the time, with choices often dictated by technical considerations and expediency. It is important not to succumb to myth-making about such procedures, and not to turn expedients into a manifesto. That said, the neorealists did make a virtue out of necessity. They did often film on location, while the decentralization and fragmentation of post-war production freed filmmakers from the prison of Roman studios, allowing them to travel all over the peninsula to shoot their films. This travelling coincided with a 'project' they shared with literary neorealism: to make known to urban Italians the material and social conditions of hitherto unknown areas of the country.

The Institution of Neorealism

This book is not *about* the critical reception of neorealism, but is, rather, a *contribution to* its critical reception. Nevertheless, an overview would be incomplete without any mention of the critical reception, and so I shall briefly outline the most important moments in the chronology of the developing 'institution of neorealism.' I shall try to keep neorealist films separate from their critical reception. Where I use terms like 'neorealism' and 'neorealist,' I am referring to films and their makers. Where I want to refer to neorealism as defined by its critical reception, I use the phrase 'the institution of neorealism.' A proper discussion of the critical reception of neorealism would require a book at least as long as this one, and fortunately such a book already exists: Giulia Fanara's *Pensare il neorealismo*.[11]

As the first neorealist films were released, the response to them was intimately bound up with the notion of a struggle of the Italian cinema industry to survive the onslaught of Hollywood imports. In the professional trade press there was a growing realization that the rebirth of the Italian cinema industry could take one of two routes. It could concentrate on popular genre cinema for the domestic audience, with the risk that no amount of success on the domestic market would generate the investment necessary for quality filmmaking capable of competing with Hollywood's resources and its international market. Alternatively, it could cultivate a 'quality' product capable of reaching a larger international market, and thereby justify consistent investment in the industry. Neorealism's success abroad was seen in the context of that second route.

In the regular press the films were at first appraised as any new film would be, but gradually an awareness grew that a body of films was being produced that challenged the 'entertainment' function of the cinema and constituted a serious contribution to cultural and political debate over the creation of the new democratic nation and over its recent history. Intellectuals on all sides started to take an intense interest in the cinema, and to assess Italian films for their political, moral, and cultural value. From that point onwards, there developed the 'institution of neorealism,' in which all Italian films started to be measured against neorealist films: a film was evaluated according to whether it posited a progressive cultural function for the cinema or was a regression into escapist entertainment. Since films *could* presuppose a serious and incisive social and cultural function for the cinema, they *should*. A battle arose in which neorealism, symbolizing a new Italy that had thrown off Fascism, faced the combined might of Hollywood and Italian industrial and commercial interests. Subsequently, with neorealism apparently under pressure from state measures, and the filmmakers being co-opted into mainstream commercial production, congresses were held   in Perugia in September 1949 and in Parma in December 1953, and de-bates were opened in newspapers such as *L'Unità*, to discuss whether neorealism was in 'crisis,' whether it could hope to continue to flourish, or whether capitalist consumerism and the Cold War were extinguishing it. Ideology played an important part in the battle for neorealism, for example between left-wing film clubs that showed and debated neorealist films and Catholic clubs that showed and debated the films of, for instance, Robert Bresson and Carl Dreyer.[12]

One of the flagships in the battle for neorealism was the journal *Cinema nuovo*, under the directorship of the Communist critic Guido Aristarco, which gradually developed a Marxist historicizing theory according to which neorealism should evolve from chronicling everyday life to being a more substantial and literary representation of the great historical and ideological movements of contemporary history. In this light, Rossellini was seen as already regressing into Catholic mysticism and consolation with *Germania anno zero*, and De Sica's *Ladri di biciclette* was faulted for not inserting its proletarian protagonist into the processes of production, but instead projecting the petit-bourgeois image of the 'victim.' For Aristarco, Visconti's *Senso* (a historical film recounting the bourgeoisie's betrayal of the democratic thrust of the *Risorgimento*) pointed the way forward. At the 1954 Venice Film Festival the entire public and the festival's administration was divided between support for *Senso* or for Fellini's *La strada*, and the two sides came to blows.[13]

Meanwhile, from France came the authoritative voice of André Bazin, defending Rossellini and Fellini against Aristarco's criticisms. Since 1948, in the journal *Esprit*, Bazin had been championing Italian neorealist cinema (particularly the films of De Sica and Rossellini) as the major new aesthetic force in the cinema, informed by a genuinely realist technique and a phenomenological approach to 'reality.'[14]

In 1974 the organizers of the Pesaro Film Festival put together a huge retrospective of neorealist films, held debates and round tables, and published a series of volumes re-examining neorealist cinema from a critical and theoretical perspective, accurately identifying its place in the cinema industry of its time, and attempting to assess what its political and cultural achievement had been, whether it could really be called a 'school,' and whether it could be said to have had a definable poetics.[15]

Fifteen years later Alberto Farassino assembled a counter-retrospective to that of Pesaro at the 1989 Turin Film Festival. The films he collected were all from the period 1945–9, many of them having neorealist traces or elements in them, without being by any means 'neorealist' films through and through. Farassino wanted to get away from the critical-aesthetic-theoretical approach to the phenomenon, and to see it in purely historical terms, not as an ideal movement struggling to stay alive and pure for a long period, but rather as a movement limited in time but with a broad reach (the metaphor he used was of a 'swamp' contaminating all Italian cinema in those five years).[16]

The collection of critical, historical, and theoretical essays that emerged in 1975 from the 1974 Pesaro meeting on neorealism received its third edition in 1999. The volume's editor, Lino Micciché, one of the most authoritative scholars of neorealism, added a new preface in which he asked, in exasperation:

> But at the end of it all, is it really possible that, half a century after the end of the phenomenon, we cannot aspire to having not just a survey of diverse and programmatically partial opinions on authors, films and problems, but (at least *also*) a compact, unifying monograph that, leaving to one side the analysis of single epiphenomena (works, authors, episodes), can analyse and historically reconstruct the overall phenomenon, which was certainly complex, but just as certainly unified even in its compound richness?'[17]

This book is not that 'compact monograph.' I am much too interested in the 'epiphenomena' – in this particular case, three actual films. To give the reader an idea of the extent of neorealism and the period it spans, however, I provide in appendix 15 a list of the fifty-five films most people would regard as neorealist, plus one, *Il Cristo proibito*, that was earnestly intended to be neorealist by its maker, Curzio Malaparte, but whose place on the list many would challenge.

We critics and historians risk little in our stance of detached observation, and so the last word in this overview shall go to De Sica who, when asked why the public prefers genre-vehicles to any other kind of film, and what this might mean, said:

> To ask me a question like that means poking a finger in a tender area of my activity as a director. And I don't think the recent success in America of my most cherished creation, *Umberto D.*, fully makes up for the indifference – almost hostility – with which it was received at the time by some critics and hence by the public. Perhaps that is why I am not the best person to reply calmly and objectively to your questions. And I hasten to point out that I am not just referring to statistics – the difference between the box-office receipts of *Umberto D.* and those of the films you mention – but also to particular episodes that reveal perhaps more clearly than the figures a certain tendency: from the Member of Parliament [he was actually the minister with responsibility for the Italian cinema] who, on seeing me for the first time, recognizes me as Sergeant Carotenuto [the protagonist of a very successful comedy film *Pane, amore e fantasia*], to Dreyer [Carl Dreyer, the film director] himself who, meeting me this summer at Edinburgh, congratulates me on *Pane, amore e fantasia*. Far, far more than the statistics, such testimony can disappoint us. And, from disappointment, to resignation, to surrender, the step is but a small one.[18]

2 Realism

If the theft of a bicycle in the real historical world is an event, and a film in which a bicycle is stolen is not the theft of a bicycle, then a film is a different 'thing' from the theft of a bicycle. This chapter sets itself the task of asking what kind of 'thing' a film is, and what might be an appropriate way of investigating it. It puts together a series of notional tools with which to investigate three Italian neorealist films – as aesthetic artefacts that are commonly qualified as 'realist.' This limits our interest to certain kinds of film: fictional narrative films of ap-proximately ninety minutes' length, made to be shown to a ticket-paying public. The chapter assembles the tools from scratch, posing, one by one, a series of questions. What is a film, what determines that a 'thing' belongs in the category of the aesthetic, and what kind of aesthetic arte-fact is a film? How does a film make reference to the real world, and what notions of 'reality' govern what a neorealist filmmaker makes ref-erence to? What do we understand by the notion of 'narrative,' what is the referent of a narrative, and are there features that characterize neo-realist narratives? How do rhetorical notions help us to characterize features of an Italian neorealist film? This chapter conducts an argu-ment in defence of taking a particular approach – an aesthetic one – to three neorealist films: *Roma città aperta*, *Paisà*, and *Ladri di biciclette*. The argument, however, does not assert that this is the *only* approach that could shed light on the films.

Aesthetics

We use the word 'realism' in a large number of different ways. We use it to refer to the belief that politics is the deployment of power rather than the search for just principles, and that each group can only hope to achieve what it has the power to obtain. In everyday life, it can refer to something akin to the philosophical position of the Pragmatists: if it works, it is true enough for me. In philosophy, realism is distinct from nominalism, from idealism, and from conventionalism, and refers to the proposition that, however difficult it may be to know truly what is 'out there,' it is there: there is a reality outside my consciousness that is not determined by or dependent upon my consciousness. Where a work of art is concerned, it can refer to the willingness of the artist to let his work be in some way determined by things existing outside the realm of art. In all cases, an appeal is made to the notion of a 'reality,' which is seen as conditioning what we believe, what we desire, or what we can achieve; it is outside our mind, and we are in some way subject to it. In our experience of life we are protagonists faced by something outside ourselves that functions as an antagonist in our drama. If our desires are not the measure of the world, it is because this antagonist forces us to measure ourselves against it.

That last sentence, in order to articulate a notion of 'reality,' uses a dramatic narrative of protagonists and antagonists, and uses rhetoric. That is what neorealist films do. Films tell stories, just as I have done. They can be realist by making the characters, the settings, and the events of the story recognizable to the viewers as having features in common with what they experience outside the cinema. Films can also be realist by articulating notions or asserting things about the world that the viewers believe to be true. The representation can be realist, and/or the discourse can be realist.

Films are real, though it is not easy or straightforward to say what a film is. What the viewer purchases, at any rate, is a viewing of the film (seeing a sequence of shadows and hearing some electronically reproduced sounds).

Let us imagine a Martian looking at Michelangelo's *Mosé* (a large marble statue of Moses) and exclaiming, 'What an extraordinary piece of hillside!' We would have to correct the Martian's assumption. He is assuming that the marble bears a record of geological and climatological forces, and so he is reading the rock as a record of the work of nature. We should want to explain that the shape of this piece of marble preserves a record not of the work of nature but of Michelangelo Buonarroti's hand, and of what we might call his 'intention.' As Michelangelo himself says in one of his sonnets, the work (which the marble now 'records') was one of 'removal' by means of a chisel of the work of nature, to 'reveal' an idea projected into the rock by the sculptor.

A marble statue (as opposed to a piece of hillside) involves the work of chiselling – of *removal* – by the sculptor. In the case of the film, we could best describe the work of the artist as one of selection and *assembly*. Let us make an enormous leap, and consider the work of the beachcomber whose 'statues' are assembled out of *objets trouvés* ('found objects'), driftwood shaped by the sea, the sun, and the wind. From an aesthetic point of view, we might find ourselves initially characterizing the work of photography as that of the assembly of *objets trouvés*. The photographer, like the beachcomber, *finds* things in the world around him, things that were *already there*, and so not created or imagined by him. He *assembles* them in front of the lens of his camera. His photograph is a record of his *assembly* of *found* objects. We only have to add the element of movement (of the objects and of the camera) to arrive at cinematography, where assembly takes place first at the level of the profilmic (what is to be filmed), and second at the level of the filmed record itself (montage). That is to say, first the filmmaker finds and assembles his objects before the lens of the camera, which he scans with his camera, and then he assembles the 'shots' he has filmed into a meaningful sequence. In the long-standing discussion over the relative merits of *mise en scène* and *montage* in the cinema, the former emphasizes the moment of assembly in front of the lens (Jean Renoir's films provide excellent examples), while the latter emphasizes the assembly of the shots once photographed (Sergei Einsenstein's films are frequently indicated as examples). Often, however, it is no more than a matter of emphasis. What we find ourselves working towards is an aesthetic perspective on the ontology of film: the *intention-to-assemble* of the artist that underlies the artefact. Any form or meaning the artefact has is the product of the assembly of 'found' components. These components themselves, in their turn, may be the product of 'intentions' – as, for example, in the performances of the actors, or in the constructions of the set designers. Multiple levels of *finding* and multiple levels of *assembly* are all held together by a network of *intentions*.

The ontology of Michelangelo's *Mosé* is that of a carved block of marble bearing the signs of the sculptor's intention. The ontology of the feature film is not so much an eight-thousand foot strip of celluloid as an assembly of sounds and images for an audience that is the vehicle and product of the filmmakers' intentions. If 'the film' is not the reel of celluloid (one of many copies) but an assembly of images and sounds, what *exactly* is the entity we are referring to when we talk about 'the film'? The American philosopher Charles Sanders Peirce, writing about logic, comes to our aid with the notions of *type* and *token*:

A common mode of estimating the amount of matter in a MS. or printed book is to count the number of words. There will ordinarily be about twenty *the's* on a page, and of course they count as twenty words. In another sense of the word 'word,' however, there is but one word 'the' in the English language; and it is impossible that this word should lie visibly on a page or be heard in any voice, for the reason that it is not a Single thing or Single event. It does not exist; it only determines things that do exist. Such a definitely significant Form, I propose to term a *Type*. A Single event which happens once and whose identity is limited to that one happening or a Single object or thing which is in some single place at any one instant of time, such event or thing being significant only as occurring just when and where it does, such as this or that word on a single line of a single page of a single copy of a book, I will venture to call a *Token*.[1]

We could say that 'the film' is a type, and a *showing* of the film is a token of the type. The notion entails that each token transmit all and only its *necessary* properties to the type. For example, the colours and shapes seen by the viewer, and the sounds heard by him, are *necessary* properties that the token transmits to the type. No matter whether we view the film on a cinema screen, a television set, or a laptop computer screen, we are still viewing 'the film': we are still consuming, so to speak, a token of the type. That is to say, while we cannot put our finger on a physical object that is the film, and must be content with the generic entity of a type, we can be sure that the properties of 'the film' are carried by each and every token. As Richard Wolheim explains, 'The Union Jack is coloured and rectangular, properties which all its tokens have necessarily: but even if all its tokens happened to be made of linen, this would not mean that the Union Jack itself was made of linen.'[2]

This account of the entity of 'the film' is nowhere near as easy to deal with as the one we can apply to Michelangelo's *Mosé* (which is a specific block of carved marble currently standing in the Church of S. Pietro in Vincoli in Rome), but it is probably the best we can come up with. The film itself is a real entity in the world, while realism is a notion we apply to the content of the viewing. There needs to be a transmission from sender to receiver for there to be a judgment about the presence or not of realism. The *fact* of transmission is simply real; it is *what* is transmitted that can be more or less, or not at all, realist.

In this book I refer to neorealist films as aesthetic artefacts, and I need at this point to clarify the implications of referring to them in this way. Most discussion of aesthetics has by now come to agree that to call something an aesthetic artefact is *by definition* the same as calling it a work of art. In everyday speech, to call something 'a work of art' is often to express a positive judgment about the value of that thing. Instead, we need to try to hold as two separate but interrelated questions the following:

(a) under what category an object is claimed to have value,
(b) how much value is claimed for it, and on what criteria.

If we take, as an example of an object to be assessed, a solid gold screwdriver, we might find the following:

(a) In what category does the object belong?
　(i) a tool for tightening and loosening screws
　(ii) a certain quantity of a rare and precious metal
　(iii) an object that, in the combination of, and conflict between, (i) and (ii), raises questions under (b).
(b) How much value is claimed for it?
　(i) a tool is valued for its fitness for a task, and a screwdriver made of soft metal is poorly fitted for the task of tightening and loosening screws – so its value is nil;
　(ii) a complex web of market considerations and conventional codification (according to which gold is 'good') means that its value is determined by its weight, and is high;
　(iii) the irony of the object being 'configured' as a tool but bereft of value in that category, and yet having high value in another category, draws attention to the object for its own sake, raising the question of its categorization under (a) (iii).

The questions (a) and (b) are separate, and yet each points to the other, ultimately drawing attention to the *nature* of the object itself. I am not insisting that this screwdriver is a work of art, but rather using the problems we face in categorizing it as illustrations.

A work of art – an aesthetic artefact – belongs in a category of objects that draw attention to themselves for their own sake by eluding any other categorization for the purpose of evaluation. A work of art belongs in the category of 'the aesthetic' because it does not firmly belong in any other category. To categorize an object as an aesthetic artefact is to remove it from other categories.

Just because we have categorized the object as an aesthetic artefact does not prevent us from then judging it to have little value, or even none whatever. To categorize the object as to be evaluated for its own sake *seems* to be attributing value to it, but in fact all it does is make the object a *candidate* for evaluation for its own sake, rather than on the basis of its fitness for some purpose or other.

The twentieth-century avant-garde played with this state of affairs. Many an artefact advanced its candidacy to membership of the category of 'a work of art' either by patently not belonging in any other category, or – very often – by having been stripped of its former categorization (which had been assigned on the basis of some purpose it served) and, as a result, having been left to be categorized as an aesthetic object for its own sake. Our solid gold screwdriver moves in such a direction. Taking a pile of bricks from a builder's yard and assembling it in the Tate Gallery is another such operation. Let us take this last example. The removal from one institution (the builder's yard) to another institution (the Tate Gallery) is a work of categorization: it is an invitation to consider the artefact as an aesthetic artefact, as belonging in the category of 'work of art.' Categorization is a matter of negotiation. A passing builder, shy of a few bricks to complete the garden wall that he is currently erecting, might eye covetously the pile of bricks in the Tate Gallery. A negotiated categorization is the product of an agreement, and agreements are subject to change and renegotiation over time.

Twentieth-century artists amassed a huge warehouse of debris in the category of aesthetic artefacts, often for the purpose of pointing out, or of asserting, *the fact that* 'the aesthetic' is just a negotiated category, a way of attending to an object.

A feature film belongs in the category of the aesthetic, and in no other, because of the disinterestedness with which we view it. Its place in the category of the aesthetic is a property of what we do with a film, or expect from it, rather than being inscribed in the object itself.

How does the discussion up to this point help us in our investigation of 'realist' aesthetic artefacts in general, of films, and of neorealist Italian films in particular? They draw our attention to three things we shall have to examine further:

1 A realist artefact can be the site of a negotiation over categorization. It can be categorized as having a task to perform (representation, or participating in a political endeavour, for example), and as therefore needing to be evaluated on the basis of its fitness for that task. It can be removed from all categories, leaving only that of the aesthetic in

which to find a home, and so needing to be evaluated for its own sake as an aesthetic artefact.

2 Since the *nature* of the object is an all-important question, the first requirement of criticism of an aesthetic artefact is to give an objective description of the artefact.

3 The characteristic of films as aesthetic artefacts is that they are the product of a process of assembly guided by intentions. The critic's objective description needs to account for the putting together of the assembly. That account will generate hypotheses about the intentions of the assembler.

It is not *because* a neorealist film is realist that it is in the category of the aesthetic. Once it has been admitted to the category of the aesthetic, we have to examine the artefact 'for itself,' as a thing in the world, *as well as*, rather than *solely*, on the basis of how well it carries out its task of 'representing' contemporary historical reality, or of 'expressing' certain political and ethical aspirations. This does not mean that it is not entirely right and proper to evaluate neorealist films for the accuracy of their representation of contemporary historical reality, or that it is not right and proper to interpret what the films are expressing and evaluate the ethical and political goals to which they aspire. The point towards which I am heading is that those things can be *separated* from objectively 'describing' the *assembly* that is at the heart of the film's aesthetic identity. Neorealist films have been extensively interpreted and evaluated, and their value as 'documents' has been extensively affirmed. The task of *this* book is to focus attention on the question of their identity as aesthetic artefacts.

Lest the argument about aesthetics up to this point seem arbitrary and eccentric, it might be well to put it in the context of a tradition of aesthetic theorizing. The argument advanced so far has affinities with Kant's explanation of the judgment that something is beautiful, in which he defines the judgment *negatively*. The pleasure in 'the beautiful,' he argues in *Critique of Judgment*, is a disinterested and free satisfaction; for no interest, either of sense or reason, here forces our assent. The judgment comes not from an object's gratifying our senses (satisfying an appetite), nor from its serving a desired purpose (being useful), nor from its meeting a moral requirement (promoting 'the good'), nor even from any vested interest we may have in the continuance of the object's existence – all of which would *constrain* our judgment. Instead, it is a *free* contemplation of the object. I have simply transferred the property of 'disinterestedness' from Kant's 'the beautiful' to my *category* of 'the aesthetic.' Membership of the category of the aesthetic is an *invitation* to value the object 'disinterestedly,' for its own sake.

The argument I have advanced up to now furnishes us with a *method* for criticizing aesthetic artefacts. Nowhere would I suggest that neorealist films themselves are 'disinterested' (because their makers may well have hoped to further political and ethical 'interests' through their films – there can be little doubt about this in the case of Zavattini, Visconti, De Santis, and Germi). Instead, I suggest that the *description of the artefacts* be as 'disinterested' as possible, and that interpretation and evaluation come *after* description. While acknowledging that the two questions are interdependent, I propose trying to keep separate what neorealist films 'are' from what they 'mean.' These might seem innocuous proposals, but so many factors surrounding Italian neorealist cinema and the culture of film study today threaten this endeavour: the 'realism' of the films, their role in a post-war Italian cultural and political struggle, and the tendency for interpretation to colonize critical scholarship and be its prime goal.

On the one hand, films belong in the category of the aesthetic because they do not wholly belong anywhere else; on the other, realism in a work of art entails some 'reference' to what lies outside the aesthetic. The category of the aesthetic does not isolate an artefact from questions of value. *Within* the category of the aesthetic are three (at least) criteria on the basis of which an artefact is evaluated: form, expression, and reference or representation. A piece of music or an abstract painting might be evaluated primarily on the basis of formal criteria; a lyric poem on the basis of formal and expressive criteria; a narrative work on the basis of all three. Realist works are particularly exposed to evaluation on the basis of criteria surrounding 'reference': for example, truth, accuracy, objectivity, and the social function of the representation. Hence, realist films not only straddle the aesthetic and the non-aesthetic by bridging art and commerce, but also because their aesthetic value is bound up with their reference to the non-aesthetic world of 'reality.' To proceed further we need to take a closer look at the notion of reference.

Reference

Let us suppose an event takes place in the real world: a man called John walks from his kitchen to his living room, tripping up as he goes through the living-room door, banging his head very hard on the door frame, wincing, and crying out in pain. His wife, Jane, who was following behind him, sees all this and, as he trips, reaches out to steady him, and then, seeing his pain, comforts him. Jane experiences the reality of John's walking, tripping, and hurting himself. Because she is present, and because she cares about him, she takes responsibility for the events unfolding before her, and tries to intervene to prevent and then reduce his suffering.

Mary, their daughter, is in her bedroom on the top floor of the house, which is wired with a closed-circuit television system in such a way that Mary sees all these events on the monitor in her bedroom. She rushes downstairs to see if her father is all right, and whether there is anything she can do.

Four hours later Peter, their son, returns home and watches the video automatically recorded by the television system. He frowns and then laughs, and says to John, who is now fine, 'Poor Dad. It's a good thing my university fees aren't paid for out of your ballet-dancing earnings.'

Jane experiences the reality in the present, Peter sees a 'sign' of what has taken place in the past, and Mary is somewhere in-between, seeing a sort of 'sign' of what is taking place in the present. Jane tries to prevent the mishap, Mary tries to remedy it, and Peter can only comment on it. Jane participates in the event, Mary responds to a reference to it, Peter views a reference to it.

That night, before going to bed, Jane writes in her diary: 'John banged his head on the living-room door,' and the next morning, John writes to his insurance company to make a claim on his medical insurance for the loss of an afternoon's wages, including in the documentation a floor-plan of his house, with a red line tracing his movement from the kitchen to the living room, and an 'X' at the doorway to the living room.

In the afternoon, David, a friend of Peter's, is in the house, and asks Peter how that dent got in the living room door-frame. Peter says, 'Dad was practising some ballet steps; I'll show you,' and enacts his father pirouetting on the threshold and banging his head. David laughs, and says, 'Do that again, while I take a photograph,' and snaps Peter's imitation of his father's accident.

The American philosopher Charles Sanders Peirce distinguished between three logical categories of 'sign,' on the basis of the way in which they are linked to their referent (the thing in the real world to which the signs refer).[3]

In the case of a *symbol*, what links the sign to its referent is a rule, or agreement. Jane's note in her diary is a collection of purely conventional symbols, which 'refer' to a real event that she personally experienced. A visitor from Mars who came across her diary, however, would not see the link between the symbols and the real event unless he knew the conventions of the English language. The agreement that we subscribe to is what forms the link.

In the case of an *icon*, what links the sign to its referent is a characteristic of the sign itself; something about the sign ties it to its referent. When Peter re-enacts his father's accident, his performance is an icon. The diagram of the accident that John sends to his insurance company is an icon, because the lines of ink on the paper correspond formally with the disposition of the spaces and walls in the house, and with the trajectory of John from one room to another.

In the case of an *index*, what links the sign to its referent is a logical or causal connection between the two; indeed, an indexical sign can be a part of the real event itself left over to indicate where the rest of the event was. The dent in the living-room door frame is an index of John's bumping his head against it: it is *part* of the impact of a hard skull against soft pine. The images on the television monitor in Mary's bedroom are an index, because they are caused by the electronic translation and transmission of the light waves reflecting off John and his environment. The video recording of his father's mishap that Peter watches is an index. The photograph that David takes of Peter's enactment of the accident is an index of Peter's iconic performance.

While the video recording of John's accident has a similar status to that of a documentary film, if we take David's photograph of Peter's performance, we have the signs of a feature film. The projected 35-mm image is indexical. It is an index, however, of the iconic performance of actors.

What is the referent of David's photograph? It records Peter's performance; but Peter's performance was not so much an icon of John's mishap as of Peter's explanatory demonstration of how his father came to hit his head on the frame. In this case, the ultimate referent has more to do with Peter's Oedipal feelings towards his father (feminizing and mocking his father in sexual competition with him, and even delighting, in a certain sense, in the bang on the head his father received) than with the accident itself; the representation is *expressive*. The referent of the photograph is, in fact, a *narrative* at a deeper level of generality than the accident itself.

Just as we can assert that a film (the transmission) is real, while the issue of 'realism' is raised by its content (what is transmitted), the same is true of a narrative. A narrative is a real object in the world. Therefore, there is yet another level of signification to be unravelled before we get (if ever we do) to the ultimate referent of a feature film. The fact that the medium of film is indexical has not brought us any closer to the ultimate referent than if we had been discussing a sequence of symbolic signs, such as those found in a novel.

It would be foolish, however, to claim that there is no difference between a film and a novel. The difference is that we are easily seduced into responding to a film as though we were Jane or Mary during John's mishap, rather than viewers of David's photograph. Indexical signs 'make reference' because of a link between cause (the referent) and effect (the sign). We distinguish between our direct experience of the referent (Jane's experience of John, in her presence, banging his head) and of its indexical sign (Peter's viewing of the video recording), because we think of signs as *referring* to their referents in the *absence* of the referent. By 'absence,' we do not mean that it never existed, but rather that it was not directly and sensorially experienced by us. The problem raised by film and sound recording is that while the referent is indeed absent, we nevertheless *appear* to have direct, sensorial experience of it. That is to say, rather than 'pointing us towards' the referent (as might the *symbols* of a novel), the cinematic sign appears to deliver to us the sensory stimuli generated by the referent itself (despite the fact that in feature films the stimuli were in fact generated by *icons* – signs referring to a referent in its *absence*). In the theatre, we directly experience the *icons*. However, whereas in the theatre we know of what stuff the iconic signs are made (flesh, in the case of the actors, papier mâché, in the case of the scenery), in the cinema the indexical signs themselves have very little physical consistency, and bear a resemblance to fantasies, dreams, and hallucinations, which we (perhaps inaccurately) think of as existing on the 'screen' of our minds.

If we were to imagine two critics confronting David's photograph (of Peter enacting John's accident), we could hypothesize two very different lines of thinking that each might follow. One critic might put a high value on realist representation in aesthetic artefacts, and feel that it is his duty to shine his critical light on the most valuable aspects of the photograph to bring out the best in it. Consequently, he might praise the way the photographer has chosen to represent a humble, entirely believable, domestic incident, and how he draws our attention and

sympathy to the little sufferings of life by underplaying the tragedy of the incident, and softening it with wry humour. The other critic might place a high value on expression in aesthetic artefacts, and see his duty as interpreting what I referred to as the 'explanation' of the accident communicated by the photograph in terms of Peter's feelings towards his father. Each critic has a different aesthetic hierarchy. Faced with the same artefact, each *seeks* a different referent for the sign and, hardly surprisingly, each *finds* a different referent.

The French film critic André Bazin argues that an important characteristic of cinematography is what I have referred to as its *indexicality* (though he does not use Peirce's terminology). Film has the special aesthetic value of bringing us into close contact with 'reality.' De Sica does not need to use narrative devices in *Ladri di biciclette*, Bazin maintains, because the 'facts' themselves carry all the power and meaning that you could want:

> [T]he film never reduces events and people to an economic or political Manicheism. It avoids cheating with reality, not just by endowing the sequence of events with a chance and almost anecdotal chronology, but also by preserving the phenomenological integrity of each of those events. *If the little boy, in the middle of the chase, needs to pee, he pees.* If a downpour forces father and son to shelter in a doorway, we, like them, have to forego the quest, and wait for the storm to pass. Events are not essentially signs of something, of a truth about which we need to be convinced; they preserve all their weight, all their particularity, all their ambiguity as facts.[4]

He is referring, in the italicized sentence, to a scene in the pursuit of the old man who has been seen talking with the thief, where the camera shoots Bruno in the foreground stopped against a wall and opening his fly to take a pee. Antonio appears from a side street in the background and shouts to Bruno, who starts in surprise, stops what he is doing, and runs after his father. (The audience invariably laughs at this point.)

Let Bazin stand for the first critic in the example concerning David's photograph. His aesthetic preferences lead him to *seek* a 'representational' referent in the scene of Bruno's 'peeing.' He not only *finds* it (the film *lists* the chance happenings in life – 'It avoids cheating with reality, not just by endowing the sequence of events with a chance and almost anecdotal chronology ...'), but he openly *polemicizes* with any alternative ('cheating with reality'; 'Events are not essentially signs of something, of a truth about which we need to be convinced ...'). Bazin sees the sequence as listing representations of things that were just there by chance.

The other critic's aesthetic preferences lead him to seek a narrative referent for the scene. Bruno does not pee. He certainly *wants* to, but his father prevents him from doing so. The referent of the sequence is not just a list of what happened to be 'there,' but Antonio's response to the theft of his bicycle: an anxiety and an obsession with retrieving *that* one, rendering him insensitive to the needs of his son, who shows unfailing devotion towards him. The listed 'facts' of the story are not the ultimate referent of the film; they form a narrative that has as its referent another narrative: the response of a particular man to a certain level of stress – and thence perhaps to another narrative concerning the nature of the human condition: solitude and vulnerability. We are gradually forced to give the notion of 'referent' a broader sense than in normal discussions of representation.

Not only does Bazin, the 'realist' critic, come to a halt at a certain stage in the process of 'making reference,' he justifies his stopping point by misreading what is in the story (whether or not Bruno actually does pee), and is thus able to conclude that the events of the story are not 'signs' of any further level of 'referent.'

In the early 1950s Guido Aristarco, in the journal *Cinema nuovo*, wrote that Visconti's *Senso* was 'realism,' because it produced a correct discourse about history, whereas *Ladri di biciclette* was *cronaca* ('chronicle'), because it merely represented everyday reality. This is understandable when one bears in mind that the philosophical tradition in which Aristarco belonged held that the course of history was more 'real' than mere sense phenomena. André Bazin protested, because his philosophical tradition, phenomenology, prioritized the direct experience of reality.

The hypothesis towards which we find ourselves being forced is that the referent of a narrative is another narrative. When I discussed the two critics disagreeing over the interpretation of Peter's photograph of David's iconic performance of his father's accident, I had the second critic conclude that the photograph recounted another narrative of Peter competing sexually with his father and transforming events into diminishments of his rival. Aristarco is privileging in *Senso* the narrative of Italian history that he thinks underlies the surface story of the film. Bazin moves in the direction of suggesting that *Ladri di biciclette* refers directly to reality, and does not have another, underlying narrative to which it refers. In dismissing *Ladri di biciclette* as *cronaca*,

Aristarco is partly agreeing with him. If our hypothesis is correct, both are mistaken.

If the referent of a narrative is another narrative, each narrative stands in a hierarchical relationship with the narratives *that are* its referents ('beneath' it) and with the narratives *of which it is* a referent ('above' it). Identifying the discourse, the 'thinking,' of a narrative is a matter of isolating one particular level and extracting from the system *that* level, hypothesizing it as being *the* level at which the *function* of the narrative communication becomes apparent. Wherever you want to find a stopping point, you can find one, as I have tried to demonstrate with Bazin.

This puts me in a difficult position, because in the name of what can I posit an alternative stopping point – other than what I myself am seeking and, lo and behold, finding? It is not a question I can answer in an entirely satisfactory manner. And yet I want to question, in a theoretical way, the assumptions often fuelling 'realist' approaches to neorealist films, according to which they use the special characteristics of their audio-visual media (photography and sound recording) to 'list' (that is to say, to 'represent') what happens to be 'there' in historical reality. These assumptions lead critics to see the artefact (the film) as assembling indexical traces of that historical reality, and inviting interpretations of the artist's discourse concerning that historical reality. The assumptions draw attention away from the artefact, and focus it either on history itself or on a discourse about that history. While it is not only legitimate but valuable and enlightening for critics to do this, I need to supply a systematic and reasoned basis for treating neorealist films (whose 'realism' I do not deny) as aesthetic artefacts that are valid independently of the accuracy of their representations of history, or of the appeal and pertinence of the discourses they articulate about it. I propose to do this by drawing attention to the referents of their 'narratives' rather than to the referents of their 'representations.'

Narrative

We need, first of all, to distinguish between representation and narrative. Since the narratives of artefacts are usually composed of representations, it will be enough to show that representation is not *sufficient* to constitute narrative. I am composing this chapter on a computer, and so I shall use my computer to suggest analogies.

Is the following a narrative?

> Chris pressed the 'control' key and the 's' key on the keyboard. He pressed
> the 'control' key and the 'p' key on the keyboard. He pressed the 'return'
> key on the keyboard.

It is a list of actions or events, represented by what Peirce would term
symbolic signs. It is not a *complete* list of the actions and events taking
place in that chronological period in that place. It omits the fly that settled on the keyboard and flew away as Chris's hand approached. It
omits the twitching of Chris's left big toe against the leather of his shoe.
It is a *selective* list, but one that does not allude to any *principle of selection*
from among all the possible things that might have been represented: it
does not offer any clues as to why those actions and events were listed
rather than others (unless, of course, the context provides strong clues).
Is a 'list' of represented events a narrative? What is necessary for a
sequence of represented events to become a narrative is a link between
the events – a perceivable allusion to the principle of selection. A list is
not a narrative, unless it somehow alludes to the principle of selection.
A narrative usually offers as a principle of selection, either explicitly or
implicitly, a sequence of cause and effect to link together the actions
and events:

> Pressing the 'control' key rang a bell in his butler's pantry, and the 's' key
> symbolically instructed the butler to write down in shorthand (s) every-
> thing that appeared on a monitor in his pantry. Pressing the 'control' key
> rang the bell again, and the 'p' key instructed the butler then to transcribe
> his shorthand on a typewriter, and bring it up on paper (p) to Chris's study
> (return).

The links are not factually correct. A nineteenth-century time traveller
to today might be fooled by them, because they conform to his expectations. A narrative does not have to be correct – 'true' – to be a narrative;
it just has to link the events. Indeed, a narrative can never be fully correct, because it is always a hypothesized 'explanation.' It is usually the
best link between events that we can come up with in the circumstances.

There can be huge variations in the level of explicitness with which
the principle of selection is made available to the 'recipient' of a narrative. If we took some shopping lists as an example, we could illustrate
this:

(a) toothpaste, apples, washing-up liquid, lemons, torch batteries, sausages, toothpicks, yoghourt, peanut butter [the list offers no principle of selection]
(b) frozen shrimp, avocado, mayonnaise, ketchup, sirloin steak, potatoes, lettuce, spring onions, ice cream, coffee [the list could be 'received' as carrying an implicit allusion to a 'narrative' of a three-course dinner]
(c) frozen shrimp, avocado, mayonnaise, arsenic, ketchup, sirloin steak, potatoes, lettuce, spring onions, ice cream, coffee [the list could be 'received' as carrying an implicit allusion to a 'narrative' of an Agatha Christie–style murder]

In both (b) and (c), the implicit allusion to a principle of selection will only work for a 'recipient' who is capable of hypothesizing shrimp cocktail, then steak-chips-salad, then ice cream, then coffee as an institution and, in (c), who knows the conventions of Agatha Christie mystery stories. A 'recipient' for whom arsenic is only a decolourizer in the manufacture of glass or a preservative for hides (as opposed to a means for doing away with retired lieutenant colonels at country dinner parties) will have difficulty hypothesizing a 'narrative' for (c); if he recognizes the three-course dinner, he will find the arsenic disruptive, extraneous, unlinked, and so will deem it an element of 'unnarrated' *listing* (mere 'representation') in what otherwise carries an implicit narrative – just as Bazin saw Bruno's peeing as an item in a list. As we shall see later, this reflection will be useful to us in considering the narratives of neorealist films.

Narrative lies in a principle of selection that explains represented (or perceived) events (perceptions being, in their turn, the product of explanations of the behaviour of our mind/body). It does not just 'represent' actions or events, but rather links represented events together according to a principle of selection. The explanation carried by a narrative does not make a narrative *because* it is a correct one. Any explanation will do.

A 'scan' of the page we are reading at the moment would be recorded by a computer as an image file, as a representation consisting of a very long *list*. That is to say, the dark marks of printing ink would be represented by black pixels. The computer stores this as a list, as a representation: pixel in position x is dark, pixel in position y is light. There are no letters, or spaces, or lines or words. However, an optical character recognition (OCR) program will recognize configurations, so that a certain configuration of dark pixels will be 'explained' as an 's,' and so on. A text-processing program will recognize groups of letters and 'explain' them as lines, words, spaces, and punctuation. At each level of 'recognition' the data becomes compressed: from image file to text file. Then I take over and further compress it into sentences, paragraphs, 'ideas,' or 'propositions.' We move through a 'hierarchy,' from the representation of surface details to ever more generalized and rule-governed explanations. At each level in the hierarchy, the amount of storage space required diminishes rapidly and identification for retrieval becomes simpler.

The referent of one narrative is not straightforwardly 'reality,' but an explanation: another narrative. Or, better, we should say that reference moves in both directions: the narrative mediates between sensations provoked by 'reality' and more general 'explanations.' Experience itself is narrative: it is an *explanation* for the behaviour of our organism (of our mind/brain/body) as it receives and processes sense stimuli. No narrative, no experience: just lists, meaningless 'behaviour' of our organism unrelated to causes. In the real world, the 'list' of stimuli that our senses give us is so vast and our behaviour so rich and complex that we are forced into drastic (and no doubt false) organization and compression in order to possess a selective 'awareness,' which we call 'experience.' The classic view of cinema is that it reproduces, 're-presents,' the original vastness.

Neorealist films are reputed to downplay, to refuse even, narrative. We shall, further on, examine episodes of *Paisà*, and discover that they result from the 'whittling down' of the narratives supplied by the scriptwriters. It may seem that Rossellini is thereby discarding 'narrative' in favour of raw 'representation.' This is a common misapprehension concerning neorealist films, according to which their 'realism' comes from their simply 'listing' what exists in reality, what falls in front of the camera (Pasolini suggested something similar when he proposed that cinema 'reproduces reality'). This view takes a limited, and limiting, perspective on 'realism,' proposing that realist artefacts, rather than subordinating representations to narrative explanation, simply *reproduce* reality. That proposition tends to stand as part of the definition of 'realism' in cinema. My argument (and we are still only in the early stages of it) is that not only is this implausible, but it also falsifies the aesthetics of Italian neorealist cinema. The concentration on a surface level of reference in realist artefacts can lead to misapprehensions of what constitutes their 'realism,' and to implausible descriptions of the *assembly* that makes them the artefacts that they are.

A narrative articulates thought by a process of one narrative having another narrative as its 'referent.' The direction of reference is from detail (the 'image file') to the general (highly compressed understanding). To illustrate what I mean, I shall give a simple example; what concerns me is to illustrate a *hierarchy of reference* and its general direction, rather than to enter into debates about the *interpretation* of particular stories.

The story of the well-known Western film *Shane* (George Stevens, 1954) tells of a gunslinger who appears at a farm, defeats the violent ranchers who want to drive the farmers off the land, and leaves. While this narrative refers 'upwards,' towards the surface of historical reality (either, on a detailed level, to the Johnson County wars, for example, or, on a more general level, to the settling of the Midwestern plains), it also refers 'downwards' to other narratives. At an early level, we could find the following: «having brought peace to the settlement of the valley through his superior deployment of violence, the gunslinger now embodies a contradiction of the very progress he has enabled, and so he must leave the valley and move on». Jumping to a 'deeper' level of narrative reference, we could find: «the resources of chaos itself are used to transform the 'wilderness' into the 'garden' of civilized, productive work». Slightly 'below' that level of reference another one operates: «the hero emerges from chaos to enable society's passage from chaos to order, but does not become civilized himself, and returns to the chaos whence he came». This narrative could feasibly, in its turn, lead us further 'downwards' in a hierarchy of reference to another narrative: «man transforms nature without becoming transformed himself». This level of narrative reference might lead to a further step in the explanatory hierarchy, in which «the creator is independent of his creation – the creator is not created by his creation». I hasten to repeat that I am merely *illustrating* the hierarchical process of narrative reference, rather than asserting a particular interpretation of *Shane*. The movement 'downwards' through the hierarchy is towards cyclical repetition. Propositions are in the present tense, statements of what is the case. Narratives are implicitly in the past tense, because they 'complete' a segment of linear time. The more you follow the sequence of referents of a narrative from the surface level to 'deeper' levels, the more you find the narrative setting up cyclical repetitions in its attempt to articulate what is the case, whereas, at the surface level, a narrative displays *difference* resulting from change over time governed by a logic of cause and effect. The progression from the superficial to the deep entails a movement from the *particular* to the *general*.

My concern is with artists who are attempting to assemble aesthetic artefacts – in this case, films. In order to explain how the component parts of their assembled artefacts are put together, I am forced to acknowledge the way in which their narrative ('sense-making') activity takes the form of a layering, in a sort of hierarchy, of reference. I need to do this in order to counter the tendency of viewers and commentators to forget that we are looking at assembled artefacts, and to treat the films as though they were carrying out an activity of listing representations or reproductions of the real world. I need to do this because so much of what is entailed in the notion of 'realism' is incompatible with an aesthetic approach to works of art in the medium of film.

Reference can point upwards towards the surface, listing the specific, the concrete, and the particular. Reference to other narratives goes in a downward direction, towards a deeper, less particular, more general, and even universal level. The effect of these combined movements, is on the one hand, to illustrate how deeper levels of understanding about reality are confirmed on the surface level of fact and, on the other hand, to make surface, particular facts and experiences conform to a more general and universal cultural knowledge. The movement upwards is towards the unique and singular; the movement downwards is towards repetition and the general. The fusion of the two movements in a narrative artefact (a single object) reconciles arbitrary experience with theoretical knowledge, and makes possible thought about and memorization of experience. Narrative brings together the particular and the general in a meaningful hierarchy.

Genre

Along the trajectory from the superficial to the deep lies a stage at which narratives are commonly characterized by notions of *genre*. In the classical and Renaissance tradition of genre theory, genres are identified on the basis of formal and stylistic criteria, and with regard to certain characteristics of the structure and content of the narrative and the social class of the protagonists. Typically, literary and theatrical works would be categorized as belonging to epic, tragedy, comedy, and mixed or intermediate categories such as romance, tragi-comedy, and pastoral. Northrop Frye was just one among many scholars who have proposed adjustments to the classical scheme according to different criteria.[5] The genre categories widely used in the discussion of the cinema are not much use to us in this discussion, because they are a strange hybrid of elements of the classical notion, of rule-of-thumb generalizations about narrative stereotypes, of characterizations of the emotional response provoked in the viewer by the style and content of certain narratives, and of labels used by the cinema industry to give a market identity to commercial products. Nevertheless, one genre that has received a great deal of discussion and analysis is 'melodrama.' Not everybody would use the category in the way in which I am going to use it, but the analyses of critics like Thomas Elsaesser and Geoffrey Nowell-Smith in the 1970s, and of other more recent scholars, all writing about the application of the category of 'melodrama' to Hollywood films, are entirely compatible with the rather radical 'mythical' sense in which I want to use the category.[6]

The more a narrative prioritizes the surface level, the more we tend to call it 'realist.' The more it prioritizes the deeper levels, the more we tend to call it 'generic.' Some types of non-fictional narrative aspire to having only one level of narrative reference, at the specific, particular surface level. Whether they realize that aspiration – and whether that aspiration is realizable – is another matter. The strongest case could be made for a scientific narrative – say, a chemist's account of what is taking place at the molecular level when a piece of paper catches fire. A legal narrative (the testimony of a witness, for example, in a trial) aspires to assemble representations according to a principle of selection that has no 'deeper' level of narrative reference. Journalists' and historians' narratives aspire on occasion to offer the one, true, principle of selection linking a series of events. Some documentary films might be considered as aspiring to having only the one, surface level of narrative reference. These considerations are relevant for 'realist' fictional narratives, because of associations that are often made between them and the types of non-fictional single-level-reference narratives I have just mentioned. By appearing, on the surface level, not to be making the conventional reference to other, deeper narratives, neorealist stories appear to prioritize representation over genre. They are commonly described as refusing narrative and offering an alternative to genre cinema. The associations made between 'realist' narratives and non-fictional narratives can sometimes hang on an implausible assertion that they function on one single level of reference only.

Part of the traditional definition of neorealism emphasizes the surface level of representation. The films are described as making reference to contemporary social and political events, with historically determined characters, and as focusing on the material conditions of everyday survival. This would explain why the films are regarded as valuable historical documents in Italy. That they are so regarded is beyond question. What is open to question is the extent to which their aesthetic value derives from their 'upward' reference to surface details or from their rehearsal of the deeper-level narratives held by Italians in a historical moment.

The genre category that characterizes neorealist Italian cinema (and specifically the films analysed in the next three chapters) is 'melodrama.' I shall often refer to it as a narrative 'matrix.' To describe the narrative matrix of melodrama, I am going quite simply to contrast it with another matrix. For the purposes of clarity, I am going to treat them as two distinct genres, even though I know as well as anybody that human life and culture are not divided into distinct categories – everything is a matter of degree. In order to contrast them, I need first to make a sharp (for the purposes of clarity, once again) distinction between two alternative metaphysical hypotheses regarding the ontology of a human being: between entities that exist in their own right and entities that only exist by virtue of the existence of something else.

1. The individual has ontological primacy, and society *derives* its existence from the primacy of the individual.

2. Social organisms have ontological primacy, and the individual exists as a component of an *organism*.

I have cast this opposition in the terms of metaphysics, where a debate has raged throughout the centuries over the status of universals and particulars. What might seem a trivial example of nominalism, former British prime minister Margaret Thatcher's proposition 'There is no such thing as Society' alerts us to the underlying implications of the political theory of Liberalism, in which human beings are seen, ontologically, as individuals.

A sociologist might articulate the opposition between what I have called 'ontologies' in different terms. Ferdinand Tönnies distinguishes between *Gesellschaft* (associational society) and *Gemeinschaft* (communal society), and examines the implications of the two alternatives. The historian Paul Ginsborg, referring to the sociologist Edward Banfield's application of the theory of 'amoral familism' to Italian society, writes:

> Banfield's theses were heavily criticized, but the term familism lived on. It
> did so because in all probability it struck a resonant chord, not simply as a
> description of attitudes in the backward and primitive South, but also for
> Italy as a whole. Familism, it emerged, was not just rural and archaic, des-
> tined to disappear with American-style modernization, as Banfield envis-
> aged. It was also urban and modern.[7]

Here we find a historian raising the notion of an opposition between
one ontology (familism) associated with Italy and another (implied in
the word 'modernization') associated with America.

The second of the two ontologies outlined above, the 'organic' one,
gives us access to how 'value' is articulated in Italian neorealist films,
and how value is intimately bound up with a notion of 'reality.' Rossellini, Fellini, De Sica, and Zavattini are neither political ideologues
themselves nor are they conscious mouthpieces for the political ideologies of others. Most people would describe them (and they would most
probably describe themselves) as 'humanists.' But what is the ideology
of this kind of humanist in this time and place? I am suggesting that
their humanism derives from a metaphysics: an ontology of what a
human being is. Their 'morality' derives from a hierarchy of values in
which the highest value attaches to that which most realizes the ontological potential of the human being: the organic. And this is clearly
articulated by them when they describe their films in terms of the love
of one's neighbour (Rossellini), of overcoming man's sense of being a
'monad' (Fellini), of the struggle against solitude and isolation (De
Sica), and of *convivenza* ('participatory living') (Zavattini).

The two contrasting ontologies give rise to two different 'deep narratives':

1. The ontological individual furnishes the components of the hero-
adventure narrative matrix, essentially *linear* in structure, and closely
related to myths of *initiation*. The heroic individual, in some sense, *is*
Nature in its dialectic of violence and production: productive violence
and violent productivity. The individual contains within him the
'chaos' of nature (individual, and leading to death) and the order of
'character' (capable of transforming nature for the purpose of sustain-
ing and promoting life). The hero must dominate chaos (by using its
very own violence against it), and so make use of it, turning chaos

against itself. Hence, the cosmos is in the individual: each individual is the product of a struggle. The individual becomes aware of his ontological grounding as an individual through the *initiation* of struggle, and it is a positive discovery. Equal and interchangeable individuals can choose to pursue their interests by forming institutions with other individuals. Society is a *man-made* institution that is the *product* of individuals acting in their own interests.

2. The 'organic' ontology furnishes the components of the melodramatic narrative matrix, typical of Italy, essentially *cyclical* in structure and closely related to myths of *creation*. Rather than the cosmos being in the individual, the individual is a *component* of a cosmos. The state of 'belonging' to that cosmos, a state of oneness and well-being (I shall refer to it as an *idyll*), has been lost. Hence, there is a desire to return to that state, to return to the completion of an ontology denied and obstructed. The mistaken belief in the ontological primacy of the individual disrupts a natural organism (producing transgression, chaos, disorder, and the loss of the state of well-being). Individuals are not interchangeable but, like pieces of a jig-saw puzzle, 'fit' into the organism from which they derive their existence (for example, in familism). 'Progress,' as such, is not possible, because the jig-saw puzzle only fits together in the configuration originally designed for it, and man's quest is for *knowledge* of that configuration. The 'organism' of society (or the family) is the only thing that is real, but it is taken from us (by our own or others' transgressions), condemning us to individualism, solitude, insecurity, vulnerability, and, above all, *sterility*.

It is as though there were two 'stories' about the struggle of human existence:

1. The individual transforms nature in pursuit of his own survival and enhancement. Society is a man-made institution regulating the individual's transformation of nature, and the product of cooperation in the transformation of nature. The individual gives rise to institutions that give rise to progress – a *linear* 'story' narrates 'action' for 'change.' The hero-adventure matrix narrates *how man progresses*.

2. The individual is the *problem*: a curse, an ontological wound, resulting from *exclusion* from the organism, an exile. The organism (society or the family) is made by nature or by God: given, archaic, original – the only entity ontologically grounded. Social organisms are a *return* to nature; nature is somehow waiting for us to return to it, understand it, be reabsorbed into it. The organism (an idyll) has been 'lost' (perhaps as

the result of transgression, of which individualism is an example), giving rise to separateness (isolation and vulnerability), which is experienced as suffering – a *circular* 'story' narrates the acquisition of 'knowledge' of 'how things *are*.' The melodramatic matrix narrates *why man suffers.*

I am not conjecturing that narrators craft their artefacts in scrupulous obedience to their ontological consciences, but rather that they inhabit the incomplete and painful reality lying between the two opposed ontological fantasies of the 'hero' and the 'idyll.'

Behind the suffering represented in melodrama lies a lost idyll. The question then arises: what does a narrative do, once it has registered the suffering of loss? Mankind cannot return to the Garden of Eden (though it is true that just because something is impossible does not rule it out from narrative). To attempt to re-establish some surrogate or imitation of the idyll on earth would offer narrative exactly the same task that the hero-adventure genre sets itself. The difference between the matrices is that, whereas the adventure hero *transforms* chaos into the garden, the melodramatic protagonist *registers* the loss and must *discover* a garden in what appears to be chaos. His job is contemplative, not active. The narrative imitates his thought, rather than describing his actions. Antonio, in *Ladri di biciclette*, encounters a problem, and what does he do? He thinks. He (a) suffers, then (b) tries to get back to where he was before, with the same bicycle, and then, having exhausted all avenues, (c) is obliged to discover the garden in Bruno, who has been beside him all the time. This brings us right back to the observation of the Italian film director Luigi Comencini, quoted in chapter 1, who explained the unpopularity of neorealism with the public by suggesting that the public wants films that 'tell a story,' while neorealist films 'illustrate a situation' instead. Exactly.

Neorealist cinema was *not* the heroic narrative of a society that, through armed resistance, had achieved a victory over chaos. It was the far, far more profound thinking of a society that had to give up the infantile illusion of heroically vanquishing anything, and instead had to discover the garden in what it had been living with all along. Perhaps that is the nearest one can get to discursively characterizing the 'value' that lay for the neorealists in 'reality.' It most certainly told a story, but not one that everybody particularly wanted to hear, because it was a little too 'realist' for comfort. You might not applaud Giulio Andreotti, the government minister who begged De Sica to stop, but he was no fool.

Idealism

'Realism' is the notion that we apply to the representation of reality. This means that, in order to characterize a particular use of the term realism, we have to bear in mind two different spheres that are united in the notion of realism: 'representation' and 'reality.' We need to turn now for a moment to look a little further into the notion of reality before we come back once again to a discussion of its representation in the cinema. We have already touched on this question in connection with the melodramatic matrix and our discussion of the ontology of a human being. We began that discussion by relating the question to an issue in metaphysics concerning the status of universals and particulars. One way in which we could characterize what I call there the 'organic ontology' would be to say that it takes a metaphysical position on the question of reality that we could describe as 'idealist.' The sense I am giving to 'idealism' in this chapter is much closer to a Platonic one than to the sense in which a philosopher like Berkeley (*esse est percipi*) used the notion. Since I have referred to the cultural context in which neorealism developed as one strongly influenced by idealist philosophy, we need to take a slightly closer look at the implications of idealism. For the sake of clarity, once again, I am going to draw sharp distinctions between metaphysical positions, even though I am fully aware that in life things are not sharply distinguished one from another. I shall start by describing what I fully admit is something of a caricature of the metaphysical position of the hypothetical reader of this book in the first decade of the twenty-first century.

He (or she) is a materialist, and believes that the basic substance of the world is matter/energy, and that this is what is real. He is also, to a certain extent, a realist, and believes that objects exist outside and independently of his mind. Indeed, a particularly prevalent belief at the moment is that the mind itself can be explained in purely material terms as the behaviour of the brain. His notion of 'history' is strongly influenced by a Darwinian materialism, in which almost random, chance, changes, *competing* to be the most successful adaptations to material conditions, 'evolve' towards no knowable or discernible goal – merely the competition for resources. Behind this thinking lies also, to a certain extent, the political ideology of Liberalism, in which individual competition for private goods, regulated perhaps by a social contract, brings about the commonweal. A person with these (possibly caricatured in the extreme) assumptions brings to the reflection about realism in cinema and literature a baggage of presuppositions. In the narrative arts, those artists whose work offers the model for which he immediately reaches are the positivists and the Naturalists of the late nineteenth century, who depicted life as being determined by material forces (for example, biological heredity and economic and environmental factors), and who tended to represent as objectively as possible material conditions. Where neorealist cinema is concerned, critics point to the writing of Giovanni Verga (a late-nineteenth-century novelist influenced by the French naturalists) as the ultimate model for the realism of the neorealists. The fact that the group of young writers around the journal *Cinema* in the early 1940s proposed Verga as a model for the Italian cinema appears to confirm this hypothesis – even though 1930s Italian theorists calling for *realismo* in Italian cinema repeatedly insisted that by this they did not mean *naturalismo*.[8] Rather than offering a multitude of quotations from pre-war critics and theorists to illustrate the idealism that Italians considered inherent in the aesthetic notion of 'art' at the time, I offer the discomfort of one critic, Fabrizio Sarazani, with the torture scene in *Roma città aperta*, when the film was first shown:

> The fiction acquires an impact that has the flavour of historical chronicle; and not through crude description, since the plot, in this first part, takes flight towards an ideal realism, towards which, henceforth, all our films should aim ... Where we are not in agreement with Rossellini is in the second part, where a harsh realism exceeds the boundaries of the aesthetic. The reality reproduced in a waxworks museum is never art. This means that in wanting to transfer into the realm of art certain monstrous realities, Rossellini has fallen into a rhetoric appropriate to Grand Guignol, which neither serves nor obeys the pure and stable laws of poetic transfiguration – laws that exclude certain appearances and facts, unless they are diluted in the inspiration of an ideal synthesis.[9]

Sarazani brings together 'art' and reality by appealing to idealist notions. The 'fiction' acquires its 'impact' from 'historical chronicle.' This is not, however, achieved by a purely surface level of representation, 'crude description,' but by being raised to the level of 'an ideal realism,' 'an ideal synthesis.' A 'harsh realism' is incompatible with the aesthetic ('the realm of art'); 'art' requires the 'laws of poetic transfiguration.' Without the idealist appeal to deeper levels of narrative reference, crude representation becomes, according to Sarazani, rhetorical Grand Guignol (nowadays we might call it 'sensationalism'), devoid of the moral component crucial to 'art.' We shall later encounter De Sica saying something similar.

Italians in the early mid-twentieth century carried a very different baggage of presuppositions from my caricatured twenty-first-century Anglo-Saxon. The two most influential philosophers at the time were Benedetto Croce and Giovanni Gentile, both of whom were idealists and dominated the ordinary education of Italians in the same way that we might describe individualist, competitive free-market neocapitalist liberalism as dominating the education of an Anglo-Saxon today.

Idealists have many ways of accounting for what we apprehend with our senses and with our consciousness, but typically use the notion of 'phenomena' – the way things appear to us, or the way our senses and our mental apparatus present to our consciousness whatever it might be in the 'external' world (the world outside our consciousness) that stimulates our senses. Idealists are typically sceptical about what we can know with certainty about what actually might exist in that external, 'real' world, because any knowledge we can have about it is exclusively the product of the processes of our mental apparatus. One of the tasks of the philosopher is to use reasoning to determine what we can and cannot have true and certain knowledge of, and to explain to what extent, if at all, we can reach beyond our imperfect apprehension of phenomena to hypothesize what truly does exist in that 'real' external world.

If cinema, as an 'art,' is to go 'beyond' phenomena, it has to do so by means of the explanatory function of narrative – selecting and organizing representations in such a way as to communicate ideas about what might truly exist 'out there' in the 'real' world external to our consciousness. The job of the artist – in this case, the filmmaker – is seen as having some similarities with that of the philosopher, but through different means (idealist aesthetics might draw, for example, on notions such as 'intuition' and 'imagination' as opposed to 'logic'). It is in this line of thinking that most Italian theorizing in the inter-war and immediate post-war years described the essential duty of cinema (the supreme medium of representing phenomena) as to strive for *realismo*. Artefacts that strove to give expression to the ideal 'realities' beyond mere phenomena were 'art,' whereas those artefacts that merely furnished the viewer with pleasure and entertainment were described as *evasione*, or 'escapism,' and were seen as having the primarily commercial goal of making profits in a particular industry. To make money, the 'industry' simply produced repetitions of stereotyped mechanisms designed to provoke an emotional response (tears, laughter, fear, sus-

pense, erotic arousal), rather than 'knowledge.' It is in this line of thinking that we find a theorist like Luigi Chiarini describing the cinema as
straddling *arte* and *industria*, being pulled in one direction by aesthetic
considerations and in another by commercial ones. The notion of *arte*
was, in fact, an ideal notion itself, and was not at all the notion I have
recounted at the beginning of this chapter, in which the work of art is
defined negatively by its belonging to a separate category of objects recognized as removed from other categories. This means that *arte* was *by
definition* associated with *realismo* in the idealist sense of the notion,
because where there was not that association the artefact was merely
evasione. It was furthermore held that where an artefact did express
ideal 'reality,' the viewer would recognize himself or herself in the
'truth' of the artefact, and would value it more highly, with the result
that films that were 'realist' would speak more truly to the public's
need to understand the reality of their own existence. I suggest that it
was this idealist notion of *realismo* as a product of narrative that informed the films of De Sica and Rossellini we shall be examining (as
well as those of other neorealists such as De Santis), rather more than
current notions of accurate 'documentary' *representation* that are so
often deployed in criticism of the films nowadays. Where Zavattini is
concerned, it might at first glance appear that he advocated a realism
quite close to that of the Naturalists, with his emphasis on 'facts'; but
we shall find, on closer examination, that it is rather more complicated
than that.

   To turn now to the 'ideal' reality beyond phenomena that Italians in
the period under consideration strove to illuminate opens a can of
worms I can only deal with by means of drastically simplified sampling
– just as I have drastically simplified the world view of my hypothetical
twenty-first-century Anglo-Saxon reader. The justification for rushing
in where a wise philosopher would fear to tread is the need to suggest
a more nuanced picture of the 'realist' poetics of the neorealists than
is normally conveyed by concentrating on verisimilitude, historical and
factual accuracy, the use of non-professional performers and of external
locations, certain techniques of *mise en scène* and montage, and the
avoidance of generic narrative and rhetorical conventions (in the sense
that discarding cinematic conventions permits the photographed 'reality' naively to reveal itself).

   Because Plato's idealism is also justifiably called 'Platonic realism,' a
simplified version of it provides a useful analogy for our purposes,

even though I am not suggesting that neorealists are Platonists. In Platonic thinking, we perceive phenomena in the form of particulars, the separate, discrete objects we experience in the world around us. For Plato, however, these are merely the way in which the universals, the Forms that unite and determine those discrete phenomena, manifest themselves in our consciousness. The universals are real, while the phenomena are merely appearances. The philosopher, in identifying the universals, achieves the goal of talking about reality, rather than about inadequate or deceptive appearances.

Using this scheme as an analogy, we could say that an artist, faced with a single, ordinary man standing in front of him (a 'particular,' in other words), perceives a series of appearances that are the product of the way in which his mental apparatus, his training, and his personal interests at that particular moment process the data provided by his senses. However, the artist has at his disposal a whole tradition of thinking that supplies him with properties to be attributed to 'man' as a universal. An artist convinced of the ultimately 'organic' nature of the human being 'knows' that the notion of the individual is defective (a deceptive appearance promoted for economic and ideological ends). The self-reliant, competitive solitude that is the glory of the protagonist of the hero-adventure matrix is for this artist an escapist fantasy. He 'knows' that solitude is *by definition* a curse, an exile from the organism. The 'knowledge' of the universal 'man' possessed by the artist informs with 'value' (in this case) the phenomenon of the particular man standing in front of him. The job of the 'realist' artist, in this philosophical context, is to portray the universal contained in the particular. He has not represented the 'reality' of the man unless he has also incorporated in his representation the ontological, moral dimension.

Marxist socialism supplies what we might call, for our purposes, other 'universals' to be taken into account, such as 'labour' (the work of transformation of nature), 'value' (in the economic sense), 'capital' (the way in which men's labour is organized), and 'class.' The artist, faced with a man at a workbench, has the duty of representing those universals in his portrayal of the particular man. These universals are contained in the Italian word *operaio*, meaning working man and member of the proletariat, and someone whose true potential as a human being (another universal, perhaps) is suppressed by the capitalist system of extracting surplus value from his labour. The artist has not represented 'reality' unless he has portrayed the particular man as an instance of a universal. To show the man happily singing at his workbench could be criticized as being 'unrealist,' superficial, and consolatory, because it does not represent the alienation of his true being by the mode of production. Vittorio Spinazzola, writing from the communist perspective of the journal *Cinema nuovo* in a 're-examination of neorealism' in 1956, criticized De Sica for not being realist in *Ladri di biciclette*, because Antonio is not an instance of the universal '*operaio*,' but rather an instance of the petit-bourgeois universal of the 'victim,' of suffering humanity, and hence a sentimental product of false consciousness:

> It is evidently very significant that no protagonist of De Sica has ever been a factory worker or a peasant or at least a male figure profoundly inserted, in whatever manner, in a determinate mode of production. His characters are shoeshine boys, pensioners, the unemployed, tramps: that is to say, they are the victims of the petty bourgeoisie according to De Sica.[10]

In all this, I am necessarily simplifying, for brevity's sake, in order to make explicit an idealist component of neorealism's approach to 'reality.' The neorealists inherit a doctrine of art in which its duty is *realismo*, and this is articulated in terms of the duty to represent the moral, political, and spiritual form of human reality. People differ in the 'universals' they apply to ethics, politics, and 'the spirit.' The way in which a film director portrays photographed phenomena as instances of universals is by means of narrative. A single shot in a film is like a scientific record, reproducing sense data, and hence phenomena. *Assembling* shots into a narrative releases the filmmaker from his imprisonment in the realm of phenomena, and permits him to represent 'reality.' Narrative, therefore, is not an impediment to 'realism' in this tradition, but is the necessary means to its achievement. How individual filmmakers have achieved their goals is something that should emerge from the descriptions of the films in later chapters. Nevertheless, I can generalize briefly here by saying that Rossellini's way of going 'beyond' phenomena is to assemble for the viewer the ways in which one or more characters 'knows' the reality of another; whereas De Sica's way of going about it is often to assemble the *mise en scène* of his shots and sequences in such a way as to force the viewer to a narrative 'reading' of the implications of the sense data supplied. Generalizing still further, I could add that Fellini typically takes up Rossellini's way, while Antonioni typically takes up De Sica's.

For the twenty-first-century Anglo-Saxon, there exists, on the one hand, a scientific model of representation, the indexical recording of material reality, exemplified in the ideal of the documentary, and, on the other hand, the imaginative or ideological projection of a fictional world, exemplified by the feature film. Idealists had a clear idea of the connection between fiction and reality: fiction can bring into focus the universal concealed behind appearances. The twenty-first-century Anglo-Saxon has no such clear notion of the connection between fiction and reality. Currently, the best he or she can do is to talk in terms of 'ideology' (a version of reality that meets the needs and fits the presuppositions of a particular person or class of persons), and to see the realm of culture as a free market in ideologies. For the early-twentieth-century Italian, *cultura* (culture) meant the struggle of thinkers and artists to identify the real universals lying behind the deceptive appearance of their particular instances.

In an idealist context, the question of technique in cinematic artefacts was a contingent, subordinate question. Both a documentary film and a fiction feature film could achieve the same goal of realism.

Realism

In any contemporary investigation of 'realist' film, the question of whether or not a film (or part of a film) is 'documentary' matters, even though the definition of 'documentary' is a thorny and much-debated issue. In an important monograph on documentary films, Bill Nichols dismisses the question of a general definition:

Of greater importance than the ontological finality of a definition – how well it captures the 'thingness' of the documentary – is the purpose to which the definition is put and the facility with which it locates and addresses important questions, those that remain unsettled from the past and those posed by the present.

However, in describing the expectations the viewer brings to a documentary he offers a starting point for such an ontology:

The most fundamental difference between expectations prompted by narrative fiction and by documentary lies in the status of the text in relation to the historical world. This has two levels. Cues within the text and assumptions based on past experience prompt us to infer that the images we see (and many of the sounds we hear) had their origin in the historical world.

Technically, this means that the projected sequence of images, what occurred in front of the camera (the profilmic event), and the historical referent are taken to be congruent with one another. The image is the referent projected onto a screen. In documentary we often begin by assuming that the intermediary stage – that which occurred in front of the camera – remains identical to the actual event that we could have ourselves witnessed in the historical world.[11]

When Bill Nichols writes that 'one fundamental expectation of documentary is that its sounds and images bear an indexical relation to the historical world,' he is referring to Peirce's category of the *index*, in which a sign is produced by, or linked to, its referent either causally or logically. By returning to the origins of photography, Brian Winston alerts us to the significance of the indexicality of photography as a medium of representation:

On July 3, 1839, M. François Arago, the radical representative for the East Pyrénées, rose in the Chamber of Deputies to persuade the French government to purchase Daguerre's patents for the world. In his arguments, he stressed the scientific uses of the apparatus; for instance, to make accurate copies of hieroglyphics and, more generally, for physicists and meteorologists. In short, the camera was to join, as Arago listed them, 'the thermometer, barometer, hygrometer,' telescope, and microscope as nothing so much as the latest of scientific instruments ... In effect, he officially (as it were) confirmed for the public that seeing is believing, and that the photographic camera never lies; or rather: the camera lies no more than does the thermometer, the microscope, the hygrometer, and so on. All these devices produce analogues of nature. That the camera can be manipulated more easily than, say, the thermometer is less significant than the fact that both instruments produce a representation of reality. It is this process of representation that is shared, and reinforces Arago's original vision of the device as being of a piece with other scientific apparatuses.

Winston then outlines Bruno Latour's defence against the 'obstinate dissenter,' who refuses to believe a result reported in a scientific paper:

'What is behind a scientific text?' he asks. 'Inscriptions. How are those inscriptions obtained? By setting up instruments.' And what happens when we are confronted with an instrument? Latour says 'we are attend-

ing an 'audiovisual' spectacle. There is a visual set of inscriptions produced by the instrument and a verbal commentary uttered by the
scientist.' I would like to suggest we have reached a place not unlike that
occupied by the viewer of a documentary film.[12]

Since documentary films have almost never been like that, we might do
better to call such films 'scientific' films (the kind used to instruct
schoolchildren about the blooming of a flower or the true motion of a
bee's wing). There are two reasons why documentary *films* do not conform to this ideal of scientific 'inscription,' one of them practical and
historical and the other theoretical.

Until the 1960s, technological problems made truly indexical filmmaking extremely difficult in the era of sound. Cameras were bulky
and noisy, and sound-recording equipment was prohibitively cumbersome (see the paragraphs on 'sound' in chapter 1). A far more important and decisive consideration, where the discussion of neorealism is
concerned, is the theoretical one (and we shall find ourselves returning
to it when we touch upon Cesare Zavattini's theories about neorealism). As Brian Winston demonstrates, it is easy for *a single shot* of film to
be indexical, in the sense of being a 'scientific inscription.' But 'a shot' is
not 'a film.' A film is an *assembly* of shots. Theorists of 'realist' film have
always known this, and it explains André Bazin's preference for *mise en
scène* over montage. Some artists have hypothesized the 'infinite'
sequence shot (for example, Pasolini in *Empirismo eretico*),[13] and Andy
Warhol could be seen as moving in that direction in a film such as
Empire. Few have wanted to make films like that, and even fewer to
watch them. The ontology of a *film* as an artefact that is the product of
assembly contradicts the unmediated indexicality of the 'mechanical'
medium of cinematography.

By briefly summarizing other factors that *remove* documentary films
a greater or lesser distance from the 'scientific' use of photography (and
sound recording) as an 'instrument of inscription,' we can begin to
identify a notional context in which neorealist films can be placed. With
this context in mind, it is easier to free ourselves from inappropriate
assumptions about the contribution of 'documentary realism' to neorealist cinema, and this will free us to take a more 'aesthetic' approach to
the films as assembled artefacts. These factors include:

1 The nature of the 'reality' recorded (which I have discussed at some
   length in the 'Idealism' section): (a) material reality; (b) the reality of

the 'spirit,' seen in an idealist perspective (can you have a 'mechanical inscription' of a universal?)
2 The semiotic means of making 'reference' (discussed in the 'Reference' section): (a) strictly indexical 'recording'; (b) iconic reconstruction ('staging,' 'acting out'); (c) purely imaginative construction, expressionist theatrical production, animation
3 The levels of narrative reference (discussed in the 'Narrative' section): (a) one single level of narrative reference (the ideal of 'science'); (b) multiple levels of narrative reference (movement in the direction of 'myth')
4 Stylistic and rhetorical choices (to be discussed later in this chapter, under 'Rhetoric'): (a) a low style (for example, Antonioni's 1949 N.U.): 'reduction' and the rhetoric of the lowered voice, or *sermo humilis*; (b) a high style (Corrado D'Errico's 1938 celebration of the conquest of Abyssinia, *Il cammino degli eroi*): 'spectacle' and the rhetoric of the raised voice or of amplification.

The neorealists inherited a tradition in which 'realism,' in the sense of penetrating behind the particular to the universal, did not give a high priority to the distinction between documentary and fiction film. An enlightening illustration of this is Antonioni's 1939 reflection on the possibility of a film about the people who live along the river Po.[14] Antonioni asks a question: 'First of all a question arises: documentary or fiction film?' He ends his reflections thus:

> It is enough to say that we would like a film with the Po for protagonist, and in which it would not be folklore, that is to say an accumulation of external and decorative elements, which would arouse interest, but rather the spirit, that is to say a complex of moral and psychological elements; in which it was not commercial requirements which prevailed, but intelligence.

It would be hard to find a better articulation of the pre-war Italian notion of the 'realist' film, and of its function to penetrate through the 'external elements' to the 'spirit' of the people, seen in terms of psychology and morality. Whether it is to be a documentary or a fiction film is almost a secondary matter.

Antonioni shot the documentary film *Gente del Po* in 1943, but damage to the negative in processing meant that only ten minutes of footage were editable into a finished version released in 1947. Apparently, it was originally intended to be twenty to twenty-five minutes in length, though it should be pointed out that all Antonioni's other early documentaries – 1948–1949 – are roughly ten minutes long. Since the conception and realization of the project spanned the years 1939 to 1947, the film is regarded as an early example of 'neorealism' (Antonioni's first full-length feature film, *Cronaca di un amore*, was released in 1950). Since *Gente del Po* is not easy to get hold of, I shall describe it.

The credits open onto men loading sacks of produce onto barges. The commentary informs us that at a certain point in its course, the river Po becomes navigable. There are shots of barges sailing down the river. We are introduced to one family living on such a barge, but the family is rendered generic by the commentary's recounting that *one* has on the boat *one's* home, *one's* work, and *one's* personal relations – and also by introducing the family as 'a man, a woman, and a child.' From the boats, the perspective turns to the folk on the riverbank watching the boats go by, and working in the fields alongside the river. We see 'staged' shots of a man hurriedly getting out of bed to go and open a pontoon bridge in order to allow the barges to pass through. Then, in a long-scale shot, we see the barges turning against the current in order to tie up at the bank. We see 'the woman' (the mother) get into a dinghy to go ashore. There follow shots of the square of a small town, followed by shots of young women on the raised banks in the early evening, and the commentary draws our attention to the tiny figure of a youth pushing his bicycle over the brow of the bank, from which we cut to a 'staged' close-up of him greeting his girlfriend on the bank. We return to the interior of the barge, where the father is baling out the bilges, from which we move to watching the mother pour out a teaspoon of medicine and administer it to her daughter, who goes to sleep in a 'staged' close-up (she turns her head and closes her eyes). The commentary informs us that as the river reaches the marshes of the delta, it becomes shallow, and this accompanies shots of men in small boats rushing to protect the straw huts in the delta marshes threatened by a storm (we hear thunder), by the rising of the river, and by the encroachment of the sea. The film ends with shots of the freshwater of the river encountering the seawater of the Adriatic.

The film, therefore, portrays two segments of river: a navigable stretch, followed by the delta marshes. It is assembled from three 'components': a lyrical-picturesque component, a narrative component, and a 'discourse' (this division into 'components' is my critical one, not the film's).

The lyrical-picturesque component comprises exquisitely composed shots of the barges sailing down the river, of women working in the fields (in one case, shot through the foreground 'frame' of a hand honing the blade of an upturned scythe), of the young women walking away from the camera on the raised bank in the evening, of the barges turning against the current, of the town shot with a pan of a man entering the background on a bicycle and passing across the near foreground, of the rippling waters of the river meeting those of the Adriatic.

The narrative component comprises the men loading the barges, the family living on the barges (the child is only shown in bed), people on the riverbank looking up to watch the barges pass, the opening of the pontoon bridge, the mother getting into the dinghy to go ashore, the boy meeting his girlfriend, baling out the barge, putting the daughter to sleep, hurrying in small boats to protect the huts against the storm.

The 'discourse' is applied externally by the commentary, for the most part. Often the commentary 'tells' us things that are not obviously communicated by the images, and the things the commentary tells us in this way function as ideological 'additions' to the film. Twice the voice-over makes the same gratuitous judgment about the life of the Po-dwellers. The first time, the commentator says: 'It is a hard life, never changing,' with accompanying shots of people working in the fields, and nothing in the footage to suggest why this might be truer about these people's lives than about anyone else's. This comment is followed by a close-up shot of a young woman, with the voice-over speculating: 'Perhaps she is thinking about happiness.' The second time, the comment follows a scene in which the mother on the barge puts her daughter to bed: 'It is a never changing life, without hope' – without any suggestion in the images of what might be the 'hope' that is denied these people. Houses overlooking the river are referred to as 'melancholy,' and shots of a quiet town, with bells tolling on the soundtrack, are described thus: 'a Po town where life flowed slowly like the seasons, like the river – this is what the bells say.' In other words, the ideological judgments are expressed in a conventionally elegiac lyrical reflection. The literary and didactic character of the original project survives in the finished film.

We are, therefore, a long way from the essentially 'cinematic' expressiveness of the artefacts that we shall be examining as the 'core' films of the neorealist aesthetic. The documentary that Antonioni made in 1948 took great steps in this direction. *N.U.* (the letters stand for '*nettezza urbana*,' literally 'urban sanitation'), is also a ten-minute documentary, but this time recounting a day in the life of the street cleaners of Rome, and has only one occurrence of this literary didacticism, early in the film: the commentary tells us how, caught up in our own 'interests' and concerns, 'we' overlook these men, and others like them in the city, whom 'no one deigns to look at.' The comment is rendered redundant by a sequence later on showing a couple quarrelling, oblivious to the street cleaner standing beside them. After this brief commentary, there is no more voice-over in the film; everything is carried by the images and by the accompanying music. The poverty of the men is eloquently carried by shots of them returning to their poor homes, eating their meagre lunch in the mid-day break, and sifting through the garbage for toys to give to their children. A parallel with *Ladri di biciclette* arises when we see the sweepers finishing their working day in front of a wall covered in large film posters. The men's *exclusion* from the prosperous culture of the city that they keep clean is eloquently conveyed by the stylistic procedure of extreme long-scale shots of the city, with their small figures traversing the cityscape.

Clearly, in the period spanning these two documentaries of Antonioni, a new approach to the medium of cinema is being forged. Late in his life, the director Valerio Zurlini recalled:

> To those of us involved in making documentaries *N.U.* revealed a master. It had an extraordinary effect on us, like the great films of De Sica and Rossellini. We did not have the eyes for looking at the reality of the city: Antonioni was the one who made us see it. All of my documentaries, and not only mine, are indebted to *N.U.*[15]

A dozen years after making *N.U.*, Antonioni described the change that was taking place in himself:

> As far as the form of the documentary is concerned, and *N.U.* in particular, I needed to get away from certain structures that had been forming, even though they were very valid at the time. Even Paolucci – who was in those days one of the best-known documentary filmmakers – made his documentaries according to determined criteria, I would say in blocks of sequences, which had a beginning, an end, and an order to them. These blocks, put together, formed a parabola that gave the documentary a certain unity. They were formally impeccable documentaries; but I felt a certain irritation with this order, the need to break up a little the organization of the material in the course of the documentary. And so ... I tried to adopt a montage that was absolutely free, ... poetically free, seeking out particu-

lar expressive values not so much through a montage that gave solidity to the scenes by means of a beginning and an ending, but in flashes, in separate isolated shots, in scenes that had no link with one another but that simply gave a more mediated idea of what I wanted to express and of what was the substance of the documentary itself: in the case of *N.U.*, the life of the city street sweepers.[16]

Discarding the logical unity of literary narrative and accepting a fragmentary, pictorial approach to the medium offered Antonioni poetic and expressive freedom. In the 'Rhetoric' section of this chapter, and in subsequent analyses of films, we shall see how central this approach is to the poetics of neorealism.

Antonioni's short documentary *N.U.* gets closer than most artefacts to Cesare Zavattini's 'ideal' of a 'neorealist film,' and it is to Zavattini's theories that we shall now turn.

Cesare Zavattini

There does not exist in English a detailed discussion of Zavattini's theories, nor are there translations of many of his writings.[17] This already large book would sorely try the reader's patience if I undertook to remedy those lacks here. Instead, I can only briefly touch upon those aspects of his thinking that bear upon the argument and the analyses of this book: his realism and its relation with morality and idealism, and his attitude towards the aesthetics of cinema.

Zavattini's realism starts from a recognition of the indexicality of the cinematic medium, and is directed towards reducing the mediation that mainstream cinema interposes between reality and its capture on film. Neorealism is concerned with 'things rather than the concept of things,' whereas 'the need for a 'story' ... and ... the imagination, as it had been exercised, did no more than impose dead schemes on living social facts.' Audiences need to be given an awareness of everyday reality with the immediacy and impact that conventional cinema wrings from 'spectacle,' from actors, and from 'stories.' Zavattini's project for the *film lampo* (instant film) entailed rushing with a minimal crew to the scene of an everyday news event, using the actual people involved to perform their own roles in the event, and hurrying it onto the screen, just as a newspaper publishes its chronicle the morning after. To this he added the notion of *pedinare*: tailing someone like a detective, not determining what the character does in the normal way of the artist, but instead seeking to find out what is about to ensue (though I should say that he never explicitly draws this implication from the notion of 'tailing').

His goal is to give the viewer 'awareness' (*coscienza*) of the reality of his fellow man, by giving him direct 'knowledge' (*conoscenza*) of it through cinema. The justification of this approach is moral: 'According to me, the world continues to go badly because we do not know reality. And the most authentic position a man of today can take up is to commit himself to articulating, right to its very roots, the problem of the knowledge of reality.'[18] At the heart of his theorizing lies an ideal notion of 'man' ('man at the deeper level' or 'man without adjectives'). What cinema can foster through *conoscenza* and *coscienza* is *convivenza* ('living in fellowship').

So far we encounter in Zavattini a theorizing that fits into the conventional account of neorealism: the inherent 'realism' of the medium of cinema exploited for disseminating knowledge in the service of social justice, and in opposition to the escapist spectacle merchandized by the mainstream commercial cinema industry. This would justify placing Zavattini firmly in the sphere of the critic Lino Miccichè's by now proverbial judgment of neorealism as having 'more an 'ethics of the aesthetic' than a simple aesthetic.'[19] The richness and variety of Zavattini's ideas are beyond the scope of these brief notes; but the concerns of this chapter require us to confront their aesthetic implications. For example, Zavattini takes the phenomenological potential of the cinema beyond mere ethical knowledge into the realm of a kind of primal aesthetic perception:

> We seem to be on the brink of discovering the original plastic value of our image. This was cinema right from the first opening of a lens to the light of the world. Everything was equal before it then, everything worthy of being recorded on a photographic plate. It was the most uncontaminated and promising moment of the cinema. Reality, buried beneath myths, slowly blossomed. Cinema began its creation of the world; there is a tree, there is an old man, a house, a man who is eating, a man who is sleeping, a man who is weeping ... But we preferred stories, to avoid the implications which emerged from this deeper knowledge of reality.[20]

The connection this notion has with the historical avant-garde, from Bergsonian intuition, through Futurism ('discovering the original plastic value of our image') and surrealism, has been noted by critics like Giorgio De Vincenti and Giulia Fanara, and has led them to propose that

Zavattini's neorealism belongs in an aesthetic avant-garde.[21] Certainly, many of Zavattini's ideas lead in an experimental direction either reminiscent of Dziga Vertov or, in a different direction, later taken up by Jean Rouch's *cinéma vérité*, by Direct Cinema, and by the New York Underground cinema of Andy Warhol. The abolition of the separation between art and life is a characteristic feature of the doctrines of the historical avant-garde, and of their late-romantic aestheticising of the whole of life. But 'life,' for Zavattini, belongs in the category of the ethical and practical. Bringing together art and life therefore means *not* the Nietzschean aestheticizing of the ethical so characteristic of the historical avant-garde, but the 'moralizing' of the aesthetic that is entirely in line with the idealist aesthetics of *realismo* he inherited from the 1920s and 1930s in Italy (see the section on 'Idealism' earlier in this chapter). Even more significant, however, and confirming Micciché's judgment, are Zavattini's repeated assertions that the aesthetic must be subordinated to the ethical ('Knowledge is not, however, enough. Artists must look at reality through *convivenza / living in fellowship*'):[22]

> We know that it is only with conscious awareness that great things can be done, yet one can get a film wrong. It is a problem people are aware of, and the Italians have tried to solve it by bringing closer together the two terms of life and spectacle so that the first devours the second. That has been their aim. And if someone says that this has always been the aim of art, the reply is that the effort to see things as they are is experienced by the Italians to a degree that approaches cruelty, and that this both goes beyond the realm of art and is more important than art.[23]

> What I mean is that there is a position, an attitude towards life, that is not just limited to the realm of the so-called artistic, but that transforms the realm of the artistic in such a way as to make it suited to present-day historical needs, inasmuch as one lives in a certain way, indeed, lives in fellowship.[24]

In his thinking lies a notion we encounter so often in realist theorizing, and one shared by the neorealists: that 'reduction' brings you closer to the 'real.' The smaller the 'facts,' the more 'everyday' they are, the humbler the protagonists, the fewer the events and the more they are preserved in their 'fullest duration,' the simpler the apparatus used for recording them, the quicker they are reproduced ..., the closer you are to 'reality.' We shall return to the implications of 'reduction' in the

'Rhetoric' section below, but in this context it is important to note how this line of thinking implies an opposition between cinema and reality at the very same time that it celebrates cinema's closeness to reality. The nature of the medium itself, and an ethically responsible use of it, are seen as being in opposition to its institutions and aesthetics. Just as André Bazin will congratulate De Sica on 'the disappearance of the mise en scène' in *Ladri di biciclette*, so Zavattini will explain his theorizing to a student in 1970 by saying 'it is with the refusal of cinema that we can make cinema':

> That is to say, the idea of the cinema ... being a way of carrying out an action that goes beyond cinema, and uses cinema as an instrument ... So a non-acceptance of the history of cinema, but ultimately a take-over of cinema, as a historical element, without the qualification of the history of cinema. We were no longer interested in the history of cinema, we didn't know how that history should be. We knew, or we thought we knew, how history should be. So it is clear that cinema was being burned up inside that history and was acquiring a value and a meaning very different from the one that it later, gradually, despite everything, ended up acquiring ... Well then, it is with the refusal of cinema that we can make cinema ... That is why I always say: camera, and not cinema, because the camera is more of a *tabula rasa*.[25]

For Zavattini, the solution to aesthetic problems in cinema are to be found in content:

> The content of neorealism almost automatically, objectively, entails forms that are always different from previous ones. If this content is strongly felt, it is bound to offer expressive solutions. To my mind one can talk of a poetics of neorealism in any movement which has a content that is as innovative and strong as that which neorealism had when it began to be talked about ... But what can distinguish us from certain linguistic experiments which are talked about today? Syntactical, stylistic, morphological novelty is a requirement common to all those spirits whom I would call 'civilised' and who have a 'morality of content.' However, if alongside this need for formal development we did not place our own particular development of content, our boundaries, our own perspective, then we would find ourselves numbered among all those who generically wish for *the development of cinema*. Whereas what we should be wishing for is *the development of a certain cinema, in a certain direction*.[26]

Zavattini's neorealism is *un certo cinema / a certain cinema*, in which the problem of style is solved by *content*, which is in turn determined by reality. Not only shall we find Zavattini's collaborator, Vittorio De Sica, meaning something very different indeed when he declares that neorealism is *un certo cinema / a certain cinema*, but the other, by now almost canonical, explanation of neorealism by the novelist Italo Calvino exactly reverses Zavattini's formulation of the problem:

> [T]hose who nowadays think of 'neorealism' primarily in terms of a contamination and co-option of literature by extra-literary concerns are putting the cart before the horse. In reality, the extra-literary elements faced us starkly and undeniably like a fact of nature; our problem seemed a matter of poetics: how to transform into a work of literature that world which, for us, was *the* world.[27]

Rhetoric

Only the close analysis of the films themselves can tell us about matters of style. Nevertheless, some general preliminary considerations, using some of the notions and terms of classical rhetoric, can help us articulate the issues at stake. It is important to note at the outset that our concern is less with cinema in general than with Italian neorealist cinema, and specifically with the three films we shall be investigating.

We have defined a film as an assembly guided by intentions. Rhetoric concerns itself with intentions. But while rhetoric strives to understand intentions directed primarily towards *communication* (the relation of the artefact to its addressee), our aesthetic priority leads us to look at intentions as they condition the fashioning of an *artefact* (the nature of the artefact for its own sake).

Aristotle distinguished three types of evidence that could be used in an address to sway the listeners: *logos* (the content and quality of the argument or thought being submitted for their acceptance), *ethos* (the character of the speaker), and *pathos* (the appeal to their emotions). These can be seen as the three cultural *functions* normally attributed to cinema: representation, ideology, and entertainment.

Logos can be associated with *truth value*. For 'realism' in general, and for Zavattini in particular, as we have seen, this is to be guaranteed by 'reality,' which is in turn partly guaranteed by the indexical characteristics of the cinema as a scientific instrument of inscription. Zavattini wants 'facts' to have the rhetorical impact of 'facts.' However much attention I might draw to the aesthetic properties of the films, we have to remember that an effective 'realist' film draws a great deal of its rhetorical impact from the fact that the viewer believes he is attending to representations of what really happened (or could happen) to real people, and it is in this area that Zavattini is most likely to talk about neorealist films, maintaining that conventional commercial cinema deploys the resources of *ethos* and *pathos* through its use of film stars and production values ('spectacle'), while remaining almost indifferent to *logos*. Neorealist cinema often eschews stars and contributes to the transfer of *ethos* to the 'authorial' director, which inevitably draws attention to the nature of the artefact itself, and hence to its aesthetic properties; hence also to expression and form, which leads in turn to style (*elocutio*). 'Realist' artefacts *by definition* deploy the truth value of *logos* – but the success or otherwise with which they fulfil that function is not obviously a measure of their *aesthetic* value. The notion of 'ideology' fuses together *ethos* and *logos*, by treating what an artist considers to be 'real' or 'true' as a function of his ethical, political, and economic orientation – and ideological criticism, fusing *ethos* and *logos*, has been a characteristic feature of the 'institution of neorealism,' evaluating neorealist films on the basis of the 'correctness,' rather than of the accuracy, of their representations.

Our aesthetic perspective must not blind us to the extent to which certain aspects of *logos* and *ethos* might have a greater rhetorical impact on the viewer the closer he or she is in time to the historical referents of the film. Zavattini's 'facts' may lose some of their impact with the passing of time. Earlier in this chapter, we drew attention to the role of *narrative* in the communication of the 'truth' about existence. Half a century after the German occupation and post-war unemployment, a present-day critic is inclined to attribute a higher priority to 'narrative' and to aesthetic considerations than did contemporary critics who were still living with the 'facts,' or than would a historian, for example. The 'nature' of the artefact itself can, therefore, appear to change over time and in accordance with the priority given to *logos* and *ethos* in its address to the viewer, which would throw doubt on the validity of a specifically aesthetic approach to the artefact. Calvino's protest – that the essence of the artefact lies in its 'poetics' – is echoed by De Sica's demand that *Ladri di biciclette* be seen as the transposition of reality onto the poetical plane rather than as *cronaca* (as we shall see when we examine the film). Rarely are the artists themselves in any doubt over the matter, *pace* Zavattini.

Pathos can be associated with *gratification*, in the context of mainstream commercial cinema. Neorealist cinema is in an ambiguous relation with *pathos*. A filmmaker such as De Santis exploits its 'persuasive' resources to win viewers over to his *logos* and *ethos* with stars and with conventional generic plots in *Riso amaro*. At the other extreme of the scale, De Sica and Zavattini disdain it in *Umberto D.*, with predictable results at the box office. It is generally agreed that *Roma città aperta* does exploit *pathos*. Whether *Ladri di biciclette* does so or not has always been a hotly debated question. *Pathos* may be the rhetorical area in which neorealism lost the battle to transform the function of cinema into one dedicated to 'knowledge.'

The five 'offices' of rhetoric (*officia oratoris*, or *partes retorices*) are *inventio, dispositio, elocutio, memoria*, and *pronuntiatio* (or *actio*), of which only the first three need concern us.

Inventio (in oratory, the discovery of the arguments) relates to the 'content' of neorealist films, and theoretically could be associated with *finding* objects, people, situations, and events in the 'real' world, and recording them in photographic and sound-recording form. The choice of found or imagined objects, people, situations, and events partly determines whether a film is 'realist' or not, and whether or not it lays claim to *logos*, or truth value. In actual fact, imagined, fictional events acquire their 'factual' credentials by possessing attributes like 'everyday,' unexceptional, and typical. Earlier, I drew attention to a notion we encounter so often in realist theorizing: that 'reduction' brings you closer to the 'real.' The smaller the facts, the more everyday they are, the humbler the protagonists, the fewer the events, the simpler the apparatus used for recording them, the quicker they are reproduced ..., the closer you are to 'reality.' To this extent, the close association in neorealism between *inventio* and *logos* is very much a matter of rhetoric, and is closely related to a question of 'style' (*elocutio*) that we could call 'reduction' (or 'lowering'), as we shall see.

Roma città aperta was the product of a careful assembly of found stories taken from historical 'fact.' *Paisà* was formed out of two processes of *inventio*: in the first, scriptwriters presented imagined stories, and this was followed by a process of erasure of the original material and its replacement by an *inventio* based on the *discovery* of the film's 'reduced' content during its shooting. *Ladri di biciclette* is based on the Zavattinian notion of *analisi*, in which fictional events were 'reduced' to the factual (the 'everyday') by being subjected to much closer inspection than would have been the case in any other medium.

Dispositio (in an oration, the disposition of its parts) can be associated with *assembly*: first, the assembly of the found or imagined items in front of the lens of the camera (*mise en scène*) or the microphone, and subsequently the assembly of the recordings in the editing of the shots and mixing of the sounds. The categories of rhetoric were devised to account for persuasive oratory, not for aesthetic artefacts with no duty to communicate or persuade. Nonetheless, a series of ideas has to be 'formed' into an oration, which therefore becomes an 'object' in the world, and *dispositio* is what gives it form, what makes an oration an 'object' in the world, an artefact. Similarly, *assembly* is what constitutes the identity of a film. Aesthetic artefacts become 'aesthetic' by being considered as objects for their own sake (rather than as having a task to perform), and this can be as true of an oration as of a film. Hence, the aesthetic is particularly bound up with *dispositio*.

Indeed, a constant theoretical stance of certain core Italian neorealist filmmakers was to protest against what they felt were pressures on them to make films *as though* they were verbal communicative utterances. They affirmed their right to reject the 'logic' of what they called nineteenth-century narrative, and to assemble their artefacts rather more as a cubist painter assembles his plastic entity on the canvas. This implies a claim that the *assembly* of sounds and images is one of the essential properties of a film as an aesthetic artefact.

It is enough to give examples of four filmmakers expressing their discomfort with conventional narrative 'logic' and their preference for the assembly of fragments.

Rossellini:

> I hate the obligations which the story places upon me. The logical thread of the story is my enemy. Passages of reportage are necessary to arrive at the fact; but I am naturally inclined to leave them out, not to bother with them. And this is – I admit it – one of my limitations: the incompleteness of my language. Frankly, I would like to shoot just episodes, like those you have mentioned. When I feel that the shot which I am setting up is only important for the logical thread of the story, and not for what I really want to say, that is where I find myself impotent: and I no longer know what to do. When, on the other hand, it is an important scene, essential, then everything becomes easy and simple ... I have made films in episodes because I find myself at ease with them; because in that way I have been able to avoid those sequences that, as I said, are useful for a continuous narrative, but that, precisely because of their quality of being useful epi-

sodes, and not crucial ones, I find – Lord knows why – supremely unpalatable.[28]

Zavattini:

[W]hile in the past the cinema made one fact grow out of another, then
another, then yet another, and every scene was created and conceived to be
immediately abandoned (a natural result of the mistrust in 'facts' I have
been talking about), nowadays, once a scene has been conceived, we feel
the need to 'stay' with the scene because we know that it has in it the
potential for enormous resonance, and for meeting all our expressive
needs.[29]

Antonioni:

What I have found most tiresome is what is commonly called the grammar
of the cinema, a certain way of shooting, a certain way of organizing sequences in reverse angle shots, pre-established camera movements, etc.;
this conventional technique, a technique thanks to which, incidentally,
many fine films have been made, no longer corresponds today to what
must be the vitality of a film. A film must be more fluid, that is, it must be
tied to particular contingencies.

...

I tried to adopt a montage that was absolutely free, ... poetically free, seeking out particular expressive values not so much through a montage that
gave solidity to the scenes by means of a beginning and an ending, but in
flashes, in separate isolated shots, in scenes that had no link with one
another but that simply gave a more mediated idea of what I wanted to
express ...

...

I have eliminated many technical preoccupations and superstructures. I
have eliminated all the potential logical threads of the story, the transitions
from sequence to sequence in which one sequence acted as a trampoline
for the next. I have done this because it seemed to me, and I am convinced
of this, that today the cinema must be tied to the truth rather than to logic.

...

Nowadays stories are what they are, possibly without a beginning or an
end, without key scenes, without a dramatic curve, without catharsis.
They can be made from shreds, fragments, unbalanced, like the life we
lead.

...

I have always been concerned to try, through a particular figurative commitment, to give a greater power of suggestion to the image, so that an image composed in a particular way might help me to say what I wanted to say with a certain shot, might help the characters themselves to express what they have to express, and might help establish a rapport between the character and the background, that which lies behind the character.[30]

Fellini:

Let us invent episodes, and let us not worry for the time being about logic and the story. Or let us attempt a Picassian decomposition. The cinema has been narrative in the nineteenth-century sense: now let us try something different.[31]

All four artists express impatience with the requirement to develop logical connections between scenes. Attention to conventional narrative logic is seen as an obstacle to the 'essentially' cinematic, or to the expression of a vision. The discovery that films could be put together out of fragments, rather as a modern painting can be constructed as a collage, was the encounter with the nature of cinema as an art of *assembly* – a film did not have to ape the nineteenth-century novel, with its smoothly articulated overall narrative coherence. Film was a medium that operated differently from prose narrative. The neorealists, not always fully conscious of what they were doing and why, were freeing cinema of its ties to an aesthetic that oppressed and constricted it. In other words, the neorealist aesthetic that we find articulated by these artists (in all cases, expressed in terms not of a programme, but of an impatience and irritation with the aesthetic expectations they feel are put upon them) concerns the nature of film as an aesthetic medium of expression (*dispositio*), rather than as some template for the accurate representation of reality. Not only Rossellini, Antonioni, and Fellini, but even Zavattini appears to be at one with Calvino in vindicating the role of 'poetics.' Not surprisingly, the filmmakers themselves are drawn to analogies with painting: the painter Bill, in Antonioni's *Blowup*, only making sense of his work when he has finished it and can stand back from it, Fellini comparing his procedures to those of a cubist, and Zavattini suggesting a similar analogy with the phrase 'a synthesis within the analysis.' None will articulate exactly what is the new logic holding together his 'fragments,' but they all agree that it is not the *confection* being applied by those around them.

Elocutio refers to *style*, whose register divides into *grande*, *medium*, and *humile*. For our purposes we need only the distinction between a 'high' register and a 'low' register. Moreover, we can adopt a metaphor, that of the volume of the orator's voice, to correspond with the two registers, and talk about *raising* or *lowering* the *voice*, giving us, for cinema:

– the *raised voice*, or 'spectacle,' corresponding to a certain stylistic register of address (and often carrying with it particular kinds of 'content'), which might be associated with Hollywood movies and the production values with which they were armed to conquer a commercial market (it includes beautiful and glamorous film stars used as performers, for example)
– the *lowered voice*, corresponding to neorealism's polemical rejection of *spectacle*, an explicit property of neorealist films (partially exemplified in the choice of non-professional performers, for example – even though that choice was also conditioned by considerations belonging in the category of *logos*).

I shall often use for the *lowered voice* the expression *sermo humilis*, because of its associations with a particularly Christian rhetoric. Erich Auerbach explains that, according to St Augustine, *sermo humilis* is the style of the Bible, and writes:

> Thus the style of the Scriptures throughout is *humilis*, lowly or humble. Even the hidden things (*secreta, recondita*) are set forth in a 'lowly' vein. But the subject matter, whether simple or obscure, is sublime. The lowly, or humble, style is the only medium in which such sublime mysteries can be brought within the reach of men. It constitutes a parallel to the Incarnation, which was also a *humilitas* in the same sense, for men could not have endured the splendor of Christ's divinity. But the Incarnation, as it happened on earth, could only be narrated in a lowly and humble style. The birth of Christ in a manger in Bethlehem, his life among fishermen, publicans, and other common men, the Passion with its realistic and 'scandalous' episodes – none of this could have been treated appropriately in the lofty oratorical, tragic, or epic style.[32]

Quite apart from the Christian associations raised by the mythical level of narrative reference that the melodramatic matrix rehearses (the loss of an organic idyll), a 'Franciscan' thread of humility runs through neorealism, owing much to the capacity of *sermo humilis* to evoke the sublime (in Auerbach's sense) in humanity, explicit in Rossellini's *Francesco giullare di Dio*, but almost as clearly developed in De Sica's *Miracolo a Milano*, in Rossellini's *Paisà* (first and fifth episodes) and *Europa '51*, and in Fellini's *La strada*.

Traditional rhetoric, applied to oratory, is the discipline of the raised voice: raised in volume, raised slightly in pitch, raised in register and with a raised, and generally repetitive, rhythmic emphasis. Words are pronounced particularly clearly, often slightly more slowly than usual, in a ringing voice. Sentences are rounded and finished, encapsulating and completing an argument, but often more than this – actually giving the argument, through the use of syntax, some kind of formal shape. These features of an 'oration' can be seen as analogous to what are called 'production values' in the cinema: extraordinary and striking events, exotic locations, meticulously recorded dialogue based on scripts honed to make every point stand out and be striking, impressive background music, glamorous performers, and so on. If these values correspond to the *raised voice*, it is easy to see how neorealism's rejection of 'production values' constitutes a *lowered voice*.

The poetics of the lowered voice is achieved in a context; the voice is lowered 'relative to ...' The lowered voice is often perceived as low in the presence of a raised one. The raised one can, however, be 'implied.' 'Realism' itself only exists in a context, and will be realist 'relative to ...' It leads us to a strange paradox, in which neorealist cinema – a visual medium – is realist by virtue of 'sounding' different from the cinema it opposes. What often happens in neorealist films is that the visual is used to challenge the raised voice, by virtue of cinema's capacity for visually magnifying, and rendering audible, the lowered voice.

When we come to examine closely Rossellini's film *Paisà*, we shall find a consistent thematic and rhetorical procedure running through the film in which Rossellini assembles a visual representation of voices that are 'drowned' by the raised voices of political, historical, social, and economic forces – the very 'sound' of war being challenged by a *sermo humilis* in which *elocutio* takes on the role of expressing the 'sublimity' of human 'being.' Rossellini often *shows* us a silenced voice. Fellini was once asked in a television interview: 'What is the feeling, the state of mind, that most inspires you, and which you feel most nourishes you?' He replied: 'I don't know. Perhaps ..., put it this way ..., the attempt to pick up, to manage to listen closely to, an utterance that has been cut off, one coming from a voice that has little by little gradually got weaker until it has become inaudible.'[33]

De Sica too made films about people who cannot raise their voices, and yet are forced to live among those who can and do. Children are, in social terms, ideal embodiments of *sermo humilis*, and ever since 1942 (*I bambini ci guardano*) De Sica has returned repeatedly to their rhetorical use in his *elocutio*. He uses them thematically, it is true; but stylistically they fit very well Auerbach's definition of *sermo humilis*: the 'sublime' (being human) expressed through a 'lowly' style, embodying a voice too low to make itself heard in the adult world. In *Ladri di biciclette* an adult, Antonio, is required to lower his voice in a place where only one voice may be raised, that of the church; and at a trades union meeting his personal concerns are literally 'silenced' by the voice of the speaker. The Santona comically adopts a raised voice to give authority to her pronouncements, incongruously articulating what can only be truly expressed in a lowered voice – and indeed, Antonio insists on whispering. At the end of the scene the clairvoyant's exchange with Adele is, contrastingly, cast in *sermo humilis*. In *Umberto D.* the 'elocution' of the landlady and her guests drowns and suppresses the voices of Umberto and Maria. In *Miracolo a Milano*, Mobbi's capacity to raise his voice and have it heard and acted upon is fundamental to his ability to usurp spaces by ejecting and suppressing their previous occupants. The film was to have had an ending in which the folk astride their broomsticks were foiled in their attempts to come to earth in far-off lands by large notices 'loudly' declaring 'Private Property' (it was censored).

The rhetorical 'office' of *elocutio* sets up a binary opposition between the *raised voice* and *sermo humilis* that functions as an ethical 'code.' We shall see how costume and diction in *Roma città aperta* are coded according to 'negative' (the sartorial high style of German uniforms and of Marina's outfits, and the Gestapo officer's impeccable syntax and pronunciation) and 'positive' (the dialect-inflected, humble speech and tatty clothes of Pina, reaching down the scale to the nakedness of Manfredi). In *La terra trema*, the coding operating between the *raised voice* of standard Italian and the *sermo humilis* of dialect is explicitly pointed out to the viewer (who is, incidentally, associated with the former) at the start of the film. Costume is used everywhere in neorealist cinema for this rhetorical function. Even if not unique to neorealism (one has only to think of Charles Chaplin), this coding of visual and aural *elocutio* is a particular feature of neorealism's poetics of style – a code in which if you are well dressed and well spoken you are in conflict with the 'organic' order of nature. Narrative (the melodramatic matrix) and style come together in the rhetoric of *elocutio*.

The poetics involves not just giving a voice to those who don't have one, but the choice to listen to some voices rather than to others. Visconti's *Bellissima* is a contest of voices, in the very texture of the film; its narrative proceeds precisely in terms of one voice prevailing over another at a given moment (for example, that of the drama coach, or the harsh, flippant Tuscan accent of the dressmaker). Zavattini's precept of *pedinamento* / 'tailing' involves *listening* to unraised voices (he wrote the story of *Bellissima*). The eminent Italian film director Alessandro Blasetti, who plays himself in Visconti's film, could sometimes be the director of a cinema with a raised voice (*La corona di ferro*, *Fabiola*), which is what Visconti used him for in *Bellissima* – the whole film is a polemic against the raised voice (Blasetti uses a megaphone and a microphone), against 'noise' and against 'rhetoric,' and an invitation to listen to the lowered voice – of a young child, among others. Fellini will return to this theme, used explicitly as a poetics, at the end of his life in *La voce della luna*, after having already engaged in a fierce polemic on the question in *Prova d'orchestra*. In *Blowup*, Antonioni's protagonist, Thomas, will not *listen* to what he is being told (by Jane and by Patricia), and acts as though only his media-sanctioned voice deserved to be heard, until finally he is wiped off the screen. Thomas, the fashion photographer, parallels the commercial antagonist against which the neorealist cinematic poetic was established, and is portrayed as unable to see the reality that his own photographs have captured. Even the 'neorealist' photographic essay he is preparing for Ron, his publisher, is the product of deceit, blindness, and indifference. *Blowup* is, therefore, a reflection upon, an illustration of, and, in its expressiveness, a deployment of the rhetoric of neorealism.

Fellini will develop the rhetoric of *dispositio* and *elocutio* in *La dolce vita*, with his assembly of fragments expressing Marcello's vision of modern Rome, and the contrast between the raised voice of the orgy and the sublime *sermo humilis* of the inaudible teenage waitress. De Sica's picture of Antonio searching for his bicycle as a fragile figure in an overbearing landscape will be developed by Antonioni in Sandro's search for meaning on the island in *L'avventura*, and in Lidia's wandering through Milan in *La notte*. There is a continuity in the way in which the resources of *dispositio* and *elocutio* are developed over time. A single-minded prioritizing of ideology (on the part of the 'institution of neorealism') in the areas of *inventio* and in *logos* and *ethos* saw in this evolution elements of 'betrayal' and 'involution.' The artists themselves staunchly maintained that the nature of the reality to be represented had itself evolved. In 1945 Rossellini and De Sica were living one reality in comfortable hotels and 'representing' another in their films. As time went on, filmmakers chose to represent a 'reality' ever closer to the one they themselves lived and knew at first hand. The films of the 1960s look very different from those of the 1940s. If the leap from *Paisà* and *Ladri di biciclette* to *La dolce vita* and *La notte* seems far-fetched in terms of 'content,' in terms of poetics there is a strong line of continuity. In the historical enterprise of carving out 'periods' in the history of cinema, neorealism tends to be considered a point of *arrival*, rather than a point of *departure*. Artists are seen as 'breaking away' from neorealism, rather than pursuing the implications of its poetics. The aesthetic perspective can help us view one aesthetic artefact as establishing a context out of which emerges another artefact.

A Note on Comedy

Comedy, as an issue, enters into every aspect of our discussion of neorealist Italian cinema: into neorealism's relation with a cinematic and cultural tradition, into the question of the functioning of narrative, into genre, and into the rhetorical procedures of neorealist films.

The 'institution of neorealism' (the historical and critical tradition surrounding the actual filmmaking) attributes a great deal of neorealism's innovative energy to its rejection of the comedies of the 'Fascist' 1930s and early 1940s (summarily dismissed as escapist 'white telephone' films). De Sica and the scriptwriters Cesare Zavattini, Sergio Amidei, and Federico Fellini all developed professionally in that tradition, and it is hardly surprising to find them using its narrative and rhetorical procedures in their post-war films. As we have seen in chapter 1, scriptwriting for neorealist films was carried out in promiscuity with writing for the music hall, for radio comedy shows, and for satirical magazines. Rossellini assigned an important role to the comedy tradition, and to music-hall performance, in the development of neorealism:

> Whether the impact of so-called neorealism on the world derived from *Roma città aperta* is for others to decide. I see the birth of neorealism further back: ... above all in certain minor films, like *Avanti c'è posto, L'ultima carrozzella, Campo de' Fiori*, in which the formula, if we want to call it that, of neorealism is being assembled through the spontaneous creations of actors: of Anna Magnani and of Aldo Fabrizi in particular. Who can deny that it is these actors who first embodied neorealism? That the music-hall scenes of the 'strongmen' or of 'Roman ditties' performed on a carpet or with the help of just one guitar, as they were invented by Magnani, or the

figure portrayed on local stages by Fabrizi, already anticipated at times certain films of the neorealist period? Neorealism is given birth, unconsciously, by the film in dialect; then it becomes conscious of itself in the heat of the human and social problems of the war and its aftermath.[34]

Federico Fellini (writer on *Roma città aperta* and co-author and assistant director on *Paisà*) was a scriptwriter on all three of the comedies Rossellini mentions: *Avanti c'è posto* (Mario Bonnard, 1942), starring Aldo Fabrizi, and *Campo de' Fiori* (Bonnard, 1943) and *L'ultima carrozzella* (Mario Mattoli, 1943), starring both Fabrizi and Anna Magnani (the leading actors of *Roma città aperta*).

A feature of the narrative function of Italian film comedies is to *validate* the heterodox world view of a character or social group, but to show that world view as incapable of *prevailing* in a social reality. A narrative that does this furnishes an overall picture of a 'figure' in conflict with a 'landscape,' and often serves to give expression to the way that figure *experiences* a landscape depicted in a multitude of small details. The distinction between the idyllic, 'deep'-level narrative references of melodrama and of comedy can sometimes merely hang on questions of rhetorical register (*elocutio*) and assembly (*dispositio*). The narrative of *Ladri di biciclette* often functions in this way, as do some episodes of *Paisà* and the depiction of the figure of Don Pietro in *Roma città aperta*.

Unfortunately, comedy as a *genre* is too large a subject to investigate here, but the use of dialect, the choice of characters from the lower classes, the costumes and locations, and the nature of the dramatic events chosen for neorealist Italian films apply the *sermo humilis* register of the *elocutio* of comedy. The *dispositio* of the assembly of fragments that characterizes many neorealist films, and most particularly those we shall be examining in detail, is a feature of comedies, whose narratives are constructed by accumulating vignettes, sketches, and illustrative episodes. Tropes characteristic of comedy, such as repetition, the incongruous juxtaposition of rhetorical contrasts, mistaken identity, and dramatic irony, are fundamental rhetorical procedures used again and again by the three films under investigation.

Alberto Farassino has suggested that neorealism, in the period 1945–49, is the product of a two-way contamination – of the neorealist aesthetic project by Italian genre cinema and vice versa – and that it is best understood through the metaphor of 'the Italian language': neorealism is the 'Italian language' permeating all of cinema in Italy in the immediate post-war period.[35] That 'Italian language,' in its turn, has many of its roots in the rhetoric of comedy.[36]

3 *Roma città aperta*[1]

Photography

The description of a film is either *true* or *false*, its interpretation more or less *plausible*, and its evaluation dependent on the *use* to which the critic wishes to put it. All three are more or less valid critical undertakings according to the context in which they are carried out. Neorealist Italian cinema is now half a century old, and has been the object of persuasive interpretation and evaluation. My endeavour is systematically to describe the artefacts. However hard I try, I shall inevitably describe them falsely, but we have to start somewhere, and we need to be prepared to accept whatever implications the description might have for interpretation and evaluation. Time and time again critics have remarked upon what they perceive to be a conflict between *Roma città aperta* as it has been interpreted and evaluated and the film as it can be objectively described.

The terms that have frequently been used to describe the 'look' of the film are 'rough,' 'raw,' 'simple,' 'direct,' and as resembling a 'documentary' or a 'newsreel.' The word 'documentary' returns again and again in criticism of neorealism, and of *Roma città aperta* in particular. These observations lead to two lines of thinking. In one the judgments have taken on the status of a description of the poetics of the film, as though they were elements of a deliberate stylistic choice. This characteristic then gets generalized to all neorealist films, and hence to the poetics of neorealism: as though the effect of 'reality' were achieved by imitating the stylistic attributes of documentary and newsreel, those attributes functioning, therefore, as a code. A related, but different, line of thinking has recourse to a heroic account of *Roma città aperta* having been shot in extraordinary circumstances and in the face of almost insurmountable technical difficulties, which account for the look of the film. This too is then extended to neorealism in general, and is offered as an explanation of a neorealist style. The question of the 'look' of the film needs dealing with a little more fully than has hitherto been the case.

A fine example of the way in which the heroic story has been used to account for the style of the film concerns the film stock used to photograph it. In a documentary film, Rossellini (by now, I would say, in his sixties), interviewed about *Roma città aperta* while he was standing at the entrance to Via Montecuccoli 17 (the apartment building in which the character Pina lived), says:

> There was no film stock to be found. I remember going to buy film from street photographers ..., you know, who took photographs with their Leicas ..., and tail-ends of film. Poor Arata, who was the cameraman, worked miracles for me, because we made use of everything, positive film, negative, internegative, anything, in fact.[2]

This description of the film stock goes right back to the earliest days, because already by 1950 Vernon Jarratt, who was in the Films Office of the British embassy in Rome at the time, in his book *The Italian Cinema*, is asserting:

> The technical difficulties were even greater. There was no proper negative and in fact the whole film was shot on odds and ends of raw-stock, bits twenty metres, fifty metres, a hundred and fifty metres long, of all sorts of mixed makes – old Ferrania, older Ferrania, Kodak, Agfa, Gaevert, and some that was quite anonymous ... It is little short of marvellous that in these circumstances Ubaldo Arata, that much-loved and much-lamented cameraman (he died in 1947) was able to turn out so quietly competent a piece of work.[3]

Having investigated the subject in some detail, I could relate a plethora of accounts, given by people present in Rome at the time, and even by one of the camera operators on the film itself, of Rossellini getting scraps of various brands of negative from American newsreel cameramen, or other stock from the U.S. armed forces, and even from the Vatican. Wherever he got the raw negative from (Ugo Pirro suggests that stock was available on the black market), the heroic story of the photographing of the film is quite simply not true.[4] David Forgacs, who put the myth to rest in his monograph on the film, *Rome Open City,* kindly furnished me with a photocopy of the report on the condition of the film before its restoration in the centenary year of the birth of cinema – a report made available to him by the Centro Sperimentale di Cinematografia.[5] The report was made for the Cineteca Nazionale, dated 12 May 1995, and is signed by Mario Calzini, who is Italy's foremost expert on the projection of films. This is what he writes:

> Examination of the original negative immediately demolishes a legend which is often brought up in connection with this film: the story goes that Rossellini and Arata shot the film using each day pieces of raw negative which they managed to find here and there, so that the photographic continuity of the film represents a kind of miracle, given the assortment of materials they were starting from. This does not turn out to be completely true: all the outdoor scenes of the film are shot with the film stock produced at the time by the Ferrania company of Savona, branded 'Ferrania C.6,' whereas when they go indoors, Arata moves to the more sensitive Agfa Super Pan, and in a few cases (reel 4) to Agfa Ultra Rapid. Without wishing to detract anything from the skill of the Director of Photography, nor from the hunt for negative, which cannot have been as easy to get hold of at the time as just buying it in a shop, it has to be said that it was already possible to find on the market at least three types of negative to be used in the appropriate conditions, and that the national industry had restarted production.

Agfa Super Panchromatic negative, at a speed of ASA 32, and the much faster Ultra Rapid, at ASA 120, were perfectly respectable stocks, and roughly comparable with what was being used in Hollywood. Since most of the film is shot in interiors, the Agfa Super would have accounted for the largest portion of the film, then the Ferrania for the exterior shots, and finally the Agfa Ultra Rapid for one reel only. Ferrania C.6 was the standard film stock in use in commercial productions and government-financed films in Italy during the early 1940s (Ferrania sold on credit, while most other manufacturers demanded cash on delivery); it was the stock Rossellini used, with Vincenzo Seratrice as director of photography, on his previous feature film, shot in 1942, *Un pilota ritorna.*

Ubaldo Arata was what we would nowadays call the director of photography (generally abbreviated to 'DP'), who chose the film stock and set up the lighting, and afterwards had a role in instructing the laboratories in the development of the film. For example, on *Roma città aperta*, rather than have the whole film developed at a constant level of contrast, Arata marked a sample section of each scene so that the laboratories could test the developing before choosing their timings for the full scene, and so match contrast levels from scene to scene. It is well known that he was worried about the inadequacy of the lighting available to him, and that in the early days of shooting no rushes were available for him to see if the exposure was correct, which may explain why he arranged for the laboratories to balance out inconsistencies in exposure between different scenes.

Calzini attributes deficiencies in the finished film to the fact that 'a heavy veil, present throughout the original negative, suggests an incomplete fixing of the film at the time it was developed.' Arata's method of arranging for separate developing times for each scene also leads to problems for a restorer who might want to balance perfectly the overall contrast of the final print: 'While in one sense this method allowed the skilled director of photography, who was fully aware of its possibilities, to stamp a certain personality on the results, in other cases it created variations in contrast between one scene and another which are difficult to correct.'[6]

Clearly, Rossellini had not only enough stock, but precisely the right stock for the filming conditions. I have dwelt on this matter for a reason. This chapter takes an aesthetic approach to the film, and asserts that such an approach requires a description of the *film*, rather than a digest of the things that have been said about it. Nevertheless, viewers have described their experience of the film using terms like 'rough' and 'documentary,' and it can be helpful to use this as a starting point for analysing Rossellini's visual 'style' in the film.

Viewers and critics might have three entirely distinct reasons for applying the word 'documentary' to their impressions of *Roma città aperta*. One is that the film 'documents' a historical period. This sense of the notion can be divided into two lines of reasoning. In one line, the film reconstructs accurately, using whenever possible the original locations and the events of the Roman resistance to German occupation: it is a documentation of historical fact. This approach uses the notion of documentary to characterize the authenticity of the *narrative* and some features of its execution. It is a line of reasoning fully and very competently discussed in David Forgacs's *Rome Open City*. Another line of reasoning, one that characterizes much Italian discussion of the film, is that *Roma città aperta* 'documents' the *meanings* that the Resistance to occupation had for the Italians at the moment in time in which the film was made and shown: notions of populism, of nationalism, of solidarity, of regeneration, of hope, of self-absolution, and so forth.[7]

We can make a theoretical distinction between 'feature film' and 'documentary' on the basis of the Peircean semiotics I discussed in the last chapter, though it will not always be applicable in practice. A documentary film is indexical: the signs recorded are directly produced by the referent. A feature film is iconic: the signs recorded are indexical recordings of iconic signs of the referent. In other words, a documentary directly records whatever is being represented, while a feature film records an imitation or reconstruction of its referent, or of an imaginary referent. At first sight, therefore, what distinguishes a feature film from a documentary is the nature of the profilmic, rather than the characteristics of the filming itself. It is not immediately obvious that you would film an icon of a referent any differently than you would film the referent itself. If your sets, locations, and actors are good enough, why should the viewer notice any difference between a fictional film of an event and a documentary film of the same event?

The third reason why viewers might reach for words like 'documentary' to describe *Roma città aperta* is more closely related to a style of filming: they recognize in the film signifying practices that they associate with documentary, and perceive in the film an absence of the signifying practices they associate with feature films. For example, we have grown so accustomed in feature films to a lighting convention in which main lights, fill light, top light, back light, and the judicious blending of hard and soft light are used to enhance the beauty of the actors, and to pick them out from their background that we interpret any absence of, or falling away from, this convention as a movement in the direction of documentary, which, we assume, does not apply these signifying practices.

I am going to use for a stylistic comparison with *Roma città aperta* a Hollywood film on a similar resistance theme, made in the same year, Howard Hawks's *To Have and Have Not*. Viewers would be perfectly correct in perceiving a big difference between the lighting used in *To Have and Have Not* and that in *Roma città aperta*. They might interpret this as Rossellini's (and his photographer, Ubaldo Arata's) refusal of the signifying practices of the feature-film, and as the conscious desire on their part to imitate the signifying practices of the documentary. This would be an aesthetic choice, and would form part of the poetics of

neorealism. Alternatively, the viewer might conclude that, in the difficult circumstances of the filming of *Roma città aperta*, it was not possible
to achieve the 'standards' of feature-film lighting, but the filmmakers
did the best they could in the prevailing conditions. In this case, the
poetics of *Roma città aperta* was not so much a conscious choice as a
product of expediency.

The nature of documentary filming at the time tends to lead to a series
of characteristics in the finished documentary film, which we can list:

– *Mise en scène:* People interacting are photographed in ensembles
  rather than in montages of shots of individuals: dialogue, for example, cannot be dismantled into sequences of reverse-angle close-up
  shots. The camera maintains a certain distance from the people being
  filmed (rather than coming in to within two feet of their faces), and
  so medium and medium-long shots predominate. Mastershots tend
  to dominate the narrative, and the need to record the complete
  action often leads to long takes (shots of long duration) – which may,
  however, then be cut at the editing stage. The viewer is oriented by
  means of panning around locations, rather than through multiple
  set-ups. The composition in the frame is determined by the location,
  rather than the location being organized or the set being constructed
  in order to permit a certain composition.
– *Montage:* The film has to find a way of overcoming a sense of fragmentation, because the 'story' is built out of components 'caught'
  rather than constructed on purpose, in which transitions cannot be
  invented and inserted. Frequently shots are repeated. In a feature
  film, by contrast, the repetition of a shot requires a narrative justification, like memory, flashback, or fantasy.
– *Sound:* Where possible, the film uses direct, synchronized sound.
  The soundtrack is not 'mixed' in the same way as that of a feature
  film: dialogue and sound effects are recorded simultaneously with
  the same microphone, rather than being fabricated and mixed together at the editing stage. But because of the practical difficulties of
  recording sound on location, voice-over and post-dubbed sound is
  used. Documentaries frequently construct a point of view 'external
  to' the events being filmed by means of a voice-over commentary
  edited in at the final stages.
– *Lighting:* Ambient light is used outdoors; one or two sources of lighting are used indoors – the problem often being one of getting *enough*
  lighting to film – from fairly broad floodlights, rather than narrowly

focused ones or spotlights. Generally, in order to capture detail, high levels of contrast in the photography are avoided, and to the same end soft (or 'diffused'), rather than hard, lighting is preferred (when subjects are in movement, the sharp shadows resulting from hard lighting would move disconcertingly). The result can be a flatter image, designed to prioritize information over visual pleasure, with some loss of the three-dimensional possibilities that in feature films are enhanced by the use of multiple spotlights.

Some of these characteristics are shared by *Roma città aperta*, but others are definitely not.

Lighting

Roma città aperta was shot in the same way that conventional feature films were shot at the time, mostly in a studio. However, the production was 'poor' for purely historical reasons: electrical power and production funding were scarce and unreliable. The 'look' of a film is largely the product of the lighting. For the interiors, mostly shot in a studio, the filmmakers had no alternative but to use large amounts of artificial light, and one problem they faced was that of getting power for the lighting units. They had a generator, but fuel was hard to obtain. Once they had solved the problem by purloining current from a nearby American forces newspaper office, there was no reason why the DP should not light his sets in the normal way (except that Arata found himself short of bulbs for the lighting units).

A lot of the film takes place at night, or it seems to, because some of the interiors lack windows (Marina's dressing room, the staircase of Via Montecuccoli – except at the top – all the rooms in the Via Tasso Gestapo headquarters, the *Unità* printing works, Don Pietro's rectory and, for the most part, his church). Hence, apart from the daytime exteriors, the room in which Marcello's grandfather is lying (which has two windows by the bed), Francesco's room (though that is mostly artificially lit), and the religious articles shop, the film is entirely artificially lit. In some cases, there are light sources in the 'diegesis' (table lamps, reading lamps, dressing-table lights, overhead lights), in others not. Even where there is a 'diegetic' light source, it is generally not used very effectively: for example, when Bergmann prepares to interrogate Manfredi by turning his reading lamp towards the prisoner's (still empty) chair, Bergmann himself does become slightly less lit, but there is no attempt whatever to create the strong contrasts that most cinematographers would have used to suggest 'the third degree.' Only Marina's bedroom, when she is alone and on the telephone, and one sequence in the torture chamber are lit in such a way as to create a particular effect. Anna Magnani was well known for being very sensitive about how she was photographed, but the only scene in which she is lit with real care is that of her dialogue on the stairs with Francesco – though, in her conversations with Manfredi in Francesco's flat, when the camera moves in for medium close-ups, she is not only lit better than Manfredi (except for one brief non-matching inserted close-up), but shots of her are in better focus than those of Manfredi.

Arata appears to have used almost no backlighting at all, and a little top lighting, with the rest coming mostly from in front of the characters to the sides of the camera, from floor-standing floodlights. Where shots` have been taken later, to be inserted into sequences, the lighting of the inserts never seems to match that of the surrounding material (a good example is a shot of Marina saying 'Che cos'è?' inserted into a more or less reverse-angle sequence between Manfredi standing and her lying prone on the bed turning back to speak to him). This may be related to the fact that in the early stages of shooting, there were no rushes available. One of the scenes in which the lighting is arranged for effect is at the end of Manfredi's torture (thrown onto the wall behind Bergmann is a shadow of what appears to be of a common domestic clothes press, which, in the context, takes on sinister connotations), but even there a non-matching shot of Bergmann is inserted into the sequence.

Certainly the photography does not strive for the richness, the beauty, the variety, and the interest that is so obviously the goal of Sidney Hickox, the cinematographer of Howard Hawks's *To Have and Have Not*. Hawks's film sets out to offer the viewer an appealing and interesting visual experience, quite independently of the narrative: its goal is the pleasure of the viewer. Performers are lit with main light, fill lights, back lights, and top lights, which 'draw' the shapes of their bodies against the background and give moulding and a tactile quality to their faces. Sets are lit with areas of light and shade (in 'pools,' so to speak), with an interweaving of highlights and shadows that gives variety and interest to the background. Some of the films photographed by Ubaldo Arata before the war also achieve a comparable effect (notably *Lorenzino de' Medici*, *La signora di tutti*, and *Scipione l'Africano*). *Roma città aperta*, in its lighting, is about as far from that aesthetic goal as it is possible to get. Light is thrown onto faces from the front, occasionally with some light from higher up, and with a fairly even level of fill lighting to reduce shadows. Faces are visible, but they are not modelled, and instead are sometimes washed out with light. Sets are lit with pools of light from floods, but otherwise with an unmodulated approach. Nothing has been done to prevent the multiple shadows that result from the floods intruding everywhere in the image. During some movements, a character's face will disappear entirely for a moment into the darkness between one light and another. In other words, not only does *Roma città aperta* 'refuse' in its lighting one of the aesthetic characteristics of both Hollywood and Italian 1930s films, it even fails to maintain a very basic minimum of conventional standards. This could be because Arata had a limited number of floods available, and because Rossellini saved time by not cutting and changing set-ups when characters moved. These features are neither entirely a product of reduced resources nor an element of the poetics of 'realism': *La terra trema* is lit entirely differently, and far better, by G.R. Aldo, with fewer resources than were available to Arata (Aldo came from still photography, and it may be inappropriate to use his exceptional work as a comparison). No other neorealist film even approaches the bland sloppiness of the lighting of *Roma città aperta* in its highly lit scenes.

Another stylistic characteristic of the film can be used in partial explanation of this frontal blandness of lighting. In a short while we shall see how Rossellini keeps his camera further back from the profilmic than is normal in cinema of the time. The further back the camera, the less freedom is offered the director of photography in placing his lights. He has to keep them out of the frame, and therefore at a certain distance from the objects they are illuminating, with the result that their light has to be spread more evenly, and cannot easily be as intense and focused as lights that are closer to (and all around) the profilmic.

A certain amount of location shooting, and particularly in exteriors, has taken place for the film, using ambient light and some 'bounced' light for softening or filling shadows. This is not, however, how feature films were normally shot. Large amounts of lighting were normally used in exteriors (in *Paisà* and *Ladri di biciclette*, for example). It is generally maintained that at that time (and some have said *until* Rossellini in *Roma città aperta* set an example) exteriors were not often used in mainstream feature films. However, contrary to received opinion, Italian films of the 1930s actually made quite wide use of outdoor and location shooting, and Arata was particularly experienced in this area (one has only to remember his work on *Scipione l'Africano, Luciano Serra pilota*, and *Passaporto rosso*). American films began exterior location shooting more regularly with the move of production to New York in the late 1940s, and it characterises the 'New York style' (a style that *may* exhibit the influence of Rossellini's film on its proponents, such as Jules Dassin, the title of whose 1948 film *The Naked City* echoes the American title of *Roma città aperta*, *Open City* – but it is not a question we can go into here). Hence, in its use of exteriors, and its reliance on available light, the troupe of *Roma città aperta* put themselves in conditions similar to those in which documentary filmmakers worked.

So far I have attempted to explain the photography of *Roma città aperta* in terms of the prevailing material conditions surrounding its filming, and this is the standard approach to the matter. However, it is inadequate as an explanation. The quality of the narrative of the film, and of its organization, the quality of its dramaturgy, and the quality of the performances of the actors (Magnani, Fabrizi, and Feist) are not matched by the quality of the lighting. The resources available to the filmmakers were not inferior to those available to the makers of *La terra trema*, where the photography is incomparably better. *Roma città aperta* is not a typical example of Arata's cinematographic style, because he photographed other films differently.

Scenes representing dark night, or closed unlit passages, are much more convincingly lit. This might suggest that where Rossellini could not see with his own eyes roughly how the picture would look on film, he was obliged to rely entirely on the professional skill and standards of his photographer, with the result that the quality of the lighting is better. It is possible that elsewhere he hurried Arata along (and this would be compatible with what we know to have been Rossellini's impatience, on occasion, with the time it took Otello Martelli to set up the lights on *Paisà*).

The photography of *Roma città aperta* most probably, therefore, owes something to its director. The accumulation of testimony to Rossellini's casual, relaxed approach to the details of filmmaking at this time, and the number of 'mistakes' we find in *Roma città aperta* all suggest that he did not put energy and attention into details of the photography. The historical evidence does not, however, suggest that Rossellini was incapable of devoting energy and attention to small details; his early animal documentaries are the product of patient and painstaking attention to detail. At the time of the making of *Roma città aperta* Rossellini had plenty of distractions, involving questions of money and his private life. It is a wonder he got anything done at all. For a while, he was making a large number of films in rapid succession. Clearly, he prioritized: some things he considered important, and others less so; but they might be different things at different moments. *Un pilota ritorna*, for example, has complex tracking shots that are almost there for the delight of their execution, while the set-up of, and transitions between, shots are sometimes very clumsy. In the period following *Roma città aperta*, Rossellini can clearly be seen to be moving in the direction of an innovative dramaturgy and narrative, starting with *Paisà*, which required a certain amount of courage and single-mindedness in the context of mainstream filmmaking of the time.

This all makes it difficult to define an 'aesthetic' that we can consistently isolate from Rossellini's work. The person who, in all the various things he has said about Rossellini (whom he clearly revered as, to some extent, his master), conveys the most complete and balanced picture is Federico Fellini. He describes coming across Rossellini in moments of painstaking craftsmanship late at night in the corner of a studio, and yet also remembers glorying in the free-wheeling improvisation Rossellini offered, unencumbered by a rigid plan to be executed, on *Paisà* (though we know that during the filming of one sequence of that film Rossellini was very intense and demanding). Film by film, we need to identify what it was that Rossellini was after at each particular moment, because it may not be possible to identify a 'constant' running through his work, except for a character of ceaseless change and enquiry. But this openness to change and enquiry might constitute an aesthetic in itself, partly defined in terms of a context. In the sphere of commercial filmmaking, to accept a fluid flexibility in matters of aesthetic priorities, rather than doggedly conforming to baseline conventional values, may be an aesthetic of 'freedom.' De Sica, who was scrupulous about formal and technical matters, found himself disconcerted by Rossellini's casual approach to such things during the filming of *Il Generale Della Rovere*. I offer all this by way of an attempt to articulate what we can deduce as an 'explanation' of the photography of *Roma città aperta*; and I offer it as an alternative to the standard explanation, which talks in terms of the 'realism' of documentary and newsreel. In a word, Rossellini was lazy. His laziness is an aesthetic position. In the economy of his artistic activity, he apportioned priorities in such a way that in the artefact certain things were attended to more energetically than others. But, of course, he was choosing among available alternatives. Laziness can be one of the most effective ways of defending one's own artistic integrity: it is a refusal of other people's priorities.

Sound

Strangely, there has been little comment on the soundtrack of the film. It makes great use of sound off. This is a device rarely used for narrative purposes by documentaries, which instead make great use of sound *over* – something *Roma città aperta* never uses; indeed, anything that might establish a point of view *outside* that of the characters in the narrative itself is rigorously eschewed, and this too distinguishes the film sharply from documentary (and also from *Paisà*, incidentally). (Sound coming from a source that exists in the world of the film's story, but is not in the frame, is considered sound coming from off-camera, abbreviated to 'sound off.' Sound that has no source in the world of the film's story, but that has been added at the editing stage – for example, background music or the commentary of a documentary film – is called 'sound over.') The loud booming sound off of the *Radio Londra* broadcast at the beginning, as the camera surveys the exterior of Manfredi's apartment, is a sound over *effect*, but it is clearly intended to be 'subjective' to the inhabitants of the apartment (to tune into the station was illegal), and is an economical way of indicating the political sympathies of Manfredi's landlady and her maid.

The images and the synchronized sound were not recorded simultaneously. Thus, from an objective point of view, the synchronized sound and the background music both have the same status, in the sense that they were both synthesized and added to the film in a similar manner at the editing stage. The normal way in which post-synchronized dialogue and sound effects are achieved is as follows: as the camera films the action, a microphone records simultaneously the sounds made by the actors and the environment as they speak and move around. This soundtrack, called a 'guide track,' is not used in the finished film, but instead serves as a guide at the dubbing stage, to enable the actors to reproduce their dialogue in accurate synchrony with their original performances (so that the words you hear fit exactly the movements of their mouths, for example), and to enable the sound technicians to synchronize the sound effects (such as doors closing, footsteps, etc.). *Roma città aperta* is unusual for the fact that it was shot without a guide track, the reason being that it cost a great deal more to develop film with a soundtrack on it than film without one, especially the variable-density type of optical track that *Roma città aperta* uses. (Interestingly, *Ladri di biciclette* was another film shot in this unorthodox way.) The camera Rossellini used, a DeVry model made in Illinois, USA, was particularly favoured by newsreel photographers for the ease of changing its magazine, and for the clarity of its lenses. A photograph of Rossellini standing beside the camera on the set of *Roma città aperta* is reproduced in Tag Gallagher's biography of Rossellini (and looks as though it was taken during the shooting of the SS round-up at Via Montecuccoli). The fact that there is no sound-deadening cover ('blimp') over the camera is further evidence that the film was shot entirely without sound – if no sound was being recorded, there would be no need to suppress the camera's noise. The result in the finished film is that the synchronization of the dialogue with the movements of the actors' lips is often poor (incidentally, it is at its best when Bergmann and Hartmann are talking in German). Generally, this does not matter, because there are not many close-ups in the film (see 'Mise en scène' below). When a dialogue has been filmed in close-up, sometimes greater care has been taken with the synchronization at the dubbing stage (as, for example, in the conversation between Francesco and Pina on the staircase outside Pina's flat on the night before her wedding). Jolanda Benvenuti had the job of rehearsing Marcello's dialogue with Don Pietro following the blow with the frying pan to the grandfather. He was required to say, 'All'anima, Don Pie', che padellata che j'ha dato.' Vito Annichiarico could not get it right, and got more and more irritated, until he eventually refused to rehearse any more. In the finished film, this is dealt with by shooting him holding the frying pan and beginning his line (his lips do not match the sounds), then quickly cutting to a shot of Don Pietro taken from behind Francesco, so that we no longer see the boy's face. Some of the actors dubbed their own performances (those playing the roles of Pina, Don Pietro, Marcello, Lauretta, and Agostino, for example), while for other roles a different actor did the dubbing (the roles of Manfredi, Francesco, Bergmann, and Ingrid, for example).

Jolanda Benvenuti also recounts that she was given the job of producing the sound effect of the machine-gun fire that kills Pina. She did this by producing a bang, and then repeating that section of soundtrack several times at regular intervals, and finally doing the same thing with a slightly softer echo effect. She also maintains that quite a number of things in the film (she does not specify which) were achieved by making use of 'special effects.' She does explain how it was possible for Bergmann to strike Manfredi in the face so violently with a whip, and how it was possible to make it look as though the flesh on his chest was burning from the blowtorch that the torturers were using on him. Immediately in front of Marcello Pagliero (Manfredi) was a sheet of glass, which Harry Feist (Bergmann) struck with his whip, and onto which pieces of hair had been stuck, which caught fire when the flame from the blowtorch hit them – to the viewer it appears that Manfredi's skin is burning. (These shots have been cut from some anglophone prints of the film.)

Many of the legends surrounding *Roma città aperta* have Rossellini as their source. Tag Gallagher quotes from a 1971 interview in which Rossellini talks about the scene of Don Pietro's execution:

> The whole scene was tremendously flat, something was missing. I saw the shots only three months [after we filmed them]. And there was very little material, because ... I had a repulsion against doing [extra] angles. I wanted to take risks, I like that. [But now] I was worrying about what to do.' The solution, he said in 1971, was 'really for me the most illuminating experience in my life. Just at the last moment I thought of giving the scene a certain kind of rhythm. It was very simple, we set up a microphone and with a finger I beat a chair, thump, thump, thump, and that little, nearly imperceptible noise completely changed the rhythm of the scene. So through that I learned that the main thing is to find the right rhythm: the [right] movement of the camera and people.[8]

It sounds as though a faint drumbeat is playing on the soundtrack: a beat, a pause, and then two beats close together. I must confess to a sneaking suspicion that Rossellini may have seen an execution scene in a film accompanied by a drumbeat – indeed, I can scarcely believe that he had not. Whether or not the drumbeat changes the rhythm of the scene, it certainly rehearses a cinematic convention. What is, of course, characteristic of Rossellini is that he exploits a conventional cinematic device *without* having a proper drumbeat on the soundtrack – just a hint: he uses a cliché and later builds a legend around it.

One of the most powerful rhetorical devices used by the film involves the soundtrack: the contrast of rhetorical register between the dubbing, by Giulio Panicali, of Harry Feist's performance as Bergmann and the humbler speech of Don Pietro and Manfredi. It is a matter to which we shall return later.

Mise en scène

In this area the film shares some features characteristic of documentary filming. However, whereas documentaries generally make great use of panning movements of the camera, the only 'scene-setting' pan in the film (such as is frequently encountered in documentaries, in the films of Visconti and De Santis and, to a lesser extent, those of Germi) is that over the rooftops of Rome behind the title credits (this shot does not appear in most anglophone copies of the film). One might have expected a pan for effect along the rows of the lined-up inhabitants of Via Montecuccoli during the German round-up, but Rossellini does not include one (this might not be a question of style, but simply of not having enough extras to convincingly furnish such a pan).

As a *general* point about the *mise en scène* of the film, it is worth noting at the outset that a Hollywood feature like *To Have and Have Not*, for example, appears to share many of the same stylistic characteristics as *Roma città aperta*, as do a large number of films of the 'realist' style of the 1940s.

Long takes (shots of long duration) and sequence shots are frequently associated with a realist cinematographic style, partly on the basis of André Bazin's critique of montage. The narrative of *Roma città aperta* is what sets it apart both from other films of its time and from other neorealist films, and that narrative strongly conditions the shooting and the editing of the film, a matter to which we shall return in detail. For the time being, it is enough to say that the film has to crosscut between storylines, between episodes proceeding in parallel, and between characters in different places. It makes for a fragmented way of shooting, and a heavy reliance on montage, and this shows in the average length of the shots in the film, which is 9.1 seconds. According to Barry Salt, the average shot length (ASL) of French and German films in the period 1934–9 is 12 seconds, while the average for Hollywood films 'went up from 8.5 seconds in the late 'thirties, to 9.5 seconds in the period 1940–1945, and finally to 10.5 seconds in the period 1946–1950.'[9] However, wherever possible, Rossellini uses quite long takes: in dialogue, for instance, he does not make much use of the reverse angle procedure. Eleven per cent of the shots in the film are twice as long as the ASL for the film as a whole, 4.5 per cent of them are more than three times as long, and ten shots are close to or well over a minute in length. As a result, a characteristic of the film is its switching from faster-cutting scenes of action and movement to a more contemplative rhythm in dialogue. Nevertheless, even this *pattern* of shot lengths conforms to the norm for both American and European films analysed by Barry Salt.[10]

To characterize accurately Rossellini's film style it is necessary to make comparisons, and so I list a few samples of average shot lengths in neorealist films (where they are not attributed to Barry Salt, they are my own calculations):

- Rossellini: *Roma città aperta*, 9.1 seconds; *Paisà*, 9.7 seconds; *Germania Anno zero*, 17.4 seconds; *Stromboli*, 11.6 seconds (Salt)
- De Sica: *Sciuscià*, 7.8 seconds; *Ladri di biciclette*, 6.9 seconds; *Miracolo a Milano*, 6.3 seconds
- Visconti: *Ossessione*, 17.5 (Salt: 16.5) seconds; *La terra trema*, 18.2 seconds; *Bellissima*, 21.1 seconds
- Antonioni: *Cronaca di un amore*, 33 seconds (Salt); *I vinti*, 45 seconds (Salt); *La signora senza camelie*, 61 seconds (Salt)

Comparisons with earlier, non-neorealist Italian films can be made with reference to the following data (kindly supplied to me by Barry Salt):

- Alessandro Blasetti: *Vecchia guardia* (1935), 15 seconds; *La corona di ferro* (1941), 5 seconds; *La cena del beffe* (1941), 8 seconds; *Quattro passi tra le nuvole* (1942), 10 seconds
- Augusto Genina: *Lo squadrone bianco* (1936), 9 seconds
- Mario Camerini: *Il signor Max* (1937), 12 seconds
- Carmine Gallone: *Scipione l'Africano* (1937), 8.5 seconds
- Ferdinando Poggioli: *Addio giovinezza* (1940), 11 seconds
- Giuseppe De Robertis: *Uomini sul fondo* (1941), 3.5 seconds
- Mario Soldati: *Piccolo mondo antico* (1941), 12.5; seconds; *Malombra* (1942), 22 seconds
- Gianni Franciolini: *Fari nella nebbia* (1942), 12 seconds

(In appendices 17–19 these figures are translated into column charts in order to make it easier to compare films.)

The figures speak for themselves. *Roma città aperta*'s average shot length conforms to the conventions of the period, particularly in Hollywood, and can by no stretch of the imagination be described as privileging 'realist' long takes. Nor, however, is the suggestion, advanced by some, that Rossellini's 'documentary' style owes something to the influence of De Robertis given support by the data regarding *Uomini sul fondo* (with an ASL of 3.5 seconds). There are notable stylistic differences between *La nave bianca*, directed in 1941 by Rossellini, with supervision and storyboarding by De Robertis (though they quarrelled over this film), and both *Un pilota ritorna* (1942) and *Roma città aperta* (1945).

Instead of being filmed in reverse-angle sequences, dialogue is generally staged in a single shot. Where more than two characters are involved Rossellini uses a three-dimensional composition, with characters in the foreground and others further from the camera, often in a 'V' formation, with its apex in the depth of the frame; in other words, two or more characters occupy the edges of the frame in the foreground, with their interlocutors in the centre of the frame further in the background (in a typical example of this composition used in an exterior the Brigadiere is accosted by the women at the bakery, and Agostino comes to find out what is happening). Comparison with *To Have and Have Not* shows that Hawks uses a similar technique for dialogue. Hence, Rossellini's avoidance of a reverse-angle procedure and his reliance on compositional strategies in a *mise en scène* procedure does not single him out from any norm that includes artists like Jean Renoir, Howard Hawks, and Orson Welles (though Renoir and Welles were precisely directors whom Bazin indicated as proponents of the new 'realist' style). Nevertheless, when Rossellini wants to contrast two characters (rather than morally unite them), he sometimes uses a different procedure. In the dialogue between Manfredi and Marina in her bedroom, and in the scenes in the Via Tasso Gestapo headquarters, he makes greater use of reverse angles. The avoidance of reverse angles in *Roma città aperta* is both a choice for its own sake and a corollary of the choice to eschew close-ups and use mainly medium shots – certainly, the procedures are two sides of the same coin. Rossellini's choices of shot length and scale of shot ('closeness' of the camera to the profilmic) appear every bit as pragmatically determined by diverse narrative and expressive requirements (the same is true for De Sica) as they are the product of poetic and stylistic principle, which cannot be said for the choices of Visconti and Antonioni, both of whom establish an entirely new relationship between montage and *mise en scène*. With the latter two directors narrative itself is conditioned by the choice of style, whereas with Rossellini, the style is fitted to the narrative and the 'vision' (which is further discussed in the chapter on *Paisà*). As a result, it has been difficult for critics to define Rossellini's style with any precision (and the same has been true for De Sica).

Rossellini's choices of 'scale of shot' are quite distinctive without, however, standing out to a large *degree* from the norm for the period. Barry Salt has tabulated what he calls the 'scale' or 'closeness' of shot for a number of films, among them *Roma città aperta*. In the column charts in appendices 20–22, each column represents the (approximate) number of shots of that particular scale (or 'closeness') out of a total of 500 shots (in the cases of *Roma città aperta* and *Paisà* the charts cover every shot in the films). The charts bear out Salt's contention that a style in which the 'medium shot' predominated was widely adopted from the middle of the 1930s to the end of the 1940s. I have included two examples of films directed by von Sternberg to show that an alternative style was certainly possible (all of his films Salt has studied show a similar pattern). *Roma città aperta* adopts the widespread 'medium scale' style. However, it does so to an extreme extent.

Labels and criteria for the 'scale' or 'closeness' of a given shot can vary from one critic to another, and from one era to another. Here I shall use those attributed by Barry Salt to 'the nineteen-forties and later': Big Close Up shows head only, Close Up shows head and shoulders, Medium Close Up includes the body from the waist up, Medium Shot includes from just below the hip to above the head of upright actors, Medium Long Shot shows the body from the knee upwards, Long Shot shows the full height of the body, and Very Long Shot shows the actor small in the frame.[11] Longer distance shots can be a relative matter, because in Westerns, for example, where outdoor shooting was common and landscape played an important part, extreme long shots were common, whereas they were less frequent in other feature films, which were mostly shot in studios. *Roma città aperta* for the most part conforms to the conventions of a studio-shot film.

Because of the height-to-width ratio of the 'classic' screen ratio (approximately 1:1.35), you really need to shoot with a medium shot before you can properly show two or more people in the same shot talking to each other. Only if they are close together face-to-face, or at an angle to each other (as in the staircase dialogue between Francesco and Pina) can you use medium close-up (or occasionally close-up) for more than one person.

Rossellini prefers ensembles to reverse-angle sequences, and hence he makes great use of medium shots. When he then cuts to one person, he usually uses a medium close-up. Once that pattern has been set up in the film, a real close-up immediately takes on greater significance by breaking the pattern (as, for example, with Don Pietro's broken spectacles or when he curses Bergmann). There are a number of occasions where close-ups have been used because Rossellini has 'inserted' into a dialogue a shot that he probably shot later (realizing that he needed some line of dialogue, or to replace a section where a mistake had been made). Examples are a shot of Pina during her first conversation with Manfredi in Francesco's apartment, a shot of Marina in her bedroom dialogue with Manfredi, a shot of Marcello (out of focus) in his dialogue with Don Pietro, and a shot of Bergmann addressing Manfredi in the torture scene, where he is clearly not against the background of the wall in the torture chamber where he says the rest of his lines (which has an 'expressionist' shadow thrown onto it), but against the wall in his office, which has a map pinned on it. In all these cases the lighting of the close-up fails to match that of the shots on either side of it.

All the films in appendices 20–22 have between 15 and 30 big close-up shots, with the exception of *Une partie de campagne*, which has fewer. There appears to be a wide range of between 40 and 80 close-up shots for most films, with the exception of von Sternberg's, which have far more, and Rossellini's, and Hawks's comedy, which have far fewer. Medium close-ups range between 70 and 90 for all films, including Rossellini's, except Hawks's, which have many more. *Roma città aperta* makes greater use of medium shots than any of the other films. Rossellini uses *more* medium shots than others to the same *degree* that he uses *fewer* close-up shots (and, when compared with Hawks, fewer medium close-ups than the American). The picture we get is of Rossellini using a fairly standard technique, but shifted towards longer (more distant) shots; he tends more towards medium and medium long, where others tend more towards medium close and close. His film's distinctive characteristic is the preponderance of medium shots, and the lack of close-up shots. This being the case, it is not surprising to find few reverse-angle sequences in dialogue (because such sequences are generally made up of close-up shots). The dialogue between Pina and Francesco on the staircase is a medium close-up shot of the two of them together, Francesco in the left of the frame looking frame right, where Pina sits in the depth of the image looking towards the camera.

On the matter of *Roma città aperta*'s style having something in common with the conventions of documentary films, it could certainly be said that Rossellini's choices of scale of shot lean away from the feature-film convention towards that of the documentary. Nevertheless, a more detailed examination of the *mise en scène* procedures that characterize the film requires us to relinquish any concern with documentary, and to start by simply describing components of the film's narrative style.

Various procedures are used to progressively open out scenes. One could be described initially as the 'pull back,' in which the camera

begins on a detail of the scene and progressively reveal
or location, or more characters. This procedure is cha
Renoir's and Orson Welles's style, though it is far less ma
città aperta than in their films. Our introduction to the Via Tasso Gestapo
headquarters starts from a shot of a map, whereupon the camera starts
pulling back to reveal first Bergmann, who moves in front of the map,
and then the Questore of Rome on the left of the frame. Similarly, but
with a different use of the camera, a scene in Via Tasso begins with a
medium close-up of Bergmann reading the headlines of the Resistance
press, and then, at the sound off of a knock on his door, the camera tilts
to show first the door at the far end of his office (with a rack-focus to
bring the door into focus, putting Bergmann out of focus in the foreground), then the NCO entering, and finally the Questore. During this
time, Bergmann has risen to his feet, and now, in the same shot, he
moves over to the other end of his office to greet the Questore, and they
both walk to the right to sit down facing each other in armchairs, with
the camera following. At this point, incidentally, there is an apparently
unnecessary cut to a very slightly different angle, which may have been
motivated by a mistake in the long take as the action subsequently progressed. Shortly thereafter, Bergmann rises and returns to stand behind
his desk, lit by the desk lamp. If you want to see how the film is lit, you
can count the shadows on the wall behind him at this point to see how
many floods are being used and where they are placed – all in order to
make it look as though he is being illuminated by the lamp on his desk
(a standard procedure in cinematography would be to throw light on
the wall to cancel out these shadows).

The same opening-out effect can be achieved with a movement of the
profilmic, rather than of the camera, as when our introduction to Don
Pietro consists of his back completely filling the screen until he runs
away from the camera after the football, revealing the boys and the
wider view. The 'pull back' device, therefore, is used to introduce two
of the protagonists into the film. It is a procedure used enormously by
Renoir in *La Grande illusion* and *La Règle du jeu*, and everything points to
Rossellini having been strongly influenced, particularly by the former.

Rossellini limits the movements (mostly panning and tilting) of his
camera for the most part to those necessary for following characters
around the interiors, the rooms: Francesco's flat, Bergmann's office,
Marina's dressing room, Don Pietro's church and rectory, the typogra-
pher's. I have already remarked on the lack of pans, and the only notable one (apart from that over the rooftops behind the credits) is the final

shot of the film, where the boys walk past the camera, which follows them, revealing the Roman skyline (a shot that Jolanda Benvenuti says was directed by her – and if this is true, it might put into question much interpretation of 'Rossellini's' ending to the film). The only really significant tracking shot is the one in which Pina makes her confession to Don Pietro beside the railway (a shot that totals a minute and a half, broken by a two-second cutaway reverse angle to look at the fascist militia who so exercise Pina). A similar, but much shorter, shot is used for Don Pietro's ideological conversation with Marcello.

The opposite procedure from the 'pull back' has the camera shooting an 'establishing' shot of the whole context, and then either cutting or developing into a closer (usually medium) shot. This is how we enter into the sequence of the assault on the bakery: with a very long shot followed by a medium one of the Brigadiere, some women, and the sacristan – to which I have referred earlier. This is also how the sequence of the SS round-up at Via Montecuccoli starts, and how the episode of the partisan attack on the German convoy is introduced.

Just as scenes develop with the profilmic moving away from the camera, so others develop with the profilmic moving in towards the camera from long shot to medium: Agostino bearing bread from the assault on the bakery, Francesco and then Lauretta returning home at night, Don Pietro arriving at the religious articles shop, or approaching the camera across the floor of his church. In one of the latter shots (at nearly 50 seconds quite a long one), Don Pietro approaches the camera together with Pina, who is holding the 'books' filled with money. They stop upon seeing something in the direction of the camera which we still do not see. It is the Austrian deserter, in uniform, who then appears in the left foreground from behind the camera, walks towards Don Pietro, and, after exchanging a word with him, passes on behind the priest and waits for him, still with his back to the camera. The reason for the shot being set up this way becomes plain as soon as you notice that the actor playing the Austrian at this point is not the same as the one who plays him elsewhere in the film (Akos Tolnay). Whether Rossellini shot the scene of the Austrian meeting Don Pietro, but something went wrong in the processing, or he simply discovered at some later stage that he had forgotten to introduce the character (by all accounts, not inconceivable) I have no way of knowing. Accounts of his having to eat humble pie with a parish priest in order to get back into his church – after he had irritated the priest, not thinking he needed the location any more – might be connected with this sequence of the film.

Rossellini appears more interested in the interaction of people, and its meaning, than in 'action' for its own sake, as the perfunctory treatment of the attack on the German convoy illustrates well. The camera angles in this sequence can be hard to reconcile, and the viewer is disoriented.[12] Admittedly, it is a 'transition' scene in the film, after the 'finale' of Pina's death. It may also illustrate something else. Tag Gallagher claims that '[i]n an innovation, for which he has never been acknowledged,' Rossellini 'discovered that when a shot's pace seemed slow, its rhythm could be sped up by subtly and painstakingly editing out single frames in the middle of the shot – the jumps would be imperceptible.'[13] I have been unable to detect any shots where this has obviously been done, but something analogous has been done in the episode of the attack on the convoy. As the German trucks go under the bridge, Rossellini has removed a whole sequence of frames, but this is because the third and fourth truck were too far behind the first two, and left us waiting with nothing happening on screen. The removal of the frames is perceptible, however, because the amount of dust hanging in the entrance to the underpass suddenly changes.

Nonetheless, an observation by Mario Calzini, in his report on the condition of the negative of *Roma città aperta* to the Cineteca Nazionale, suggests that there may be more to Gallagher's account than I can detect:

> In the body of some scenes, there are a few frames missing, and these omissions are repeated in successive texts [he is referring to subsequent prints and negatives struck from the original negative], which are a sign of problems arising during the original editing. In these cases it is not possible to guess how many frames are missing.

Apart from the SS round-up at the apartment building and the torture scene in Via Tasso, the rest of the film mainly consists of people coming in (or going out) through doorways: this is how scenes of dialogue are endowed with dynamism, and because of this there are only two *temps morts* in the film: the dialogue between Pina and Francesco, and the first minute-long shot of Marina in her dressing room. The latter scene develops first with Marina's own entry through the door, then with that of Lauretta, who goes back out again (very disapprovingly) when Ingrid comes in. Incidentally, the two long takes of Marina in her dressing room (each a minute long) have mismatched lighting, owing to the change of camera set-up, and hence of lighting, when the camera moves to the wall where her mirror hangs.

Dialogue in Francesco's apartment takes place in a continual entry

and exit through the door to the landing with, on two occasions, pre-
cipitous entries by Pina (the boys' sabotage and the SS round-up). Similarly, Bergmann's office has NCOs coming in and out, the Questore,
Ingrid, and, during the torture scene, Bergmann himself repairing to
the salon to discuss matters with Hartmann. The peace of Marina's flat
after Pina's death is broken by Lauretta, who insists on entering the
living room, and later rushes out of the bedroom when Manfredi
enters. Don Pietro's various haunts are the site of continual entries and
exits (perhaps the most effective one – and the nearest to 'realistic'
lighting the film gets – being the arrival of the children for catechism,
where he scolds Marcello: 'Ma tu sei sempre l'ultimo ..., a lodarlo').
Don Pietro's encounter with the Resistance organization surprisingly
makes unnecessarily heavy demands on sets: he enters the shop, then
a passage stairway, then the printing shop, and finally an office within
the printing works. During the SS round-up, suspense is maintained
by both Don Pietro and the fascist soldiers entering and exiting rooms
from the landings (the blow with the frying pan being signalled by
sound off).

   Rossellini tends not to make a 'theatrical' use of his sets (as does
Renoir, for example): they are not self-contained stages, but communicate with other spaces into which the camera frequently penetrates.
We are made aware that each room has an 'outside' surrounding it
(Francesco's flat by means of the landing, Marina's dressing room by
means of sound off, Bergmann's office by virtue of the adjoining rooms
and the sound off that comes from them: screams and Chopin). As we
shall see when we come to discussing montage, the film sets itself the
task of linking disparate characters and events, and the articulation of
space in the film (helped, where Marina is concerned, by the use of the
telephone) succeeds in doing that in quite sophisticated ways. In Via
Montecuccoli, the landings play an important role in 'institutionalizing'
the environment. There is an excellent analysis and interpretation of
how the city of Rome is viewed institutionally in the film, from above
by Bergmann and from below by Pina, in David Forgacs's monograph
devoted to it.[14]

   The way in which the filmmakers have institutionalized space, and
then used that institutionalized space, is not merely a matter of representation, but has a fundamental role in creating the narrative. The film
tells the story of the German *occupation* of Rome, that is to say, of a
'transgressor' intruding into Italian space. Had the 'story' really been
about the *Resistance*, this *mise en scène* would not have been enough. The

armed Resistance in Rome involved attacks on German and fascist troops, on plant and equipment. In fact, apart from the attack on the convoy, which is really just the freeing of prisoners, and the sabotage of Romoletto's band of boys, we see little of what Bergmann is actually fighting against. Instead, the film concentrates on the Germans' intrusion into the private spaces of Italian civilians – Manfredi's landladies' apartment, Via Montecuccoli, Marina's dressing room, Don Pietro's rectory (which is referred to, rather than shown). The Brigadiere stands out because he will not trespass or intrude into private space, and the Italian Fascist militia are uncomfortable doing so. True, the Germans are searching for the partisans who have been involved in actions, but those military actions are neither shown nor referred to (with the exceptions already mentioned). The result elides some aspects of 'war' and 'armed conflict' between two antagonists, and emphasizes an illegitimate, oppressive, and unjustified *trespassing*.

This has a number of effects. First of all, it tends to hide some of the historical realities of the war. Second, it makes possible the 'melodramatic' narrative we have continually referred to, and removes the elements of hero-adventure that a 'battle' would have entailed. The children are a source of comedy for the incongruity of their adult posturing (Marcello in particular), rather than of heroism. They are more like mascots condescendingly used as emblems of 'family' in the Italian melodramatic tradition than the well-developed and problematic figures presented in De Sica's neorealist films. The death of Pina is a product of the convergence on one person of the products of several different institutionalized spaces, and so the film's first half functions as an accelerated montage leading up to her fall (a matter discussed in the section on plot). This is how an ethical discourse is articulated in the film, and is what endows a frequently conventional melodramatic narrative with such extraordinary impact.

The film's designation of space, therefore, carries much of the ethical weight of the narrative. Don Pietro's domination of the grandfather's bedroom 'protects' it from the intrusion of the Fascists and Germans. Similarly, his domination of Bergmann's space in Via Tasso (as well as the ethical connotations of the juxtaposed salon and torture chamber) carries much of the ethical weight of the second half of the film.

The film's narrative opens with a masterly use of space and light for expressive effect. The first two sequences are primarily interiors, in gloomy dusk or artificially lit, and carry the German elements of the story: first the SS search of Manfredi's apartment, and then Bergmann's dialogue with the Questore of Rome in Via Tasso. Suddenly the film introduces the *popolo* of Rome in a big wide shot, set outdoors in sunlight, of the assault on the bakery. Everything opens up; the oppressive, artificially lit space connected with the German occupation is replaced with open, free space, full of people, gestures, sounds. This scene develops into Pina's dialogue with Manfredi in Francesco's apartment, whence she sends Marcello to fetch Don Pietro. Again we plunge into open, sunlit space, full of the movement and sound of children playing football. Gradually, from then on, the film pulls us inexorably back into the windowless, alien confinement of Via Tasso, until, in the coda to the film, Don Pietro's execution and the boy's response to it return us to open space and full daylight. In other words, the introductions into the narrative of Pina and Don Pietro both involve sudden 'openings-out' of the spatial dimension, together with brilliant lighting contrasts. They are both 'escapes' into sunlit open spaces from oppressive, dark interiors.

The use of space, and characters in it, may have something to do with why the film is often described as having a 'choral' quality. The impression may have been reinforced by something Rossellini said in reply to Mario Verdone's question in a 1952 interview ('What are the constant elements that you feel you have kept up in your films?'):

> I do not have formulae and preconceptions. But if I look back over my films, I undoubtedly encounter elements that remain constant in them, and which are repeated in them, not programmatically but, I repeat, quite naturally. Above all the *choral element* [*coralità*]. The realist film is, in itself, choral. The sailors in *La nave bianca* count as much as the refugees in the hut at the end of *L'uoma dalla croce*, as much as the populace in *Roma città aperta*, as much as the partisans in *Paisà* and the friars in *Giullare*.[15]

This is not an impression that stands up to closer inspection of *Roma città aperta*. Certainly, the way the apartment building is used, the SS round-up, and the assault on the bakery can be seen as having choral elements. Elsewhere, however, the film works to create threads uniting a series of protagonists, rather than depending on a choral performance. A lot of what passes for 'choral' depends on what Pina tends to 'signify' – she is used as a synecdoche for 'the people,' and her fatal run takes on any choral significance only from its place in the narrative. The film is not choral in the way that *Caccia tragica*, *Riso amaro*, *La terra trema*, and *Il sole sorge ancora* are.

Performers

The choice of actors was partly determined by questions of money. In order to get financial backing for the film, it was necessary to have some actors whose popularity could be used as a guarantee of future success at the box office. Both Aldo Fabrizi (Don Pietro) and Anna Magnani (Pina) met those requirements. They both asked for quite a large sum for their services. As a result there was little money left over for other actors, which partly accounts for the choice of inexperienced non-professionals, chosen from among the circle of friends of Rossellini and Sergio Amidei (the scriptwriter). Where Anna Magnani is concerned, the fact that she was to be well paid for her work turned out to be a good thing, for as filming began her son fell gravely ill with polio, which badly upset her. The need for money to pay for her son's treatment was a strong incentive for her to remain working on the film, and her distress may have given intensity to her performance. We could consider Rossellini as having incorporated a documentary approach to Magnani's personal condition into the fabric of his aesthetic object: he filmed *her*, and used her as Pina. He used this approach with Magnani in *Amore*, with the friars in *Paisà* and in *Francesco giullare di Dio*, with Ingrid Bergman in *Stromboli* and *Siamo donne*, with George Sanders in *Viaggio in Italia*, and with De Sica in *Il Generale Della Rovere*. The dangers of following this line of interpretation lie in obscuring some of the realities of commercial feature-film making.

While Fabrizi appears to have been the choice to play Don Pietro all along, for quite a while Clara Calamai was seriously considered as a candidate for the role of Pina, but negotiations with her broke down, and Rossellini was persuaded that Magnani was right for the part. Of all the people approached in connection with the proposed film, the two who were immediately the most positive about it were Fabrizi and Magnani, and both straightaway understood its power and beauty from having its story recounted to them.

The choice of leading actors, however, also belonged to a large extent in the realm of conventional commercial expediency, and to that extent cannot be included in a notion of the film's neorealist 'poetics.' Nevertheless, when Fabrizi demanded an exorbitant sum for his participation, and Magnani insisted on matching his fee, Rossellini and Amidei did not immediately look elsewhere, and instead set about raising the necessary money. To this extent, therefore, the choice of performers enters very much into the 'poetics' of the film. For a dramatic story of this nature, bearing these national historic overtones, the choice of two music-hall comedians, with a background in popular dialect theatre, was deliberate. The implications of the choice were numerous, but most significantly in the sphere of rhetoric. It was a deliberate refusal of the rhetorical register conventionally associated with adventure and historical films of a 'civic' nature, and was a deployment of the rhetoric of *sermo humilis*.

Fabrizi immediately took to the script, but the role was not in his normal professional 'range.' Rossellini told an amusing story once about getting the required intensity out of his performance at the end of the torture scene. However embroidered this story might be, it does shed light on the poetics of Rossellini's approach to the use of Fabrizi; the actor fitted into the total picture, the 'whole' artefact, that Rossellini was striving for, and details of his performance were merely 'mechanical' problems to be solved:

> Thirty years later, when someone asked about the wonderful 'emotional quality' of Fabrizi's performance, Roberto was ready.
> 'You remember,' he answered, speaking English, 'the scene when Fabrizi realizes Manfredi [Pagliero] is dead and he blesses him? Well, Fabrizi said to me, "You must do me a favor. I want to cry. I want really to cry." So I said, "Okay, cry, then."
> 'We spent half a day waiting for him to cry. Then we said, "How can you cry?" "Well, you know, I think, for example, of a little white flower." So he said, "Be ready! When I snap my fingers, start shooting because I will be crying."
> 'And so we wait for hours. Then he says, "May I have a cognac?" "Yes, okay, you can have a cognac." So finally after twenty cognacs, he gets totally drunk and he thought about that little white flower and starts to cry.
> 'I called him later into the projection room, and I said, "You can see what a masterpiece you have made." It was absolutely disgusting. The tears were coming out of his nose in balloons, from his mouth. Exploding! It was absolutely a disgusting scene!
> 'He said, "But I really cried!"
> '"I know you really cried. But what does it mean to really cry? It means nothing at all!"
> 'So we had to do the scene again. And it was very easy. With a few drops of glycerin he was crying. It was nothing at all!
> 'How can an actor in a studio with the lamps, the electrician around, and

everybody tired of waiting – how can he get into the mood? Actors know just two, three, or four tricks, and they always play on those kinds of tricks. But if you want something else, you must invent things and you must make them at ease. To "feel" to "participate" to me means nothing at all.'[16]

Any experience of research into accounts of the making of *Roma città aperta* counsels caution. Just because Rossellini tells the story about Fabrizi's performance does not make it true. But Rossellini did *tell* the story, and it is revealing about his response to the admiration for the 'emotional quality' of Fabrizi's performance. He does not explain the meaning of Fabrizi's tears, nor does he accept their 'ontological' value: 'I know you really cried. But what does it mean to really cry? It means nothing at all!' Instead, he concentrates on the poetics of his art. His little story asserts that he was engaged in creating an 'object,' a film, and he accepted the contribution of others in its construction. Fabrizi's desire to cry did not conflict with the *rhetorical* goals of Rossellini's 'object,' and so he granted Fabrizi's request. Rossellini did not have some picture in his head of a 'reality' to which he had to be faithful, nor was there some kind of 'realist' *means* to be used in the construction of his 'object.' Crying was a rhetorical device that had value for its *meaning*, yet no 'meaning' derived from Fabrizi *actually* crying. There was a chemical means of achieving the effect that was far more expedient.

This story, and the meaning I have attributed to it, goes directly *counter* to the point I made earlier about Rossellini's 'documentary' use of actors. This apparent contradiction should not cause alarm, because one of the striking features of *Roma città aperta* is the way in which Rossellini will use different devices and styles at different moments for different purposes.

Tag Gallagher makes the point about the film's conventionality succinctly:

It is true that *Roma città aperta* was a challenge to the industry: it abandoned certain traditions of quality, assumed a political stance, portrayed recent events, dealt with controversial issues, and took license in language, drugs, sex, violence, and choice of heroes. But, though independently produced at a time when a once flourishing industry was disorganized, *Roma città aperta* was not made to spite the establishment, nor even despite the establishment, but rather by established filmmakers with established methods of production and financing. It was not shot on the street by improvisation with non-professional actors, as Rossellini's legend would later insist, but mostly in a studio with famous stars and a detailed script. *Roma città aperta*'s revolutionizing innovations were in content rather than technique.[17]

From Magnani Rossellini needed the authenticity and spontaneity of passion and instinct (instinct may not have lain behind Magnani's *method*, but it was the effect *achieved*). From Fabrizi he needed 'contamination' with self-deprecating humour (a certain humility forced upon Fabrizi by the fact that he was performing in a range over which he was not fully a master). For a film that was attempting in its 'content' a rather delicate operation of reconciliation between the Church and communism, a film whose completion probably depended on the goodwill of Vatican figures for the supply of film stock necessary to shoot it, in a context where filmmakers had thoroughly disgraced themselves in the Church's eyes over the shooting of *La porta del cielo* (to such an extent that parish priests were forbidden to allow filming in their churches anymore, a ruling that caused problems for Rossellini too) – for such a film, in such a context, to choose a rather unprepossessing music-hall buffoon who specialized in dialect, vulgar slapstick, and sexual innuendo to play the one priest whose personal sanctity would outweigh in Catholics' eyes his political compromises could hardly be called 'expedient.' If not exactly revolutionary, it was a significant and innovative rhetorical choice.

Rossellini discussed the extent to which he saw *Roma città aperta* as an aesthetic construction, deriving from an existing artistic tradition and owing a great deal to the actors and the use he made of them:

Whether the impact of so-called neorealism on the world derived from *Roma città aperta* is for others to decide. I see the birth of neorealism further back: above all in certain novelized war documentaries, where I too had a part to play with *La nave bianca*; then in real and proper fictional war feature films, which saw me involved in the script, as in *Luciano Serra pilota*, or in the direction as in *L'uomo dalla croce*; and finally and above all in certain minor films, like *Avanti c'è posto, L'ultima carrozzella, Campo de' Fiori*, in which the formula, if we want to call it that, of neorealism is being assembled through the spontaneous creations of actors: of Anna Magnani and of Aldo Fabrizi in particular. Who can deny that it is these actors who first embodied neorealism? That the music hall scenes of the 'strongmen' or of 'Roman ditties' performed on a carpet or with the help of just one guitar, as they were invented by Magnani, or the figure portrayed on local stages by Fabrizi, already anticipated at times certain films of the neorealist period? Neorealism is given birth, unconsciously, by the film in dialect; then it becomes conscious of itself in the heat of the human and social problems of the war and its aftermath. And while we are on the topic of dialect films, it would not be out of place to refer, historically, to our less immediate predecessors: I am talking about Blasetti with his film using 'types,' *1860*, and Camerini with films like *Gli uomini che mascalzoni*.[18]

Rossellini is attributing an element of 'authorship' to the actors. In hindsight he is seeing the films *Avanti c'è posto*, *L'ultima carrozzella*, and *Campo de' Fiori* as teleologically *leading* to neorealism. *Avanti c'è posto* (Mario Bonnard, 1942) starred Fabrizi and *Campo de' Fiori* (Bonnard, 1943) and *L'ultima carrozzella* (Mario Mattoli, 1943) starred both Fabrizi and Magnani, with Fellini as a scriptwriter on all three. Yet everything Amidei says leads in the other direction: that the choice of actors was an element of continuity with the theatrical and economic values of conventional Italian filmmaking of the early 1940s (Amidei was for Magnani, Rossellini for Clara Calamai, both conventional box-office 'draws' at the time).

The role of Agostino, the sacristan, is a comic one from start to finish: it was written as comedy, the actor chosen to play the role (Nando Bruno) came from comedy, and he plays it for comic effect (even, on occasion, as a 'stooge' in a duet with Fabrizi – for example, over the bread, over boiling cabbage, and over money). The narrative convention in which the priest's helpers are burlesqued goes back at least to Manzoni's *I promessi sposi* a century earlier.

Marcello is very different from the children in *Germania anno zero* and in De Sica's *Ladri di biciclette*. As Gallagher recounts: 'Roberto also signed Vito Annichiarico, a ten-year-old shoeshine boy working in Largo Tritone across from the Countess's office [she was financing the film on the basis of its being about the life of Don Morosini], whose father was missing in Africa and whose mother was in hospital, to play Pina's son for 13,200 lire a day.'[19] Annichiarico was to have played Pasquale in *Paisà*, but Rossellini chose Alfonsino Bovino from Maiori at the last moment. It is revealing that on at least two occasions Rossellini was unable to get Annichiarico to say his lines properly on camera, and had to use devices to cover up the fact (in both cases they were scenes with Don Pietro: the discussion of ideology, where an out-of-focus close-up is inserted into the sequence, and the scene after the frying pan, where

Marcello is made to face away from the camera). Marcello is used – as the youngster aping the adults – for comic and melodramatic effect; he looks younger than he really is, and than the role required him to be. Hence, Annichiarico as an actor and the role he is required to perform have something of the rhetorical about them. Rossellini makes Marcello innocent by satirizing the incongruity between his ideology and actions, on the one hand, and his age, on the other. Marcello is playing a role that is too grown-up for him.

De Sica does not create this gap between the 'role' and the 'reality' in his children, certainly not in *Ladri di biciclette*. His child is not innocent, he just is what he is, looking with his feelings and needs upon the adult world. He is young, sensitive, and vulnerable, in need of care and protection. The child does, indeed, supply a perspective on society, but only in so far as his youth makes more apparent the failure of society to meet basic human needs. Besides, in De Sica, the qualities of the child (sensitivity and vulnerability), are shared by adults: Antonio, Maria, and Umberto. De Sica adds children fully to his *dramatis personae*, as characters sharing equally in the expression of social need; he does not use any devices to make them special. De Sica is not sentimental, whereas in *Roma città aperta* Rossellini is. Whether, between *Roma città aperta* and *Paisà* and *Germania anno zero* Rossellini learned from De Sica, or whether the changes just reflected Rossellini's artistic development, I have no way of knowing.

Less attention has been paid to the performance of Harry Feist as Bergmann than to those of Magnani and Fabrizi. To a large extent, he carries the weight of the second half of the film, after Pina has been eliminated from the story. Feist's impatient and fastidious gestures and speech are what most communicate Bergmann's indifference to human values in the pursuit of his professional goals. If we pay close attention to his speech, we realize that a great deal of the effect is achieved by the choice of an Italian actor to dub his dialogue – Giulio Panicali, who dispenses with a German accent and instead bestows upon Bergmann's diction the same fastidious precision (a beautifully precise and correct Italian) that is expressed in his costume and deportment. Panicali's diction belongs in a higher rhetorical register than that of anyone else in the film, and there is a literary quality to his syntax. As a result, he contrasts 'rhetorically' with Manfredi's, and in particular with Don Pietro's, humble diction. Their accent, dialect, and diction carry so much meaning in the film partly because they are so violently contrasted with the beautifully controlled work of Harry Feist and Giulio

Panicali – the meaning, in this case, is constructed out of a binary opposition between two different rhetorical registers of performance from
the actors.

Feist plays Bergmann as a dandy: elegantly turned out and self-conscious in his movements, gestures, and speech. Significant also is his effeminacy (apparently a reference to a characteristic of one of the two
historical figures on which his figure is based, Major – subsequently
Lieutenant Colonel – Herbert Kappler of the Gestapo and Colonel
Eugen Dollman of the SS) – Feist was chosen *because* he was homosexual and camp.

Bergmann is depicted as efficient, and as applying studied strategies
to achieving his goals. Herbert Kappler was generally regarded as having been very effective at carrying out an extremely difficult job in
Rome. In counter-terrorism, routine torture is used as much as a
weapon for deterrence as for actually getting accurate information from
prisoners. It was the Italian Fascist police lieutenant Pietro Koch who, it
appears, relished torturing prisoners. Koch was also a dandy, but not,
as far as I know, homosexual (indeed, it was his girlfriend who led to
his eventual capture in Florence). These speculations are directed to the
question of whether any 'sadism' was *intended* in the make-up of the
character of Bergmann. If a reference was being made to Koch, then that
might have been the intention. However, *Roma città aperta* as a whole
avoids drawing attention to the Fascists, treating them with burlesquing tenderness (as bungling) or even compassionate understanding
(the humiliation of the Questore of Rome), and sets up the Germans as
the real antagonists. The dramatic power of the interrogation scene
depends on the conflict being simple: between Bergmann's desire to get
information and Manfredi's refusal to give it. Sadism and exaggerated
'evil' in the portrayal of Bergmann would have complicated this simple
dramatic conflict.

Instead, the narrative of the film projects his character as fastidious,
impatient, and irritable. While he is fully aware of the humanity of his
prisoners, that humanity is depicted as an irritant, making people stupidly (as he sees it) refuse to tell him what he wants to know and putting him to the trouble of having to torture them to extract answers.
Torture is itself a disordered business, because it can lead to frustrations
such as the source of information dying before you have got what you
want out of him (another source of irritation to Bergmann). Then prisoners have the stupidity to commit suicide, a further minor irritant.
Humanity, on the one hand, and the ordered, efficient achievement of

Bergmann's goals, on the other, are portrayed as being in conflict, producing in him irritation, which is carried through into the salon in his dialogue with Hartmann. The film surrounds Bergmann with these 'irritants,' disturbing his ordered world (his obsession with order is set up earlier in the film in his dialogue with the Questore of Rome about the Schröder Plan). To a certain extent, it is the order of the dandy, and is a product of the poetics underlying Bergmann's representation.

The shallowness of his dandyism and his effeminacy are easily related to the whole scheme of the film, in which sexuality, morality, and political approval are intertwined. It is done with a crudeness that would be entirely appropriate in a genre vehicle, or a film of political propaganda: the good are 'naturally' good and the 'bad' are bad because they are 'naturally' bad (and sexually either perverted or simply promiscuous). There is no explanation. Therefore, it is entirely understandable that the film should be seen as expressing an essentially populist political message, in which political value is the product of the natural, spontaneous goodness of 'the people.'

Magnani's personal style of acting is particularly appropriate within this scheme, because she projects her characters (in all her films) as driven by passionate instincts rather than reasoned thought. Indeed, in *Roma città aperta*, Pina's death is 'unrealistic,' in the sense that she has hitherto been depicted as one who knows how to cope with the realities of the German occupation. Only passion and 'instinct' (along with the plot element of it being her wedding day) justify her futile pursuit of the German truck. In other words, her fatal dash after the truck teeters on the brink of being 'out of character' in the *logical* scheme of the film, and is redeemed by a *histrionic* element in the performance of a particular actress. Magnani launches herself through the passage leading to the street, and then at the departing truck, with a wild fury that is extraordinary in the literal sense. Normally, if you run and rerun a struggle or a fight in a film enough times, you begin to see how it was choreographed. No matter how many times you rerun this scene, at whatever speed, Magnani seems out of control. There are conflicting reports about how much the scene was rehearsed, and small details of each account indicate that each one is unreliable. Certainly, Magnani's performance at this point in the film has become legendary, partly for its historical meaning and partly for its slightly shocking authenticity. There are a number of flaws in the sequence's filming (a point to which we shall return), but the viewer is too involved in Pina's frenzy to notice them. The viewer would not have been satisfactorily convinced had any other character portrayed in the film behaved in a similar fashion.

Hence, moral and political values are coded in the film not just in terms of sexual orthodoxy and the family, but also in terms of acting styles: when we come to the torture scene, Bergmann is already negatively coded for his cool dandyism in comparison with the positive pole of Magnani's passionate instinctiveness in the film's first half. While the contrast is between almost caricatured stereotypes of 'humanity' and 'inhumanity,' the viewer's responses and suspension of disbelief depend on the performers' professional qualities rather than on the 'realism' inherent in the scenes.

Costume

Costume supplies an important contribution to the narrative devices of the film. There are two significant costume 'gifts' in the film: Marcello's gift of his scarf to his new *'papà,'* Francesco, which saves the latter's life, and Ingrid's gift to Marina, in payment for the life of Manfredi, of a fur coat, which is retrieved once it has served its purpose. The two gifts fit, moreover, into a coding system in the film that creates a scale ranging from Pina's unbecoming cardigan to Bergmann's impeccable uniform. The fur coat donated to Marina is merely an extension of the silk stockings and the elegant outfits she is able to wear as a result of prostituting herself with the Germans.

The film displays a scale of different registers of dress. Pina's family and the other tenants of Via Montecuccoli, as well as Manfredi and Francesco, are dressed in one 'register,' all civilian (and their speech has much in common, something that becomes significant when we take a closer look at the portrayal of Bergmann). Marina's costume at Flavio's restaurant, after the shooting of Pina, belongs in a quite different, and much higher, register, and therefore signals her alienation from solidarity with the community, the suspect nature of her morality, and her affinity with the Germans. In the case of the civilians, the register of costume is associated with money, and hence directly with morality. Where uniforms are concerned, a similar parallel applies, so that in the film overall, the higher the register of dress, the lower the ranking in the moral scale.

The rhetoric of *sermo humilis* sets up an association of a quartet of highly valued and interrelated characteristics: poverty, low register dress (and speech), high moral standards, and realism (in the sense of 'reduction,' as discussed in chapter 2). To this extent, the notion of 'realism' is partly an *evaluative* term, defining superficial and rhetorical characteristics of the iconography of the narrative.

Since the film's story concerns war, uniforms play an important role. The next step, in the scale of uniforms, is the crumpled greatcoat of the Brigadiere, along with, slightly further up the scale, the rather sloppily uniformed Fascist police who stop Francesco on his way home from work (their conversation, about women, is also casual, and yet they are joking about prisoners they have seen brought in for interrogation by the Gestapo in Via Tasso). Next up the scale are the members of the firing squad, incongruous and clumsy in uniforms that appear too big for them. (In contrast to Hartmann's self-confidence, they have difficulty taking and lighting a cigarette with gloves on.) Quite a large jump brings us to the Tuscan fascist NCO who follows Don Pietro upstairs to check on the sick grandfather, and whom we have already seen checking papers during the dialogue between the priest and Pina (her 'confession'). Up to this level on the scale, the Fascists have been distinguished from the Germans, on a level hovering between the political and the moral, partly through the use of costume. Precisely by means of the 'register' of his costume, however, the Tuscan Fascist alludes to the involvement of the Fascists with the Nazis (a fact that tends to be glossed over in the film). He is, if anything, 'redeemed' somewhat by being rather stupidly overawed by Don Pietro's pantomime with the grandfather, just as the Questore of Rome's political coding is softened by being dressed in civilian clothes and being insulted by the stiffly uniformed Bergmann. A similar adjustment to 'coding' applies to Hartmann, drunk and slouched in a chair. Then come the German soldiery who surround Via Montecuccoli, one of whom is 'demoted' in the hierarchy by having his helmet knocked askew by a slap from Pina – a minor rebellion on her part, but one that gathers significance from its subversion of the costume code. Finally, there is Bergmann, the dandy in uniform, perverse in his smartness. The whole interrogation and torture sequence is played around the contrast in costume between the uniformed and the un-uniformed, and climaxes in the nakedness of Manfredi.

Don Pietro is a case apart, 'uniformed' at different levels of register, the highest being at the Via Montecuccoli round-up (and at Benediction in church after Pina's death). The initial coding is at the comic level of 'disguise' (he has already been introduced into the film, incongruously, as humbly and clumsily refereeing a football match in his clerical 'uniform'). But when he (and Marcello, similarly 'uniformed' in clerical garb) rush to the fallen body of Pina, the uniform takes on a higher register, so much so that the episode ends with an added, narratively superfluous, shot of Don Pietro cradling the body of Pina in a way that many have recognized as alluding to the Renaissance iconography of the *Pietà*, Christ's deposition from the cross. Uniform, where Don Pietro is concerned, is exploited both to raise him in status and to signal his humility in setting little store by his uniformed persona (he is the only one who wears spectacles, apart from Gino, the partisan commander in the printing shop, and shows no irritation when the Germans cause them to be broken). The Austrian deserter signals his conversion by his change out of uniform into civilian dress.

The coding of dress is motivated by the story, and by its historical 'referents.' Nevertheless, in the case of Bergmann, Marina, the Brigadiere, and Agostino, the narrative coding of costume is used emphatically, one might say 'rhetorically,' as a means of persuading the audience to respond to the characters in a certain way. Moreover, costume is used to 'institutionalize' characters in a noticeable manner.

Reflecting on the use of costume can take us from the uniforms worn by men to the luxury of the clothes worn by women according to their sexual behaviour (wives and mothers or prostitutes), and from there to a thematic complex revolving around sex.

Sex is a 'theme' in *Roma città aperta* that is intimately bound up with the film's generic nature as melodrama. The family is established as an anchor in the chaos that is the storm of war. While the episode of the boys being spanked for returning home late is one of many scenes using the narrative and rhetorical procedures of comedy, its narrative emphatically affirms 'organic' values in a context of disorder. Pina's marriage to Francesco and Marcello's endorsement of it have a similar function. The typical melodramatic narrative has a family threatened and destroyed by some act of transgression, usually sexual, with a resolution involving either the reconstitution of the family or some sort of expiation. This basic narrative characterizes hundreds of Italian films in the period 1936–56, and *Roma città aperta* fits the pattern. Marina's transgression threatens to destroy Pina's family and the 'community' held together by Don Pietro and defended by Manfredi. The kernel of the melodramatic narrative is suffering, but something is done to endow the suffering with a 'cause,' however perfunctory or remote.

It may not be going too far to say that sexual pleasure is always, or always eventually becomes, transgressive in melodrama. What is significant about *Roma città aperta*, and about neorealism in general, is that there is a 'flight' from pleasure. In this film and in *Paisà* sexual pleasure is 'denied' by the very narratives that propose it. In *Paisà* the sexual sentiments of Carmela, Francesca, and Harriet are truncated by the stories. Few films, however, thematize sex as much as *Roma città aperta* does. 'Good' and 'bad' is coded in sexual terms, such that slight ambiguities are raised in the logic of the narrative. When the Germans come to search Via Montecuccoli 17, they are looking for the saboteurs of the night before, and so it is Marcello who indirectly brings about his mother's death. However, it is easy for the moral signifiers of the film to lead the viewer to attribute her death to Marina's betrayal of Manfredi.

Lauretta is 'stripped bare' by the director of the film: in Marina's dressing room she displays more of her breasts than was usual in Italian cinema because of the dress she is wearing; as she comes home late, she bares her upper thigh to stash her money; in Marina's apartment she runs out of the bedroom when Manfredi enters while she is undressing. The other two times we encounter her, she is unprepossessingly in curlers. The actress who plays her, Carla Rovere, was having an affair with Rossellini during the making of the film, while the actress who dubbed Ingrid was Rossellini's 'official' mistress, Roswitha Schmidt. Pina's 'sacrifice' is, in fact, a foolishly passionate impulse with no practical, 'Resistance' purpose, whose cinematic representation was based, apparently, on the passionate attachment of Anna Magnani – later to become Rossellini's mistress – to Massimo Serato, her lover; and this representation was deliberately chosen instead of the originally scripted one, which followed the historical chronicle of Maria Teresa Gullace's death (see page 163). In Magnani's performance, Pina's death is tightly bound up in a mesh of sexual conflict. 'Realism' is not exactly the first explanation that leaps to mind. It is worth remembering that in 1945 Roberto Rossellini was every bit as much a historical 'fact' as Maria Teresa Gullace.

It has been suggested that the matrix within which to understand the treatment of sexuality in *Roma città aperta* is that of patriarchy: 'Pina is a threat to patriarchy, and must be killed off.'[20] There is something implausible in the suggestion that *Roma città aperta* is about the struggles of feminism and the Oedipal complex, and yet perhaps this perspective furnishes a clue to a deeper thematic level of narrative upon which the film draws.

In melodrama the family often has the function that in other types of narrative has been characterized by Curtius's notion of the topos of the *locus amoenus*.[21] He identified the 'garden' (*hortus conclusus*) as a recurring topos (or commonplace). If melodrama is the narrative of suffering occasioned by loss, then the idyll denied could well have something to do with natural fertility and growth, which would, in turn, identify it with the feminine. What is not so clear is where the masculine might come into the picture. In hero-adventure, the initiated male makes possible the fertile garden (from which he is then frequently excluded). Nevertheless, we can start with 'Italy' as a feminine entity, linked to the earth and to fertility, in which fertility is a resource fought over, and in which the feminine acts as a symbol of what has to be distributed and yet, at the same time, preserved. It must be remembered how much Italy was, until the end of the nineteenth century, more a literary entity than a political and geographical one. This literary entity was, in its turn, composed of ingredients taken from culture, from historical experience, and from peasant agricultural reality. Italy was a woman who had once been mistress of the world; she was now a handmaiden or, even worse, a concubine, forced to yield her produce in order not to be totally despoiled. This is how Italy is represented by Dante, Petrarca, Ariosto, Machiavelli, and Leopardi, indeed, by the entire major canon of Italian literature. Rossellini in *Roma città aperta* is attaching himself to a tradition that was the acquisition of every Italian schoolchild.

The First World War brings about a radically new approach to war, both in literature and in cinema, symptomatically embodied in the latter case by Jean Renoir's *La Grande illusion*. War ceases to be seen in spiritual terms as an initiation, and begins to come under the umbrella of the economic. If the role of the male is to die in war, what is wrong with war? In a sense, this is the question embodied in the figure of von Rauffenstein in *La Grande illusion*, and which is resoundingly answered in the final section of Renoir's film set at Elsa's farm. War interferes with biological production. War is a malfunctioning of society, indeed, a denial of what its true function is. *Roma città aperta* does not argue so much the politics of war as the economics of war. Notions of national tradition come to be replaced with notions of class. Instead of being represented in epic and heroic terms, war becomes the subject of satire (we see foretastes of this in Ariosto's treatment of the battle of Ravenna, in Voltaire's *Candide*, and in Stendhal's treatment of Waterloo in *La Chartreuse de Parme* – it certainly did not all start with the First World

War). In Italy, a good example is Emilio Lussu's novel *Un anno sull'Altipiano*, which contrasts so radically with a regressive, eroticized war novel like Marinetti's *L'alcova d'acciaio* that it is hard to imagine the two coming from the same culture and the same period (they are both memoirs, having rather the same relation to their historical referents as *Roma città aperta*). It is as though the whole culture of right-wing, nationalist bourgeois heroism embodied in Futurism and D'Annunnzio, glorifying a mythical masculinism, had in fact, as Renoir perceived, been jettisoned as outdated and irrelevant or, even worse, become the butt of satirical mockery. In *Roma città aperta* part of the treatment of Bergmann can be categorized as satire, with the figure of Hartmann serving partly to satirize Bergmann. Hartmann (aware of the problematic nature of his role, and questioning of hierarchy) is to Bergmann (unquestioning of hierarchy) what in Renoir's film de Boëldieu is to von Rauffenstein. The new protagonists, against whom the old appear slightly ridiculous (both Bergmann and von Rauffenstein are *physically* caricatured), are Maréchal and Rosenthal in Renoir's film, and Pina, Don Pietro, and Manfredi in Rossellini's. The impact of *Roma città aperta* all over the world may have owed more to its reflection on the war, and its embodiment of an attitude to war in general, than to what it had to say specifically about Italy (which may explain why the satirical, pacifist, Renoiresque *Vivere in pace* of Luigi Zampa was, outside Italy, often rather implausibly seen as its twin).

Realism entails the choice of the melodramatic matrix over the hero-adventure matrix. The melodramatic matrix (concerned with 'why man suffers') could be seen as less progressive than the hero-adventure matrix (concerned with 'how man progresses'). In fact, however, it turns out to be rather more complicated than that. The hero-adventure matrix, in its thought, hypothesizes the turning of chaos against itself (violence against violence) through the setting up of an antagonism (heroes against villains) in order to thwart the monopolization of resources (by the villains) and facilitate the productive social use of those resources (by the institution of society). Inevitably, the hero-adventure narrative concentrates on the moment of antagonism in that logical sequence: the conflict. With the defeat of the villains, the narrative ends. Any narration of the productive social use of the resources, now made possible by the work of the heroes, belongs in the matrix of melodrama. However, in melodrama the impediment to production and reproduction is 'chaos' – and the chaos brought about by the heroic conflict every bit as much as anything else.

War is an affliction, regardless of what the war is over, and regardless of what the war is designed to achieve. War stops production and reproduction – even though, in the hero-adventure matrix, war is a means of facilitating and enabling production and reproduction. In other words, in the context of the Italy of 1942–5, the two narrative matrices themselves are in conflict. In social (class) terms the hero-adventure matrix posits an elite (heroes) persuading society to accept chaos and the suspension of production for a future benefit. The melodramatic matrix, concentrating as it does on *any* chaos as the cause of suffering, constitutes a critique of the very notion of an elite. It shows up the elite as validating itself at the expense of the community, and very often uses satire to this end. (There was intense debate in occupied Rome over the appropriateness of the G.A.P. partisan attack in Via Rasella that brought about the German reprisal of the Fosse Ardeatine massacre.) From a political point of view, this matrix fatally leans towards populism – as is the case with *Roma città aperta*. The politics of Rossellini's film derives as much from the generic matrix underlying the narrative as from anything else.

What we are finding is that the narratives of war that we are discussing contain a *metanarrative* component. *La Grande illusion* starts with the hero-adventure narrative of the conflict and mutual respect between von Rauffenstein and de Boëldieu and gradually replaces that way of 'thinking' with a narrative belonging to the melodramatic matrix, with the empty table in Elsa's farm. The film itself constitutes both a critique of one narrative matrix and its polemical replacement with another. In Italy, neorealism is part of this general metanarrative activity. It is not so much that neorealism 'abolishes' the primacy of narrative as that it polemically asserts the primacy of one matrix over another. This is one of its important contributions to 'thinking' in the twentieth century: shifting and adjusting the narrative matrices according to which 'thought' is articulated.

This metanarrative side to neorealism was enormously influential. In Poland, Andrzjei Wajda, who acknowledged a huge debt to Italian neorealism, will make the polemic between the hero-adventure and the melodramatic matrices the kernel not only of his narrative treatment of the Polish experience of the war (in *Kanal* and *Ashes and Diamonds*), but also of his explanation of Polish history in general, that is to say, of the Polish people's way of 'thinking about' reality and politics.

In *Roma città aperta*, Marina's and Lauretta's femininity is monopolized by the enemy, while Pina's is truncated (interestingly, on the morning of her wedding to a man who, the night before, has confessed to being unable fully to articulate the reason for fighting). Once the Germans left Rome, the monopolists became the Americans, as represented in *Paisà*. Even though *Roma città aperta* codes values in terms of sex, it studiously avoids outright condemnation. Marina and Lauretta are explicitly coded as more stupid than evil (Lauretta says so to Marina at one point), and Bergmann's inhumanity is caricatured and satirized rather than demonized. Sex is supposed to function not just as a morality, but as an investigation into the dynamic of fertile, productive social life, and how war interferes with it.

At the core of *Roma città aperta* lies the death of a pregnant woman, one that the heroism of Manfredi and Don Pietro was powerless to prevent, and one for which their sacrifice fails to compensate. Manfredi loses Marina, and pays for it, but his heroism in the torture chamber is like closing the stable door after the horse has bolted. He is being tortured – emasculated – while Marina is being wooed by Ingrid – the sexual needs that Manfredi refused to meet being met by the Germans, who represent 'war.' There is a 'theme' in Italian cinema, everywhere apparent, in which the male fears being unable to meet the sexual – or reproductive – needs of women. The acting personnel of post-war Italian cinema mirrors this remarkably accurately, with a cult of the female star recruited from the fertility festivals of beauty contests and of heroic dramatic male leads imported from Hollywood. The theme of masculine inadequacy is in continuity with the theme, inherited from the literary tradition, of Italy being a woman abandoned by her menfolk to foreign invaders. In some ways, this is also emblematic of the narrative representation of the Italian Resistance as a whole. Calvino's novel *Il sentiero dei nidi di ragno* gets very close to all the ambiguities of the Resistance in its mixture of opportunism, sexual anxiety, and desperate idealism, and the theme is present in Pavese's *La casa in collina*. Aldo Vergano's film *Il sole sorge ancora* opens with Cesare failing to complete his contract with a prostitute in order to flee from the Germans, and develops into the story of a male 'shamed' out of opportunism and into armed rebellion by the demands of the young, fertile heroine, Laura. A pagan idealization of feminine sexuality is accompanied in neorealism by the association of masculine sexuality with shame and impotence, from the novels of Calvino and Pavese, through the films of Rossellini (throughout the war trilogy of *Rome città aperta*, *Paisà*, and *Germania anno zero*), to those of De Santis (in *Caccia tragica* the male loses his wife to the fascists on their wedding day) and of Zavattini/De Sica (in which an almost childlike sexual *pudeur* operates).

Another theme running through early post-war Italian cinema is prostitution. No matter that sometimes it is investigated seriously, and sometimes merely exploited for audience gratification; it functions like a shorthand. Already Visconti has built the melodrama of *Ossessione* around it. Rossellini takes it up in *Roma città aperta* and *Paisà*, and then develops it in *Stromboli* and *Europa '51*. Dozens of mainstream Italian commercial films make it the central theme of their narratives, and it is one of the favourite plot elements of the *strappalacrime* formula. Fellini picks it up in *Le notti di Cabiria*, Visconti once again in *Rocco e i suoi fratelli*, and Antonioni in *Cronaca di un amore* and, more obliquely, his 1960s trilogy. It is taken up by Pasolini in his first two films, *Accattone* and *Mamma Roma*, and even by the young Bertolucci in his first film, *La commare secca*. This is not mere sensationalism, nor is it gender politics. At the heart of melodrama lies the question of what is the fundamental economic resource providing security, and what is necessary to preserve it. The fusion of this generic matrix with narrative material from the war led to the examination of women's sexuality as an economic resource in a time when masculinity was impotent to sustain the world's productive equilibrium. The men were too busy with death. 'Warfare is to men what childbirth is to women' was an oft-used fascist classical quotation, dear to Mussolini. Prostitution is like women doing the work that men had failed to do. Moreover, women having to use their femininity as a resource for survival in a time of scarcity is equivalent to their being raped by whatever it was that caused the scarcity. If you see the 'cause' as the Germans (or in *Paisà* as the Americans), that is one thing (and it is the subject of two of the most famous and powerful Neapolitan songs of the era, *Munasterio 'e Santa Chiara* and *Tammuriata nera*). If you see the 'cause' as the political failings of Italians themselves in harbouring Fascism and bringing down the war upon themselves, it is another thing altogether, and gives another twist to the notion of the 'transgression' that devastates the 'organism' in the melodramatic matrix. Don Pietro's allusion to that political 'transgression' (precisely during the pregnant Pina's premarital confession) has been unwisely dismissed by critics as conservative bigoted piety. Pina's pregnancy, her fertility, and the children in her apartment function as powerful binary opposites to the theme of prostitution in the scheme of the melodramatic narrative matrix. To see heroism in *Roma città aperta* and fail to see the shame involves a selective 'use' of the film, and does not fully account for the impact the film had on audiences coming to it with very different perspectives. In his next two films, Rossellini begins to examine the theme of shame so lucidly that he ends by losing the support of his audience.

The Narrative: Story and Plot

In a monograph on literary neorealism, Lucia Re proposes that an ideologizing or mythicizing process operates in the bringing together of isolated 'chronicles' of the Resistance:

> The texts of Resistance writing recount episodes and scenes of what is implicitly a single narrative; they are subplots that converge ideally into a single governing plot, which is that of history itself. The teleological perspective of the Liberation as the end of the conflict is what gives these mini-narratives the sense of an ending; it allows the partisans themselves to narrate the immediate past and the present as causally motivated and oriented towards a meaningful conclusion. The structural principle of causality which motivates Resistance narrative and informs the plot coincides with the partisan *cause* itself, that is, the *mythos* whereby historical time, geographical space, and human action are imaginatively grasped together in the form of a tale unfolding towards the recovery of (lost) freedom. This *mythos* is in turn what motivates the very act of writing as a perlocutionary speech act, intended to elicit action on the part of the reader in the form of solidarity and participation in the partisan struggle.[22]

The process that Re describes could be seen as operating in *Roma città aperta*, but its scope is most appropriately applied to the 'whole' of Resistance narrative, taken as a corpus. With this one, particular artefact, this single film, viewed as an aesthetic object, our perspective requires that we look first at the generic narrative shape that is given to the fusing together of a number of separate 'stories.' In this perspective, we need to follow the 'aestheticizing' process, as well as the 'ideologizing' process that Re describes; that is to say, the factors that contribute to the 'beauty' of a narrative made out of raw, fragmented chronicle, whose elaborated 'form' is supplied by its ideological function. A persuasive suggestion has been made by Marina Zancan, who develops a 'cognitive' hypothesis in many ways remarkably similar to the one that I have, in the chapter on realism, been applying to neorealist cinematic narrative. Rossellini, Amidei, Fellini, Zavattini, De Sica, and Calvino are all on record as maintaining that their artefacts arose out of their own experiences, and those of everyone around them, as though that *explained* them and justified them. What kind of *explanation* is that? Zancan's argument is long and detailed, and we can only sample it here. The disorder of war, she asserts, puts into crisis the family/social ontology of the subject, interfering with what is regarded as the function of human existence, reproduction.

> This triggers a process of socialisation of knowledge and of discourse-production, linked in its turn to individuals, to material needs and to life lived in the present. This mechanism of production in circulation of knowledge is characterised by at least three important features: 1) a direct relation between knowledge and practical life ... 2) a tendency to abolish the distance between addresser and addressee ... and 3) legitimation becomes self-legitimation, within the cognitive process itself.

She quotes Italo Calvino's contention (in the preface to his novel *Il sentiero dei nidi di ragno*) that narrative seemed to come from 'la voce anonima dell'epoca' ('the anonymous voice of the epoch'), and continues:

> It is within this process that there arises, during the two years of clandestine struggle, a diffuse and continuous narrative practice, carried out by many voices, at the oral level, that has devised expressive forms dictated by the 'immediacy' of people's needs: a practice that lies objectively at the basis of written narrative ... Episodes of combat, people dying, killings, get communicated in story-form: the writing of these two years is produced by a community that *tells its own story*, and this continual story, first oral and then written, is an integral part of the daily life of the community itself ... The passage from the oral to the written, in the years 1943 to 1945, takes place, therefore, in a context in which the *protagonists* have a determining function: *the person who is writing* is firmly integrated in the community that produced both action and communication (first he is the combatant and then, on top of that, the writer); the *addressee* is directly present, and it is the *community* itself that *legitimates* the discourse produced; the *means of production* belong to the same community that produces the discourse.
> ...
> However, between wartime narrative and the neorealist novel come two 'minor genres,' the *memoir* and the *short story*, that need to be analysed as intermediary forms between the narrative and the novel, that still bear the

strong marks of the themes and forms of resistance writing, but which are also already within the literary institutional sphere ... The writing of memoirs offers the immediate postwar Italian literary context two key ideas, recognised as principles operating in the previous two years: a) that it was historically, culturally and politically necessary to socialise, through writing, one's own experience and the knowledge that it had produced; b) that between the true and the beautiful there existed a relationship of equivalence deriving from the value inherent in the true-lived-narrated.[23]

Applying Zancan's reasoning to cinema (and to *Roma città aperta* in particular), therefore, it would not *just* be a matter of professional filmmakers organizing diverse narrative materials into a coherent dramatic artefact, guided by the signifying practices of the cinema. Particular factors were at work at a primary level, at this historical moment, giving both the raw material and its aesthetic elaboration a special 'truth' status (which the artists themselves *refer to*, but do not articulate discursively). However, it is with the secondary elaboration (corresponding, in Zancan, to the steps from oral to written narrative to 'novel'), involving the signifying practices of the cinema, that I want to start.

Roma città aperta, a single, coherent narrative, is very different from *Paisà*, which consists of six separate narratives told one after the other. The first film recounts one story; the second film recounts six stories. However, the genesis of the two films was very similar. Originally, *Roma città aperta* was to have been very like *Paisà*, a film in episodes, consisting of four different, separate stories, with the title *Storie di ieri* (*Stories of Yesterday*). I shall give each one a title (using the name of its protagonist in italics) for easy reference:

1. *Don Pietro:* A priest helps the partisans, is arrested by the SS, condemned to death, and put before a firing squad. This story conflates two different figures:

(a) Don Giuseppe Morosini, who was arrested on 4 January 1944, condemned to death by a German military tribunal on 15 February for aiding the partisans, and executed on 3 April at Forte Bravetta – where Don Pietro's execution was filmed. The firing squad did not kill him, and the Italian officer commanding it finished him off with a pistol shot to the back of his head. At an entirely separate execution on 2 February 1944, eleven partisans were being executed at Forte Bravetta when the Italian firing squad deliberately aimed away from the prisoners. The German officer commanding the squad finished off the prisoners with his pistol.

(b) Don Pietro Pappagallo, who was arrested on 29 January 1944 for supplying false papers to partisans, and helping them get across the German lines to refuge with the Allies, and was shot on 24 March together with 334 other prisoners in the Fosse Ardeatine in reprisal for a partisan attack on a German regiment the previous afternoon.

2. *Manfredi:* A partisan leader escapes across the rooftops of Rome when the SS come to his lodgings to arrest him (a story based on the experiences of the scriptwriter Sergio Amidei, and generally regarded as portraying a partisan leader, Celeste Negarville, who was never, in fact, arrested).

3. *Pina:* A woman tries to make contact with her husband, who is being held prisoner by the Germans in an army barracks, and is shot by a German NCO (a story based on the true events surrounding the death of Maria Teresa Gullace recounted later in this chapter (p. 163) – Aldo Fabrizi, who will play Don Pietro in the film, was an eye-witness to this shooting). Pina (not Gullace) lives in an apartment in a block of flats, Via Montecuccoli 17, off Via Prenestina (the building still looks much as it did when the film was made).

4. *Romoletto:* A band of children carry out acts of sabotage against the Fascists and the Germans in occupied Rome (there are conflicting accounts of the origins of this story, but it was probably based on a Hungarian novel of the turn of the century).

However, these *four* stories, the four originally intended as the *Storie di ieri*, are merely the ones conventionally recognized as being the sources of the film. If we look at the narrative, we can see other narrative components that have, at least part of the time, their own autonomy:

5. *Bergmann*: A German Gestapo officer, with the help of the Italian police, hunts down and interrogates partisan leaders in order to break up their organization. This story refers to Major (later Lieutenant Colonel) Kappler, who operated from offices and cells in a building rented by the German embassy, located in Via Tasso. The Italian chief of police (the *Questore* of Rome) refers to Pietro Caruso, who was tried and shot at the end of the war, and whose actual death was somewhat gruesomely recorded by Visconti in what is definitely a documentary section of the part-documentary, part-re-enacted film, *Giorni di gloria*.

6. *Marina*: A working-class girl climbs the social ladder by working as a nightclub entertainer and prostituting herself with German officers. She becomes both the girlfriend of a partisan leader and the object of the lesbian attentions of a Gestapo officer, Ingrid, who feeds her cocaine habit in exchange for information leading to the capture of the partisan

boyfriend, with whom she has quarrelled over the drug habit. Her closest friend, Lauretta, is the sister of Pina. Marina lives in the wealthy Parioli district of Rome, but she is, in fact, the daughter of the concierge of
a commercial building in Via Tiburtina, a working-class district.

Stefano Roncoroni, Ugo Pirro, and Tag Gallagher chronicle the way
the various threads are brought together into one narrative.[24] There
is no doubt that the central figure in the operation is Sergio Amidei,
whose role in neorealism is an interesting one. On *Roma città aperta*,
besides being perhaps the main source for the film, he is also credited
with the role of assistant director (Jolanda Benvenuti says he was
hardly ever on the set and, independently, Vito Annichiarico – the boy
who plays Marcello – says he never saw him). Certainly, Amidei was
both a promoter of the neorealist aesthetic and an obstacle to some of its
features. As time passed, it became clear that he was not entirely in harmony with Rossellini's aesthetic aims. When it came to making *Paisà*,
he was gradually distanced from more and more of the episodes, and
he more or less ejected himself at an early stage from the writing team
on *Ladri di biciclette*. By all accounts, Amidei was a prickly person, but
that cannot explain all his differences with his neorealist collaborators.
When Rossellini got Fellini to smarten up the dialogue on *Roma città
aperta*, Amidei appears to have recognized the value of the contribution
(though this may have had a lot to do with Amidei's awareness that,
coming from Trieste in the north, he had difficulty with good Roman
dialogue, whereas Fellini wrote material for popular Roman stage performers every day). He remained a close collaborator with Rossellini
throughout the neorealist period (though not on *Europa '51, Dov'è la lib-
erta?, Amore, Viaggio in Italia*, and *Francesco Giullare di Dio*). Apart from
his work with Rossellini, and on Lizzani's *Cronache di poveri amanti*,
however, the other films he wrote for in this period tended to be comedies or films bearing a strong element of 'contamination' with conventional genre cinema – even though they might have often contained an
element of social-political satire. He himself describes his approach to
Roma città aperta as having, at the outset at least, few ambitions to innovation. If we put all these things together, we might conclude that the
large role Amidei played in the conception and execution of *Roma città
aperta* is one of the factors accounting for the elements of conventionality that critics have detected in the film. Amidei brought the 'subjects'
of the partisan leader, and of the Gullace shooting, while Alberto
Consiglio furnished the subject of Don Pietro. It could be, as Gallagher
tends to suggest, that the highly scripted, compact character of *Roma*

città aperta's narrative owes much to the dominant influence of Amidei at a time when Rossellini was just beginning to develop his own aesthetic. Certainly, a study of the genesis of *Paisà* shows a film shifting, in its filming, a great distance from the conventionality of the original sections scripted by Amidei, Alfred Hayes, and Klaus Mann, and indicates that Rossellini made more and more use of Fellini as the production progressed.

In discussing the narrative of *Roma città aperta* it is helpful to distinguish between 'story' and 'plot.' Victor Shklovsky pointed out that a narrative recounts a series of events that are supposed to have taken place in chronological order over a period of time. To this order he gave the name *fabula*. However, the order in which the written or filmed artefact presents these events to the reader or viewer may not preserve the chronological order in which they are supposed to have happened, and the reading or viewing experience probably will occupy the reader or viewer for a very different period of time than that covered by the events recounted. To this order he gave the name *syuzhet*. It has now become commonplace to use 'story' for *fabula*, and 'plot' for *syuzhet*, which is what I shall do. However, since it can be difficult for the untrained reader to remember which is which, I am going to add a mnemonic device to each term, giving 'event-story' (the events as they happened) and 'recounted-plot' (as they are recounted to the viewer in the plot of the film), so that the reader will not have to keep returning here for a reminder.

In the case of *Roma città aperta*, not only are the six event-stories we have identified above merged into one recounted-plot, but each individual event-story is fragmented and dispersed in its own recounted-plot in order that the four event-stories may proceed in parallel in the overall recounted-plot.

Nowadays, we are accustomed, in novels and in films, to following parallel stories told in disjunctive blocks, which converge in a dénouement. John Grisham's or Elmore Leonard's novels are typical examples. Raymond Chandler did not tell his stories that way. If we compare *Roma città aperta* with *To Have and Have Not*, we can see that neither did Hollywood in those days (which is one reason why Orson Welles's *Citizen Kane* is extraordinary for its time). Hawks's film could have followed the Free French story, Slim's story, and Steve's story in parallel, bringing them eventually together. Instead, the narrative remains with the protagonist, Steve (Humphrey Bogart), who holds together all the subplots, sometimes in a merely formal way by being a 'witness,' and always constitutes a coherent point of view on the various threads of the narrative. *Roma città aperta* uses montage to keep its parallel 'chronicles' separate to a large extent in the first half, each block establishing a different person's perspective (Bergmann's, Marina's, and Don Pietro's), with 'links' formed in particular by Pina, who more and more serves as a unifying point of view for the viewer, and whose death, for that very reason, leaves the viewer with a sense of loss and disorientation. Pina, however, drops out of the story altogether in the middle, and this is one of the reasons why the actress Clara Calamai would not make up her mind to take the role when it was offered to her. Calamai's reluctance is a 'symptom,' as it were, of conventional cinema's discomfort with what Rossellini and Amidei were doing, an explanation of which is suggested in the reflections of Marina Zancan I have just quoted. The parallel threads come together, as both the climax and dénouement of the parallel montage narrative process, in the sequence of the SS raid on Via Montecuccoli and the killing of Pina. This sequence brings the narrative to an end, after which it has to be 'restarted.' This is effected through the rather arbitrary (from the recounted-plot point of view) attack on the convoy carrying away German prisoners – a sequence not really 'linked' to anything else in the film, neither prepared for nor taken up later – which serves as a transition into the scene that properly restarts the narrative, that in which Manfredi and Francesco meet Marina in Flavio's *trattoria*. In fact, the climactic music continues, without a break, from the shooting of Pina to the end of the scene of the attack on the convoy, whereupon the scene of Flavio's *trattoria* takes up the story with diegetic sound only. Clearly, the filmmakers were aware of the need for some device to maintain narrative continuity. All that remained thereafter was to bring together the Manfredi–Don Pietro thread and the Bergmann thread. Gradually, Don Pietro takes over as the unifying point of view for the viewer. Once again, the film comes to a stop with the death of Manfredi, the curse of Don Pietro, the removal of the fur coat from the prostrate Marina, and Hartmann's epilogue: 'We are the master race!' The execution of Don Pietro is a 'coda,' required by the exigencies of *chronicling*, and is told through a dispersal of points of view, finally settling on that of the boys.

The film, therefore, breaks into three: (1) up to Pina's death, (2) up to Manfredi's death, (3) Don Pietro's execution. Each dénouement is a death.

In order to get a clear picture of how *Roma città aperta*'s narrative is constructed, it is useful to separate event-story and recounted-plot, and lay them out one after the other. The description of the recounted-plot (table 1 on p. 153), in particular, will be decidedly indigestible for the reader, but any conclusions must be based on complete data made openly available – even though some readers may prefer to glance at the data, and then take my word for it. To proceed, we shall need to give a status to historical 'referents' that are not explicitly referred to in the film, but which the Italian (and especially the Roman) audience of 1945–6 would see as being components of the event-story. Moreover, for brevity's sake, we shall apply this analysis only up to the shooting of Pina, merely mentioning what happens afterwards. Since the event-story involves (as we have seen earlier) six parallel actions, we shall lay them out one after the other, and then, at a second stage, see how the recounted-plot transforms them into one narrative. Each of the six 'threads' of the event-story will be identified by the name we gave it at the beginning of this section, which is the name of a character, and will be in *italics*, to distinguish it from a reference to the actual character himself or herself. The recounted-plot we are going to concentrate on, therefore, moves from one point in time (the SS raid on Manfredi's landlady) to another point in time (Don Pietro cradling the body of Pina in his lap). However, the event-stories contain material *previous* to the start of this chronology, referred to or alluded to in the narrative. Sometimes, it is slightly arbitrary as to which of the six 'threads' we shall attach this *previous* material, and sometimes the same material belongs to more than one thread.

Italian films are split, for showing in cinemas, into two halves (*primo tempo* and *secondo tempo*), to permit the selling of confectionery (from which cinemas derive much of their profit margin) in the interval. *Roma città aperta* is split after the attack on the German convoy; the *secondo tempo* begins with Manfredi and Francesco arriving at Flavio's restaurant. Hence we shall be examining all but the last scene of the *primo tempo* of the film.

In what follows, each numbered 'paragraph' of event-story (i, ii, iii, etc.) refers to a continuous 'section' of recounted-plot in the film (an unbroken sequence of 'scenes'). However, we follow each event-story 'thread' one by one. In a subsequent part of this chapter, on the 'plot' of the film, we shall see how these 'thread-sections' of scenes are interwoven (through cross-cutting or parallel montage) in the recounted-plot of the film. In other words, we analyse the narrative structure of the film by first dismantling and then reassembling it.

1. *Don Pietro*

(a) Previous event-story material referred to or implicit in the recounted-plot:
Don Pietro Pellegrini has contributed 'much' to the Resistance in Rome
– this 'much' is referred to in the recounted-plot (at the printing shop) –
but we are not told what has been involved. He is the parish priest for
the working-class Prenestina quarter of Rome, his church is San Clemente, he lives in the rectory beside the church, and he is trusted by his
parishioners.

(b) Event-story material covered by the chronology of the recounted-plot:
(i) Don Pietro organizes and referees a football match for the boys of his
parish. Marcello comes to tell him that he is needed in Via Montecuccoli. En route, he discusses with Marcello whether piety or political
commitment is the highest priority in the current circumstances. The
two of them encounter Agostino, the sacristan, bringing home bread
from the raided bakery.

(ii) Don Pietro is let into Francesco's apartment by Pina to meet
Manfredi, who has an appointment that evening with a representative
of a band of partisans in the hills above Tagliacozzo, which it is no
longer safe for him to keep. He asks Don Pietro to keep the appointment instead, at the Tiburtina bridge, and to pass money to the representative.

(iii) Don Pietro goes to a religious articles shop and is taken into the
basement, where he meets first Francesco (whom he informs about
Manfredi's having been hidden by Pina in his flat) and then Gino, a partisan leader, who gives him two books in which the pages have been
replaced by banknotes.

(iv) He enters his rectory, where Agostino is boiling cabbage, and Pina
is waiting to make her confession. He makes a package that Pina insists
on carrying. He accompanies Pina out of the rectory and through the
church of San Clemente, where he is approached by the Austrian
deserter, whom he promises to help. He then returns to Pina, and they
converse as they walk along beside the railway. He meets the representative of the partisans and hands over the package of books.

(v) Don Pietro admits the children into the church for catechism.

(vi) He is arranging pews with the other children in the church when
he is informed by Marcello that Romoletto has bombs in the attic.

(vii) Don Pietro and Marcello, wearing surplices and carrying the Holy
Sacrament, arrive at the entrance to Via Montecuccoli 17, claiming that
there is a dying man upstairs, and the Brigadiere supports their story.

They climb to the attic, where Don Pietro tears open the door to the roof and takes the mortar bomb and the machine gun from Romoletto.

(viii) Don Pietro and Marcello hurry down the stairs carrying the weapons.

(ix) Don Pietro sees the Fascist soldiers coming up the stairs below him and slips into Pina's flat.

(x) In sound off, the Fascist soldiers hear the sound of the frying pan with which Don Petro hits the grandfather to quieten him.

(xi) He prays over the apparently sleeping grandfather as the Fascist soldiers enter the room, look around, and go out again.

(xii) Don Pietro and Marcello are emerging into the passage between the street and the courtyard of the apartment building, when Pina dashes through.

(xiii) Don Pietro grasps Marcello tightly to him, and covers Marcello's eyes with his hand.

(xiv) Don Pietro lifts Marcello from Pina's body and passes him to the Brigadiere. He kneels down and takes Pina's body in his lap.

(c) Subsequent to the death of Pina:
Don Pietro takes Marcello to his rectory, and lets him sleep on the sofa. He celebrates Benediction in church. He arranges false documents in the name of Giovanni Episcopo for Manfredi, and refuge in a monastery for the Austrian deserter. He is about to lead Manfredi, the deserter, and Francesco into hiding when the Germans arrest him, take him to their Via Tasso headquarters, interrogate him, and make him watch the torture of Manfredi. He curses the Germans and then repents for his outburst. He is shot at Forte Bravetta.

2. *Manfredi*
(a) Previous event-story material referred to or implicit in the recounted-plot:
Viewers would know certain historical facts – in addition to those recounted in appendix 2 ('Historical background for neorealis'):

(i) In August 1943 the Badoglio government declared Rome an *open city* (Athens, for example, was so designated), which was not to be militarily occupied or fought over – but no one properly observed this agreement, and in fact the Germans occupied the city, and the Allies bombed the rail depots in the San Lorenzo quarter, causing destruction in surrounding quarters (Via Montecuccoli is located beside the main rail shunting yards).

(ii) By January 1944 the Allied military advance had reached an area north of Naples and south of Rome – for various reasons, the Allies failed to occupy the Rome area as soon as they might.

(iii) The city was nominally governed by Mussolini's Fascist republic, its bureaucracy, and its police, but the Germans had the real control.

(iv) Partisan bands, organized by the Committee for National Liberation (in which the Communist Party, whose clandestinely printed official newspaper was *L'Unità*, played a prominent role), operated against the Fascists and the Germans in the city.

(v) The Germans combatted these groups by using informers and spies, capturing one member, and using torture to get him or her to give them details about other members, a strategy in which they were very successful.

(vi) The Gestapo interrogation headquarters were in a building in Via Tasso.

(vii) The action of the event-story would have taken place in the period between January and April 1944 (Maria Teresa Gullace was killed on 3 March 1944, Don Morosini was arrested in January and shot in April).

(viii) The Allies entered Rome in June 1944.

Luigi Ferraris was born in Turin in 1906, was arrested in Bologna in 1928, and was sentenced to twelve years' imprisonment for conspiracy to subvert the state. He escaped in transit, and hid in France (information from his police dossier is given to Bergmann by the Questore of Rome). He now calls himself Giorgio Manfredi, is working in Italy as a leader of the Committee for National Liberation, and is a member of the Communist Party. (He starts to tell Don Pietro that he is a communist in Via Tasso, but is taken away before he can say it all.) He has made an appointment to meet in Rome a member of a partisan band that is operating in the hills outside Rome, in order to pass them money from the committee (he tells Don Pietro this). During an air raid, he started a romantic liaison with a nightclub singer called Marina Mari, but the relationship is going sour (he tells Pina this). He has been avoiding her, and she has been trying to contact him. He has at some point expressed disapproval of her cocaine habit, and tried to get her to stop taking the drug (this comes out in the quarrel between them after Pina's death). A Gestapo agent has photographed the two of them together in Rome, and Bergmann has connected his face with that of a man in a group photograph of Communists (Bergmann shows the two photographs to the Questore of Rome).

(b) Event-story material covered by the chronology of the recounted-plot:

(i) Manfredi is listening to a BBC news broadcast on the radio in an apartment by the Piazza di Spagna when the SS arrive to arrest him. He escapes across the roof to the Spanish embassy.

(ii) The next morning he turns up outside Francesco's apartment in Via Montecuccoli. He asks to speak to Don Pietro.

(iii) Manfredi talks with Pina about the assault on the bakery. He gives Lauretta a message for Marina. He recounts his affair with Marina to Pina.

(iv) He asks Don Pietro to take money to Tiburtina for the partisans, as in *Don Pietro* ii.

(v) Manfredi is waiting for Francesco in his apartment that night. He is warned to lie low. He reads *L'Unità*. When Pina rushes in, they look out the window in alarm together with Francesco at the explosion in the rail depot.

(vi) The next morning Manfredi is shining his shoes in readiness for his friend's wedding, when the Brigadiere knocks to salute the bridegroom.

(vii) He and Francesco open the window and look down at the street when Pina rushes in to warn them about the Germans.

(viii) They withdraw from the window.

(ix) Manfredi escapes from the building through the window of the laundry room.

(c) Subsequent to the death of Pina:

Manfredi leads the attack on the German convoy that frees Francesco. They go to a *trattoria* to eat that evening, and are informed that there has been a big round-up of partisans; they meet Marina, who invites them to stay at her flat. Manfredi quarrels there with Marina over her drug habit, and afterwards she overhears him discussing their meeting at Don Pietro's the next day to escape from Rome to a monastery in the hills. He tells Francesco to lie low because he is too upset by the death of Pina to be useful to the Resistance at the moment. Manfredi meets Don Pietro and the Austrian at the priest's rectory, and is arrested on the street when they leave. He is taken to Via Tasso and tortured to death by the Gestapo without revealing any information about his associates.

3. *Pina*

(a) Previous event-story material referred to or implicit in the recounted-plot:

Pina is the daughter of a plumber, brought up in a working-class quarter of Rome, a widow with a son (Marcello), who until recently worked at the Breda engineering works, but was made redundant when the Germans confiscated the machinery to take to Germany (she tells Manfredi part of this). She got to know Francesco, her neighbour, from his hammering a nail in their party wall and knocking a mirror off the wall on her side (she reminisces in the conversation with Francesco on the stairs). They have been planning their wedding for a long time, but have kept having to put it off, and she is pregnant from him. Pina believes in God, and is about to be married in church by Don Pietro (she tells Manfredi this). She has been involved in two raids on bakers' shops in the past week. She lives in the flat next to Francesco's with her sister, Lauretta, and two other couples: one couple about whom we never learn anything, and another (the wife is referred to by the 'grand-father' as Elida) who have four children (Otello, who is Marcello's friend, Andreina, another younger girl, and a toddler boy) and the eld-erly father of one of them, just referred to as the 'grandfather.' We are not told if, and how, these people are related to each other, but it was the rule for homeless refugees to be lodged in existing households. From an exchange between Lauretta and Elida, the mother of Otello, we learn that the apartment is the latter's home, in which Pina and Lau-retta rent a room and the use of the kitchen. The grandfather sleeps in the same room as the other, unnamed couple.

(b) Event-story material covered by the chronology of the recounted-plot:
(i) Pina participates in the assault on the bakery. She gives some loaves to the Brigadiere. She sees Manfredi waiting, approaches him with caution, and lets him into Francesco's apartment. She calls Marcello down from Romoletto's attic, and sends him to get Don Pietro. She talks to Manfredi. She goes out to prepare some coffee in her own flat.
(ii) She returns with coffee, and talks with Manfredi some more until Don Pietro arrives, at which point she leaves. She catches Marcello eavesdropping at the door and sends him off to get water.
(iii) At Don Pietro's rectory she waits for his return, then accompanies him out (see *Don Pietro* iv).
(iv) When Don Pietro comes back from talking to the Austrian, they continue as in *Don Pietro* iv.
(v) In the evening, she bursts into Francesco's apartment, as in *Manfredi* v.
(vi) Angry scenes between Pina and the boys returning home after their exploits, and involving Lauretta.
(vii) Her conversation with Francesco on the landing.
(viii) She rushes into Francesco's flat the next morning to warn him and Manfredi about the Germans.

(ix) Together with the other tenants Pina is herded into the courtyard by the Germans, and slaps a soldier who flirts with her. She sees Francesco being taken away, and chases after him, eventually being gunned down by the Germans.

4. *Romoletto*

(a) Previous event-story material referred to or implicit in the recounted-plot:
Romoletto is guided by the Communist Party's policy for all anti-fascist parties to lay aside their political differences and unite in the struggle against Fascism and Nazism (Marcello quotes him to Don Pietro). He believes women are 'trouble,' and will not admit the girls to his conspiracies (Marcello quotes him to Andreina). [Note: in the narrative thread I am calling *Romoletto* I include Marcello and the friends who live with him, Otello and Andreina.]

(b) Event-story material covered by the chronology of the recounted-plot:
(i) Romoletto has a hideout on the roof of the building, where he plots with the children of the Via Montecuccoli tenants to carry out actions against the Germans and the Fascists (Marcello sneaks up there when he can).

(ii) Marcello interrupts Don Pietro's football match and walks to Via Montecuccoli, as in *Don Pietro* i.

(iv) He eavesdrops on the conversation between Manfredi and Don Pietro in Francesco's apartment, and is sent to get water by his mother, but he sneaks upstairs to Romoletto.

(v) Romoletto commends his fellow-conspirators for their action in blowing up a petrol store at the railway depot.

(vi) The boys are afraid of the scolding and spanking they will receive from their parents for being out after dark. Marcello and Otello are scolded by Pina. Marcello talks to Andreina about the role of women in the Resistance. Marcello refuses to divulge secrets to Francesco, and asks if he can call him 'papà' from the next day onwards.

(vii) Marcello arrives at the last minute at Don Pietro's church for catechism.

(viii) He is arranging pews with the other children in the church when Andreina rushes into the church with two little ones, and tells Marcello that the Germans and the Fascists are at their house.

(ix)–(xv) This event-story material corresponds to *Don Pietro* (vii–xiii).

(c) Subsequent to the death of Pina:
Marcello sleeps at Don Pietro's rectory, and the next morning is in the

churchyard, saying goodbye to Francesco, when the men leave for the monastery in the hills. By calling Francesco back to give him a scarf, he saves him from being arrested by the Germans. The boys watch the execution of Don Pietro.

5. *Bergmann*

(a) Previous event-story material referred to or implicit in the recounted-plot:
Bergmann's application of the Schröder Plan is producing results, and large numbers of Resistance organizers are being rounded up (Flavio, the restaurateur, tells Manfredi of some cases, and Francesco tells him of others).

(b) Event-story material covered by the chronology of the recounted-plot:
(i) The SS raid Manfredi's apartment, but cannot pursue him across the rooftops because the Spanish embassy is next door.

(ii) Sturmbannführer Bergmann explains to the Questore of Rome the Schröder plan for dealing with terrorism, and for rounding up deserters in occupied cities. An NCO informs him that the SS have not found Manfredi at his apartment, and Bergmann shows the Questore a photograph of Manfredi and Marina taken on the Spanish Steps. The Questore says that Manfredi is known as one of the leaders of Committee for National Liberation. Bergmann shows him another photograph in which Manfredi appears. They are interrupted by a scream of pain from a *'professore'* who is being interrogated in another room. They discuss Marina.

(iii) Ingrid visits Marina in her nightclub dressing room, bringing cocaine.

(iv) Bergmann is reading the clandestine Resistance press when the Questore arrives with a file on Manfredi (Luigi Ferraris). Bergmann tells the Questore that Manfredi has been seen in the Prenestino quarter, and about the sabotage in the rail depot. Bergmann goes into the salon to get Ingrid, and shows her the file.

(v) The SS carry out a raid on Via Montecuccoli as a result of what Bergmann has found out in (iv).

(c) Subsequent to the death of Pina:
Ingrid finds out from Marina where Manfredi will be (at Don Pietro's) the next morning. The prisoners are brought in and interrogated. Bergmann gives Ingrid a flask of cocaine for Marina, whom Ingrid entertains in the salon. Hartmann tells Bergmann that the Germans are hated

for spreading only death and destruction. Hartmann supervises Don Pietro's execution, and finishes him off with a pistol shot when the firing squad fails to kill him.

6. *Marina*
(a) Previous event-story material referred to or implicit in the recounted-plot:
Marina Mari is the daughter of the concierge of the building in which Pina's father had his plumber's shop, and a friend of Lauretta. She works (together with Lauretta) as a well-known nightclub singer (the Questore admires her). She and Manfredi started a relationship when she showed no fear during an air raid. Manfredi disapproves of her drug habit, and wants to break off the relationship. Marina is supplied with cocaine by a lesbian Gestapo officer, Ingrid, who hopes to prise out of her the whereabouts of Manfredi. Marina prostitutes herself to the Germans to support her comfortable lifestyle, because she despises the life of ordinary families (she tells this to Manfredi). Before Pina is shot, it is not made entirely clear whether she has, at any point, told the Gestapo where to find Manfredi (the SS expected to find him at the apartment in Piazza di Spagna, and then at Via Montecuccoli).
(b) Event-story material covered by the chronology of the recounted-plot:
(i) Marina telephones Manfredi's lodgings while the SS are searching the place.
(ii) Marina paces her dressing room, needing more cocaine. Lauretta tells her that she has seen Manfredi at Francesco's, and gives her Manfredi's message. Ingrid enters. Marina leaves the room to perform.
(iii) Marina telephones Manfredi's lodgings.
[Note: As far as the event-story is concerned, Marina's is the least carefully thought out thread. It is not clear from the *story* whether Marina is weak or is an opportunist: on the questions of Marina's motivations and of her precise actions, the *story* is incomplete, and leaves the viewer to surmise.]
(c) Subsequent to the death of Pina:
Marina meets Manfredi at Flavio's restaurant, where she has been waiting, hoping to catch him. She invites them to stay at her apartment, quarrels with Manfredi over her cocaine habit, overhears his plans, and tells Ingrid over the telephone (with Bergmann listening in) that she will call again later. We next see her receiving a fur coat from Ingrid in Via Tasso, confirming that she told the Gestapo where to arrest Man-

fredi. Hartmann brings her from the salon to the torture chamber, and looks on in alarm when he realizes what he has brought her to. She faints. Ingrid retrieves the coat, instructing the NCO to 'hold her for a while, and then ...'

7. Miscellaneous
(b) Event-story material covered by the chronology of the recounted-plot:
(i) Francesco is returning home from work when he is stopped by Fascist soldiers, and his papers are checked. Arriving home, he pauses in the passage and sees Lauretta delivered home by a German officer and stashing away the money she receives from him. Francesco turns and walks away.

The laying out of the plot (table 1) reveals a number of empirical features. Before thread-section 21, most thread-sections are of at least 1.5 minutes' duration; from number 21 onwards, none is that long, and most are of less than half that duration. Therefore, the parallel montage (cross-cutting between thread-sections) accelerates considerably on the morning of the wedding and of Pina's death. This is partly because threads have been brought together, to a large extent, in one time and place, but the rate of cross-cutting is also a rhetorical and stylistic device. Indeed, because of the rapid cross-cutting, the viewer gets the *impression* that from 21 onwards plot-time and story-time are coinciding in the real viewing-time, whereas in actual fact this is not the case at all. Plot-time considerably compresses, or elides, story-time: some two hours of story-time are compressed into ten minutes of viewing-time. (The relationship between plot-time and viewing-time in the cinema is too complicated to go into here; one could easily *expect* them to be the same, but because of editing conventions, they almost never are. In other words, there is a further level of adjustment to add to Schlovsky's two categories of 'story' and 'plot' before we can accurately talk about what the viewer actually perceives. The problem does not arise in literary narrative, because no one would dream of expecting plot-time and 'reading-time' to coincide, whereas in the theatre, one would expect them to *have to* coincide. In the cinema, if a man gets up out of a chair and starts towards a door, whereupon a cut takes us to him closing behind him the door we 'know' he has just gone through, it is hard to say that 'plot-time' has elided 'story-time,' and that we have not been 'shown' him going through the door.)

In order of total (accumulated) duration there are three groupings of

Table 1 The plot of *Roma città aperta* (*primo tempo*)

Scene* nos.	Thread	Duration**	Number of each thread-section and description	Event-story references
2–9	*Manfredi*	3.3	1. SS raid on Manfredi's apartment	2bi, 5bi, 6bi
10	*Bergmann*	2.5	2. Bergmann with Questore; photos of Manfredi and Marina	2bi, 5bi, 5bii, 2a, 6a
11–18	*Pina*	6.0	3. Assault on bakery; Brigadiere; black marketeer; lets Manfredi into Francesco's; calls Marcello to get Don Pietro; Lauretta; talks to Manfredi	3bi, 3a, 2a, 2bii, 2biii, 4bi, 1a, 6a, 6bii
19–21	*Don Pietro / Romoletto*	2.6	4. Football; Don Pietro summoned by Marcello; conversation with the boy; Agostino and the bread	1bi, 4bii, 3bi
22	*Pina*	1.1	5. Pina tells Manfredi about herself	3a
23	*Manfredi / Don Pietro*	0.2	6. Manfredi meets Don Pietro in Francesco's apartment	2biv, 1bii, 1a
23–4	*Pina / Romoletto*	0.4	7. Pina catches Marcello eavesdropping; Marcello goes to Romoletto to tell him something important	3bii, 4biv
25	*Manfredi / Don Pietro*	0.8	8. Manfredi asks Don Pietro to collect and deliver the money to the partisans	2biv, 1bii
26–9	*Don Pietro*	3.4	9. Don Pietro collects the money from the printing shop	1biii, 7bi, 2biv, 5biv
30	*Marina*	3.7	10. Marina in nightclub needing drugs; getting news of Manfredi from Lauretta; meeting Ingrid	6bii, 2biii, 5biii
31–6	*Pina / Don Pietro*	6.2	11. Pina waits for Don Pietro in the rectory; the books with money in them; the Austrian deserter; culpability for the war	3biii, 3a, 1biv, 1biii
37	*Don Pietro*	0.5	12. Hands over the money to partisan	1biv, 1bii, 1biii, 2biv
38–9	*Miscellaneous*	1.3	13. Francesco is stopped by Fascist soldiers on the way home; he sees Lauretta returning	7bi, 1biii, 6a
40–1	*Manfredi / Pina*	1.8	14. Francesco returns home to find Manfredi; Pina comes in looking for Marcello; the explosion at the rail depot	2biv, 2a, 3a, 3bv, 1biii, 5biv, 4bv

Table 1 *(continued)*

Scene* nos.	Thread	Duration**	Number of each thread-section and description	Event-story references
42–5	*Romoletto*	1.5	15. The boys return from their sabotage mission, and fear for their families' reception	4bv, 4bvi, 5biv, 3bvi
46–7	*Pina / Romoletto*	3.2	16. Pina scolds the boys; Lauretta quarrels with Otello's parents; Marcello tells Andreina that girls cannot fight; Francesco respects Marcello's secret; Marcello expresses love for Francesco	3bvi, 4bvi, 4c
48	*Pina*	2.8	17. Dialogue with Francesco on the landing	3bvii, 2a, 3a
49–50	*Marina*	0.6	18. Marina telephones Manfredi's lodgings	6biii, 2biii, 2bi
51–4	*Bergmann*	2.7	19. Bergmann looks at the clandestine newspapers; the Questore shows him Manfredi's dossier	5biv, 2a, 6a
55	*Don Pietro*	0.4	20. Don Pietro lets the children in for catechism	1bv, 4bvii
56–7	*Pina*	0.3	21. The Brigadiere congratulates Francesco	3a, 3bii, 3bviii
58–9	*Pina / Manfredi*	0.6	22. Pina warns the men about the Germans surrounding the building; they look down at the street	3bviii, 5bv
60–1	*Bergmann*	1.1	23. The Germans surround the building and bring out the inhabitants	5bv
62–3	*Don Pietro / Romoletto*	0.5	24. Andreina arrives at the church to summon Marcello	1bvi, 4bviii
64	*Bergmann*	0.3	25. The SS empty the building	5bv
65	*Manfredi*	0.2	26. Francesco and Manfredi escape	2bix
66	*Bergmann*	0.1	27. The SS line up the inhabitants in the courtyard	5bv
67–8	*Manfredi*	0.2	28. Francesco and Manfredi escape	2bix
69	*Bergmann*	0.3	29. Fascist soldiers look at the women's legs in the laundry room	5bv
70–2	*Pina*	0.7	30. Pina with the others in the courtyard	3bix

73	*Don Pietro*	0.7	31. Don Pietro and Marcello arrive with the sacraments, and start up the stairs	1bvii, 5bv, 4bix
74–5	*Don Pietro / Romoletto*	0.9	32. They reach Romoletto's attic and take the weapons from him	1bvii, 4bix
76	*Bergmann*	0.3	33. The Fascist officer starts up the stairs to check out Don Pietro	1bvii, 4bix, 5bv
77 parallel montage	*Don Pietro / Romoletto / Bergmann*	0.4	34. Don Pietro and Marcello come down the stairs, the Fascists climb up	1bviii, 4bx, 5bv
78	*Don Pietro / Romoletto*	1.2	35. Don Pietro and Marcello enter Pina's apartment, hide the weapons, and sit by the grandfather, who wakes up and protests	1bix, 4bxi, 5bv
79–80	*Bergmann / Don Pietro / Romoletto*	0.8	36. The Fascist soldiers enter Pina's apartment and start searching it; they enter the grandfather's room and see him moribund, receiving the last rites	5bv, 1bx, 4bxi
81	*Don Pietro / Romoletto*	0.5	37. Don Pietro and Marcello comment on the frying pan episode	1bx, 4bxii
82–5	*Pina*	1.0	38. Pina sees Francesco captured, and runs after him; she is gunned down; Marcello, Don Pietro, and the Brigadiere rush to her body	3bix, 1bxi, 1bxii, 1bxiii, (2bix), 4bxiii, 4bxiv, 4bxv, 5bv, (6b)

* Here, a scene is what would in a script be a 'scene': a sequence of shots taken in one location and one story-time. However, where there has been a to-and-fro (for example, in a telephone conversation), I have arbitrarily called it two 'scenes.' Number of scenes: 85 (add one scene for the attack on the convoy, and you have the number of scenes in the *primo tempo* of the film). Average scene duration: 39 seconds.

** Duration in minutes and tenths of minutes of following the *thread* (which may be made up of more than one scene). Average duration in minutes and tenths of minutes of following one *thread* before picking up another: 1.5. Number of *thread-sections*: 38. Roughly 2 scenes per *thread-section*.

– Approximate duration of the film up to the death of Pina: 55 minutes.

– Main *threads* in descending order of total duration (in minutes and tenths): *Don Pietro* 19.1, *Pina* 17.9, *Romoletto* 9.4, *Bergmann* 8.5, *Manfredi* 7.1, *Marina* 4.3.

thread-sections: (1) *Don Pietro* and *Pina*, (2) *Romoletto, Bergmann,* and *Manfredi*, (3) *Marina*, with each grouping getting twice as much time as the grouping that follows, so that twice as much time is devoted to the *Don Pietro* and *Pina* threads, for example, as to the other four threads. The picture would be different, of course, if we calculated the total duration of threads for the whole film (including what follows Pina's death). *Manfredi* and *Bergmann* would start to catch up with *Don Pietro*. However, given that the film breaks into two at the death of Pina, the first self-contained half greatly privileges the melodramatic genre surrounding *Don Pietro* and *Pina* over the Resistance hero-adventure genre surrounding *Manfredi* and *Bergmann* (though, as we shall see, *Don Pietro* is very much concerned with the Resistance theme). This is even more marked if we bear in mind that the *Romoletto* thread is tied to *Pina* and to *Don Pietro* by Marcello (and appears in the 'Event-story references' column for nearly half of all the thread-sections). Moreover, the *Romoletto* and *Manfredi* Resistance threads are also linked to the rest of the film by *Don Pietro*, while *Manfredi*, partly through Francesco, creates the link with *Pina*. Nevertheless, the assault on the bakery and the whole story of Lauretta are only anchored in the plot by *Pina*. To a certain extent, Pina the character, and hence the thread *Pina*, are superfluous to the film *as a whole* (i.e., to both halves put together), and are only justified by the *historical* fact of the death of Maria Teresa Gullace, which, at the level of chronicle, caught the imagination of the people of Rome as emblematic of 'family' crushed under the cruel and indifferent jackboot of the German occupation (it was so reported in the newspapers of the time). Her death occasioned a demonstration and partisan attack later the same day in which an innocent bystander, a woman coming out of the church of San Gioacchino, was killed by a stray bullet. Gullace's death historically *provoked* armed Resistance activity (none of which is alluded to in the film, unless we see the attack on the convoy as being analogous), but in itself was a chance by-product of the Occupation. The film's plot, however, makes this thread the climax and dénouement of the first half, which thereby becomes a self-contained plot, a 'film' of its own. Not only that, the scene of Pina's death becomes one of the most celebrated sequences in the whole of the history of the cinema.

The *Don Pietro* thread in the first half of the film, based on the Resistance activity of Don Morosini and Don Pappagallo, contains three 'Resistance activities': giving the money to the partisans, arranging the escape of the Austrian deserter, and rescuing Romoletto's weapons, but these activities are intimately interwoven with *Pina* (the books and the Austrian with Pina's confession, the weapons with the 'grandfather'). Don Pietro 'acts' in the Resistance because three people ask for his help: Manfredi, the Austrian deserter, and Marcello. The *Manfredi* thread is mainly filled by Manfredi's relationship with Marina and by his hiding from the Germans. It is only when he leads the attack on the convoy that he carries out any 'Resistance activity.' This attack, extremely significant in historical terms, is understated in the narrative rhetoric of the film.

The attack on the convoy is treated almost elliptically, from a cinematic point of view. It is made up of a few shots, mostly in very long scale, that sometimes make it difficult for the editor to reconcile the angles of viewpoint. An analogous assault on a German patrol in Via Rasella led to the reprisal of the Ardeatine massacre, in which ten Italians were executed for each German killed. Manfredi's attack on the convoy would be reminiscent of the Via Rasella ambush, and could evoke the same controversy over whether such exploits justified the terrible price paid for them. Manfredi's attack more closely resembled that of Via Rasella in the script than it does in the film, where it passes as an action primarily directed towards freeing the prisoners held by the Germans. By having this attack in the film, the filmmakers appear to endorse and even celebrate the partisan action in Via Rasella. Its elliptical treatment may be an attempt to avoid too much controversy, and to weave the historical event into the film's narrative threads.

If, therefore, we see *Roma città aperta* as breaking into two 'films,' the first combines the 'Resistance activity' of a priest with the melodrama of an innocent pregnant mother's death, while the second transfers the 'Resistance activity' role to Manfredi (besides the attack on the convoy he stops the Germans arresting more partisans by dying under torture without revealing information) and the domestic 'melodrama' role to Don Pietro, who embodies compassion and sanctity (as opposed to Resistance defiance), and dies innocent (he is not explicitly accused of any 'Resistance activity'). He is not really interrogated by Bergmann, but rather is 'tortured' by being forced to watch Manfredi's torture. However, this is used by the narrative's dramatic machinery for manipulating the emotions of the viewer, rather than as the equivalent of the military tribunal to which Don Morosini was subjected. In other words, in the second 'film' Manfredi becomes what Don Pietro had been, and Don Pietro what Pina had been, in the first 'film.' Thus, the first 'film' is *repeated* to a certain extent by the second. In the first, Pina's (domestic) values are immune to the Occupation, while in the second Don Pietro's values are immune to the Gestapo. It is, of course, an exaggeration, but there is a grain of truth in the suspicion that the 'Resistance' functions almost as a pretext for a moral melodrama. There is nothing remarkable about *Roma città aperta* in this regard, because it is a feature of most Resistance narratives (particularly cinematic) of the immediate post-war period in most countries. In Italy, for example, a *political* perspective on the Resistance only began to feature widely in the cinema in the 1960s.

We have observed earlier how the melodramatic matrix characteristically sets up a narrative that moves in repetitive circles, cyclically repeating itself in order to 'illustrate' a situation, a condition, or an experience (whereas a hero-adventure narrative generally moves from one situation to a 'changed' new one). In *Roma città aperta* the narrative has repeated 'movements' (we earlier called them two 'films' and a 'coda'), in each of which a civilian (denoted by his or her costume) dies at the hands of, and in a situation dominated by, 'uniformed' (once again, costume does the work) soldiers. In order to make its 'reference' to the Occupation and the Resistance, *Roma città aperta* narrates a melodrama of human suffering brought about by the irruption of transgressive chaotic elements (war, in this case, as in so many) into an idyll (connoted by the 'humanity' of Pina and Don Pietro and their roles in the 'organic' Prenestina community).

In the first half of the film Pina offers the viewer a point of view (ethical and emotional) and in the second half Don Pietro serves this purpose. As I have already said, *Roma città aperta* is not like *To Have and Have Not*, with the protagonist always present, serving as a continuity of consciousness; the Italian film cross-cuts between separate threads not linked by the on-screen presence of a continuous consciousness. *Roma città aperta* therefore has to create the effect of a point of view for the viewer and supply a linking consciousness, and then shift it from one character to another mid-way through the film.

If Pina is to a certain extent superfluous to the 'main' narrative of the whole film, Don Pietro is, in a similar way, superfluous to the film's second half. However, each functions as a consciousness that is characterized by being innocent and a victim (Don Pietro is not innocent in actual fact, but various means are used to project him in this light). From this perspective, it starts to become clear how the film has functioned historically in the social narrativizing of the Second World War.

Pina and Don Pietro establish a point of view for the viewer: they are innocent victims, rather than involved combatants – their 'resistance' is on the human, compassionate level. The point of view constructed by the film defines the viewer's vision of himself or herself as *innocent victim* (and is reinforced by the viewer's identification with Don Pietro's point of view on the torture of Manfredi). At the film's showing at the Rome Festival (24 September 1945), a fairly elite audience felt the emotional impact of the film, but was dubious about its message, and about the film's roughness. In some ways, this is an entirely appropriate response to the film: to see it precisely for what it is.

Rapidly the point of view on the war carried by Pina and Don Pietro became a cult expression of how Italians needed to narrativize the war, and its 'truth' or acceptability was reinforced by foreign responses to the film. Even the elite gradually began to accept it as the 'story' of the Resistance. However, critics could not help finding the film's adoption as 'realist' a little unconvincing. Hence, the myth of the film coexists with perplexity about that myth.

The same generic (melodramatic) narrative is rehearsed with less obviously manipulative means in *Paisà*, and bears the same message. This time Rossellini's camera sets up an 'objective,' ironic point of view, rather than offering a particular character as a 'position' for the viewer. The effect is that of a 'reality' *caught* or *discovered* by the camera, rather than one *produced* by a consciousness. This 'effect' is precisely what characterizes the 'realism' of neorealism as it emerges from the interpretations and evaluations of a phenomenological critic like André Bazin. *Paisà* is thus deemed more realist than the earlier film, but in fact it reinforces, retrospectively, the 'truth' of what in *Roma città aperta* was communicated by means of the viewer's identification with a character who was the bearer of a point of view. *Paisà* proves that what *Roma città aperta* narrates is 'true' (real).

Rossellini does the same for Germany in *Germania anno zero* that he had done for Italy in *Paisà* – but without provoking anything like the same response in the Italian public or in Italian criticism, because Italians no longer saw it as acceptably narrativizing their own experience (i.e., it does not articulate their thought about the war, and so does not meet a *need* for narrative). It was necessary for Italians to have their experience narrativized as that of innocent victims. For Rossellini to do that for the Germans was (a) going too far in contradicting other narratives, which portrayed the Italians as the innocent victims of the Germans, and (b) of no particular interest to Italians anyway (those small touches of 'humanity' Rossellini gives to Germans in *Roma città aperta* and *Paisà* have gone entirely unremarked in Italian writing about the films – with the exception of Indro Montanelli's contemporary review).[25] *Roma città aperta* and *Paisà* were box-office successes, while *Germania anno zero* was a flop; critics began to find Rossellini becoming 'involuted.'

The plot of *Roma città aperta* moves rapidly and economically, and the viewer does not receive the impression that he or she is just watching talking heads involved in dialogue, even though our analysis of the film's event-story content shows the enormous amount of information conveyed in a short time. However, if we used the classical distinction between *mimesis* (what we are shown taking place) and *diegesis* (what we are told about – though this is not the way the word is currently used in film theory), we would immediately notice how much the plot relies on *diegesis*. For example, the relationship between Manfredi and Marina is pivotal to the action of the plot, and conventional mainstream cinema would probably have exploited that romantic and erotic material in the *mimesis*. Instead, the first half of *Roma città aperta* consigns it to brief mentions in the *diegesis*. Apart from the attack on the rail depot by Romoletto's band (even here, the actual attack itself is 'elided'), and the handing over of money to the partisan, 'Resistance activity' receives little *mimesis*. Indeed, to follow the plot properly, the viewer needs a large amount of knowledge, which reinforces the persuasiveness of Marina Zancan's and Lucia Re's discussion of the way in which neorealist Resistance narratives built upon already existing, elaborated narratives. Precisely because *Roma città aperta* is formed out of a number of *threads* based on well-known and already narrated 'events,' its blending of them into a single whole creates a three-dimensional plot that *alludes* to much of its own content rather than painstakingly playing it out.

A feature of almost all Resistance cinema is that the real 'war,' with its 'professional' soldiers, takes place off-screen. Indeed, the distinction between 'the military' and 'the civilian' is an important characteristic of Resistance cinema.[26] By this means *Roma città aperta* creates the 'inhumanity' of Bergmann (and it is in contrast with this inhumanity that Hartmann's speech, and his alarm at bringing Marina to see Manfredi's corpse, carry significance). *Paisà* investigates in some depth the very different experiences and mentalities assigned to 'professionals' and 'civilians,' and gradually breaks down the barrier separating them. The profoundest, most significant, and most 'realist' films about 'war' do not *depict* battle, and this is because of the 'thinking' function of narrative and the choice between the two genres (hero-adventure or melodrama) facing an artist wanting to deal with the subject. 'Thought' has less to do with facts and more to do with structuring a generic narrative: melodrama, a world view that embraces and gives a meaning to experience through *contemplation*. And if, as sometimes occurs, the melodramatic myth involves a transgression precipitating chaos, the meaning of the disturbance of the idyll is often evoked by means of a senseless tragedy that is not really part of the war, but involves somebody who is 'good' being needlessly, and possibly accidentally, killed, followed by the struggle to reassert order, the idyll. Pina's death amply fulfils this requirement. In other words, part of the definition of chaos is meaninglessness and arbitrariness. This is typical of all resistance narrative. The antagonists are the 'idyll' (order) and 'meaninglessness' (disorder), and this goes for German representations of the war too.

If we remember that the function of narrative is explanatory, then it is clear how narrative connotes 'meaninglessness' as negative a priori, as it were. The accelerated montage procedure creates the senseless death of Pina, and motivates it as a product of 'disorder,' making it hurtle down unexpectedly and accidentally: she becomes the figure for the garden of the idyll. The senselessness of Pina's death is also a product of generic contamination, involving comedy and incongruity, producing a modulation of the viewer's state of tension through the device of mixing genres (see the following section on 'Dramaturgy'). Moreover, there is no indication of who shot Pina, no writhing and dying in pain, nor any blood. Her death is completed with an allusion to the Christian iconography of the Deposition from the Cross and later, at Benediction, to the recital of the 'Litany of the Blessed Virgin.' Pina represents the idyll abruptly snuffed out.

The second half of the film moves a little in the direction of the hero-adventure matrix, and is the section less remembered and celebrated, even though it may well be factually very accurate. Manfredi versus Bergmann is the mainstream antagonism of the war that normally runs off-camera. They are antagonists in the struggle over what Don Pietro signifies – he is the melodramatic element, the link with the first half of the film – the senseless destruction of the garden. Pina and Don Pietro are the film's real protagonists (note how they statistically dominate the first half), even though the subject-matter of the film is Manfredi versus Bergmann.

The Manfredi and Bergmann threads raise more political issues in the film than most people notice:

- Class: Manfredi's relationship with Marina would have been better if he had met her 'in those days' – when she was true to her social origins; betraying them has a metaphorical relationship with the betrayal of Manfredi, and hence of the democratic Resistance.
- The political background to the war is referred to when Bergmann and the Questore discuss Manfredi's activism against Fascism back in the 1920s, which briefly shines a light on the Fascist police state.
- Bergmann's contemptuous treatment of the Questore of Rome brings the story of Fascism up to date.
- Bergmann's taunts and arguments concerning the inherent incompatibility between the left-wing and the right-wing elements of the Resistance allude to its more problematic areas and those of the postwar reconstruction.
- Bergmann's comment that searching Don Pietro's rectory was a mistake alludes to the position of the Vatican and of the Catholic Church in the context of its Concordat with the Fascist state.
- Manfredi's questioning of Pina about how the women are coping with conditions, and her recounting to him of how the Germans have requisitioned her engineering factory's means of production allude to the working-class struggle for economic survival that constituted a large element of the Resistance.

However, a list of political observations carried by the film does not change its basic narrative matrix. It is the film's narrative that characterizes it, rather than a collection of details occurring in individual dialogues. At most, this list demonstrates that Amidei and Rossellini are by no means as politically naive and rooted in the generic as the 'popular' narrative they are assembling. Nevertheless, if you give importance to these elements, the film comes closer to the standard ideological definition of realism (as 'analysis').

These details apart, the politics of *Roma città aperta* are more those of narrative than what is normally thought of as a politics of realist representation. If we were discussing political parties and their programs, this argument would be considered perfectly normal and acceptable. But to suggest that a *cultural* monument like *Roma città aperta* is in an *iconic* relationship with the referent of the Resistance, and in an *indexical* relationship with the referent of the post-war reconstruction (rather than the other way round), challenges the very basis of much Italian reception of the film. It suggests that the film does not so much 'index-ically' represent the Resistance as function as a direct symptom of what Italians *needed* from the Resistance after it was over. It requires that we pay at least as much attention to the film's narrativizing function (and hence to the 'downwards' direction of its reference) as to its representa-tional function (the 'upwards' direction of its reference to historical events). While this suggested perspective may seem to be a criticism of the film's 'realism,' it draws attention to the craft of the narrators, and to the aesthetic status of the artefact as an object, which is something that theories of realism tend to neglect. The film's impact is the same for those who experienced the Second World War as for those who know next to nothing about it. Is this because of the 'accuracy' of the subject matter, or because of the aesthetic qualities of the artefact?

Dramaturgy: Analysis of the Episode of the Shooting of Pina

1. Ingredients

The historical basis for the episode of Pina's death lies in the death of Maria Teresa Gullace:

> In the morning, in front of the barracks of the 81st infantry in Via Giulio Cesare, mothers, wives, and daughters of men who had been rounded up by the Germans are loudly demanding the release of their dear ones, who have been locked up there prior to being deported ... A young prisoner tries to escape through an opening on the first floor. He is killed with a burst of machine-gun fire. Teresa Gullace, the mother of five children and six months pregnant, is trying to throw a package with a piece of bread and cheese in it to her husband whom she spies at a window. She tries to push through, and is killed by a German NCO.
>
> In the afternoon, two bands of G.A.P. partisan guerrillas respond to the killing of Teresa Gullace with an attack on the garrison of the same bar-racks. In the firefight an officer of the fascist militia gets killed. A woman also dies, hit by a stray bullet as she was coming out of the church of San Gioacchino.[27]

Before *Roma città aperta* was conceived, Giuseppe De Santis, together with a group of writers from the journal *Cinema* and members of the Roman Resistance, had included this episode in his script for a film on the Resistance called *G.A.P.* (the Gruppi di Azione Patriottica were the urban guerrilla partisan formations). Antonio Parisi, in his monograph on the director's work, recounts a conversation in which De Santis told him:

> One of the things that most appealed to us as a way of celebrating the work of those comrades who were daily risking their lives in the G.A.P. squads was to write a film treatment having them as protagonists. It was the first film to be conceived about the resistance, even before *Roma città aperta*. I would say that Rossellini's film copied it, I do not know whether deliberately or by chance, because an episode in the Roman Resistance featured the woman, like Magnani, killed by the Germans, which actually took place in Viale Giulio Cesare outside the barracks of the 81st infantry, and it was one of the most important episodes in the script for *G.A.P.*[28]

Rossellini had come close to the *Cinema* group during the making of his own 1942 film *Un pilota ritorna*. De Santis and others of the group had then collaborated on a film that Rossellini started making in July 1943, a melodrama set in the San Lorenzo railway yards just beside Via Montecuccoli (Pina's home in *Roma città aperta*), called *Scalo merci*. De Santis was both scriptwriter and Rossellini's assistant director on the film. Soon after they had started shooting, the Allies heavily bombed the railway yards, and Rossellini moved the troupe to Tagliacozzo in the Abruzzi hills (where Manfredi will be charged with sending money in *Roma città aperta*) and changed the script to set it among foresters, while De Santis stayed on in Rome. In the cast were Francesco Grandjacquet (who will play Francesco in *Roma città aperta*) and Roswitha Schmidt (who will dub Ingrid). The production ran out of money, was abandoned, and was taken up and completed in 1945 by Marcello Pagliero (who plays Manfredi in *Roma città aperta*), with a new title, *Desiderio*, and released in 1946. The finished film has a first part made by Rossellini, and the rest by Pagliero. Carlo Lizzani, a member of the group of younger artists and writers (who will later be Rossellini's assistant on *Germania anno zero*) recalls:

> At the time of the resistance to the dictatorship, conversation, dialogue, and personal contacts provided great terrain for debate, a formative network of which almost nothing remains for successive generations. In our case it is a patrimony that has never been committed to written documents, but that counted enormously for Rossellini, just as for De Sica and

Visconti. I remember that those of us who were the younger ones placed a lot of faith in this cultural guerrilla war conducted through private dialogue and debate. The evenings passed chatting at the editorial offices of *Cinema*, the fraternizing on the set of *Scalo merci* ..., I think these things gave that director a decisive push.[29]

Much discussion has taken place over Rossellini's transformation from a maker of the regime's patriotic films (*La nave bianca* with Francesco De Robertis, *Un pilota ritorna* with Vittorio Mussolini, and *L'uomo dalla croce*) to anti-fascist 'resistance' films like *Roma città aperta* and *Paisà*. The issues involved are beyond the scope of this book. Nevertheless, it should be clear how the movement took place and, more importantly for our purposes, how *Roma città aperta* itself grew out of the contacts Rossellini's work brought him with the younger generation of partisans and film theorists, the melodrama of *Scalo merci* acting as a halfway house. All along, Rossellini wanted the freedom to make films his own way, something that government productions allowed far more than commercial ones, and it was a freedom he never thereafter renounced. De Santis had started out with the formal, traditional, literary Visconti on *Ossessione*, and as a *Cinema* critic admiring the literary, formal filming of the French tradition. His collaboration with Rossellini, whose approach to cinema was closer to the freer, less formal, documentary approach of De Robertis, earned De Santis the wrath of Visconti, a director very different from Rossellini. In the genesis of the episode of Pina's death we are watching the development of more than just the neorealism of Rossellini.

Tag Gallagher makes an interesting observation concerning Pina's pursuit of the truck: 'Roberto surely recalled a similar scene in King Vidor's 1925 *The Big Parade* – one of the most famous scenes in movies – where Renée Adorée chases the truck taking John Gilbert away.'[30] Vidor was one of the directors championed by the *Cinema* group in the early 1940s; his *The Big Parade* and *The Crowd* were paradigmatic examples of 'realism' in the cinema. Rossellini himself admired Vidor. In *The Big Parade* Jim, part of the American contingent arriving in France to fight against the Germans in the First World War, is billeted in a farm where he falls in love with the owners' daughter, Mélisande, and she with him. Jim's battalion is suddenly ordered to move up to the front, and Mélisande sees all the soldiers hurrying onto trucks to be transported away. She looks in vain for Jim among the masses of men, and finally the two catch sight of each other, Jim aboard a truck that is about to move off. Mélisande runs to the truck, pulls Jim down, and tries to stop him from leaving, but an NCO tears them apart and good-naturedly bundles Jim back onto the truck, which starts trundling off down the road. Mélisande clutches Jim's hand, then a strap hanging from the truck, and is dragged along until she lets go. The scene closes with her standing alone in the road, looking after the departed battalion, and finally sinking, sobbing, to the ground.

The girl trying to hold back her lover from going off to be killed at the front is a commonplace of war narratives, and forms part of the 'back at home' melodramatic motif that endows stories of battle and bravery with poignancy. To call it a cliché belittles the profundity and authenticity of the theme, but if Pina's death were a variation on that theme, it might not deserve to be called as innovative and historically meaningful as it has frequently been described. Certainly, one sometimes gets the impression that the 'institution of neorealism' wilfully forgets that other good films had ever had anything profound or ethical to say about war before 1945, least of all American ones. If Pina's pursuit of the truck carrying away Francesco were 'intertextually' linked to Mélisande's pursuit of Jim's truck, the implications could be deemed profound. Even assuming Amidei's original idea was inspired by seeing Anna Magnani run after Massimo Serato (Magnani's biography does not confirm the story, but then it might not be the kind of story she would pass on to a biographer), then Rossellini's acceptance of Amidei's suggestion, and his decision to move the episode from Viale Giulio Cesare (in the Prati district of Rome, very different from the railway district) to Via Montecuccoli might have been partly motivated by his recollection of *The Big Parade*, its thematic connotations, and the enormous audience response it evoked. Rather than being a component of the rejection of convention in neorealist cinema, it would constitute the exploitation of a conventional narrative motif of melodrama.

However, to see ourselves faced with such an interpretive choice would perhaps mean embracing precisely the kind of evaluative criterion concerning *Roma città aperta* that has hitherto obstructed analysis of the film. It is characteristic of Gallagher's iconoclastic appreciation of Rossellini's art that he makes his observation with no further comment. We could certainly decide that the artist finds his material wherever he can, and that what matters is the use he makes of it. Rossellini could be seen as 'transforming' rather than 'exploiting' the American motif. Magnani is no Renée Adorée, no 'ingénue,' no fiancée holding her lover back from fighting. Her fury belongs in another register. If Vidor's film lies somewhere behind Pina's pursuit of the truck, then Rossellini and Magnani made very good use of that material.

The scene of Pina's death grew in conception during the actual shooting of the film. From being one short story among many, it became woven into a single long story made up of numerous threads. It was a late decision to have it take place in Via Montecuccoli, rather than in another part of the city. All the threads come together in her death, and some threads end with that event. We only fleetingly return to the community of the Prenestina (in Manfredi's arrest at Don Pietro's rectory); Romoletto and his band drop out of the film, only to return at the very end. It was a complex and expensive scene to shoot, because it required a large number of extras, uniforms, and vehicles, all of which had to be managed and coordinated.

It has been said that it was shot with three cameras. While being costly in film stock, this would have been economical in time and organization, and permitted the makers to remedy mistakes at the editing stage, as we shall see.

A parenthetical note may help some viewers to grasp the scene more clearly, because the topography of the apartment block on Via Montecuccoli may not be clear to all. On the building's frontage to the street is a tall entrance, with double doors that are left open during the day (in a night-time scene, we see Francesco and then Lauretta come through these doors, which are closed for the night). The doorway leads to a large passage, which goes right through the building to a courtyard inside, surrounded on all sides by the wings of the apartment building. From the middle of that passage lead off large spiral staircases, laterally going into the wings of the front section of the building, the one on the right (looking from the street) being where Francesco has his apartment, overlooking the street. At the back of the same front wing of the building, with windows onto the courtyard this time, is the apartment where Pina lives. The entrances to those two apartments face each other across a landing on the spiral staircase, beyond which the two apartments have adjoining walls (which explains how, two years beforehand, Pina and Francesco had got to know each other as the result of an argument about banging on the adjoining wall: their love grew from a quarrel between neighbours).

This all could have been made much clearer to the viewer than it actually is with careful continuity and choice of camera angles, both inside and outside the building, and it is typical of the film (and perhaps of Rossellini's directorial style) that such care has not been taken. This might seem mere pedantry on my, the critic's, part. However, a cinema screen is essentially two-dimensional, and left and right are the most important orienting factors for the viewer. A scrupulous *narrative* film director will either include 'establishing shots' in his montage, to orient the viewer topographically, or he will avoid the need for this by one of two methods: either by choosing his angles so as to preserve a coherent point of view or by developing his scenes in long takes in which characters move around the location. Rossellini does neither of these things. Let me quote from a conversation held much later between an interviewer and Jolanda Benvenuti, who edited the film (Jolanda rarely completes a sentence, and it can be hard to render her nuanced syntax in English):

Did you pay attention to how the preceding shot ended, so that ...?
No, but don't you see how each scene is on its own? Look at them closely, it's not as though there are cuts from angle to angle ... [*she means:* it is not as though the camera angle for one shot has been chosen to match that of the shots that were to precede and follow it]. We would [*meaning:* the shot would] stop where the dialogue ends.
How many takes did he make for each scene?
Very few. We'd use everything [*meaning:* all the footage we shot]. There wasn't the film [*meaning:* there was not enough raw film stock for multiple takes]. That's the way the film was shot. No clapperboard. He would tell me: 'Do it this way.' I would ask: 'Why?' He would say: 'Can't you see?' Me: 'What d'you mean, can't I see? I don't know!' We were always arguing like that.
If a scene was complicated, how many takes would you make of it, maximum?
Oh, no, he didn't find them complicated; if it was a long scene he would shoot it all, and then do little pieces. He would do one master shot, and then lots of pieces.
...
When Rossellini wasn't there I did the shooting. The final scene with the children, that one I shot. Then I did another one. But more or less, they were scenes with no dialogue.
Was there direct sound?
It was shot silent, and then dubbed.
...
So if a sequence shot had a mistake, it was a mess? You only had one take?

If it was a long shot, I just left it alone.
How did you edit the scene of Pina's shooting?
Oh, we spent a month, just on the machine-gun. I had one bang, and I just multiplied it frame by frame. We worked with nothing.
Who was the sound-effects man?
Me.
You did the machine-gun burst?
Sure, I did lots of them.

...

I'd wonder how we were going to put these pieces together, really. Because, the way it was shot, I didn't see how to edit them. I'd be incensed. I'd say 'This is impossible.'
Did you do all the editing yourself?
Yes. Eraldo [Da Roma], who should have done it, was in jail, something to do with the Germans [she makes some gestures, indicating that we would know what she was talking about]. And I always used to edit for him [Rossellini]. I liked it.
And when somebody [she means Rossellini] is fixated [about/on something], and the scene has been shot out of sequence, I just didn't understand.
Did Rossellini come when you were editing?
Rossellini would say 'This evening we'll see it [*meaning:* we'll see what you – Jolanda – have managed to put together]; if it's not right, we'll do it over again.' Then he'd see the scene [*meaning:* the montage I had put together], and say [her gestures imply that he was not satisfied] 'We'll shoot another scene.' Rossellini was never there, it drove me crazy. Rossellini would say 'Try whatever you like.'
Often I wouldn't even have a copy of the script. It had disappeared, nobody knew where it was.
What were the practical problems in the editing?
He shot as the whim took him and I needed to match the shots. Then he'd say 'Damn it,' and I: 'What do you expect?'
Rossellini would improvise, he would shoot when he felt like it. He would come and say 'Here's some footage.'[31]

The Germans round up the inhabitants in the courtyard (where Pina slaps the flirtatious soldier), and take the men out through the passage into the street. Pina sees Francesco being led through the passage, and gives pursuit, fighting her way through the Germans, who try to stop her. Once she has reached the doorway on the street, she sees the truck carrying Francesco drive off, and chases it. Don Pietro and Marcello, meanwhile, have come down into the large passage from the staircase, and have started to leave the premises through the front door on the street, and hence witness the shooting (which those in the courtyard cannot see).

There are a number of 'mistakes' in the filming of the actual shooting:

(a) Pina looks at the truck and sees Francesco; she struggles with the Germans at the doorway on the street; she looks again, and Francesco calls out to her; but the truck, which was already in movement, has not got any further away.

(b) Pina's run after the truck is too short, because she falls too quickly; it does not provide enough footage to create the required effect. The filmmakers solved this by inserting, into the shot taken from the truck of her running after it, a shot taken from across the street in front of the doorway of that same chase. Basically, the same action is run twice, from different angles.

(c) In the shot from the back of the truck, Pina is too far away for the viewer to see her eyes. But in the shot from across the street, Anna Magnani can clearly be seen to look down at the ground to check that she is not going to stumble over a rut in the road. If the viewer were to perceive this, it would greatly detract from the impression of passionate instinct propelling her pursuit.

(d) Marcello rushes over to his mother's fallen body, followed by Don Pietro, who has a black cloak fully covering his white surplice. In the transition from one shot to another, the cloak disappears.

(e) The position in which Pina's body lies in the roadway changes from shot to shot.

From our perspective, studying the film, these details provide insight into the roughness of the film and of Rossellini's way of shooting: there are a lot of mistakes in 22 seconds of film. Yet Rossellini tolerated them. However, they equally indicate the dramatic and aesthetic power lying behind the *assembly* of the scene, and behind the whole technique of parallel montage storytelling that leads up to it, for that cinematographically 'flawed' sequence is one of the most admired and celebrated in the whole of European cinema.

This sequence contributes to the 'myth' of neorealism as a heroic cinema, overcoming insuperable technical obstacles and deriving all its impact from the 'truth' of the representation: a cinema of 'content' rather than of 'form.' That myth belongs in the realm of reception and interpretation, but under the close examination of 'description' becomes decidedly questionable.

2. Genre

Part of the effect of the scene is its suddenness and unexpectedness, a result in part of the mixture of genres interwoven throughout the whole episode. Not only does the scene weave together *narrative* threads, it also makes a single whole from diverse *generic* patterns. The viewer's being slightly bewildered and disoriented contributes to the ultimate effect. Up to this point, the character of Pina has furnished the main unifying point of view for the viewer on the multiple strands of the narrative between which the film intercuts. Her death constitutes a 'loss' to the viewer in relation to his or her viewing experience, and thereby gains in rhetorical impact. More importantly, perhaps, the juxtaposition of generic patterns is directed to a powerful rhetorical *pathos* through the manipulation of the viewer's emotional responses.

The episode as a whole deploys the genre of melodrama in the casual and meaningless death of a pregnant woman on her wedding day, the result of a transgression on the part of Manfredi's slighted lover, Marina (though this rather depends on how the viewer understands the logic of the narrative leading up to the episode). It also deploys the melodramatic theme of 'non-organic' trespassing into the intimate territory of the 'organic' community (reinforced by the women's concern for each other's family members).

Adventure and suspense give form to the partisan's flight from the SS, and to Don Pietro's intervention to prevent the discovery of the weapons held by Romoletto in the attic. Most of all, Rossellini uses the stereotyped cinematic convention of suspenseful parallel montage by cutting between Don Pietro descending the stairs and the Fascist militia climbing up them, and then releasing the tension with comedy.

The largest generic ingredient in the episode is supplied by comedy:

- the Brigadiere arriving with flowers for the bride;
- Pina slapping the amorous SS trooper and dislodging his helmet, playing with the rhetorical coding of costume;
- the women telling the Fascist NCO that they trust him to take care of their belongings;
- the Fascist militiamen looking up the skirts of the women instead of in the direction in which the partisans are escaping;

- Don Pietro's arrival 'in disguise,' as a priest come to deliver the Last Sacraments to a dying man;
- the Brigadiere commenting on how times have changed since the days in which priests would arrive with the promptness of the fire brigade;
- the broad Tuscan accent of the Fascist NCO telling the Brigadiere that he does not like his face (this 'encodes' the NCO as 'different' from the Roman populace, and draws once again on the rhetorical coding of costume, as well as exploiting regional stereotypes according to which Tuscans are both sarcastic and rude and had the reputation of being the fiercest and hardest of the Fascists);
- the slapstick choreography of Don Pietro with the mortar bomb and the barrel of the machine gun;
- the comic dramatic irony of the grandfather's protest against death;
- the clever sound-off slapstick of the blow with the frying pan, followed by Don Pietro's frantic attempts to revive the grandfather;
- the comic bewilderment of the Fascist NCO overawed by Don Pietro's pantomime.

Just as the film as a whole is 'repetitive,' in the sense I have described in the section on narrative (a similar story 'told twice'), so this first half of the film has cyclical features to it. The generic contamination in a narrative context of 'suspense,' which we have just encountered in the episode of the shooting of Pina, is itself a repetition of an earlier scene, that in which Pina goes to Don Pietro's rectory to make her confession on the evening before her marriage (in table 1 it is 'thread' number 11, scenes 31–6). The comic role here, corresponding to that of the Brigadiere, is played by the sacristan Agostino (performed by an ubiquitous character actor of Italian film comedy, Nando Bruno), who this time is sarcastic towards Don Pietro and downright snide towards Pina. The element of comic disguise for a serious purpose is constituted by the 'books' containing money for the partisans. Pina's feminine and instinctive – but rash – humanity lies in her insistence on carrying the books for Don Pietro, and the suspenseful threat comes from the appearance of the Austrian deserter. In its formal, generic, and narrative features, this scene is 'repeated' in the killing of Pina. The thematic pattern of 'disguise,' or misrecognition, is soon after taken up by the episode of the spanking of the little boys on their return home from blowing up a German railway petrol wagon ('thread' number 15). This feature of proceeding by means of cyclical, repetitive vignettes belongs to the narrative structure of Italian film comedy, and is a notable characteristic of the first half of *Roma città aperta*, constituting one of the structural devices whereby the filmmakers bring together in a unified assembly the fragmentary and diverse elements of the film's multiple event-stories.

The deliberate intention to create a generic *assembly* is indicated by the decision to add Federico Fellini to the scripting team. The extent to which the episodes deploy the rhetorical resources of *logos* (in their realism), *ethos* (in their melodramatic moral and political referents) is overshadowed by their deployment of *pathos* (the appeal to the viewer's emotions).

3. Aesthetics

The artist creates an object that satisfies him (or her). He may not know exactly why it satisfies him, but he accepts that the object configured this way is more satisfactory than when it is configured in some of the other ways he has tried out. Similarly, the viewer is satisfied. Critics have the job of hypothesizing what might account for the satisfaction, usually in terms of the formal properties of the object, what it manages to communicate (its expressiveness), and what it succeeds in representing. A simple example might be the 'superfluous' shot, at the end of the sequence of Pina's shooting, where the camera changes its position on Don Pietro cradling the lifeless body of Pina across his knees, and holds this almost 'still' image for a few seconds (just over five, to be precise). The filmmaker's and the viewer's satisfaction might be accounted for by the critic in terms of the image's formal resemblance to the traditional iconography of Christ's body being received by his mother, Mary, after having been taken down from the Cross. In expressive terms, it could be seen as connoting martyrdom, or Pina sacrificing herself for the Resistance (even though Pina's rash pursuit of the SS in the attempt to retrieve her bridegroom hardly belongs in the realm of a martyr's self-sacrifice). It could be hypothesized that the image represents (or has as its narrative referent) a fertile and innocent Italy persecuted by a sterile and inhuman Nazism – which is a drastic and inaccurate simplification of the real historical context, but one infinitely more palatable than some of the available alternatives. From a purely aesthetic cinematic perspective, we could describe it as the conclusion to a parallel montage procedure bringing about a fortuitous convergence of logical elements on a senseless outcome. Pina and Don Pietro occupy the great bulk of the footage in the rapid inter-cutting of the first half of the film, and it is appropriate that this self-contained narrative culminate in an almost still image of the two of them together in an emblematic pose.

It is very likely that Rossellini was at most only partially aware at the conscious level of what he was doing when he set up the shot, and that it was at the editing stage that the shot became useful as a rhythmic device to bring this section of the film to a satisfactory close. Continuity errors in the shots at this point in the film suggest that Rossellini had gone back to collect 'coverage' (shots designed to offer flexibility at the editing stage) after having shot the main narrative material. The viewer never has to contemplate the sequence without the shot of Pina and Don Pietro, and so perceives a total unity and continuity of narrative and representation. The critic, by contrast, perceives a work of *assembly*. Viewers find the whole sequence entirely coherent, which confirms the appropriateness of the filmmakers' choice on formal grounds, 'shaping' the assembly for the purposes of the whole artefact. The filmmakers were concerned with the aesthetic qualities of the artefact, but it was only after they had completed it, and seen the response of viewers, that they realized what it was they had assembled. It is unlikely that they thought for one moment that half a century later a film historian (Gian Piero Brunetta) would say about the sequence:

> Indeed, one is more and more inclined to think that in future it will be possible to recognise, study and understand the meaning of the Italian and European Resistance struggle from a single sequence of *Roma città aperta* (that of, for example, the death of sora Pina) much more than from consulting dozens of history books and thousands of pages of documents.[32]

If what Brunetta says is true, this is due to the aesthetic properties of the artefact, and to the 'deeper' levels of narrative reference, rather than to the 'surface' level of 'realist representation,' because the actual events surrounding Maria Teresa Gullace's death bore only a limited resemblance to what is depicted in *Roma città aperta*. In order to describe the *nature* of the artefact at this point, we need rhetorical and narrative notions. Notions of 'fact' and indexical representation, proper to cinematic 'realism,' are of little use to us.

Via Tasso

When the film first appeared, there were a number of critics who expressed reservations about the torture scene in the Via Tasso Gestapo headquarters. One contemporary newspaper review is particularly revealing because it condenses in a single paragraph many of the notions applied to 'art' and 'realism' that we examined in chapter 2. Rather than send the reader back to that chapter, I shall repeat Sarazini's comments here:

> The fiction acquires an impact that has the flavour of historical chronicle; and not through crude description, since the plot, in this first part, takes flight towards an ideal realism, towards which, henceforth, all our films should aim ... Where we are not in agreement with Rossellini is in the second part, where a harsh realism exceeds the boundaries of the aesthetic. The reality reproduced in a waxworks museum is never art. This means that in wanting to transfer into the realm of art certain monstrous realities, Rossellini has fallen into a rhetoric appropriate to Grand Guignol, which neither serves nor obeys the pure and stable laws of poetic transfiguration – laws that exclude certain appearances and facts, unless they are diluted in the inspiration of an ideal synthesis.[33]

Sarazani brings together 'art' and 'realism' by appealing to idealist notions. The 'fiction' acquires its 'impact' from the 'truth value' (*logos*) of 'historical chronicle.' This is not, however, achieved by a purely surface level of representation, 'crude description,' but by being raised to the level of 'an ideal realism,' 'an ideal synthesis.' A 'harsh realism' is incompatible with the aesthetic ('the realm of art'); 'art' requires the 'laws of poetic transfiguration.' Without the idealist appeal to deeper levels of narrative reference, crude representation becomes, according to Sarazani, rhetorical Grand Guignol (nowadays we might call it 'sensationalism').

Indro Montanelli also demurred in his review of the film: 'Of the two hours of the film show, only ten minutes left us dissatisfied: those of the torture, which we would have preferred less explicit.'[34] Rossellini apparently would have preferred not to show the torture itself, but Amidei insisted that it was a historical fact that needed documenting. French viewers of *Roma città aperta* were enormously impressed by a film that finally represented the hard reality (torture) that lay behind so much of the Resistance struggle. Rossellini was right to worry about the decorum that too much 'realism' would infringe. Torture is a very intimate physical act, and to portray it in film to an audience is pornographic. But having it witnessed by Don Pietro, and giving the audience a position alongside Don Pietro, emphasizes the public, political, and theatrical nature of the event, and prevents it from becoming pornographic.

Amidei countered Rossellini's reluctance with the assertion of a documentary *function* (that of making known historical facts) for the scene. Hence, it has two functions: one dramatic and expressive, the other documentary. Both the 'expression' of a national response to the German occupation and the 'documentation' of what that occupation involved were features of the film that contributed to its being considered the inauguration of neorealism.

Partisans were frequently arrested on the basis of information received from informers. Both Lieutenant Colonel Herbert Kappler (who operated from a building in Via Tasso) and the Fascist police lieutenant Pietro Koch (who operated in a commandeered hotel, Pensione Oltremare in Via Principe Amedeo, and later in the Pensione Jaccarino) made routine use of torture, in which the victims were frequently disfigured, crippled, blinded, and killed. Successful and unsuccessful suicide attempts by prisoners were not uncommon. The number of detainees who refused to divulge information even under the most atrocious torture was high. On one occasion, Fascist troops aimed wide in a firing squad, and the condemned men had to be finished off by the German officer present with a pistol shot to the back of the head. Don Morosini (one of the models for Don Pietro) was dispatched in this way, but by an Italian officer.

In critical evaluations of *Roma città aperta* there has been a tendency to see the first half of the film as 'realist,' and the second half as 'generic,' whereas in fact it is the other way round.

The drama of the interrogation scene works by contrasts. An essentially theatrical dynamic is constructed out of a small number of ingredients: the set (three adjoining rooms: Bergmann's office, the torture chamber, and the salon), the action (the torture as an act, the torture as spectacle, and Bergmann's movements between the rooms), and the three characters (Bergmann, Manfredi, Don Pietro). To these ingredients are added secondary ones (Ingrid and Marina, Hartmann, the Austrian deserter hanging himself) that serve to tie up the narrative – though Hartmann's speech serves a function in the play of dramatic contrasts, as we shall see. After Don Pietro has delivered his curse and then repented, an epilogue to the whole sequence is furnished by Hartmann, seated on a chair and looking into space: 'We are the master race!'

The drama hinges on the way Harry Feist performs the role of Bergmann, which contributes to generating meaning in the scene. Just as the first half of the film gathers much of its impact from the histrionic talents of Anna Magnani, the second half relies heavily on those of Harry Feist. Manfredi and Don Pietro do not change in this scene. They are endowed with 'heroism' by the actions and behaviour of Bergmann, and by the fact that they do nothing; they remain the same. It has to be admitted that Don Pietro does change a little, at one point, where he pronounces his curse on Bergmann, but he quickly retracts it, and returns to being 'the same.' Hence, the drama and its meaning (variously interpreted as 'quiet heroism' and 'humanity') are produced by the context in which the two Italian characters remain 'the same.' Bergmann's role is to provide the context in which this steadiness acquires meaning, and it is the job of Harry Feist (and the dubber, Giulio Panicali) to project that role.

The attributes with which the scene endows Bergmann can be listed without recourse to much interpretation. He is presented as at first polite and well mannered. The real Herbert Kappler admitted that he had once struck a prisoner, but claimed that he had immediately apologized. Certainly, for the purposes of the drama, it would slightly drain the scene of meaning if Bergmann were portrayed as being totally *unaware* of the humanity of his prisoners. For example, the tactic of forcing Don Pietro to watch Manfredi's torture depends on Bergmann's knowing and appreciating the suffering this would cause. Bergmann's portrayal is given impact by the way he abruptly switches from being humane to indifferent.

As a narrative event, making Don Pietro watch Manfredi's interrogation is not 'realistic' because, where it really is important to get information from two prisoners, letting one know what the other has or has not told you is about the worst tactic you could use. The drama and its meaning, however, depend on Don Pietro's response to a *context*, and the device of having him watch the torture creates precisely that context. Moreover, the viewer is given a reason for watching the torture by this dramatic device – not only a reason, but also a point of view, that of Don Pietro. Manfredi is led to another room behind a closed door. Sound off would have *signified* adequately the torture (as it did in the earlier scene of the torture of the 'professor'). Bergmann's action in opening the door and then leaving Don Pietro with this vision is the dramatic device that endows Don Pietro's passivity with meaning. Later, while Bergmann watches and frets in irritation and frustration, Ingrid comes in to get a cigarette, and at one point goes over to watch the torture. She is satisfied that Manfredi has not spoken, because it is like a bet she has won with Bergmann: 'I told you it wouldn't be easy.' When, however, Hartmann enters, together with Marina, he is immediately shocked at what he sees, and looks over at Marina in concern to see what effect it is having on her. Hence, the drama builds up layers of contrast as it progresses, and uses Hartmann as an ethical foil to Bergmann and Ingrid.

The theatricality of the scene (both in the dramatic conflict and in the three-winged stage of the adjoining rooms) derives partly from the theatricality inherent in interrogation and torture themselves: they are a formalized ritual, with a predictable course, and essentially repetitive. The first step in the ritual is Bergmann's turning his desk light to shine in Manfredi's face. It is understandable, therefore, but not necessarily correct, to suspect that this scene was a product of generic construction. Although he is not the most valuable human being in the scene and his knowledge is deliberately coded as being of low quality, Bergmann is the scene's dramatic pivot; it all revolves around him, and is, in a way, a play, a ballet, a performance directed by him. To judge the scene's theatricality as falling into genre misses the point that the theatricality is thematic; it is as much a part of the content as of the style. The fact that there is interrogation and torture in the film is pure chronicle, almost documentary. This floor of a building in Via Tasso is where the partisan war in Rome was played out – anything *else* would have been a generic device. To emphasize its theatricality, to portray it as a matter of display, is a rhetorical device. But it is a motivated device, because torture *functions* as display in a strategy of terror. To this day, prisoners are regularly tortured as a deterrent. Part of the result of the expressive device is to fashion a message that the theatrical display did not work on either Manfredi or Don Pietro. Their 'humanity' is given poetic expression, is enshrined in an image: that of being immune to theatricality. The *sermo humilis* of their lowered voices, quiet tones, and unremarkable dress (in contrast with Bergmann's rhetorical display) functions as a sign of their humanity (Auerbach's 'sublime' – see the section on 'Rhetoric' in chapter 2) in a code of binary opposites. Bergmann, in his fastidious, rhetorical self-consciousness, sets up one pole of this opposition; all you need are a few touches to set up the other pole. A slight messiness, a lack of self-consciousness, and you have created the 'opposite' of Bergmann: you have evoked a man of great humanity and depth compared with an icon of shallowness. It is the lightness of touch with regard to Bergmann – indeed, endowing the dandy with his own shallow humanity – that endows Don Pietro with his profound compassion. 'Lack of rhetoric' in the portrayal of Don Pietro, in other words, is part of an essentially rhetorical deployment of *sermo humilis*.

The torture also functions at a deeper level of narrative reference, that of the melodramatic matrix. Bergmann makes a wager with Ingrid: that Manfredi will give a higher priority to his own, individual interests (survival and the avoidance of pain) than to the interests of the 'organism' (the Resistance) of which he is a part. The two 'ontologies' that we schematically identified in chapter 2 are placed in conflict. Manfredi, by accepting pain and death, chooses the 'organic' ontology and, by being certain that he is acting for the best, affirms it as metaphysically 'truer' than the new 'modernizing' ontology of individualism that Bergmann confidently champions (and propounds to Hartmann in the salon). For this reason, Ingrid's coming into the office and positively crowing over the likely outcome of Bergmann's wager, and Bergmann's extreme irritation, are not just 'realistic' psychological details of the narrative, but are elements emphasizing the scene's profounder ethical implications. Similarly, earlier on in the interrogation, when Bergmann questions Manfredi's alliance with 'monarchists,' and Don Pietro's alliance with atheistic communists, Rossellini does not have the Italians respond with arguments. This is because Bergmann is portraying 'Italy' as an institution constituted by *competing* individual political interests. Merely by ignoring his blandishments, Manfredi and Don Pietro attest to the metaphysical notion of 'Italy' as an ideal organism. With hindsight, we might view Rossellini's representation more sceptically, but it is easy to see how *at the time* it was taken as a representation of the 'truth' about the kind of 'universals' that lay behind the Italian resistance to the German occupation. Independently of the 'realism' or otherwise of the *representation* lies the 'truth' of the *discourse*.

Two points of view operate for the viewer: that of Don Pietro, seated in his chair, with whose eyes we see into the torture chamber (a matter of *mise en scène*), and that of Bergmann (a matter of montage, as we follow him into the salon). The cutting of the sequence carries Bergmann's impatient irritation. The drama comes from the torture itself, and two different reactions to it, and depends to a certain extent on Bergmann's *awareness* of the difference between the two responses (which he expresses to Hartmann, in terms of its being 'interesting'). This is effective, very economical dramaturgy. The 'triptych' stage on which it is composed (Bergmann's office, with on one side the salon and on the other the torture chamber) similarly has the qualities of economy and effectiveness.

This economy has led to the characterization of Rossellini's work with the word 'simplicity.' The rhetoric can be understated: there is no need to make Bergmann a monster; just make him a dandy, and set up a contrast with a humble priest, whose broken spectacles function as a sort of 'opposite' to dandiness. Neither Don Pietro nor Manfredi ever show irritation. They are not distressed at their treatment. Instead, they accept profound suffering. The contrast has been set up between superficiality and profundity.

The 'meaning' of all this for the history of the Resistance is a matter for interpretation. Description has done its job when it has shown how the effect has been created. The dramatic work is an aesthetic achievement; the interpretative response is a matter of reception. Aesthetics must concern itself with the 'object,' rather than with the use to which it is put, which is a matter of cultural history.

It is clear that *Roma città aperta* is not a documentary; it is a fictional film. However, the narrative *refers*, by means of iconic signs, to events that actually took place and to people who actually existed. We could call the direction of this reference 'upwards' towards the surface, towards the specific, the concrete, and the particular. We could describe the film's generic, melodramatic reference to other narratives as going in a 'downward' direction, towards a deeper, less particular, more general, and even universal level. The fact that *Roma città aperta* carries both movements, upwards and downwards, accounts for how it can be seen as both realist, documentary representation and ideological 'myth.' This ambiguous reception of the film concerns its 'content,' and is dependent on whether the movement of reference upwards is privileged, or the movement downwards. It is essentially a question of interpretation. However, the oscillation between two views of the film as 'document' or 'rhetoric' also concerns the 'form' of the artefact itself, as an object, and to that extent is essentially a question of aesthetics. This question is then contaminated with the question of evaluation insofar as a critical context has existed in Italy in which a 'documentary' *form* is given positive connotations (neorealist innovation, authenticity) and a 'rhetorical' *form* negative ones (conventional commercial cinema, Hollywood, genre, escapism). Similarly, 'document' would privilege the movement upwards of the reference, and 'rhetoric' the movement downwards. Thus it is that description, interpretation, and evaluation are bound up together, and interpretation and evaluation tend to colonize description.

Roma città aperta and Neorealism

> For us, the important thing was to be able to start working and begin to recount what had happened, what we had seen. We were not thinking of renewing who-knows-what ... When the Americans arrived here, everybody emerged from the woodwork, very keen to get back to work and also very hungry, to tell the truth. This is what influenced the birth of neorealism! ... When – it was 1945 – I went to her house in Via Amba Aradam, where she was living at the time, to show her and read to her the script of *Roma, città aperta* [*sic*], she told me – I remember it as though it were yesterday, and I remember everything, even what others have forgotten – she said: 'It is the most beautiful story that I have ever read and also that I have ever seen.' Well, if I have to be honest, Anna's feeling was one which neither I nor Rossellini had at the time. We made that film because we had stories to tell, certainly, but above all because we badly needed to work and to eat ... For example, the fact of Fabrizi and Magnani. Actors taken from the street, my eye! Certainly, there were those too, but the film could only get made because Fabrizi and Magnani were in it, and were already very famous, and together assured us a minimum guarantee [at the box office]. The bottom line was these two names, who were basically the only ones, I have to admit, ... to have a strong feeling that it was a great film, much more than either of us.
>
> Sergio Amidei[35]

Our discussion of *Roma città aperta* has consisted of fragmentary approaches, looking at the film from different perspectives, as the product of a large number of experiences and aspirations that were in the air at the time. The filmmakers (Rossellini and Amidei) describe themselves as not having been aware of what exactly they were doing. They were trying to put together a film, but what kind of film they were trying to put together was something that they discovered as they made it, and then when the public responded to it. One thing that was clear was that they were *assembling* the film from diverse fragments. Other artists were doing the same around them at the time: De Santis assembling partisan stories for his script of *G.A.P.*; he, Visconti, and Serandrei assembling almost journalistic, documentary accounts of the last days of the war in *Giorni di gloria*. Behind these activities lay the thinking of the 1930s, of Visconti and Antonioni, about how film had the capacity to make 'idealist' narrative (in the sense referred to in chapter 2) out of

the direct recording of ordinary life, and about how the lessons of documentary could be applied to feature-film making. De Robertis, Rossellini himself, Antonioni, and Visconti had been involved in various
forms of documentary filmmaking. The war, the German occupation,
the Resistance, and the Liberation had thrown up a multitude of micro-
narratives, all with broad and profound general implications. Everyone
has noticed how the neorealist filmmakers themselves produced virtually no theorizing about what they were doing, and that the theorizing began around 1950, on the part of critics, after the films had been
made. Zavattini's own theorizing begins mainly after the completion of
Umberto D., and as a response to obstacles placed in his way.

There was a *tension* between, on the one hand, the characteristic pull
of indexical filmmaking and documentary towards the shot, towards
the briefest narrative, towards the fragment (as we have seen in chapter
2) and, on the other hand, the feature film's need for traditional narrative and dramaturgy, and for an overall form in which the assembly
could articulate the ideal and the universal in human experience. The
ninety-minute feature film was in tension with the five- or ten-minute
chronicle. Sergio Amidei, the professional adapter of literary texts, the
master of crafting the well-formed feature film, stood in the middle,
resolving the tension between the explosion of indexical micro-narrative and the tradition of the ninety-minute feature film. Whatever kind
of artefact *Roma città aperta* constitutes, Rossellini stumbled upon it in
the urge to get back to filmmaking, to simply make a film. That is what
filmmakers do: they make a film. They discover what kind of film it is
as they make it. Subsequently, with Fellini at his side, Rossellini broke
further away from the formal constraints represented by the pull of
Amidei and 'discovered,' as he made *Paisà*, the potential of the fragment itself, through whittling away at the scripts provided for him. A
process of rhetorical 'reduction' towards *sermo humilis* (drawing on the
narrative conventions used by comedies to link fragments into a whole)
characterizes both Rossellini's work and that of the partnership of De
Sica and Zavattini that gave birth to *Ladri di biciclette*. Both Rossellini
and De Sica stumbled upon poetic self-expression without necessarily
trying to do so, or without necessarily knowing what it was they were
trying to achieve, but rather by exploring and discovering the possibilities made available by rhetorical 'reduction' and a more pictorial (or
photographic) approach to narrative *dispositio*. They were *discovering*
essential characteristics of narrative *film* as a medium by gradually freeing themselves from what one could call 'literary' conventional expec-

tations. The freedom to explore and discover was furnished by what I have called, in the 'Overview' chapter the *hiatus* in commercial producers' control of filmmaking. The struggle they had to go through to get films made meant that the films were *their* films, rather than films answering to producers' commercial requirements.

The 'content' of their films – both the stories and the political and social impulses they articulated – were, as Calvino said, just 'there' around them, thrown up by the aftermath of the war. The problem was how to make films out of them. *Roma città aperta* is the product of the confused multitude of ideas Rossellini was receiving from all around him as a result of his contacts with the younger generation around the journal *Cinema*, the left-wing Resistance circles he met through them and through Amidei, and his own past experience as a maker of fictionalized documentaries for the government – all this encountering the fierce narrative crafting of Amidei.

Without bothering himself too much with what he had created in *Roma città aperta*, Rossellini ploughed on making more films, *discovering* where his own aesthetic and moral inclinations were taking him, maturing as a man and as a filmmaker from *Paisà* to *Viaggio in Italia*. The young Federico Fellini had started as a graphic caricaturist and journalist, and then moved into comedy-scriptwriting for Mario Bonnard and Mario Mattoli. Through the contacts this had given him with Aldo Fabrizi he got roped into writing the comedy scenes in *Roma città aperta*, made his first neorealist film with Rossellini on *Paisà*, wrote more for Pietro Germi, went back to comedy with Lattuada on *Luci del varietà*, got pressured into directing his first comedy by Rizzoli on a subject by Antonioni, *Lo sceicco bianco*, turned his comedy approach to the satire of provincial bourgeois domestic life in *I vitelloni*, and then explored and discovered his own way through *La strada* and *La dolce vita* to *8½*. Visconti started with projects for literary adaptations of Verga's stories, finally made it into production with a traditional, intense, and pessimistic melodrama in the French manner in *Ossessione*, was commissioned to make an election documentary for the Communist Party in Sicily and 'discovered' the fusion between this subject and his literary adaptation of Verga in *La terra trema*, went back to stylized, theatrical comedy for *Bellissima* and *Siamo donne*, and finally pulled together the traditional melodrama and the political-historical allegory in the highly formalized *Senso*. Meanwhile, De Sica and Zavattini moved out of comedy, picking up the whole country's taste for the same intense and pessimistic melodrama that produced *Ossessione* (and Rossellini's *Scalo*

the dark days of the war, and made *I bambini ci guardano* and *La
.l cielo*. They then picked up from the post-war climate the urge
tʊ   ʌ into film the micro-narratives of the war's aftermath in *Sciuscià*
and, combining that urge with the narrative and rhetorical procedures
of comedy, produced *Ladri di biciclette*. They then applied the procedures of comedy to an allegorical fable in *Miracolo a Milano*, after which
they consciously distilled the 'realist' implications of their work up to
then in *Umberto D*.

Who is to say at what point any of this constitutes 'neorealism,' or
that *Roma città aperta* is any more a 'transition' from one sort of film to
another than any of the other films I have listed? The 'institution of neorealism' has valiantly tried to take a snapshot of the process of exploration and discovery at a certain point, and stamp on it a name and a definition, but the artists themselves continued imperturbably to make
one film after another, constantly exploring and discovering the artistic
potential of the medium. Cultural or film history gnaws away at the
enigma, while an aesthetic approach to the artefacts can find no slot
into which to stuff a 'definition' of neorealism.[36]

4 *Paisà*[1]

Whereas the writing, shooting, and editing of *Roma città aperta* involved the development of 'found,' pre-existing narrative components, what is notable about the making of *Paisà* is that much of the final film resulted from the progressive whittling away at the original narrative material. This leads us to hypothesize that what Rossellini was aiming for in the film will be identifiable in the characteristics and qualities of what is left at the end of the whittling process. We could use an analogy, and say that he was like a painter presented with a heavily painted canvas prepared by his assistants (the writers), and that to transform it into 'his' painting he set about systematically erasing more and more of the original painting, until the canvas bore only and exactly what he wanted.[2]

The project's original working title was *Seven from the U.S.* (in English). Work began on the script in June 1945, and the film was shot between January and June 1946. There were to have been seven episodes. A synopsis, which is hard to date precisely in the progress of the project, but was certainly early, goes as follows:

> This film aims to illustrate in a certain number of episodes the campaign of the V Army in Italy and the life of Americans in Italy.
>
> The episodes have been constructed so as to describe the most representative types (an infantryman, a Negro M.P., a nurse, a Catholic Chaplain, a tank driver, a secret service officer parachuted into a Garibaldi brigade) and, at the same time, the fundamental stages of the American advance in Italy (the Sicilian campaign, Naples, the bridgehead at Anzio, the capture of Rome, the North).
>
> The aim of the authors is not to describe military actions, but to offer as

realistic and faithful a picture as possible of the life of the Americans in Italy and of their relations with the Italians.

The six heroes of the six episodes die, and each of the six episodes ends with a white cross in a military cemetery. This means that the film aims to pay respectful and affectionate homage to the memory of those Americans who lost their lives for the liberation of Italy, and is intended as a message to their Nation.[3]

A prospectus, describing how the film might open, was written by Klaus Mann at least in time for Rod Geiger to take it to America in August 1945. The protagonists of each episode are shown one after the other, in each case involved in speculation about their coming encounter with Italy and the Italians: 'While these people are wondering about Italy, the ITALIANS are anxiously waiting for the arrival of the Americans. We see groups of Italian soldiers and civilians, women and children, in various Italian cities and villages – breathless with expectation, hopeful and apprehensive, whispering to each other The Americans are coming ... What are they going to bring?'[4] Mann's prospectus evokes an expectancy, among both the Americans and the Italians, concerning an imminent encounter. The film will move from an entirely different premise.

Klaus Mann (son of the novelist Thomas and attached to the American liberating forces) wrote a script (in various versions) of more or less the whole film, a lot of which was never used, but the first episode of the eventual film stays relatively close to his script; Alfred Hayes (an American playwright and poet, working as a journalist for the military) wrote a draft of the *Naples* and *Rome* episodes (later turning the latter into a novel, *The Girl on the Via Flaminia*, published in 1949, from which an American film, *Act of Love*, was made in 1954); Sergio Amidei wrote stories for a number of episodes (for example, discarded versions of the monastery episode and of a partisan story to close the film set in the Alps), and was mainly responsible for the final screenplay of the *Rome* episode; Marcello Pagliero wrote an episode that was discarded. Responsibility for how the final version of the script turned out, however, belongs to Federico Fellini, working together with Rossellini throughout the shooting of the film. Everything developed during the shooting. The first *Sicily* episode changed slightly but significantly; the *Naples* episode was completely transformed by Fellini and Rossellini when they found the actors and saw the caves at Mergellina; the *Rome* episode followed closely Amidei's script; the *Florence* episode used a mixture of materials from the original script, greatly pared down, and rewritten by Fellini in collaboration with ex-partisans who had fought in the actual struggle being depicted and with the help of the Florentine novelist Vasco Pratolini; the *Monastery* episode was written by Fellini at the time of shooting; the *Po delta* episode was written by Fellini and Rossellini, with help from ex-partisans, at the time of shooting.[5]

The genesis of each episode will be discussed as it comes up only where I feel it is appropriate, but there are one or two general points that emerge. Henceforth, 'the film' will refer to the finished artefact, while 'the project' will refer to various treatments, storylines, scripts, and intentions that preceded its shooting.

In order to sell the *project* to the (American) backers in the first place, its main subject matter prioritized the Americans' experience and their suffering during the Italian campaign. The *film* shows no such priorities, and indeed totally reverses them. In each episode the perspective of the American protagonists constitutes a viewpoint on the nature and experience of the Italians with whom they come into contact. Italian culture had a very real contribution to make towards rehabilitating Italy in the eyes of its own citizens and in those of the rest of the world at the war's end, and particularly with the Americans. Narrative in Italy, and particularly in the cinema, had a precise cognitive social function, partly conditioned by the peculiar position of Italy in the war. Indeed, the ideological slant that the 'institution of neorealism' invariably takes on neorealist films is further evidence of the primacy of that function. *Paisà* cannot really be likened to any other film, and yet its function, while broader and far less stereotyped, followed a trend in Italian cinema – one considerably at odds with the descriptions of the project that we have just recorded.

The structure of the overall film is straightforward. It consists of six independent episodes. Each has a voice-over introduction spoken by an unseen commentator, who narrates the events in the Italian campaign that have taken place between the time of one episode and the next. All these 'introductions' except the final one are accompanied by what has generally been called 'documentary footage,' apparently of events recounted by the voice-over narrator. In the *Po delta* episode, there is no such footage, but a viewer could be forgiven for momentarily mistaking the first shot of the episode for documentary footage. In some cases, it is hard to be persuaded that the footage is more than emblematic and token, and British and American distributors have felt free to interfere with these parts of the film, removing footage. However, each introduction has its own particular characteristics, as we shall see.

There is a standard way of describing *Paisà*: Rossellini's camera follows the advance up the peninsula of the Allied liberation armies. Two aspects of this description simplify matters that are in fact rather more complex. First, Rossellini did not shoot the episodes in the same order as that in which they appear in the film (the episodes were shot in the order I, V, II, IV, VI, III – and the last actual shot to be filmed was that of Carmela lying dead on the rocks in the *Sicily* episode), and therefore not in the same order as the events would have taken place chronologically in time, nor in a progressive geographical movement northwards along the peninsula. If part of *Paisà*'s reputation rests on its being a faithful record of the Allied, and then Rossellini's, journey up the peninsula, then that reputation is ill founded, because both the episode 'set' in Sicily, and that 'set' in the Appenine mountains west of Rimini (the *Monastery*) were actually shot just south of Naples (Rossellini was introduced to a Franciscan monastery near Salerno). (See appendix 23, 'Map of settings and locations for *Paisà*.') The American tanks liberating Rome were filmed in Livorno (in a sequence directed by Rossellini's assistant Massimo Mida). In the *Florence* episode, the rooftop scene was filmed in the fashionable Parioli quarter of Rome (in an apartment building in Via Lutezia inhabited by members of the family of Rossellini's other assistant director, Federico Fellini), while the shooting of the captured Fascists was done on Rossellini's behalf at the Rome Scalera studios. The partisans of the final *Po delta* episode were filmed being drowned in the Tiber near Fiumicino, and the flares they set for the Allied arms and supply drop were filmed further up the coast, at Orbetello, north of Civitavecchia.[6] Second, each episode chooses a slightly different moment in the process of liberation. A brief survey of the episodes shows that the notion of forward progression contained in the standard description does not do justice to what is a more complex operation upon time. If we might be permitted a metaphor, the film *moves* forward, but *leans* backwards.

In the *Sicily* episode, the film does exactly what the standard description says that it does: it accompanies the Allied liberating armies in their first encounter with the Italian civilian population in July 1943. In the *Naples* episode, set in early October 1943, the Liberation has already taken place, and the Americans are now established as the occupying force in Naples – there is neither conflict with the Germans nor conflict between Italian partisans and the German army, nor any reference to an Italian Civil War. In other words, the transition from Sicily to Naples, rather than 'accompanying' the American advance, tarries a little in order to let the Americans get ahead of the film, whereupon the film catches them already established in Naples.

The two time-segments of the *Rome* episode cover the two different periods I have just described above as being those covered separately by the *Sicily* episode and the *Naples* episode respectively: in the flashback, the arrival of the Americans in June 1944, and in the 'present' of the story, the period in which they were the established ruling force in the winter of 1944 – in other words, it jumps in time ahead of the following two episodes. In the first case, there is a moment of encounter, of change, and of renewal. In the second case, a moment of misrecognition and of shame. However, the device of the flashback enables Rossellini to *reverse* the order of these two moments. From the disappointment and shame of the Allied occupation, we 'step back' into the moment of hope and purity of the Liberation itself that preceded it.

Sicily was an exception in the history of the Liberation. In many other parts of Italy, the arrival of the Allies was preceded by the struggle of Italian partisans both against the Germans and against their fellow Fascist countrymen (the Germans had been forced out of Naples by an uprising of the Neapolitan populace before the Allies arrived). The fourth episode, set in Florence, combines these two moments by choosing a particular time and place. The Allies have arrived in Florence, but only control the city south of the river. In early August 1944, to forestall the Allies, the Germans have just blown up all the bridges across the River Arno except the Ponte Vecchio. It is enough to cross the river for one to be in a previous historical and political situation, in which Italian partisans are fighting the Germans and the Fascists. These two moments are both depicted in the *Florence* episode and, as in the *Rome* episode, the narrative permits Rossellini to 'step back' a moment in history simply by having his protagonists cross to the north side of the river.

The *Monastery* episode set on the eastern edge of the Apennines (the actual location, Savignano di Romagna, lies in the coastal plain between San Marino and Rimini, on the Gothic line) corresponds more to the standard description of the film, and describes a moment that is the continuation of the same situation as that described in the first, *Sicily*, episode: the initial arrival of the Americans to replace the German occupiers. However, by entering the monastery, the chaplains 'step back' in time a great deal further than in the other episodes, in this case to a notional 'time' of simplicity and spirituality.

The final episode is set in the delta of the River Po, north of Ravenna, at the very end of 1944 – in other words, at exactly the same time as the 'present' of the *Rome* episode (indeed, Francesca, the protagonist of that episode, darts into a cinema that is showing at that moment newsreels of the fighting going on in the north of Italy – that is to say, what is to follow on from this episode). It goes back a stage in the process of the war and the Liberation in Italy, even though it takes place a year and a half after the *Sicily* episode. Here, the Allied armies have yet to arrive. Rossellini is describing the Italian partisan struggle against the German army. The Allies have been held up, and cannot advance and take advantage of the work that the partisans are doing in the way the partisans were hoping they would, nor can they come to the rescue of the partisans who are being overwhelmed by the Germans. Rossellini could have described events a couple of months later, and only a few miles to the south of the location of this episode, where the two forces depicted in his episode (the partisans and the Popsky units), amply supplied by the Allies, defeated vastly superior German forces and captured Ravenna – but he chose not to. One could see this choice as one between two narrative matrices, the heroic and the melodramatic, and as developing an elegiac, almost liturgical honouring of the Resistance already begun in the *Florence* episode.

The progression of the film from start to finish could be looked at in terms of the succession of episodes as they are ordered in the final editing of the film or, alternatively, it could be seen in terms of the gradual construction of the film itself, as it was shot episode by episode (in the order *Sicily, Monastery, Naples, Florence, Po delta, Rome*) – which might provoke an interpretation of the film as being a gradually deepening analysis of a complex web of experiences. For example, the first three episodes *to be shot* deal with the effects of the war on ordinary Italian civilians, and with the ways in which they cope with this. These episodes search for, and find, moral values at the most basic and simple level of humanity. The fourth and fifth episodes *to be shot* constitute together an elegiac commemoration of the Resistance, a theme absent elsewhere in the film, and only separated by the *Monastery* episode as a result of the decision to edit the episodes together in a 'geographical' order (a northerly movement). *Paisà* can be seen as telling the story of the emergence of its own narrative; the film gradually discovers the story it has to tell. A third possibility would be to see a historical progression, starting from the political and historical situation described in the final episode, proceeding through the encounters of the *Sicily* and *Monastery* episodes, and arriving at the shame and degradation depicted in the *Rome* and *Naples* episodes. It is clear that only one of the three possibilities is compatible with what I have referred to as the standard description of the film, and even that compatibility depends on an element of simplification. The first choice (the succession of episodes as ordered in the film) could be looked at from the point of view of the function of the overall narrative for its audience, meeting its need for explanation, rather than as purely a matter of historical representation: the film starts with an invasion by the Americans of a degraded nation – what appears on the 'surface'; it ends by penetrating behind the surface to the population's resistance to Nazism and Fascism to discover the 'truth' about Italians. In the first three episodes, the Americans see only the 'surface'; in the last three they encounter the 'truth.' However, it is very probable that the final ordering of the episodes was dictated by the desire to give a simple 'geographically' progressive succession to the six stories. The film is concerned with *values*. It is as though the film, as it *moves* forward, *leans* backwards to reach out for those values.

Since *Paisà* is made up of short episodes, the tendency hitherto has been to treat it as a collection of 'essays,' each with its own 'meaning.' Because the film also deals with important historical events, the comment on those events has been seen as the function of each of the essays. Paradoxically, even while acknowledging that Rossellini gives less importance to conventional narrative than does the commercial cinema around him, commentators have tended to reduce the episodes to what have been identified as their narrative nuclei. A symptom of this approach is the way in which the *dramatis personae* have been referred to: by their reduction to protagonists operating in the context of undifferentiated groups of characters. In the *Sicily* episode, the protagonists are Joe and Carmela, while the groups are the American soldiers, the villagers, and the German soldiers. In the *Florence* episode, the protagonist is Harriet, while the group is the partisans. In the *Monastery* episode, the protagonist is the Catholic chaplain, while the group is the Franciscan friars. We shall see that this collapsing of episodes into narrative nuclei has limited the descriptive possibilities of the artefacts, reducing and restricting their aesthetic identity.

Anglo-Saxon viewers may have seen a version of the film different from the one Rossellini prepared in Italy. In the introduction to each episode, anglophone prints of the film have a map show the movement of Allied forces up the peninsula. These are explanatory additions for the British and American markets that do not appear in the Italian version. To make room for these additions, some of the documentary footage in the introductions has been cut. The introduction to the *Florence* episode, and its opening scene, have been severely pruned. Moreover, some American critics have pointed to the shooting of the American soldier by a German sniper in the *Sicily* episode, remarking that his fall forward is filmed in slow motion. This is not the case in the Italian version of the film. Indeed, the cut back and forth, between Joe from Jersey being hit and the Germans doing the shooting, is absent in Rossellini's version, which just shows Joe being hit and falling forward, and then cuts to the German soldiers. The scene in which Francesca, in the *Rome* episode, takes refuge from the police in a cinema, and is protected by the usherettes, is missing from the anglophone version.[7]

All references to the film in the following discussion will be to the best-known Italian version – though even that choice does not solve all problems, because various Italian editings of the film exist.[8] The episodes will not be discussed in the order in which they appear in the final film, but *in the order in which they were shot* – though with one exception: the *Rome* episode (number III in the final film and the last to be shot) will be discussed first of all. This is because the *Rome* episode lies outside the 'grouping' that can be applied to the other five episodes. The 'groups' are (a) the episodes shot in and around Naples (I, V, II) and (b) the 'Resistance' episodes (IV, VI). Because the conclusions one is led to draw from the film as a whole unfold from the gradual build-up to the *Po delta* episode (which we know was shot with particular care and intensity), rather than from the *Rome* episode (which is the least characteristic one in the film), it is best to discuss the *Rome* episode on its own. Moreover, a number of features of the *Rome* episode show continuity with *Roma città aperta*, and so it makes sense to start our analysis with that episode.

The *Rome* Episode (III, shot last)

The Rome episode of *Paisà* (shorter than most at seventeen minutes – only Naples, at nearly fifteen, is shorter) has the longest documentary introduction, lasting two minutes and five seconds, about one-eighth of the whole episode, and containing forty-three shots. It might be best to call it a 'prologue,' because we shall need the term 'introduction' for something more specific. The longest shot is six seconds long (a pan over the city from the Pincio), but the average length of the shots is about three seconds, and most are of about that length, giving the montage a regular rhythm of cutting that is very different from that of the story itself. The body of the story has an average shot length (ASL) of sixteen seconds (made up of a number of sequence-shots in dialogue scenes, with shorter shots in action scenes). Hence, there is a complete separation, stylistically, between the 'prologue' and the 'story.' Indeed, reference to the ASL chart of *Paisà* shows the prologue as having a very low ASL of three seconds, and the body of the episode as having a far longer ASL than any other substantial portion of the whole film. (See appendix 24, 'Average Shot Length for different sections of *Paisà*.')

The shots in the first half of the prologue (the Germans leaving Rome) have the camera at a greater distance from the action than those in the second half (the Americans arriving) – in the latter case, the camera photographs from eye level, street level, close into what is being photographed. Shots of the Germans leaving, by contrast, have been done in a longer scale, and sometimes convey the impression of being snatched clandestinely (for example, from a window above the street, with the window frame in shot). The footage is neither haphazardly chosen nor haphazardly put together, and functions to add an iconic element of expression to colour its indexically represented content.

Quite a lot of the footage is located around Piazza di Porta San Giovanni and the Via Appia Nuova, with vehicles going left to right. The voice-over commentary describes the Germans as fleeing, which in fact they did, towards the north. A Roman viewer familiar with the area, who accepts that they are shots of the Germans *leaving* the city and who imagines the cinema screen as having metaphorical compass points, with north at the top of the screen and east to the right, would think that the German vehicles were moving *towards* the Allies, in a south-easterly direction, rather than leaving Rome. Another explanation would put the cameramen across the 180° line of the Germans' movement, and filming the Germans *retreating* from the lines of defence against the Allied advance to the south-east of the city, and *coming into* the city, in order to leave it towards the north – which explains why the commentary merely says: 'Passano per le vie di Roma le truppe di Kesselring in fuga' / 'Kesselring's retreating troops pass through the streets of Rome.' Some of the shots of the Allies entering are located in the same place (Via Appia Nuova). It is just possible that some of this latter footage was shot by the cameramen working on De Sica's *La porta del cielo* in the Basilica di San Paolo who, it appears, rushed out to record the arrival of the Americans.

These rather pedantic details provoke a reflection on exactly what function Rossellini intended for this archive footage in the prologue. That it was important is attested to by the fact that he devoted 12 per cent of the episode to it. In all the other episodes, the 'documentary' footage (in the final episode there is none) accompanies the voice-over commentary, as though 'illustrating' it. In this episode, the footage lasts much longer than the commentary, and is therefore included for its own sake. Of the 43 shots, only 12 contain commentary; of the 125 seconds of footage, only 39 have voice-over. The rest of the footage has music and/or diegetic sound that tellingly contrasts the sound of vehicles for the German part with jubilant crowds, vehicles, and bands playing for the American part. Footage of the departure of the Germans shows empty streets, or scattered civilians taking no notice of the passing Germans, whereas footage of the Americans populates the screen with citizens reacting to their arrival. However, the prologue taken as a whole has it *own* 'introduction' supplying the conventional description of the Allied campaign to which the viewer has become accustomed from previous episodes in the completed film: two shots of Montecassino, followed by two shots of shelled villages, accompanied by commentary saying: 'Lunga, tragica sosta a Cassino. Il 22 febbraio 1944 sbarco alleato ad Anzio.' / 'Long, tragic halt at Cassino. The 22nd of February 1944, Allied landing at Anzio.' This is followed by the slightly longer pan over the city from the Pincio, and a shot of a shelled tank near Castel Sant'Angelo, accompanied by the words 'Angosciosa attesa di Roma. Dopo una serie di battaglie durissime, sanguinose, lo schianto tedesco.' / 'Rome waits anxiously. After a series of very fierce, bloody battles, the German collapse.' Then begin the shots of the Germans moving into the city around San Giovanni, introduced with the words 'Passano per le vie di Roma le truppe di Kesselring in fuga.' / 'Kesselring's retreating troops pass through the streets of Rome.' Then follow 47 seconds of three-second shots of Germans in flight without commentary, in only the last shot of which comes the voice-over starting up again: 'Miracolosamente ...' / 'Miraculously ...' – and the footage of the populace greeting the Americans begins (in the same streets in which we have just seen the Germans) – '... intatta, la città saluta i liberatori. 4 giugno 1944' / '... intact, the city welcomes the liberators. 4th of June 1944' – after which there is no more commentary to accompany the ensuing 16 shots (lasting 51 seconds).

The episode clearly has, therefore, in its first few shots, the normal brief, commented introduction, bringing us up to date chronologically and geographically, after which an extended prologue (mostly uncommented) of archival footage starts to function as an establishment of the story itself, by evoking and depicting the mood and, in a general way, the characters who will form the drama about to unfold, and in which the German retreat and the American liberation get equal but significantly different treatment – all this followed by a shorter 'story' than usual, which is characterized by a much slower rhythm than anything else in the film. When the story goes into its flashback, and we see Fred dismount from the turret of a tank, surrounded by jubilant and welcoming crowds, we are watching footage that could be a continuation of the prologue (in fact, Rossellini sent the assistant director to shoot the scene in Livorno). The 'story,' therefore, returns, in the flashback, to its prologue, with momentarily anonymous characters, who proceed to step into the 'story.' The prologue, uniquely in this episode, has a status half-way between the 'introductions' to the other episodes and the 'story' of this episode.

Shortly, I shall propose that the decision to edit the episode in *non*-chronological order (that is to say, with a flashback in the middle) was a late one. Had the *syuzhet*, or 'recounted-plot,' of the episode retained the chronological order of the *fabula*, or 'event-story,' the prologue we have just been discussing would have led seamlessly into the story of the episode: Fred would have emerged to meet Francesca from one of the vehicles seen liberating Rome in the prologue, and the relationship between 'documentary introduction' and 'story' in this episode would have been far closer and more meaningful than in any other episode – hence its length and character. The distinction between indexical documentary footage and iconic fictional footage would have been heavily marked by the contrasting rhythm bestowed upon each (an ASL of three seconds for the documentary part, and an ASL of sixteen seconds for the 'story' part).

The flashback structure of the *Rome* episode might seem to invite a level of interpretation in which going into the past implies both the past of the Italian experience of the war and the past of Francesca's innocence, linking the two in a simile. Normally, Rossellini's approach entails a commitment to a phenomenology of 'the things themselves' (as we shall see in the *Naples* episode), rather than to a reduced, conceptual 'meaning' of which they are supposedly the vehicles: the characters and the settings are unique and irreducible, which is partly why viewers are so tempted to see a documentary element in the film. Nowhere except in the introductions to the episodes is *Paisà* a documentary, but its creation and discovery of meaning operates *as though* it were documentary, *as though* those bodies and those locations were what held meaning, rather than the narrative. All this is often said to be much less true of the 'story' part of the *Rome* episode, where place and characters do not speak for themselves. However, this feature of the episode is counterbalanced by the bodies and locations being so unique and irreducible in the prologue.

Because the *Rome* episode does not function in quite the same way as the other five, commentators have gone to extremes, describing it as 'Hollywood' filmmaking, using 'Hollywood' as a term of critical abuse (just as they might use the description 'Fascist cinema' for pre-war films). Whether the discreet deployment of classic cinematic narrative procedures merits critical abuse is questionable, but it is the context of the *Rome* episode that has led to its being so denigrated: commentators are pointing to a stylistic, narrative, and dramatic contrast between the *Rome* episode and the others in the film. If this episode had just 'looked at' a prostitute going about her work, walking along the streets, and *through that* allowed her true nature and history to *emerge*, it would probably now be deemed every bit as much of an artistic achievement as the rest of the film. Instead, the revelation of the simple innocence, the hope, and the suffering lying behind Francesca's appearance is carried by the rhetorical device of a flashback.

Stylistically, the episode recalls *Roma città aperta*, and not coincidentally is principally the work of Sergio Amidei's scripting of Hayes's story. The theme of prostitution is used as a metaphor for Italy's circumstances; the settings are for the most part interiors (much of the episode was shot in the same studio in Via degli Avignonesi as that in which *Roma città aperta* was shot); much of it takes place at night; most information is conveyed in the dialogue; the story is told by means of montage, and at the end in parallel montage – all of these features being notable characteristics of the earlier film. Nevertheless, the goal of the narrative is still that moving forward in history while leaning backwards in time towards an idyll that characterizes much of the whole film, and all of it is narrated, acted, and filmed with dignity, economy, and restraint, above all with a restrained use of rhetoric. It is only because of what Rossellini does in the other episodes that this one has brought down upon itself so much unjustified condemnation.

It is an actress's film, in that the story depends on the many changes in the performance of Maria Michi, who was the girlfriend of Sergio Amidei, the writer mainly responsible for scripting the episode (though the original story comes from Alfred Hayes). She was, however, also involved with Rossellini.[9] Hence, the episode is partly an offering to Michi, who was not a trained or experienced actress. It consists of a number of narrative sections, in each of which the character Francesca has to transform herself emotionally and show a different aspect of her 'personality.' During her squabble in the bar, the police raid and her taking refuge in the cinema: (a) she is initially presented as distracted and slightly ashamed of being associated with the rather vulgar girls at the next table; (b) she is required to change to being touchy, aggressive, vituperative, and vulgar; (c) to the policeman who tries to put her on the police van with the other prostitutes she plays at being a proper, well-behaved young woman (in contrast with what we have just seen), and so appears deceitful and slippery; (d) in the cinema she is depicted as frightened, and then ashamed when the usherette refuses her money (this scene has been removed from some distributed anglophone prints of the film). At the first meeting and dialogue between Francesca and Fred: (a) she begins the scene walking rather aimlessly through the streets; (b) when she encounters Fred, she becomes the opportunistic, manipulative prostitute; (c) in the hotel room, she becomes the seductive prostitute (but not completely); (d) when he recounts the story of 'Francesca,' she becomes sensitive, delicate, and pensive. In the flashback to six months earlier and their first meeting: (a) she starts off being presented as welcoming, happy, fresh, and youthful; (b) in mid-conversation with Fred she suddenly becomes despondent, and starts talking of her suffering; (c) in her farewell to Fred she is portayed as poignant and tender, displaying an innocent sexuality. Back in the present, leaving Fred in the hotel, she is solicitous and efficiently practical, while during the parallel montage between Fred leaving Rome and Francesca waiting for him, she is shown as eager and hopeful, but disappointed.

All of this is 'written into' the episode, and needs to be 'acted out,' rather than emerging from a location and a situation, as in the other episodes. This theatrical quality distinguishes it from the other episodes in its conception, its performance, and in the style of its filming. Nevertheless Rossellini, who discarded much of the original material prepared for the film, retained this episode. It has been suggested that once he returned to Rome from his intense labours in the Po delta (see the discussion of that episode below), he fell once more under the influence of Amidei. We have hinted that he might have had personal reasons for offering a role to Michi. This all implies that a question of authorship lies behind the distinctive character of the *Rome* episode. Rather than springing from the collaboration between Fellini and Rossellini, the episode involved the execution of Amidei's script based on Hayes's story. Rossellini translated a narrative into images, rather than discovering a narrative through the progressive erasure of a 'story.' Nevertheless, having translated that narrative into film, he then adjusted it at the editing stage so that the episode might retain the superimposition of two different experiences, characteristic of the whole film, and their relationship in historical time, which allowed Rossellini to penetrate behind the superficial appearance of a prostitute plying her trade out of dire necessity in the centre of Rome and a GI cynically exploiting opportunity. The episode retains the cognitive function of the film as a whole, compassionately examining and explaining the shame of Italy, and uncovering the values which have survived the social and material devastation of the war. It entrusts its message, as did *Roma città aperta*, to the rhetoric of its dramatic performance. For the critic, it offers a nice contrast with the style and approach of the other episodes, and shows a transition from the structures (script, studio, performers) underlying *Roma città aperta* to the very different structures and approach that characterize the rest of *Paisà*.

The use of the flashback has given many critics pause for thought. The episode was originally intended to tell a chronologically ordered story of Fred meeting a girl when he entered Rome, and then, six months later, trying to find her again, disconsolately accepting the solicitation of a prostitute, and not recognizing that it was the girl he had been searching for.[10] In all the other episodes, the 'documentary' introductions lead seamlessly into the time of the start of the stories. In the *Rome* episode, the prologue (set in June 1944) takes us to the time of the *flashback* in the story, *not* to the beginning of the story, which is set in December 1944, six months after the Americans have entered Rome. Thus if you see the episode in continuity with its prologue, its main body, which is generally referred to as being a story told in the present with a flashback in the middle, is in reality made of two *flash-forwards* (to December) surrounding a 'present' (in June). Otherwise, you have to see the flashback as returning us to the prologue.

The closer you look at the episode, the more plausible it becomes that the flashback construction was imposed *after* the shooting of the material. In the finished version the flashback serves to change the emphasis given to different aspects of the original story. What is the real heart of the episode is the moment of 'coming out' of the flashback. The way in which Rossellini has restructured the material that Amidei gave him permits him to *reverse* the order of the narrative material: to have us *step back* from the degradation of December 1944 into the idealism of June (that 'leaning backwards' towards the idyll that characterizes the whole film). Moreover, just as we saw Rossellini and Amidei contrast closed, artificially lit interiors with the boisterous 'people' in sunlit outdoors in *Roma città aperta*, so they contrast night for December with day for June in this film: daylight illuminating the dark. With this procedure Rossellini picks up a rhetorical device we have seen deployed in the previous film.

The 'story' starts with a superimposed 'title,' 'Sei mesi dopo' / 'Six months later,' and a contrast, working as an analogy, of the jump from Scottish bagpipers to Glen Miller's Orchestra on the soundtrack, as well as a significant jump from bright sunlight to night-time. This pseudo 'flash forward' is brought to an end by means of the camera entering the consciousness of Fred, who brings us 'back' to the time of the prologue (June). However, we cannot use the terminology of a 'flash forward' for the December setting, because this 'return' to the time of the prologue (June) uses all the recognizable procedures and all the narrative devices (Fred's describing the past in voice-over, for example) of an entry into a flashback. The first part of the story (December) has Francesca as its centre and point of view. In the hotel room, the camera comes down to a close-up of Fred lying on the bed, delivering his monologue, and then dissolves into his memory, with his monologue continuing for a few sentences in voice-over into June. The flashback takes us to the prologue – the arrival of the Americans – and rigorously maintains Fred's point of view with shots keeping him in the foreground and Francesca deeper in the frame (there is one lapse, where we see Francesca outside the bathroom). During their scene together, music starts up in the background, rising at the end of the scene, and stopping with the dissolve back into December. The return to December is *not* back to the close-up of Fred, but to a close-up of *Francesca* hearing his account, with Fred's voice now dubbed in a sort of voice-over (he is off-camera), almost as though it were sounding inside Francesca's head (this shot becomes an extended sequence-shot, lasting nearly two minutes). The flashback does not quite return to where it started (in Fred's mind), but instead to Francesca's mind. This would be compatible with an original plan to narrate the story in chronological order, because if a flashback had been envisaged during the shooting it would have been more orthodox to both enter it and exit it through Fred's memory. As Francesca starts to reply to Fred, music gently rises on the soundtrack. The camera backs off from Francesca, and we see Fred on the bed, but his voice, still dubbed, retains its close acoustic. In the middle of this dialogue-in-one-shot, Fred's speech returns to being direct sound, in a particularly jarring acoustical mismatch (further evidence that the flashback was devised at the editing stage). The camera keeps Francesca (who has come forward) in the foreground, and Fred out of focus in the background, as she and Fred discuss whether the past can be retrieved. This shot dissolves into a longish sequence-shot of Francesca making arrangements and leaving the hotel, with Fred seen only in a mirror. There are only four shots left until the end of the episode: three of Fred departing, and one of Francesca waiting in the rain. The superimposition of individual experiences one upon another is to a large extent carried by Rossellini's decision to *begin* the flashback with Fred's point of view (Fred always in the foreground, Francesca in the background), and then *come out* of the flashback with Francesca's point of view (Francesca in the foreground, Fred in the background).

My job is to draw attention to the film rather than to 'defend' it. However, our closer look at this episode offers an understanding of what the filmmakers were trying to do, which is something rather more complex than has generally been conceded. Earlier I alluded to what I judge to be Rossellini's interest in a superimposition of two experiences. At the start of the 'story' proper in the final version (in December, six months after the prologue), Francesca's experience is the exclusive focus. In the hotel room (approaching the flashback), Fred's experience is the focus, or so it seems. Coming out of the 'flashback' we focus on Francesca's experience of Fred's experience, which has, as it were, *given her back her own* – superimposing the past on the present. The entry into Fred's consciousness has been a device to enable us to enter Francesca's, and to penetrate 'behind' her superficial appearance as an opportunistic whore. As usual, the film is looking for the values preserved by the Italians in 'disordered' circumstances, values not fully perceived by the Americans, but provoked by the encounter with them. The sudden opening up of depths is, in fact, located in one person (Francesca), in one place (the hotel room rented by the hour), and in one moment (that of 'coming out' of Fred's reminiscence – the close-up of Francesca with the voice-off coming from the bed). The way in which the camera, the dialogue track, and the music track are used indicates a great deal of care and thought, with a clear purpose. By the way in which he has chosen to shoot and then edit these scenes, Rossellini has started to 'erase' Fred from the story, to whittle down the narrative he was given by the script, and to 'lean backwards' to reach out for values while moving forward in history. It is no longer the story of Fred's search for Francesca, but of Francesca's loss. Even though Rossellini has allowed his work to be substantially conditioned by the material Hayes and Amidei furnished, he has nevertheless persisted in transforming and reducing the original material, moving towards the erasure of the more conventional parts and drawing the viewer into a contemplation of Francesca's 'thinking.'

Once Rossellini had carefully shot Francesca reacting to Fred's reminiscences in that way, the decision to rearrange the narrative at the editing stage into a flashback has the effect of emphasizing that moment of the story and the perspective that the director has given the viewer upon it. The episode makes unusual demands on criticism of Rossellini's craftsmanship, because criticism has traditionally looked above all at the way he *shoots* his material, and is unused to analysing the way in which he might transform, using *editing* for rhetorical purposes, material conceived differently at the shooting stage.

The *Sicily* Episode (I, shot first)

The film as a whole starts with music playing behind the credits – the passage that will accompany the Mergellina section of the *Naples* episode. The credits end with the music reaching a climax, whereupon there is a cut to the 'documentary footage,' accompanied by the following voice-over narration: 'On the night of the first of July 1943 the Anglo-American fleet opened fire on the southern coasts of Sicily. Twelve hours later the huge operation of the Allied landing on the continent of Europe was under way. Under cover of darkness, Anglo-American patrols push into Italian territory.' The 'documentary footage' is clearly organized narratively, and the commentary narrates what we see in the footage. On the climax of the music behind the credits, and the cut to images, as if in some kind of match of image to sound, we see a large plume of water rise from the explosion of a shell from the 'Anglo-American' bombardment. We cut to various shots of ships, barrage balloons, and landing craft at sea, in sometimes poor quality footage. Then we see a much better-quality shot of one landing craft full of men, followed by good-quality shots of troops wading ashore. There is a dissolve to the dim figures of tanks in silhouette against the sky, seen through grass in the foreground, with an accompanying commentary about 'patrols pushing into Italian territory under cover of darkness.' Hence, a certain amount of care has been taken not only in the organization of this footage, but also in the transitions both from the credits to the introduction and from the introduction to the 'story' proper of the episode.

The beginning of the *Sicily* episode raises suspicions, shared by Giulia Fanara, who writes: 'The long-scale shots that precede the landing are referred to by Roncoroni as archive footage (but there is talk of footage shot in Livorno relating to a "landing").'[11] This is the only mention I have encountered of doubts concerning the footage. It is inconceivable that Rossellini could have faked the footage that *precedes* the landing (showing veritable flotillas of large ships), and highly unlikely that he would have made it of such poor quality. It is just possible that the better-quality footage of the single landing craft, and of the men wading ashore, was shot by, or on behalf of, Rossellini (the shots elsewhere in the film taken in Livorno, representing Fred's first encounter with Francesca in Rome, were directed by Massimo Mida, one of the film's assistant directors), and is no more 'documentary' than the fictional parts of the film. The reason Mida had to go to Livorno was because only there was a tank available, and it is conceivable that the silhouette shots of the tanks were specially filmed there too. Most probably, it is all archive footage except for, possibly, the shot of the tanks.

The *Sicily* episode was the first one to be shot, not in Sicily but on the Amalfi coast south of Naples – which is also the location used for the *Monastery* episode supposedly located between the Apennines and the Adriatic. The very last shot of the film to be taken – more than six months later – was, however, the shot of Carmela's body on the rocks, taken at Anzio, further north up the Italian peninsula.

The story proper is announced by a sort of staccato chase motif in the music, and by the fact that we move from what has been natural lighting to what is clearly artificial lighting. It is not entirely convincing 'night-time' lighting, and slightly resembles day-for-night photography (putting filters over the lens to darken daylight or even sunlight), which the director of photography, Otello Martelli, might have considered an acceptable code for an audience used to watching a Hollywood western every Saturday night. In the first shot there are highlights on the rocks, but a strong light, throwing clear, sharp shadows, from the right of camera. Certainly, elsewhere in the episode, large amounts of artificial light were used, and Martelli slowed progress with the time he took to light each shot, making use of a great deal of lighting equipment (which attracted the curiosity and awe of the villagers, and cluttered up the church). This first shot does not, therefore, attempt to create the illusion of following on from the introduction (least of all, the shot of the tanks), which is significant, because it means that even if the introductory footage was specially shot, Rossellini intended the audience to treat it as it would later learn to treat the documentary footage before each episode. As a result, there are not just six separate films (one for each episode), but a seventh made up from the sequence of interrupted 'documentary' passages, and by creating this separation of material, Rossellini prevents the viewer from reading the 'stories' as having a documentary code of address (a logic applies: if they are different, they cannot be the same). Nevertheless different episodes offer different transitions from the introduction to the story, with different degrees of separation between the two types of material.

The first shot of the 'story' is in the long scale, of a steep mountainside, into which the small figure of a soldier enters from an unusual direction, the top of the frame, and comes down towards the middle ground. Another soldier enters from the right, and more enter the foreground, gradually building an ensemble. The next shot is from below, with a burning house in the background and soldiers in the foreground. In the next shot the camera pans to follow the soldiers entering and leaving the foreground as they climb the steep steps into the village. Then there is another shot, following which the next two shots of the soldiers are brightly lit – the first of them so much so that it looks like sunlight from above – and thus in no way match the previous footage. All the while, the soldiers are discussing what to do, with their sergeant wisecracking unconvincingly as he gives orders. The performances of the American actors are very wooden. This has its effect on anglophone viewers of the film, but the effect goes further than that. In this first episode we enter the story in the middle of the action of the American soldiers' reconnaissance into the village. None of them yet has a name, and the sergeant's lines, written for an actor such as Eli Wallach, are performed by a vastly less competent player with no sense of humour. As a result, critics see this episode almost exclusively in terms of the events that unfold in the tower, particularly between Joe and Carmela – as though the early part of the episode were just a necessary preparation for what is the 'real' story: its meaning and importance is measured in terms of its quality as spectacle. Everything tells us that if Rossellini did not think something was essential, he did not shoot it. Hence, viewers have allowed certain characteristics of the film to prevent them from paying sufficient attention to what Rossellini *did* choose to shoot. It has meant that the American soldiers have been seen as a homogeneous group and the villagers likewise.

When a woman looking for her child comes out of the church and sees an American soldier, her response brings out the other villagers. This is shown as distressing the soldiers, which leads the viewer to understand that the Americans were not intending to have this 'first encounter' with the Italians at all, and were hoping to get through the village in pursuit of the Germans without coming into any relationship whatever with the inhabitants of Sicily. The soldiers and the villagers form up either side of a boat outside the church, neither group knowing what to do, a situation that the sergeant defines as 'a mess.' The villagers are made to see the Americans merely as soldiers at first, and to assume logically that they are German. Next they see them as Americans, and then finally the two groups begin to come into focus as individual human beings, a process that accelerates in the church. Around the boat, Rossellini has created his 'first encounter' between the Italians and the Americans, a meeting neither desired nor expected, at which neither group has anything to say to the other. This contrasts eloquently with Klaus Mann's prospectus, which we quoted earlier: 'While these people are wondering about Italy, the Italians are anxiously waiting for the arrival of the Americans. We see groups of Italian soldiers and civilians, women and children, in various Italian cities and villages – breathless with expectation, hopeful and apprehensive, whispering to each other "The Americans are coming ... What are they going to bring?"'

One of the villagers, a distinguished-looking middle-aged man called Luca, is clearly an authoritative figure and a Fascist, incredulous and then angry at the arrival of the Americans. Once we are inside the church, and once Tony Mascali starts questioning the villagers in Sicilian-accented Italian, relationships start to develop. A mother, worried about her son in the Fascist Italian army now that the balance of power has changed, is reassured by Tony. As soon as he speaks Italian, and identifies himself as originating from Gela, he becomes an individual for the villagers – Rossellini acknowledges the ontological orientation of Italian culture that we pointed to in chapter 2: the Americans become humanized as soon as, and only inasmuch as, they can be seen as part of an organic community or family (Carmela's concern for and interest in Joe increases in proportion to the amount she learns about his family). The sergeant wants Tony to hurry up and get information about the Germans, but Tony is interrupted by questions as to his identity and origin. He does not brush these aside, and is made to assert that the Italians want to know who they are talking to before they will talk freely, replying to his sergeant, 'You just don't speak Italian in a hurry.' So there is a dramatic dynamic between the sergeant wanting information and no contact, and Tony's sense that you need contact to get information (the scene between Joe and Carmela in the tower will be a magnification of this observation of the birth and growth of contact). Tony, through his speech and background, is the cultural bridge between the Americans and the Italians, and Joe will become the moral bridge. But already in the church Joe is distinguished from the group by his recognizing the human reality and individuality of Carmela, meeting the sergeant's suspicion of the Italians by saying that she is just a girl, and not to be feared. One other older GI stands out from the group by intervening between the sergeant and Tony, telling Tony to take as much time as he needs in talking to the Italians. Together with the impatient, sceptical, pushy, and slightly cynical wise-cracking sergeant, this makes four GIs who have developed an individuality. On the villagers' side, there is the smart, alert youth who takes the Americans into the church and then introduces them to Carmela; there is Luca, the glowering Fascist; there is the enthusiastic old man from Gela; there is Carmela herself, and others who stand out less. The sergeant wants information about the Germans, while the villagers want to talk about the hardships they are suffering – they have been bombed, they dare not leave the village, the terrain around is mined, and they are keeping vigil over the body of the daughter-in-law of one of the women present, whom they cannot bury. Insistently, Luca, the Fascist, is in shot, glowering at the Americans and, whenever he can, impeding their progress (Tony pushes him aside with a smile of satisfaction as they leave the church).

The film's production could not only afford Martelli's lighting equipment, it could also afford to record dialogue in direct sound. Much of the completed *Paisà* preserves the direct (as opposed to post-synchronized or post-dubbed) sound of the dialogues recorded during shooting; where that could not be used, and speech was dubbed in later, one can hear the difference in the acoustic quality of the sound. Carmela's lines are dubbed, for example, while, during her dialogue with Joe in the tower, Joe's parts of the dialogue are in direct sound, the difference (a lack of echo to Carmela's voice) giving their scene an odd quality for a viewer who listens closely, further flattening Carmela's already slightly affectless speech (the girl who plays her was not Sicilian, but from near Naples, and so had to be dubbed). This switching from direct sound to dubbed and back again is a feature of much of the whole film, and we have already remarked upon a particularly crude and obtrusive example in the *Rome* episode. The *Monastery* episode had to be wholly dubbed (except where the friars were speaking in Latin) because the friars performing the roles spoke Neapolitan, while the episode is set in Romagna – where an entirely different dialect is spoken. *Roma città aperta* had been shot very cheaply without sound (for 10 million lire), while *Paisà* was an expensive production, costing 56 million lire (the Lux Film production company, the largest in Italy at the time, was spending on average around 15 million lire per film in 1946).[12]

The filming in the church uses the camera differently from the way one expects from Rossellini, mixing medium-scale shots, sequence shots, and reverse angles. The viewer is less detached than normally with Rossellini, because of the way in which the camera moves around among the characters, whereas Rossellini usually uses a static camera (though he might pan and tilt it), and in fact one such move is rather clumsy (the shot in which Tony is asked for a cigarette by a man who shows no interest in actually getting one). It may be that Rossellini shot insufficient footage in the church, and had to use flawed takes at the editing stage. Overall, this 'first encounter' is richer and more nuanced than commentators' neglect of it would lead us to believe. Nevertheless, it has flaws, which Rossellini tolerated.

As the episode developed through the stages of treatment, script, and final film, seemingly small changes transformed it totally. In an early treatment it is a straightforward love story between a tall, handsome blonde American and a Sicilian girl named Assunta, starting in the church and initiated by the girl, and ending with the death in the tower of the handsome American and the disappointment of Assunta, who tries to take out her anger on some wounded Germans.

The next piece of evidence we have is a version of the script telling much the same story as the finished film. A platoon of GIs walks through a village, and is drawn into the church by the moans, ignored by the villagers, of wounded Germans inside lying against the wall. One of the Germans recognizes the soldiers as American, whereupon the villagers crowd round them to shake their hands. When Tony starts speaking in poor Italian, they question him, but when he says that his parents are from Gela, a comic old man with an unreliable memory but unshakeable confidence in it, called Uncle Luca, declares that no one with their names ever lived in Gela, which embarrasses the other villagers' sense of courtesy. Carmela is attracted to Joe by his compassion for the wounded Germans. She volunteers (to the scandal of Uncle Luca) to lead the Americans to the tower, and is left there with Joe. (As the platoon leaves the church, Uncle Luca's memory is refreshed, and he tries to tell Tony long funny stories about Tony's father's exploits in Gela.) In the tower, it is Carmela who initiates conversation with Joe, drawing him out. Joe is shot by a sniper. The Germans arrive in the tower to find just Carmela, who treats them coquettishly to distract them from Joe's hiding place in the cellar. In a longish sequence, the Germans rape Carmela, a virgin, one after the other. She escapes, and goes to the cellar to find that Joe has died trying to climb the ladder to rescue her from the raping going on over his head. She takes his gun and goes back into the tower to shoot at the Germans, but is overwhelmed by them. Joe's platoon returns to the tower to find just Joe's body there, and they assume that he was betrayed. A final sequence shows Carmela's body along a roadside with a bullet-hole in her forehead.[13]

In the short treatment, the girl's name is Assunta. In the script it is Carmela. The script, therefore, belongs to a fairly advanced stage in the project, by which time Rossellini had already selected Carmela Sazio, a shy and unsophisticated fifteen-year-old from a very backward Neapolitan village, for the part (her not being Sicilian is part of the reason why her dialogue has to be dubbed). This script, however, has not yet accepted all the consequences of the choice of actress, for the girl is still more socially self-confident and articulate than Joe. The film drains almost all the eroticism and sentimentality from the script we have summarized. Neither protagonist acts flirtatiously towards the other. Joe is not at all happy at being selected to stay with Carmela, and protests that Tony would be the appropriate choice. Carmela, on being told that Joe will stay with her ('Guarda quanto è carino!' / 'See how good-looking he is!' says Tony), replies: 'Vogghio tornare 'a chiesa. Posso tornare 'a chiesa?' / 'I want to go back to the church. Can I go back to the church?' Slightly incongruous with all this, and a remnant of the script, is Rossellini's retention of Carmela's moment of jealousy when she thinks Joe is showing her a photograph of his wife, but it is brief and scarcely emphasized, and provides a pretext for emphasizing the word sorella, 'sister.' Nor are the Germans portrayed as particularly threatening – though once again Rossellini retains a reduced element of incongruity in that, despite one of them having declared himself too exhausted for sex, they are throwing dice to see who will take Carmela first when she fires upon them with Joe's rifle. In other words, Rossellini changes the original story, but fails fully to strip out the extraneous remnants of the earlier version (we shall encounter an even more clumsy example of this failure in the *Florence* episode).

We have seen how much detail is packed into the encounter between the Americans and the villagers. The next element to receive a certain measured treatment is the insecurity of the Americans in the tower. It reminds one GI of a Frankenstein movie, while another tries to reassure the group by jokingly giving a real estate agent's tour of the premises.

The conversation between Joe and Carmela is cast as two young people trying to get to know each other across a language barrier – it functions almost as a language class, rather than as an erotic-sentimental encounter. Their first topic of conversation is that of the shooting stars, which imply wishing: wishing that they were not in the present situation, one in which the melodramatic 'disorder' of war has placed them (Joe talks of home, attempting to restore the order of life). When we cut to the German who has shot Joe, his companions are not sure that he really saw a light, and attribute his action to the nervousness of the situation making him excessively jumpy. Rossellini is portraying Joe's death as something very close to a *senseless accident*, a product of the disorder of the times, rather than as an act of conscious warfare (and in this, it bears comparison with Pina's death in *Roma città aperta*). Not only that, it occurs when a relationship between two individuals has been established on the basis of a natural, organic identity: Joe is now not a 'soldier,' but a young man who is part of a family.

The moment the platoon leaves Joe and Carmela in the tower, the sound of the sea rises on the soundtrack together with, after a few seconds, as Joe pulls out a cigarette, a soft musical motif (which only lasts a few seconds). The fast cutting that at first characterized the episode has already taken on a slower rhythm, with more sequence shots.

Most commentators describe the scene between Joe and Carmela as an incipient love scene. Our job here is not to interpret the film, but an empirical listing of the features of the scene suggests a slightly different interpretation (words in Italian are in italics).
1. Joe asks Carmela, 'Are you a Fascist? I bet you are a Fascist' (Joe applies his preconceptions about Italians to Carmela).
2. As he starts to light his cigarette, she strikes him sharply on the hand, like an elder sister might to a careless child, whereupon Joe pats her encouragingly on the shoulder and answers his own question: 'You're a good girl. You're not a Fascist really.' There is direct physical contact

throughout the scene, but with overtones of family (the informality of children) rather than of sexuality.

3. Joe assumes her name is Maria (Joe applying his preconceptions once again). They exchange names, again with Joe touching her.

4. Joe looks out at the sea and admires the scenery. Carmela understands that he is referring to the sea, and mentions that her missing father and brother were at sea – she immediately connects it with her family. Joe understands '*mare,*' and immediately thinks of the sea at home in New Jersey. Both of them, in other words, think of where they would rather be – with their families.

5. Carmela uses this understanding as an excuse to go and look for her family, and starts off, but is restrained by Joe, who warns her of the danger outside. Carmela, frustrated and irritated, says that all soldiers, Americans, Germans, and Fascists, are the same (Carmela applies her preconceptions to Joe).

6. Seeing her irritation, Joe tries to calm her down, protesting that this situation is not of his choosing, that he doesn't want an argument, and tries to make her smile by grunting. Frustrated, he throws away his cigarette, and wishes he were at home. He sees a shooting star, and tells Carmela about making wishes.

7. Carmela understands him, and says, '*Ah, stella cadente.*' But Joe, not understanding that she has understood him, is further frustrated by the language barrier, and says, 'No stella cadent, shooting star!' and continues wishing. (Music starts up in the background, and continues until the shooting of Joe.) He admits his fear, and his desire to be home. Carmela picks up the word 'home,' and misunderstands it as '*come.*' (This is not in the script we have, and is an implausible confusion of two words.) Even more frustrated, Joe takes up the topic of the Italian language, and lists the Italian words he knows. He then tries out Carmela's English, and promotes her to 'the head of the class' for getting his name right. He tries 'boy' and 'girl' with her, and praises her for saying 'girl.' Under his encouragement (a handshake, a pat on the shoulder) she starts to smile. His next achievement in the lesson is to get her to say 'friends.' He then tries 'me blonde, you dark,' but relapses into wishing for 'home.'

8. Carmela says '*Come – in America si dice istesso?*' [*Come* (= 'how' or 'like') – in America it's the same word?]

9. Joe takes this as a cue to tell her that back home in America he drives a milk truck, and imitates milking a cow, which Carmela interprets as bell-ringing. He does some more mime, and Carmela understands him

this time, relating it to her Uncle Luca's cows (is this a remnant of the comic Uncle Luca of the script, or does it refer to the Fascist Luca, into which the film has transformed him?). Luca sat seven children on a cow once. Joe picks up *'bambini,'* and asks her 'You *bambini*?' When Carmela says no, he pulls out his wallet to show her his sister's child, and shows photographs of his whole family. The photograph of his sister and nephew leads to Carmela's face darkening, and to reassure her he says, 'You don't understand. It's my sister.' As he shows his face and the photo in the flame of his lighter, Carmela says *'Sorella'* and smiles. It is on the mutual understanding of the words 'sister/*sorella*' that Joe is shot.

The growing relaxation between the two youngsters on the image track is paralleled by the progression in linguistic understanding on the soundtrack: sea, Carmela, Joe, girl, friends, blonde, milk, children, sister – items of the common language of humanity, but restricted to the biology of nature, and in opposition to the circumstances in which they find themselves. The erotic material of the script is replaced with the melodramatic narrative matrix.

Similarly, the Germans are allowed to resolve into relatively normal individuals, worried about their future, about home, and thirsty rather than libidinous – which gives a role to the female, Carmela, that of getting them some water. From that, the rest of the episode unfolds rapidly and elliptically. The dramatic events are either rapidly shown (Carmela opening fire), or merely alluded to (the killing of Carmela), and this belongs to a procedure of narrative elision and understatement that we shall find to be a feature of much of the whole film. What Rossellini devotes footage to is the establishment of what I have elsewhere tried to define as the melodramatic matrix of his narrative: the situation of human beings trying to cope with the 'disorder' of the war and to restore a natural order (we shall find this to be particularly true of the *Po delta* episode). However, in this episode, he introduces two important elements: one is the theme of the Americans' flight from the suffering of the Italians, and the other is the rhetorical device of dramatic irony with which he deploys the theme.

The first three episodes of *Paisà* (as assembled, not as shot) end with the Americans failing to understand the perspective of suffering of the Italians, and running away from it. This theme enters the film late in the project, presumably near the shooting stage, and therefore must be at least partially Rossellini's modification of stories provided by others. In the *Sicily* episode, the American soldiers looking down at Joe's body say: 'Why, that dirty little Eyetie!'; in the *Naples* episode, the black MP avoids Pasquale's gaze, and flees the caves of Mergellina; in the *Rome* episode, while the script has Fred searching for Francesca, the film has him fleeing from a rendezvous with 'a whore,' unmindful of the suffering she has recounted to him.[14] The fourth, *Florence*, episode has Harriet more concerned with her sentimental life than with the suffering around her. The last two episodes invert this theme, and depict the Americans understanding, accepting, and participating in the suffering of the Italians. In all episodes, therefore, the enduring central fact is the suffering of the Italians, and what is developed is the perspective of the Americans who are brought into contact with it. In this first episode, the device of dramatic irony is deployed, in which the Americans, on their first encounter with the Italians, are *ignorant* of the Italian 'melodramatic' experience of the war, whereas the viewer is given knowledge that the protagonists do not have, the result endowing the narrative with a rhetorical impassivity that we shall discover to be a feature of the film.

The episode is recounted with two different rhythms: one extremely elliptical, the other more measured. The encounter with the villagers, the Americans in the tower, the dialogue between Joe and Carmela, and the sojourn of the Germans in the tower are given time and space, while everything else is treated very briefly and elliptically. The average shot length of the episode is 8.2 seconds. However, two shots during the conversation between Joe and Carmela last one and a half minutes and four minutes and twelve seconds, respectively. Put them to one side and the average shot length of the episode is 6.2 seconds. From the beginning of the episode (indeed, from the documentary introduction onwards) until Joe is shot, the editing of the shots links them in strict chronological order. Gradually, the rate of cutting slows, until the long, four-minute shot of their conversation against the seascape with its calm music, paralleling Joe's reminiscences of home and family. Joe's death, bringing about the 'disorder' of war, functions like the shock of Pina's shooting in *Roma città aperta*, and from that moment until the end of the episode, the editing uses parallel montage, cutting between the Germans and Carmela, between the interior of the tower and the cellar where Joe lies dying, and then adding the platoon to the texture, all resolving in the one final shot of Carmela's body spread over the sharp, pointed rocks. The form of the montage imitates the content of the story.

By erasing much of the erotic sentimentality of the 'project,' Rossellini has stripped down Carmela's sacrifice to being motivated by the *value* of Joe as a human being (identified as being part of a family), rather than as an erotic love-object. He is shot, arbitrarily, by a gunman responding to jitteriness, as he talks about his family. We shall repeatedly find that Rossellini's 'whittling down' of the stories prepared for the film takes the form of highlighting and isolating the *values* held by and embodied in the Italians, preserved by them in the midst of war, as though from a pre-war, or non-war 'past' (not subject to 'disorder'), towards which the film 'leans back,' as it were.

The choice of Carmela Sazio to play the young woman (called Assunta in the original treatment) made it impossible to preserve certain elements of the original story. Carmela could not plausibly have been, as she is portrayed in the script, the more outgoing and sophisticated person in the couple, drawing Joe out of his shyness by chatting him up. This meant abandoning some of the elements of the erotico-sentimental story, and replacing them with a portrayal in *sermo humilis* of Carmela, directed towards evoking the 'sublime' elements of her humanity, and hence her value as a human being. To this extent, Rossellini adopts a *stilnovista* approach to her portrayal.[15] Even so, in this episode, as elsewhere in the film, Rossellini did not fully erase the incongruous leftovers of the original plot. Residual story elements from the script (her moment of jealousy and the Germans' belated decision to throw dice for who will rape her) protrude into, and contradict, the direction in which Rossellini was moving during the episode's shooting. We shall see that Rossellini became much surer of himself, both on the level of narrative and on the level of the film's technical execution, as he shot the next two episodes (*Monastery* and *Naples*).

This is not just the first episode of the assembled film, but the first one Rossellini shot, and shows us the director groping towards both his themes and his style, which are intimately bound up together. As we have seen, he does not entirely strip out the plot's extraneous elements, and there are mistakes and clumsiness in the shooting. The lighting is a mess, continuing the lack of concern we have noticed in *Roma città aperta*. In the episode's early sequences, as I have mentioned, the lighting does not cohere. As the GIs and Carmela come out of the church, one of the soldiers casts a sharp shadow over Carmela's face – normally the director and the cinematographer would agree to discard a shot marred by such an error, but it seems not to have bothered Rossellini (and he accepts a shot with a similar error in the *Naples* episode). In the tower scene between Joe and Carmela, the lighting is strong, throwing clear shadows on walls where there should be none and rendering unconvincing from a visual point of view the 'danger' associated with showing a light. In its favour, the multiple-source lighting outlines the characters against the background, but it makes almost no attempt to give a coded analogue of the darkness in which the scene takes place. The viewer must rely on the narrative, rather than the photography, for that. When the two characters sit by the opening in the wall, however, the lighting becomes more convincing (they are backlit from outside the tower). As he progressed in shooting the film, Rossellini began to accept Martelli's presence, and to accept the role lighting can play in his eloquence, partly, perhaps, because of the way *location* began to become a *protagonist* of the episodes.

Choices of photographic style are not always coherent: Carmela's discovery of Joe's death and her subsequent decision are carried by two close-ups of her with lens diffusion, giving a soft focus to her face, that owe more to Martelli's background in earlier filmmaking than to the more austere style used for the rest of *Paisà*. Indeed, during the scene with the Germans in the tower, shots of Carmela alone use a softer more diffuse lighting than those for the rest of the scene, suggesting that they were taken on a different occasion and not properly matched with the rest of the sequence. Rossellini's direction of the non-professional American actors is still unsure, and by choosing to use the direct sound recorded at the time of shooting, especially for the Americans (perhaps because he could not be sure of getting them into the studio later to dub over their dialogue), he preserves a rather crude and wooden delivery, and an acoustic mismatch between Carmela's lines and Joe's. When the rest of Joe's platoon returns to the tower, four men gather in a medium shot to look down at his body through the trap-door, but in the following close-up shot where the sergeant says, 'Why, the dirty little Eyetie!' there are five of them – a continuity error. In a worse error, Carmela climbs the ladder from the cellar where she has hidden the wounded Joe. As we see her from below climbing up, she is carrying Joe's carbine, but in the following shot from above, when she emerges through the trapdoor, she is not. The story requires her to take up the gun from beside his body *later*, when she finds Joe dead. Elements of the 'roughness' that also characterized passages of *Roma città aperta* will persist throughout the film, standing alongside passages shot and put together with meticulous care.

This first episode uses narrative not so much for explanation (placing events in a chain of cause and effect), as for knowledge: holding events suspended in front of our *attention*, while we learn and take in their implications. The viewer watches a character acquire knowledge. This establishes a pattern for the whole film, throughout which, generally, it is the Americans whose knowledge is inferior, and who either acquire knowledge from and about the Italians, or flee a situation they do not understand. The values, therefore, are located in the Italians, and Rossellini creates an artefact in which the viewer appears to accompany the Americans in their acquisition of knowledge, their encounter with those values. By watching the Americans learn, we learn. What we learn is how to watch, to look at what we see.

The first episode has a particular version of this recurrent pattern. Ignorance is particularly located in the sergeant: he is suspicious of the Italians, does not want to make contact with them, is impatient to prosecute the war, calls Carmela 'that dirty little Eyetie.' Tony, Joe, and the older GI are counterbalances to the sergeant. Tony is the first to make contact, reassuring a mother about the safety of her son. Joe then takes on the positive role of 'erasing' Carmela's ignorance, by revealing himself as a 'brother' to her. Her sacrifice is an index of the natural human values according to which she acts. The knowledge that the viewer has acquired is then given dramatic impact by the rhetorical device of irony (by comparing it with ignorance). Far more important than the *events* we have witnessed is the *knowledge* Rossellini has made available to us, the *values* that flow from that knowledge, and the *imagery* – containing that knowledge – he has held up to our gaze. Rossellini has whittled down his story to serve its essential narrative referents, grasping the artistic freedom to jettison the cinematic narrative conventions contained in the project, and to erase from his canvas all but what is essential to his search for values. In *Paisà*, just as in his previous film, he is meeting a need for narrative, or for what narrative can do: to explain Italy and Italians as being not opportunists, but moved and inhabited by profound human values. Rather than synthesizing those values through the deployment of narrative conventions, Rossellini appears to uncover them in the process of erasing narrative.

Clearly, a theme central to the *Sicily* episode is 'trust.' Can the Sicilians trust the Americans in the way that they could not the Germans? Can the Americans trust the Sicilians? Can civilians trust soldiers (Carmela says that soldiers are all the same, implying that she doesn't trust them), and can soldiers trust civilians? Luca is not someone the Americans can trust, and Rossellini has them show that they don't trust him.

Gradually, this theme centres on Carmela, and on what it is in her that makes her trustworthy. The 'story' and 'drama' of a narrative is normally what an artist would use to make matters clear: events would be organized to demonstrate treachery or trustworthiness. In the *Sicily* episode, however, this theme is partially developed almost *in opposition* to the action of the story, in the intervals between events. The events, viewed by the Americans, lead to their interpretation of her as untrustworthy ('that dirty little Eyetie'). The rhetoric of drama leads in one direction; it is on another narrative level, that of the rhetoric of *sermo humilis*, the lowered voice, in which Carmela is observed phenomenologically, that the contrary interpretation is articulated.

When she makes the gesture of slapping Joe's hand, like an elder sister to a younger brother, Rossellini has identified what it is that makes her trustworthy, namely, the simple, spontaneous humanity of 'organic' ontology. To this extent, the *soupçon* of love interest in the film detracts from the analysis of the theme, because the fact that she could be trusted to look after the young man she had fallen in love with would say nothing about how trustworthy she was with regard to those with whom she was not in love. Rossellini carefully avoids using any of the cinematic conventions available to him to make Carmela appear trustworthy when she is first introduced, and the sergeant does not trust her. Joe spontaneously does trust her. Later, in the tower, he questions her: 'Are you a Fascist?' The question suggests that he is not sure to what extent she can be trusted, and yet the direct and ingenuous way it is posed reveals his openness to whatever her reply might be. Her sisterly slap completely reassures him.

The theme of trust, however, is just the overt narrative pretext for the examination of *what it is* in Carmela that makes her trustworthy. This 'something' emerges from the way Rossellini shows how she looks at the world: relating to everything as though it were part of her family. The darkness of the tower (somewhat spoiled by Martelli's lighting) elicits protectiveness; Joe is treated as a sibling; the sea reminds her of those members of her family who are out there; milk reminds her of the cow on which she sat together with other children.

Virtually all the stereotypical elements attaching to a young girl in the cinema (coquetry, sexual attractiveness, ingratiating small talk, girlish movements of the body), and present to a greater or lesser extent in the script, are stripped away by Rossellini (or drastically reduced), to leave an essential 'organic' (in the melodramatic sense we have discussed) human being, on whom tragedy will descend. Everything is directed towards *her way of knowing the world* as the viewers' only route towards our way of knowing her. Similarly, up to a point, with Joe. Indeed, the final shot of Carmela's body on the rocks is an index of *Joe's* knowledge of Carmela, contrasted with that of the other GIs. Rossellini does not show Carmela being killed. Instead, he concentrates on his characters' *knowledge* of her. It would be quite difficult to give a 'character sketch' of Carmela, because we know very little about her – except that a certainty is communicated about the nature of her 'being.' Carmela 'says' less than anyone else in the episode, and yet hers is the 'voice' to which Rossellini's *elocutio* of *sermo humilis* gives the greatest resonance.

Notwithstanding all these observations, it must be remembered that the Germans are shown as mistakenly trusting her too. Just as in the *Florence* and *Monastery* episodes, there are two levels of narrative and dramatic rhetoric at work in the episode: one a conventional rhetoric of 'action,' the other a phenomenological rhetoric of 'contemplation.' Rossellini's artistic trajectory is, starting particularly with *Paisà*, from the first to the second. His characters are not really faced with 'choices' in this film, they simply 'are' what they are, and the film sets about finding out what they 'are.' Rossellini's 'movement' is away from action for the achievement of change and towards contemplation for the acquisition of knowledge.

Rossellini's irony, the rhetorical device of denying to the other characters in the episode the knowledge he has given to the viewer, adds emphasis to the knowledge the viewer has, and as the filming of *Paisà* progressed, he gradually discarded the device (until his only partial erasure of the script in the *Rome* episode, shot last). The *Sicily* episode might not be a great piece of cinema (and we have encountered flaws both in its plotting and in its formal execution), but it was distinctly different from what cinema-goers were used to at the time. The next episode he shot left even sympathetic critics flummoxed.

The *Monastery* Episode (V, shot second)

Rossellini's son died in Spain while he was preparing *Paisà* for its presentation at the 1946 Venice Film Festival, and his brother, Renzo (who wrote the music), took over supervising the last stages:

> My brother left for Spain with whatever means he could, to collect the body of his son. I found myself having to replace him, more out of brotherly love than because I was competent to do so: the film was programed for the opening of the Venice Festival and we had to finish working on it ...

None of us – least of all myself – were aware of the importance of the cinematic event we were involved in. I anxiously followed the showing of the film: I could feel, and it was real, the isolation that enveloped us. For Paisà passed off, like Roma città aperta, amid the scepticism and indifference of everyone ... Paisà was presented at the Venice Festival and it is true that it passed unobserved, receiving, even, stupid reviews in the daily newspapers. A year later it triumphed on screens all over the world.

But the wide and steady distribution that the film received in the farthest flung countries, and the immense popularity its merits earned for it were, here in our own country, very relative. The film's release was in starts and stops, and without the attention it deserved. Only when the increasingly astonishing news of the praise and response of the public arrived from France and America could *Paisà* finally be relaunched here. But its first release was, as I said, left to chance. Indeed, I remember that exhibitors, in the tumultuous, disordered and ravaged Italy of the time, found it appropriate, given the episodic structure of the film, to mutilate it freely at will. *Of* Paisà's *six episodes, the very delicate one of the friars was the most butchered, and even cut altogether* [my italics].[16]

Renzo is only slightly exaggerating the poor reception at the critics' screening. At the screening for the public, however, it was voted the best film of the festival. We have already noticed how this was the pattern of reception for *Roma città aperta*: sceptical critics and an enthusiastic public. It is what Renzo says about the *Monastery* episode that is particularly interesting for us in this part of our discussion of the film: exhibitors (cinema managers) cut the episode from the film when they showed it. Suppressing an episode altogether is the most negative aesthetic judgment of an artefact that it is possible to make, implying that it furnishes the viewer with none of the disinterested 'satisfaction' that Kant attributes to aesthetic artefacts.

Post-war Italy saw a struggle between the Right and the Left over the direction that the reconstructed nation should take. The Catholic Church demonized the Left, and was regarded by the Left as an enemy. The *Monastery* episode of *Paisà* aroused controversy. Umberto Barbaro, one of the prime movers of neorealism in the cinema, reviewed the film's Venice press showing for the Communist Party newspaper, *L'Unità*, on 19 September 1946:

Entirely convincing the Sicilian and Neapolitan episodes, where the director treats with heartfelt tenderness the destinies of people caught up in the tragic fury of the war, while the Florentine adventure, hinted at rather than recounted, and the monastery episode, more ambitious than clear, leave the viewer perplexed and dissatisfied.

In a letter to *Bianco e Nero* (number 4) in 1948, Rudolph Arnheim brought up the ending of the episode: 'Faced at the end with a speech in which the liberal Captain extols the spiritual serenity of the Italian monks at precisely the moment in which they display the very intolerance that was one of the causes of the war, the viewer cannot understand "what it is all about," and goes away confused and dissatisfied.' Pio Baldelli, twenty years later, agreed: '[The friars'] votive offering is completely devoid of "spiritual serenity" and a "moving lesson in humility": instead it amounts to a *war*, different from one fought out in the open, but equally rooted in intolerance and childish fanaticism.'[17]

Both Barbaro and Arnheim claim that the episode leaves the viewer 'dissatisfied,' and blame that dissatisfaction on a lack of clarity (Barbaro is 'confused' and Arnheim 'perplexed'). Baldelli is provoked to anger. It is clear that all three disagree with what they take to be the 'meaning' of the episode. The job of this chapter is not to try and persuade the viewer to 'agree' with any particular 'meaning' that can be derived from the artefact, but rather to describe it in such a way that the intentions behind its assembly emerge, and the viewer can gain 'satisfaction' from watching it.

Two entirely different stories were originally prepared for what was to become the monastery episode:

1 Near the Anzio bridgehead, an American military chaplain dressed in civilian clothes knocks at the door of a Trappist monastery, seeking retreat after having killed two Germans. Following a crisis of conscience, he returns to the front to be with the men who need him.
2 The setting was transferred to Predappio, the birthplace of Mussolini, by Amidei, with a story in which some military chaplains bring tinned food to a monastery. The monks, to prove that their food is better, kill a pig (the other 'pig' from Predappio) and treat the chaplains to a feast.

But Rossellini encountered some real monks in a real monastery while he was filming the *Sicily* episode on the Amalfi coast, and the original stories were to a large extent erased. What replaced the erased stories at the core of the episode was what the crew found at the monastery. From the first story (number 1 above) the episode preserves the element of 'contradiction' contained in the figure of a man who is at one and the same time a priest and a soldier. However, this is not achieved by means of a dramatic conflict, but rather by quite simply bringing military chaplains from a modern war into the secluded world of a monastery. The contradiction concerns no longer the conflict between killing a man and honouring the Ten Commandments, but rather between a relativist modern world and an absolutist archaic world. From the second story (number 2 above) the episode preserves the theme of personal hunger, one of the features most frequently described by Italians as characterizing their experience of the later stages of the Second World War. In both cases, what is preserved from the stories creates an opposition between an organic human community on the one hand and antithetical phenomena thrown up by the war on the other.

The aim of this chapter is to describe the text of *Paisà*, not its making. However, in this case knowing something about what it was that Rossellini 'found,' and around which he built his episode, and seeing its relationship with the episode itself helps to understand the assembly that constitutes the artefact.

There are conflicting accounts of how the monastery was discovered. Rossellini says that the German prisoners of war who were acting in the *Sicily* episode took refuge in it, and 'When I went there to collect the prisoners I met the monks, who were moving in their simplicity.'[18] Rod Geiger says that he and Fellini found it:

> The fifth episode, which was the second to be shot, was completely different from how it had been envisaged. It was rewritten by Fellini and a bit by me. One day, Federico and I – Roberto was in Rome – were going around Maiori and we saw an old monastery. We decided to go in, and we met those wonderful friars. They invited us to eat. The father superior said: 'We have a rule: no talking during the meal. We would be grateful if you would observe it.' We found it all very amusing. And the only things there were for us to eat were greens. The monks had nuts and wine. One of the friars read the Gospel while the others ate. It was all so funny that we started to laugh, nervously, and we couldn't stop. Out of this experience the episode was born.[19]

Fellini does not remember whether or not Geiger was with him when he came upon the monastery. '"Since I had often been placed in religious pensions when I was little" [Fellini has admitted that his mother's response to autobiographical fictions like this was 'Quando mai?' / 'Really?'], Fellini said, "I went inside with great interest, and I encountered an atmosphere of infinite grace, almost like a pastel. There were five or six monks, very poor and extremely simple ... I got Rossellini to come and eat one evening in this little convent," said Fellini, and, after discussions with him, "I wrote [the treatment for the episode] during a stay I made there."[20] Gallagher says Fellini encountered the monastery while walking on the beach at Maiori. Some say the friars came from the monastery at Baronissi, which is several miles inland from Salerno, and a long way from Maiori, but others say the monastery with its friars was on the Lungomare Amendola at Maiori. The monastery we see in the opening shots of the episode, at any rate, was certainly not on the sea-front.[21]

Massimo Mida – he and Fellini were the assistant directors on the film – wrote a location report for the periodical *Film d'Oggi* in July 1946 (just after the whole film had been shot):

[T]he two authentic American chaplains (one Jewish and the other Protestant), who were performing in the episode alongside the American actor William Tubbs (in the part of the American Catholic chaplain), had brought a novel air of vacation into the monastery with their good manners and their compliments: the Americans and the Franciscan friars exchanged smiles and warm handshakes. And yet their spontaneous welcome and these little infractions (and they weren't even infractions, only seeming such to our outsiders' eyes) revealed the authentic nature and the hidden spirit of this ingenuous and reserved religious community. Everything and everyone offered an occasion of wonderment and surprise; so much life suddenly flooding in baffled the friars in the early days, but after a while they were no longer reticent. The community opened up to our eyes in its entirety and authenticity; and after our vague and hurried first impressions we had soon to form a more mature and firmly based judgment. An isolated world that had remained therefore simple and spontaneous: we were never able to discern in the attitude of the friars a single sign of affectation or of studied virtue. In their monastic life, in their human relations, and in the rules of their faith they consciously followed a course convinced that they were following the best path to the truth. And no one would ever have been able to convince them that, probably, in order to arrive at the truth, other paths might also exist, and not only within the same faith and according to the same rite. For this reason relations between the American chaplains and Father Vincenzo who, as we said, stood out from among his brethren for his personality and intelligence, never went beyond a frank and cordial formality. And with us Italians the relationship was only human and psychological; it never broke through those barriers, not just because none of us wanted to push it further, but because, even if it had seemed appropriate, we would have encountered difficulties beyond the scope of our resources; and anyway, isolation had created in the friars a mentality as closed and impenetrable as the crater of a volcano. Besides, it was all Rossellini needed for his episode, and you can be sure that the director of *Roma città aperta* knows how to exploit to the utmost the personality and human characteristics of his actors. After a few days the friars had become extraordinarily authentic pawns of his imagination. Actors, precisely that, true and authentic actors.

And so our friars were transformed; it was not hard to perceive a liveliness in their eyes, open smiles on their faces, usually so severe and composed. Padre Salvatore, the oldest, and Father Angelico, who was reserved and rather shy (he couldn't hold back, and snorted like a train if a draught caught him), both ended up overcoming their inhibitions before the camera. For Padre Claudio, the youngest and the organist of the monastery, it was like going back to the time of his seminary: he relived among us his happy schooldays, talking of football and books, caught up in his role, intrigued by the unusual task. He asked us to explain all our movements, he wanted to understand the mysteries of the camera, he told us of his childhood as a provincial boy growing up with the irresistible, natural, and sincere vocation to serve the Lord.

The one who remained unmoved by the new experience, changing neither his character nor his way of life, was the Padre Vicario. His thin and strident voice would turn, towards the end of his discourse, into a whispered sigh; his hearing was not what one could call perfect, and for this reason perhaps he smiled continually, tilting his head a little to one side. When he was supposed to be in a scene, he would turn up at the last moment, and every so often, in the inevitable pauses in shooting, evanescent, he would disappear without anybody realizing it. Once, with the lighting ready and the scene already rehearsed, we wasted a lot of time searching for him: he had gone to the bottom of the garden to water, as he said, certain little plants that were thirsty. His sideways glance was gentle and at the same time slightly wicked: but it must have been a nuance that didn't correspond at all to his character. He had been forty years in the monastery. I would love to have seen him suddenly in a great metropolis, New York, say.

As for the lay brothers, the modest, obedient, and timid little mendicant friars, I always had the impression that none of them had really understood what was going on in the monastery; without batting an eyelid, as though following a rule of their order, they carried out our instructions with visible excitement: Fra Pacifico would run from one end of the monastery to the other with his swift little steps; Fra Raffaele would offer to the Lord his bizarre and personal prayers, composed in who knows what imaginary ravishment, before the camera, as though it were the altar or the image of the Madonna; he always looked unwell, and complained to all of us of his bad health; Fra Felice, Master of the kitchen, carried on distributing for us the modest victuals of the monastery between the pans and the stove-top with great diligence and seriousness: but he did not lose heart when faced with the American tinned food. I don't think he ever fully understood the reason for these preparations ... Only the next day [after the last day of filming] did I learn that Padre Claudio, from whom I had concealed my membership of a party of the Left, had spent all night weeping. Someone, I don't know for what reason, had contravened my instructions to keep silent on the matter.[22]

Padre Claudio's distress in real life at learning that Mida was a communist uncannily parallels the response of the friars in the story of the episode to the creed of the two non-Catholic chaplains.

The monastery in *Paisà* is set at Savignano di Romagna, inland from Rimini. The friars of Maiori or Baronissi spoke in Neapolitan, and so to conform with the new setting their dialogue was dubbed into Romagnolo. The Padre Guardiano was dubbed by Carlo Ninchi, a film star whose voice is instantly recognizable, and it creates an effect analogous to having someone's voice dubbed by Orson Welles in an English-speaking film. Ninchi may have been chosen to imitate what Mida calls the 'rotund' voice of the real Guardiano. There is one point in the film where I think we hear the real Padre Guardiano's voice, a very different one, and that is where he leads the *Ave Maria* and gives a blessing (in Latin) before the meal, which appears to have been recorded in direct sound (in other words, for that sequence, Rossellini used the originally recorded 'guide track').

The members of the community in the film correspond closely to Mida's description of the actual monastery, except in one particular. Viewing the episode is made easier if one identifies the friars in it, especially because much criticism of *Paisà* tends to lump them together into an undifferentiated group. The Padre Guardiano (whose name, Padre

Vincenzo, is never used in the film) is the head of the community, and the one who challenges Captain Martin over his failure to try and convert his colleagues.

When he is introducing his community to the American chaplains on their arrival, the Padre Guardiano gestures with his hand to one friar (who is given no other designation in the episode) as being 'Il Vicario.' This is the youngish, fair-haired friar who asks after the village of San Leo, who picks up and nearly puts on the helmet, who looks on eagerly at the cooking, who tells Fra Raffaele that there is nothing to fear from having a Jew in the monastery, and who asks Captain Martin if he has examined the consciences of his colleagues. However, he is too young to correspond to the description given by Mida of the Vicario ('forty years in the monastery,' 'head tilted to one side,' 'poor hearing'), and he does not seem to have the indifference to the film that Mida describes. The only explanations I can suggest are that the gestures of the Padre Guardiano in the scene of introduction got out of synchronization with the words he was reciting, or that the dubbers later made a mistake, or that Rossellini in fact gave the role of the Vicario in the 'story' to a different friar. The Padre Guardiano's hand, after gesturing towards the younger, blonde-haired friar while he pronounces the words 'Il Vicario,' then turns round and gestures towards Padre Salvatore, while he pronounces the words 'Il Sostituto.' Padre Salvatore is an elderly friar with spectacles, who later shows great interest in the tinned food. He offers a better candidate to fit Mida's description of the Vicario, but you would have thought that Mida would have made it clear that Padre Salvatore and the Vicario were one and the same person, if that were indeed the case. Padre Salvatore can be seen to show a certain indiscipline as an actor in Rossellini's film, because during the scene where the chaplains take a liqueur in the Guardiano's office, he talks to another friar while the action is going on – a piece of 'dialogue' that is not registered on the soundtrack by the dubbing.

Padre Claudio is the organist, young and with spectacles. He has told Captain Martin that he is twenty-five years old, and that since the age of ten he wanted to join the monastery, and this occasions the discussion between the chaplains about the appropriateness of entering a monastery so young. He is always alert and interested in everything that is going on. Two friars are not identified by name in the film. One is a tallish, grey-haired older friar who expresses disapproval over the Americans' being invited to supper, and who may fit Mida's description of Padre Angelico (but who might just as well fit the description of the real Padre Vicario).[23] His disapproval is one sign of the theme of 'hunger' that I mentioned as being preserved in the episode from the otherwise discarded first 'story.' There is one younger friar whom we only see entering the refectory at supper.

Those I have so far mentioned are the ordained friars, below whom in the hierarchy are the lay brothers. Fra Pacifico's status is that of a servant in the monastery: he is the one who comes to meet the Americans at the entrance to the monastery, who maintains an impassive, slightly scowling expression throughout, who sometimes waddles in a Chaplinesque way when he is in a hurry, who learns that two of the chaplains are not Catholic, is scandalized, and runs through the monastery telling all his fellow monks, and who is, as we shall see, a protagonist of the episode. Fra Felice is the imperturbable, down-to-earth cook, and Fra Raffaele the older friar whose promise of prayer in thanks for the Hershey chocolate bar goes on too long, and who is frightened by the news of Feldman's being a Jew.

The Americans are Captain Bill Martin, a Catholic priest, played by the actor Bill Tubbs, brought over from the States by Rod Geiger, Captain Jones, the Lutheran pastor, and Captain Feldman, the rabbi – the last two are played by real U.S. army chaplains stationed at a military base near Naples.

There are three long-scale shots of the monastery, taken from afar and all from the same angle (in fact they are two different shots, one from slightly closer that is edited twice into the film), but there are no other establishing shots to orient us in the building complex. Captain Martin, from the entrance to the monastery, looks up at and remarks upon the bell-tower, but that shot is not followed by a reverse-angle shot (we must remember that the monastery used for the film is not the monastery it is supposed to be in the 'story,' and so the long-scale shots that introduce the episode are probably not of the same monastery as that used for the filming of the rest of the episode). The part that we see most of is the main hall on the first floor (where the Guardiano greets the visitors) with a stairway at one end going down to the entrance. Downstairs is the kitchen and, presumably, the refectory. The chapel is adjoining, but we are not shown where exactly. There is a veranda leading off the first floor, onto which Fra Pacifico shoos the chickens, and which is also referred to as a garden, where the three chaplains talk to Padre Claudio.

Federico Fellini wrote a treatment for this episode which, while betraying his authorial contribution, also carries all the hallmarks of Rossellini's poetics.

From a technical point of view, there is in this episode very little of the 'roughness' that we encounter in the other five episodes. There are several complex and beautifully executed sequence-shots, and the lighting of the episode is assured (the episode has the longest average shot length of the film, at 10.1 seconds, except for the 'story' section of the Rome episode). True, there are two flawed moments, but they do not intrude. When the Americans first arrive at the door to the monastery, Captain Martin gives his little speech about the age of the place, and Captain Feldman taps him on the shoulder to ask whether it was a quotation from Shakespeare. He jumps his cue for doing this, and even starts saying his line before Martin has finished his lines, but Bill Tubbs carries on undaunted, and Feldman re-says his line, the error being covered by the dubbing. Much later, when Martin is defending himself against the criticism of the friars, behind his back Jones and Feldman appear in the doorway visible in the background. Halfway through what appears to be one shot they suddenly disappear (shot 93 of the episode). It looks as though Rossellini has cut a number of frames out of the shot, and those discarded frames showed Jones and Feldman moving away. We are reminded of a similar procedure in *Roma città aperta*, where Rossellini removed a number of frames from the shot of the German convoy going under a bridge, because the gap between two of the trucks was too great and made the shot overlong (see the preceding chapter).

Concern has been expressed over the slight ambiguity of genre in the episode: serious and delicate while at the same time appearing to have comic moments. Comedy is inherent in the allusion to the New Testament story of the feeding of the five thousand, for example (where the Padre Guardiano's impossible demands of Fra Felice, the cook, are immediately followed by fortuitous gifts of bounty), but it belongs in a structural feature of the episode, which we shall identify as a contrast between two stylistic registers (the *raised voice* and *sermo humilis*), and, in this case, paralleling the incongruity of the chaplain's intrusion into the alien world of the friars, highlights the imperturbable steadfastness of Fra Felice, who must cope with whatever life sends his way. In fact, the comedy invariably involves the distress caused to the subordinate lay friars (Fra Felice, Fra Pacifico, and Fra Raffaele) by the chaplains' visit, and relates to a simplicity that is the central theme not only of the episode but also, as we have seen, of the historical reality that prompted the making of the episode.

In the introduction to the episode the documentary footage and the commentary start simultaneously. The voice-over commentary says:

'The Gothic Line is a natural obstacle that cannot be eradicated. Each tiny village must be bitterly contested with the enemy, who defends himself with desperate determination.' The footage is a rapid montage (most shots are of two seconds' duration) of the following: (1) A shot of a hilly landscape, (2) a shot in which a tank fills the bottom half of the frame, and fires its gun to right of frame, (3) a shot of three American soldiers lined left to right and away from the camera, the furthest one firing a machine gun to the right of frame from behind a protective mound, (4) a medium shot of an American soldier lying away from the camera slightly towards the left, firing a machine gun, (5) a closer shot of what appears to be same tank, in the same position, as shot number 2 (except that the soldier in the turret is not wearing a helmet this time), firing again to the right, (6) a very long shot of a valley taken from on high, with shells exploding on the ground far in the distance (presumably from the tank we have seen firing) – the commentary ends at this point – (7) a long shot of the monastery on its hillside, (8) a shot very similar to number 7, but from closer (the transition made with a rapid dissolve).

All these shots are accompanied by the sound of the tanks and guns firing, with further explosions audible. Once the commentary ends at shot 6, the sounds of gunfire and explosions become louder and move to the forefront. Continuing the episode, shot 9 is a carefully composed shot, taken from roof height, of Padre Claudio standing at a window, listening to the gunfire, and looking over the valley, lit from below him (i.e., lit artificially – a shadow is thrown up and to the right of him), and the camera proceeds to a montage of various friars, in various parts of the monastery, pausing in their duties to listen to the loud gunfire: (10) Fra Pacifico sweeping the altar steps in the church, lit in a complex and quite careful way, (11) a medium close shot of Padre Guardiano reading at his desk, carefully lit from multiple sources, and (12) Fra Felice and Fra Raffaele in the kitchen, very brightly lit.

Shot 13 is of the monastery, from a distance, identical to shot 8. However, now there is no gunfire on the soundtrack, but instead the pealing of church bells. This shot is held for ten seconds. There is a dissolve to shot 14 (again very carefully and evocatively lit) in which Fra Felice is ringing the big, deep-toned bell in the bell-tower, though we also hear the pealing of a higher-pitched bell at a faster tempo. This shot dissolves to the main hall of the monastery, on the first floor (shot 15), with the ordained friars emerging from various directions, embracing each other happily with the kiss of peace (the friar whom I have tentatively identified as Padre Angelico positively runs into the picture and shows far greater animation and bonhomie than anywhere else in the episode). The hall is lit to give it arches, doorways, and diagonals of shadow in a variety of areas of light, through which the friars, in their black habits, enter and exit. In shot 16, Fra Pacifico shoos chickens up some steps and out onto the veranda, and there are a few cuts between the inside and the outside, as the other friars go out onto the veranda, where the 'story' proper begins with prayers of thanksgiving for their deliverance – they kneel and are photographed in a half-minute shot (with a four-second cutaway to a close-up of the Padre Guardiano leading the prayers), far longer than anything so far.

The transition from documentary footage to story footage is more complex and subtle than in any other episode. The documentary footage illustrates the voice-over commentary, though only emblematically. The long-scale shot of the monastery is not obviously any different from the documentary footage of the landscape in which the battle is set. The montage of shots around the interior of the monastery are 'story' material, even though they may 'document' the real life of the monastery. However, the soundtrack (artillery barrage) behind that first montage of interior shots of the monastery carries on unchanged from the documentary footage. The two categories of film overlap through the use of a 'sound bridge' (the noise of battle). Nevertheless, the montage of monastery shots were not made in a 'documentary' way, because, as we have seen, they were carefully posed and very carefully lit with artificial lighting. The pattern of 'homing in' on the story setting is the same as that of the *Naples* episode. However, if we look a little further into the episode, we find that there is more to it than that.

After the villagers come and reclaim their chickens, there is another montage of shots around the monastery, repeating the pattern of shots 10, 11, and 14: shot 24 is of Fra Pacifico sweeping the altar steps (similar to, but not the same as, shot 10); shot 25 is of the Padre Guardiano at his desk, as in shot 11 (followed by a detail shot, 26, of the letter he is writing); shot 27, of Fra Pacifico walking through the main hall, parallels shot 15. Music has started up on the soundtrack just before we enter this montage, and comes to an end just after it finishes. Jumping a lot further into the episode, we come to the end of the scene in which the friars challenge Captain Martin over his duty to convert his colleagues to Catholicism. The monks kneel down to pray in the church, and there is a wipe to shot 97. On the soundtrack is the voice-off of a friar reciting: 'Benedicite. "Tristis est anima mea, usque ad mortem." La mia anima è triste fino alla morte.' / 'My soul is sad unto death.' Shot 97 is of the empty refectory, shot 98 is a shot of the Catholic chaplain's empty cell, and shot 99 is a repeat of shot 15, but with the main hall now empty.

In other words, *four times* in the episode (of 20 minutes' length) there are pauses in the action for a montage of shots around the monastery. (In actual fact, there are *six* tours of the monastery, but the other two are linked to the story, and not 'inserted' montages, like the four I have described.) On the soundtrack behind the first montage is the gunfire of war, behind the second is the pealing of bells, behind the third is gentle music, and behind the fourth montage is the prayerful chanting of a friar. There are a number of repeats throughout the episode of shot 15, the main hall of the monastery, filled by different friars doing different things (but most often by Fra Pacifico). The friars themselves are, of course, all dressed similarly in their habits. The result is that the central 'character' of the episode is *the institution itself*, with its 'uniformed' community. The episode gets close to being a 'documentary' of this institution, this *place*, and of the community of men who form it and are formed by it – acting as a frame for a 'story' brought about by the entry into it of the Americans. The monastery and its community have a special status, because of the way they are photographed, and because of the way that the shots are edited into the episode. Apart from the shots in the 'introduction' to the episode, the viewer is given no 'establishing' external views of the monastery, but only montages of particular *parts* of the monastery associated with the friars themselves, viewed from *within* the institution itself.

There appears to be no privileged narrative point of view in the *Monastery* episode. This is a feature shared only with the *Sicily* episode, because in each of the other episodes the narrative is 'focalized' through a character (Pasquale in *Naples*, Francesca in *Rome*, Harriet in *Florence*, and Dale in the *Po delta*). Rather than attribute a point of view to an objective 'camera' in this Franciscan story, it would be more accurate to see it as being formed by an institutional and architectural entity, as though the age and the unchanging nature of the monastery endowed it with a timeless objectivity, like that of nature itself. A tendency towards a rhetorical portentousness (a rhetorically *raised voice* of *ethos*) in this perspective is counterbalanced by the comedy adhering to the simplicity (*sermo humilis*) of the current members of the monastic community. Shots in the relatively long scale are rendered intimate by the architecture's bond with the friars themselves, institutionalized, as so often in Rossellini's films, by the 'uniform' they wear. It is as though Rossellini were asking what the war would look like to the monastery if it had eyes to see with and a voice to speak with. Twice Captain Martin emphasizes the age of the monastery, and its existence before the beginning of what he thinks of as 'modern life.' The arches of the entrance at the bottom of the stairs, and of the main corridor at the top of the stairs, form part of an organism by virtue of their link with the institution of the community, and with each individual friar's place in it, and are always used to frame compositions in those parts of the monastery. Hence, there appears to be no real hierarchy of discourse in the episode, no authority to cue a reading for the viewer, other than that of the institution itself. Repeatedly, throughout the episode, the 'story' is anchored by these montages around the monastery. The 'origin' of the discourse is made to appear to be the *place* itself and its relations with its inhabitants.

The entry of the American chaplains raises questions about the monastery at two points: in the discussion between the chaplains themselves and in the discussion between the friars and Captain Martin. This is the dialogue in the first discussion:

JONES: They are really fine fellows. I only wish I could speak their language well. So I could talk to them ... ask them a few questions.
MARTIN: No need to ask any questions ... you'll find everything very clear and simple here.
JONES: He ... he's very young [referring to Padre Claudio, the organist, who has just left].
MARTIN: He's twenty-five.
JONES: Don't you think he's too young to be in here?
MARTIN: No ... he told me that he always wanted this vocation ... that since he was ten he always wanted to enter this monastery.
JONES: I think one can really be in peace with his Lord, without relieving himself from the world ... after all it was created for us. The world is our parish.
FELDMAN: How can they judge us and life if they don't know what it's all about?

The problem the episode poses the viewer is how to respond to the judgment that the friars do, in fact, make later in the episode – how to interpret it. As I keep repeating, interpretation is not the job of this analysis of the episode, but I cannot resist the temptation to wonder whether the following passage in Michelangelo Antonioni's collection of projects and ideas for films, called *Quel bowling sul Tevere*, might not have owed something to a viewing of *Paisà*:

I had managed to convince an influential priest to get me into an enclosed convent dressed as a builder. To spend a few days within those walls, and to breathe the same air that kept alive those women who had renounced life, seemed to me the first step to take. The priest agreed and even found the ideal place, a little convent in a northern city. He did not, however, agree with me that the nuns were women who had renounced life. He was an educated person and the terms of the dilemma did not escape him. On one side, everything which gives a meaning to our existence, on the other side, the denial that any of that has any meaning at all. On top of this, a profound contempt for our values, our goals, and our feelings.

Enclosed convents, they say (the priest in question and others), are communities of prayer, of sacrifice, and of love. To find in these three values an answer to the practical relevance of their existence one needs to grasp the meaning of prayer, of sacrifice, and of love. The enclosed sisters gather up the implorations of the world and translate them into a dialogue with God. There seem to be countless reasons why a life spent in voluntary segregation is substantially useless, and why a commitment to the salvation of the world, but which avoids the world in the most complete way, is illusory. But on the religious level, the usefulness of a thing is not measured according to our vision of reality nor according to our convenience. What response can these nuns give if they have chosen as a discipline not to give a response? The difficulty of understanding their life comes neither from the rigour of their Rule nor from the way in which they put it into practice. It comes from us who do not seek a pause for reflection on the mystery of their experience.[24]

The 'story' of the *Monastery* episode in *Paisà* proposes that Captain Martin, even though he may not have been seeking it, *finds* 'a pause for reflection on the mystery of [the friars'] experience,' and it elaborates the theme, developed during the shooting of the film, of the Americans gaining knowledge of a specifically Italian ontological experience. Most neorealist narratives recount the *loss* of the 'organic' ontology, of the 'idyll,' at the hands of 'modernization.' The *Monastery* episode is unusual in portraying Captain Martin *finding* it – just as Rossellini did when he 'found' the monastery and its community while shooting the *Sicily* episode of *Paisà*. Already, as we have seen, this encounter with an Italian 'ontology' is what is narrated in the story of Joe and Carmela in the *Sicily* episode, and it is hardly surprising that Rossellini, in developing the next episode he shoots, should elaborate on the theme he has just initiated (although, for the viewer, this is partly hidden by the different ordering of episodes in the finally assembled film). This is part of what I am getting at in suggesting that *Paisà* tells the story of its own making. We shall try and identify the way in which Rossellini expresses this 'story,' but first we must indicate the second area of controversy in the episode.

The other discussion follows on from the discovery by Fra Pacifico that Jones is Protestant and Feldman Jewish (when they fail to respond to the Angelus – it must be remembered that the Angelus was an institution founded by the Franciscans). He races round the monastery (the occasion for another 'tour' around the institution) communicating his alarm to the brethren. The Padre Guardiano engages Captain Martin in conversation before prayers in church:

PADRE GUARDIANO: Forgive me if I ask you a question, Reverend ...
MARTIN: Why certainly, Father.
PADRE GUARDIANO: Have you spent much time together with the other two priests?
MARTIN: We have been together throughout the whole Italian campaign. Twenty months, twenty-one months ... Sicily, Salerno, Rome, Florence. They are good friends, very dear friends. I have great admiration for them.
PADRE GUARDIANO: Have you never tried to lead them towards the path of the true religion? Have you never tried ...
MARTIN: (after a moment's hesitation) But ... Father, the Protestant and the Jew are just as convinced of being on the path to truth.
PADRE GUARDIANO: And yet we know that they are in error.
PADRE VICARIO: Yes, we know that.
MARTIN: Oh, yes, most certainly.
PADRE GUARDIANO: But we must do everything we can to try and find a way of saving those two souls who could become lost.
MARTIN: I am a Catholic, Father, and I am a priest, and I humbly believe that I am a good Catholic.
PADRE GUARDIANO: Forgive me, Father, my intention was not to remind you of your duties ... I meant to say ..., you are all military chaplains ... In the mission that you practise you are all exposed to the same risk, to the same dangers as those of the soldiers. Have you never thought that your two companions could depart this life from one moment to the next?

FRA SALVATORE: Saint Paul says: 'Omnes quidem resurgemus, sed non omnes mutabimur in gloria' ('We shall all indeed rise again, but we shall not all be changed in glory').

MARTIN: But he who is in good faith 'In novissima tuba surget in gloria' ('At the last trumpet he shall rise in glory').

PADRE VICARIO: That is true, but have you examined their consciences?

PADRE CLAUDIO: But are you sure that they are in good faith?

PADRE GUARDIANO: Have you ever spoken to them about these matters?

MARTIN: No, I have never examined their consciences, I have never discussed the matter with them. I have never asked them anything, because I have never thought that I could judge them. I know them too well, they are good friends of mine. Perhaps you, in this peace, in this atmosphere of undisturbed meditation, consider me at fault. I do not feel guilty. I have nothing on my conscience.[25]

At this point the other monks enter, and they kneel and pray, whereupon the camera makes another tour around the monastery. There follow some shots of Fra Felice preparing dinner, with friars looking on desirously, after which comes the final scene, set in the refectory, in which Captain Martin gives his response to the conversation, which is how the episode ends:

A one-minute shot shows Fra Felice entering bearing a tray of food which is placed in front of the guests. Cut to a medium close-up shot of the three chaplains preparing to eat. Cut to a medium close-up shot of Captain Martin and the Padre Guardiano, who invites them to eat. Martin says, 'We want to wait for you, all of you, Father.' The Padre Guardiano says that they are fasting, and as he does so, we see three friars in a line sitting silently. Back to Martin and the Padre Guardiano, where Martin asks, 'Why?' and the Padre Guardiano says: 'Because Divine Providence has sent into our asylum two souls on whom the light of the Gospels has yet to descend ..., [cut to close-up of Padre Guardiano] we dare to hope that with this humblest of (turning to Martin) sacrifices we may obtain from heaven a great gift.'

Back to a medium close-up shot of the three chaplains. Cut to a close-up shot of Martin, taking his spoon to his mouth, stopping, putting it down and saying: 'Forgive me if I do not observe your rule, but ... I want to speak to you ... I want to tell you ...'

Here he stands up, and we cut to a long shot of the whole refectory: '... that what you have given me is so great a gift that I feel I shall always be in your debt ...'

Then, as he goes on, we start cutting around: to the two chaplains, rather bemused, to two friars, then to more friars, then to a close-up of Martin, and then, when he finishes his speech, on the words *Pax hominibus*, the long shot again: '... I have found here that spiritual serenity which I had lost in the horrors and sufferings of the war ... A beautiful, moving lesson in humility, simplicity and pure faith ... Pax hominibus bonae voluntatis [Peace to men of good will].'

As we saw in the introduction to our discussion, this element of the 'story' has given rise to polemic. Rather than attempt to solve the problem by means of interpretation (what the episode 'means'), it might be better to try and identify what the episode *consists* of, what forms it. Just because Rossellini shows the friars doing something, and just because one character interprets it in a certain way, does not mean that the episode is being used by Rossellini to express an 'opinion.' It is not an essay, it is a film, and Rossellini is showing something in an almost documentary way – he is showing what he 'found.' What is it that he is showing?

To answer that question, let us pay careful attention to Fra Pacifico. The second person we see in the episode is Fra Pacifico: after the shot of Padre Claudio surveying the battle from the window, there is that of Fra Pacifico sweeping the sacristy and listening to the gunfire (10). He is chosen as one of the elements of the montage of the monastery, and a similar shot of him sweeping occurs again (24). The rejoicing at the Liberation is represented by Fra Pacifico shooing the recalcitrant chickens up from downstairs and out onto the veranda/garden, and he remains in the *foreground* when the friars kneel down to give thanks (16–21). He is the one who answers the doorbell, welcomes the Americans, and ushers them in, leading them upstairs to the main hall to meet the Padre Guardiano, and imperturbably personifying the 'five hundred years' of history about which Martin is lecturing his colleagues – indeed, he is in the *foreground* during that speech (27–33). His job is to prepare cells for the guests, and he announces that they are ready (48). When the Padre Guardiano goes down to the kitchen to ask Fra Felice to work the miracle of the loaves to feed the guests, Fra Pacifico is behind him, looking on (53), and it is Pacifico who answers the doorbell to receive the miraculously appropriate gift of chickens (61–4). The 'miracle' continues, with Captain Martin's piling cans high in the impassive Fra Pacifico's arms, and hastily adding a box of toothpicks, whereupon Pacifico scurries down to the kitchen to announce to Fra Felice the new bounty, and to admire the testing of the condensed milk

(67–9, 74, 76). At the beginning of the two-minute sequence-shot in which the chaplains discuss the friars in the garden, Fra Pacifico is watering some plants in the background (77), and it is he who kneels and starts saying the Angelus in the midst of the chaplains and, amazed that the others are not imitating him – Captain Jones responds to his questioning look with 'Buonasera!' – asks Martin why not, and claps his hands in horror at the light-hearted reply of the American. His Chaplinesque waddle through the monastery announcing the news occupies shots 78–80, and in the ensemble where the friars discuss the matter with the Padre Guardiano, Fra Pacifico is in the *foreground* (83). Later, at the end of the conversation between the Padre Guardiano and Captain Martin about the non-Catholic chaplains, the monks enter the church to pray, and Fra Pacifico swings round into the *foreground* of the image to kneel down nearest the camera (96). Shortly thereafter, when Fra Felice pulls the roasting pan out of the oven, Fra Pacifico is in the *foreground*, watching with interest (100–1). When the friars process into the refectory for supper towards the camera, Fra Pacifico is at the *head* of the procession (104), and as the camera cuts to them moving away towards the tables, he manouevres himself to the back of the file to be the friar closest to the camera (105), then takes his seat in the right *foreground* of the frame.

The episode consists of 119 shots; Fra Pacifico appears in one-third of them, and often in a very prominent way. Fra Pacifico is the lowliest lay brother, with a servant's role in the community, and yet he is statistically the protagonist of the episode. In other words, while the 'story' has as its protagonists Captain Martin and the Padre Guardiano, the episode as a whole has as its protagonists not just the monastery itself, but also Fra Pacifico, who functions as the human manifestation of the institution and the community, almost as a synecdoche. Despite the statistical prominence of Fra Pacifico in the episode, and the subtle way in which he is foregrounded, he is treated with a total absence of cinematic rhetoric: he is never given a real close-up, nor is he ever for a moment picked out and isolated from the environment of which he forms a part (all the other friars receive more than one close-up).

Paisà is formed from a number of rapid short stories, each of only twenty minutes' duration, allowing little time for the development of characterization. However, one thing does emerge quite strongly, and that is that certain characters are all of a piece, without self-consciousness, and that those characters are in *contrast* with others. In the *Sicily* episode, for example, the sergeant of the platoon and the mature Fascist villager play particular roles, and assume certain attitudes, while Joe and, in particular, Carmela are 'simple.' In the *Naples* episode, the military policeman plays a role and adopts attitudes (his legalistic one, for example), while Pasquale simply 'is.' In the *Monastery* episode, the Padre Guardiano, the Vicario, and Captain Martin are aware of the roles that they have to play, whereas Fra Pacifico, Fra Felice, and Padre Claudio (the organist) are 'simple.' In the *Po delta* episode Dan, for example, is self-conscious, while Dale and Cigolani are 'simple' – they 'do.'

The bearers of the rhetoric of the *raised voice* in the *Monastery* episode are the Padre Guardiano and to a lesser extent Captain Martin. The Padre Guardiano receives reverent treatment from the camera, in a number of brightly lit close-ups, sometimes taken from slightly below. He is always shown moving in a slow and dignified manner. His speech is dubbed by one of the most important actors in Italian cinema at the time, whose voice was redolent with dignity and substance. What he says is couched in pondered, almost liturgical, language.

However, the friar we see most of is Fra Pacifico, with his impassive, disgruntled face and his comic gait, who is scandalized by this alien intrusion into his simple world. Yet he is the servant of the monastery, whose job is to greet and welcome whatever and whoever appears at the door, be they villagers bearing chickens or Martians from another planet. His job is to accept and to cope with what arrives – which is precisely the task set the protagonist of the melodramatic matrix. The monastic community is the organic 'idyll' in the melodramatic matrix, and the Americans are 'modernization.' If you want a 'hero' of the melodramatic narrative, it is Fra Pacifico. He is the bearer of the rhetoric of *sermo humilis*. The element of comedy that the episode carries derives from the contrast between two registers of *elocutio*.

The task of the melodramatic matrix is not change but knowledge: not to combat and transform chaos and the wilderness, but to discover therein a garden. Narrative and rhetoric are the two sides of an aesthetic coin. The garden proposed by Fascism had been a 'rhetorical' one, and the question now was, Was 'rhetoric' (in the sense of *incoscienza* that we discussed in chapter 2) actually extinguishing real human values? In Italy the end of Fascist 'rhetoric' had been brought about by a foreign invasion. At the end of the war, priests were being shot for being priests, and partisans were being shot by communists for not being communist. Was the 'rhetoric' of political sectarianism extinguishing human values? There was a real concern in Italy that one 'rhetoric' was being replaced by another. Indeed, soon the question arose as to whether political sectarianism and its 'rhetorical' nature had extinguished the ability, in aesthetic criticism, to distinguish a good work of art from a bad one; in other words, there also existed a problem of 'rhetoric' in aesthetics. At the beginning of our discussion of this episode, we quoted Barbaro, Arnheim, and Baldelli as examples of those for whom a correct ideological position obscured the aesthetic qualities of the artefact.

Paisà tries to face as squarely as possible a reality, and to uncover in it a garden. The film is both impassive and enormously impassioned, which is something that narrative allows you to be: to show things one way, and to have a character in your narrative interpret them in another way. In the *Po delta* episode, you can show the heroism of the group, and have members of the group despair. In the *Sicily, Naples,* and *Rome* episodes, you can use dramatic irony. In the *Monastery* episode, you can show the backwardness of the friars, and have an American chaplain recognize in them an organic ontology that is beyond the reach of 'modernized' man. The title Rossellini gives to his next film, *Germania anno zero,* could properly be applied to Italy in *Paisà,* because the film strips away 'rhetoric,' politics, and history to see what is left standing. In the *Monastery* episode, as he climbs the stairs to meet the Padre Guardiano, Captain Martin comically goes on about the monastery's five hundred years of history, while Rossellini's camera impassively focuses on Fra Pacifico and what is present in year zero. The friars' talk of the other chaplains' being 'lost souls' is, yes indeed, 'rhetoric,' ideology and intolerance. But what is it that the monks *do*? They renounce their first good meal in months, and pray. They take in and feed these military chaplains, these walking contradictions, and pray for them. A film about the war, the defeat of one side and the victory of another, a civil war won, should, you would expect, be about change. But in the melodramatic matrix it is about discovering what lies beneath 'rhetorical' appearances.

The rhetoric of the *raised voice* is the vehicle of what is desired and striven for. *Sermo humilis,* the rhetoric of the lowered voice, embodied in Fra Pacifico, is the vehicle of the reality that must be accepted. It is an *aesthetics* of realism. Its philosophical and political status can certainly be questioned, but in its narrative construction and articulation it is an expression of the human mind making sense of experience. Humility, forbearance, and simplicity may be universal Christian virtues, but Rossellini distils them from an international encounter as being especially Italian, 'organic' virtues. Captain Martin is endowed at the outset, to a certain extent, with the simplicity and integrity that enable him to respond to the environment of the monastery in which he finds himself placed. He shows an immediate warmth in his response to the monastic community, and a complete tolerance of what he finds to be their entirely understandable intolerance, secluded as they are from the 'modern' world. My drawing attention to the centrality of Fra Pacifico is not intended to draw attention *away* from Captain Martin. The qualities with which Fra Pacifico is endowed – faith, simplicity, and humility, and possession of an 'organic' ontology – are qualities that Captain Martin is shown as recognizing. Pacifico and Martin are the result of a procedure of comic, contrastive 'doubling,' to a certain extent, with the aim of creating an object, an artefact, that can be the vehicle of a vision that communicates a response to experience – or, more simply, an experience. Fra Pacifico is the objective correlative of what has moved and impressed Captain Martin, the *Italian* values of which the war makes a gift to the Americans. In this episode we are watching Rossellini sketch out the beginnings of his grand theme of the 'contrast' between the cultures of the 'North' and of the 'South,' which will grow to become more explicit and prominent in *Stromboli* and *Viaggio in Italia*. The reaching out towards the values that Rossellini is groping to articulate is carried by the tendency of the film to 'lean' backwards in time even as it pushes forward in history. Celebrating Italy's progress out of tyranny and oppression, the film paradoxically, in accordance with the melodramatic matrix, sings an elegy for values located back in time past.

It is in the two episodes (the *Monastery* and the *Po delta*) that are based on the impact of an environment on the filmmakers that we find the overall effect not only being to a certain extent an expression of the nature of the moral atmosphere of the Italians, but also incorporating the American protagonists, and functioning to pull in the viewer too. You could compare the *Monastery* and *Po delta* episodes with the *Naples* episode, where the viewer is educated by seeing first one point of view then another, and in both cases learning and going deeper behind the immediate appearances; in contrast with which, in the *Monastery* and the *Po delta* episodes, the setting, and the relations of the characters with that setting, function as the means of enlightening and winning over the viewer. At the heart of the *Monastery* episode lie the four (or more properly six) 'tours' around the monastery and Fra Pacifico – and this is not an interpretative assertion so much as an empirically verifiable fact emerging from an objective description of the episode.

The narrative components of the assembly that constitutes the *Monastery* episode are the 'contradiction' and the 'hunger' preserved from the original two 'stories,' giving us the clash of creeds and the fast of the final story, integrated into the representation of an organic community contrasting in every way with the values of modernization brought by the war – that community 'represented' by means of a montage of shots and mixing of sounds, and by the 'synecdochal' prominence given to the figure of Fra Pacifico. The *dispositio* of the components is so subtle, and the rhetoric of *elocutio* deployed in the episode so *humilis*, that many viewers have failed to attend either to the components of the assembly or to their interrelation, and have reached immediately for an 'interpretation' of the episode, achieving only confusion and dissatisfaction. The viewer must notice the *transition* from the fighting on the Gothic Line to the seclusion of the monastery (by means of overlap and a sound bridge), and the establishment of the institution of the community as the source of the discourse (by means of the montages and the soundtrack). In addition, the viewer must see the comedy of the episode as deriving from the interplay between the *raised voice* and *sermo humilis*. Attention to *all* the components of the episode creates a point of view from which to view it, and provides the foundation on which the melodramatic narrative matrix generates 'knowledge.' The episode is a good example of Rossellini bringing nothing to what he *found*, but instead seeing his job as that of revealing its nature.

It is not easy to explain exactly how Rossellini's 'simplicity' is achieved. The simple characters do not explain themselves or their actions; they exist purely in what they do; they do not theorize, they act; hence, the viewer's experience of them is not a product of thinking about them (for example, about their motives, their desires, their goals), but of seeing them. Thus, they are not opposed to the world they inhabit, they are not in polemic with it, they do not represent an alternative principle to it, nor do they comment on it. Instead, they are part of the reality; and thus they take on the function of defining reality: they become the indicators for the viewer of what that reality is.

Fra Pacifico (like Carmela in the *Sicily* episode) says very little. His 'performance' is almost pure mime. From a professional actor, we would judge it a performance of enormous skill. What is Rossellini's role in the creation of this performance, this construction of a complete and yet simple character? Surely, a 'complete' and 'simple' character comes under the heading of what we would call 'realism.' The hypothesis that Fra Pacifico's performance is a product of Rossellini's 'direction' is not entirely plausible – it would place us back in the realm of his being a supremely competent actor. A more plausible hypothesis is that Rossellini assembles his artefact out of 'found' elements. Massimo Mida, in his description of the real monastery at Maiori/Baronissi, devotes just one sentence to Fra Pacifico: 'Fra Pacifico would run from one end of the monastery to the other with his swift little steps.' We have already seen how *Roma città aperta* is to a large extent a work of assembly, making a homogeneous whole out of heterogeneous parts. The basic materials assembled were, in that case, 'found' narrative components from the chronicle of Rome under the German occupation: the task was to select and combine. Rossellini's art in *Paisà* lies partly in his ability to 'find' a thing (to see it), to recognize what he has found, to 'leave it alone' in the sense of not interfering with it or modifying it, and to create a space for it in his artefact. He does this not just with people, but with places – for example, the caves of Mergellina, the monastery, and the marshy river delta (in the *Po delta* episode).

It may appear that I am giving a 'reading' of *Paisà*: interpreting the film, saying what it means, and showing how this was, at the time, a representation of a felt reality. That is not what I am trying to do. *Paisà* is a film (it is six films, actually) that represents (points to referents) and narrates (explains the referents), but that also forms an object, an artefact, which is not fully described as a representation and a narration. André Bazin concentrates on the representation of referents, which determines their explanation because the explanation is something already contained in the referents represented (which Bazin calls 'facts'). Ideological criticism concentrates on a *pre-existing* 'explanation' as *determining* the choice of the referents. A concern with aesthetics, by contrast, draws attention to representation and narration as activities in themselves, independently of the referents represented and of the explanations narrated, and asks questions about how those activities give rise to an artefact, rather than what that artefact might mean (interpretation) or what uses might be made of it (evaluation). Certainly, in the artefact referents are depicted and explanations hypothesized, so we cannot treat the film as a purely formal construction, as we might a string quartet of Haydn. Nevertheless, that is the direction in which I should like to lean, not in order to challenge the 'realism' of the film, but in order to highlight the extent to which the film is something other than the 'reality' it depicts or the explanation it gives of that 'reality': it is an artefact, a real object in the world which exists independently of the reality it depicts and explains, and an object that is new in the sense that it did not exist until its creators made it. Its justification, in other words, is different from that which would apply to a historical-documentary representation and narration of the Second World War. This is not to say that such a documentary would not have form, nor that *Paisà* is not 'historical' in many ways. Nor is it to deny that the artefact was created by historically determined beings, and is viewed by historically determined beings. It is merely a matter of emphasis. Can we look at it as an object, rather than seek in it what we want from it? The answer is probably no, not easily and not fully, but that is not a reason for not trying.

Is this merely an attempt to erase 'history' from neorealist cinema? To see neorealist cinema as a practical activity directed towards the development of a cultural contribution to the reconstruction of a war-ravaged Italy is a received wisdom so well entrenched as to be immune to any excesses of aestheticism that I might fall into. Giulia Fanara quite rightly says: 'The political themes of the Reconstruction became for the the artists a terrain for practical intervention and participation'[26] I do not question the validity of that perspective. However, it is a perspective that has so totally dominated treatment of neorealist cinema that one can be forgiven for suspecting that buying a ticket to see a neorealist film entails donning a hardhat and taking up a hammer to tackle a recalcitrant roof beam in the edifice of Italian society. Indeed, the Catholic establishment laboured hard and cunningly to see to it that as few Italian Catholics as possible saw a neorealist film: they censored films, they manipulated investment and subsidy, they encouraged American imports, and they built up an alternative exhibition circuit, all in order to strangle neorealism. This is the *other* face of a film criticism that sees films primarily in terms of politics, ideology, and practical action. If you support that action, you praise the films; if you do not, you try to burn them. Perhaps an Anglo-Saxon critic of the third millennium needs neither to praise nor to burn *Paisà*.

The *Naples* Episode (II, shot third)

Phenomenology does not seem to amount to much of a philosophy if you just describe its basic positions and methods. However, in the context of some of the other movements reigning at the time of neorealism (for example, positivism, idealism, historicism, dialectical materialism), Phenomenology becomes a clearly distinct position. Herbert Spiegelberg furnishes the most succinct summary I can find of what unites phenomenology's adherents:

All those who consider themselves Phenomenologists subscribe, for instance, to [Husserl's] watchword, *Zu den Sachen selbst* ('To the things themselves'), by which they meant the taking of a fresh approach to concretely experienced phenomena, an approach as free as possible from conceptual presuppositions, and the attempt to describe them as faithfully as possible. Moreover, most adherents to Phenomenology hold that it is possible to obtain insights into the essential structures and the essential relationships of these phenomena on the basis of a careful study of concrete examples supplied by experience or imagination and by a systematic variation of these examples in imagination. Some Phenomenologists also stress the need for studying the ways in which the phenomena appear in men's object-directed ('intentional') consciousness.[27]

That account of phenomenology would describe remarkably well what we experience when we view the *Naples* episode of *Paisà*. It was French critics and intellectuals strongly aligned with phenomenology who had the greatest respect for what Rossellini was doing in the cinema. This is not to say that Rossellini was a phenomenological philosopher. Perhaps the most eloquent description of Rossellini's approach to filmmaking comes from his assistant, Federico Fellini. It is a completely different kind of description from one that identifies a philosophical framework supporting his approach, and yet it is compatible with the phenomenological method. Indeed, Fellini's seemingly metaphorical, psychologizing account uses words that build towards a very precise analysis of Rossellini's 'vision.' *Everything* counts in the quotation which follows, but I also want to draw the reader's attention to particular words, and so I shall italicize them (even translating rather clumsily to preserve as much as possible of the original):

Following Rossellini while he was shooting *Paisà*, it suddenly seemed clear to me, *a joyous revelation*, that you could create cinema with the same *freedom*, the same *lightness of spirit* with which you might draw or write; you could make a film *enjoying it* and suffering it day by day, hour by hour, *without worrying too much about the final result*; and having the same intimate, anxious, and exciting relationship with it that you have with your own neuroses. I realized too that the obstacles, the doubts, the second thoughts, the dramas, the travails were not that different from those suffered by a painter trying to fix a tint on the canvas or a writer crossing out, rewriting, correcting, and starting again, looking for a mode of expression that, impalpable and elusive, *lies hidden* among a thousand possibilities. Rossellini *sought out and followed his film in the streets*, with Allied tanks passing only feet away from us, people shouting and singing from the windows, hundreds of people milling around trying to sell us things or steal things from us, in that raging bedlam, that teeming lazaretto that was Naples, and then in Florence and in Rome and in the endless marshes of the Po, with problems of every kind, permits revoked at the last moment, plans thwarted, money disappearing mysteriously, in the frantic carousel of self-styled producers ever more greedy, infantile, deceitful, and opportunistic ...

What I think I learned from Rossellini – a tutorship never translated into words, never expressed, never planned – was how to *keep one's balance* in the midst of the most adverse and difficult conditions, and at the same time the natural ability to *turn those adversities to one's own advantage*, and to turn those difficulties into a feeling, into emotional values, into *a point of view*. This is what Rossellini did: he lived the life of a film as *a wonderful adventure to be simultaneously lived and recounted*. His ability to *let himself go* in front of reality, always attentive, lucid, and impassioned, his way of naturally placing himself at an indefinable but unmistakable *mid-way point between the indifference of detachment and the clumsiness of commitment* enabled him to capture and hold on to reality in all its dimensions, *to look at things from the inside and from the outside simultaneously*, to photograph the air around things, to reveal what is elusive, arcane, and magical in life ...

There is always that moment in which you come across *his look*, his feeling for a reality ever suspended in a firm inevitability, in an aura of tragedy that is unbroken, almost sacred, precisely because it is veiled in the heartrending familiarity of the most banal gestures, of the most common habits, of the most everyday things. It was as if Rossellini's almost *distracted and casual way of looking* at the most terrible situations enabled them to *preserve uncontaminated* their awful power, and the anguish seemed to be nourished by the very *transparent irresponsibility of the eye that beheld it*. This gaze, this way of observing things, coincided with a period in which what was happening already had in itself the form of a story, it was already narrative, it was already character, it was already dialectic. As long as reality retained that painful, fractured, tragic, elusive quality that it had in the aftermath of the war, there was a miraculous harmony between that reality and *the dry eye of Rossellini which observed it*.[28]

Phenomenology requires 'an approach [to concretely experienced phenomena] as free as possible from conceptual presuppositions, and the attempt to describe them as faithfully as possible.' Fellini depicts a side of Rossellini's personality which looks upon the world with a light, detached, dry, irresponsible, disinterested gaze. The approach and the gaze are more than compatible. Indeed, Rossellini's film is a veritable assault on conceptual presuppositions, as we have already seen.

The *Monastery* episode of *Paisà* was the second to be shot. *Naples* was the third. The original story was apparently the work of Alfred Hayes – 'I agreed to write two episodes: a story about a negro MP in Naples and a drama about the liberation of Rome.'[29] Rossellini used virtually none of Hayes's story, of which a brief 'treatment' has reached us in this form:

A black M.P. is on duty at a petrol dump on the outskirts of Naples. He has made friends with a Neapolitan shoeshine boy, Pascà.

Pascà often asks him about America, and the black man describes it. Pascà also asks him to take him to America with him, and the black man promises to. On this basis, they are very good friends.

One night, the black man is on guard duty. Pascà is keeping him company. In the dark, the boy sings Neapolitan songs which the black man tries to repeat with his deep, vibrant voice.

Two unsavoury characters turn up out of the dark, and draw near. They start out obliquely, then they offer the black man money: they want petrol, and they are prepared to reward him. The black man chases them away and resumes singing with the boy.

The other two rejoin their mates, and together decide to do without the black man's help. They have all they need: the truck, the cans, a length of rubber tubing, and something to pierce one of the petrol tanks.

Suspicious, the black man gets up and calls 'Who goes there?' Two or three shots ring out, the black man falls to the ground. While other soldiers arrive, opening fire, Pascà throws himself on the body of his friend, desperate with grief: he must not die; if he dies he won't take him to America. Dying, the black man smiles, and tells him not to make too much of a thing of it. He is a poor negro, in America he counts for nothing, he's like a shoe-shiner. He's better off not going with him to America. It wouldn't amount to much going there with a poor negro. He's better off staying in Naples ...[30]

Rossellini takes the two characters, and to a large extent erases the story.

The final shot of the *Sicily* episode – Carmela's body on the rocks –
fades to black, while the terminal, climactic chord of the music ends.
Immediately there is a rapid fade-in to a slow panning shot (right to
left) across the temples of Paestum, accompanied straightaway by gentle music and the following voice-over: 'The war passed rapidly
through the regions of southern Italy. On the eighth of September the
guns of the Allied fleet were trained on Naples. Having broken through
the German defences at Salerno, the Anglo-Americans landed on the
Amalfi coast, and a few weeks later Naples was liberated. The city's
port became the most important logistical centre of the war in Italy.'
Between the words 'Salerno' and 'the Anglo-Americans landed' there is
a wipe (one image gradually replaces the previous one in a progressive
invasion of the screen from right to left) to a pan (right to left) over a
misty Vesuvius seen from a distance, the pan ending against a dark
mountainside in the foreground. After the words 'Naples was liberated,' there is another wipe from right to left, revealing a sort of picture-
postcard static view of the Bay of Naples, with a picturesque plume of
smoke rising from Vesuvius in the background. Between the words
'most important' and 'logistical centre' there is a dissolve to the first of
three shots of cranes unloading material onto the quay, and the music
stops. What is plainly intended as diegetic sound of the port starts up
on the soundtrack, but it does not match very accurately what we see.
Then there is a rapid dissolve to a shot of the city's busy Porta Capuana,
with a truck passing in the foreground, its sound clearly diegetic on the
soundtrack (it may even be direct sound at this point). A shot of a market is then followed by one of a fire-eater performing in the street and
calling out to his audience, from which we cut to an admiring *scugnizzo*
(the word used for street urchins in Naples). By now we have established dialogue on the soundtrack, and the 'story' has begun.

The voice-over commentary gives a chronicle of the Liberation so far,
finishing with a characterization of Naples's status at that point. The
images do something else. From a formal point of view, they form an
accelerated montage: the first three shots are of twenty-seven, eight,
and three seconds' duration respectively, and remain short until the
end of the passage we have just described. It is not immediately obvious that all of it is archive footage, and that we can call it 'documentary,'
in the sense of having a different status from the footage of the story.
The first three shots are essentially of 'landscape.' The first long panning shot begins on a meadow, with a white cross on a grave in the foreground, and gradually reveals in its movement two of the three temples

of Paestum, with more crosses in the foreground. The second shot preserves the slow panning movement from right to left, and supplies a landscape establishment of the mountains around Naples. The third shot could be of a still photograph of the port of Naples. Thereafter, the shots of material being unloaded by cranes on the quayside (beginning with a pan right to left, to match the previous footage) that illustrate the voice-over commentary appear to be archive footage. However, the process of progressively homing in on the small part of Naples in which the story begins continues, with shots of streets, and so it is not clear where 'documentary' footage ceases, and 'story' material begins.

The long shot of Paestum could be fulfilling a number of functions. It illustrates the breakthrough at Salerno (Paestum is just to the south), and the crosses illustrate the fighting involved in that breakthrough. However, it also functions as an image of a timeless Italy with ancient traditions, now overrun by a modern war between two foreign occupiers. The shot of Vesuvius from a mountain vantage point has a similar function of evoking a timeless landscape, and Rossellini's later work will develop on this particular use of Naples as embodying profound and eternal values. These two shots could be archive footage, or they could have been expressly taken for the film. Since the story is set in the real streets of Naples, all shots that set the scene are compatible with the world of the 'story.' Even the cargo being unloaded on the dockside will reappear later in the story. Only the voice-over commentary stands outside the story, recounting a supposedly 'true' narrative that acts as a frame in which is set the fictional one. As the camera penetrates into the market and the streets, it remains high at first, with overhead shots, from an 'impossible' vantage point, and then views events through crowds in the foreground in a more 'documentary' way. The result of all these features is to supply the episode with an expressive, informative, scene-setting transition both from the previous episode to the new one and from the historical facts of the war to the fictional story about to unfold. Distinctions and transitions are, in other words, gently but rapidly smoothed out. The rhetorical effect is to endow the story with aspects of the status the historical material has, enhancing the story's aura of authenticity.

Pasquale is established in a social environment of children scouring for money. He, like some of the other boys, wears a military cap too big for him, down over his ears, similar to that worn by the black military policeman, and a jacket too small, similar to a military jacket, so that when he drags Joe through the streets, he seems a miniature version of the adult. This play of adulthood against childhood will be a theme of the episode.

We first see Joe, the MP, from Pasquale's point of view (in a reverse-angle sequence), having his upper lip drawn back to examine his teeth (as though he were livestock) by the boys bidding for the right to exploit him (his shoes, his jacket, and the wallet in an inside pocket). An adult intervenes, and declares himself the winner in the auction ('Tec-cot'e tremila lire' / 'Here, take three thousand lire') even though Pasquale has bid more (Pasquale: 'Aggio ritto tremila lire e ddui pacchett'e sigarette' / 'I bid three thousand lire and two packets of cigarettes'; Man: 'Vattene, vattene. Tremila lire abbasteno' / 'Go away, three thousand's enough'). Pasquale feels cheated ('Ma te n'abusi che so' pic-cirillo' / 'But you're taking advantage because I'm little'), which motivates his ruse of pretending that the police are coming in order to scatter his rivals. Thus, the ambiguity of this tall, strong, wealthy representative of a conquering army coming from a background of slavery and oppression is introduced from the very first moment we, the viewers, see him, while at the same time Pasquale's youth is presented as an obstacle to his survival in the Neapolitan economic jungle. Joe's power is diminished by drink; Pasquale's lack of power is compensated for by intelligence. As they go through Naples, the pair are very similar to Antonio and Bruno in *Ladri di biciclette*, both as a visual motif (their contrasting height and gait) and psychologically: in De Sica's film Antonio's wits are dulled by obsessive anxiety, while Bruno is alert, resourceful, and protective of his father. Costume is important in *Paisà*: Rossellini has Pasquale put on a military coat (when he gets to his shoe-shine box) that is far too big for him, which emphasizes his smallness and his vulnerability, along with a military cap – the two together functioning as an index of his admiration and *need* for the paternal, which he projects onto the American military. Joe will interpret Pasquale's clothes as an index of his predatoriness. In both *Paisà* and *Ladri di bici-clette* the adult is too self-absorbed to notice the needs of the child, and both films use that dramatic irony to generate meaning.

The scene in the puppet theatre preserves the perspective already created of Pasquale upon Joe: cuts to Pasquale are of him observing Joe's childlike response to the performance. Joe's spontaneity gives him affinity with the popular culture and social atmosphere of Naples, while his interpretation of the performance sets him apart. Pasquale's role remains that of protecting Joe, despite his diminutive size. Joe's response to the romance-epic narrative material of the puppet show continues the theme of his race, contaminated with the moral judgment already introduced at the auction (while Joe has every right to object to black skin being equated with evil, he himself is drunk and in search of a prostitute). As they wander through empty squares with coiled barbed wire, Pasquale bullies and chivvies Joe along. When he tries to rouse the American from the ground, Joe drops a harmonica that he had grabbed from Pasquale's pocket, and the boy picks it up and blows through it. Joe, like a child, wants to play it himself, and Pasquale, instead, somewhat contemptuously throws Joe's hat, which he has been carrying, on the ground, moving Joe along by getting him to pick it up. On the one hand, the scene functions like a walking tour through bombed-out Naples, the narrative almost a pretext for documentary-like footage, culminating in the dialogue on the pile of rubble in a ruined building, against a church bell-tower looming between wrecked walls. On the other hand, it develops the reversal of roles between child and adult. With his harmonica, Pasquale has taken on features of a Pied Piper, leading the innocent and unaware.

The conversation on the pile of rubble is assembled out of a number of elements. Most of it is in direct sound, with Pasquale's lines dubbed in, to all of which are added sound-off effects. One of Joe's lines on the soundtrack bridges two shots, in the first of which he is not seen to speak, an error introduced at the editing stage. The shots of the two of them together come in basically two forms: one a general shot, with natural lighting, but leaving Joe's face slightly in shadow, and another from a little closer, in sunlight with fairly strong fill light from left of frame (on occasion Joe blocks this fill light, casting an incongruous shadow over Pasquale's face in the right of the frame). There are cut-away reaction shots of Pasquale responding to Joe, in dubbed sound. There are close-ups of Joe, generally in direct sound. The centrepiece of the sequence is a one and a half minute two-shot of monologue from Joe with enthusiastic supporting interjections from Pasquale (the boy's attention is directed at Joe, at whom he looks, while Joe's attention is directed towards himself, looking straight ahead or 'into his imagination'). The average shot length of this episode (the shortest in the film at 14 minutes and 50 seconds) is overall 6.5 seconds, but with that long sequence shot removed, it comes down to 5.9 seconds. At the beginning of the sequence, there is a continuity error in which Pasquale has the harmonica in his mouth, while in the next shot he is holding it in his hand. From the differences in lighting, one would deduce that there were about four set-ups, plus inserted close-ups. The sequence was shot with care and attention to its meaning, and yet quite noticeable errors were tolerated, which could have been corrected. Dots Johnson's acting is weak in one of the shorter close-ups, where he becomes discouraged in his fantasies: he makes the transition from imitating the train to saying 'I don't want to go home' too rapidly, and it would have been easy to reshoot that isolated 15-second shot. Once again, we find Rossellini prepared to accept a certain 'roughness' of presentation, provided he can capture the feeling and imagery that he wants.

The sequence serves a number of functions. It invites the viewer inside, so to speak, the experience of Joe (Pasquale's and his own eyes, as well as the viewer's, are on Joe): his hopes and desires, his susceptibility to the rhetoric of the Liberation (by victorious heroes), and his bitter awareness of the reality of his position in society back home. The idea derives from Hayes's treatment (quoted at the beginning of this section), but it is removed from the treatment's conventional narrative context of an armed robbery, and anchored in a historical moment. The way in which Rossellini has chosen to carry this out is by making Joe's fantasies arise out of the historical environment in which he finds himself at that particular moment. As Joe sprawls on the mound of rubble, we hear the sounds of the city in the form of 'sound off.' These sounds off provoke in Joe the fantasies of a hero's return home and welcome: he associates in his inebriated mind the sounds of a train or a ship with the kind of narrative usually found in Hollywood cinema, and elaborates upon that narrative in a conventionally generic way, only to reject it, finally, as an illusion in violent conflict with his actual social status as a black man. The viewer acquires his or her knowledge together with Pasquale, signified by the boy's warning to Joe not to fall asleep. Across the language barrier (Pasquale repeats 'che dici?' / 'what are you saying?', 'che fai?' / 'what are you doing?'), using gesture, Pasquale participates in Joe's fantasy. Pasquale is not, however, just the viewer's surrogate in the scene. The scene is located in a *place*, a bombed building: a somewhere that has been reduced to nowhere, an identity that the war has defaced, changed, violated – and these characteristics are, as it were, transferred to Pasquale: he finds a key, but no longer has a door to open. The place gives expression to what lies within the experience of both Joe and Pasquale, just as the monastery does with the friars, and the Po delta with the partisans. This means that when he leans over the supine American and says 'Joe! Joe! Si tu ruorme io arrubb'e scarpe' / 'If you fall asleep, I'll steal your boots,' the boy's gesture is laden with significance concerning the values that have survived within him, despite the devastation of his circumstances. The scene ends with a rapid fade-out on his words.

The episode breaks into two halves at this point, with a jump in time and place, and yet with the second half constituting a repetition, in formal terms, of the first. The first half establishes Pasquale's point of view on Joe, through which the viewer gains knowledge about Joe. The second half emphasizes Joe's point of view on Pasquale. Implied is a sort of common experience of poverty and oppression. Sentiment and instinct – even a sort of nobility – enable Pasquale to cross the language barrier, and experience undermines Joe's preconceptions. The conflict between Joe and Pasquale is over morality, in the legalistic sense of theft (even though Joe starts off drunk in search of a prostitute), and develops into a much more ambiguous understanding of a historical and political situation (the thief is stealing from those who have impoverished and orphaned him). The episode answers the question Joe puts to Pasquale: 'Why do you steal?'

There is a fade to black followed by a fade into an establishing shot of Joe's jeep entering the frame and proceeding down a wide street, followed by a through-the-windscreen shot of Joe intent on battling with the traffic, then a dissolve into a high angle shot of traffic in a street, and finally a return to the through-the-windscreen shot of Joe looking up (shading his eyes), this time at something that has caught his attention just ahead. This last is the first in a reverse-angle sequence of six shots alternating between the viewer (and it is important that it is *not* Pasquale) looking through the windscreen at Joe, and Joe's point of view (the camera jerks) on Pasquale, the pilferer. After the reverse-angle sequence there is a master shot of Joe's jeep drawing alongside the truck, which then dissolves into a through-the-windscreen shot of Joe driving in his jeep with Pasquale in the passenger seat.

The fade into and out of black and the dissolve that start off the second half of the episode denote elision, a jump in time and space, and the consequent omission of 'action.' What has been elided is Pasquale's theft of Joe's boots and Joe's arrest of Pasquale – the key actions in a dramaturgy of preconceived rights and wrongs. The ensuing dialogue between Joe and Pasquale is, this time, shot in a single sequence-shot lasting fifty-two seconds, through the windscreen of the jeep, from the 'observer's' point of view that Rossellini has created for the viewer. What Joe says reinforces our understanding of his viewpoint on Pasquale, which has been established in the immediately previous reverse-angle sequence: he is a systematic, opportunistic thief, ungrateful for what the Americans have brought with them. Our 'detached' observation of Joe's viewpoint continues while Joe goes through Pasquale's pockets (saying 'Why do you steal? Why do you steal?'), until we are offered another shot from Joe's point of view, of Pasquale running away crying. Joe himself then enters this shot to catch the boy, and brings him back to the jeep for a 34-second sequence-shot from a detached viewpoint, in which he now starts to treat Pasquale as a little boy ('Put this coat on before you catch cold'). When he finds the harmonica, his anger returns, and Pasquale once again defends his integrity (as he had done over the auction) saying: 'Te l'aggio ditto che nun aviv'a durmì' / 'I told you not to fall asleep.' By now, however, the disproportion of power between the adult and the child has come home to Joe, who demands to be taken to the boy's parents at home (Pasquale protests: 'Io nun a' tengo' / 'I haven't got one').

We can move to the entry of Joe and Pasquale into the cave at Mergellina. Outside, Joe has been surrounded by children, has distributed sweets, has been offered one of, evidently, many pairs of boots – all filmed from the observer's point of view. When he enters the cave, the camera alternates between Joe looking and what he sees (one of the shots of Joe being twenty seconds long), establishing his point of view. At a certain point the procedure changes. There is a shot from behind Joe taken at the level of Pasquale's head – it is a head and shoulders close-up of Pasquale, with Joe's left hip out of focus in the right-hand edge of the frame; Pasquale's head is tilted back to point up at Joe's face, but his eyes are lowered to look at the boots held at thigh level in Joe's hand; Joe is swivelling away from the view of the interior of the cave. There is a cut to a close-up of Joe's head from adult height. He has turned past Pasquale below him, and lowers his eyes to the ground, asking: 'Where's your mother an' father?' There is a cut to Pasquale's level, where he moves around Joe's body to face him, looks up, and says, 'Nun te capisco' / 'I can't understand you.' There is a cut up to Joe's head and shoulders in which he raises his eyes away from the boy who has come round in front of him, and starts turning away from him towards the interior of the cave, then a cut down to Pasquale who, looking up, sees that Joe is turning away, and lowers his gaze to the boots. A cut back up to Joe continuing his turn away, and saying, now with his back to the boy, 'Dov'è mamma e pàppa?' is followed by a cut back down to Pasquale, who walks round Joe to his front, to face him from below, looks up at his face, and says, 'Mamma e papà non ce stanno chiù. So' morti.' 'E bombe' ... / 'Mummy and Daddy aren't here anymore. They're dead. The bombs ...' The camera cuts up to Joe again, while the voice of Pasquale continues off-camera to say: '... Bum, bum! Capisci? 'E bombe. Bum, bum!' – Joe's head is turning back away from Pasquale, his eyes looking up and down. The camera cuts back down to a close-up of Pasquale looking up once more at Joe's back. Then it cuts to a medium, *piano americano* shot of the two of them in that position, Joe leaning away from Pasquale, dropping the boots and starting to move out of the frame to the left, meanwhile Pasquale's eyes going from Joe's head to the boots in his hand, then on the ground, and bending forward to pick them up, the camera tilting down to follow him. As he begins to rise from his bending position, the camera cuts to a close-up of him rising back erect, looking towards the camera in the direction of Joe's exit, motionless with huge wide eyes. There is a cut to Joe in his jeep driving fast away from the camera down the hill through a tunnel of arches, gradually being obscured by the dust thrown up by the wheels, and this shot fades to black. Ever since we have seen the interior of the caves, there has been music on the soundtrack, rising to a crescendo finale at the end of the episode (music that was, as we have said, behind the film's opening credits).

The sequence in the cave is carefully choreographed, with the lighting accurately set up to illuminate Pasquale's face in particular, and his little figure outlined against the gloom by backlighting. Though the camera rises to Joe's level to shoot him, and descends to Pasquale's level to shoot him, we neither see Pasquale from Joe's point of view nor Joe from Pasquale's. Pasquale's attention is equally divided between trying to get Joe to look at him (in which he is unsuccessful) and keeping the boots, which Joe evidently no longer wants.

The elisions in the narrative, the choice of camera angles, decisions about *mise en scène* and editing have all been directed towards delving behind superficial appearances and exploring the complexity of the two protagonists' experience. The viewer watches the characters learn: Pasquale, that the power and wealth of the American is only temporary and apparent, that Joe is no 'father,' and that he must rely on himself; Joe, that his belief that he, as Liberator, was bringing bounty and security to inveterate thieves hid the reality of the Allied bombing and its consequences for the civilian population, and that Pasquale and others like him were young, orphaned, and destitute. What 'happens' in Rossellini's new narrative is that the viewer progressively sees more clearly; in his dramaturgy a complex understanding gradually displaces simple appearances.

The beginning of the episode establishes Joe's view of Naples, and establishes Pasquale's view of Joe. They each have intentions towards the other: Joe to be taken to a prostitute, Pasquale to rob Joe. They each have intentions regarding what will be the relations between them. The episode overturns those intentions, functioning like a lesson in phenomenological method: to strip away interests and preconceptions, and open up each character (and the viewer) to a full experience of the other. In this the episode is schematic, like the Rome episode. However, from a narrative point of view, it is the least schematic of all the episodes: the 'story' merely puts the two in each other's company, and takes them around Naples. This, in its turn, merely assembles on film the genesis of the episode: Rossellini decided what he would film when he saw Alfonsino Bovino and Dots Johnson together, and when he saw the caves at Mergellina.[31] The drama, therefore, is found in what is simply seen, and given articulate cinematic expression in order that the viewer might 'see' what Rossellini saw. Rossellini's 'vision' is not simple at all, and Fellini's careful and acute analysis of the extraordinarily ambiguous balancing act needed to reach it should be a warning. But the *poetic* achievement of the artefact is one of simplicity. Claude Chabrol recounts happening on the set of Rossellini's *La paura* and being inspired to the following reflection: 'Everything was obvious in the simplest way possible. It was the invention of the straight line. A straight line is very simple, but you have to know where it starts and where it ends. That's what I learned from Rossellini: to go directly for the simplest thing, because the simplest thing permits you to express what is essential.'[32] For example, the scene between the protagonists in the caves at Mergellina derives much of its impact merely from the difference in height between the two characters, which Rossellini's use of the camera preserves. This does not mean that each detail in the episode does not bear narrative importance. For example, the film is careful to supply explanations for Pasquale's behaviour (the ruse of pretending that the police are arriving in response to having been cheated at the auction of Joe; his warning to Joe not to fall asleep; his willingness to return the boots). Similarly, at the end of the episode the little boy's material needs are made very clear by the way in which he eyes the boots, which, if they are no longer wanted, he must not let out of his sight. The episode is neatly constructed around a 'contrivance' in the narrative: that of making Pasquale and Joe meet, coincidentally, on two separate occasions, with the power roles reversed (at the first meeting, Pasquale is in control, but learns about Joe; at the second, Joe is in control, but learns about Pasquale). From the narrative point of view, the episode is a well-formed artefact, a carefully constructed assembly. What makes one want to characterize it as 'simple' is the fact that it appears not formed for the *purposes* of illustrating a predetermined 'theme,' but as a *result* of registering the minor details of a historical moment. The episode appears to assemble the product of a *flânerie*, consisting of a movement through Naples, from the display and show on the street and at the puppet theatre to the ultimate signifiers of a historical moment, the bombed building and the caves of Mergellina. At the level of *dispositio* it is an assembly of the microscopic narrative indices linking places with people, history, and politics, its simplicity deriving from an *elocutio* of *sermo humilis*.

The *Florence* Episode (IV, shot fourth)

Both André Bazin and Gilles Deleuze have identified a characteristic of some neorealist films that we called, in chapter 1, the *film balade*, and for which, in our discussion of the *Naples* episode, we used the word *flânerie*. Could the French recognize it more easily than we can because they have words for it and we do not? The *Florence* episode of *Paisà* offers a fine example of the phenomenon. Nothing important happens to either of the protagonists, Harriet or Massimo; instead, they are witnesses to what unfolds as they 'travel' towards their destination. Nothing much happens to any of the other characters in the episode either: the partisan from Lucca, the partisan leaders Gigi and Marco, the policeman, the British officers, and the 'Major' on the rooftop (who is played by one of the film's producers, Renato Campos, and whose daughter is played by Giulietta Masina, in a scene shot in the street where Fellini and Masina lived in Rome, Via Lutezia). Four people are killed on camera, but these deaths are in the margins of the story. The death that matters, that of Lupo, is mentioned in passing in the last shot of the episode. The only character we learn much about is one we never see: Lupo.

In no version of the 'project' for the film does the city of Florence appear. The American nurse Harriet was to have been the protagonist of a Neapolitan story that was eventually discarded. The execution of some partisans by the Fascists figured in Amidei's abandoned project for the last episode. In fact, it was during the shooting of the *Florence* episode that the idea of the *Po delta* episode, which was to replace Amidei's original story, was developed. Massimo is played by Renzo Avanzo, the son of the Baroness Antonietta Avanzo, who was Rossellini's aunt, and who owned land in the delta. As they ate and rested in Florence after shooting, they discussed setting an episode on her estate. In just such a way, as Rossellini and Fellini rested in Naples from work on the Sicilian episode, they met Vasco Pratolini, a Florentine novelist who was working on his latest book, *Cronache di poveri amanti*, and asked him to help work out the story for an episode set in Florence. When Rossellini and Fellini finally got to Florence, they met partisans, and consulted with them on details. It emerged that the men they were talking to had not done much fighting, and the real fighters had mostly dispersed. Thus was born the 'absent' Lupo.[33]

Something we remarked upon in our discussion of *Roma città aperta* applies also to this episode: the huge amount of information we, the viewers, are given, not through what we see, but through what we hear.

While Harriet is treating wounded partisans, we learn: that the British Eighth Army is halted on the south side of the city; that the partisans are moving to meet them; that the fighting has been, and still is, intense; that only one river crossing survives (Ponte Vecchio); that the fighting is intense along the Lungarni; that the partisans find the American nurses attractive; that Harriet has lived in Florence for a few years, speaks Italian, but with a strong English accent, and that she had many friends in Florence; that Harriet has done a long tour, and has been assigned rest in Rome, but does not want to go. From the policeman we learn about the route across the river through the Galleria degli Uffizi. From the British officers we learn that they are trying to assess the situation across the river.

From the point of view of the dialogue, the subject matter is: the strategic situation in Florence – the parts that the partisans dominate, the Fascists sniping, and the Germans controlling the rest; the disruption and suffering this causes the populace; the fact that the British are waiting, when they could and should be advancing and liberating the city; the fact that the bridges are down (which is not the reason the two British officers give for waiting); Massimo's need to get to his family, and the foolhardiness of this; Massimo's knowing the partisans personally. The action, and what we see, introduce us to the following: the impetuousness of both Harriet and Massimo; the lack of urgency of the British; a 'tour' of the city centre (ruins, a deserted city, Germans dominating, sniper fire, difficulties of meeting basic domestic needs like water); the shooting of the partisan in the doorway; the execution of the Fascists.

I have deliberately left out what we learn about Lupo. A picture is gradually built up. In a dialogue between Harriet and the partisan from

Lucca we learn that her friend (we quickly start to assume that he is her boyfriend) is a partisan leader and that he is 'famous.' From other partisans at the medical post Lupo acquires an aura of mystery, which is reinforced when Harriet questions two partisans at Palazzo Pitti. In her first dialogue with Massimo, Lupo grows to being 'legendary.' From the newspaper, and in the discussion between Harriet and a man and his daughter, we gather that Lupo was once a normal man (but an artist, so already connoted as exceptional), known personally to various people, but has now become something more. The last account we have of him comes from the partisan dying in Harriet's arms. In death, and in his relationship as commander to the dying partisan, Lupo's dual nature, man and spirit, is completed and closed off as being a recounted one. No concrete physical reality can now interfere with the narrative of Lupo. He is the product of diverse discourses: sentimental, social, political, and mythical.

The episode starts and ends with Harriet tending a wounded partisan. In the episode's final shot the scene bears some resemblance to a *Pietà* scene (Mary holding the body of Christ), which we have already seen imitated by Rossellini in the shot of Don Pietro holding Pina's body in *Roma città aperta*. It is in this shot that she learns of the death of the man she has been seeking, who, while never shown in the film, has been elevated to a symbol of the spirit of the Resistance by the almost religious way people speak of him.

The *Florence* episode bears traces of the changes in the story that occurred during editing. While Harriet is treating the partisan from Lucca (their dialogue takes on a completely different acoustic when she brings up the subject of Lupo – indicating that it was filmed and dubbed separately from the rest), and while she discusses with the doctor whether she has to go to Rome or not, more partisans enter the room from a side door, and sit on a bench. Among them is Massimo, dressed in the clothes we shall later see him wearing, which a doctor starts to take off in order to examine his wounded arm. The partisan sitting next to him turns to him and says: 'Go on, stop looking like an undertaker. You'll find her, that little wife of yours' – suggesting that the intention had been at some stage to bring up Massimo's quest (to get back to his wife) in this part of the episode, rather than a little later on. Harriet's breakaway from the doctor and nurse who are trying to persuade her to take her rest in Rome occurs as Massimo passes in the background, and it is to go off with Massimo that she rushes out, holding up her hand towards him. In the following sequences in Florence, when Harriet comes up to him, he exclaims: 'Harriet! How strange to find you here, since when have you been in Italy?' (and yet ..., they have just been in the same room together, a few feet apart, and she has just run out after him). This strange loose end is left over from a stage in the editing at which Harriet and Massimo were supposed to meet at the American medical post. Cutting out their meeting and dialogue at the beginning and having them meet later may have had the result of slightly reducing the footage devoted to Harriett's and Massimo's self-absorbed indifference to the history unfolding around them, which is one of the main themes of the episode. If Harriet and Massimo's encounter is delayed, it means that their central 'story' is very slightly demoted in importance to promote the depiction of the general situation of Florence, and of citizens who are not part of the main story. This would be further evidence for the notion that the private quests of Harriet and Massimo are, to a certain extent, in contrast and opposition to a historical situation; that their movements through Florence function as a sort of *flânerie*, in the margins of which profoundly significant events are taking place; and that the more conventional material has been whittled away in the editing – though *to what extent* it was to be whittled away changed as the episode was assembled.[34]

Florence is the episode most full of events, strung out like 'beads' along a 'string' formed by Harriet's and Massimo's attempts to reach their loved ones: wounded fighters arriving at the medical post; partisans recounting their activities; Harriet finishing her tour of duty, but not wanting to go for a rest to Rome; refugees milling around Palazzo Pitti; the hardship of inhabitants of the still unliberated zones; the British distributing flour; the growing legend of Lupo; news from north of the river reaching the south by newspaper and by telephone; two British officers supposedly reconnoitring, but actually sightseeing; partisans trying to keep the route across the river secret from the Germans; a tour of German-occupied Florence; a First World War veteran keeping lookout over enemy action; frustration with British delays; confused apartment dwellers; ingenious devices for keeping life going under sniper fire; partisan actions against the Fascist forces; the Fascists shooting a partisan, and his death; the summary execution of Fascist snipers; news of the death of Lupo.

The introductory footage consists of six short shots, gradually growing in length from two seconds to six seconds. They are, in order: two shots of military vehicles driving towards the camera (from left to right) along a hilly mountain road; a shot of a file of mules going away from the camera (left to right) in hilly terrain; a shot of a tracked personnel carrier passing along a dusty road (left to right) in the foreground, with a hilly landscape in the background; and two shots of American tanks manoeuvring (in both there are three planes of depth, in each of which a tank is moving in the opposite direction to the tank in the adjacent plane – the second of these shots is rather striking). These shots accompany the first part of the voice-over commentary: 'The German troops, pressed by the Allies, retreat across Lazio, Umbria, and Tuscany. Battle is rejoined for a while on the hills around Florence. But during the first few days of August the troops of the Eighth Army were liberating that part of the city that lay south of the Arno.' The footage is certainly illustrative, but not precisely of anything recounted in the voice-over. We do not see footage of German troops retreating, or of battle, or of the liberation of southern Florence. The 'documentary' footage is, therefore, rather more arbitrary in this episode than in the others, linked to the story that follows only by the fact that the Allied forces are advancing, and by the fact that we cut from military vehicles on the battlefield to their consequences: military ambulances on the home front.

At this point, there is a wipe to a road on the outskirts of Florence (it was actually shot near Lucca) where U.S. military vehicles are passing in both directions in front of the entrance gate to the American medical post. The voice-over, having paused, restarts and concludes: 'On the other side of the river the Italian partisans who had risen up were fighting against the Germans and the Fascist snipers' – but, of course, what we are seeing is the beginning of Harriet's story, not footage of what the voice-over is recounting. This sequence in front of the gates to the medical post is poorly established. There are two cutaways from ambulances and a jeep arriving to a largish group of Italian civilian onlookers (mainly men and children), but this group is never visible in the establishing shots, and so it is hard for the viewer to understand where they are. Not only that, one prominent character in the group looks at the camera and later makes a sort of sighing gesture, neither of which has any connection with the narrative. The reason why the viewer cannot make sense of where the onlookers are is because the camera has crossed to the opposite side of the road and, for those cutaway shots of onlookers *only* (and without this fact being made clear), is pointing in a reverse angle towards the side of the road where the camera is positioned for the rest of the shots. Those onlookers are where the camera is in all the other shots, but this fact is nowhere established for the viewer.

The very 'roughness' that disorients the viewer in this first sequence is, instead, exploited to great effect in the execution of the Fascists, which we see in the margins, so to speak, of another narrative event (the death of the partisan). Massimo has impetuously dashed across the street, and the partisan who comes out of a doorway to give him covering fire gets shot by a sniper. Marco and Harriet pull him back into the doorway. The camera cuts to a long-scale shot of the whole street, for no apparent reason, until we see some tiny figures appear from the other end. The line of trees, the pavement, and the buildings all accentuate the impression of perspective, adding to the depth of the image in a way that will become the almost obsessive hallmark of Antonioni's compositions (starting with *Cronaca di un amore*), but which is uncharacteristic of Rossellini's style of shot-composition. From the left, in the distance, and from the foreground, partisans run towards these figures, which can just be made out to be three captured Fascists in the midst of partisans, one being dragged along backwards by the armpits with his heels scraping the ground. There is a cut to a camera in almost the same position (a little bit forward), but this time with a long-focal-length lens (telephoto). The action is a direct continuation of that in the previous shot, but this shot was taken at another time, and there are continuity errors, including a complete change of sunlight on the building behind. Unlike the compositions one associates with Rossellini, this telephoto shot gives the viewer little sense of where exactly he or she is viewing from. The partisans push and pull the Fascists to the right along the street, towards and to the right of the camera, with the camera panning to follow them, until they are nearly level with the doorway holding Harriet and the dying partisan. There is a cut to a very slightly changed camera position (the same as that in which Marco and Harriet pulled the partisan into the doorway), but still with a telephoto lens. Marco stops the tallest Fascist and makes him look into the doorway, saying: 'Pigs, look at what you've done ... Move!' and then forces him, followed by the others, across the street towards the camera, looming right up into the lens and across it to the left. There is a cut in which the camera appears to look down 'behind itself' to the left, so to speak, to where the Fascists have been flung on the ground, but we can only see them through the heads, necks, arms, and bodies of the partisans crowding around them. Rapidly the partisans step away, and we hear 'No, no, I don't want to die, no!' shouted in terror (but it is not clear from which Fascist); there is a puff of smoke in the foreground, and the bodies jerk (this whole shot lasts three and a half seconds), whereupon there is a cut to Harriet and the wounded partisan in the doorway.

The summary execution of the Fascists by the partisans carries a great deal of historical impact. Rossellini has deployed, throughout the episode, various devices to create a representation of what is seen, what is 'happened upon,' in the margins of an essentially conventional romantic story. In this particular sequence, his seemingly casual style creates an extraordinary effect. From the change in daylight it is clear that the long shot and the ensuing telephoto shot were taken at different times of day (or even on different days), suggesting that it was not merely a case of two shots being taken in the same filming session of the same action, with the decision of how and whether to use them left to the editing. Definite decisions were taken to shoot one of the shots and then, at some later time, to supplement it with the other (though there are not enough clues to tell us in which order they were shot). The long shot in depth creates an unexpected event intruding on the story, glimpsed but not completely discerned (the perspective effects accentuate the viewer's distance from the events photographed). The telephoto shots disorient the viewer, bringing him close enough to the action to see clearly all the details, but at first denying him any point of view on them. Then, however, the second telephoto shot brings the events right up into the viewer's face, around the camera, as though the camera were not there (even though it is so obviously there). The rapid, 'glimpsed' shooting of the partisans (the view obstructed) denies the action the rhetorical treatment it would seem to deserve, and preserves a sort of 'discretion.' The cut between the two telephoto shots is almost imperceptible to a viewer at first, because it is done on the move, and with an object passing in the foreground (as the trees have been doing up to now), so that the result is similar to a single sequence-shot.

The shooting of the Fascists is what a 'person' sees who is standing in the midst of the characters; but the film has created no such 'person,' because hitherto the point of view has been narratively (though not always optically) associated with Harriet and Massimo – in this case, Massimo has departed, and Harriet is across the street busy with the wounded partisan. Consequently, the only 'person' left to be 'seeing' the execution from that point of view is the viewer himself. The shot of the Fascists being executed was done on contract for Rossellini by Basilio Franchina at the Scalera studios in Rome. Whatever was the length of footage Franchina supplied, Rossellini cut it down to almost nothing, and used it in a characteristically *almost* off-hand way. The gap between the importance of the event and its cinematic treatment amounts to a kind of rhetorical 'elision,' of which we have already seen examples in *Paisà*. We shall encounter others. Part of the impact of the sequence derives from its all happening so rapidly around you that you cannot be quite sure what you have seen. It would be easy to say that this looked like 'documentary,' but in fact it is nothing of the sort; it is a very ingenious solution, deploying devices for creating point of view and a rhetoric of understatement for dramatic effect. It may also have been shot and edited that way partly to get past the censor, or to avoid provoking too much controversy.

The style of filming used for the capture and execution of the Fascists contrasts markedly with one used for the 'story' of Harriet and Lupo. From the shooting of the Fascists – a shot lasting three and a half seconds, not a millisecond longer than absolutely necessary – there is a cut to Harriet and the dying partisan in the doorway lasting twenty seconds, followed by a close-up of Harriet with the partisan's head on her shoulder as she reacts to the news of Lupo's death, lasting thirty-three seconds, with the background music swelling to a crescendo at the end of the second shot (the final one of the episode). In fact, the whole sequence has music, but it rises and falls drastically in volume (sometimes almost disappearing) according to what is being photographed and what rhetorical character Rossellini wishes to bestow upon it.

The Harriet-Lupo story is joined with the story of Massimo trying to reach his family. The two combine the motif of the reassembly of the family-organism fragmented by the 'disorder' of war. The two protagonists transgress prudent limits: Harriet rushing for the Galleria degli Uffizi despite the entirely persuasive reasons the partisans have given for keeping the passageway's existence secret for really important expediencies, Massimo rushing across the street and so causing the death of the partisan – a death that is, therefore, ultimately the consequence of the protagonists' impetuous desires. Those desires are the 'string' that bears the 'beads' of the many events we have listed. It is a story displaying the form of the melodramatic matrix we have identified elsewhere, and it is told with emotionally manipulative close-ups, swelling music, and much exclamation. The 'string' is the part of the film most compatible with a conventional tradition of Italian narrative cinema. The 'beads,' by contrast, display a variety of styles, one of which we have just examined in the case of the killing of the Fascists.

A completely different style is used for the two British officers in the Boboli gardens, probably the best-known sequence in the episode for the interpretation that is generally put on it. We have seen the two officers strolling nonchalantly around Palazzo Pitti, smoking cigarettes, ear-lier in the episode (the helmet worn by one of them in that scene has been replaced by a beret in the Boboli dialogue). The Boboli scene starts with Massimo and Harriet passing, and stopping just behind them, while Massimo points out his house to Harriet. The camera cuts to a medium two-shot from in front of the seated officers, with Massimo squatting behind them. The officers' parts of the dialogue are in direct sound, whereas Massimo's lines are post-dubbed. On two occasions Massimo's lines are contained in cutaway close-ups of him, possibly suggesting that an original version of the scene may have been shot in ensemble shots, with altered dialogue incorporated later by means of the cutaways. The latter may, however, have been used because in the ensemble shot Massimo tends to slip out of the right of frame at times.

The British are burlesqued, in the style of comedy. Ensemble shots are characteristic of comedy, and so the inserted close-ups of Massimo are a little out of place. Still, they serve to underline the serious implications of the comic nonchalance of the British, and their incongruous detach-ment from the realities of war (claiming that Ghiberti is anticipated in Salisbury Cathedral, and that the Germans are out of their depth). This treatment of the British is a stereotype Rossellini has already used in *Un pilota ritorna*, where they are pipe-smoking, easy-going flying officers, treating their Italian prisoner with courtesy and good humour (when the Italian pilot tries to escape and is recaptured, they apologize and hope he hasn't caught a cold), switching off the radio when it starts to broadcast tiresome news about the war, and fondly tending a cat in the battlefield. The policeman indicates that these British officers are not to be taken seriously by the slight exaggeration (binoculars-telescope) with which he dismisses them: '... and these two are still here looking at Giotto's campanile through their telescope!'

The interpretation given in Italy to this scene does not focus on com-edy, but rather sees the bitter expression of resentment towards the Allies' unwillingness for the partisans and the Communist Party to emerge politically strong from the war: the British are deliberately let-ting the Fascists mop them up before advancing, and so the scene is making a historical point. Whether this interpretation is entirely correct or not – whether the 'use' subsequently made of *Paisà* is entirely justi-fied by the substance of the film – is an interpretative and evaluative question that lies outside the scope of this 'description.' Certainly, if we remember that the scene is the work of Rossellini and Fellini, and that the British officers have already been glimpsed strolling nonchalantly

among the crowd, there is evidence for giving their caricaturesque portrayal (the stereotype being exploited is that of the rather eccentric
English 'gentleman') rather more weight than has usually been the
case. Not only is there a precedent for this portrayal of the British in
Rossellini's earlier *Un pilota ritorna*, but it is to be found in Renoir's
seminal *La Grande illusion*, where the French prisoners about to be
transferred to another camp are unable to get their British replacements
to understand the importance of the escape tunnel they have excavated.

The two perspectives on the scene – as comic burlesque or political
polemic – are not incompatible. Just as the fleeting glimpse of the killing of the Fascists may have been an expedient deemed necessary to get
such politically sensitive material into the film, so the satirical comedy
may have been the most sensible way to raise a delicate and controversial political issue in 1946 (the most audacious treatment of Fascism, the
war, and the Liberation in the Italian cinema of the period was also a
satirical comedy, Luigi Zampa's *Anni difficili*, which, right up to the
moment of shooting, was to have been directed by Carlo Ludovico
Bragaglia, the absolutely archetypal director of conventional commercial comedies of the period).

Comedy also appears in the longest shot of the episode, that detailing
the activity of the First World War major (an Italian 'gentleman' this
time) keeping a lookout on the rooftop – a complex sequence-shot shot
lasting a minute and a half. An expressionist style not found elsewhere
in the film characterizes the sequence directed by Fellini of the demi-
john of water being hauled across the street, and Otello Martelli was
very reluctant to photograph it in the way Fellini wanted. These are just
samples of the different styles deployed in the 'beads' strung along an
essentially conventional, melodramatic 'string.'

The Florence episode has the most 'normal' average shot length of
the whole film, 9.5 seconds – nearly the same as that for the film as a
whole (9.7 seconds), and uses a mixture of different scales of shot, from
close-up to very long shot. It displays elements of the way in which its
construction was improvised – a rather arbitrary documentary introduction, sequences shot in direct sound have lines of dialogue over-
dubbed, and close-up sequences are inserted into ensemble sequences
with background and lighting betraying a different location. The episode hovers a little uncomfortably between several clashing modes of
cinema, and sets out to fulfil conflicting functions: historical witness,
political polemic, legend, melodramatic emotional manipulation, comedy entertainment. The partial and imperfect 'erasure' of the 'story' in

the re-editing has not been completed, leaving fragments incongruously protruding. It is perhaps the episode that most completely, but
most uncomfortably, articulates cinematically the process of making
the whole film.

The *Po delta* episode (VI, shot fifth)

The *Po delta* episode was the result of yet another erasure. Sergio Amidei had set his ending for the film in the Alps – in the Val d'Aosta – with
tall Italian partisans looming over the American OSS operative para-
chuted into the snow to help them, and showing him what the Resistance really meant. *Paisà* was already some months into shooting (it
took six months), and there were practical problems with an Alpine
location and the melting of the snow. Rossellini and Renzo Avanzo
(with Fellini), during pauses in the shooting of the Florentine episode,
toyed with the idea of making use of their aunt's estate in the Po delta,
with which both were familiar from childhood. The nationalist rhetoric
was discarded, they tramped the marshes in search of remembered
spots, and enlisted a local poacher, Cigolani, to help them. Both assistant directors remembered it as the most intense period of the shooting:
'In these days, at Comacchio, Roberto is unusually tense and concentrated. He shoots one shot after another without letting himself be distracted, following an intense thread of inspiration: Federico [Fellini]
and the others attentively and rapidly work to keep up with him.'[35]
Massimo Mida later wrote: 'Together with that of the friars, it was one
of the most improvised episodes. But Roberto had it very clear in his
mind, and any time-wasting irritated him. The only time he got angry
with Federico and me was in the scene with the corpse floating by ...,
where the women had to move up to the edge of the river. We were supposed to give the order on a signal, but we got distracted, and so we
had to retake the shot.'[36] Jolanda Benvenuti (JB), who as usual did the
editing for Rossellini, was interviewed in the 1980s by Ivo Barnabò
Micheli (IBM):

IBM: So this is one of the last sequences of *Paisà*, a film that you edited,
when you were very young?
JB: Yes, yes.
IBM: It is one of the most edited films of Rossellini.
JB: Yes, in fact, Rossellini threw himself body and soul especially into
this episode. I don't know ... he felt it more strongly, this episode of

these partisans. And in this case, he was always present at the editing. Because normally he just told me what I was supposed to do. For this episode he stayed in person.

The *Po delta* episode is characterized by *fragmentation, repetition,* and *circularity* (incidentally, these will be fundamental characteristics of the structure of Fellini's films). The episode has two distinct narrative parts:

(a) the melodramatic narrative of the rescue and burial of the dead partisan, that is to say, his re-incorporation into the social organism from which the German atrocity had severed him;
(b) the typically Rossellinian 'stepping back' to narrate the process that led to the partisan's being severed from the social organism in the first place: the 'suffering' (and in this, the episode repeats a formal narrative pattern that determines a large part of *Paisà* as a whole).

The episode consists of ten 'sections': (1) the retrieval and burial of the dead partisan, (2) collecting the radio, (3) the visit to Casal Madalena, (4) the night-time supply drop, (5) the return to Casal Madalena, (6) rescuing the British airmen, (7) the meeting with the men from Popsky's Army, (8) the defeat and capture by the Germans, (9) the conversation with the German officer, (10) the dumping of the partisans in the river and the shooting of Dale and the British airman.

However, the episode is in two 'parts,' corresponding to the division between (a) and (b) to which I have just referred:

(a) the 7-minute 'section' of the retrieval and burial of the dead partisan, which maintains a continuity of time and place, and consists of 46 shots, producing an average shot length (ASL) of 9.1 seconds;
(b) the *remaining* 9 'sections,' separated by disjunctions in time and place, occupying 15 minutes, consisting of 134 shots, producing an ASL of 6.7 seconds.

The episode's two parts, narratively moving forward, but 'leaning backwards,' are each characterized by a slightly different cinematic style (for example, the first part by a slower rhythm and a *mise en scène* that assembles multiple points of view). As we have seen in the case of *Roma città aperta*, the episode comes to a narrative close at a certain point, and is then 'restarted.' Critical evaluations over the past sixty years have almost unanimously privileged the first 'part' (just as they have tended to do in the case of *Roma città aperta*).

This structure, the critical tradition, and the testimony of the two assistant directors to Rossellini's particular engagement in the filming of the first part prompt us to examine closely the first 46 shots of the episode, that is to say, part (a).

This is the only episode to have no introductory 'documentary' footage. But there is voice-over commentary accompanying the first shot (1), saying: 'Beyond the battle-lines, Italian partisans and American OSS soldiers, fraternally united, fight a battle that the bulletins do not record, but one that is perhaps harsher, more difficult, more desperate.'

The viewer has come to expect documentary footage to precede the 'story,' and can easily assume that the body floating down the river is 'documentary.' Indeed, until it is absorbed into the 'story,' by about shot 6, it seems that way (except that previous documentary footage had normally been cut more rapidly). Moreover, the commentary is very slightly different from that hitherto, in that it contains an element of self-reference – 'which the bulletins do not record' – and a comparative judgment – 'perhaps harsher, more difficult, more desperate' – expressed with a personal element ('perhaps') not present in other commentaries. The viewer is likely to interpret it as meaning that this battle is 'harder' than the ones referred to in previous introductions (in fact, the English airmen, when they are rescued, fail to realize the true nature of the situation into which they have fallen). Hence, the episode is announced as a climax. Hitherto, the commentary did not offer 'interpretation' of the film as a whole, whereas this one signals the final coming together of the Italians and the Americans, 'fraternally united.' Everything, therefore, is subtly announced, in these few words, as different from previous episodes, and one interpretation ('desperate') is immediately suggested to the viewer. The partisan's body floating past is scene-setting, but not in the same way as in any of the other episodes. The scene being set is an intrinsic and essential part of the action, bearing much of the episode's meaning, and this initial commentary is completed by the voice-over at the end of the episode (the only such case in the film): 'This was taking place in the winter of 1944. By spring the war was already over.'

Throughout the film, the voice-over commentary is conveyed through the crisp, precise, emotionally detached diction of Giulio Panicali, who so magisterially dubbed Harry Feist's performance of Bergmann in *Roma città aperta*. Much critical commentary has been devoted to these words, as though they were intended as some final, closing 'irony.' This may be the effect of their coinciding with the drowning of the partisans, but in fact the voice-over is merely continuing the chronicling role it has had at the beginning of each episode. Its explicit reference to the content of the 'story,' however, ('*this* was taking place') is unique in the film, and is the only occasion when the voice-over becomes not documentary, but is contaminated by the fiction of the story.

Episode V of the film (*Florence*) ends with an image of one dying partisan (in Harriet's arms) and reference to the death of another (Lupo). The *next episode to be shot* (though not the next in the final film) begins with the body of a dead partisan. The two Resistance episodes are linked by an almost liturgical iconography of death and worship (the Florentines revering Lupo and the watchers on the bank of the Po paying homage to the dead partisan in the river). The *Po delta* episode brings to centre-stage and analyses what, in the *Florence* episode, we have merely encountered in the margins of the central story.

Shot 1 is a long-scale shot that develops into a close-up, with the body floating towards the camera from the depths of the image, and across the frame from right to left (with a tower on the bank 'closing' the image on the right, leaving the composition open on the left). The camera pans left and tilts down to follow the body, which finishes, at the end of the shot, by passing out of the bottom left-hand corner of the frame. The last shot of the episode (180), with its similar voice-over, has the bodies of the partisans falling from the top right of the frame down to the bottom left. A symmetry unites the first and last shots of the episode, enacting the 'repetition' of the melodramatic matrix. The episode cyclically starts and ends with dead partisans in the river. The placing of the camera in shot 1 on the river itself brings the viewer close to the body, as though a participant in some action that is taking place. On the soundtrack, in addition to the voice-over, is the sound of lapping water and music. The music consists of a held tremolo chord in the strings, punctuated by a three-note arpeggio phrase from the low brass section, widely spaced, that changes pitch in a 'series' (a pattern repeated at different points of the scale), and this very slow but regular melody continues until shot 13. The music effectively creates a sense of slow, quiet, steady flowing. This first shot lasts twenty-two seconds, and initiates an accelerated montage for the first seven shots of the episode (22, 6.5, 5, 3, 1.5, 1.5, 1.5 seconds respectively), after which this section of the episode settles into the steadier rhythm it will maintain. But in this accelerated montage, the cutting of the shots briefly almost surpasses the rhythm of the music, giving the viewer a rapid series of points of view over a musical base of steady movement.

Shot 2 looks across the river, with a village on the far bank, the river going across the frame, and the partisan's body in the middle of the frame, passing right to left, its swift movement in the current measured by the village passing in the background as the camera pans left to follow the body. Crossing the cut to the next shot, the sound of the wind – hooting and whistling – starts on the soundtrack, and this sound will be used throughout the episode, sometimes more, sometimes less prominently. The viewer has the impression of standing on the bank, watching the body pass. Shot 3 is taken from the water's level: women and girls, with two German soldiers among them, standing motionless on the bank, watching the body, with the camera tracking right to left along the row of watchers. The camera's low position, pointing up towards the watchers on the bank, makes the horizon behind the banks too low to be visible, causing the people to stand out against a completely bare sky and, because the line of watchers has younger girls on the right, accentuates the impression of perspective back and away on the right of frame. This is taken by the viewer to be a reverse-angle of shot 2, namely, of the people looking at the body floating past that is contained in shot 2.

Shot 4 must have been the one retaken because Fellini and Mida got distracted. From head height, the camera, looking parallel along the bank, pans slightly to the right to follow a group of women and children who, having crossed the road that stretches out away from the camera, step forward (rightwards across the camera) up to the riverbank, looking towards the body. They are in close-up, and so the camera (and hence the viewer) appears to be in their midst. The viewer is now ready once again to interpret the next shot (5) as showing what these women see: which is very similar to shot 2.

Shot 6 is taken from a similar camera position to shot 3, looking up at the Germans standing among the women in shot 3 – from rather closer this time – one of whom points to the middle of the river and says '*Partizanen*,' the other replying '*Banditen*.' There is a reverse-angle cut to the body in the river (7), similar to shot 2 – indeed, rather too similar, because the body now passes in front of the same church on the opposite bank that it passed in shot 2. The reverse-angle sequence continues in shot 8, this time with a shot from water level of the people seen in shot 4 – a young boy in a balaclava prominent in the foreground – walking left along the bank and looking towards the body, with the camera tracking along with them.

The insistent reverse-angle procedure (showing someone looking, and then turning the camera on what is seen) sews the viewer into the story, putting him or her together with the body's watchers, and inevitably inviting him or her to share the watchers' feelings (which are given a point of contrast by the Germans breaking the reverent silence and calling the dead man a 'bandit'). 'Stepping up' to the bank and then 'walking' along with the body has a ritual, almost liturgical air of formally paying homage to the man's sacrifice. The emptiness of the frame, especially in shot 1 (with only a tiny line of vegetation halfway up the screen indicating a far-off horizon), gives connotations of solitude and despair to the death of the partisan. The solidarity expressed by the watchers on the bank takes on the significance of incorporating back into the human social 'organism' the solitary, isolated dead man, and belongs in the narrative matrix of melodrama – the iconography bears comparison with that of Mara and her mother and sister waiting on the rocks for the Valastro men to return from the storm in *La terra trema*: there too solitude and nature's indifference to man are opposed to the social and family organism. Throughout the sequence, either the body in the water, or the camera, or the people on the bank are in continuous motion from right to left (with the exception of shot 4), and the sound of the lapping water, the whistling of the wind, and the steady notes of the background music all contribute to a single, overall sense of inexorable flow. It is not difficult to understand why the sequence has attracted so much attention.

But there is something logically wrong with part of the sequence. Given that the viewer would find it hard not to see it as a reverse-angle sequence, and that the body is moving downstream towards the left, then when the watchers on the bank, seen from the river, walk to the left to accompany the body, they are moving in the wrong direction. Whether this was a mistake, or whether Rossellini decided to sustain a harmonious leftward motion in every shot (something that we shall see he maintains for the whole first section of the episode) is a matter for speculation. It is not a mistake he repeats in this first section of the film, which preserves a great sensitivity to movement, direction, and sight lines. (If the logic of the shot from the river of the people on the riverbank derives from their being on the *opposite* bank of the river, this fact has been inadequately 'established' for the viewer, and does not cohere with the implied logic of reverse angles that is everywhere established.)

To proceed with our description of the episode's first section: shot 8 of the people on the bank ends with a rapid dissolve into shot 9 of the body moving right to left, away from the camera towards the left, with some reeds just visible in the foreground. The dissolve signifies a jump in time or place, and means that shot 9 is not what the people on the bank (8) see. Shot 9 ends with a more marked dissolve into shot 10, which suggests that it is not what the people in shot 10 see either. This is my cumbersome attempt to point out that the viewer not only shares the viewpoint of the characters on the partisan's body, but also has a detached perspective of his own, as in shot 1, which might tend to be associated with that of the voice-over commentator, a kind of voice of history.

Shot 10 has the camera down at the level of the reeds, through which we see Cigolani and Dale. Cigolani rises and points towards and slightly to the right of camera, saying 'Un altro partigiano morto ...' / 'Another dead partisan ...,' and the shot is followed by a reverse-angle shot (11) of the body in the river, similar to previous ones, but with the body slightly moving towards the camera – still from right to left, of course. Dale and Cigolani have their 'own' view on the body, different from that of the Germans, of the villagers on the bank, and of the viewer. This reverse-angle 'introductory' sequence of the two men is made of very brief shots, whereupon the rhythm becomes more mea-sured as they get into action. Shot 12 has them manoeuvre the boat with Dale in it out of the reeds looming into the camera, so that we appear to be right in their midst (as in the killing of the Fascists in the Florentine episode). Cigolani says that he will get the body ('Lo vado a ciapare' / 'I'll go and grab it') and Dale warns him to beware of the Germans in the tower, saying that he will explode a mine to distract them. Cigolani is the one who decides to get the body, rather than (as elsewhere) taking orders from Dale, and responds to the latter's warning with 'Non m'interessa. Io vado lo stesso' / 'I don't care. I am going anyway.' Dale talks in English, Cigolani in Italian; each understands the other (in a way that has not hitherto characterized relations between the American military and the Italians, and later in the episode an interpreter trans-lates Dale's orders to the partisans). Dale and Cigolani have a special relationship, and their deaths are the only ones clearly identified in the episode. There is no language barrier between them; each speaks in his own language and is completely understood by the other. Dale is the commander, but the first action is decided upon and led by Cigolani. In this opening 'section' of the episode, Dale collaborates in an essentially

Italian action to retrieve the body, an action driven by moral ('melodramatic') motives, rather than by tactical or strategic ones.

A wipe to shot 13 very economically takes us to Dale arriving at the bank, in a match with shot 12 – they almost seem one shot, but the wipe signifies an elision. The music takes the three-note melody into the high woodwinds, and a rocking accompaniment starts up very gently. Through the reeds we see Cigolani rowing from right to left (14), and we cut to a shot 15 of the body moving gently right to left in the middle of the river as we look across to the thin line of the farthest bank. Shot 16 has Dale running towards the mine in the foreground, right to left, followed by a closer shot (17), with the mine looming in the right of frame, the camera looking down at him as he sets his detonator. In shots 18 and 20 the Germans are seen in their tower from below, in 18 one of them pointing to the right and crying '*Schau!*' with an inserted reverse-angle shot from slightly above of the body in the water (19), and in 20 the German on the right passing a cigarette to the one on the left (the movement goes from right to left again), and starting to light his own. There is a cut to Cigolani (21) rowing close towards the camera and slightly left to right (one of the few cases of movement in this direction), and then to Dale (22) using a cigarette to light the fuse of his detonator. As he gets up and runs back away from the camera out of the top of the frame, the camera tilts down slightly to a close-up of the burning fuse. There is a dissolve to a long-scale shot (23) across water of the riverbank, with a large explosion going off in the distance, raising smoke up into the horizon, and Dale lying down for cover behind a dune in the foreground, followed by a shot (24) through reeds of the distant German tower.

Rossellini has gradually set up a parallel montage. Starting with the cutting from the partisan's body drifting down the river, he added the people on the bank and German soldiers. Then he added Dale and Cigolani, giving them their own view of the body in the water. In shot 25 Cigolani reaches the body and, with the people on the bank now gone from this section, Rossellini has reduced the 'threads' from four to two. But with Dale and Cigolani separated, he now cross-cuts between Dale, the Germans, and Cigolani. This is, in miniature, the procedure used for the first half of *Roma città aperta*.

Shot 25 is held for longer than those around it, and is strikingly composed: a pale sandbank cuts from the middle of the right edge of the frame down to the bottom lefthand corner, while from the middle of the right edge of the frame, the thin, dark line of the riverbank curves across the middle of the frame, in deep perspective. Cigolani's boat enters from the left, a third of the way up the frame, and makes in a straight line for the body, which is exactly in the centre of the frame. The image is sparse, bare, yet made of planes of very slightly differing paleness, with the bank going into the distance giving a sense of wide space and of the isolation and vulnerability of the two men. As Cigolani reaches the body, and starts to take off the lifebelt, there is a cut to a shot (26) taken from the same place as shot 20 of the Germans in the tower, looking to the right, shouting '*Shau! Feuer!*' and raising their guns. The sound of their firing is over the cut to a one-second shot (27) of Cigolani, with the camera at medium distance, manoeuvring the body, then a cut to a medium long shot (28) of Dale standing up and firing to the right, then to shot 29 (a closer version of 26) of the Germans turning to the left, saying '*Verfluchte schweinerei!*' and firing in that direction, followed by a shot of bullets hitting the reeds where, we presume (we can't see him), Dale is taking cover (30). Shot 31 repeats 28 of Dale shooting; shot 32 is a more distant version of 29 (in fact, it is taken from the same position as 26) of the Germans shooting; and shot 33 is a close shot of Cigolani getting the body into his boat and starting to paddle it – he starts to move out of the bottom right corner of frame, but turns the boat to the left, and this is followed by a dissolve to a shot (34) of him rowing in the middle of the river from right to left, with the camera panning to follow him as he poles to the reeds. This dissolves rapidly into a sequence-shot (35) of him rowing towards camera and from left to right down a channel between reeds, reaching a sandbank beyond which is Dale's boat, the two getting out of the boats to haul Cigolani's over the bank (37 seconds), with a cut to a closer shot (the camera on the sandbank beside them) of their efforts (36), and of the two boats pushing off again. The music has at times lowered to being almost imperceptible, and the sound of the whistling wind is strong. The sound effects of the men's oars being thrown into the boat are clearly post-dubbed, and very poorly synchronized with the action, which is a clue to the extent to which the soundtrack is deliberately 'constructed' for effect, and is not a direct recording of real sounds.

The very brief shot (27) of Cigolani getting the body has the camera slightly above the scene, looking slightly down at it, and parallels shot 1, which started 'detached,' showing the utter isolation of the dead partisan, but ended with its closeness forcing a 'participation' on the viewer. Shot 27 shows, narratively, the redemption of that solitude, the reabsorption into the 'organism' of human fraternity.

Next come shots of Dale and Cigolani each moving right to left through the reeds in their boats (37, 38), the latter (38) being remarkable for the way Dale disappears behind reeds and the camera pans to follow his invisible progress behind a wall of reeds in the foreground. In the next shot (39) Cigolani's boat looms into the frame from the left (unusually), followed by Dale's, passing very close to the camera and going away, with the camera panning as they move away, towards the shore, where small figures of men approach to greet them as they get out of their boats. The camera has often been held very low, and this is particularly noticeable in the next shot (40), to which there is a dissolve, still of the meeting on the shore, with the camera down at the level of the gunwhales of the boats, looking up at the backs of the men standing on the other side of them. The next shot (41), from just above head height, a *piano americano* of Dale and Alan talking about the latest communication from headquarters, raises the horizon in the background to make the sense of space less broad for the conversation that ensues. The dialogue crosses shots 39 to 42, and starts among the Italians:

PARTISAN: What's happened?

CIGOLANI: Another partisan in the Po.

PARTISAN (*to other partisans*): Lads, another partisan in the Po.

DALE (*to Alan*): What've you heard from Fifth Army Headquarters?

ALAN: General Alexander's Headquarters have the message to cease all operations and for all partisans to return immediately to their homes.

DALE: There's another partisan in the Po.

DAN: These people aren't fighting for the British Empire, they're fighting for their lives.

DALE: What else did Headquarters have to say?

ALAN: I told them we were completely cut off and that from one moment to the other ...

DALE: What the devil do they expect us to do? Have you told them we have no ammunition, no food and no possible means of defence?

ALAN (*off-camera*): I told them our entire situation ... Their answer is still: 'Cease all activity'!

DALE (*off-camera*): What do they expect us to do? We're entirely surrounded by Germans!

ALAN: I'm expecting a confirmation for my last message ... There's supposed to be a plane coming over tonight to make a food and ammo drop over at Cannarin. (*To Dan*) So that there will be no mistakes, we'll light three seconds' signal fires on the beach.

DALE: But don't you understand? If we light those fires, the whole German army'll be down on our necks!

DAN: Well, we'll all die one way or another ... but that's a small matter for Headquarters.

ALAN: I didn't want to get our food supplies by sea because it'd take too long ... so I made arrangements for a plane tonight.

DALE: Alright, alright! Nothing can hurt us now anyway!

Dan's words 'These people aren't fighting for the British Empire, they're fighting for their lives' form the other point in the film that has led to much critical interpretation (similar to that surrounding the British officers in the *Florence* episode). In fact, later in this *Po delta* episode, when two British airmen are rescued from their ditched plane, the partisans are not overjoyed at the men turning out to be British rather than American, but resign themselves to it being 'megio che gnente' / 'better than nothing.' The OSS operatives' words here are seen as an indictment of Alexander, and of British policy towards Italy, usually identified in terms of political conservatism, but here characterized as colonialism. Certainly, resentment towards the British comes up often enough in the parts of *Paisà* scripted by Fellini and Rossellini together for it to be a theme attributable to them – though we shall note that the man killed together with Dale by the Germans at the end of the episode for protesting the drowning of the partisans is one of those British airmen, rather than another of the Americans. In any case, the filming of this section of the episode suggests a separation of the destinies of the Allies and the Italians, as we shall see if we finish our examination of the episode's first forty-six shots.

Hitherto the story has been told through the use of parallel montage and reverse-angle editing. From shot 39 onwards, the emphasis moves to *mise en scène*, with more complex compositions embracing more than one action. All the 'threads' of the story have now been united in one place, Cannarin: the dead partisan, Dale and the Americans, Cigolani and the partisans. Although these threads are brought together in shot 39, with a progressive accumulation – first Cigolani with the dead partisan, then Dale, then the other Americans on the shore, then the other partisans – the two groups, of Americans and Italians, remain distinct and hierarchically separated. In shot 40 Dale goes over to talk to the other Americans, while the partisans go over to Cigolani's boat to collect the body. The 'action' now consists of two things happening in parallel: Dale discussing the situation with the Americans and the partisans burying the dead man. But rather than cross-cutting between the two, Rossellini uses *mise en scène*: first one group entering the frame and then the other, or one group in one part of the frame and the other in a different part.

Shot 41 is just of the Americans, who walk across the camera from left to right as they talk, coming close as they pass, with the camera panning to follow them as they start to walk away to the camera's right. There is a cut to shot 42, a close shot of the partisan's body being carried by his comrades, again from left to right, passing very close to the camera – putting the viewer 'in their midst' – which follows the movement. From the left, close to the camera (at about waist height), enter the Americans, walking once again away from the camera and forming up in a triangular threesome in the right of the frame facing out of the frame to the right of camera. Behind their backs, in the left of the frame, further in the background, are the partisans, who have put down the body and, beyond it, are digging with their hands in the sand to make him a grave. It is a careful composition of left and right, foreground and background. There is a cut to a close-up (43) of Dale, from straight in front, delivering his last lines, whereupon he looks over towards camera left. There is a cut to a medium close-up of the dead partisan's head and shoulders (44), which is logically what Dale was turning to look at, and so is the second half of a reverse-angle sequence – except that the image of the partisan is not how it would look from the distance and angle at which Dale is standing. In 43 Dale looks, but while in 44 we see what he is looking at, we do not see exactly what he sees, but instead are placed very close to and 'in the midst' of the partisans. The arms of partisans reach into the frame to lift up the body. There is a dissolve, eliding time, to a medium shot (45) of the mound of the grave running away from the camera with, on either side, rows of partisans in the frame's edges, kneeling and shovelling sand onto the mound with their hands. In the top of the frame (i.e., at the head of the grave), Cigolani's hand enters the frame, placing the lifebelt on the grave, then sticking in the pole of the 'PARTISAN' sign, which the camera tilts up to show him doing, and, as the camera reaches his head, taking off his balaclava, whereupon the partisans at the side of the grave rise to their feet. Shots 44 and 45 are 'related' to the Americans by 'developing' out of shot 42, and being 'announced' by Dale's glance to the left in shot 43, but at the same time, shot 42 is an intimate shot of the partisans' 'private' experience. Rossellini's procedure has created a quite complex point of view, contrasting an element of 'detachment,' provided by Dale, and yet identification with the partisans, through closeness and intimacy.

Shot 45 parallels in reverse, visually and in the tilting movement of the camera from detail to a larger picture, shot 22, in which Dale used a cigarette to light the fuse of his detonator to explode the mine and distract the German sentries. As he got up and ran back away from the camera out of the top of the frame, the camera tilted down towards the burning fuse sticking up out of the sand. If we took shot 1 of the body drifting towards and past the camera, then shot 22 of Dale, which tilts down to the detail of the fuse sticking up out of the sand, then shot 27 of Cigolani collecting the body, and then shot 45 of the grave mound in the sand, which tilts up to Cigolani putting the sign in the sand and taking off his balaclava, we would have two pairs of matching shots: 1 / (a) the body in the river and (b) the tilt downwards from Dale to the fuse; 2 / (a) Cigolani collecting the body from the river and (b) the tilt upwards from the grave to Cigolani. These four shots 'sum up' the first section of the episode, establishing its basic, underlying iconography and, even though wordless and with little action, establishing its melodramatic narrative.

Shot 46 is of the scene around the grave. The camera has been placed further back from the grave, and about forty degrees to the left of its head. The partisans (three along either side of the grave), taking off their hats, are finishing rising to their feet. The three Americans enter the frame at the foot of the grave from the left, taking off their helmets, and stand in a line to the left, perpendicular to the lines of partisans along the grave. In other words, they 'participate,' but are visually 'separate.' The partisans start moving away from the grave, into the depths of the frame and also leftwards towards the Americans, who then start moving leftwards and away from the camera, the two groups, slightly separated in space, returning towards the boats on the shore. The camera is set at such a height that the perfectly flat, straight horizon cuts exactly halfway across the height of the frame, leaving an image that is half light sky and half darker sand.

As in the *Florence* episode, with the deaths of Lupo and the shot partisan, death in the cause of the Resistance is given a ritualistic, almost liturgical character, bearing religious overtones, both here and in the sequence of the watchers on the riverbank. (All three deaths in *Roma città aperta* were also visually associated with religious iconography.) In the *Po delta* episode, this is combined with the theme of solidarity, and with that of the melodramatic matrix in which the individual is 'saved' from the solitude of disorder and is re-incorporated into the social organism.

The sequence's dialogue appears to be partly in direct sound, and when the Americans are speaking together we can hear the wind picked up by the microphone. This is not, however, the same sound as the whistling wind to which I have already referred, which is also present in these scenes. The latter sound gives a sense of space to the image. These distinctions make clear how the soundtrack is constructed to enhance the effect of the visual image and to express a feeling: it is built up of the music, the lapping of the water, and the whistling of the wind as a continuous background, on top of which other sounds are mixed when appropriate.

The average shot length for the whole of *Paisà* is 9.7 seconds, whereas that for the *Po delta* episode is 7.3 seconds. Hence, the *Po delta* episode's ASL is 25 per cent shorter than that of the film as a whole, and 17 per cent shorter than the ASL for *Roma città aperta*, half of which is constructed in parallel montage. But the fact that the first story segment we have examined, even while seeming to be made up mostly of parallel montage, is more leisurely paced than the rest can be seen from the fact that its 46 shots in 7 minutes produce an ASL of 9.1 seconds. The ASL of the *remaining* 15 minutes of the episode (134 shots), 6.7 seconds, is even shorter than that of the whole episode (there is particularly fast cutting during the battle between the partisans and the Germans). (See appendix 24, 'Average shot length for different sections of *Paisà*.') These figures help us to see statistically how the overall rapid flow of the episode is gradually set in motion, preparing for a progressive acceleration in a way similar to the build-up to the death of Pina in *Roma città aperta*. The forty-six shots we have examined form the first narrative 'section' of the episode, and have a steadier rhythm than will become normal for the episode, functioning stylistically as an introduction.

The sense of fluidity in the episode is empirically illustrated by two features that emerge from the description of this first section: the consistency of slow movement from right to left across the frame, and the movement in depth away from and towards the camera. The overall effect is made possible by the frequent use of medium long, long, and very long shots (in terms of scale rather than of duration). Landscape has not been an insignificant feature of Rossellini's cinematography hitherto, but in the final episode of *Paisà* it assumes a particularly prominent role, which henceforth will persist for a while in his work, and it is a question we shall return to shortly. The sense of space is conveyed by the unusually large number of shots in the 'long' scale and by the low position and tilt upwards of the camera to create a huge horizon (and we have seen in shot 41 how Rossellini will raise the camera to reduce that horizon when he feels it appropriate). A comparison between the scale-of-shot charts of this episode of *Paisà* and of *Roma città aperta* (see appendices 20–22 and 25) shows the *Po delta* episode tending much more towards medium and long shots than *Roma città aperta* (which already used longer scale shots than was normal in the cinema of the time). Moreover, we must bear in mind the way in which the 'calibration' of our classification of scale of shot is dependent on context. What would have been a 'very long shot' in *Roma città aperta* is merely a 'long shot' (relative to other shots) in the *Po delta* episode of *Paisà*.

Our analysis of the first forty-six shots was prompted by suggestions from people intimately involved in the film's shooting that Rossellini was more concentrated on this passage than he usually was in filming, and that he had a particularly clear idea of what he wanted. I think that looking closely at the passage has shown us what that 'vision' was, and how he set about communicating it cinematically. The passage has formal symmetries that do not appear frequently in Rossellini's films (the movements from right to left across the frame, the patterning of characters moving right up to the lens and then away from it, and the patterns of panning and tilting of the camera). It is just one of the episode's ten story sections, yet, at seven minutes of screentime, it occupies a third of its twenty-two minutes. Hence, it is a rather calmer, drawn-out opening section to the episode, which then accelerates rapidly, with far greater ellipsis in the narration. It establishes the environment and its topographical and emotional feel, the flowing movement, and a certain distance from the events photographed, combined with a sense of the viewer's participation in them. It sets up one main event, the executed partisan drifting down the river, on which it then constructs a series of points of view: (a) the German soldiers, whose reaction is very different from that of (b) Italian civilians, (c) an Italian partisan, Cigolani, (d) an American OSS officer, and (e) the viewer himself, somewhat detached and partly associated with that of the voice-over commentary.

It is a critical commonplace to say that Rossellini (as he himself indicated) derived the *Po delta* episode from one specific image: that of the body floating down the river. The whole thrust of this book's argument is that, rather than the 'surface' level of representation, it is the 'deeper' levels of narrative reference that contribute most to the *aesthetic* status of film artefacts as assemblies. Hence, that one, single image of the corpse in the river does not just 'represent,' it 'narrates.' And what it narrates belongs in the melodramatic narrative matrix: how 'modernization,' expressed in this case by the war, conflicts with an 'organic' ontology of the human being. The body of the partisan floating in the river, photographed in a wide, empty landscape, 'narrates' the destruction (or loss) of the 'organic' ontology at the hands of a 'modern' civilization. The retrieval of the body is the spontaneous response of the Italians to that loss. The theme, therefore, of this episode is coherent with that of the others we have examined, especially of the *Sicily* and *Monastery* episodes, and with a theme that Rossellini will elaborate in *Stromboli, Francesco giullare di Dio, Europa '51,* and *Viaggio in Italia.*

This episode and the *Florence* one deal with the partisan struggle: *Florence* with the civil war, and with the Allies not helping, except with medical support; the *Po delta* with the OSS, deliberately identified as American and not British, participating in the Italian struggle against the Germans (there is no sign of civil war in this episode). The OSS and the partisans are cast in an intermediate zone between civilian and military. They are not portrayed as being completely military by identifying themselves with a disciplined 'army' (note Dan's remark 'Well, we'll all die one way or another ... but that's a small matter for Headquarters'). The partisans are not completely civilian (they are distinct from the people on the riverbank, and from those we later encounter at Casal Madalena – even though they have their support). The episode deals with war, but not with the chaos-creating war of armies; instead, it is the struggle for survival of the melodramatic matrix. The Germans are never attacked; the partisans just try to survive and bury their dead. In the section we have analysed they shoot at the Germans just to make it possible to get the partisan's body – to deal with the suffering, rather than to oppose it by fighting or attacking. The episode's protagonists are depicted as the avant-garde of the suffering civilian population. Perhaps one of the reasons for the episode's importance in the history of Italian cinema is that it meets, by the way it uses the melodramatic matrix, all the 'needs' for narrative that we have identified. Another reason could be its aesthetic qualities.

The first 'section' of the episode we have just discussed establishes a narrative and expressive basis for the episode as a whole, which subsequent sections will elaborate: (a) the environment, (b) a sense of defeat, (c) the fact that the Germans dominate the area and (d) that the civilians are oppressed, (e) the partisan struggle against the Germans, (f) the homage to the dead partisan as a form of 'resistance,' and the willingness to risk life to bury him, signifying that the struggle is as much symbolic as material – the upholding of human values in the midst of disorder, (g) the isolation of this partisan band, (h) the role of the OSS, alternating between cooperating and commanding, (i) the bureaucratic approach of Headquarters, the disastrous approach of British policy towards the partisans, and its cost in Italian lives, (j) a sense of vulnerability and lack of hope, combined with (m) a moral determination to restore human 'order.'

The rhythmic 'flow' set up by this first section establishes the link (often created by the movement of boats along the water among the reeds) between the other nine 'sections' I listed earlier, in an episode that is itself episodic, made up of micro-stories. The first section is far and away the longest and most developed, occupying seven minutes, with fifteen minutes left for the other nine sections.

The first section shows Rossellini when he is most patient and conscientious in translating his vision into film narrative. In ensuing sections, he can be less careful, and it might be worth making a list of the elements of 'roughness' that start to appear in the episode. To start with the sound, we have already mentioned how sometimes sound effects are only very approximately linked with the visual image: when Dale and Cigolani pull the boats over the sandbank the sound effects match the action in terms neither of accuracy nor of timing. Sometimes the dialogue is in direct sound, and on one occasion when Dale gives orders to his OSS colleagues, the actor stumbles over the words – it is a brief piece of dialogue, and could easily have been reshot. The shouted dialogue between Dale and the Popsky officer, on the other hand, is post-dubbed, and poorly synchronized. A little after that sequence, Cigolani gives orders to the partisans, but no longer with the voice we have associated with him, and no longer in dialect-inflected speech, but in a clipped, crisp standard Italian – presumably a different performer was used to dub him at this point. Towards the very end of the episode, when the partisans who have been taken prisoner are talking to each other, Rossellini has made a specific choice to dub their muttered lines in a 'close' acoustic that sounds more like voice-over than men talking in the open air (after all, part of the significance of the scene is that the Allied soldiers are seated on chairs in the hut, and the partisans on the ground outside). This was probably less a mistake than a deliberate choice to give intimacy to their exchanges, but it slightly disorients the viewer.

Similarly, inside the hut, during the dialogue between the German officer and the Allied prisoners, the viewer can be slightly disoriented as to the point of view being created by the camera positioning. After the introduction to the whole *Po delta* episode, Dale becomes the point of focalization of the narrative. In the hut the camera creates a point of view for the German officer, which goes counter to how the viewer has been receiving the episode. Shots of the Americans are closest to what the German sees. Admittedly, at this point he is expressing the German experience of the war (the destruction of German cities). Gradually the sequence resolves into a more even-handed treatment, when the German starts uttering Nazi propaganda, and when Dale and he discuss what will be done with the partisans outside, shot in a straightforward reverse-angle sequence.

When Dale and Cigolani are stashing their weapons in order to go to Casal Madalena to get food, they fumble indecisively over what they are going to hand to each other, with which hand, and where to put it. Cigolani at one point finds himself having taken up too many things (the sickle and the gun), and having to put down the sickle and start again, in order to tuck the gun into his belt. It is a tiny detail, but one which suggests that there had been no rehearsal, and therefore no decisions over exactly who would hand what to whom and with which hand. It could be claimed that this fumbling improvisation is more 'realistic.'

After the gun battle between the Germans and the partisans, the Germans lead their prisoners away from right to left (and towards the camera). This maintains the 'general' movement of the episode, to which we have amply referred, and so echoes the connotation of defeat carried by the partisan's body drifting right to left down the river at the beginning. It does not, however, entirely make sense in the context of the end of the battle, where the Germans arrived from the right and the partisans fled towards the left. One would have expected Rossellini to have had the Germans lead the prisoners off to the right, in the direction from which they (the Germans) had come, and to which they were returning. Right and left are important markers of orientation for the viewer of a film, and we have already noticed a similar incongruity in the opening 'section,' where the watchers on the riverbank move in the 'wrong' direction. In both cases it could be claimed that Rossellini was prioritizing the *stylistic* choice of movement from right to left in defeat, over the *logical coherence* of montage. A similarly casual attitude towards the need for coherence in right and left orientation – without any apparent stylistic justification – characterizes the gun battle between the Germans and the partisans, and in particular the suicide of the partisan who puts a shotgun to his own head.

It is worth noting that when the Germans win the battle in the marshes, Rossellini shows the different meaning capture holds for the different groups by having a partisan commit suicide, Dale cast aside his weapon in frustration, and the Popsky officer light a cigarette. In this context, a puzzling narrative choice is that of having a British officer be one of the Allied men killed by the Germans at the end. First of all, the partisans' exchange over the rescued British pilots ('They are not American, they are British' – 'Better than nothing') continues the whole film's negative portrayal of the British, particularly in comparison with the Americans, and may be a residual trace of the American production finance and ideological thrust behind the initial project. The British airmen do not seem fully to understand the situation into which they have by chance fallen. One of them says that if he can be given civilian clothes, he will get out on his own. Dale tells him that he will be shot if he is caught in civilian clothes. He replies, 'Better than staying here.' Dale says, 'I can take you over to the Popsky people if you don't like it here' (Popsky's Army was a British unit, led by a Polish officer, operating at the time in the Ravenna area to prepare for the Allied advance). The next scene in the episode – indeed, the next shot – is of the partisans meeting the Popsky unit. In other words, it appears that it is the dissatisfaction of the British with the partisans, and of the partisans with the British, that leads to the next scene. This negative portrayal of the British cannot simply be dismissed, and yet the Allies who die are not just the Americans. Indeed, the one you would expect to die, Dan (who said they were all going to die anyway), does not. Dale is shot, and with him one of the rescued English airmen. This is a strange choice, because this man has only just arrived in the place, and all he knows is what Dale has told him. Initially, he had totally misunderstood the situation. He wants to get away from the partisans as soon as possible and, speaking no Italian, cannot communicate with the Italians, who do not seem to have a high opinion of the British anyway. This raises questions for the interpretation of the film's ending. It has generally been assumed that the 'sacrifice' of Dale was a product of his intimate relations with and respect for the Resistance, the partisans, and Italians, which lead him to react spontaneously (in a noble but foolhardy gesture comparable to Pina's in *Roma città aperta*) to the cruelty of the Germans. When the man who responds in exactly the same way, and shares the same fate, turns out to have none of the same 'established' motivations, the standard interpretation loses some of its force.

After the lengthy 'introductory section' of the body in the river, there is a lot of story material to pack into fifteen minutes of film, which can lead to great ellipsis (as André Bazin noticed, interpreting the ellipsis as reinforcing the viewer's sense of seeing 'facts'). The parachute supply-drop (shot at Ortebello, not far from Rome) is a case in point. It is a good example of a sequence 'assembled' out of several disparate elements, but the result, while evocative, is only just satisfactory. There is a shot taken from a high angle, with a wide-angle lens, taking in a fairly large area. It is dark but with some reflected sky, giving the areas of water a lighter colour so that we can understand what is happening. The fires light very quickly, whereupon we see people moving in the water. Then we see the fires going out, after which we only see the landscape very dimly indeed, and it is the soundtrack alone that carries the story. The soundtrack is made up of the aeroplane above, and of machine guns firing, of voices calling across a distance, but also of voices whispering. The sound of the guns firing is followed by that of voices trying to call out in something like a shouted whisper. The sequence ends with Dale calling Alan, both more or less in silhouette against the horizon, to go to Casal Madalena. The problem facing Rossellini was to film a scene in which 'darkness' and the inability to 'see' (because the fires lit for the aeroplanes' vision attracted German attention) are the main theme. He solved it by using the soundtrack.

The human attachment of Dale to the Italians is narratively established most strongly by the two 'sections' of the episode concerning Casal Madalena. His association with the people there is connoted by a feature on the soundtrack. On his first visit, as Cigolani calls him to come over, we hear a baby crying. He will offer ointment against mosquito bites (which is the only story element that might explain how the Germans could know that the partisans had visited the place – and therefore his gesture has terribly ironic consequences). When he returns after the massacre, the sequence is announced by a baby crying on the soundtrack (at a higher and more desperate pitch). The baby's role is not just a sentimental device, but anchors the two sections in the melodramatic matrix of the natural family order being destroyed by the meaningless chaos of war, and functions narratively in a similar way to the death of Pina in *Roma città aperta*. The sound of crying supplies a poetic and rhetorical link between the two Casal Madalena scenes.

The first visit to Casal Madalena, in search of food, provides a contrast and moment of repose in the middle of the episode. The friendly welcome (and the intermediary role of Cigolani), the food, the eels, the signs of family life, a large kitchen (with a ceiling lamp blocking part of the shot, casually left there almost as a rhetorical device) function as signs of the natural 'order' that war disrupts. Not only does this element of contrast bring out the nature of the partisans' situation, but it sets up a brutally dramatic contrast with the second visit to Casal Madalena.

The return to Casal Madalena after the massacre is done visually with the assembly of four elements: (1) a static shot of the child standing over a body, (2) two tracking shots (moving right to left) of the child moving right to left towards a body and then, as the camera nears him, looking at the camera (presumably at the Americans) and then away; (3) shots of the two Americans, fairly close, and dimly seen in the dark, moving towards the camera, slightly right to left; and (4) the soundtrack, with the child's crying. The lighting comes from the left (from the dawn). The Americans approach the child from the right. Therefore, what is on the left is lighter than what is on the right. Since the camera approaches the child from the right, the child is backlit (markedly so in the first static shot). To go into greater detail: we enter the scene with the sound of the child crying and the shot of the two Americans dimly coming in towards the camera. This is followed by a static-camera shot of the backlit child standing still, but with a dog coming towards him from the left. After this the sequence alternates between shots of the Americans and tracking shots of the child.

It is clear what effect is being sought. The camera looking at the child is supposed to be the gaze of the Americans. However, the material that has been shot of the child is rather messy, and rather messily put together. Not only that, the time when the shots of the child start to be tracking shots coincides with that when the Americans *stop* walking towards the camera (which is inappropriate, given that the tracking movement of the camera is supposed to be imitating the American's movement towards the child). Not only that, the tracking shots of the child do not match. There is one, first, then a cut to the Americans (hence we are in a reverse-angle sequence), then a cut back to the tracking shot of the child, but it is a different one, even though it is supposed to be a continuation of the previous one: the child is not in the right place in the frame for this second shot to match the first – or, if you prefer, the viewpoint is not the right one to coincide with the Americans approaching. Moreover, the child is not imitating the same action: he does not quite have the same response, in the second tracking shot, as the one he is showing in the first one. The assembly of the three elements is enormously economical, and quite rightly drew the critical attention of André Bazin, resulting in famous paragraphs on Rossellini's 'ellipses,' which he interprets in terms of 'factual' realism. We have pointed out that ellipsis was forced upon Rossellini by the amount of narrative material he had to cover in a short time, and that the material narrated is intimately connected with the hierarchy of narrative reference appropriate to the melodramatic matrix. But the sequence could have been filmed and edited more carefully.

My observations might seem trivial. But we must remember that the second Casal Madalena scene is one of the moments of highest tension, and of greatest significance, in the whole film. This is where the ordinary civilian population pays a terrible price for giving help to the partisans. It is an element of narrative 'content' that is very important, both dramatically and for a representation of historical fact. We are seeing the repetition of a pattern. In *Roma città aperta* the sequence of Pina's shooting was full of mistakes, but it does not matter. In *Paisà*, one of the most important scenes is flawed, but it does not matter. Are these two scenes sloppy because Rossellini was lazy or uncritical of his own work? Or is it because Rossellini, at high dramatic moments, was only concerned with expression, and not very much with form? Is it because he felt that leaving his assembly of images with rough edges actually gave them greater immediacy? Or is it because Rossellini, at the moment of shooting, was not completely aware of the dramatic centrality of the footage he was collecting and, precisely because these sequences were *assembled*, it was only later, at the editing stage of putting the assembly together, that he had to do the best he could with the footage available (and would the first 'section' of the *Po delta* episode be an example of his knowing exactly what he was doing right from the start of filming)?

To explain it all, as is so often done, in terms of the difficulties of filmmaking in the immediate post-war years, with shortage of resources and personnel, does not tally with the fact that *Paisà* had invested in its production more than three times the sum normally invested in Italian productions of the period, that its shooting extended for six months, that it had the finest director of photography and cameramen Italy possessed, as well as an experienced director with, standing constantly by his side in the role of assistant director, the episode's scriptwriter. Nor is the standard explanation compatible with the great care lavished on the initial 'section' of the episode. To a certain extent, these questions bear on the issue of Rossellini's poetics, which is the focus of our analysis of the film, but they are not questions to which it is easy to supply an answer.

Our analysis does seem to offer plausible answers to other questions regarding Rossellini's poetics. We referred earlier to the increasing role of landscape in Rossellini's cinema during this, his 'middle period,' and the *Po delta* episode is revealing in this regard. The episode bears comparison with Robert Flaherty's *Nanook of the North* for a number of reasons. Flaherty's film measures man against his environment and the hardship he has to overcome; like the *Po delta* episode, it is about the struggle for survival in an extreme and hostile environment. Flaherty's film is considered a documentary, but we have already discussed the inadequacies of such a label. Its aim was both anthropological/ethnological and narrative/expressive: Flaherty desired to make a record of the life of the Inuit hunter, but also to communicate his perception of the humanity, heroism, and profound happiness of the Inuit people. Rossellini was similarly trying to record a historical moment in a specific time and place and, at the same time, to pay homage to the courage and humanity (and, by means of the rhetoric of *sermo humilis*, the simplicity) of the partisans and of their OSS companions. Both directors achieve their aims by narrating a struggle for survival, and by dramatizing it through the use of a 'sublime' landscape as an antagonist. There are even visual parallels between the water, the reeds, and the boats that ply them, on the one hand, and the ice, the snow, and the sleds that traverse them, on the other. Both films make great use of shots in the long scale, and seem merely to observe their characters moving within them.

Landscape used in this way has become codified in the cinema, in epics set in the desert or the African savannah, in westerns set in the prairies, and in road movies like those of Terrence Malick. All these films have two things in common: human beings are dwarfed by the landscape and the landscape itself is characterized particularly in terms of monotony. From the aesthetic point of view, this kind of representation comes under the heading of the sublime (in the eighteenth-century sense of the distinction between the 'beautiful' and the 'sublime'). The sublime is not an objective quality of anything so much as a man's view of himself in relation to it, and so can pertain to the grandeur of nature (relative to the human observer); or it can be used relentlessly in opposition to man – to efface him by conjuring up the 'not-man' quality of nature (rather as one might use outer space). In this landscape the protagonist constitutes a fragile, heroic assertion. Moreover, the landscape can give expression to, or even actually contain, an enemy such as the Indians in the prairies, the Bedouin in the desert, and the Zulu in the savannah. These enemies constitute 'hordes,' vastly outnumbering the protagonists and forming part of the monotony of the natural landscape; they are part of the threatening sublime. In the *Po delta* episode, this is how the German occupation is represented: it is pervasive, mostly invisible, ever a threat to life.

Rossellini will make a similar use of landscape in *Germania anno zero* and *Stromboli*. It is a romantic use of landscape, and contrasts with the classical, Virgilian use made by Visconti in *Ossessione*, De Santis in *Riso amaro* and *Non c'è pace tra gli ulivi*, or Zampa in *Vivere in pace*. Germi, by contrast (many have suggested under the influence of the American western), moves more in the direction of Rossellini in *In nome della legge* and *Il cammino della speranza*. For Visconti and De Santis, in particular, their approach was theoretically based upon what they held to be photography's capacity for showing the relations between man and his environment, as formed by and maker of it; the idealist notion of labour as the transformation of nature plays a role in their conception. Rossellini uses landscape for signifying the 'other,' against which 'being' a man is heroic. In *Stromboli* it carries religious overtones that, in an existentialist philosophical climate, held great significance. Antonioni uses landscape in this way – both natural, in *L'avventura* and *Professione reporter*, and urban and architectural, in *La notte*, *L'eclisse*, and *Il deserto rosso*. As we shall see later, so does De Sica in *Ladri di biciclette*. Interestingly, Rossellini can exactly invert this relationship between man and landscape: in *Viaggio in Italia* the desert is *inside* his protagonists, while it is the landscape that contains the human. The film narrates the gradual penetration of the internal by the external.[37]

My theorizing in the 'Realism' chapter might seem to exclude the possibility of the existence of heroism within melodrama, but the heroism of Dale, Cigolani, and the others in the *Po delta* episode is that of suffering with great dignity and *coscienza* (awareness) the struggle for survival in a broken world. The ruins of Berlin in *Germania anno zero* have often been interpreted as a metaphor for the moral condition of Germany at the end of the war, and something similar could be said about the marshes of the Po delta. There is no need to go as far as drawing a parallel between the landscape and a moral condition, for the mere fragile presence of a human being in the sublime monotony of a landscape is expressive enough on its own. Existentialism, as a postwar philosophical fashion and mood in response to the German occupation, is associated particularly with France, and it was the French phenomenologists who were the first and most articulate champions of Rossellini's cinema. It was a matter not just of philosophy, but also of poetics. Italian neorealist cinema, in its poetics, corresponds to French existentialism, and what Sartre and Camus were to France, Rossellini, De Sica, and later Antonioni were to Italy.

The heroism Rossellini celebrates is one often characterized as 'quiet heroism.' Rossellini uses a rhetoric of *sermo humilis*, the lowered voice, to present his partisans and OSS operatives (and contrasts it with the grandiloquy of the German officer). His marshes are not photographed with broad sweeps of the panning camera from a high vantage point, with his tiny heroes isolated in a vast, picturesque landscape, as in the epics we have referred to earlier. Alfred Hitchcock uses the sublime monotony of the American Midwest in *North by Northwest* (1959) to express the vulnerability of Roger Thornhill (Cary Grant) to a pervasive and invisible threat, in the famous crop-dusting sequence. He enters the sequence with two highly rhetorical shots, one from a very high vantage point, followed by a cut to an extremely low vantage point, and the procedure achieves its rhetorical effect. Rossellini, by opening his episode with the body of the partisan floating down the river, seen from the bank, deploys a more subtle and profound rhetoric, putting the viewer in the midst of the landscape, and alluding at the outset not only to the menace but also to the defeat held within it. This rhetorical stance is then reinforced by the narrative, in which Dale and Cigolani put themselves in considerable danger in order to endow with the dignity that it deserves (the derogatory sign that the Germans attach to the body becomes the memorial to his life) the human suffering and defeat contained within that landscape.

Concluding Remarks

The film as a whole, in its different episodes, uses a variety of very different devices to achieve different effects. It illustrates what I referred to in connection with *Roma città aperta* as Rossellini's stylistic eclecticism. The *Sicily* episode has at its centre a long sequence-shot of dialogue in the medium scale, in which the characters create contact with one another; the verbal aspect is reinforced by the continuity of the unbroken shot. The *Naples* episode has another key dialogue at the end; but here speech is relatively unimportant, and everything hinges on the camera cutting from low-placed camera close-ups on Pasquale's face to a higher-placed camera for close-ups of Joe – the very opposite of contact. The *Florence* episode assembles fragments, stumbled upon as though the camera just happened to be present filming Harriet's 'journey' when an event took place. The *Rome* episode depends for most of its impact on the sequence-shot close-up of Francesca at the moment of 'coming out' of the flashback. In the *Monastery* episode, shots in the fairly long scale, embracing the architecture and the community, are extremely important in creating the effect, particularly the repeated montages of fairly static shots of different parts of the institution. In the *Po delta* episode, movement across, towards, and away from the camera, followed by the panning movement of the camera itself, often in the long scale, are what characterize the style in important parts. Moreover, while speech is relatively unimportant in this episode, the contribution of the soundtrack – sound effects and music, but also the child's crying at Casal Madalena and the shouted whispers during the supply drop – is an important element in the construction.

For all sorts of financial and institutional reasons, films enter the womb of their making already formed in most of their important aspects. The stories, the performers, the locations, and the general shape and function of the final object are already determined at the start of shooting. For more than six months before the start of shooting of *Paisà*, many hands were at work on the script, without this having had more than a peripheral effect on the finished product. *Paisà* is interesting because it records the work of its own making. The film grew from episode to episode. Shooting the *Sicily* episode on the Amalfi coast led to the discovery of the monastery, to the choice of location and performers, and thence to the narrative itself of the *Monastery* episode, which completely discarded its various 'scripts.' It also led to the conception of the *Florence* episode, and shooting that episode led to the conception of the *Po delta* episode. The sojourn in Amalfi also led to the discovery of Alfonsino Bovino (Pasquale was originally to have been played by Vito Annichiarico, Marcello in *Roma città aperta*), the caves at Mergellina, and, for the *Naples* episode, a totally different approach to narrative and setting from that originally proposed. Only *Sicily* and *Rome* survived, even in those cases with the former transformed by the discovery of Carmela Sazio and, in the latter case, with the flashback structure imposed during the editing. If *Paisà* were a painting, one would have to say that one can see the brush-strokes, the erasures, and the fillings-in. As usual, the artists themselves are their most reliable critics, and in this case Fellini identifies the joy in the progressive creation of the film:

[T]he obstacles, the doubts, the second thoughts, the dramas, the travails were not that different from those suffered by a painter trying to fix a tint on the canvas or a writer crossing out, rewriting, correcting, and starting again, looking for a mode of expression that, impalpable and elusive, lies hidden among a thousand possibilities.[38]

This is the purely aesthetic principle borne by the film. It is fused with an ethical principle, in which human dignity and respect flow from 'simplicity.' The fusion of the aesthetic with the ethical principle is created by the fact that the ethical principle of simplicity is communicated by the artistic deployment of the *elocutio* of *sermo humilis*.

I have deliberately avoided, for the most part, quoting Rossellini's verbalizations of his poetics, in favour of allowing them to emerge from the film itself, because it is as artist that he interests me in this investigation, rather than as critic (even of his own artefacts). It is, however, necessary to make an exception, because of the extraordinarily revealing nature of the *language* Rossellini uses to describe what I have elsewhere called his 'laziness,' and which I have qualified as being his way of defending his artistic integrity against the expectations of others. I have quoted earlier an interview for the journal *Bianco e nero* in February 1952, in which Mario Verdone asked Rossellini about his love for 'films made up of short episodes,' to which Rossellini replied:

It is true. And that comes about because I hate the obligations which the story places upon me. The logical thread of the story is my enemy. Passages of reportage are necessary to arrive at the fact; but I am naturally inclined to leave them out, not to bother with them. And this is – I admit it – one of my limitations: the incompleteness of my language. Frankly, I would like to shoot just episodes, like those you have mentioned. When I feel that the shot which I am setting up is only important for the logical thread of the story, and not for what I really want to say, that is where I find myself impotent: and I no longer know what to do. When, on the other hand, it is an important scene, essential, then everything becomes easy and simple ... I have made films in episodes because I find myself more at ease with them; because in that way I have been able to avoid those sequences that, as I said, are useful for a continuous narrative, but that, precisely because of their quality of being useful episodes, and not crucial ones, I find – Lord knows why – supremely unpalatable.[39]

He calls it 'one of my limitations'; he does not justify it, he simply confesses his spontaneous ('Lord knows why') inclinations: 'I no longer know what to do,' 'I find myself impotent,' 'supremely unpalatable.' The elements that provoke in him a sense of constraint and conflict ('the obligations,' 'my enemy') appear to obstruct him in reaching for some unexpressed goal. The elements that obstruct him are defined as 'the story,' and the shots ('the shot') whose function ('important for ...') is 'the logical thread,' and which for him seem 'useful' but 'not crucial.' Counterposed to the negatives in his confession are the stated or implied positives. Once again, they are expressed in terms of spontaneous inclinations, rather than a programme: 'everything becomes easy and simple,' 'I find myself more at ease.' The qualities that define the elements towards which he is spontaneously drawn are 'the fact,' 'just episodes,' 'what I really want to say,' 'simple,' 'essential,' 'crucial.' In this whole passage, Rossellini keeps his discourse on an emotional level, except for one abstract, theoretical observation, which he does not so much proclaim as apologize for: 'the incompleteness of my language.' This incompleteness is a kind of laziness that he uses to defend his aesthetic choices against the demands and expectations of others.

Rossellini's whole reply to Mario Verdone is either uncannily astute rhetoric or else it is a groping for words to express a poetics that Rossellini discovers in his behaviour, rather than one he proposes as a program. The Frankfurt School philosopher of aesthetics Theodor Adorno famously claimed the modern age to be that of the 'fragment,' in which 'all completeness is a falsehood' (Adorno proclaims what Rossellini apologizes for). *Paisà*'s fragmentary, 'incomplete,' lyrical ('what I want to say') approach to narrative heralds a new aesthetic in Italian cinema that will have considerable influence outside Italy.[40]

5 *Ladri di biciclette*[1]

Vittorio De Sica and his films have been poorly served by criticism. Lino Micciché offers four reasons for this: (1) the quantity and variety of De Sica's contributions (accredited director of thirty-one films and probable 'director' of a number of others, all of which, combined with his work as an actor, make a total contribution to nearly two hundred films, plus his role in more than one hundred and eighty theatrical shows of various types); (2) the uneven quality of the oeuvre; (3) the difficulty of distinguishing De Sica's contribution to the unquestioned masterpieces from that of the screenwriter Cesare Zavattini; (4) a critical orthodoxy in which 'De Sica's (and Zavattini's) passionate and outraged humanism, and their commitment to bearing poetic witness to a period of great hopes and great disappointments, cannot help seeming obsolete.'[2] In the case of *Ladri di biciclette* in particular, I would add a fifth reason, namely, that prevailing notions of realism have led viewers to see it as a transparent film representing a historical reality, and hence as an object offering few points of access for critical analysis. It appears to tell a coherent story immaculately and straightforwardly, while any meanings that can be derived from the film appear to be carried by the story itself, rather than by the aesthetic means with which it is recounted. The object, the aesthetic artefact, with which the viewer appears to be confronted is that 'story,' fashioned more by Zavattini than by De Sica, who could appear to be merely the faithful executor of the instructions laid out in the script.

The best way to approach an understanding of the film is to start by clarifying its gradual genesis at the script stage. At some time in the first half of 1947, the novelist Luigi Bartolini received a telephone call:

'One fine day, Zavattini telephoned me to say that he had spent the whole night awake, absorbed in the pleasure of reading my "marvellous" book; and so he suggested that I send De Sica a copy.'[3] De Sica recounts: 'One day Zavattini says to me: "A book by Luigi Bartolini has come out, read it, the title and the concept are worth using." It was *Ladri di biciclette*. Bartolini grants us the title and the right to take the idea for a film from the book, for a certain price.'[4] In July 1947 Zavattini writes to a friend: '[De Sica] is asking me to give him a friendly price for the work of adaptation and the screenplay I am doing for him.'[5]

Luigi Bartolini's novel, *Ladri di biciclette*, was first published in 1946 by Polin, in Rome, and then republished in 1948 by Longanesi (Milan), and again, more recently, in 1984. All Bartolini's writings, *Ladri di biciclette* included, are autobiographical, and derive from his chequered life and career as a painter and engraver who maintained that his art was pure, and that he made his living giving lessons. In *Ladri di biciclette* he weaves a web of reflections, impressionistic descriptions and diatribes around the account of having not just one but two bicycles stolen, searching for them in the popular quarters of Rome, and ultimately recovering both. The first-person narrator is motivated by anger at being robbed, by a determination to retrieve the stolen bicycles, and by a condescending disdain, mixed with affection, amusement, and delight, for the low life of Rome. Nested within the story of the theft and recovery of a particularly cherished aluminium bicycle lies, among many other things, the theft and retrieval of the other. His search throughout Rome for both (using yet a third bicycle to get around) is the occasion for his sketches and reflections on the lives, mores, and environment of the populace. Rather than a linear narrative, it is an assembly of digressions, returning from time to time to a central thread – in other words, it is more like a diary than a novel. He finds the second bicycle being transformed for resale in a bicycle repair shop and, after submitting the culprits to charges and interrogations at the police station, decides that since he has got his bicycle back, and has made them suffer, he no longer wants to pursue the matter. Regarding the cherished aluminium bicycle he has lost, he briefly contemplates, and immediately rejects, the suggestion that he simply steal another. Bartolini finds the thief of the aluminium bicycle (in Via di Panico), but is unable to get the bicycle itself. He eventually has recourse to a prostitute who knows people in the street, and arranges for the return of the bicycle in exchange for a ransom. His closing reflections put a retrospective interpretation on the whole saga:

There was plenty for me to get angry with myself about, for having given importance to retrieving (or rather paying a ransom for) a bicycle. But I repeat that there is no finer pleasure than that of retrieving something we have lost or had stolen. And as a corollary you could deduce from this that in our everyday search for pleasure it might be a good thing for somebody to steal something that we are attached to. Steal it from us, of course, as a joke; but without letting it show that it is a joke. And the person who has been robbed runs around just as we did for our bicycle. For besides, no weightier nor greater are the joys to be found in the world in normal times.

Life is nothing but finding what we have lost. We can find it once, twice, three times, just as I managed to find my bicycle twice. But the third time will come along and I shall not find anything. So it is, I say, with the whole of existence. It is a running backwards, to finally lose or die. A running backwards right from infancy! We come out of the womb and we start missing the comfortable bed we have lost; the newborn baby's eyes are closed and already it is seeking, feeling, with its rose petal nose, at the mother's breast, the sweet erect nipple; then, having lost the milk, it searches for its father's hand to guide it in its first steps. We look for too many things before we die. And I shall look for a friendly face and shall see only Luciana's, if I see that: for it would be, in my last hours, already to die with the sun before my eyes.[6]

Probably the best comment on the differences between the novel and the film come from Bartolini himself:

While the film was being shot I learned, from the news items which the publicity offices send around to cinema magazines, the following: that I was no longer the person who had been robbed nor the searcher for, and the finder of, the bicycle; nor was the bicycle retrieved; it was not a case of a gentleman, of a bohemian poet and artist who, caught up in the 'pleasure of the chase,' had cleverly managed to nab the thieves; rather, it was a case of some poor devil of a billposter predestined to crime, a billposter unimpeachably honest in the first part of the film (so much so that to get a job he pawns pans and sheets) but who, as soon as he realises that it is difficult to get a bicycle back once it has been stolen, steals one himself.[7]

Zavattini, presumably working on his own at this stage, produced a treatment (called *soggetto* in Italian), which he later referred to as having been written in August 1947. Retaining a good deal more of Bartolini's novel than the film itself will, it starts by taking an external, middle-class viewpoint on its social material, and neither places Antonio in the social isolation so characteristic of the film's portrayal, nor does it raise the issue of unemployment:

> Every morning hundreds and hundreds of workers leave the suburb of San Basilio for Rome: the majority cover the miles that separate the suburb from the city by bicycle, a few walk or take the bus. Antonio has a bicycle. He is a billposter. He leaves home early and returns around sunset. He lives with his wife and son in two shabby rooms: in San Basilio they all know hardship. They live like dogs because of the lack of running water, the communal toilet facilities, the prices which are higher than in the city. But Antonio, his wife, and his son are almost used to this hardship. Not that San Basilio is bursting with cheerfulness, but those who live there have neither the time nor the desire to take note of the discomforts that someone coming there for the first time from outside notices. A panel of journalists arrives at the beginning of the film to investigate the living conditions of the quarter. They look around, they ask questions – going around with them we see many striking aspects of the neighbourhood. They interview Antonio too. All he wants is for the roof of the house where he lives with two or three other families to be fixed. The panel leaves, promising to publish what they found in the newspapers. Antonio hurries off because it is late, and they have held him up.

At work sticking up posters, Antonio has his bicycle stolen, and finds himself in the company of many similar victims at the police station, where he is accompanied by a friendly and helpful policeman. The next morning he returns to the city to look for the bicycle with his son, Ciro, a rather helpless, tearful child towards whom he is habitually violent. The pederastic encounter is more harshly treated than will be the case in the film, and is situated in a general criminality and corruption:

> Suddenly [Ciro] thinks he sees a saddle just like that of their bicycle. He goes up to it and touches it. The owner of the stall starts shouting, thinking he is pilfering, and gives him a cuff. The boy starts crying; a bystander consoles him, and takes him behind a cabin they are putting up (perhaps he is the foreman), clearly with obscene designs: in fact, here comes Ciro running away wide-eyed; we see him come out from behind the cabin terrified, fleeing. He is not interested in looking for the bicycle anymore, and searches for his father; he sees a hand stealing a purse from the handbag of a woman doing her shopping. A frightening and fantastic world opens up

in front of him. He finds his father and starts crying. Antonio would like to get his hands on the man Ciro tells him about. He is undecided; time is getting short. He ends up going to the cabin. A few labourers are working there. And over there is the man himself. Antonio is embarrassed. He challenges him. The man defends himself with the biggest show of hypocrisy imaginable. The labourers defend him: 'The boy was crying and he called him over to comfort him." Antonio is made to look like a fool and, coming away from the group, gives his son a kick in the bottom, telling him to be more careful what he says. We know that his son was telling the truth. Now Ciro is crying; he cries on the bus, he cries in the tram, quietly but insistently. Antonio loses his patience and tells him that if he does not stop he will smack him.

Antonio accepts advice to visit 'a woman who is in contact with Padre Pio,' who tells him that 'he will find his bicycle, but he must pray.' He takes Ciro to a tavern to 'make peace' with him, and 'with a piece of chalk works out the sums on the table.' Thinking he sees the thief, Antonio follows him to a brothel, where a prostitute, who knows where the 'fences' hang out, offers to sort out the matter for him (following the story of Bartolini's novel). She fails in her endeavours, and Antonio takes the bus back home, together with Ciro, 'who has received another smacking and is crying.'[8]

Zavattini shows the treatment to De Sica:

> My work as a director requires above all an initial anchorage: I have to feel enthusiasm for the subject right from the first words, the first few lines, I would say. The content, the substance of the story, as I think it over, has to raise in me a feeling of happiness, a warmth coloured with enthusiasm and revelation at the same time. The essential features of the story, the basic situations, set off in me a sort of play of vibrations and resonances; and that is the signal that I am participating instinctively and emotionally in even the obscure vicissitudes of these still undefined and imprecise characters who I already feel to be mine.
>
> When I come to translating into images a story like that, I can perhaps get it wrong; and it is not for me to say whether and how often I have made such mistakes. But one thing is certain; that the story, as such, must be that one and none other than that one, with regard to the particular moment, orientation, and I would say state of mind governing my work as a director. This has always been the case with the stories of Cesare Zavattini, my precious collaborator. With this inexhaustible inventor of stories

for films, I follow, step-by-step, the work of developing the plot, weighing up, living through, discussing with him and defining together with him, often for months at a time, every detail of the screenplay. With the result that when it comes to 'shooting,' in my mind the film is already complete in every feature and every detail.[9]

What De Sica says here is very revealing of his way of conceiving a film as a 'whole,' as a complete object rather than as an accumulation of narrative details and characters. The *soggetto* (story) that he claims to have immediately grasped as a whole is very different from the film, taken as a whole – from which one is tempted to deduce that De Sica's contribution to the script, producing that complete artefact expressing a sublime, existential vision, enormously modified Zavattini's proposal for a film that mixed political criticism with a slightly grotesque depiction of local colour.

A team of scriptwriters was assembled, but it did not consist of all the people whose names appear in the film's credits. Suso Cecchi D'Amico explains:

It started out with Zavattini and Amidei. Amidei withdrew because he did not find the film congenial, and so they brought me in. And we did it, De Sica, Zavattini, and me. Then there is the name of Gherardi, whom I never met, and who was in the credits because De Sica had told him: 'We will make the next film together,' and he had died around that time. Then there was an old friend to whom he had to find an excuse for giving some money, Franci. He put that name in too! It did not worry us in the least.[10]

According to Maria Mercader (De Sica's companion at the time, and later his second wife), Sergio Amidei worked on the script for a month, and all agree that his withdrawal from the team was stormy, though two reasons are given for it. His friend, Ugo Pirro, tells the story this way:

At his house, for example, they worked on the screenplay of *Ladri di bici-clette*, at least up until the moment at which, after a fierce argument, and in a fit of temper, he threw De Sica, Zavattini, and Suso Cecchi D'Amico out of the house and refused to work on the film anymore.

As we will recall, the journalist Lianella Carrell, whom De Sica had chosen to play the role of the unemployed billposter's wife, appeared in the first sequences of the film, but from the moment when the billposter and his son started to go around the city in search of the stolen bicycle, until the end of the film, that character, in Zavattini's plan, was no longer to appear. Her presence was considered, basically, superfluous.

Amidei, on the other hand, claimed that no, the wife could not disappear after the first sequences without her absence being justified. Basically, he saw the story as hinging on a relationship between three people. Amidei had no intention of giving up a narrative structure that was correct, but also traditional, and day after day the discussion ran aground, each person clinging to his convictions, until the day when Amidei literally grabbed De Sica and Zavattini by their coat collars and shoved them out of the door.

So, together with Amidei, the billposter's wife dropped out of the film after the first sequences.

On the evening that *Ladri di biciclette* was released, Amidei went to the cinema, bought his ticket and watched the film. When the words 'The End' appeared and the lights went up, he rose to his feet, turned to the friends who had come with him and to Maria Michi, who was sitting next to him, and said: 'I am a shit!' publicly recognizing that he had been wrong. This was Sergio Amidei.[11]

Clearly, the overall structure of the script was already sufficiently firmly sketched out for Amidei to find himself in a minority, and this cannot have been much before the middle of December 1947, because he was present at a location scouting trip for the Messa del povero episode on 7 December 1947. Amidei's own account concentrates on a more crucial point, and, interestingly, he claims to recognize in the film contributions that he made:

My name is not on *Ladri di biciclette*. I can even recognize my work on this film, but the fact remains that my name is not there and officially it is not one of my films. I had worked on *Sciuscià*, with Viola, Franci, De Sica, and for a bit Pagliero. And with Zavattini, whose collaboration had been a bit external because Zavattini at the time was doing *Fabiola*. And so then when it was decided to make this *Ladri di biciclette* taken from Bartolini's book, and we started working on it, I was a bit irritated over Zavattini's lack of participation, his failure to be present at the meetings for *Sciuscià*, and so I had asked for him to be present. And we went ahead, all of us together. But then certain things I did not agree with upset me, I was a bit ill, and in bed, and I told them to go away. De Sica went downstairs and bumped into Rossellini, who told him that I tended to have these outbursts, but later would get over them. Perhaps I really did get over it, but much later, and so I did not do any more work on the film. Suso Cecchi came in for the first scenes, I think those of the Monte di Pietà [pawnbroker] ... I basically had doubts about the whole film, in the sense that I did not find it 'Italian,' I did not find it right at that moment in time that a comrade, a Communist, a worker who lives in the suburbs, and whose bicycle is stolen, should not go to local party headquarters and that they should not find him a bicycle. They were ignoring this type of solidarity, which existed at the time. Why? Because in the background, even if it was changed, remained Bartolini's character, who went off in search of the thief.[12]

More than one commentator on the film has observed that Antonio had only to borrow a bicycle for there to be no film left. In the original novel, Bartolini did not even need the stolen bicycle, but pursued its recovery at first out of anger and bloody-mindedness, and then at the end justified it on philosophical grounds. If the theft of Antonio's bicycle is really to be taken as an ultimate material deprivation (which is not yet what emerges from the first version of the treatment, where the theme of unemployment does not appear), then the 'story' is, indeed, fragile. As we proceed to analyse the film closely, we shall see that there may be more to the story than merely a search for the means of earning a living, and this may be as much a product of themes that De Sica constructs by means of the *mise en scène* as of what is in the script.

Amidei's objection to Maria dropping out of the story is a clue to the tendency towards conventional 'well-made' films that we have already detected in Amidei in connection with *Roma città aperta* and *Paisà*.

In the passage we have quoted from Amidei, there is the suggestion that the episode of the pawnshop owes something to the contribution of Suso Cecchi D'Amico, and all agree that the ending, with Antonio attempting to steal a bicycle, was her idea:

On *Ladri di biciclette* we spent entire days together, because we went around collecting places and situations to describe the Rome of that period. Zavattini has even written a fine diary of those peregrinations.

Perhaps he would have been satisfied with just lining up the episodes and ending the story as Bartolini does, with the protagonist's melancholy return home. I need a sound architecture, carefully to draw the parabola of the story in order to work on it. So I proposed the ending with the attempted theft of the bicycle; the proposal was accepted with enthusiasm, and from that moment on I felt more sure about the work remaining to be done.[13]

A glimpse – how accurate and reliable is hard to tell – into the working of the team is given by Sergio Leone, who recalls:

About *Ladri di biciclette* I also remember one of the first scriptwriting sessions, at which I was present almost by chance. Amidei and Zavattini were there. Then of course the thing collapsed and Amidei dropped out. But what really struck me, in the twenty minutes I spent with them, was Zavattini saying in his northern accent: 'I think the protagonist should go out with his mortadella sandwich wrapped in a newspaper on which one can clearly read the word "*Unità*."' Total silence reigned in the room. De Sica had his back to everyone else and kept his eyes concentrated on the square of sky framed by the window. Amidei and Zavattini were seated opposite each other across a table, and I stood over in a corner ready to proffer cigarettes to the first person who asked for some. After a moment, Amidei exploded: 'Christ almighty! *L'Unità* has got damn all to do with it! If anything, just "tà"!' There followed a long pause of general silence, and then De Sica's voice could be heard saying: 'My dear friends, according to me, what is needed is an apple, a red apple, one of those multi-coloured ones, half red and half pale, and he leaves the house taking a bite out of this apple!'[14]

This account gives support to Suso Cecchi D'Amico's more general reflection:

When *Sciuscià* had come out in Italy ..., it had led to critics, and not just them, in a way detrimental to De Sica himself and to the scriptwriter Sergio Amidei, to place the emphasis on the undeniable contribution of Cesare Zavattini, a noted intellectual of the time, an innovator, a well-known writer of the first rank, the only one among the people listed in the credits of the film to have his papers in order in the scale of values of the artistic world, which relegated cinema to the bottom of the scale.

And Zavattini was again talked about a lot in Italy with regard to *Ladri di biciclette*, weighting the scales in his direction ... Zavattini has never been able to accept the supremacy nowadays universally accorded to the film director, particularly where De Sica is concerned, and this is a matter over which we have never been in agreement.

I had been working with him for more than a year when he asked me to take part in the screenplay of *Ladri di biciclette*. We had already had the sat-isfaction of an Oscar for Best Foreign Film won by René Clément with *Le mura di Malapaga*, for which we had written the script. Zavattini and I were a very experienced team and we complemented each other. As is well known, Zavattini had great intuition and a very fertile imagination. To get the best out of him you had to let him ramble, and be ready to capture the sparks from his rapid fire. Like every true writer, he did not like the patient work of getting the screenplay down on paper, something which I instead, as a craftswoman, enjoyed very much. His passionate attention to detail, to tiny observations, sometimes distracted him from the overall structure, which I instead have to have clearly defined from the outset, and which I always keep in mind.[15]

This was De Sica's comment on his approach to the film:

I had no intention of presenting Antonio as a kind of 'Everyman' or a per-sonification of 'the underprivileged.' To me he was an individual, with his individual joys and worries, with his individual story. In presenting the one tragic Sunday of his long and varied life, I attempted to transpose real-ity onto the poetical plane. This indeed seems to me one of the most important features of my work, because without such an attempt a film of this kind would simply become a newsreel. I don't see any future in our neo-realism if it does not surmount the barrier separating the documen-tary from drama and poetry.[16]

From the scarce and scattered data we have available, we could hypothesize the following contributions to the film:

– from Zavattini, the original idea, the basic story, the capacity for imaginative invention, a passionate involvement with the moral and political implications of the material, the relentless pursuit of con-crete detail;
– from Suso Cecchi D'Amico, a concern with overall structure, and with the shape of the narrative;
– from De Sica a detached, self-controlled perspective on the material, the characters, and events, a craftsman's concern with linking them elegantly together and a striving for the poetic.

What others may have contributed to the film is hard to guess. Oreste Biancoli's presence is mentioned by Zavattini in his diary account of the location-scouting trip to the brothel in Via di Panico in September 1947, and is named by Zavattini as one of the writers when he consigns the 'definitive' version of the story to his diary in April 1948, although no one seems to attribute any particular contribution to him.[17] A month of scriptwriting was spent in Sergio Amidei's apartment, presumably in the period from the end of November to the beginning of December, and including work on the Messa del povero episode and on the overall shape of the story.

By the time we reach the stage of what Zavattini called the 'definitive' version of the treatment (see below), Suso Cecchi D'Amico's ending has been incorporated. Meanwhile, between September 1947 and February 1948, a team consisting of De Sica himself, Zavattini, Suso Cecchi D'Amico, and one of the two assistant directors, Gerardo Guerrieri, with sometimes Amidei and Biancoli present, had been doing research in the field, visiting a brothel in Via di Panico, a 'Mass for the poor' in the Church of Saints Nereo and Achilleo, and a clairvoyant dispensing advice from her living room in a small street off the Via Nomentana.

On 20 April 1948 Zavattini records in his *Diario cinematografico* that he has completed the script of the film (together with, he adds – interestingly – Biancoli, De Sica, Suso D'Amico, Franci, and Guerrieri), and writes: 'I am transcribing the story in its definitive version,' adding in parentheses that 'the first pages remain the same as those I wrote in August last year' – which I have assumed refers to what we earlier called the 'first version' of the treatment. This is odd, because rather than merely *completing* the 'first version,' this 'definitive version' quite radically adds to, subtracts from, and changes what was in that first version. The impression that Zavattini's presentation of the piece leaves is that this 'definitive version,' rather than being a 'treatment' that *preceded* the completion of the script, is a sort of précis of, and commentary on, what has been laid out in the script. It claims to lay out 'the issues in play' before then 'proceeding more rapidly with the bare facts.' It starts with a theoretical justification of the subject matter of the film (coherent with Zavattini's theorizing discussed in chapter 2) by comparing the unexceptional nature of the events recounted with the hierarchy of the media's values:

> What is a bicycle? Rome is full of bicycles just as it is of flies. Dozens and dozens are stolen every day and the newspapers do not dedicate to it even a line in six-point type. Perhaps the newspapers are no longer capable of establishing the true hierarchy of facts. If somebody stole Antonio's bicy-

cle, for example, the newspapers ought to, according to us, devote to the theft a four-column headline.

It then introduces a more politicized Antonio than we encounter in the film itself, which makes a much different use of the posters Antonio sticks up than does this treatment:

> Antonio is about forty years old, he lives in the suburbs and earns the bare minimum to feed himself, his wife, and his son Bruno. They have just given him a job, after a long period of unemployment, working for the Council. And he has had to pawn the family's sheets to redeem his bicycle ... He sticks up his posters with the greatest care possible and sometimes he reads them. He is active in the parties of the left but he sticks up just as carefully the posters of the right.

The bicycle is not synonymous with a job, but is rather a comfort to Antonio, and something that saves him money on bus fares. This means that when Zavattini writes, 'to grasp the full meaning of this event [the theft of Antonio's bicycle] you need to make an effort to put yourself in Antonio's place,' he is referring more to the hardship of life on the Valmelaina estate than to the despair of unemployment. Zavattini is much closer to Bartolini than to De Sica when he devotes a couple of paragraphs to the heartlessness of thieves, for whom he is sure the reader 'would have immediately demanded the death penalty.' At the police station, Antonio receives sympathy from others amid a general agreement that the police's response to crime is in direct proportion to the monetary value of the stolen objects.

From this point on, the narrative of the 'definitive version' of the treatment corresponds closely with that of the film, with the one exception that the ending follows that of the 'first version,' rather than that of the film itself (in other words, Antonio and Bruno are seen riding home on the bus – this will be discussed in the detailed analysis of the film towards the end of this chapter).[18]

The script was in development, therefore, for nine months from July 1947 to April 1948, and shooting began in mid-May. In the meantime, De Sica had been searching for the money with which to produce the film. De Sica himself describes the production environment in which he saw himself as embarking on that quest:

> In a period like that which the life of our nation was going through, and in

the total absence of an organized cinema industry, only individual initiatives could start up and come to fruition. I mean that the problem of costs was without a doubt the determining factor that encouraged these aspirations, these attempts to create a cinema, no longer drawing on fiction but on real life, on a reality already identified and circumscribed.[19]

Suso Cecchi D'Amico recalls how David O. Selznick offered to finance the film, provided it used an American star in the main role: 'The Americans had offered to finance *Ladri di biciclette* if we chose for the main role, in place of Maggiorani, Cary Grant. Today it makes you laugh, but at the time we held a full meeting, and turned down this substantial backing.'[20]

Maria Mercader recounts in her memoirs how, after fruitless quests throughout Europe, De Sica was offered financial backing for the film when he was least expecting it:

We came back to Milan pretty depressed. In the hotel foyer Fabrizio Sarazani introduced us to Count Cicogna, with whom we started the usual halting conversation, full of smiles, of people trying to get to know each other. After a while Vittorio went to make a telephone call to Rome and I found myself telling the story of *Ladri di biciclette*. The Count was such a good listener that I also told him about going the rounds of the producers of half the world in search of alms. Vittorio came back from his call and spoke in his own entertaining and moving way. The result: a man whom we had only met an hour earlier committed himself fully where the professional producers had held back: Count Cicogna declared that he would finance the film fifty per cent.

The rest of the money was offered to Vittorio by a great friend, the lawyer Ercole Graziadei; Sergio Bernardi, another friend in good times and bad, took care of the accounts and of the administration of the company PSD [*sic*, for PDS (Produzioni De Sica)].[21]

De Sica confirms the freedom that this allowed him: 'I found men courageous enough to finance the film in three friends: Ercole Graziadei, Sergio Bernardi, and Count Cicogna of Milan. They were three extraordinary partners. They let me do whatever I wanted. Indeed, they gave me all the money I needed, which was, anyway, very little.'[22]

The shooting began in May 1948, post-production was more or less complete by the end of October, and the film had its first public showing in November (a very warm reception from the Circolo del Cinema of Rome); it got its disastrous initial release in the December Christmas holiday period, being quickly chased out of its downtown Rome cinema by King Vidor's *Duel in the Sun*. Already, in mid-September, Zavattini was at work on a first draft of the treatment for *Miracolo a Milano*.

Having established the film's independence of any authorial contribution from its financial backers, we can return to an initial, preliminary, and *general* discussion of the partnership between De Sica and Zavattini. While for the general public *Ladri di biciclette* is known as a film 'by De Sica,' in the world of Italian film scholarship, the *tendency* is almost the opposite: that is to say, to see Zavattini as the source of the ideas, the story, the ideology, and the realist theories that lie behind the film. There are two reasons for this. One is the 'cultural' prestige that Zavattini as writer (not just for the cinema) and theorist has, as well as the role he played in the institutions of Italian cinema, and in the 'institution of neorealism' (contributing regularly to the journal *Cinema nuovo*, for example, speaking at conferences, running organizations, representing professional bodies). The other reason is that most of the documentation we might use to examine the question of the partnership between him and De Sica comes from Zavattini himself: his own letters to De Sica, De Sica's letters to him, and a large number of his writings, interviews, and declarations. There is plentiful documentation in which Zavattini accuses De Sica of taking credit for a film that in fact was mostly Zavattini's work, and in which De Sica, rather than asserting his own contribution, tries to placate Zavattini, reassuring him that anything good he, De Sica, had done owed everything to Zavattini. The latter will *say* that it is entirely appropriate that a film should be regarded as the work of the director, and that De Sica deserves all the recognition that he is getting; but he never actually concedes authorship of any particular element of *Ladri di biclette* to De Sica – it all evaporates into a rather general notion of the director giving Zavattini's work cinematographic existence. Both De Sica and Zavattini agree that theirs was an equal partnership, and yet Zavattini never seems to credit De Sica with any concrete contribution, except that of admirably executing the script. In short, the documentary evidence we have is not entirely reliable. If we want to know what was the nature and extent of De Sica's contribution to *Ladri di biciclette*, we ultimately have to judge from the film itself.

De Sica qualified his loyalty to 'reality': 'these attempts to create a cinema, no longer drawing on fiction but on real life, on a reality already identified and circumscribed. Naturally a transfigured reality, from which to gather its secret human values, and therefore universal ones, a reality transposed onto the plain of poetry, of absolute lyricism.'[23]

'True,' 'reality,' 'identified,' 'circumscribed' are all compatible with Zavattini's notion of the potential of the camera to give impact, intensity, and meaning to the everyday, taken-for-granted material reality around us. 'Its secret human values,' 'universal,' 'transfigured,' 'poetry,' and 'lyricism' all belong to a philosophy of idealism, to a metaphysics directed not to the particular, but to the universal. If what De Sica says is not just rhetoric, then we should expect him to be carrying out a particular operation on the material supplied by Zavattini – one not necessarily in conflict with Zavattini's contribution, but superimposed, as it were, upon it, and in harmony with it. And when we examine *Ladri di biciclette* closely, this is exactly what we do find. Neither De Sica without Zavattini (films made in collaboration with other writers) nor Zavattini without De Sica (scripts directed by other directors) ever reached the aesthetic achievements that they reached together.

After *Ladri di biciclette*, the two together made *Miracolo a Milano* and *Umberto D.*, which De Sica occasionally referred to as his most cherished work, but whose screenplay was the work of Zavattini alone. In the post-1949 reactionary political climate, and in the restored world of the commercial cinema, *Umberto D.* was avant-garde, and marginal, as were Visconti's *La terra trema* and Rossellini's *Francesco giullare di Dio* – 'art films' in a market not yet set up for them, and not really to be set up until 1960. In this perspective, we could venture that *Ladri di biciclette* got the balance exactly right, and that the esteem in which it has been held for half a century attests to the fact. Indeed, we should be faced with a situation slightly similar to that which we have encountered above with *Roma città aperta* (which Rossellini subsequently 'rejected') and *Paisà* – an artistic movement, not in the sense of a 'school,' but in the sense of change, development and progression ahead of the rate of viewers' ability to keep up.

When De Sica describes Zavattini's first approach to him regarding the novel of *Ladri di biciclette*, he says, 'it is worth taking the title and the idea' – not the 'story,' but the *title* and what might nowadays be called 'the concept.' From a letter of Bartolini to the editor of *L'italiano*, we learn, in fact, that De Sica only actually acquired the rights to film the novel on 13 November 1947, well after the first treatment had been written (August), some scriptwriters had started work, and location and 'event' scouting had taken place (September).[24] Everything indicates a gradual process of pruning away ever more residues of Bartolini's novel, and accumulating small self-contained narrative episodes, like 'sketches,' which then had to be linked coherently together and fitted into an overall structure.

The film's title indicates, with no qualification or context, a common, banal feature of everyday life in Rome at the time. After the war, cars and fuel were scarce and expensive, and bicycles a common way of getting around; indeed, a bicycle took on particular meaning when the Germans, during the occupation of Rome, prohibited their use, because they had been used in terrorist attacks against German troops (there is an allusion to this in Zavattini's 'first version'). Easy to steal and then to sell, their theft was part of the thriving and essential black-market economy on which Rome survived. As 'a concept' for a film, the subject might be entirely appropriate for the comedies set among the *popolo* (of which Mario Bonnard's films are a good example), but incongruous for a serious dramatic work. The kind of comedy that a Bonnard, a Righelli, or a Bragaglia might have made around the subject would have told of the lives, the environment, and the vicissitudes of the community in which bicycle thieves worked, their loves, their run-ins with the police, their relations with their clients and victims – *not*, in other words, what we find in *Ladri di biciclette* (with the exception of the scenes set in Trastevere), but rather more like what Bartolini gives us in his peregrinations through popular Rome. Zavattini leapt on the concept of a man desperately searching for the bicycle that has been stolen from him, and on the *title*, claiming later to have discarded everything else of Bartolini's.

When we look at the two 'soggetti' that Zavattini wrote, especially the first, we find a great deal more than just the title lifted from Bartolini: the meaning of the bicycle, its pecuniary value, the stubborn determination to retrieve the stolen one and none other, the prostitute, and the attitude towards thieves as parasites who offend against notions of human fellowship. One wonders whether De Sica might not have been the one who most thoroughly brought about the real discarding of Bartolinian material.

Ladri di biciclette breaks down the barrier between comedy and serious artistic cinema. De Sica's and Zavattini's cinematic background and training lay in the upper reaches of comedy, while their social, moral, and philosophical consciences demanded something more ambitious, already developed quite highly in *I bambini ci guardano, La porta del cielo*, and *Sciuscià*. From *Scuscià* onwards (with the exception of the fable of *Miracolo a Milano*), the titles of their films heralded their lowering of the rhetorical register towards that of comedy – *Sciuscià*,

Ladri di biciclette, Umberto D., Il tetto – and towards the magnification of the microscopic details of everyday life that lay at the heart of Zavattini's project for a socially effective cinema.

Locations

Since one of the aims and achievements of *Ladri di biciclette* the film is to set the character of Antonio against an urban social landscape, and measure his experience of it, it is appropriate to see how that landscape is assembled and endowed with expressive status. Everything in the film bespeaks a specific time and place: 1947, and not just Rome, but clearly defined zones and social classes in Rome. The time and place are denoted and connoted by location shooting and, on the soundtrack, by the fact that almost every line of dialogue in the film is spoken in Roman dialect (the exception is the church mission to the poor, where the middle-class characters speak standard Italian). I have decided to approach the question of location by providing the reader with a map of Rome, with numbered locations marked on it, and to discuss briefly the locations used in the filming in the order in which they appear in the narrative. (See Appendix 27, 'Map of locations in Rome,' pp. 454–5).

The numbered locations on the map are where the respective scenes were actually filmed, and are clearly recognizable to this day. Some of them are actually named in the film: (1) Valmelaina, (2) Via della Paglia, (6) Via Francesco Crispi, identified by Antonio as 'al Florida,' the name of a cinema in that street, (7) Piazza Vittorio, and (8) Porta Portese. Location 10, the Church of Saints Nereo and Achilleo, of the Mass for the poor, was a well-known and eminently recognizable institution. Some of the locations actually used for the filming are not compatible with the movements of the characters in the story, and are not named – for example, location (12), the Ponte Duca d'Aosta (*ponte* means 'bridge'), where Antonio fears Bruno has ended up in the river, is much too far from locations 10 and 11 to fit with the story. Other locations are not named, but are perfectly compatible with the unfolding of the story – for example, locations 4, Porta Pia, and 5, Porta Pinciana, or location 8, Porta Portese, followed by 9, the Ponte Palatino. There are some locations about which I know neither where they were supposed to take place nor where they were actually filmed, such as the Monte di pietà (the pawnbroker's) and the municipal billposting office.

(1) Valmelaina, is about seven miles from the centre of Rome, off the

map diagonally to the top right. In 1947 it was in the middle of a sort of waste-countryside. Now the city has extended to meet it. Valmelaina figures much more prominently in Zavattini's original 'treatments' for the film than it does in the finished film. In the first treatment, he located the Ricci home in the suburb of San Basilio, which is an urban resettlement area similar to Valmelaina slightly to the east and just a little closer to the main city: there was to be a commission of journalists investigating conditions in the community, as well as explicit political activity originating from the quarter (see the description Zavattini gives of San Basilio earlier in this chapter). In the second treatment, less importance is given to conditions in Valmelaina: ('in Antonio's flat, it drips right onto the bed when it rains. He lives in one of those glum apartment blocks in Val Melaina that do not even have a toilet. I admit that there are those who are worse off than our Antonio'). Instead, the film allows the *mise en scène* to carry much of the expressive weight of the use of the location.

A present-day, non-Italian viewer of the film can benefit from the explanation of the significance of Valmelaina, and of the social and topographical disposition of the city of Rome, given by Pierre Sorlin in his study *European Cinemas, European Societies 1939–1990*:

Rome is the largest city in Europe with a municipal territory almost as wide as Greater London. In *Shoeshine* the two boys often sleep in a barn with horses and on one occasion they enter the centre of the city on horseback. This was 1946, but four decades later there were still farms, barns and small groups of houses which could only be reached along unasphalted roads but which were nevertheless 'in Rome.' The Italian capital has for a long time been a city, plus suburbs, plus a no man's land.

When the kingdom was unified in 1871 Rome had only 200,000 inhabitants. The city, kept inside the Roman wall, was divided into three sectors. The West was the traditional, popular, overcrowded district ... The South was composed mostly of Roman ruins. The East was occupied by sumptuous mansions surrounded with parkland. The regal government decided to transform the old, half-ruined city into a modern capital. As it needed ground to erect a central station, offices and blocks of flats it spent enormous amounts of money to buy the parks and lay out rectangular streets ... Before the war Rome had 1,200,000 inhabitants, many of whom were unemployed immigrants settled in shanty towns hastily established all around the city. Fascism, irritated by this unpleasant image, had promised to demolish all shanty towns and build proper housing for everyone.

Some construction sites were set up quite far out from the city walls, because land was cheaper there and also because this would remove the proletariat from the city centre. Val Melaina, where *Bicycle Thieves* begins, is a full five miles from the Roman wall. Later, the entire stretch along the road was built up, but in 1947 this was an urban desert, a gap of several miles. Distance is a fundamental feature of the film. There are no jobs in a new neighbourhood, a neighbourhood that is not even finished yet. The distance from the centre prevents the men from going into town to look for work. From this point of view fascism has been successful and even in 1947, three years after the Liberation, the administrative delegation at Val Melaina checked all proposals and controlled the labour force ... The Val Melaina estate is not finished, there is no running water in the flats, the streets are not paved, but there is no money and no will to complete it.[25]

(2) Via della Paglia, right in the centre of the old popular quarter of Trastevere, is where the film situates the apartment of the Santona (her name means literally 'the big holy woman,' but idiomatically it denotes her link with the spiritual, her mature age, and the respect in which she is held). In reality, the real Santona, on whom the figure is based, did not live in Trastevere, but in a narrow winding street called Via delle Isole, in a tiny quarter surrounded by the more comfortable, modern residential area of the city on the Via Nomentana opposite Villa Torlonia, slightly north-east of location 4 on the map.
(3) Monte Sacro is where Bruno works at a petrol pump, and where Antonio drops him off on the way to his first day of work. It is a commune part-way between the 'satellite' settlement of Valmelaina and the established city itself. Antonio arrives here by bus to collect Bruno after the theft. As an identifiable half-way point, it partly establishes the distance separating Valmelaina from the main part of the city.
(4) The next shot of Antonio, after he has dropped off Bruno at Monte Sacro (3), shows him cycling through Piazzale Porta Pia, a gateway in the original walls of the city, at the edge of the more modern, established, comfortable central zone of the city. This is also where he comes, after reporting the theft to the police, to catch the bus home. In the film's narrative, it is depicted as the threshold of the zone that the working classes enter to carry out official (in this case, council) work, but which they must leave in order to return to the centrifugally located residential zones set aside for them. Porta Pia is used by the narrative for Antonio's arrival and departure in this zone from which he is socially excluded.

(5) Antonio is given his lesson in sticking up posters in Porta Pinciana. The two boys are begging from the business and bureaucratic denizens of this area (the man they approach dressed in a 'uniform' denoting his status).

(6) Antonio's bicycle is stolen from him in Via Francesco Crispi, he chases the thief into Largo del Tritone, and is carried by the taxi into the Traforo del Quirinale (the tunnel). This zone, close to the institutions of the government of Italy, is the political and business centre of the city, which the poor are shown as entering in order to serve, to beg, and to steal. When Antonio has recourse to the organs of that government to protect his property and his livelihood, their representative (the police) has more important things to do, namely, to control and suppress the working classes by policing a workers' rally.

Zavattini's 'definitive' treatment of the film locates the police station at the Fontana di Trevi, which is a couple of hundred yards from Largo del Tritone (6). I do not know whether the scene was actually filmed there.

(7) Piazza Vittorio Emanuele II is where the first second-hand market is held. This market constitutes a 'transition' from the conventional, official, law-abiding world to the 'underworld.' It is in the wealthier East of the city, part of the more modern city centre, and Antonio is brought to it by municipal employees. The younger dustman wonders whether they should not have gone to Porta Portese (8) first, if what they were looking for was stolen goods.

(8) Porta Portese is where the second market is held. It grew up there at the end of the war, in 1945, when the old popular market in Campo de' Fiori was closed down. Antonio and Bruno shelter from the rain, and are surrounded by German seminarians, under a cornice of the nearby Istituto San Michele, which had served for a time as a penal institution. The Campo de' Fiori market had been hitherto the traditional location for the *popolo* of Rome in the cinema. The square is in the western, popular district, close to the river. Its market was immortalized in Mario Bonnard's popular and successful comedy starring Aldo Fabrizi and Anna Magnani, *Campo de' Fiori* (1943), and we have already quoted (in the chapter on *Roma città aperta*) Rossellini attributing the genesis of neorealism to the depiction of the *popolo* in that and other films, and to the role of the performers in the depiction. Porta Portese is in Trastevere, an older, popular quarter of Rome. An 'underworld' is depicted here, and it is by penetrating into this world that Antonio begins his descent towards crime himself. The failure of the search in Piazza Vit-

torio starts off the theme of failure and isolation (he is no longer accompanied in his search by friends), and the exploration of the popular underside of Rome. This is the main theme of Bartolini's novel: the artist is a middle-class bohemian whose search for the stolen bicycles is in large part an exciting travelogue through the Roman social undergrowth. The film, however, uses this 'transition' for another purpose, that of assembling its existential 'vision,' and not principally for a lively presentation of 'local colour.' Here, at Porta Portese, in fact, Antonio immediately encounters the thief, who partly stands for that undergrowth; and a large part of the rest of the film involves contact with this underworld of deprivation (the Messa del povero, the clairvoyant's apartment, the brothel, and the poverty of the thief's home). Bartolini's perspective of amused curiosity at the vitality of this world is partly preserved in the film; but the viewer is also prompted to give it a 'reading' through Antonio's eyes, as pulling him down to its level – precisely one of the things against which the possession of a job and a bicycle protected him. Hence, the move to the location of Porta Portese is an important transition in a narrative in which Antonio's anxiety is given concrete, visual, social form, and towards which the sublime, existential 'vision' of the film as an overall artefact is reaching.

(9) Antonio and Bruno follow across the Ponte Palatino the old man whom they had seen talking with the thief at Porta Portese.

(10) Don Luigi Moresco, who died in 1942, established a Messa del povero in the church of Saints Nereo and Achilleo, an ancient basilica beside the Caracalla baths. The church is located in the classical, archaeological zone of Rome, and in the spacious centre of the city (rather than in the 'popular' periphery). The poor have to leave their zone, and enter the zone of the comfortable, secure middle classes and tourists, in order to receive temporary charity and indoctrination in the spiritual necessity of their suffering. To get from the Ponte Palatino to the church, Antonio and Bruno would have had to follow the old man through some of the most famous classical and archaeological landscapes in the urban world. Nowhere does the film photograph this conventional, picturesque, and 'cultural' Rome. From the point of view of topography, the dissolve from the old man walking onto the bridge to him going up to the door of the church is a major ellipsis (the distance to be travelled is considerable, and would take quite a long time). But it is made necessary by the film's choice to 'elide' a conventional representation of Rome as spectacle.

The film's most drastic distortion of topography takes place when

Antonio and Bruno quarrel in the garden of the church. Antonio looks around for the old man, whereupon the camera cuts to a reverse-angle shot of what Antonio 'sees': the Ponte Duca D'Aosta (shot 433 in the film, and location 12 on the map). A little later, after the slap he administers to Bruno in the garden, we see Antonio admonishing his son to start walking, with the bridge in the background. De Sica uses montage to conflate two entirely different parts of the city in a single reverse-angle sequence.

(11) After Antonio's slap, Bruno and he, apart, cross Piazzale Numa Pompilio, close to the church.

(12) Antonio searches for the old man along the banks of the Tiber, and fears that it is Bruno who has fallen into the river, at the Ponte Duca d'Aosta. As we have seen, from a topographical point of view, the choice of location is implausible. Not only that, Antonio and Bruno, after emerging from the church, would have had to walk to the northernmost edge of the main city, and then return to the centre once again to eat in the restaurant. The bridge and its location were probably chosen for their expressive potential in the narrative. Back in the centre of the city, the banks of the Tiber are massively built up with masonry, and would look unconvincing as a place where a child might accidentally slip into the river. Here, instead, the river is easily accessible. Perhaps more important are the architectural features of the bridge itself, with its stiff, perpendicular, monumental construction. This makes possible the striking telephoto shot of a tiny Bruno at the top of the enormous ramp of steps to the side of the bridge, which the viewer is prompted to read as Antonio's point of view on his son at that moment (solitary, abandoned, tiny, overwhelmed by the city). It also permits De Sica to photograph Antonio rushing into the tunnel (which carries the towpath) in fear for his son's safety. The tunnel repeats the motif of Antonio rushing into a tunnel (at the Largo del Tritone) in pursuit of his purloined bicycle, and in despair at the implications of its loss. De Sica here may very well have been exploiting the viewer's memory of the earlier sequence, for the expressive purposes of superimposition, since it is a resource he uses throughout in his assembly of the film's narrative and of its overall 'vision.'

(13) The restaurant where Antonio takes Bruno to make peace with him is on a street called the Passeggio di Ripetta, close to the eastern bank of the Tiber, in a respectable (rather than 'popular') residential zone of the city. The location itself partly reinforces the narrative content of the scene that takes place there, for Antonio's low social rank makes him out of place in the restaurant.

The walk from the restaurant to Via della Paglia (2) to consult the Santona is elided in the film by a dissolve. Since Antonio encounters the thief as he comes out of her apartment, and follows him to a nearby brothel, the brothel must also be in Trastevere; and since Antonio collars and harangues the thief immediately after coming out of the brothel, and the thief's neighbours congregate around them, the ensuing episode must be taken as also occurring in a street in the same part of Trastevere. Hence, the low life of Rome is firmly given its home in Trastevere. While, for the purposes of the film's narrative, the Santona, the brothel, and the thief's apartment have to be in neighbouring streets, in many accounts of the film's story and its making (and in Zavattini's first treatment), the encounter with the thief's neighbours is supposed to take place in Via di Panico (partly because this street figures prominently in Bartolini's novel and partly because the real brothel that the filmmakers visited while they were researching the script is located in Via di Panico), which is not in Trastevere, and instead is situated within a couple of hundred yards of location 14 on the map. This too is an old, popular quarter of the city.

(14) After the unsuccessful encounter with the thief, there is a dissolve to Antonio and Bruno walking down Via della Rondinella.

(15) After another dissolve, eliding time and space, Bruno is shown nearly being knocked down by passing cars as he crosses the Lungotevere Flaminio (a wide street, contrasting markedly with the small, narrow streets of the previous scenes). This is consonant with their progress north along the Tiber towards the stadium, although, if they were walking home, they would not be taking a plausible, direct route. Zavattini's definitive treatment explains something that is only implicit in the film when Bruno is sent off to catch the tram: 'Here they are in Via Flaminia, in the neighbourhood of the Stadium, where they will catch a tram, then after the tram a bus, then another bus to Montesacro.'

(16) The film ends with Antonio's botched, improvised attempt to steal a bicycle in the vicinity of the Stadio Flaminio, also called at the time Stadio Nazionale. Bruno sits on the kerb, and tries to catch a tram in Via Flaminia.

Performers and Costume

De Sica's concern not to recycle the same faces in the cinema pre-dates neorealism, for he is already declaring in 1942:

I like above all faces that are, so to speak, as yet unseen: actors who are not actors, who have not yet been corrupted by the profession and by constant practice, in whom everything is genuine and fresh. If I could, I would choose my performers from the streets, from among the crowd.

...

I mean to say that, convinced as I am that the cinema needs faces that are new and have not been over-exposed (whereas in our films we always see the same faces, which, made up or photographed slightly differently each time, come round and round with the monotony of carousel horses), I have done my best – helped in this by the scripts I have chosen – to show in my films little-known or totally unknown faces.[26]

He is already theorizing a desire for 'movement' away from repetition and convention in the cinema. Interestingly, experience of working closely with Zavattini, whose theories, as we have seen, privilege the use of 'real' people, rather than icons who imitate them, does not lead De Sica to the same 'theorization' of the use of actors 'taken from the streets.' Instead, he describes his choices as being determined by artistic – aesthetic and technical – considerations. When he talks about *Sciuscià*, one even finds a question of taste interfering with what seem more important questions of authenticity:

The problem of the performers arose. Actors or non-actors? I should like to declare at this point that the choice of so-called actors 'taken from the streets' is never preordained for me, and is not the result of a rigid attitude. There are characters which require professional actors, there are others which can only come alive in a certain particular face, irreplaceable, and only to be found in real life. It was very difficult to find the two boys for *Sciuscià*. Cappellone and Scimmietta could not play them: too ugly, almost deformed. The long search began; hundreds of parents brought their children along, the same weary procession which would be repeated for *Ladri di biciclette*.[27]

Nevertheless, his ideas are clearly taking a turn towards those of Pudovkin, for whom the cinema, by its nature, requires performers who visually embody a type (a matter to which we shall return):

The faces for a film's characters must at all costs, I believe, be sought outside the circle of professional actors. The cinema captures from the actor that moment and those nuances which are not possible in any other kind of performing art: this permits the effective use of non-professional actors. And it is among them, in most cases, that you find the perfect correspon-

dence between the face of the actor and that of the character you are creating. The question of the typage of the characters, whose essence is defined
by their specific characteristics, should never be ignored: otherwise, if the
character were not to find its actor, it would be better not to create it.[28]

De Sica's virtuosity and versatility as an actor was legendary. Hence
he could be seen as having precise technical reasons for preferring
material that he could more easily mould to his intentions than would
be the case with professional actors. Massimo Mida recalls:

I have two indelible memories of him. The first is tied to certain screen
tests that he was doing – this was in 1942 – at Cinecittà, to choose the protagonist for *Teresa Venerdì* (the choice was Adriana Benetti, my companion
at the Centro Sperimentale di Cinematografia). Well, I shall never forget
how Vittorio, before the astonished eyes of the girls, performed the scene
which had been prescribed; no other director, at least at that time, could
count on such a direct, immediate technique. He was so good that he imitated the gestures and movements of an adolescent in such a way as to
completely transform himself, with his talents as an actor, and get inside
the psychology of a young and inexperienced woman. All that was necessary, therefore, was to imitate him, to follow him, to use the same mimicry
he did. When he later came to get performances from the actor taken from
the streets for *Ladri di biciclette*, Lamberto Maggiorani, or the boys for
Sciuscià, Vittorio De Sica carried on using that system, and we all know
with what fine results. Certainly, this was not the only way to get a performance out of an improvised actor: Rossellini ... used something different,
the stick and the carrot, until he was satisfied with the results.[29]

Nevertheless, De Sica gave importance to the 'authenticity' deriving
from the spontaneity of the performers' own personalities: 'As for my
way of directing actors, I should like to point out that it is not always true
that I show them the scene, acting it out for them; on the contrary, I fear
that this can have its dangers, leading to a depersonalization of the actor.
Therefore, whenever I can, I limit myself to explaining what I want.'[30]

By the time he was making *Il tetto*, and later *L'oro di Napoli* (in which
he acted himself), he was talking in terms of mixing professional and
non-professional actors in the same film: 'Mixing professional actors
with those taken from the streets is something I have already tried once
in *Miracolo a Milano*, where Stoppa, Bragaglia, and the others did not
look out of place beside the "tramps." Thus, I think the result was sufficiently positive to merit a second try.'[31]

The implication is that in a film like *Ladri di biciclette*, there was no such 'mixing.' It is important, therefore, to make clear that the minor characters in all De Sica's films have been predominantly professional actors. When the filmmakers and subsequent commentators say that *Ladri di biciclette* was shot with actors 'taken from the streets,' they are referring only to the three protagonists (the three members of the Ricci family, Antonio, Maria, and Bruno). As far as I can tell, the other characters are played by professional actors, with one or two possible exceptions. Even Massimo Randisi, who plays the middle-class boy in the restaurant, acted in a major Italian production in the same year. De Sica told Zavattini: 'If the Santona herself played the role of the Santona in the film the result would be something superb.'[32] In fact, a highly experienced actress, Ida Bracci Dorati, performs the role in the film.

The search for the right 'faces' for the protagonists was a long one, as De Sica's assistant, Luisa Alessandri, recounts: 'The search for the protagonist was long and laborious: for months I went around construction sites looking for the right face. We made lots of screen tests, even on Ferzetti, at that time a young and unknown actor: he was good-looking and very talented, but he resembled so much Laurence Olivier!'[33]

It was while they were auditioning children, brought by their parents, for the role of Bruno that they found the person they were looking for: 'One day a lady came with a photograph of her son, but De Sica was immediately interested in the father, photographed standing next to the boy. It was Maggiorani.'[34]

De Sica tells the story slightly (but significantly) differently:

Suddenly in the queue of parents I saw a workman who was holding his little son by the hand. I beckoned him to come forward, and he approached hesitatingly, pushing the boy in front of him as if on a plate, and smiling wistfully. 'No,' I told him, 'you are the one I am interested in, not the child.' It was Lamberto Maggiorani. I gave him a screen test straightaway; and his way of moving, how he sat down, how he moved his hands covered in callouses, a workman's hands, not an actor's, everything about him was perfect ... I made him promise that after the film he would not think any more about the cinema, and would return to his job. He kept his word faithfully, but then there were redundancies at the Breda factory, he found himself unemployed, and returned to the cinema as a last resort.[35]

The search for Bruno continued, and De Sica's reasons for rejecting the various candidates are partly in line with what we have already recounted about his criteria, but also in contradiction with his reasons for not using the 'real' shoeshine boys for *Sciuscià*: 'The big problem was the child. They brought me hundreds: they were either pretty, romantic, smarmy or useless.'[36]

He started shooting the film without a performer for the role of Bruno:

> In desperation I decided to start the film anyway. I began with the scene of Antonio in search of the friend who will help him find the bicycle. We were shooting in that kind of little theatre in the working men's club. I was telling Maggiorani something when I turned around in annoyance at the onlookers who were crowding around me, and saw a odd-looking child with a round face, a big funny nose and wonderful lively eyes. Saint Gennaro has sent him to me, I thought. It was proof of the fact that everything was turning out right. A man's life has these happy days when everything goes well and everything proceeds simply and naturally. Well, on *Ladri di biciclette* that was my happy day.[37]

The person to play Maria Ricci was found just as fortuitously, as Lianella Carell, a young journalist at the time, relates:

> I had come to interview him. I had won a poetry prize and felt myself to be a woman of letters, and they had given me this job. I arrived and there was a terrible confusion, a huge roomful of girls. I went to the production manager and told him: 'I have to speak with De Sica,' and he replied: 'You'll be lucky, young lady, don't even think of it, because De Sica still has not found the protagonist for his film.' 'But I have an appointment, and I have to speak to him.'
>
> De Sica appeared and with great determination I went up and said to him: 'Excuse me, I am here.' He looked at me and said to me: 'But this is Maria,' and turning to the others: 'Don't you realize that she is Maria?' Nobody had realized it, but everybody started saying: 'Yes, yes, she's just right,' and I: 'I'm sorry but no, no, I am not doing it, I am not an actress, I am a journalist.' He took my hand and said to me: 'The cinema needs you, your face. I need you.' Won over and charmed, I said: 'Yes.' De Sica turns to the cameraman and says to him: 'Listen, tomorrow we will give her a screen test and see how it comes out.'[38]

These accounts of the 'finding' of the protagonists suggest that De Sica chose his actors for their immediate *visual* appearance, without knowing them as people, and without seeing how they behaved or hearing how they spoke. He was carrying out the stage of 'finding' the pro-filmic components of his essentially visual and pictorial assembly. This leads us to pay attention to the selection of the professional actors for the other roles. He chose actors with a certain plumpness of physique for those whom he wanted to portray as more or less 'secure' in the social landscape he was about to depict: Baiocco (the dustman friend), the man whose bicycle Antonio steals at the end of the film, and who forgives him, the policeman who intervenes in the dispute beneath the thief's apartment, the lawyer at the Messa del povero, the middle-class customers at the restaurant, the managers of the brothel, the Santona. He chose more gaunt figures for those threatened by that social landscape: Antonio, the old man seen talking with the thief, the thief himself, the clients of the Santona. Without wanting to push the point too far, I draw attention to the way in which De Sica is assembling a specifically *visual* artefact, using a code of typage for his performers that involves, in this case, the binary opposition of fat and thin. As we shall see when we come to look in detail at the film, De Sica presents Antonio to the viewer as inhabited by an a priori anxiety (as an index of his vulnerability to the threats contained in the landscape), and this may have been partly what struck him in the photograph of Lamberto Maggiorani (Luisa Alessandri's recollection is the more plausible).

It is important also to remember that De Sica's concern for 'authenticity' did not extend to using the performers' own voices: 'There was a bit of a scandal over the dubbing, when the Queen of England at an Italian Cinema Week [a promotional event put on by the Italian embassy] learned that the Italian actors were dubbed. Even Maggiorani was dubbed in *Ladri di biciclette*! Later they began to have the actors dub themselves, but it was not until halfway through the 1950s.'[39]

We shall be noting aspects of the soundtrack in different parts of the discussion of the film, but here I remind the reader that the film was shot entirely without any sound being recorded (not even a guide track), and the dialogue was recorded by professionals in a dubbing studio at the end of shooting – laboriously, as Luisa Alessandri recalls: 'How many hours we spent at the moviola reconstructing the dialogue, which had to follow exactly Zavattini's original text.'[40] Hence, the voices and the accents of the characters are a matter separate from that of the choice of performers, and constitute a transition to an issue that I would call 'costume' (how the characters were dressed), an issue related to that of 'location.' The film is set mainly in lower-class Rome, where Roman dialect, rather than what is called 'standard Italian,' is used. Dialect was an essential ingredient of Zavattini's realist polemic against traditional Italian cinema, which had generally avoided using it in the cinema, preferring to make gestures in the direction of popular speech without confronting all the cultural connotations attached to the historical and sociological fact of dialect. Neorealism is credited with the entry of dialect into the Italian cinema, and *Ladri di biciclette* is noteworthy for its consistent use. Once again, it permitted the establishment of a code of binary opposition. The middle-class characters who dispense charity at the Messa del povero speak standard Italian.

Moreover, throughout the film, the informal *tu* form of address is used by everyone in almost every situation. Only at the Messa del povero do we encounter characters who use the formal *Lei* form of address and, in one instance, the *voi* for the second person singular, which carries inevitable overtones of the fascist regime's prescription of that form of address. One exception to this general rule is where Baiocco uses the *Lei* form of respect to Maria, but in a scene where he dismisses her concerns (at the *dopolavoro*).

The question of 'register' applies also to costume in the film. For most of the film, Antonio is dressed in a register that places him at the bottom of a hierarchy of 'costume': in a jacket, dark sweatshirt, and trousers that are markedly dirty and tatty. He shares this register with the mendicants at the Messa del povero, but not really with any other character in the film. There is, however, a parallel drawn with Bruno, who also wears a jacket and is made a small imitation of his father. When Antonio first reports to the Ufficio affissioni (the depot for the billposters), he is dressed in a much higher register, with a hat, a smarter jacket, and a white shirt buttoned at the neck, which gives visual emphasis to this more positive moment in the narrative of his experience. This is the register of the characters in the street where the thief lives, for example (with one notable exception, which we shall come to later), and of the vendors at the Piazza Vittorio market. A higher 'civilian' register than that is attributed to the middle-class dispensers of charity at the Messa del povero, the other diners at the restaurant, and the man whom the two boys beg from during Antonio's billposting lesson. Antonio and Bruno are dressed in exactly the same overalls – a sort of uniform – on the day they leave for work, the son a smaller version of the father, and

Antonio's cap an important symbol of 'belonging' to the supportive institution of regular employment. We have already noticed the use of 'uniform' for visually modulating the 'moral' and political register in the chapter on *Roma città aperta*. In *Ladri di biciclette*, the register connoted by costume relates not only to social class, rank, or condition, but also to a sort of existential condition: in the social landscape constructed by the film, those protected from anxiety wear 'uniforms' signifying their attachment to social institutions: policemen, municipal employees (e.g., street-sweepers and dustmen), clerks (at the Ufficio collocamento, at the Ufficio affissioni, at the police station) or political party officials (the man giving a speech at the dopolavoro), the businessman with his briefcase and umbrella.

The density of representation of social institutions in *Ladri di biciclette* is remarkable (in the order that they appear in the film): public transport (buses and trams intrude everywhere, and are used deliberately for their connotations), public housing, employment centre, pawnbroker, municipal publicity, the Santona as a sort of social worker, police (on three different occasions), working-men's club, political party, municipal sanitation, markets, the clergy, prison, church charitable work, public works (the bridge), restaurant, state radio, brothel, municipal sports stadium. These are components of the urban social 'landscape' in which Antonio is placed as a fragile, vulnerable figure, and part of the *visual* representation of this landscape is carried by 'costume.'

Perhaps nothing better exemplifies casting for type than the round-faced, open-eyed, boneless, complacent self-satisfaction of the Santona's daughter – another character whom the camera picks up in the margins of the narrative, quite literally follows for the purposes of weaving together minor threads, and then drops. Her concern is with the coffee, and it functions as comic bathos. It is easy to see *Ladri di biciclette* as relentlessly focusing on its protagonist and his anxiety, and to forget how much that anxiety is a product of what De Sica puts around him, to act as a context and a foil. Gilles Deleuze is right to refer to a notion of the *film balade* (from *se balader*, to stroll around). For Deleuze, the notion is connected with a phenomenological approach to the representation of reality, and a break with classical narrative, and is possibly better at describing the effect than the means used to achieve it.[41] I often prefer to identify the 'means' in the classical narrative procedures of comedy, and perhaps Italian critics like Spinazzola are correct when they describe De Sica's procedures in terms of *bozzettismo* (made up of vignettes): 'However, we are at the level, substantially, of the sketch, in which the social tension of the story gets dissipated, losing its goal and its purpose.'[42] Spinazzola's characterization of the film, however, is inadequate as a description of the *function* of De Sica's use of the procedures of the comedy sketch. I shall devote particular attention to De Sica's use of a procedure of *following* things or characters with the camera. This procedure is his way of weaving together a multitude of minor threads so as to assemble a total picture, what I shall call a 'landscape' into which he inserts his 'figure,' Antonio, with the overall purpose of articulating with great delicacy how that figure *experiences* that landscape. *Ladri di biciclette* has a larger and more finely detailed active – even speaking – cast than appears at a first viewing, and De Sica uses the narrative devices of comedy and of the 'follow shot' to weave them together with extraordinary fluidity into a coherent whole that is far more than the sum of its parts.

Narrative

An account of the main lines of the story of *Ladri di biciclette* could make everything in the film flow logically from the initial premiss of Antonio being poor and unemployed: he is offered a job requiring him to have a bicycle; the bicycle is stolen; he searches for it in vain; when he steals a bicycle, he is apprehended and humiliated in front of his son, who gives his father his hand. Everything else in the film could be seen as filling in this basic template, prompting an interpretation of the film as a realist picture of post-war poverty and unemployment, with the direction of narrative reference going 'upwards' to the surface level of historical reality. Alternatively, the film can be read as having as its referent the psychology and emotions of a particular individual in those historical circumstances, and as appealing to the viewer's sympathy for the suffering of the protagonist. The film could be either *cronaca* (chronicle) or a sentimental appeal to the emotions of the viewer, or both.

The comedies and melodramas of the 1940s and 1950s Italian cinema are full of characters who desire, and whose desire affirms their humanity and vitality (the novel by Bartolini that prompted *Ladri di biciclette* is a case in point). Their actions may achieve little more than compounding their problems, but they are expressions of desire and self-affirmation. The stories that Zavattini prepares for De Sica, however, adhere to a particularly austere melodramatic scheme, setting up situations in which characters are deprived of the ability to deploy basic features of their humanity, which is blocked, stifled, or even erased. Circumstances (often, but not always, poverty) force the characters to the margins of society, where decision-making is taken away from them, and where their humanity is negated, in such a way that they cannot act upon their desires or in their own defence.

Zavattini's stories function like laboratory experiments. He creates plots in which the scope for desire to be expressed in action is closed off. In *I bambini ci guardano, Sciuscià, Ladri di biciclette*, and *Umberto D.* events and circumstances progressively strip the protagonists of the autonomy on which the free exercise of their humanity depends, and the viewer is left with knowledge not only of the vulnerability to which their progressive diminishment exposes them, but also of the characters' experience (their own acquisition of knowledge). The viewer grasps the full implications of the experiment that is unfolding, and watches the character gradually grasp them too. This knowledge of the character's experience restores, as it were, in the viewer's eyes, the humanity of the character, so that the narrative functions first to diminish the character (at the hands of a defective 'society,' for example) and then to rebuild him or her as the human being experiencing that diminishment. The viewer acquires knowledge of the character's way of experiencing his or her condition, while always remaining 'outside' the character, observing. De Sica's stylistic procedures are directed towards both observing from the outside and offering the viewer a reading, from inside, of the experience.

We could take two very disparate judgments of the narrative of *Ladri di biciclette*. The first is by André Bazin: 'The screenplay, to begin with, is diabolically clever, for, starting from the alibi of its social topicality, it handles several systems of dramatic co-ordinates that back it up in every sense.'[43] The second is by Vittorio Spinazzola:

> But its initial very persuasive premiss comes out in a plot overflowing with coincidences and novelistic twists, and in the unfolding of a series of episodes that line up a number of very picturesque circumstances and places: the second-hand market of Porta Portese, the 'Messa del povero' in a pious institute, a brothel, the bathing areas along the Tiber, the surgery, so to speak, of a santona. The various separate sections constitute a credible fresco of the 'other' Rome, unknown to tourists. However, we are at the level, substantially, of the sketch, in which the social tension of the story gets dissipated, losing its goal and its purpose.[44]

Both judgments are correct, it seems to me. The film does become increasingly fragmented and episodic as it progresses. And yet, these fragments are fluidly and seamlessly sewn into a whole in which the story of a stolen bicycle is given resonance. In the language we are using in this book, we would call this 'reference.' We would say that the film succeeds in making reference to things that are wider in scope than those logically entailed by the sequence of events surrounding the story of a stolen bicycle. How does it do this, and in what sense can it be said to do it?

The film does this by creating an urban and social landscape around Antonio, *while* recounting the main 'story,' and by making this landscape appear 'other' in relation to Antonio. As a result the filmmakers can offer the loss of, and search for, the bicycle as an evocation of Antonio's *experience* of that landscape and its 'otherness.' It is the whole, assembled artefact that achieves this wider sphere of 'reference,' but we can see how the assembly achieves this overall picture, and how it modulates it, by paying close attention to the assembly's details (particularly the *mise en scène* and the soundtrack) at each moment. In other words, the film does not achieve its overall effect by giving the reader a certain list of pieces of information, but by endowing the narrative with a deeper and wider frame of reference. The overall 'picture' assembled by the film could be associated with the aesthetic notion of the 'sublime' (in the eighteenth-century sense of the distinction between the beautiful and the sublime). We have already used this notion to characterize the first 'section' of *Paisà*'s final episode, the rescuing and burial of the corpse of the dead partisan in the river Po. There, the 'landscape' was vast, anonymous, and threatening, and the 'melodramatic' heroes constituted fragile and vulnerable human figures overwhelmed by that landscape. *Ladri di biciclette* does the same by depicting Antonio as an isolated and vulnerable figure in a huge, threatening social and urban landscape.

To Zavattini's 'experiment,' and its goal of 'knowledge,' De Sica adds a poetic dimension, using the visual composition and the soundtrack to place a 'figure' in a 'landscape' that excludes and overwhelms him. Anticipating the detailed examination of the film that follows these introductory considerations, we can identify four major cinematic procedures that De Sica uses to achieve his poetic ends, involving three distinct ways of using the camera. For his 'observational' portrayal of a figure in a landscape, De Sica uses the 'follow' shot, where the camera is pulled across the landscape by the movement of a character. This procedure is so frequent as to be one of the defining stylistic characteristics of the film. To portray visually the 'experience' of a character (usually one of defeat) he uses, in this case less frequently, a procedure of 'accompanying' the character with a tracking shot (the camera tracks back in front of a character walking forward). A pervasive stylistic characteristic of his *mise en scène* is composition in depth (organizing the pro-filmic in planes of foreground, middle ground, and background), and this is combined with a particular use of camera-positioning to portray the fusion of the observational and the experiential, so as to furnish the viewer with a 'reading' of how his character is experiencing 'diminishment.' Here the camera angle itself (rather than the pro-filmic, or what is before the camera) functions as a signifier in the narrative. The result of these four procedures and three uses of the camera is that the viewer both acquires the 'knowledge' imparted by Zavattini's relentless experiment and also contemplates De Sica's overall pictorial 'vision' of human experience.

The basic organization of the film's narrative is summarized in table 2, which follows at the end of this section. For purely practical purposes, I have divided the film into 'narrative sequences,' not fully corresponding to 'sequences' or 'scenes' in the technical sense of the terms. In the 'function' column, I have divided the 'narrative' into 'threads.' The 'main narrative thread' develops from the basic story of the job, the bicycle, the theft of the bicycle, and the search for the bicycle **(A)**, into the search for the thief rather than the bicycle **(B)**, and then into a flight from a hopeless situation **(C)**. In each of these subdivisions of the main thread, I identify a 'sub-thread' relating to the help from others that Antonio either seeks or is given. I identify as a 'secondary thread' the story of the unfolding of the father–son relationship. Some scenes I identify as 'transitions' and some as 'digressions.' In this column I have added – not very systematically – some of the recurring themes raised by the 'threads,' preceded by a plus sign (+).

Although not strictly relevant to the narrative structure of the film, I have exploited the economy of the 'table' format to draw attention to two aspects of the film that benefit from a synoptic view. One concerns the wealth of depictions of social institutions in the film (in the column 'Institutions'). The other concerns questions of genre. I use the label 'melodrama' to refer to what I have elsewhere defined as the 'melodramatic narrative matrix.' Where the label 'comedy' appears in this column, I am referring to the cinematic procedures and conventions of comedy, rather than in all cases to a scene being 'comic.' For example, during the theft of Antonio's bicycle, the accomplice diverting the taxi away from the thief and into the tunnel has many of the characteristics of cinematic comedy.

Main narrative thread (A): Unemployment, the offer of a job, the job, the theft, the search for the bicycle. This narrative thread follows a fairly logical cause-and-effect course, while still allowing room for the depiction of 'a figure in a landscape.'

Main narrative thread (B): The pursuit of the thief. **(A)** transforms itself into **(B)**, in itself a logical transformation. This narrative is less consequential, more a matter of evocative and expressive 'scenes' linked by chance, and offering a great deal of scope for the depiction of 'figure in a landscape.'

Main narrative thread (C): The flight into fantasy, resulting from awareness that the bicycle is gone forever. This thread serves almost exclusively for the depiction of 'a figure in a landscape.' It often features the procedures of comedy.

Sub-thread: This concerns, for each of the variations on the *main narrative thread*, attempts to get help from the society around, and whether or not help is granted. This thread inherently characterizes Antonio's relations with the social 'landscape.'

Secondary narrative thread: The father–son relationship. This thread develops out of the *main narrative thread*, taking on a life of its own in the final third of the film, and complements the depiction of 'a figure in a landscape,' partly by offering Bruno as a foil to Antonio's experience.

Transition and *Digression:* These are scenes that often constitute the *film balade* or *flânerie* element of walking through Rome and its social landscape (characteristics of the film identified by French phenomenologist commentators from Bazin to Deleuze). The narrative is assembled progressively more from fragments as the film proceeds, with more and more subtlety required in assembling them with coherent fluidity; the procedures of comedy are one means to this goal.

What this table lacks is a sort of graph of the changing 'mood' of the film as it progresses over time, like a musical composition: starting low at the beginning, rising with the securing of the bicycle and the job, plummeting with the theft, and then being modulated in its second half, until its final drop in the last scene. Such a 'graph' would show how scenes and sequences relate to each other in terms of contrast or reinforcement.

Table 2 Narrative structure of *Ladri di biciclette*

Narrative sequence	Institutions	Generic elements	Function
1. The bus, the Ufficio collocamento	Municipal employment office; public transport; communal water source		*Main narrative thread (**A**)*: unemployment, offer of job + Antonio's isolation + Antonio's anxiety *Sub-thread*: help spontaneously given
2. Antonio and Maria outside, and then in their flat	Common standpipe; public housing; siren (?)	Melodrama	*Transition* + Antonio's anxiety + effect on marital communication + Antonio's helplessness and lack of resources
3. Monte di Pietà.	Pawnbroker	Melodrama	*Main narrative thread (**A**)*: pawning sheets; redeeming bicycle from pawn *Sub-thread*: request for help from Clerk (granted) + Maria's resourcefulness + Family re-established + Society can be understanding and responsive
4. Ufficio affissioni	Municipal poster office; fellow-worker greets Antonio as colleague		*Main narrative thread (**A**)*: the job + family re-established + solidarity of colleague + Antonio's fear for the bicycle
5. Santona first time (Via della Paglia)	Sort of freelance social service	Comedy	*Transition* or *Sub-plot* (relating to Maria) *Sub-thread of main narrative thread (**A**)*: Request for help + sets up contrast with second visit + Antonio's condescension + Antonio's fear for the bicycle + social suffering
6. Ricci apartment, preparing to go to work	(Family); Giro d'Italia	Melodrama	*Transition* + family established + Antonio's obsession with bicycle overshadowing Bruno + Bruno's care for infant *Secondary narrative thread:* Father–son relationship

Table 2 (*continued*)

Narrative sequence	Institutions	Generic elements	Function
7. Antonio and Bruno going to work	Public transport; Bruno's work	Melodrama	*Transition* + sets up contrast with end of day *Secondary narrative thread:* Father–son relationship
8. Bill posters go out; the lesson	Municipal public services	Comedy	(a) *Main narrative thread (A):* bill-posting *Sub-thread:* help spontaneously given (the 'lesson') (b) *Digression:* the boys begging + social hardship, indifference, complacency, class, poverty
9. The theft	(Predatory society of theft); taxi (public transport)	Tragic, but with comedy elements: the thief's accomplices	*Main narrative thread (A):* the theft + Antonio's anxiety + lack of social support + predatory individualism
10. The police station	Police; political and social control	Melodrama	*Main narrative thread (A):* reporting the theft *Sub-thread:* Request for help (denied) + society's indifference + social and political conflict and oppression; society not doing its duty
11. Antonio catches the bus at Porta Pia	Public transport		*Transition:* consequences of theft, travel through Rome
12. Antonio's journey home	Public transport	Melodrama	*Transition:* walking through Rome + Antonio falls in Bruno's eyes + Antonio's lack of resources
13. Antonio lets Bruno into their apartment			*Transition* + effect of Antonio's anxiety on marital communication

Table 2 (*continued*)

Narrative sequence	Institutions	Generic elements	Function
14. The dopolavoro	Working men's club; party politics; public cultural activity	Comedy	*Main narrative thread (A)*: the search for the bicycle; *Sub-thread*: Request for help (implicitly denied by political party; granted by Baiocco) + Antonio's helplessness + poor marital communication; *Digression*: political meeting: the variety act + political action in social solidarity + social ignorance and indifference to Antonio's plight + social conflict
15. Piazza Vittorio	Municipal sanitation; public market; police		*Main narrative thread (A)*: search for stolen bicycle; *Sub-thread*: help given by street-sweepers + social solidarity (the dustmen) + social solidarity (excluding Antonio – vendors of stolen goods) + threats from society (pederast) + Bruno's need for care and Antonio's neglect, an index of anxiety
16. In the dustcart and to Porta Portese	Municipal sanitation; 'Sunday' as holiday; public market; clergy; 'underworld' of black market	Comedy	(a) *Transition*: ride through Rome; (b) *Digression*: dustman's thoughts; (c) *Main narrative thread (A)*: search for bicycle; *(B)* sight of thief (chance encounter) + human comedy (vendors' remarks as they flee rain); (d) *Digression*: German seminarians + Bruno's need for care and Antonio's neglect, an index of anxiety (his fall) + Antonio falls in Bruno's eyes
17. Chasing the old man		Comedy	*Main narrative thread (B)*: NB – now search for thief, rather than bicycle + Bruno's need for care and Antonio's neglect, an index of anxiety (Bruno trying to pee)

Table 2 (continued)

Narrative sequence	Institutions	Generic elements	Function
18. Messa del povero	Catholic Church; soup kitchen	Comedy	*Main narrative thread (B)*: search for thief *Sub-thread*: request for help (from old man, mostly denied) *Digression*: portrait of society + poverty + satire of middle-class complacency and indifference (ineffectual help to poor) + middle-class concern for form
19. The slap in the garden of the church		Melodrama	*Secondary narrative thread*: Father–son relationship + Bruno's need for care and Antonio's neglect, an index of anxiety
20. The 'drowning'	Spontaneous social co-operation	Melodrama	*Secondary narrative thread*: Father–son relationship + social solidarity (bystanders rescuing boy) + Antonio's isolation (he does not help) + Antonio's knowledge of his neglect of Bruno
21. On the Lungotevere	Football fans; soldier in background	Melodrama	(a) *Secondary narrative thread*: Father–son relationship (b) *Transition*: pausing in the walk through Rome
22. Restaurant	Restaurant	Comedy Satire	(a) *Secondary narrative thread*: Father–son relationship + Antonio's lack of resources + social class divisions + satire of middle-class complacency and concern with form + filmmaker adjusting moods + social indifference (song) (b) *Main narrative thread (C)*: NB – now it is Antonio's knowledge: that the bicycle is gone for good
23. Santona (second time)	Public radio; freelance social service	Comedy	(a) *Main narrative thread (C)*: lack of resources leads to flight into fantasy *Sub-thread*: request for help (implicitly futile) (b) *Digression*: social suffering + concern with form (quarrel over the queue) + pure comedy (ugly man) + burlesquing of the Santona

Table 2 (*concluded*)

Narrative sequence	Institutions	Generic elements	Function
24. Encountering the thief		Comedy (thief round corner)	*Main narrative thread (B)*: search for thief (renewed by chance encounter)
25. The brothel	Brothel	Comedy	*Main narrative thread (B)*: search for thief *Digression*
26. The thief's street, the policeman	Community of Trastevere; Police	Comedy	(a) *Main narrative thread (B)*: search for thief *Sub-thread*: request for help (from policeman – ineffectual) + Bruno helps his father + Antonio falls in Bruno's eyes (b) *Digression*: social deprivation – particularly relating to thief's family + social solidarity (excluding Antonio – criminal world of Trastevere) + society's rules ineffective (policeman, sympathetic but unable to help)
27. Wandering, the Stadium, the failed theft	Public sports facilities; football fans; public transport; community supports owner of bicycle; sporting cyclists	Melodrama (tragic)	(a) *Transition*: walking through Rome + Bruno's need for care and Antonio's neglect, an index of anxiety (b) *Main narrative thread (C)* *Sub-thread*: help granted spontaneously (owner of bicycle dismisses charges) + social solidarity (excluding Antonio) + Antonio's helplessness and despair (c) *Secondary narrative thread:* Father–son relationship

Analysis of sequences

Any suggestion that De Sica's directorial style, by association with neo-realist conventions, is characterized by 'long takes' is contradicted by the fact that *Ladri di biciclette*, at one hour and twenty-five minutes in length (excluding the final credits), and consisting of 737 shots, has an average shot length of 6.9 seconds.[45] In the preceding section I divided the film into twenty-seven 'sequences,' which do not correspond strictly to what would be called 'scenes' in a shooting script (separated by a change of location or of time of day), but rather to units of the narrative.[46] I shall be taking only a selection of these sequences for analysis, starting with a close look at the first three, and discussing different aspects of the film in different sequences. Where I refer to a shot, I shall give its number out of 737, and for clarity sometimes put that number in parentheses.

One of the aims of this description of *Ladri di biciclette* is to identify De Sica's directorial style. Both André Bazin in 1949 and, more recently, Guglielmo Moneti in 1992 have suggested that his style is nearly unidentifiable, constituting, if anything, an absence of marked, distinguishing stylistic characteristics, especially in the use of the camera and in the *mise en scène*. Both critics are clearly emphatic in this regard:

André Bazin (1949):

> To the disappearance of the notion of the actor into the transparency of a perfection that seems as natural as life itself, corresponds the disappearance of the *mise en scène*. Let us be clear: De Sica's film took a very long time to prepare, and everything in it was as minutely pre-planned as in a studio super-production (which is what permits there to be last-minute improvisations). And yet I cannot recall a single shot in which a dramatic effect resulted from the '*découpage*,' strictly speaking. [*Découpage* refers to the way a narrative is broken down in the shooting script into 600–700 'shots' from different angles and distances, which are then assembled in the editing to make a film.] The latter seems as neutral as in a Chaplin film. And yet, if one analyses the film one discovers in it a number and a typology of shots that do not noticeably distinguish *Ladri di biciclette* from an ordinary film. But the choice of shots is directed only towards bringing out the value of the event in the clearest possible way, while allowing the lowest index of refraction [i.e., the least amount of distortion or interference] through the style. This objectivity is very different from that of Rossellini in *Paisà*, but it belongs to the same aesthetic. One could see it here as par-

alleling what Gide and above all Martin du Gard say about narrative prose in the novel: that it must tend towards the most neutral transparency. Just as the disappearance of the actor is the result of superseding a style of performance, so the disappearance of the *mise-en-scène* is similarly the product of a dialectical progress in the style of narration. If the event is sufficient in itself for there to be no need for the director to emphasize it with particular angles or positions of the camera, this is precisely because the event has reached a level of perfect luminosity that permits art to unmask a nature that ultimately resembles it.[47]

Guglielmo Moneti (1992):

A uniform series of stylistic procedures, basically fairly simple, comprises the regular fabric of the film. The camera movements always have a descriptive function, reducible to essential pans frequently combined with tracks following the action, never rapid or designed to emphasize a particular element of the image, but always trying to give a linear character to the narrative ... In the course of the entire film, there is very rarely recourse to figurative deformation resulting from an oblique shot, but instead frontal shots, with a normal inclination, give a natural vision at head height. The role of the camera, whether it is static or in movement, is above all to expound: its placing always depends on what must be framed, and its movement traces out the territory most congenial to the action. It is, in short, a secondary role with respect to that of the profilmic. Thus the whole image works to the advantage of the object of the representation, without references to the act of representing. It is an object that tends to detach itself from the act of *mise-en-scène*, to free itself from the play of cinematography, to break its rules ... In short, the director tends more to hide himself than to show himself, refashioning his formative intervention into a mediation that can hardly be noticed ... It tries to conform to the spontaneous spatial perception of the viewer ... De Sica seems not to want to choose a characteristic construction of the shot, to build up a personal poetic approach; he does not make precise choices, in other words, but opts for an approximation which reduces his own authorial impact ... His tendency towards an expressive neutrality of cinematic language is evident and explicit.[48]

To avoid unnecessary repetition, I shall gradually accumulate shorthand labels, in italics, to identify stylistic features of the film.

Sequence 1: Set and filmed at the Ufficio di collocamento (employment office) of Valmelaina. Antonio is given a job, requiring him to have a bicycle.

(1) [Behind the opening credits] Right from the start of the film (though not from the start of its shooting, because this was not the first shot to be filmed), De Sica establishes his procedure of *'following'* something in the pro-filmic assembly: the camera pans (and tilts) to *follow* some thing or character as they move. The first shot follows (a) the bus coming in from right to left, curving with the road, and coming to a halt facing the camera; (b) men who converge on the bus to surround the Clerk, who gets off the bus and comes round the front of it from left to right towards the Ufficio di collocamento (employment office). A typical feature of De Sica's style is to *balance* a movement of the camera or of the pro-filmic in one direction with a simultaneous or immediately successive *balancing movement* in the other direction – in this case: left to right, and back to right again.

A feature of De Sica's style is the *'follow shot.'* Simple panning with the camera is rhetorical display. It is something the *director* does to lay out the pro-filmic before the viewer. Neither De Sica nor Rossellini do it. In the 'follow shot' it is the *character* or the pro-filmic that moves the camera. The 'follow shot' is a movement of the camera deriving from the narrative, rather than from the director's pictorial flourish. Visconti and De Santis pan all the time, because in their cinema 'characters' are a product of the setting. In De Sica's rhetoric, the camera moves because the world that the viewer sees is the product of the characters' experience. An additional 'reality effect' resulting from the follow-shot procedure is the implication that the viewer is seeing, metonymically, parts of a whole that extends outside the framework of the film, whereas in fact the viewer is seeing what De Sica has assembled.

(2) [Behind the credits] There follows a dissolve to a closer shot of these people, from a camera position to the right of (1). The people go up the outside stairs of the office (they move towards the right, and then go left up the stairs); then they come back down again, followed by the Clerk [*follow shot*], continuing the procedure of *balancing movement*: up to left, then back down to right.

(3) Dissolve to a closer shot of this, bringing the Clerk more into prominence. He asks: 'Ricci. C'è Ricci?' A young man turns round, more or less towards the camera, calling out 'Ricci?' and comes through the crowd towards the camera.

(4) Cut to a long-scale shot, with the camera placed high, of the pro-filmic content of shots 2 and 3 seen from a long way back, with the

young man running towards us, while the camera pans to *follow* him to the right and downwards to Antonio seated at the water pump, with a woman doing washing on the other side and to the right. The woman doing her washing endows the pump with the quality of a social institution, an element of the urban *social* landscape, from which Antonio is excluded by his absorption in his anxiety at the vulnerability to which his lack of employment exposes him. This is conveyed to the viewer by the narrative's setting Antonio apart from the other unemployed men, and seated in passive isolation.

A general point I want to make about the *mise en scène* of the film is that De Sica is constructing a visual, pictorial representation of a *figure in a landscape*. The film's narrative functions to articulate Antonio's experience of his (the figure's) relation to that landscape (one of isolation, exclusion, fragility, and vulnerability). While the discursive logic (cause and effect) of the narrative articulates Antonio's suffering at being unemployed and therefore poor, I want to draw attention to how the audio-visual assembly (*dispositio*) of the film itself constructs a *pictorial* evocation of an experience. I suspect that this is part of what De Sica is referring to when he talks about his 'poetic' intentions in making the film. I further suspect that it is to this assembly of a figure in a landscape that commentators are referring when they talk about the power of the film not being fully accounted for by its 'narrative.'

Shot 4 reveals the architecture of the blocks of housing taking up the left of the frame, with a sort of wasteland in the right of the frame (which is the part occupied in the foreground by Antonio), emphasizing the location of Valmelaina in a vacant, waste area far from the city, and contributing to the construction of a figure in a landscape.

My analysis of the film is not intended as a polemic against a 'realist' reading of the film as a detailed and accurate representation of a plausible historical and social 'reality.' Nor do I put into question the necessary convention whereby viewers make sense of a film narrative by treating as 'persons' with a 'psychology' the characters in a film narrative. However, in reality, there are no 'persons' in a film, just actors paid by the hour to stand in a certain place, to carry out certain actions, and to deliver certain lines of dialogue – all of which are assembled into a sequence of sounds and images for the viewer. In drawing attention to the assembly of the *film* as an 'artefact,' I shall therefore try to avoid treating the 'characters' as 'persons,' though I fully acknowledge that I shall have lapses from this austere ideal. I shall sometimes mark items that contribute to the scrupulous, detailed 'realism' of the film with a capital 'R' in brackets [R].

The young man calls to Antonio: 'Ricci? Annamo, te vonno! Ma che sei sordo? Annamo' / 'Ricci? Let's go, they want you! Are you deaf? Let's go.' Antonio rises and brushes dust off his clothes, and the camera tilts to *follow* him and the other man running back to the Ufficio di collocamento, in a sort of reverse movement of the beginning of the shot, held for quite a long time (a *balancing movement*: down towards us, then back up away again). (On the soundtrack we hear the bus start up off-camera [R], and it appears from the left in the end of the shot, and again, moving left to right, in the beginning of the next shot [*sound/image background* – see explanation below].)

(5) The camera returns to the position of shot 3, with the young man and Antonio entering from the left, and going up to the stairs (so shot 5 is symmetrically the reverse of 3 [*balancing movement*]). De Sica accumulates a great deal of data in the background of his narrative images, which both contributes to realism [R] and constitutes a procedure to which I shall give the label of *sound/image background*: (a) the bus goes off; (b) the workers argue in an irritated way among themselves and with the Clerk about who most deserves a job, and whose fault it is that they have no work.

Then follows a much faster sequence of shots (20 shots, 6–25, in 58 seconds, giving a very short average shot length of 2.9 seconds), mostly in reverse-angles. The effects achieved by framing are (a) to separate the Clerk from the men, either with the Clerk alone in the shot, or sometimes with Antonio to one side of it, and generally from *below*; (b) to show the unemployed men always as a group, shot from *above*; (c) to separate Antonio from the other men, in different ways, and to different extents, and to put him in a half-way position between the Clerk and the others – sometimes on his own, sometimes in a two-shot with the Clerk (shot from *below* and in profile in right of frame), and sometimes coming forward out of the group of men (shot from *above*). Antonio starts on a step well *above* that of the other men, more or less at the height of the Clerk, and then steps down to an *intermediate* height between that of the Clerk and that of the men.

(26) Then a shot similar to shot 5, of Antonio coming down the steps, pushing through the men with no regard for them [*figure in a landscape*], and moving off left. Meanwhile he continues his dialogue with the Clerk. As Antonio pushes through the men, the Clerk offers a job to another man, amid the protest of his fellow job-seekers in the *sound/image background* [R].

The sequence from shot 3 to shot 26 was photographed in sunlight. From close attention to the shadows, and to the disposition of the extras playing the job-seekers, one can hypothesize that the whole scene was shot first in two mastershots, one with the camera in the position of shots 3, 5, and 26, and the other with the camera a long way back for shot 4. At a different time (one presumes after the mastershots had been taken – the sun being lower in the sky suggests that it might have been later the same day), the reverse-angle sequences of shots 6–25 were taken, using three different camera set-ups, containing much of the dialogue originally contained in the mastershot (5), and replacing most of it (as well as incorporating material from the mastershot, 5), with the job-seekers placed differently from how they had been in shots 3, 5, and 26. If this hypothesis is correct (the move from mastershot to subsequent closer 'coverage' is a standard filming procedure), then we can see De Sica approaching Antonio's receipt of the job first from a simple detached perspective, tending to isolate him, and then elaborating, with the closer reverse-angle 'coverage,' a more subtle and complex articulation of his relation to the others. In the mastershots, the composition was mainly in one plane, from left to right. In the assembly of reverse-angles, De Sica has developed a *composition in depth*: Antonio in a middle ground, with a foreground and background made up of the Clerk and the other unemployed men, photographed from camera positions at different heights. At the very least, De Sica gave himself at the shooting stage the option of carrying out this elaboration at the editing stage. The procedure of *composition in depth* will, as we progress through the film, turn out to be one of the most distinctive characteristics of De Sica's *mise en scène*.

Sequence 2: Valmelaina. Antonioni collects his wife, Maria, at the communal standpipe, and the two return to their apartment.

This is not a very important sequence for the main narrative of the film, and in the narrative table presented earlier in this chapter I labelled it a 'transition' sequence – it takes us from one event (getting the job) to the next event (pawning the sheets in order to redeem the bicycle). However, if we examine it closely, we see how expressive are De Sica's directorial procedures.

(27) Dissolve to a very long-scale shot of a tiny Antonio coming towards the camera along the façade of one of the apartment blocks, towards the standpipe in the foreground, at which Maria is collecting water in the midst of other women who are talking among themselves (see plate 1). For his construction of a *figure in a landscape*, De Sica uses in the composition of his image architectural features of the urban land-

scape to dominate or overwhelm the small figure, both by the size and shape of the buildings themselves in relation to the figure in the vertical and horizontal dimensions, and also by the emphatic use of perspective (shooting along the façade of a building) in the third dimension of *depth* of the image.

Antonio turns to his left, around the fencing, comes level with the camera, and walks left to right across the frame, with the camera panning right to *follow* him. A feature of De Sica's filming procedure is to have a character walk in a *'V' movement* towards and then away from the camera placed at the apex of the 'V,' usually passing from left to right – typically, later in the film, Antonio will come down a street towards the camera, turn a corner, and walk down another street away from the camera. It is a procedure we shall see used to great effect in the scene of the second visit to the Santona. It permits the director to use a stationary camera, to avoid tracking, and to depict the character coming into the camera from one place and going away from the camera towards another, in the *depth* of the image, rather than just panning from left to right to follow him in a single plane. It combines the features of the *follow shot, balancing movement*, and *composition in depth*, characteristic of De Sica's *mise en scène*.

Antonio stops, at the bottom right-hand corner of the frame, with the women at the standpipe in the centre and left of the frame. The standpipe is fenced in with strands of barbed wire going across the frame, stapled to tall posts, and Antonio rests his hand on a strand and looks towards Maria on the left. Meanwhile, a woman carrying a bucket has walked right to left across the foreground and goes off left of camera, giving a counter-motion to that of Antonio and the camera [*balancing movement*] (see plates 2 and 3), and in the midst of the babble of the women can be heard a siren (like that of an ambulance) [*sound/image background, R*]. Antonio calls out: 'Mari'.'

(28) [23 secs.] Cut to the camera placed in Antonio's position (hence, a point-of-view shot) directed towards Maria at the standpipe. Now a woman is pushing other women's buckets away from the standpipe (a sort of *sound/image background* of quarrelling and conflict repeatedly used in the film – a struggle of egotisms that De Sica makes a recurring feature of the social landscape). Since a feature of De Sica's *mise en scène* is *composition in depth*, I shall also need short-hand labels (*foreground* and *background*, and sometimes *foreground/background*) to draw attention to his compositions. Shot 28 both starts out and is subsequently developed with very careful composition. In the *foreground* are the

strands of barbed wire. Just a little beyond them are placed some women in the *foreground* of the right half of the frame. Beyond them, raised up head and shoulders higher than them, is Maria, just left of centre of the frame, with two women a little lower than her to the left of the frame, whose edge is marked by the post to which the barbed wire is attached. Maria is against the sky, shot from below head height, and behind her are more strands of barbed wire. The sky is framed to the right by the descending perspective of the buildings, seen along their façade [*composition in depth*]. This is how we first see Maria, in a striking composition, making her stand out from the other women (see plate 4). As she is subsequently brought into the sphere of Antonio's anxiety, she is reduced in stature by the mise en scène, and by the way this shot itself develops (this 'reduction' of her is helped by having her carry with difficulty two heavy buckets of water). Antonio repeats: 'Mari'.' The shot then develops into a medium-close two-shot of Maria and Antonio, because she turns to camera right and comes round towards the camera, passing behind the women in the foreground to where Antonio is standing. For part of this movement, she is framed alone, holding the buckets, in medium to medium-long shot, moving to the right, with the building behind her (see plate 5). The camera, panning to *follow* her, arrives at Antonio's shoulders (his back is to the camera) in the near *foreground*, and as he moves right, and the camera *follows* his and Maria's movement, a very large post in the immediate *foreground* fills the whole frame (see plates 6 and 7), for a while completely erasing Maria from the image. It might not seem significant at this moment in the film, but when we find De Sica repeatedly, throughout the film, 'erasing' a character (either Bruno or Maria) from shots connoting Antonio's point of view, we begin to realize how the director is using this as a stylistic device, to be *read* by the viewer as an expression of Antonio's self-absorption and isolation from those closest to him. Maria comes out from behind that post to be in the left half of the frame in an aspect between profile and three-quarters face, looking slightly up directly at the taller Antonio, who is in the right half of the frame in pro-file (looking towards her, though in fact part of the time with his eyes down), slightly nearer the camera. Beyond Antonio is the fence, but Maria stands in a gap in the fence, so that a thick post, fully in focus, rhetorically divides the frame in half, right between Antonio and Maria (see plate 8). A dialogue starts. Maria: 'Che c'è? Che è successo?' / 'What's up? What's happened?' Antonio: 'Ma dimme se nun so' disgraziato!' / 'If I'm not the unluckiest ...!' Maria: 'Che c'è Anto'?' / 'What's the matter, Antonio?' Antonio: 'C'è er posto e nun lo posso prende' / 'There's a job and I can't take it.' As he says the last two words, Antonio turns away from Maria (see plate 9), and starts to walk out of frame to the right, with the camera *following* him (panning to the right), leaving Maria off-camera, as he now walks vigorously away from the camera (which stops its pan), along the wasteland, with the apartment blocks on the left. In other words, Antonio has turned his back on, and walked away from, Maria (taking the camera with him). A character turning his/her back on, and walking away from, his/her interlocutor, taking the camera with him/her, will be one of the most characteristic moves in Michelangelo Antonioni's *cinema dell'incomunicabilità* (cinema of the impossibility of communication) (I shall take up this point shortly). Maria, following him, enters the frame from the left, and walks after him, the two of them rapidly changing the scale of the shot from medium-close to long scale as they get further from the camera (see plate 10). Maria's movement, and then the movement of the couple together, have executed the characteristic '*V*' *movement* I referred to earlier. Maria has difficulty keeping up with Antonio, because of the two buckets of water she is carrying, and among the other things she says to him she asks him to stop, but he carries on.

(29) The camera now moves to a point perpendicular to Antonio's progress, but ahead of him, and pans to the right to *follow* him and Maria move from left to right, getting closer to where the camera is placed (see plate 11). The camera is, in fact, placed at the top of a steep bank that falls down to the level of the apartment blocks in the *background*. Antonio does not heed Maria's pleas (she says: 'Senti, che hai detto? C'è er posto?' / 'Wait, what did you say? There's a job?') and continues striding on, but now he executes a complex turn. He turns back towards Maria, waving the work document he has been given (and replying to her question with 'E bono, pure, municipale!' / 'And a good one too, with the Council!'), but also changes direction by turning his body towards his left – in other words, away from the camera – striding down the bank towards the apartment blocks (see plate 13), and then turning his head to look to the front. This has the effect of making him drop rapidly into the background, so that we are left with Maria in full shot, level with the camera in the left half of the frame and, much smaller, just the top half of Antonio visible (at about the height of Maria's knees) right at the bottom of centre-frame in the background, having turned his back on, and walked away from, his wife once again [in a '*V*' *movement*]. He has, in fact, turned first towards her and then away from her, in order rather abruptly to move away from her, and this is emphasized by the fact that he drops away into the distance,

340 Italian Neorealist Cinema

while she now has difficulty, encumbered by her buckets, in starting the descent down the steep slope to follow him (see plate 14).

Meanwhile, De Sica has added two other elements to the scene, one in the *foreground* and one in the *background*. In the close *foreground*, a couple arm in arm (out of focus) walk across the frame from right to left, in a counter-motion to that of Antonio, Maria, and the camera (see plate 12). One can only presume that De Sica made the couple do this to provide an expressive contrast to the positioning and gestures he is showing with respect to the Ricci couple (as well as to create a *balancing movement*). In the *background*, a group of children dressed up to imitate an adult wedding procession, in front of the apartment block on the left, come forward towards the bank to start walking up it in a band [*balancing* Antonio's movement away from the camera and downwards] (see plate 14).

(30) There is a cut, with the camera now placed at the bottom of the bank, beyond Antonio, looking back at Maria at the top of the bank, with Antonio in the *foreground*, completing his turn towards her (see plate 15), and going back to help her by taking one of the buckets from her. Meanwhile, the children mount the bank in the right-hand *background* of the frame [*balancing movement*], and when they get to the top, they turn right and walk along it. As this happens, the camera pans right to follow Antonio and Maria as they pass from left to right, coming towards the camera, with the result that the the rest of the shot has Antonio and Maria in the *foreground* moving from left to right and, in the *background*, at the top of the frame against the sky, the children moving towards the right along the bank in unison with the whole movement (see plate 17). The point at which the children's 'wedding procession' climbing the bank passes closest to Antonio and Maria is the moment when Maria tries to defuse the tension by saying in a softer voice: 'Embè, se rimedia, Anto.' Che non se po' rimedia'?' / 'Oh well, we'll sort something out, Antonio. Can't something be done about it?' – as though the nearness of the children in the *background* were provoking a gentleness and optimism (see plate 16). To this Antonio replies: 'Ma che te voi rimedia'! Ce vo' la bicicletta, subito, si nun me presento subito, er posto se lo pia 'n altro.' / 'What do you want to sort out! I need the bicycle, straightaway, if I don't show up straightaway someone else will take the job.' All the while, in the background of the soundtrack we hear the shouting of children and the barking of a dog [*sound/image background*]. When they get level with the façade of the apartment block, and move into its shadow, their faces can no longer be seen clearly because the film is now underexposed, and there is a cut.

(31) At the cut, the camera moves to a position behind Maria and Antonio, as they walk towards the entrance and staircase of their section of the apartment building – with the lighting and exposure corrected. Now they are both seen from behind, Antonio as usual in the right of the frame, and Maria a little ahead of him in the left. There has been a tendency throughout this sequence to keep Antonio in right of frame, Maria in left, for coherence. As she gets close to the steps, Maria turns to her right and looks back and up at Antonio (who turns slightly to look at her), gently shaking her head, and asks: 'Che se po' fa' allora?' / 'What's to be done then?' to which Antonio replies: 'E che voi fa'!' / 'What's the use!' Meanwhile, De Sica has added another element to the scene, and once again it involves both *foreground and background*. This time, it is a woman who comes down the stairs in the *background* towards the couple and the camera and as she gets close to Maria, says: 'Buongiorno signora Ricci' (to which Maria replies: 'Buongiorno signora'), and then carries on, passing between the couple into the *foreground*, and walking out of the frame in the left foreground (you can see the woman looking over to someone who is directing her towards the end of her movement) [*balancing movement*: as the Riccis go away from the camera, the woman comes towards it] (see plates 18 and 19). As this woman comes forward, she completely covers Maria (*erasing* her from the image), who has gone ahead and is now standing on the first step of the stairs (see plate 20). As Maria reappears from behind the woman neighbour, she is turning leftwards right round to look at Antonio in the right of frame (thus keeping her back to him and yet turning her face towards him at the same time), and aggressively exclaiming: 'Non te la dovevi impegna' 'sta bicicletta, Antò!' / 'You should never have pawned that bicycle, Antonio!' (see plate 21).

(32) The camera cuts to an almost 180-degree reverse-angle position, set up on the landing at the top of the stairs visible in the previous shot, looking down towards Maria in the *foreground* on the lower steps in the gloom of the stairwell, with Antonio still outside the archway down in the brighter daylight in the *background*. Antonio raises his arm high and replies to Maria's challenge: 'E che te magnavi?' / 'What did you think you were going to eat?' Maria now turns to look up the stairs, but also to look from side to side (concerned that the neighbours will hear them quarrelling), saying: 'Statte zitto' / 'Be quiet,' while Antonio continues exclaiming loudly and angrily: 'Mannaggia a me quanno so' nato' / 'A curse on the day I was born.' Maria again tries to quieten him, looking back and down towards him and then around: 'Nun te fa' senti' / 'Don't let people hear you,' but Antonio carries on letting off steam:

'Vie' voglia de buttasse a fiume ...' / 'Makes you want to throw yourself in the river ...' (Maria: 'Te voi sta' zitto' / 'Will you shut up.') Antonio: '... vie' voglia' / '... it does.' In other words, Antonio has negated her by turning and walking away from her, while she now negates him by trying to silence him out of shame. This shot is again very strikingly, and eloquently, composed. The *architecture* of the staircase, with its harsh edges and angles, the framing of the arch at the entrance, Maria placed above Antonio in the *foreground*, with him on the ground, raising his arm and his voice, in the *background* ..., all of this, shot in deep focus, combining to express the stress and anxiety that is setting them against each other, and that Maria tries to hide from the neighbours (see plate 22).

Balanced and symmetrical compositions, exploiting architecture, enacting a 'ballet' of the characters turning away from each other, provoking the viewer to a 'reading' of the way in which anxiety is obstructing marital communication ... will all be characteristic features of Antonioni's *mise en scène*.

Other features might appear to be just 'realism,' but they turn out to be much more carefully thought out than that, and to be used for expressive and formal purposes. The protagonists are portrayed in the midst of other things going on, being done by other people: the woman carrying her bucket across the foreground in front of the standpipe; the woman pushing other women's buckets away from the water tap; the couple walking across the foreground arm in arm; the neighbour coming out of the apartment building and passing between them; the playing children climbing the bank as Antonio and Maria come down it. A 'realist' explanation would see these things as merely 'inserting' Antonio and Maria in a world carrying on its activities beyond the borders of the frame (the approach to 'representation' that I have elsewhere characterized as the notion of the 'list' – things are 'there' in the film because they really were there in reality). In fact, these added elements work on the formal level to give balancing counter-movements to those of the protagonists and of the camera. They also bear a relation, on the semantic level, to what is going on between the protagonists: the children at play, for example, almost seeming to 'prompt' the softer, gentler reassuring tone of Maria at that moment, the couple arm in arm passing in the foreground contrasting with Antonio and Maria, and the neighbour bringing out the 'wrongness' of this family quarrel. The background details (which might, in fact, be placed in the foreground) create relations of either contrast or reinforcement with what is at the centre of the 'story.' De Sica tends to balance the composition, with material (often in itself either interesting or meaningful – for example, the women fighting over the standpipe) placed both in the background and in the foreground.

I probably do not need to remind the reader that nothing was 'there' to be filmed until De Sica put it there; no relations of foreground and background existed until De Sica created them with his assembly of profilmic figures, objects, and events, and until he chose to place his camera, and to move it, in such a way as to produce those compositions (quite apart from the fact that the entire soundtrack – dialogue and sounds of any kind at all – was assembled in a dubbing studio). Just as the statue of Moses is not the result of the work of nature but of Michelangelo's chisel guided by his intentions, so the sequence we have examined is the result of De Sica's *work* of assembly. The instructions carried by the script – whoever may ultimately have been responsible for it – could have been executed in any number of different ways. De Sica's filming turns out to be every bit as formally rigorous and lyrically expressive as that of a director like Antonioni, who is generally regarded as a far more 'pure' poet of the cinema. What has got in the way of viewers' and critics' appreciation of this fact is the sheer quantity of data that De Sica's *mise en scène* supplies, and the subtle force with which his montage presents it, and above all the ease with which the final product can be (or certainly has been) absorbed into the notion of 'realism.'

Understandably, a filmmaker will take particular care over the first sequences of his film, where he has not only to capture the viewer's attention and interest, but also to communicate rapidly enough information to identify his protagonist as a character, and to give the viewer a sense of the way he approaches life. Even where a sequence has been assembled at the editing stage from 'coverage' material integrated into material shot with mastershots, as in the dialogue between Antonio and the Clerk of the employment centre, it has all been coherently thought out for its expressive value. Not all the sequences in *Ladri di biciclette* have been shot and assembled with such attention to formal and expressive coherence and elegance. The first sequence of the film that the crew shot, for example, that set in the *dopolavoro* (the working men's club), while being complex in content and meaning, does not achieve the same stylistic elegance – perhaps because it took De Sica a while to get into his stride. The sequence of Antonio being accosted by the thief's neighbours, assembled from what we might call 'coverage' (shots designed to integrate details into the overall narrative of the sequence), does not have the coherence of perspective and composition that we find in the material we have just examined. But we shall encounter more than enough sequences in the film bearing the signs of this subtle coherence and elegance to contradict the common notion of De Sica as a *mestierante* (anonymous competent craftsman) lacking an identifiable style.

I have encountered no viewer or commentator who says that Antonio is presented as a selfish, unpleasant person. Clearly, therefore, De Sica achieves his goal of prompting the viewer to a *reading* of the narrative and the camera's perspective on it. Antonio's behaviour could be explained by two years of frustration and unemployment, except that in these early scenes the viewer only gradually acquires that knowledge. His relationship with his wife acts as an index of anxiety. He is shown as overreacting to the need for a bicycle out of anxiety (the Clerk tries to calm him: 'Aho, non famo a cojonasse' / 'Don't let's be stupid') – and anxiety will characterize him throughout the film. But more than that, Antonio is presented as 'isolated' and anxious a priori. The viewer accepts this, without feeling provoked to moral judgment, as an *existential* feature of the vision offered by the artefact. De Sica uses the composition of the image and the placing of the characters to create a visual spectacle for the viewer of the sublime (in the eighteenth-century sense of the term), in which a small and isolated figure is overwhelmed by the 'landscape.'

The sequence concludes with a scene of the couple entering the apartment. Maria takes the initiative, gathering the sheets, while Antonio looks on listlessly. I shall not describe the scene, except to note that here the background music starts up a melancholy motif in a minor key, which comes to a natural end, finishing a cadence, in synchrony with the end of the scene.

Sequence 3: Monte di pietà – the pawnbroker. Maria pawns the sheets, and Antonio redeems the bicycle.

De Sica's task in this sequence is to establish a contrast in every way with the previous sequence. Here, therefore, he is exploiting the viewer's *memory* of the previous sequence (and he uses this procedure of exploiting the viewer's *memory* on a number of occasions throughout the film, as we shall see). He establishes his contrast with the montage, the *mise en scène*, the acting of the performers, and the soundtrack. To begin with, I shall concentrate just on the pawning of the sheets (shots 38–52), a reverse-angle sequence with an average shot length of 4.6 seconds, contrasting rhythmically with the shots I analysed from Sequence 2 (27–32), which had a much longer average shot length of 12.6 seconds, and in which the camera observed the characters in a detached way, from the 'outside,' with both figures in the frame. Sequence 3 uses a procedure of reverse-angles, in which the camera points first at character A in close-up or medium close-up, and then swivels to photograph character B similarly. The reverse-angle procedure tends to assemble two point-of-view shots: the viewer is given character A's point of view on character B, and vice versa. Reverse-angles do not *inevitably* prompt the viewer to identify with characters, and where they do, they do so in different degrees (as we shall see in this case), but the procedure is a stark contrast with the 'detached' two-shots of 27–32.

The dissolve from the Riccis' apartment to the pawnbroker is accompanied by the background music, which had come to a conclusion at the end of the previous sequence, starting up again immediately in a slightly brighter harmonic mode. At the moment where the Clerk offers slightly more money than the sheets are worth (shot 47; see plate 25), a new, bell-like, stepping motif starts up in the music, and will be used by the film as a 'code' to emphasize the 'optimistic' elements of the story, in contrast with the rest of the music. Throughout the sequence the voices of other customers waiting in line can be heard in the *background*. These customers can also be seen peering forward through the counter-window, and when Maria and Antonio leave with their money, an elderly man steps up to the window and pushes through a pair of binoculars, which are picked up by the hands of the Clerk, visible in the shot [*sound/ image background, R*]. The man with the binoculars is in fact a case of the camera 'staying' on what is not part of the 'story,' and is therefore part of the *'follow'* procedure, which we shall see taken further later in the film.

The counter-window is an index of the 'institution' of the pawnbrokers. De Sica does not start the scene with a wide, establishing shot of the pawnbroker's premises, but rather launches straight into a medium-close reverse-angle sequence of the dialogue between Maria (and later Antonio) and the Clerk, through that counter-window, which functions as 'establishing' the location and the situation. In shots of Maria, the counter-window is a dominant feature of the image, 'institutionalizing' her relationship with the Clerk (see plate 24). To begin with, De Sica establishes a parallelism, by including the counter-window in shots from Maria's point of view of the Clerk (see plate 23). He does not, however, preserve that parallelism.

The dialogue bridges the cuts between the two components of the reverse-angle assembly, and I shall collect it all together here. Maria pushes the sheets through the window and, as the Clerk helps her and starts unpacking them, says: 'Sono lenzuola ... sei pezzi ... sono di lino, lino e cotone, roba buona, roba de corredo.' / 'They're sheets ... six pieces ... they're linen, linen and cotton, good material, from my trousseau.' The Clerk: 'Uhm. So' usati.' / 'They're used.' Maria: 'Quattro so' usati, due so' novi.' / 'Four are used, two are new.' The Clerk: 'Quanti pezzi sono?' / 'How many pieces are there?' Maria: 'Sei, tre matrimoniali e tre a 'na piazza.' / 'Six, three double and three single.' In shot 43 the Clerk (examining and counting the sheets) says: 'E tre.' / 'That makes three.' He pushes the sheets to right of frame along the counter (to a figure we have just seen working beside him). He looks at Maria, thinking a little, making a bit of a grimace, and says: 'Settemila' / 'Seven thousand.' Maria looks at him, repeats, 'Settemila?' and turns to her left (camera right), so that we see her looking slightly up in profile. Antonio enters the top right of the frame of the counter-window, turning from Maria to the Clerk, and asks: 'Nun se potrebbe fa' 'n po' de più?' / 'Couldn't you make it a bit more?' In shot 45 the Clerk looks at the sheets, picking at one, looks towards Maria, smiling and shaking his head (as if to say 'there's only so much I can do'), with his eyebrows raised (in a sort of appraisal of the sheets) and replies, 'Eh, so' usati, so' usati' / 'Eh, they're used, they're used,' in a rising pitch expressing 'it is difficult to offer more' (in other words, in a very expressive, communicative way, in real dialogue with the question Antonio asked – can he give a bit more? he would if he could). In shot 46, with the camera further back behind the Clerk so that we see him clearly from behind, he pushes the sheets over to his assistant, saying: 'Be,' metti dentro sta' roba.' / 'OK, put this stuff away.' Something in the way he says it expresses that he will give a little more – his tone contains a consent to the request. He turns back to the window and leans forward, putting his hands on the counter. In shot 47 the Clerk (seen from Maria's side of the counter), nods his head forward as he says with a smile: 'Settemila e cinquecento' / 'Seven thousand five hundred' (see plate 25). As he says this, there is a cut to Maria and Antonio, through the window, smiling.

De Sica has required from the actor playing the Clerk a warm, human, sympathetic expressiveness in his body language, in his facial expression, and in his tone of voice that no one else in the film except Antonio's friend Baiocco ever directs towards a member of the Ricci family. The bell-like, stepping motif in the music reinforces this. Moreover, at the moment when the Clerk responds to Antonio's request, De Sica *eliminates* the counter-window from shots of the Clerk taken from Maria's side of the window (compare plate 23 with plate 25, which is of shot 47).

De Sica wants in this scene to raise the mood, and to show the Riccis positively affirmed, while still dominated and conditioned by the social institution. To that end he eliminates the counter-window in the reverse-angle shots of the Clerk. Shots of the Clerk play down foreground and background by using shallow focus. The background of the wall of shelved sheets (which will be important shortly) is so out of focus as scarcely to register in the image. The foreground of the ticket-window is merely implicit in the viewer's memory. But the shots themselves create an image of Maria's point of view on the Clerk as a person relating to her with kindness and understanding, and they achieve this by *no longer* including the counter-window. The shots of the Clerk use, in fact, the conventional shallow-focus medium-close language of emotional engagement that is one of the cinema's tools for prompting the viewer to identify with the characters whose point of view that shot encodes. De Sica is creating his change of mood not just by giving the viewer 'knowledge' through the narrative and the dialogue (the Clerk giving Maria the extra five hundred lire with a smile), but also through the manipulation of the viewer's emotions (reinforced by the change of mood in the music).

This procedure could be judged, from the point of view of the overall narrative of the film, as slightly opportunistic, because the viewer is identifying with Maria, a character who will shortly be dropped from the story. However, that judgment depends on what we take to be the overall narrative of the film. If the 'story,' and total 'vision,' assembled by the film is of the material suffering of Antonio resulting from poverty and unemployment (a 'realist,' logical, cause-and-effect analysis), then the procedure is an opportunistic narrative device: the viewer's spirits are raised when he is shown Antonio 'up,' and not raised when Antonio's fortunes change. Maria's point of view and feelings are merely being exploited for the sentimental effect of raising the viewer's spirits, rather as the background music is used.

If we were to give De Sica's poetic claims the benefit of the doubt at this early stage in the film, and were to approach the film taken as a whole artefact (rather than as a sequence of 'episodes'), as well as hypothesizing that the 'intention' of the artist is to assemble an artefact that makes deeper levels of narrative reference (to the suffering caused by isolation deriving from exclusion from an organic ontology – 'solitu-dine,' in De Sica's words), then De Sica could be seen as evoking, as he needs to, aspects of the lost Utopia, the 'idyll,' in this and subsequent scenes in the film. Maria's 'pleasure' is a part of Antonio's experience, and the family as an icon of the 'organism' communicates and shares in a relation of interdependence. In the anxiety of isolation, Antonio is carefully depicted as cut off from communicating and sharing with oth-ers (and we have seen how the *mise en scène* has been used to achieve this depiction in the previous sequences). In the present and subsequent scenes De Sica posits the hypothesis of 'organicity' that he will subse-quently show 'society' to lack. The lack will be registered in the form of an 'absence,' and through the anxiety this absence causes in Antonio. For the viewer to register an 'absence,' the viewer must hypothesize a 'presence' that is denied.

Once again, I am tempted to draw parallels with Antonioni. In an early scene of *L'avventura*, Sandro and Anna make love. While they are doing so, Claudia is shown in the art gallery below their bedroom look-ing up at the ceiling and smiling. The viewer reads this as her ironically imagining the couple's unity, despite the indifference Anna has imme-diately beforehand expressed to her. In the shots of the couple making love, an 'absence' (of what lovers should feel for each other) is depicted by means of a contrast with the 'expectation' attributed to Claudia, and thereby hypothesized for the viewer. Claudia is used as a device to pro-vide the viewer with a 'reading' of the shots of the couple making love. Her 'expectations' are then used in a similar way throughout the rest of the film. An example of Antonioni's depiction of an 'absence,' in which the viewer has at first to furnish his or her own hypothesis (because a hypothesized 'presence' is only gradually established), is the opening sequence of *L'eclisse*, of Vittoria and Riccardo in his apartment. Anto-nioni assembles fragmented, disjointed shots of the apartment and of the characters. What would give 'meaning' to this location, and the characters' presence in it, would be their love affair. But this is no longer. Hence, Antonioni's (uncharacteristic, in this sequence) *mise en scène* and montage assemble the depiction of an 'absence.' The common interpretation of scenes like this as 'expressing lack of communication' is misleading, because the characters are communicating extremely powerfully their distress and bewilderment at this sudden, unex-plained 'absence.' Antonioni is 'narrating' the withdrawal of sense and meaning experienced by characters who are over-reliant on the ephem-eral fragility of erotic-sentimental bonds. His films extend this to a

Plate 1, shot 27

Plate 2, shot 27

Plate 3, shot 27

Plate 4, shot 28

Plate 5, shot 28

Plate 6, shot 28

Plate 7, shot 28

Plate 8, shot 28

Plate 9, shot 28

Plate 10, shot 28

Plate 11, shot 29

Plate 12, shot 29

Plate 13, shot 29

Plate 14, shot 29

Plate 15, shot 30

Plate 16, shot 30

Plate 17, shot 30

Plate 18, shot 31

Plate 19, shot 31

Plate 20, shot 31

Plate 21, shot 31

Plate 22, shot 32

Plate 23, shot 39

Plate 24, shot 40

Plate 25, shot 47

Plate 26, shot 99

Plate 27, shot 105

Plate 28, shot 483

Plate 29, shot 484

Plate 30, shot 485

Plate 31, shot 486

Plate 32, shot 504

Plate 33, shot 505

depiction of the 'absence' of more solid moral, political, and existential bonds.

I have dwelt on the comparison with Antonioni because I believe it helps us to see more clearly how De Sica's procedures operate, and what they assemble. De Sica fills his images and his narrative with a great deal of social 'data.' Zavattini's contribution to this must be considerable, to judge by everything we have seen about his 'poetics' in chapter 2. If we apply Zavattini's privileging of realist 'content' to *Ladri di biciclette*, we are led towards a predominantly political and sociological reading of the film, and can make the mistake of judging certain of De Sica's *mise en scène* procedures as being examples of a 'sentimentality' laid over the rational, realist 'content.' If, however, we train ourselves as viewers in a broader reading of the assembled artefact, we can be more receptive to the lyrical, poetic level at which De Sica's *mise en scène* assembles the 'absence' lying behind and generating Antonio's anxiety. Antonioni does not load his image with social 'data' in anything like the way De Sica does, and depicts an absence by means of the viewers' and the characters' desires and expectations (for example, on the rocky island in *L'avventura*). De Sica depicts the absence of 'organicity' by filling his frame with other things *instead*, 'presences' that the viewer is prompted to read as being negative alternatives to what *should* be present. The 'absence' of supportive, communicative, interdependent human fellowship (Zavattini's *convivenza* as the product of *conoscenza*) is depicted by its substitution with competitive individualism (characters quarrelling in the background, for example) and complacent, indifferent ignorance. The depiction of Antonio's anxiety ('tailing' him in his journey through Roman society) functions to register that subsitution as a negative 'absence' – not merely as a critique of a particular society in a particular historical moment, but also as a feature of the contemporary human condition: a need for fellowship and solidarity in the hardships of life. The 'individual' is by definition isolated and solitary. In the hero-adventure narrative matrix, the hero's solitude is a mark of his being equal to the forces of nature and society, which he dominates, bringing order out of chaos. The solitude of the individual is not coded as negative, a form of suffering. In the organic ontology of the melodramatic narrative matrix, solitude is *by definition* a deprivation and a loss. The individual is *not* equal to nature and society; only as a component of an organism can he satisfactorily survive. The self-sufficiency of the protagonist of the hero-adventure matrix is what the neorealists call the 'escape' into fantasy. The 'realist' image of post-war Roman society assembled by *Ladri di biciclette* furnishes a total artefact expressing a vision of an existential experience of lack. It does so by assembling a vision that corresponds to 'the sublime': a fragile individual in an awesome and threatening landscape – in this case, not one of craggy mountain peaks and storm-tossed seas, but an urban social landscape ordered according to the laws of economic competition and class interests. The 'data' that De Sica adds so densely to his image, and which has often been interpreted as a realist 'listing,' in actual fact functions in *opposition* to Antonio, as a negation of what it is to be fully a human being, and as we go through the film I shall often use a shorthand for elements of this 'background' by referring to them as *foils* to Antonio.

Hence, it would be wrong to reduce to a stereotyped, opportunistic, sentimental procedure the evocation of positive organicity through the institution of the family (Maria's point of view at the pawnbroker's).

The second half of the sequence depicts Antonio redeeming his bicycle, using a similar reverse-angle procedure through the counter-window. It is in this sequence that occurs one of the shots that have remained most powerfully etched in viewers' memories: the pawnbroker's assistant carrying the Riccis' sheets to a high shelf. This shot too 'eliminates' the counter-window, and is emphasized as a shot of the point of view of Antonio. It therefore tends to detach itself from the strict sequence of exchanges through the window, and becomes a poetic metaphor for Antonio's 'experience' of that existential *landscape* to which I have been referring. The shot is a fine example of De Sica's camera integrating a poetic, expressive image into the narrative by appearing to *follow* a *digression* that crosses the *foreground* of the frame (we shall encounter further examples). The Ricci family's sheets have to be carried higher and higher, past shelf after shelf of other sheets, a tiny, fragile emblem in the midst of a sublime, monotonous 'sea' of surrendered linen. Even the 'idyll' (the job secured, the bicycle redeemed, the harmonious solidarity of the family re-established) is haunted by De Sica's evocation of an alien 'landscape' *experienced* by Antonio.

Sequence 6: Saturday. Valmelaina, the Riccis' apartment, preparing to go to work.

The lighter mood of cooperation and family solidarity, supported by Cicognini's background music, and particularly the stepping bell motif, continues from the Monte di pietà right through to the lesson in billposting. In the scene where the family gets ready for the working day, the solidarity is visualized in the affectionate play between Antonio and Maria, and in the parallel costume (and omelette in the top pocket) of Antonio and Bruno. Once again, composition in depth and *mise en scène* play a very important part in modulating the potential sentimentality of the scene.

The sequence introduces Bruno into the film, but it does so in a particular and characteristic way, using composition in depth. In the very close foreground is the bicycle, in the middle ground Bruno, and in the background Antonio (see plate 26). To get this shot, the filmmakers had to place the camera between the wall of the room and the bicycle, and the lighting had to be so low as to make the shot almost unacceptable for a feature film (in fact, Bruno quickly opens a window). This shot is one of a number in the film in which De Sica forces the viewer to a 'reading' of Antonio's point of view on his family. In Sequence 2 Maria, seen from a point of view approximating Antonio's, is momentarily erased from the image by a huge concrete post as she approaches Antonio from the standpipe, and later she is once again erased by the passing neighbour. In the restaurant scene, Bruno is erased from the image by the waiter bringing wine for Antonio. In the shot we are examining now, the camera is not taking up the physical position of Antonio – quite the opposite – but the 'reading' to which the viewer is subtly prompted is to see the effacement of Bruno by Antonio's anxiety about the bicycle as an analogy of Antonio's point of view on his son. It is something that is 'narrated' by the logic of the *mise en scène*, without yet forming an important part of the narrative for the viewer. It plants a seed that will be cultivated by the film as it develops. However, it does introduce Bruno in a way that helps us to understand a feature that runs through the whole of De Sica's cinema: his use of children. In this shot, and right throughout the film, Bruno both devotes himself to, and depends on, Antonio. The narrative of the film will emphasize this relationship frequently by means of composition in depth – Bruno vulnerable in the foreground, with Antonio oblivious or neglectful in the background: when Bruno is pestered by the pederast at Piazza Vittorio, when he falls at Porta Portese, and when he is nearly run over on Viale Flaminio near the end of the film. During the chase after the old man, Bruno is constantly shot stopping and looking up at his father, ready to respond to him.

The ontology of a child is *by definition* 'organic.' It is not so much that children are 'innocent' in De Sica's films as that they are dependent, collaborative, oriented towards the 'other,' at the opposite pole from the 'individualist' ontology. The child forms a contrast with the corrosion of the organic ontology brought about by modernization. Antonio, by acting in awareness of the 'individualist' alternative to the organic ontology, makes 'mistakes.' The child never makes a mistake. Bruno, like other children in De Sica's films, constitutes an instance of an ontological universal that functions as a lost ideal, an evocation of the 'idyll' against which De Sica's portrayal of contemporary society acquires its morally critical tone.

This scene in the Ricci apartment also contains an example of De Sica's *formal* composition in depth. When Maria hands Antonio his cap, and the two of them affectionately scuffle, the camera is set up to photograph them against the window, and therefore against the light – not a choice a cinematographer would spontaneously make, because it requires so much careful 'fill' lighting (see plate 22). In the foreground, the table with the plate and the *frittata* (omelette) on it extends towards the middle ground and background. In the middle ground are the two figures, while in the background is the window, with a bottle on the ledge, through it the arch of the apartment block, and through that first the arches and then the windows of the opposite block. De Sica has left the walls on either side of the window bare. The result is a formal symmetry in all three dimensions. I am not suggesting any particular interpretation of De Sica's choice, but just pointing out what his compositional choices are.

De Sica will often, however, use the background for narrative information, and this is the third example of composition in depth that I want to indicate in this particular scene. As Bruno finishes combing his hair, we see his bed in the background with, above it, a poster of the *Giro d'Italia* (a cycle race) and photographs of celebrated cyclists, and across these a religious poster – typical examples of the 'data' De Sica includes in his image, functioning in *opposition* to Antonio. Bruno's 'effacement' is a 'reading' of Antonio's anxious self-absorption offered to the viewer, but Bruno is by no means effaced for the viewer.

Sequence 8: Porta Pinciana. Antonio is taught how to stick up a poster.

This short scene contains three sequence-shots (119–21), with continuous diegetic sound throughout: the accordion-playing of one of the two begging boys and the running commentary of the expert bill poster. These two features of the soundtrack reappear several times in the film. Diegetic music (by which I mean music whose source is in the story) occurs in the *dopolavoro* scene, in the Messa del povero, in the restaurant scene, and perhaps in the scene in the thief's neighbourhood. I say 'perhaps' because the music is of a barrel organ, the kind found on the streets; but if there was once such an organ in the scene, the shots in which it appears have been cut from the final film. The 'running commentary' is a peculiar feature of *Ladri di biciclette*. It occurs here in the billposting lesson, in a shortened version in the *dopolavoro* scene (the party or union official's voice), in the Piazza Vittorio market (Baiocco's voice), in the dustcart trip to Porta Portese (Meniconi's voice), in the thief's apartment (the mother's voice), and later in the brothel (where the running commentary is maintained by two women: the concièrge and the madame). In four of the cases (not the *dopolavoro* scene, nor the thief's apartment), the 'dialogue' has some of the characteristics of 'voice-over' (non-diegetic sound added at the editing stage, typically the 'commentary' of a documentary or newsreel): the acoustic does not correspond consistently with the spatial setting in which the characters utter the words and with the position of the camera in relation to them, and the sound often comes from off-camera. In the *dopolavoro* scene, the voice has the plausible acoustic of a 'background' and as Antonio distances himself from the source, it dies away.

One of the functions of music in a film (both diegetic music and non-diegetic, 'background' music) is to hold together the continuity of the viewer's time frame while the film assembles disjointed and sometimes elliptical shots. Running commentary can have the same function, and in *Ladri di biciclette* only in this scene and in the *dopolavoro* scene is there both music and running commentary. At Piazza Vittorio and at the brothel, the running commentaries are non-essential additions to the narrative, in the sense that they do not add important or necessary information. Here the commentary complements the sense of the narrative (a 'lesson'). But both here and in the case of Baiocco's running commentary at Piazza Vittorio, the intonation of the speaker has a stylized formality to it, while in the brothel scene, the two women are decidedly agitated. In this case, however, it also has another function, that of framing the 'digression,' which consists of the boys begging from a passing businessman.

Shot 119 shows the billposter rapidly attaching the top half of a poster of Rita Hayworth. (Commentators have made much of this poster, so I shall remark no further on its obvious contrast of two cinematic traditions. 'Cinema' is referred to three times in the 'story' of the film: here with a Rita Hayworth poster for *Gilda*; later, when Antonio refers to his bicycle having been stolen from outside the Florida cinema – linking the theft with the poster, perhaps, but too subtly for the viewer to make the connection; in the dustcart en route to Porta Portese, where Meniconi denigrates cinema as entertainment.) Shot 120 changes the angle, and is in a longer scale. The boy playing the accordion approaches the ladder to prop himself on the bottom rung, and is booted off by the expert, who does not break his verbal rhythm, but merely inserts an 'A' regazzi'' / 'Hey there, young lad' into his running commentary. At this point, a man dressed in a dark suit, with a hat, a briefcase, and an umbrella, passes into the frame from the right *foreground*, and proceeds down the street. The camera abandons the posting lesson, and *follows* him and the two boys as one of them falls into step with him and begs from him (the accordion player lags behind). When the man takes no notice of them, the boy keeping step with him turns back. The camera cuts back to the billposting, now complete, where the two adults are taking down their ladders and riding off on their bicycles. As Antonio rides away (in a 'V' *movement*), the two boys are proceeding down the street.

A *foreground* detail (the businessman) and a *background* element (the diegetic music, related to the boys) are developed as an expression of what Antonio's job is protecting him against: poverty and begging and, above all, the indifference and exclusion of society, represented by the man dressed in the 'uniform' of bourgeois power and security. All of this is articulated with the procedures of comedy, of which the running commentary is an important ingredient. When Antonio's bicycle has been stolen, his despair is conveyed by *him* sitting on the bottom rungs of his ladder, reduced now – in his own eyes – to the condition of those two boys. Society will now kick him off the ladder, which represents a socially integrated means of earning an independent livelihood. The 'background digression' of the two boys has endowed the ladder with a meaning that the viewer now 'reads.'

The episode's relation to the narrative is as a digression, and in this case, a quite striking and remarkable one that it is very unusual to find in a feature film. And yet the reading of it to which the viewer is prompted belongs in the development of visually articulated themes (as opposed to discursively articulated, for example in the dialogue or in the dramatic encounters the protagonist has) that bear upon the main story, and the total vision that is the ultimate product of the aesthetic artefact. De Sica fills the film with data that is presented in the background, but that is a great deal more than 'realist setting,' for it constitutes the narrative assembly of the vision. It would be easy to see the data as 'realism' in the sense discussed elsewhere of the 'list' – things represented because they were 'there' – but that would be to forget that De Sica has assembled this 'list' for a purpose, according to a precise principle of selection. This small example of De Sica's approach to the narrative assembly of the film can be seen as a feature of much larger portions of the film: the Santona, the seminarians at Porta Portese, the restaurant, the brothel, the Messa del povero, and to a certain extent the football crowd in the stadium. Not often is such a digression so completely detached from the main narrative, but I shall later be describing one other example approaching this effect, that of the smartly dressed neighbour of the thief.

It is interesting to note that shot 121 was taken at a different time from shots 119 and 120. A continuity error is the clue to this fact (nothing else betrays it). The billboard onto which the poster of Rita Hayworth is being posted in shot 121 has different posters on either side in the other two shots. Moreover, from shot 120 to shot 121, the bottom half of the Hayworth poster has implausibly materialized on the billboard. I wonder whether De Sica first shot the 'lesson' without the digression of the businessman, and then later – another day – added the digression as an unscripted elaboration (this would imply, for example, that shot 121 was taken *before* the previous two shots). The same continuity error appears in the next sequence of the bicycle theft: the billboard acquires different posters from one shot to the next.

Sequence 9: Via Francesco Crispi. The theft of the bicycle.

The sequence of the bicycle theft consists of 37 shots in 2 minutes and 56 seconds, giving an average shot length of 4.8 seconds. The sequences of the film that are most comparable are that of the vendors hurrying out of the rain at Porta Portese, that of the argument in the thief's neighbourhood, and that of Antonio's theft of a bicycle at the end of the film. In these sequences De Sica makes use of montage to assemble the narrative.

In this sequence, of the first bicycle theft, there are some principal, anchoring shots, around which are assembled reverse-angles and different perspectives. The first of these principal shots, which also ends the sequence, looks down the wall of Via Francesco Crispi on which Antonio is sticking the poster. During the preparations for the theft, a longish shot of the young thief reconnoitring between the cars is broken into with a return to the shot down the wall, in which his accomplices are also reconnoitring. The theft itself consists of continuations of these shots, intercut with shots of Antonio reacting. As Antonio chases the thief into Largo del Tritone, the addition of an overhead shot is notable. Then De Sica uses Antonio's point of view, through the windscreen of the taxi, during the pursuit into the tunnel, with cutaways to the accomplice. The realization that the pursuers have been chasing the wrong cyclist is carried by a fragmented sequence of reverse-angles, after which the anchoring shot becomes that of Antonio walking out of the tunnel close into the camera, intercut with reverse-angles of the streets he looks down. The sequence ends with a return to the initial 'anchoring' shot, where he returns to the wall, dejectedly throwing down the bucket, flicking a loose corner of the poster with his brush, and sitting down on the ladder rubbing his thigh, at which point the camera concludes the sequence by tracking into a close-up. The overall effect is to convey Antonio's *experience* of the events, without always limiting the camera to giving only his visual perspective on them.

The shots of the wall and of the tunnel use architecture and perspective to give the viewer a sense of being closed in, despite the size of the cityscape, and the tunnel itself sows a *memory* in the viewer's mind that is taken up in the sequence where Antonio thinks Bruno may have fallen in the river. The beginning of the theft sequence uses the viewer's *memory* to contrast it violently with the previous one of the 'lesson': the silence resulting from the absence of the diegetic music is particularly effective. The sense of things running away from Antonio and eluding him is taken up in the scene at Porta Portese, where everyone else is moving with a purpose while Antonio stands bewildered, wanting things to freeze. These links and cross-references are a feature of De Sica's style: the assembly of his fragments into a fluid and coherent evocation of Antonio's fragile hold on the landscape in which he is set. Moreover, the theft sequence primes the viewer for scenes that follow later in the film. When the thief and his neighbours portray a hopeless, impoverished innocence, the viewer *remembers* the coolly planned theft by an organized gang, incompatible with a desperate lone gesture, and not comparable with Antonio's theft at the end. At both the narrative and figurative levels, this scene sets up contrasts with important scenes later in the film, in which the depiction of Antonio's solitude is visually made more stiking by the contrast with the effective help given first to the thief by his neighbours, and finally to the victim of Antonio's own theft, at the end of the film.

Sequence 14: Valmelaina. Antonio seeks help from Baiocco at the *dopolavoro*, or working men's club.

This was the first scene in the film to be shot. Towards the end of the sequence, the dialogues between Antonio, Baiocco, and Maria are shot with close-up, frontally lit reverse-angles, in which faces loom in a frame devoid of background, a style that is uncharacteristic of the rest of the film. Other aspects of the sequence, however, are more characteristic of the way in which the film as a whole is assembled.

The scene is announced by a 'sound bridge' in the shot that precedes it, of Antonio approaching the building in which the *dopolavoro* occupies the cellars. The instrumental introduction to the Neapolitan song *Ciccio formaggio* can be heard before we actually cut to Antonio entering the location. This diegetic music constitutes a background (for a while coming into the foreground) for the whole sequence, playing throughout. Not only that, as Antonio enters, the voice of a trades union or communist party official can be heard addressing a meeting of Valmelaina residents, and this 'background' sound continues until Antonio gets out of earshot. In some ways, this voice-off (whose source then enters the frame for a moment) functions rather like what I characterize as a 'running commentary' accompanying other sequences in the film, such as in the lesson about posting bills (sequence 9), in the Piazza Vittorio market (sequence 15), and in the brothel (sequence 25). The search for the thief in the later part of the film will often involve Antonio arriving in the midst of ongoing activities (Porta Portese, the Messa del povero, the restaurant, the Santona, the stadium), which portray a social 'background' that the narrative appears to stumble upon in a journey through a particular place at a particular historical moment. While this procedure establishes a 'realist' setting for the film (appearing to assemble a 'list' of items 'represented' because they were 'there' in reality), it is also one of the ways in which De Sica assembles the 'landscape' into which he is placing his 'figure' and thereby establishing the narrative's deeper levels of melodramatic reference.

The sequence is assembled from three narrative, dramatic, and figurative elements: the union or political meeting, the variety act, and Antonio's dialogue with Baiocco and then Maria. There takes place a gradual 'nesting' of the three elements within one another, culminating in the third. The viewer is offered a multiple perspective in which values, established by what has preceded the scene, can shift according to the perspective. I shall crudely identify the values in terms of 'positive' (things being the way we feel they ought to be) and 'negative' (things being other than the way we feel they ought to be). The values of 'positive' and 'negative' are from the viewer's perspective, which is both *with* Antonio (the viewer is brought into the *dopolavoro* by Antonio) and *on* Antonio. As will almost always be the case, De Sica's procedures maintain a detached, objective perspective on Antonio while at the same time offering the viewer an overall picture that expresses his personal experience of the world.

The first element of the sequence is an address concerning unemployment by a trade union or communist party official to the residents of Valmelaina. Earlier, we quoted Sergio Leone's account of a scriptwriting session in which it was proposed to have Antonio's sandwich wrapped in a copy of the Communist Party newspaper *L'Unità*. In some ways, this address serves an analogous function. Its insertion as a casually overheard piece of 'background' may have been the furthest the filmmakers dared to venture in the reactionary climate overtaking the Italian cinema in the aftermath of the 1948 elections. What we hear is this:

> [*Off camera*] Here it's not a question of the employment office. If there's no work, people can't be given jobs. Besides, we as a cell have brought the matter up in the local section and with the chamber of employment. Benefits don't solve anything; they just humiliate the worker. They get used up in no time, and leave everything else as it was before. Here what is needed [*the speaker appears in shot*] is a major program of public works. And today, basically, at the rally, what did they say? The same thing. [*Here the camera reverses its angle to the audience, and we see the cigar-smoking labour exchange Clerk listening and nodding his approval.*] From us you can't expect miracles. We're keeping our eyes open all the time. [*Here Antonio causes an interruption, looking for his friend Baiocco. The speaker calls for silence:* 'Keep quiet over there!' *One of the listeners points to Antonio, saying,* 'It's him, it is!'] As soon as there's a possibility [*as Antonio moves away, the speaker's voice continues off camera*] of fixing you up, we won't let it pass, you can be sure of that ... I know, you are right, the main thing is to find work, because once a fellow is working the world starts to function properly ... [*The speaker's voice becomes inaudible as Antonio rounds the corner into the space where the variety act is being rehearsed.*]

This speech 'nests' the politics of unemployment into a scene in which human solidarity and affection are the problematic element at the centre of the scene, endowing the whole sequence with two levels of discourse, articulated by De Sica's customary superimposition of foreground and background elements. Moreover, the whole sequence is characterized by a sort of grumpiness and conflict between the people, having quite the opposite effect to one of a moral and sentimental idealization of the working man. Antonio has come to the *dopolavoro* in search of help from a friend who is politically and culturally active. The political and cultural activities are shown as background elements of a social 'landscape' from which Antonio is excluded, and by which he is rejected. The 'positive' value is carried by the workers' solidarity and their analysis of their situation. Is the 'negative' value carried by the indifference of the union or party official and of the other workers to Antonio's suffering, or is it carried by Antonio's self-absorbed, isolated, individualist refusal to see his predicament in a wider social and political context? The whole sequence is ambiguous in this sense, both here with the political speech, and in the next section involving the variety act. What we could affirm is that while the film raises political questions, Antonio's isolation is located in an existential space separate from questions of politics.

In the second section of the sequence, where Antonio interrupts Baiocco rehearsing a variety act, it is hard for the viewer to decide what is the function in the narrative of the quarrel over the cadence in the song, beyond the fact that it is one more element of the social landscape which excludes Antonio's concerns and experience. The 'positive' value could be being carried by the communal cultural activity, while the 'negative' value is being carried by the quarrelling over the song, and by the domineering irritability of the singer. It is almost as though we had Zavattini's political discourse (see his versions of the *soggetto* earlier in this chapter) in a dialectic with De Sica's melodramatic discourse. In the first section of the sequence, the political and the melodramatic discourses are in conflict; in the second section the variety act functions as a contrastive 'foil' to Antonio's predicament; in the third section the melodramatic discourse is at the centre and all the other elements of the *dopolavoro* are at the periphery. The 'positive' value is carried by Baiocco's sympathy, empathy, and solidarity with Antonio's predicament, while the 'negative' value is carried by Antonio's behaviour towards Maria and his isolation from the solidarity uniting his fellow workers. One thing, however, that the whole sequence does achieve is to introduce Baiocco into the film through the veil of Antonio's experience, just as Bruno was introduced earlier in the film behind the bicycle. Both Bruno and Baiocco offer representations of the 'organic' ontology whose *absence* Antonio experiences in terms of anxiety, and with which Antonio's human diminishment is contrasted.

This is the scene where Maria is dispatched from the film. Antonio is shown as avoiding her anxiety, while Baiocco is made to dismiss her condescendingly:

ANTONIO: Don't let's start moaning! I didn't come home because I didn't want to hear moaning.

MARIA: Moaning? And who's moaning, excuse me? It's not something that happens every day! Have you done something? Have you looked for it?

BAIOCCO: Don't start crying like that! You look like a little girl, you do. It's not the first one to be found ... They'll change the saddle and the handlebars, but it's got to be there at the market tomorrow. And if it's there, we'll bring it home, won't we, Antonio? Maybe tonight you won't be sleeping so well, but the important thing is that we'll get it get back. Don't worry.

Maria's dispatch takes almost the form of a suppression. As we have seen earlier in the chapter, it was a scripting decision hotly contested by Sergio Amidei. Furthermore, as the Riccis go out of the *dopolavoro*, it appears that Zavattini asked for some frames, of Maria crying, to be cut: 'Here, Zavattini requested the removal of about ten frames that paused on the face of the woman dissolved in tears.'[49] There is a rather too abrupt cut where this has been done – and I suspect it was more than ten frames that were cut. Amidei's other reason for dissatisfaction with the film can also be related to this scene, where the local Communist Party section could have resolved Antonio's predicament by rustling up a temporary bicycle for him. Speculating about why Maria is dropped from the film could be asking the wrong question, which might instead be, what is her function in the first place? In considering how she is used to establish the idyll whose loss the rest of the film evokes, we identify a function for her that, from this point onwards in the film, has outlived its purpose. Amidei might have, once again, been attached to a 'logical' convention of narrative that neorealist films were in the process of transcending.

Sequence 18: The Church of Saints Nereo e Achilleo. Antonio follows the old man into a 'Mass for the poor.'

This sequence is yet another 'episode' bracketed off from the rest of the film by diegetic organ music that starts up before the camera cuts to the inside of the building, and continues until the action has already begun outside in the garden. It is an episode assembled with an enormous amount of background detail, making great use of the follow shot and of sound-off, and constructed, in part, out of the procedures of comedy (the old man swearing loudly in church within earshot of the supervisors – 'Ma portamece col diavolo che te s'encolla, che me ne frega a me!' [something like: 'Take me there with the devil sticking to you, for all the shit I give!'] – the chase through the church, Bruno's smack on the head from the priest dozing in the confessional, the young supervisor shouting demands for Antonio to keep his voice down). The presentation of the middle-class supervisors is at times satirical (pedantic dosing of the *minestra*). The possible overtones of the episode are worth investigating.

The episode is given a real, historical setting: the 'Messa del povero,' set up by Don Luigi Moresco in that actual church. On the release of the film, the Vatican newspaper, *L'Osservatore romano*, harshly criticized the episode's satirical approach:

Right on the fifth anniversary of the death of Don Luigi Moresco, his 'Messa del povero' has been brought to the screen – albeit as an incidental episode. But rather than screen, it is a case of scorn. In the film reviews section above, an ethical and aesthetic judgment of the film in question is expressed – because for us, humanistically speaking, art is the completion, the integration of life – while here we add just a few words, on a note of regret and reproach. Reproach on finding that even Italian artists have dared to insult, with caricatures of low, anticlerical taste, a charitable institution that brings together in fellowship beggars and better-off people, and that not even the political police of the 'clandestine period' dared to interfere with even minimally. A note of blame, finally, for those who, giving the ecclesiastical authorities the fullest assurances of their intention to respect the poor and the work of charity, insinuated themselves into the temple, instead, in order to describe the 'poor' brethren as an inert flock supinely receiving handouts and absolutely devoid of soul or human dignity; and in order to describe the brothers of the 'poor' as fatuous benefactors.

It would remain, finally – restraining our anger for the offence given to the religiosity of the Roman people, presented as superstitious and ignorant – it would remain, as we were saying, to express a judgment on the actions of those who approved such a film, and gave it access to the public. But we prefer to abstain from doing so. At least for the time being. *Piero Regnoli.*[50]

The *Osservatore romano*'s interpretation of the episode is not tendentious, because it coincides with that of all successive commentators on the film. However, neither Zavattini's account of the location scouting

trip to the church (dated December 1947) nor his 'definitive' treatment
of the film (dated 20 April 1948) suggest criticism or satire of the benefactors, even though his well-known political opinions would make
him critical of the Catholic Church's approach to social problems.
Meanwhile, however, the Christian Democrats have thrown out the
parties of the Left from the governing coalition (May 1947), have been
elected to an outright majority in parliament during the making of the
film (April 1948), and have installed a fervent Catholic, Giulio Andreotti, in the under-secretaryship to the cabinet in charge of the state's
dealings with the cinema. The last paragraph of Regnoli's note is worth
picking up. It suggests that the 'those who approved such a film'
should not have allowed the film's release in that state. The authority in
question would have been Andreotti, whom both Zavattini and De Sica
were later to blame for many of the trials that belaboured neorealism in
successive years, and their own cooperative endeavours in particular.
Zavattini was active in a number of bodies defending the independence
and vitality of Italian cinema at the time. Giulio Andreotti was a disci-
ple of the very eminent Christian Democrat politician, Giorgio La Pira,
who had entered parliament as a deputy at the end of the war, and was
nominated after the April 1948 elections to De Gasperi's cabinet as
under-secretary in the Department of Labour (unemployment is one of
the themes of *Ladri di biciclette*). Giorgio La Pira was a devout Christian
Democrat lawyer, who was famous for having instituted a 'Messa del
povero' in Florence before the war, and for setting up an even more
well-known one than Don Moresco's in the church of San Girolamo
della Carità in Rome. Years later, in a memorial to La Pira in his own
perodical, *Trenta giorni*, Andreotti wrote:

> La Pira in person established in the church of San Girolamo della Carità in
> Rome the Messa del povero, which he had conceived a few years earlier in
> Florence. It was a new experience that complemented for us that of the
> Conference of San Vincenzo (with weekly visits, two by two, to the suburb
> of Pietralata). Communal prayer, a short homily, coffee and sandwiches,
> and the rest of the morning spent talking with these people unblessed by
> fortune. Bolder colleagues turned themselves into barbers, gradually
> acquiring a certain professional skill in smartening up the guests who for
> the rest of the week were ignorant of razors and – not all of them – even of
> soap. But more than anything, these poor creatures were grateful to us
> because we listened to them, and they could unburden themselves,
> dreaming together with us about possible changes of direction in their

uneasy lives. When the Professor arrived, they would all try to get close to him, and his smile would light up the faces of so many who did not benefit from other moments of attention, and bore the burden of complicated family histories.[51]

It is not inconceivable that the 'avvocato' (lawyer) in the episode, who shaves the old man's chin, and who leads the congregation in a prayer, might be an allusion to the Christian Democrat party, through parodies of La Pira and Andreotti. Even the words of the prayer the 'avvocato' intones are open to an ironical interpretation:

Io voglio uscire da questo luogo santo / I wish to leave this holy place [*repeated by the congregation*], sentendomi purificato nell'animo / feeling myself purified in my soul [*repeated by the congregation*] e rasserenato nello spirito / and calmed in spirit [*the lawyer's words start to get covered by the dialogue between Antonio and the old man, but he repeats himself, to combat the disturbance of Antonio*] ... e da ripercorrere ... e da ripercorrere le strade del dolore e della privazione / ... and from retracing the paths of sorrow and privation.

The episode of *Ladri di biciclette* set in the church of Saints Nereo and Achilleo may be using the satirical devices of comedy to make more precise 'reference' than at first meets the eye.

Sequence 22: Passeggio di Ripetta. Antonio and Bruno eat in a restaurant.

The restaurant scene is bracketed off from the rest of the film by a feature of the soundtrack, the Neapolitan musicians playing a Neapolitan song of the period *Tammurriata nera*, and then continuing to play instrumentally right through to the dissolve at the end of the scene, whereupon the state radio, broadcasting sports news, replaces it. That this bracketing is deliberate is suggested by the fact that the first chord of the song starts in the previous shot on the Lungotevere, forming a 'sound bridge' that announces a change of location and mood. The dissolve from the Lungotevere to the inside of the restaurant entails an ellipsis, which is 'hidden' by the montage. Antonio moves to the right across the screen and across the street, whereupon the next shot shows him and Bruno, from inside the restaurant, opening the door and entering, making it appear that they have entered a restaurant on the opposite side of the street. In fact, they have had to make their way to a street parallel to the Lungotevere, and what is hidden in the montage is not in fact hidden by the *mise en scène*, because through the open door we see the cityscape clearly.

Although neither born in Naples nor of Neapolitan parents, De Sica spent a significant period of his childhood in the city, and thereafter always identified himself as 'Neapolitan.' As a singer he frequently performed Neapolitan songs. He inserts two into *Ladri di biciclette*, *Tammurriata nera* in the restaurant scene and *Ciccio formaggio* in the *dopolavoro* scene.[52] Despite the popular Roman setting of the film, he uses for his diegetic music not popular Roman songs, but Neapolitan ones. In both cases, he uses their ironic, light-hearted tone to contrast with the tone of the film's narrative content at the point where the song is inserted.

Introducing his blistering performance of *Tammurriata nera* (captured on film in the documentary *Cuore napoletano* [Paolo Santoni, 2002]), the Neapolitan performer Peppe Barra addresses his listeners thus:

> Behind the ironic and jocular lyrics of this song ..., think that it was written in 1945 [in fact, 1944], when Naples had suffered, as well as a war ..., was daily suffering the raping of her women. They were raped, and after nine months black babies were born, to whom the people nevertheless gave traditional names: Peppe, Ciro, Ntuono. Behind the gay, laughing mask of a people lay hidden, as always, anger, despair, and anguish.

The words of the song are printed in appendix 26.

It is just possible that, rather than a rape victim, as Peppe Barra asserts, the mother in the song might be the 'Angelina' to whom Joe, the black MP in the *Naples* episode of *Paisà*, wants Pasquale to take him, in which case the song would be alluding to prostitution rather than rape.[53] The distinction may be less significant than at first appears, and I have discussed the ambiguous relationship between prostitution and rape in the chapter on *Roma città aperta*. The song makes comedy out of a social tragedy – the rupture of the organism – and narrates a society indifferent and complacent in the face of the mother's exclusion and isolation. The tension between form and content is an *expressive* aesthetic procedure, creating, as does *Ladri di biciclette*, the evocation of a figure (the mother) in a landscape. The 'melodramatic' corrosion of an organic ontology is attributed, in the song, to a historical cause: the violent irruption of modernization into an idyll. The 'voice' from which the discourse of the song issues is not just ironical, but downright sarcastic, cruelly consigning to an irretrievable past an idyll that has now been supplanted.

Contemporary Neapolitan songs were among the most eloquent expressions of the overall perception of 'modernization' (in this case the Allied invasion/liberation) ripping apart the organic fabric of Italian society. Two of the most famous dealt with rape. De Sica baptized one of them, *Munasterio 'e Santa Chiara*, with his performance as a singer, and inserted the other, *Tammurriata nera*, into *Ladri di biciclette*.[54] This should alert us to De Sica's detached, ironical way of assembling an artefact with profound resonance. The restaurant scene in *Ladri di biciclette* employs, as do other scenes in the film, the procedures of comedy, but, rather than with a comic function, with the aim of setting up a contrast between tone and content. This is part of the way De Sica articulates the expressive background of his film, which in turn configures the landscape in which he is inserting his figures. De Sica's use of the song, therefore, nests within the film a mirror image of his own artefact that contains it, while also giving that mirror image other functions in the assembly.

The restaurant scene is ostensibly offered to the viewer as a self-contained interlude, a respite from Antonio's troubles, and a moment where he gives expression to his humanity (his relations with his son) and acts upon his and Bruno's desire (for food, wine, and music), rather than being driven and impelled by social circumstances. In reality, the filmmakers have arranged it so that this is the stage where the narrative portrays Antonio as reaching a full awareness of his situation: that he will not find the bicycle, which is gone forever; that the society is competitively individualistic and not organic, structured in such a way as to consign him to a class whose scope for self-realization and self-affirmation is virtually nil (which is partly the narrative function of the middle-class family at the adjoining table). In the background, the Neapolitan song narrates the irrelevance of a person's desire to social reality (the mother's desire can achieve no more than a 'name' for the child, whose social potential and whose integration into the social organism are stifled by the circumstances of his birth).

Having been shown acquiring this 'knowledge,' Antonio is then portrayed as taking two actions, neither of which are true expressions of free autonomy in the context of the characteristics with which the filmmakers have hitherto endowed him. The first is to regress into fantasy from what little knowledge and autonomy he does have, by visiting the Santona, the clairvoyant whom he has already been shown as not respecting; the second is to steal a bicycle, even though the film has hitherto set him up in opposition to the aggressive, self-affirming lawlessness of ruthless competitive individualism. Indeed, when he does steal a bicycle, even the avenue of ruthless self-affirmation is seen to be denied him by social mechanisms for maintaining equilibrium, in which bystanders unite in solidarity to thwart him. The narrative contrives always to isolate him from those mechanisms, so that when he is robbed, and when he later catches the thief, bystanders are made to negate his needs, but when he turns to theft himself, they are made to assert their own needs for social solidarity.

A 'realist' approach to the film concentrates on *the viewer's* knowledge, and how it is supplied. But the film narrates *the characters'* acquisition of full knowledge of their condition. One way of achieving that aim would be to have characters who *reflected* (though in a film it is much harder to represent that reflection than it is in a novel). Instead, De Sica and Zavattini *narrate* the characters' acquisition of knowledge about their situation. In *Ladri*, there are three scenes where this takes place in Antonio, scenes occurring one after the other: the restaurant scene, followed by the scene at the Santona's, where he articulates this knowledge by his action, and the scene in the thief's neighbourhood, where he decides not to press charges against the thief, and where he is thrown out by the neighbours. He finds the thief, but (a) this does not get him his bicycle back; (b) it does not improve his position; and (c) social forces defeat and isolate him. The loss of the bicycle is a *pretext* for a series of narrative 'images' of a human condition or situation. On the level of realism, the *logic* of the bicycle must carry everything. On the expressive level, the search for the lost bicycle creates the opportunity for a series of expressive 'scenes,' which the film as a whole *assembles*.

The 'nesting' procedure I have already referred to is developed in the *mise en scène*. The entry into the restaurant is filmed in a reverse-angle sequence, showing first Antonio looking (see plate 28), then what he sees (see plate 29), and then, to confirm the perspective, a closer shot of Antonio looking (see plate 30). This prompts the viewer to see what ensues through Antonio's eyes, and gives emphasis to Antonio's experience, rather than to the viewer's. The viewer's more objective experience would have been emphasized had De Sica *introduced* the scene differently (for example, with the shot in plate 31). The *mise en scène* then 'reduces' the restaurant to a small section of the premises, and sets up one three-dimensional composition 'nested' within another. The 'external' composition has Antonio and Bruno in the middle ground, with the orchestra on one side and the middle-class family eating on the other side. Since much of the scene develops in reverse-angles between Antonio and Bruno across the table, the orchestra and the wealthier family alternate as 'background.' Nested within that composition lies the table, with the wine in the middle ground, and Antonio and Bruno alternating as 'background.' We could describe it this way: (1) the orchestra; (2a) Antonio; (2b) the wine on the table; (2c) Bruno; (3) the table of wealthier customers generally being served by two waiters simultaneously. The 'landscape' is constituted by 1 and 3 (incorporating the song on the soundtrack and the whole restaurant as a social institution), into which De Sica places his 'figures' 2a and 2c, with the wine – 2b – between them. However, the order in which he develops these nested constructions is opposite to the one I have described. First, he exploits the inner set-up of Antonio and Bruno around the wine to establish the self-absorption of Antonio, and then he expands the narrative to embrace the outer composition, starting light-heartedly with the musicians, and then darkening the episode by introducing Antonio's comparison of his own circumstances with that of the other diners. In this way, De Sica first prompts the viewer to take a critical perspective on the scene, and then gradually winds it up to a crescendo of anxiety.

The bare narrative content of the scene is as follows: father and son enter and sit down. Antonio cheerfully proposes that they get drunk, to which Bruno responds with a bemused expression. Antonio summons a waiter and orders a litre of wine and a pizza, to which the waiter, wiping off the table, replies that this is a *trattoria* not a *pizzeria*. Antonio sees Bruno look over his shoulder to exchange glances with the boy behind eating a *mozzarella in carrozza* with his hands, and orders two of them, and the wine 'immediately.' Bruno looks over again at the boy behind, who turns away haughtily. Antonio taps the table with his hand in time to the music, enjoying it. The waiter places the carafe of wine and two glasses on the table, and Antonio fills the two glasses. He empties his in one go, and tells Bruno to drink up, which the boy does reluctantly, until Antonio remarks on how his mother would react to knowing that his father was making him drink, at which Bruno smiles. Antonio turns to enjoy the music. The singer leans forward and sings first to Antonio and then especially to Bruno, who smiles bashfully. The waiter brings the dishes, and father and son attack their plates with knife and fork. Bruno has difficulty, and starts eating the food with his hands, pulling out the string of cheese, and looking over in triumphant fellowship to the boy behind. Antonio, starting to pour himself more wine, notices where Bruno is looking, and we see two waiters depositing dessert and champagne on the table behind. Bruno's curiosity is met with haughty disdain by the other boy. Antonio says that to eat like those people costs a million lire a month. Bruno, crestfallen, puts down his food, but Antonio encourages him not to think about it, and to carry on eating. But after a moment, Antonio takes a pencil out of his pocket to write on a napkin, and laments how well-off they would have been with the money from his job. He passes pencil and paper to Bruno to continue the accounting. Bruno says that they should go to Porta Portese every day, because they must find the thieves. Antonio says that they will never find them, not even with Bruno's mother's saints and candles.

Clearly, the restaurant as a whole, the other family, the music, and the waiters act as *'foils'* to Antonio. The scene calibrates the fragility of Antonio's and Bruno's participation in this social institution: first, they nourish an ephemeral participation, enjoying the meeting of their needs, and then they gradually register its ephemeral nature and their exclusion. Society's indifference to their needs is articulated not so much by polemic (though partly so) as by burlesque and caricature – the procedures of cinematic comedy.

The comedy, the music, and the fact of eating suggest that the scene could be experienced by the viewer as a 'respite' in the relentless wearing down of Antonio, and one in which the father–son relationship is reaffirmed after its breakdown under stress – a sentimental interlude. But I am not sure that De Sica is as sentimental in this film as some commentators have suggested. We have looked at the structure of the 'external' composition of the *mise en scène* (musicians – father and son – wealthier family); now it is time to pay attention to the 'internal' composition nested within it (Antonio – wine – Bruno).

That deep focus was available to De Sica, even in this interior (the large amounts of artificial lighting used are detectable in occasional sharp shadows), is shown by its use at times. Given the importance of the 'background' throughout the scene, one would have expected De Sica to choose deep focus. Instead, for the reverse-angle sequences of Antonio and Bruno across the table, De Sica chose to move the camera in close, with shallow focus, visually isolating them, so that he could concentrate the viewer's attention on his depiction of their relationship. A shot taken from rather farther back than normal, of Antonio quaffing his wine, allows us to see how the camera set-ups were arranged (see plate 33). Antonio is shot from over Bruno's left shoulder, but usually from closer in. Bruno is shot from a point close to Antonio's right elbow (left on the screen) – in other words, at table-top height, and not really from Antonio's physical vantage-point. This set-up enables De Sica to photograph Bruno as dominated by the foreground, just as he was dominated when he was first introduced into the film by Antonio's bicycle. Not just dominated, however, but erased (see plate 33). De Sica has Antonio take his son to a restaurant to make up with him, and then he immediately shows Bruno erased by his father's desire to escape from stress into inebriation ('C'ubriacamo, va!' / 'We'll get drunk, come on!'). While the shot from Antonio's right elbow of Bruno erased by the delivery of the carafe and glasses is not from Antonio's *physical* point of view, De Sica's *mise en scène* and montage prompt the viewer to *read* it as Antonio's awareness of his son. De Sica, a scrupulous craftsman, would have discarded a shot where something in the foreground completely blocked out the main subject of the shot – *unless* that is precisely what he intended. Since it is a procedure he uses *four times* in the film (the concrete post erasing Maria in plates 6–7, the neighbour erasing Maria in plate 20, first the bicycle and now the wine erasing Bruno – see plates 26, and 33), it qualifies as a characteristic stylistic procedure, directed not towards 'realist' representation, but towards the viewer's *reading* of Antonio's state of mind. Moreover, for the camera to be that close to table level is to be closer to the child's point of view than to the father's, and the 'erasure' of the child is what Bruno, not the father, experiences. Hence, the viewer's 'reading' of the shot contains not only Antonio's awareness of Bruno, but also Bruno's experience of that awareness. The 'reading' that shot number 504 stages for the viewer is a synthesis of the 'experience' of Antonio and that of Bruno. It functions metaphorically, as a poetic image, given visible and 'photographic' articulation, while not being something that anyone present in the restaurant would 'see' (unless they leaned down to peer past Antonio's right elbow).

It is relatively easy for a filmmaker to articulate an 'experience' of the world in characters who are free to act: their actions can be used as 'indices of' (because they are 'caused by') their perceptions and aspirations. In the melodramatic narrative matrix, where characters are 'acted upon' – where their 'experience' is precisely one of having little or no scope for action, and where the 'content' of the narrative is their 'contemplation' of their situation – the filmmaker is obliged to resort to metaphor and analogy in order to give cinematic expression to moral ideals that are negated by, or absent in, the 'reality' being represented. This applies as much to episodes in *Paisà* and *Roma città aperta* as to *Ladri di biciclette*, and should make us cautious about describing the filmmakers' styles as being either straightforward 'realism,' on the one hand, or 'sentimentality,' on the other. This scene in the restaurant is an example of neither.

It is instructive to pause for a moment and reflect on the implications of this example of De Sica's use of the camera in a procedure of composition in depth. At the start of our analysis of sequences, the two most authoritative analysts of *Ladri di biciclette*, André Bazin in 1949 and Guglielmo Moneti in 1992, suggested that De Sica's use of the camera, of *mise en scène*, and of montage (Bazin's *découpage*) are neutral and objective, subordinating all stylistic procedures to the straightforward exposition of the pro-filmic (meaning, what is in front of the camera to be photographed). The 'erasure' of Bruno in the shot we have just been discussing (as well as the other 'erasures' we recalled elsewhere) is not something existing in the realm of the pro-filmic that has simply been 'photographed' by the director. Viewed from anywhere else, Bruno is not erased. Viewed even from the position of the eyes of Antonio, Bruno is not erased; nor is he erased in a viewpoint from the position of his own eyes. That erasure does not exist in the pro-filmic, but is, instead, a *product* of the combination of *mise en scène* and camera position (of the composition in depth, and of the camera being placed at Antonio's right elbow) – assembled for the viewer's eyes alone.

We could leave the matter there: a debating point, in which a tiny victory is scored by paying close attention to the film's *mise en scène*. Already, however, this debating point raises implications for critical method. Bazin's and Moneti's *descriptions* of the film start from an *interpretation* of *Ladri di biciclette* as 'realist.' That interpretation produces an emphatic and peremptory description of the film that, in a circular argument, reinforces the original interpretation – one that flies in the face of every declaration of intent coming from De Sica (his insistent prioritizing of 'poetry' over 'realism'). Where does their interpretation come from? It comes from 'theory.' Where Bazin is concerned, it comes from his teleological theory of the aesthetic development of the cinema as an art form. In Moneti's case, I think it owes something to a *cultural* tendency in Italy to privilege the role of Zavattini in the making of the film (and hence his 'theory'). I have proposed an alternative critical procedure. The 'theory' from which it starts is a remarkably banal one that is empirically verifiable, namely, that a film is 'an assembly guided by intentions.' The method deployed is 'description.' In chapter 2 I proposed that the critic's objective description needs to account for the putting together of the assembly which, ideally, will generate hypotheses about the intentions of the assembler. Where those hypotheses coincide with the explicit and repeated declarations of the 'assembler' (De Sica, in this case), there are plausible grounds for believing that we have accurately described the assembly. At the start of the analysis of *Roma città aperta*, I proposed that 'the description of a film is either *true* or *false*.' On the level of what I have called the 'debating point,' Bazin's and Moneti's descriptions are false. More significant, for an aesthetic approach to Italian neorealist cinema, is *how* and *why* they came to produce false descriptions. They put the theoretical and interpretative cart before the descriptive horse.

Talking of horses, the extent to which a film is *assembled*, rather than being a performance that is photographed as it unfolds, is illustrated by shots 483 and 485 (plates 28 and 30). The camera has been moved from one place to another. The production secretary has made sure that the horse outside is present in both (though the angles do not completely correlate). During the wait, the horse has become as hungry as the characters in the story, and so in shot 485 (plate 30) it is wearing a nosebag! Tiny misalignments of continuity like this pervade the film as witnesses to its slow and painstaking assembly. Nowhere in the film has De Sica just set off his performers and filmed them. The whole film is assembled from short shots, in which even two adjacent shots of the same 'action' have been taken on quite different occasions. The reverse-angle sequences do not simply repeat a shot in their alternation. One way of filming a conversation in reverse-angles is to have a static camera film A saying all his lines, then a static camera film B saying all his lines, and at the editing stage cut them up and glue the pieces together in alternation. De Sica certainly does this. Often, however, he changes the scale of the shot (the distance of the camera from the performer) both during and between shots, to modulate the expressiveness of the dialogue and of the interaction between characters, as happens in the reverse-angle sequence between Maria and the pawnbroker's Clerk near the beginning. We could therefore say that De Sica's style involves not just the 'follow-shot,' which tracks a character across or into the frame, but also a 'following' of the mood and emotions of the character. At the end of the concluding reverse-angle sequence of the restaurant scene, the camera pulls into a close-up on Antonio's desperate face, which is then 'matched' by the first shot of the next sequence having him run away from the camera into Via della Paglia, seeking release from his anxiety. Simultaneously, the Neapolitan orchestra is 'matched' on the soundtrack by the EIAR radio station's identification signal of twittering birdsong. De Sica's style lies not just in what he shoots and how he shoots it, but also in how he puts it together, and how he manages the transitions that become progressively more important as the film assembles progressively more fragmented scenes.

Sequence 23: Via della Paglia. Antonio consults the Santona.

It is Sunday, and De Sica strews his image and his soundtrack with elements that anchor them in a particular day of the week: the Sunday markets, Meniconi's complaint of rain on his day off, the Messa del povero, the Modena football fans passing on the Lungotevere, the radio broadcasting sports news, a church bell tolling, the crowd at the stadium, amateur racing cyclists, people at leisure. The landscape in which he places his figures bespeaks the very release of stress Antonio is denied in his struggle to find the bicycle before Monday. So he *runs* into Via della Paglia, with the diegetic sound-off (amplified to a volume and acoustic more like sound-over) drumming society's recreation into his and the viewer's ears.

There are two visits to the Santona in the film, and I shall discuss both together. They differ in only a few, but significant, respects. In the first visit, Antonio is smartly dressed, and self-confident. He mocks the Santona, but De Sica does not mock her (or scarcely). In the second visit, Antonio is dressed in the lowest register possible, and has lost all his self-esteem. Here De Sica mocks the Santona, but Antonio does not. But there is an ambiguity in the treatment of the Santona. In both visits, her scenes contribute to the 'background' of suffering that is portrayed in various parts of the film (Valmelaina, the Messa del povero, and the thief's apartment). With the exception of Valmelaina, all these portrayals of suffering are proposed by De Sica with elements of scepticism, satire, burlesquing, and comedy.

In the first visit to the Santona, the suffering is portrayed in the background of what is *already* the background to the narrative. Antonio is led into her apartment by background elements which De Sica *follows*. Down in the street, the boys who are playing a game of *bocce* appear to be in the very margins of the narrative, and yet Antonio intervenes in the game with a gesture, and asks one of them to watch his bicycle for him. The women come in to see the clairvoyant, and Antonio goes upstairs because he is drawn up there, *following* the women who go upstairs. Things *lead into* other things, which are then picked up. So 'follow' is a procedure not just of the shot, but of the narrative too. It seems as though we are 'glimpsing' things outside of the narrative, of the 'story,' but this is, in fact, precisely what some of the narrative is composed of. As Antonio walks towards the door of the Santona's room, suffering appears in the background of the soundtrack, in a dialogue between the Santona and the mother of a crippled boy (the mother does not understand what the Santona means when she talks about leaves falling). Antonio tries to get Maria to come away with him, and eventually calls her away, mocking her for her gullibility.

Zavattini and De Sica depict Antonio as overconfident, playing a patriarchal role. Clearly, this is a case of the filmmakers priming the viewer's *memory* in preparation for a contrast in the second visit. The only touches of mockery of the Santona that the filmmakers add are to have the mother ask what 'the leaves' mean and to have the Santona's daughter dryly twirling a flower in the kitchen when Maria pops in to deposit her money. In the second visit to the Santona, De Sica uses the daughter to hold together his *mise en scène*.

Antonio's second entry into the Santona's apartment is similar to the first. This time, the radio in sound-off on the soundtrack gradually dies down in volume as he proceeds along the corridor to her room, to be replaced with, still in sound-off at first, (a) a dialogue at the doorway between an older woman and a younger mother of a boy on crutches, who all come into the frame as the camera follows Antonio to the door; (b) when Antonio enters the room, a dialogue between the Santona and the young man. Dialogue (a) belongs in the theme of suffering; dialogue (b) belongs in a comic thread that De Sica progressively weaves into the scene.

The transition to the comic thread is carried by the Santona's daughter and the coffee. Antonio passes her in the corridor pouring out a cup of coffee in the kitchen. Once he is in the room, the camera cuts away from him, and from the scene he is watching, to frame the daughter, as she enters the room, following her into and across the room with the coffee, with the Santona glancing behind her as it is put down on a dresser. This supplies the transition to the shot, from the Santona's point of view, of the ugly man in front of her. By following the daughter and the coffee, De Sica makes the otherwise difficult transition from one reverse-angle sequence, between Antonio looking and the scene in the bedroom he sees, and the next reverse-angle sequence, between the Santona and the ugly man. In the counter-shot to that of the young man seen from the Santona's point of view, namely, the shot of the Santona from the man's point of view, the daughter stands behind her mother looking on dryly, indifferent, above it all, and as soon as she can interrupt, she proffers the coffee, saying: 'Mammà, se fredda.' / 'Mamma, it's getting cold.' The reverse-angles continue, of the young man sniffing, reaching into his pocket for money, and then rising. But rather than follow him out, the camera, from over the Santona's shoulder, follows the daughter, who emerges from behind the camera, and follows the man to the door, looking back dryly at the scene as she goes out. This takes the camera over to Antonio and Bruno at the door, and the camera can now follow Bruno in the same shot to the chair in front of the Santona, which leads to the comic dispute over places in the queue. A reverse-angle to the Santona shows her finishing her coffee, and assuring all of her attention, calling for calm, and indeed eventually having to shout. An otherwise disjointed *mise en scène* is held together and rendered fluid by means of the daughter and the coffee, and by De Sica's readiness to colour the whole episode both with comedy and with the dispassionate superiority of the daughter. But both the element of the daughter and that of the client's failure to understand the Santona's oracular pronouncement are taken over from the first visit. The Santona's status as an oracle is conveyed with enormous economy by the repetition of just two phrases in the dialogue: the second daughter saying, 'Quella sì e quella no' / 'That one yes and that one no,' and the Santona saying, 'Dammi la luce' / 'Give me light.' These almost emblematic indices of a higher register are contrasted with the Santona's dropping into broad dialect and very direct address (for example, with the young man), contradicting her 'spirituality,' and revealing, as it were, her real role in this place of last resort for the community. Antonio's question about the bicycle leaves her at a loss for rhetoric, but she rapidly finds a solution, with her pronouncement. Ironically, it turns out to be exactly accurate, because Antonio finds the thief immediately, but never the bicycle. As he reaches for his money, she strokes her hand, making a show of being above material things, but snatching a quick glance at his offering just the same. At this point Antonio rises, and the camera follows him and Bruno in a single shot as they get up, cross the room, go through the door, down to the end of the corridor, and turn through the door of the apartment. By keeping the camera in the room, De Sica is able to let us hear the Santona's dialogue with Adele, obviously a regular client, with its complete absence of rhetoric:

SANTONA: 'Adele, che c'hai da dimme oggi?' / 'Adele, what have you got to tell me today?'
ADELE: 'Eh! Mi' marito s'embriaca sempre!' / 'Eh! My husband's always getting drunk!'
SANTONA: 'Eh, fia mia, è 'na croce. Tu nun je da' li soldi!' / 'Well, my dear, it's what we have to bear. You shouldn't give him the money!'

ADELE: 'E che ce posso fa', s' 'i prende!' / 'And what can I do, he takes
   it!'
SANTONA: 'Eh, s' 'i prende! Eh!' / 'Yeah, he takes it! There you go!'

Both the shot of the Santona's daughter entering with the coffee and
that of Antonio and Bruno leaving the Santona's apartment are examples of De Sica's characteristic '*V*' *movement* procedure, discussed above
in the section on Sequence 2.
   The soundtrack has, during the scene, developed from the overheard
dialogue in the corridor to the dialogue with the ugly man, to Bruno's
loud cry to Antonio to take the empty seat, and then to the crescendo of
the dispute, with people talking over one another and the Santona
shouting over everybody. Then the sound drops very low, to Antonio's
whispered query, rises with the Santona's pronouncement, and drops
into silence again, only to resume with the quiet dialogue with Adele.
The whole scene is modulated by the volume and density of the
dialogue track, and De Sica pursues this resource in the following
sequences. The camera cuts to the stairwell outside the apartment, with
Antonio and Bruno emerging and starting down the stairs in silence. As
they do so, a church-bell starts slowly tolling, forming a sound bridge to
the scene of the encounter with the thief, which takes place with not a
word spoken. The slow tolling continues until Antonio enters the
brothel, when there starts up one of De Sica's 'running commentaries,'
which continues throughout the brothel scene, carefully modulated,
starting with the porteress and being taken up by the madame.
   The narrative of the final third of the film is in fact not unitary at all,
but extremely fragmented and episodic, depending on chance encounters and threads brought into the film that are then dropped. It is all
sewn seamlessly together by De Sica's camerawork, his *mise en scène*,
and his assembly of the soundtrack.

I shall bring together sequences of Antonio's 'search,' sometimes disturbing the chronological ordering of the analysis of sequences in this
chapter. But before dealing with the 'search,' it is worth drawing attention to the way in which De Sica uses the *memory* of the viewer, in combination with a characteristic procedure of composition in depth, to
create a 'signifier' out of two shots, a device that will be a characteristic
of Kieslowski's later cinema. In this case, the contrast between the two
shots 'signifies' a 'wrongness.' When Antonio, on his way to work,
drops Bruno off at Monte Sacro (sequence 7), the camera shoots the boy
with his back to the camera saying goodbye to his father (who pedals

away into the depth of the image) and moving over to the petrol pump at camera-left, to start his own work. When Antonio returns to collect his son at the end of the day (sequence 12), the camera is placed where Antonio was last seen disappearing, and Bruno stands beside the petrol pump to camera-right, looking in the direction of the camera for his father's arrival on his bicycle. Instead, Antonio appears on foot out of the background from behind his son's back, startling him. The later shot 'mirrors' the earlier one, signifying the 'wrongness' of the inversion, and the matching of the two shots even extends to the unusual swooping crane movement of the camera towards Bruno.

Sequence 15: The market at Piazza Vittorio Emanuele.
The search for the stolen bicycle begins at the market in Piazza Vittorio Emanuele at dawn. De Sica's son, Manuel, recalls stories his father told him about filming the sequence:

> I really think Papà particularly liked the dawn ... It seemed to have always attracted him more than the rosy sunsets. Papà told me about coming across, early in the morning, the director of photography of the film Carlo Montuori, completely frozen, clinging to his camera, devotedly waiting for the fleeting moment. He had stayed there in order to protect with his whole body the *châssis* (the magazine of film mounted on the back of the camera) from the rigours of the night. Dawn has a brief duration, and for this reason several days were needed to sew together long sequences which had cost many early forced awakenings for the entire troupe just to get a few minutes of footage. My father would often speak of the painstaking work of his collaborators. During the filming in Piazza Vittorio, he required the production secretary, Roberto Moretti, to stop the trams passing. Poor Moretti, who did not even have a permit to set up the tripod of the camera on the square, with great presence of mind disguised himself as a tram conductor, and began to redirect all the trams bursting with workers that happened to pass in proximity to the square. Before anyone guessed the reason for the existence of this man in the middle of the crossroads, the shooting was finished and Roberto arrested.[55]

In fact there is a jump from dawn to early sunlight in the first cut to the porticos of the square (with Baiocco's voice continuing over the cut). The fifteen-year-old future film director Ettore Scola was on his way to school:

> That morning I found Via Emanuele Filiberto blocked by barriers: Piazza

Vittorio seemed deserted; only a worker, a street sweeper and a child were crossing the street, going in the direction of the market. A low and strangely close voice, like that of a prompter amplified by a megaphone, reached the actors and the crowd gathered behind the barriers: 'More slowly, Lamberto. Let Gino go ahead. Enzo, keep behind Papà.' The whisper was coming from a small tower on top of which, in a little wooden armchair, was seated a gentleman wearing a hat, a scarf, and a camel hair coat.[56]

(Given that the film was shot between May and October, mere pedantic curiosity prompts me to ask whether De Sica's scarf and camel-hair coat, and the fact that Scola was going to school, suggest that Piazza Vittorio was one of the last sequences to be shot, in the autumn, when dawn occurred later.)

De Sica populates the background with 'uniformed' employees of the municipality – a *'foil'* to Antonio's vulnerable condition. Each sweeper has barely a square metre to clean, creating an almost surreal choreographic effect. Further evidence that De Sica is deliberately constructing the background of his images to act as a 'foil' to Antonio and Bruno comes from a tiny detail later in the scene. When Bruno is accosted by a pederast, De Sica has a man walking back and forth in the background blowing bubbles. Since this figure appears in two different scenes separated in time, it is clearly intended as an important component of the construction of the *mise en scène*.

Where there is no music early in the scene, this is replaced by a comic *running commentary* on the dialogue track. Baiocco not only gives instructions to Antonio and Bruno, and to Meniconi and Bagonghi (the three dustmen forming a comic trio of the fat one, the thin one, and the dopey one), but also mutters the thoughts that pass through his mind (about pretending to be disinterested window-shoppers, and exclaiming at the quantity of goods on sale) in an acoustic on the soundtrack that does not correspond with his distance from the camera. Baiocco is a character straight out of the Roman comedy that *could* have been made out of Bartolini's story, and that lies in the background of De Sica's film.

As the vendors bring out the bicycles, two traders quarrel fiercely in a *background* that is carefully placed in centre-frame. This has by now become a recurring motif in the background – the women at the standpipe at Valmelaina, and the variety act in the *dopolavoro* – and so clearly constitutes a deliberate characterization of the social landscape in which the figure of Antonio is placed (in the fragment of screenplay quoted at the end of this chapter, Zavattini makes explicit reference to it). De Sica uses the gradual assembly of the market as a metonymical account of the city waking up and starting its social and economic life around a bewildered and excluded Antonio. As the men scan the bicycles, a tremor of low music starts up on the soundtrack. The search is developed with a systematic use of tracking shots in reverse-angles: the men are tracked as they walk and look, and this alternates with tracking shots following their gaze. This use of an 'accompanying' tracking camera is reserved for portrayals of Antonio's (and later Bruno's) 'experience' of defeat: in Largo del Tritone, here, and after the humiliation at the stadium. Towards the end of the search, one shot cuts back to a larger view, gaining a distance, as though showing the hopelessness of it all. Montage is used to swiftly convey the passing of time and the piling up of frustration. Parallel montage is used to follow the episode of the bicycle frame being painted and that of Bruno being pestered by a pederast. This scene, one of Bruno trying to take a pee during the chase after the old man in Trastevere, one of him later trying to catch a tram in Via Flaminia, and one of him picking up Antonio's hat after the final failed theft are the only cases of parallel montage in the film, and draw attention to Bruno, creating for him a point of view and a separate space in the film, and hence an 'experience' of the landscape, and prompting the viewer to a 'reading' of Antonio's neglect of him as an index of the latter's anxiety.

Sequence 16: The Porta Portese market.

The ride in a dustcart from Piazza Vittorio to Porta Portese is accompanied by another comic *running commentary* on the soundtrack, this time Meniconi's, complaining colourfully about the rain on his day off, about the cinema being no attraction on a rainy day, and about pedestrians. On the cut from inside the dustcart to the shot of the dustcart arriving at Porta Portese, the music starts up.

Although quite short, the sequence at Porta Portese is complex, and deserves attention. Guglielmo Moneti has given a detailed analysis of the beginning of the scene to demonstrate that 'the shots reveal to us particular portions of reality and hide others. The movements of the shot produce those of our knowledge, and hence the itinerary of meaning.'[57] I am not sure that De Sica's procedures here are concerned with the articulation of spaces so much as with weaving together a number of different narrative threads.

Antonio and Bruno's first moments in the square are treated with a rapid montage mixing the following elements: (1) reverse-angles between Antonio and the vendors packing up (everything moving away from the camera); (2) longish-scale shots of Antonio and Bruno with the market dispersing behind them; (3) medium-scale, shallow-focus telephoto shots of Antonio, and then down to Bruno, in the midst of the hubbub, looking this way and that; (4) overhead shots of the square. Since the 'story' at this point concerns the search for the bicycle (not the thief), the montage procedure functions to narrate Antonio and Bruno's disappointment, and to put them in the midst of a reality that is in flight from them, eluding their grasp. It shows them lost and disoriented, alone in the midst of a busy social landscape.

However, already De Sica is devoting some shots to a camera placed at (or tilted towards) Bruno's level, developing a place for him in the narrative which the next section of the sequence develops further. A shot from Antonio's point of view of people sheltering under the cornice of the Istituto San Michele is followed by a reverse-angle shot of Antonio deciding to go there, followed in turn by an overhead shot of the two making for the building, in the direction of the camera. This is followed by a use of composition in depth to prompt a 'reading' of Antonio's perspective on his son (while not taking up Antonio's point of view): Bruno falls down in the foreground, while Antonio at the wall in the background looks the other way. After a brief dialogue between them, the camera concentrates on Bruno cleaning himself and looking around (in a medium shot of him from his height). The music stops and is replaced with the sound of bicycle bells and a facetious exchange (One man: 'Oh! Hai paura de 'e tarme?' / 'Oh! Are you afraid of moths?' The other: 'No, nun me vojo bagna' er fracche!' / 'No, I don't want to get my tuxedo wet!').

Then comes another of De Sica's 'digressions,' with the arrival of the German seminarians, seeking shelter from the rain. It is an unscripted scene added by De Sica during the shooting, which has attracted the attention of many commentators. Its appealing gratuitousness raises the question of its function. Sergio Leone, who was helping on the film, gives this account:

> I was helping out for nothing on *Ladri di biciclette*, and I also had a tiny and much-noted part in the film. And with regard to this part, I have to say that I saw the birth in De Sica of the idea for a scene that was not even in the script. We were at Porta Portese, shooting the sequence in which the father of the boy wanders around looking for the bicycle. I was sixteen at

the time, and was in the second year of grammar school. I was watching De Sica, rather I was drinking him in with my eyes, when all of a sudden he said: 'Ah, here I'd like to see a group of ten or fifteen red priests, those of the Propaganda of the Faith, it has started to rain, and I'd like to use this stupendous light.' So he stopped the shooting, and the next day we shot the marvellous scene – from the choreographic point of view as well – of these red priests who, caught by the storm, shelter under a cornice, and two of them talk to each other, so that the child, fascinated by this strange language, is distracted and stops to listen to them. There you are: I was one of the two red priests engaged in conversation, a conversation that in fact consisted of reciting numbers, because we couldn't speak German, while the rest of the group was made up of school-friends of mine whom I had gone to recruit when De Sica had said that he didn't know at the time where to lay his hands on fifteen youths.[58]

Red comes out as black in panchromatic film, and De Sica was too expert a craftsman not to know it – only on colour stock would the red costume of this clerical order come out differently from any ordinary priest's black costume. Stopping shooting and resuming the next day was hardly the best way to capture 'this stupendous light.' Besides, the scene against the wall is lit with large amounts of artificial floodlighting, as can be seen from the multiple sharp shadows on the wall behind the figures. Leone's references to 'the child' are a more plausible explanation for the insertion.

The scene with the pederast at Piazza Vittorio has already been an enormously softened version of Zavattini's original treatment. Pio Baldelli, in his 1969 long essay on the film, discusses the general tendency of De Sica to soften the harsher polemical notes in Zavattini's proposals for this scene at Porta Portese, for the restaurant scene, and for the scene in the thief's neighbourhood. Baldelli takes a 'psychologizing' approach (as opposed to what one could call my rather austere 'functional' approach) to the portrayal of Bruno, and it has the virtue of highlighting how the point of view that De Sica gives Bruno (an innocent wonder) can endow what I have been calling the landscape with 'the lightness of a fairytale.'[59]

Here against the wall, De Sica builds up a contrast between medium shots of Antonio, taken from his height, which exclude Bruno, and medium shots of Bruno, from his height, which exclude Antonio (in the previous chapter we saw Rossellini using a similar procedure at the end of the Naples episode of Paisà). When the seminarians crowd around, he has Bruno push them away from him, asserting his own space. De Sica shoots Bruno looking around at them, from Bruno's height, without either Antonio's or the seminarians' heads being in the frame – the image frames just Bruno's response of open fascination (and here Moneti's reflections on the creation of narrative space for 'sense' would be entirely apposite). This functions narratively to set Bruno's open response to the 'landscape' in contrast with the exclusion and rejection that Antonio's anxious self-absorption induces. This 'digression' could be a sentimental distraction from the main thrust of the film, but instead viewers and commentators remark on this tiny episode because, I think, it assembles an image in which the organic idyll is opposed to the exclusion of the individual, in accordance with the melodramatic narrative matrix. The young clerics offer a pretext for focusing on Bruno's experience. Leone's testimony alerts us to the extent to which De Sica is positively choosing to assemble his own (rather than just Zavattini's) melodramatic narrative from 'fragments.'

The third section of the sequence develops the more straightforward narrative of the search, which transforms into a search more for the thief than for the bicycle. We first see the thief in a reverse-angle long-scale shot from Antonio's point of view against the wall (trilling music starts up on the soundtrack). But then, in a medium shot carrying the dialogue between the thief and the old man, both the camera and the microphone are much closer than Antonio, contradicting the coherence of the reverse-angle sequence. It looks as though this shot might be left over from some previous plan for shooting the whole sequence (perhaps before it was decided to add the digression of the seminarians). This is what takes us from the German seminarians to the pursuit of the thief (which in turn transforms into the pursuit of the old man).

Sequence 17: Trastevere. The pursuit of the old man.

The pursuit of the old man is shot with the very procedures that are generally ascribed (elsewhere often implausibly, I would maintain) to neorealism as a 'style': long takes and long-scale shots in deep focus. The music imitates the action with its trills and rapid scales. The attention to Bruno is continued in this sequence, developing what I earlier characterized as the 'secondary narrative thread' of the father–son relationship. Bruno is made continually to stop and look up at Antonio for an indication of what to do next. He is made to act on his own initiative, giving rise to the micro-narrative 'digression' of his attempt to take a pee, which comes into conflict with Antonio's self-absorbed, isolated single-mindedness. Once again, parallel montage separates the two characters, and when Antonio rejoins him, and shouts at him, making him jump, this is synchronized with a phrase in the music. De Sica's digressions, his chance events, his micro-narratives are all highly integrated components of an overall narrative assembly, as often as not deployed with the procedures of comedy.

Sequence 20: Ponte Duca D'Aosta. Antonio fears for Bruno's safety at the river.

On a figurative level, this sequence makes effective use of architectural compositions. In the section in this chapter on 'locations,' I remarked on how Antonio desperately plunging into the tunnel (the soundtrack giving his cry an expressive echo) mobilizes both the viewer's *memory* of the tunnel immediately after the theft of the bicycle and its associations for Antonio. Moreover, Bruno is twice shot as a tiny figure against a vast architectural feature of the bridge. On one occasion this is in a telephoto shot that conflicts with the point of view established by the reverse-angle of Antonio looking at him. The viewer is not shown what Antonio would actually see from his vantage point, but is offered, instead, an image whose *mise en scène* prompts a 'reading' of Antonio's state of mind.

One could question the narrative coherence of the portrayal of Antonio's guilty fantasy of harm coming to Bruno. The 'secondary narrative thread' of the father–son relationship functions perfectly adequately in the overall structure of the film by merely prompting the viewer to 'read' the neglect of Bruno that results from Antonio's obsessive anxiety over the bicycle. De Sica's *mise en scène* permits Antonio's isolated self-absorption to run in parallel with the *viewer's* perception of its consequences. To have Antonio himself realize the extent of his neglect at one point in the film (this sequence and the beginning of the restaurant scene), and then for the film to *resume* the procedure of offering 'readings' of the neglect is, I suspect, a slight flaw in the austere coherence of the film's narrative.

Sequence 24: Trastevere. Coming out of the Santona's, Antonio encounters the thief.

While Antonio's first sight of the thief and the pursuit of the old man were shot with long-scale long takes, accompanied by expressive background music, the chance encounter with the thief outside the Santona's, in complete *contrast*, is shot in close-scale reverse-angles in utter silence, which is only emphasized by the soft, slow tolling of the church bell on the soundtrack. Antonio's diminishment and bewilderment at this stage in the narrative is conveyed by bringing the camera in close and having him not utter a word.

Sequence 25: Trastevere. The brothel.

Continuing the play of contrasts, once Antonio enters the brothel an intense verbal *running commentary* starts up on the soundtrack, and continues throughout the sequence, with the dialogue track rising to a crescendo in the dining room of the brothel. The running commentary starts with the concièrge, and is picked up by the madame, while in the middle – where Antonio argues with the thief and the girls in the dining room – a confusion of voices takes over.

If we pause for a moment, and consider all the running commentaries together from a stylistic point of view, we can see De Sica incorporating in the *soundtrack*, as part of the same procedure of accumulation of *background* data that he uses in the *mise en scène*, the essentially *literary*, comic-poetic (colourful dialect speech is a significant component) contributions of Zavattini as a *writer*. This is done in a distinctive and striking way *four times* in the film (the billposter, Baiocco, Meniconi, and the brothel), and is a procedure that, in one form or another, is used to a lesser degree in a number of other sequences (the *dopolavoro*, the Messa del povero, the restaurant, the Santona, the thief's mother's apartment, and the stadium) – a total of *ten times* altogether. In every case, the procedure *opposes* the 'landscape' to the figure of Antonio contained in the *image* that the soundtrack accompanies, and constitutes what I have called a *'foil'* to the character. It is such an intrinsic part of De Sica's cinematographic style that it forms a major component of the procedures he will deploy in *Umberto D.*, where the *image* will show Umberto putting himself to bed with a cold, while the *soundtrack* will carry in the *background* all the elements of the 'landscape' that oppose and thwart him.

Sequence 26: Trastevere. Antonio confronts the thief, and is in turn confronted by the thief's neighbours.

This sequence is the richest in micro-narratives of the whole film: (1) the neighbours gathering around Antonio and the thief; (2) the well-dressed neighbour; (3) the epileptic fit and the mother's response; (4) the scuffle; (5) the bucket of water thrown from an upstairs window; (6) the search of the apartment; (7) the policeman's sympathetic but powerless response; (8) Antonio's ejection from the street. Each of these micro-narratives is developed in great detail, and all are fluidly integrated into the main narrative threads of the film. I shall draw attention to just one or two features of the sequence.

The sequence is constructed around a contrast between the defiant masculine display down in the street and the wretchedness this hides up above in the female zone of the apartment – the filmmakers' customary procedure of offering the viewer a dual perspective tinged with comic irony.

Costume plays a role in the assembly of one of the micro-narratives. When Antonio accosts the thief, one of the bystanders who takes a particular interest is a man dressed in a dark sweatshirt, with tousled hair, carrying a small baby. He hurries back into a doorway, and emerges implausibly soon thereafter, minus baby, dressed in a white shirt and tie, smart striped jacket, with his hair carefully smarmed down with brillantine, wearing sunglasses. He is led through the crowd by a companion to come right up to Antonio and challenge him. When the argument looks as though it might be turning into a tussle, he carefully removes his sunglasses, and puts them in his top jacket pocket. When the policeman, in an even higher 'register' of costume arrives, the smartly dressed civilian retires to the back of the crowd, and from that point onwards plays a less prominent role in events. In other words, De Sica uses this man and his costume to function as part of the *visual* assembly of his social landscape (forming a binary opposition, a '*foil*,' to Antonio, for example). The unnamed man is used for the visual 'costume' part of the assembly of this episode, whereas the development of the dialogue (between Antonio, the bystanders, the thief, his mother, and the policeman) is carried by other figures who come forward to replace him. He fulfils a role in the assembly assigned to costume, until the arrival of the policeman in *his* costume renders him redundant. This micro-narrative is also, of course, an example of the procedures of comedy being used by the filmmakers for the assembly of their artefact.

However, if we look closely at the episode, we can detect clues that betray how these micro-narrative episodes were assembled progressively, rather than having been fully determined at the script stage. Well before the smartly dressed neighbour is rhetorically led into the dispute between Antonio and the thief, we can quite clearly see in the background that very same character approaching the scuffle, and standing to watch it in curious, detached observation. His appearance here is completely incompatible with the micro-narrative I have just described.

It is out of the question to imagine De Sica *adding* him, incongruously, to an earlier scene, when he had already decided to use him in an entirely different way. It follows, therefore, that the micro-narrative was filmed *afterwards*, and inserted into the whole episode, with De Sica relying on the fact that the viewer would not notice the incongruous presence of the background bystander. This confirms what we notice in other episodes, namely, that at the shooting stage the film gradually assembles fragmentary 'digressions' (micro-narratives) that De Sica *almost* seamlessly (because in most cases there is a clue somewhere to what has been done) weaves into the overall narrative texture of the film – and that usually these insertions display the stylistic features of cinematic comedy.

The search of the apartment depicts the other side of the coin presented by the masculine display in the street (reinforced by a woman and child across the street who are framed through the window during Antonio's dialogue with the policeman). It is accompanied by another brief *running commentary*, this time from the mother, who remarks on everything Antonio and the policeman see and touch, and projects an image of poverty and innocence which the viewer, as well as the others, know to be not entirely candid. The viewer knows that the thief is a member of a well-organized and successful gang, and we have seen him comfortably astride a bicycle disbursing money at Porta Portese. The commentary of the mother is the vehicle of yet another 'display' in which the soundtrack plays ironically against the visual image.

This fragile, poverty-stricken zone is rendered even more fragile when the policeman asks the mother to step outside her own apartment for a moment to allow the men to talk. Meanwhile, voices from the masculine 'display' down in the street can be heard loudly entering through the window. To cap it all, as Antonio leaves the apartment the daughter arrives with matches, crossing into the foreground, while Antonio eyes her in embarrassment as he closes the door in the background.

Antonio has the thief in his grasp, and yet his greatest defeat comes at the hands not of the well-to-do middle classes, nor of the institutions of the capitalist state, but of this minutely described social 'landscape' that, in its compact struggle for survival, quite literally ejects him. From a thematic, iconographic, and *generic* point of view, this is less 'drama' than *comedy*. It is from a *poetic* point of view that it takes on its impact as the overall pictorial portrayal of a figure in a landscape.

There remain, in the film, just two sequences of Antonio and Bruno walking dejectedly through the streets of Rome, before the climax of Antonio's attempted theft at the stadium.

Sequence 27: Walking through Rome, the stadium.

From the thief's neighbourhood to the stadium there are three 'transition' shots, all '*V*' *movements*, of Bruno and Antonio walking, dejected and tired, down streets left to right towards the camera, turning a corner, and proceeding away from the camera. In the third of these, Bruno is twice nearly run over by cars, as Antonio carries on oblivious. This shot ends with a wipe to yet another '*V*' *movement* shot of them turning the corner into the street near the stadium. They stop. Antonio looks along the street, while Bruno goes to sit down on the kerb. This shot is all the viewer has to establish the location and its layout.

This final sequence in the film has moved audiences for half a century. One way of accounting for this response would be to interpret the narrative in order to identify the emotions and psychology that the viewer attributes to the characters as though they were 'people'; but that is precisely the kind of approach that this book is trying to avoid – not so much because it is 'wrong' as because it gives us little insight into the filmic work that brought about the sequence. Instead, it might be instructive to identify and list the components that make up the sequence, and to examine the way in which they are assembled.

The sequence is assembled in coherent montage blocks, making use, above all at first, of reverse-angle sequences (or sequences that function as reverse-angles). In the first part of the sequence, the blocks of reverse-angle shots deploy De Sica's characteristic construction of the *mise en scène* in depth: foreground, middle ground, and background. Within this first part, De Sica starts to establish a significant use of the vertical plane: what is 'up' (Antonio) and what is 'down' (Bruno). When Antonio rides off on the stolen bicycle, De Sica makes effective use of the horizontal plane (right and left) and the panning camera. To conclude the episode and the film as a whole, the director abandons reverse-angles, and deploys the tracking camera, just as he has done elsewhere in the film, to accompany father and son walking away from a 'defeat,' and emphasizes the vertical plane in a series of parallel shots of Bruno (down) and Antonio (up). If we thought of the components as 'words,' and their assembly as a 'syntax,' we could see De Sica as constructing 'sentences' that construct a narrative that needs very little interpretation.

The sequence does, however, raise problems of orientation for the viewer. It starts with an establishing shot of Antonio and Bruno at a street corner in the vicinity of the Stadio Flaminio, looking in the direction of the stadium. This is followed by reverse-angle sequences of Antonio looking – and seeing the stadium, the football spectators, and their bicycles ranged round a curve in the street. However, the positions from which those things would be clearly visible bear no relation to the position from which Antonio is looking, and are irreconcilable with any perspective that the viewer could hypothesize from the establishing shot. To see what Antonio is shown as looking at, he would have to be a good distance further up a street more or less parallel to the one he is shown as standing in. Bruno's appalled stare at Antonio racing past him on the stolen bicycle is incompatible with where Antonio is shown to be (in a street not included in the establishing shot). Moreover, changes in the planning of the sequence are betrayed by discontinuities. At one point there is an abrupt cut between two shots of Antonio, where the continuity of his position from one shot to the next is completely implausible: in the first shot he is at the corner turning to look down the side street at the bicycle, while in the second he is further up the main street to the right, walking left towards the corner.

Various clues alert us to the fact that the shots depicting Antonio at the corner – looking repeatedly at the lone bicycle and then grabbing it – were taken at two completely different times at least. Near the corner with the main street, on the wall of the building against which the bicycle is leaning there are a number of posters in some shots, and none at all in others. The gutter of that same street is dry as Antonio sets off to grab the bicycle, and full of water in the next shot, when we see passers-by start up the street to chase him. I think it is true to say that posters on the wall, and no water in the gutter – as well as other tiny details – characterize shooting time A (which includes the first establishing shot and the majority of the shots in the scene, right through to the very end – as Antonio and Bruno complete their last 'walk' together out of the film, the posters are on the wall). No posters on the wall and water in the gutter characterize shooting time B. Shots from time A and time B are interspersed in a single reverse-angle sequence, with no break in continuity otherwise. These are only my hypotheses, and give us little to go on, certainly not enough to guess whether A preceded B or vice versa.

We can only speculate. One possibility is that one (or more than one) original plan for filming the whole sequence determined the shooting of the bulk of the material, while a subsequent decision was taken to assemble the scene differently, and the material already shot was recut and reassembled, possibly with the addition of newly shot material. We do know that the whole sequence was originally intended to continue for longer than it actually does, but at a late stage was truncated – and I discuss this below. Furthermore, the sports cyclists passing in front of Antonio and Bruno seated on the kerb were most likely an 'insertion' added to an existing planned scheme (one of De Sica's frequent expressive 'digressions'). The most likely explanation for the viewer's slight disorientation is that the script required locating the Riccis in a busy street with a side street for the theft of the unattended bicycle, whereas no such street existed with an eyeline to the stadium itself. The end result is a final sequence that works, and is coherent; but the viewer lacks the full orientation he or she really needs.

I am being pedantic because my job is to describe the artefact's assembly, not to praise it. However, the lack of coherent establishment of the location may work to the advantage of the scene's effectiveness. Since viewers cannot properly see and orient themselves in what Antonio and Bruno are shown as seeing, the landscape and the events become that much more a product of the characters' state of mind. The links between 'looking' and 'what is seen' are imaginative. The shortcomings of the scene as a 'realist' representation of Rome may actually enhance its lyrical and expressive properties.

On the soundtrack there is music throughout the sequence. At the wipe from the walking 'transition' to the establishing shot in the street by the stadium, the music changes from the familiar looping melody characterizing the film, and is replaced by low minor notes, with a high trill above, not really a melody at all, but just assembled phrases. There follows a wave-like, repeated melodic motif in the lower strings, and with the increase in Antonio's agitation it develops an ominous sound heightened by the roars of the football crowd, modulating into tense, built-up motifs in series (that is to say, phrases repeated at different points in the scale). The music closely accompanies and highlights the mood of the images in this part of the film, contributing to the creation of atmosphere, as though prompting the viewer. The trills with built-up chords accompany Antonio looking agitatedly at the unguarded bicycle. As he rides away, the rhythm accelerates to a climactic chord at the moment of his capture. Then the music fades to let the dialogue take over, and returns to a version of the standard, looping melodic material, as Antonio and Bruno walk away into the evening. However, as they walk amidst the football crowds, the voices of the people around can be plainly heard, and the viewer could listen to them if his or her mind were not attending to the protagonists, just as is the case with the men's voices below the apartment of the thief's mother. De Sica sometimes uses the soundtrack to 'isolate' Antonio precisely by allowing the viewer to participate in the life of the social landscape around him.

With the establishing shot, the 'transition' thread of walking dejectedly through Rome gives way to a new 'transition' scene of stasis, in the midst of a landscape characterized by the football supporters and their roar, populated by bicycles, with nowhere for Antonio to go but home. His anxious movements back and forth indicate a need to take action, which generates a sequence of 'events,' after which the story returns to, and ends on, the original 'transition' thread of the two walking dejectedly through the landscape, which has now been further defined by their experience. The 'events' are: (1) Antonio seeing the bicycle and thinking of stealing it; (2) his attempting to send Bruno home; (3) Antonio stealing the bicycle, being pursued and apprehended; (4) the owner of the bicycle looking at Bruno, and deciding not to prosecute Antonio. Both the transitional 'stasis' and the 'events' are carried for the most part by 'blocks' of reverse-angle sequences, resolved by a return to the 'transitional' walk through the streets.

Immediately after the establishing shot, (669) of their entry into the main street, the first and longest 'block' begins (shots 670–96). The scene is set up in De Sica's usual three-dimensional assembly, emphasizing the dimension of 'depth': in front of Antonio is the stadium, with its crowd and their bicycles. Behind him is the tempting unguarded bicycle. In the middle is Bruno squatting on the kerb, and Antonio himself. De Sica cuts between Antonio and one or other of the three elements: the stadium, the bicycle, and Bruno. Shots of the stadium, the crowd (accompanied by its roar), and their parked bicycles are 'virtual' reverse-angle shots, in the sense that these things are not clearly visible from where Antonio is standing, theoretically with the 'camera.' They are what is 'there' in his experience rather than what the viewer observes him looking at. Shots of Bruno emphasize the vertical dimension, for the camera comes down to ground level to shoot him in a spatial dimension that is reserved for him almost throughout the whole final sequence of the film – only in a small minority of shots henceforth will Bruno share the frame with the head and shoulders of an adult. The vertical dimension is emphasized also by a very high shot of the crowd starting to leave the football stadium. On one occasion even the shot of the unguarded bicycle behind Antonio (678), is a 'virtual' reverse-angle, because it is taken with a telephoto lens (678), and does not encode Antonio's true perspective so much as his state of mind. At times the bicycle is shot over Antonio's shoulder. The horizontal dimension of the layout will be emphasized when he steals the bicycle and attempts to outrun his pursuers, passing in front of Bruno.

De Sica inserts one small 'digression' in this first 'block' of reverse-angles, where Antonio sits beside Bruno on the kerb, with the camera at their level (shot 685), and a group of sporting cyclists pass from right to left out of focus in the *foreground*. The two turn their heads to follow them passing (shot 686). Tiny clues indicate this that shot was filmed at a different time from shot 685, and the 'digression' of the passing cyclists may have been an afterthought on De Sica's part, rather like the seminarians at Porta Portese.

Shot 696 is a sequence-shot, in which Antonio turns from the bicycle in the side street (having made a decision), pulls Bruno to his feet, gives him money, sends him off to catch a tram back to Monte Sacro, starts out in the direction of the unguarded bicycle, has to turn back and dispatch Bruno who has followed him, and then proceeds towards the bicycle. With Bruno sent off to the tram, Antonio pursues his struggle in utter solitude; the emptiness of the street where the bicycle leans beside the doorway is a deliberate feature of the *mise en scène*. There is a cutaway to Bruno failing to get onto a tram (a tiny narrative 'fragment' in parallel montage, as usual, of a 'defeat' of Bruno at the hands of the adult world), after which the next 'block' of shots begins, starting with Antonio riding off on the bicycle and the owner, implausibly, dashing out of the doorway immediately and shouting for help. This is followed by a reverse-angle shot of passers-by responding to his cry and running up the street towards the camera. The camera cuts around the block to follow Antonio's progress, until he (supposedly) re-enters the main street, whereupon there is a reverse-angle shot of Bruno seeing him pass.

This shot of Bruno (703) has his body facing to camera right, towards the tram stop, his head turned towards the camera, his eyes widening. The camera tracks right, panning to stay on Bruno, meanwhile pulling into a close-up of just his face. This has the effect both of dramatizing the image and of imitating the passage of Antonio's flight in front of him. The camera tracking past Bruno's horrified face functions as an analogy of Antonio's movement on the stolen bicycle and of his fleeting point of view on Bruno. By tracking past his face, the camera offers the viewer both Bruno's view of Antonio and a *'reading'* of Antonio's view of Bruno, abandoning him as he takes flight into compulsion. It is a very dense shot rhetorically, and a still from it is one commonly used to illustrate the film. This is followed by a reverse-angle (implying what Bruno sees) of Antonio passing from right to left and in a *'V' movement* curving off towards the stadium. In actual fact, Antonio has not sped along the street where Bruno is standing, and so this too is a 'virtual' point-of-view shot, following the 'story' rather than the topography. The camera cuts closer to Antonio's pursuers dragging him off the bicycle, and this too is followed by a shot of Bruno looking on in distress, and starting forward towards the camera in the direction of his father.

The next 'block' of reverse-angles starts ambiguously with a shot of the owner retrieving his bicycle and approaching the camera with his arm raised. Only when there is a cut to Antonio's head and shoulders in the midst of his captors, and the gesture of the owner is completed by a hand cuffing Antonio (to shouts from the owner), is it clear that this is a reverse-angle sequence starting with Antonio's point of view on the owner. However, this is interrupted by Bruno, who enters the throng of men, with the camera preserving his space and showing the adults only from their knees up to their lapels. He passes behind some figures, and emerges in the centre of the throng to tug at his father's jacket, crying 'Papà, papà.' Shots of Bruno, always at his height, are now alternated with shots of Antonio's head receiving cuffs and insults. The sound of a tram bell announces a cut to a long-scale shot, in which the tram splits the group into two, one of which contains Antonio, some captors, and the owner coming over to the pavement towards the camera. The tram, an interference from outside the story, is a device typical of De Sica's style (and just such a device is used in the opening scene of *Umberto D.*). It functions to open up the group around Antonio and allow the camera to cut back to a longer-scale shot to carry on the narrative, as well as adding a characteristically intrusive *background* interference and a *'foil'* to Antonio. The camera cuts back to Bruno, stranded on the other side of the tram, photographing him from the front as he bends down to pick up Antonio's hat and starts walking towards the camera (which tracks back in front of him), crying. This is an example of De Sica's use of the tracking shot to 'accompany' his character in defeat (an earlier example occurs in Piazza Vittorio). This scene gave rise to the story of De Sica stuffing cigarette butts into Enzo Staiola's pockets and scolding him for smoking (see chapter 1), but actually involved De Sica shaking him roughly and slapping his face, saying 'Piangi! piangi!' / 'Cry! cry!' (the documentary that records this also shows Enzo proud of his performance afterwards).

A new 'block' of ten very rapid reverse-angle shots (716–26) starts between, on the one hand, the owner of the bicycle looking from father to son and back again and, on the other hand, either Antonio (head and shoulders) or Bruno (in his own space between the adults' knees and lapels). The owner decides not to take the matter further (he says, 'Lascia stare' [Let it drop], despite the protests of the captors), quite clearly as a result of seeing Bruno standing beside his father. The captors send Antonio away. All this has taken place by the pavement holding parked bicycles that Antonio saw from the main street in the first block of 'virtual' reverse-angles. This 'block' of the sequence ends with Antonio and Bruno walking left along the pavement (Bruno handing his father the hat), with the camera tracking along beside the two, who leave the frame to the left.

The final 'block' of shots returns to the main street where the whole sequence began. The camera, on the pavement where Antonio and Bruno had stood at the outset (but a little further up the street), shoots the pair as they cross from the other side of the street towards the camera, now coming from left to right, through the departing football crowd. This 'reversing' of the camera's position (the camera has crossed from one pavement to the other, so that they left the previous frame towards the left, and re-enter this one from the left) is repeated in the next shot, when the camera moves over to the other side of the pair, Bruno in the foreground shot below adult shoulder height, the two walking from right to left and slightly towards the camera, at which point the camera tilts up to leave Bruno and shoot Antonio's head and shoulders in medium-close scale.

The last eight shots of the film pick up the alternation between Bruno shot at his height and Antonio at his, and 'wrap' this in two shots of them both from behind, walking away from the camera down Via Flaminia. The first 'wrapping' in the envelope shows Antonio from behind, too apathetic to move aside, being bumped by a truck, carrying football supporters, edging through the crowd (like the one that passed them earlier in the day outside the restaurant, and so prompting the viewer's *memory* of the contrast). They are now at the corner where the whole sequence originally started. There follow three matching 'pairs' of shots, taken from in front, of father and son walking towards the camera, which tracks back in front of them. As suggested earlier in this chapter, this is a case of De Sica dropping the 'observational' procedure of the 'follow' shot in favour of his less frequent procedure of 'accompaniment' (the tracking shot), associated with defeat. Each pair consists of a shot first of Antonio only in head- and-shoulders medium-close scale, then of Bruno with his father visible only knee-to-lapel in the left of the frame. In the first matching pair of shots Antonio looks straight ahead while Bruno looks up at him. In the second pair Antonio looks down to Bruno (camera right) and then away as he starts to cry, while Bruno slips his hand into that of his father, who grips it tightly to his body. In the third pair Antonio looks straight downwards (not to Bruno) while Bruno looks up at his father. The final 'wrapping' in the envelope shows the two figures having passed the camera, which has stopped tracking and now watches them from behind go off in the midst of the crowd. Antonio is reabsorbed into the landscape from which he first emerged at the beginning of the film. But the crowd into which he is shown merging is the very crowd that De Sica has, with enormous eloquence, shown rejecting and 'ejecting' him a short while earlier in the sequences of the *dopolavoro*, the Messa del povero, the thief's neighbourhood, and the stadium. Antonio has nowhere else to be except in the social 'landscape' that negates him.

De Sica's camera and *mise en scène* imitate the 'content' of the film at this point. He has abandoned reverse-angle shots from Antonio's point of view from the moment of his apprehension after the theft. There is nothing more for Antonio to look at; the landscape no longer holds out anything for him (in the last few shots, the 'landscape' is carried most particularly, for the viewer, by the *soundtrack*). Instead, Bruno is shown as looking at him. But progressively this too has ceased to be in reverse-angle shots from Bruno's point of view. Instead, just as in the final scene of the *Naples* episode of *Paisà*, the viewer is offered Bruno in separate shots taken from his height, which contribute to defining the relationship between father and son. Apart from Bruno, the only person who is looking at Antonio anymore, as he walks back to the 'start' of the film, so to speak, is the viewer – but now with a profound 'knowledge' of what he or she is seeing.

De Sica greatly admired King Vidor's 1928 silent film *The Crowd* when he first saw it as a young stage actor.[60] In interviews, writings, and declarations, he frequently used the words 'la folla' (which is how Italian translates the title of Vidor's film) when talking *both* about the environment he was depicting in his films *and* about the viewing public to whom his films were destined. In *The Crowd*, John's compulsive, anxious insecurity, his irritability, and his isolationist comparison of himself with others deplete the social resources that would enable him to com-

pete adequately in the social environment in which he tries – and fails –
to assert himself. He gradually has to learn the value of the human solidarity offered by those close to him. De Sica and Zavattini depict Antonio Ricci as a similarly flawed social being, with much to learn about
human values. John's son, in *The Crowd*, plays at times a role beside his
father very similar to Bruno's beside Antonio. The logical and inevitable
trajectory of both protagonists is downwards. But whereas Vidor ends
his film optimistically with a sentimental scene in which John and Mary
dance together and attend the vaudeville show where John's advertis-
ing slogan is successful, De Sica and Zavattini do no such thing. While
both directors take the same tender, respectful stance towards the
'crowd' they *depict*, De Sica extends this respect to the 'crowd' to whom
he *destines* his film. When the film was released, he stood anxiously in
the foyer of the Metropolitan cinema in Rome to hear the response of the
viewers as they emerged from the auditorium. *Ladri di biciclette*'s run at
the Metropolitan was drastically cut short in order to replace it with
Vidor's *Duel in the Sun* (1948). It would be hard to find a better illustration of neorealism's place in the history of cinema.

At the beginning of this chapter I said that the shooting script of *Ladri di
biciclette* is not available (because of an expressed wish of Zavattini's). A
notion of what was planned in the script has to be deduced from Zavattini's 'soggetto definitivo' (discussed earlier in this chapter). From that
we know that the film was originally supposed to continue a little
longer, after the failed theft of the bicycle, to show Antonio and Bruno
riding home on a bus, but that a final decision was made to end the film
earlier.

   In his essay on the film, Pio Baldelli makes frequent reference to its
'sceneggiatura.' In almost all cases it is clear that he is actually referring
to either the first or the 'definitive' *soggetto* published by Zavattini.
However, for the original planned ending to the film Baldelli actually
transcribes from a 'script,' containing scene and shot numbers (suggesting far more shots in the film than the actual 737 in the final version).
Unfortunately, Baldelli does not cite any published source for this
'script,' and I have been unable to verify the status of his text. Even
though it describes a scene that does not exist to be viewed, the text confirms so much of what we have observed about the way the film assembles its narrative – the concern with details, suggestions for actual shots,
the attention to 'background' elements (the repeated 'quarrels' taking

place in the background), the care given to the soundtrack and the way it is used to characterize the figures in a landscape – that I quote it in full from Baldelli:

> In the screenplay there followed 24 more shots, sc. LXXIV, 1137–1156: 'They get to the tram stop and wait. A tram arrives bursting to the seams. Using their elbows and shoving, amid people protesting, Antonio and Bruno manage to get onto the running board. The boy is about to fall at the last moment, his foot slips. Antonio catches him and pushes him inside. Bruno manages to get inside the tram. He manages to find a seat next to the window.
>
> 'Through the glass of the window he sees his father who is still on the running board holding on with difficulty, with one foot along the side of the car. Bruno is beside the window and looks straight ahead, sadly. Close-up of Antonio who looks straight ahead, distraught. His face also betrays the effort of holding on to the tram. Detailed shot of Antonio's hand trembling from the effort. Close-up of Antonio who is very sad and exhausted. Close-up of Bruno looking at his father. The father looks at his son. Detail: the son looks at the father. The tram stops, some people get off. Bruno notices that the seat in front of him is free. He climbs over and sits on it, takes off his hat and places it on the seat next to him.
>
> 'A man would like to take it. Bruno: It is taken. Bruno turns towards the window and without enthusiasm, without joy, beckons to his father to join him. Antonio tries to make his way through the crowd on the running board and on the platform. Voices of passengers: What are you pushing for? ... Aoh! ... Listen to me ... Antonio seems not to hear the people's protests and carries on forward. He grabs onto the handrail and with his shoulders and his elbows clears some space. Antonio gets next to the empty seat. He gives a gentle shove to a man standing in front of it intensely reading a newspaper.
>
> 'He finally gets to sit down, his expression that of a man who needs a rest. He looks at his son. Behind them starts up one of the usual stupid quarrels between passengers, which acts as a sound background to the solitude of Antonio and Bruno. Bruno slowly leans on his father and looks straight ahead. His face too shows signs of weariness and sadness. Close-up of Antonio who cannot hold back his tears, wipes his eyes with his hand, and adjusts Bruno's scarf, which is hanging down, around his neck. Long-scale shot of the tram going off towards Piazza del Popolo. The first lights of the evening turn on.'[61]

Concluding Remarks

De Sica and Zavattini paid their mortgages, so to speak, from the Italian commercial cinema industry. I, the critic writing this book, have devoted much time to studying the workings of that industry. Nobody harbours any illusions about what factors were involved. Yet De Sica and Zavattini, on their own, wrote and produced *Ladri di biciclette* within that context, using all the resources of the industry – it was not a cheaply made, unprofessional film, nor was it marketed and distributed outside the normal commercial structures. As an 'object,' the film belongs in 'the cinema,' with all the economic and institutional associations that attach to that entity.

The story of the film's initial release in December 1948 is instructive in this context. The Italian state distribution company, ENIC, released it in the 'Christmas holiday' period. A family visit to the cinema was (and often still is) a traditional part of the ritual of the Christmas / New Year break in Italy. As Maria Mercader, De Sica's partner, recounts:

> I do not know who had the idea of arranging the opening of the film in the whole of Italy for the 22nd of December. Caught up in the circus of Christmas films, *Ladri di biciclette* certainly did not have the qualities that would recommend it to a holiday public determined to forget its troubles ... In Rome we went a couple of evenings to spy on the reaction of the spectators coming out of the Metropolitan cinema. We were talking quietly with the manager when we saw coming out of the auditorium a man who looked like a working man, with his wife and children, who came up to us and said to the manager: 'Give us our money back and put a warning on the posters for big families when the film is a rip-off.'[62]

The story is taken up by Alfredo Guarini, who was at the time heading ENIC:

> Once the film was completed, the moment arrived to release it, and I had set up various private showings that it was my intention would serve first of all to acquaint those who worked in our business with the film, and to create around *Ladri di biciclette* an atmosphere of interest which would lay the basis for a new type of publicity launch. Unexpectedly – in my absence – and flouting the good faith of De Sica, the offices of ENIC decided to release the film in a few Italian cities. It was a huge flop, because a normal public could not guess from the simple posters of a film like *Ladri di bici-*

clette that they were being offered the masterpiece that De Sica's film in fact was.

As soon as I heard the outcome I hastened to Rome, suspended the showings of the film, and agreed with De Sica on a new system of release. Starting from Milan, the director personally introduced the film and explained it to the public in all the major Italian cities. So much interest was born from this that it brought about a considerable increase in box-office receipts, and today – at least as far as *Ladri di biciclette* is concerned – we have no reason to complain, as we do for so many other neorealist films, about the lack of public response and thus of poor Italian receipts.[63]

One critical approach to *Ladri di biciclette* is to interpret its *content* as a denunciation of social conditions in post-war Italy, as though some photographically identifiable institution or system were to blame for poverty, unemployment, and crime: the government, the middle classes, capitalism. Certainly, both De Sica and Zavattini would criticize these entities, and would offer the film as a source of knowledge (*conoscenza*), to disturb complacency and promote a social awareness (*coscienza*) in its viewers. However, to take the film this way is to break it up into its components, and interpret each fragment as directed towards a critique of the government (in the *dopolavoro* scene), the Church (in the *Messa del povero* scene), the police and the middle classes (in the restaurant and *Messa del povero* scenes), and the lack of solidarity among the poor (in the market scenes and those in Trastevere). This approach does not adequately account for the *film* as a whole, whose critique is directed ultimately at the *cinema* as an institution and an industry – for offering to its viewers artefacts providing gratifications that are meretricious, shallow, and false. The film is not a 'discourse' in a polemic, but an aesthetic artefact introduced into a context made up of other aesthetic artefacts. Many of the readers of this book, accustomed to the cinema as neorealism *enabled* it to become, will find it hard to imagine how, in 1948, *Ladri di biciclette* was like a hand grenade thrown into a cocktail party. Its aesthetic act was not primarily to denounce specific evils in the Italian social order, but to enact what the aesthetics of cinema could be. To the question of whether the aim of the film is to put an end to unemployment or to make the viewer feel sorry for Antonio the answer is clearly that it is neither. The man who produced and directed that film was no mere technician competently executing the instructions of a scriptwriter who was the real artist. That charming, sweet, modest De Sica, during the last stages of completing the script, was capable of tearing Zavattini's pages out of the poor man's hands, ripping them into little pieces, hurling them onto the floor, and stamping them into his living-room carpet.[64]

We need to add together Zavattini's realist theorizing (summarized in chapter 2) and De Sica's almost contrary insistence:

> Neorealism is a certain cinema, it is a way of feeling. Unfairly, Chaplin himself and Clair himself place our cinema on a plane of reality. No, that is not right. It is a transfigured reality. It is a transposition onto the lyrical plane, onto the poetic plane, onto an elevated plane. Woe betide it if it were reality! If it is reality, then it is chronicle, it is a banal truth.[65]

Both men insist that they are talking about 'a certain cinema' (see the section in chapter 2 devoted to Zavattini), but that specification has one meaning for Zavattini ('reality' and 'morality') and a slightly different meaning for De Sica ('poetry,' 'lyricism,' and 'a way of feeling').

Our analysis of the film began, in the section on 'Narrative,' with the observation that Zavattini's plots function like 'laboratory experiments.' The sphere of autonomous action is progressively tightened around the protagonists, to the point where they can no longer act, but only 'know.' Their knowledge of their own situation becomes the viewer's knowledge. In Zavattini's theoretical scheme, the viewer's knowledge gives rise to his or her moral responsibility, which should lead in due course to action. This is what Zavattini means by 'a certain cinema': a *convivenza* (living in fellowship) involving direct participation in reality. De Sica's understanding of 'a certain cinema' is entirely compatible with Zavattini's. At the same time, it is entirely different. It sees the cinema as a medium even better suited than literature to *expressing* a particular sensibility he regards as 'modern' (and it is for this reason that attention was drawn earlier in the analysis to parallels with Antonioni). In the section of chapter 2 devoted to 'Rhetoric,' we noted how the rhetoric of *sermo humilis* functioned to bring about a 'reduction' in the form and content of films. This means that 'realism' can be a product of 'reduction': what is narrated is more 'real' because it is unexceptional, ordinary, and everyday. Zavattini sees realism in this light, as the rejection of the amplification of 'spectacle,' and therefore as bringing the viewer into contact with *reality*, the 'facts' of which he or she can have solid, sound 'knowledge.' This very same 'reduction' is for De Sica the pathway to *poetry*, enabling his camera to assemble imagery expressing feeling and experience ('states of mind').

Without wanting to make too strong a point out of it, we can say that the two different senses of 'a certain cinema' encapsulate the tension we discerned between 'realism' and 'the aesthetic' in chapter 2.

All of this is contained, between the lines, in De Sica's sweetly reasonable explanation, given around the time of the film's completion, of why he was making it:

> Why am I making this film? Well, since *Sciuscià*, I have had in my hands thirty or forty film scripts, each perhaps more beautiful than the next, full of facts, of striking circumstances. But I was looking for an event that was less extraordinary in its appearance, one of those events that can happen to all of us, and particularly to the poor, and that no newspaper deigns to cover ... My aim is to draw out what is dramatic in everyday situations, what is marvellous in the smallest, indeed the tiniest, news story, in things regarded by most people as uninteresting material. In fact, what is the theft of a bicycle, one far from shining and new besides? In Rome a large number are stolen every day and nobody bothers about it because, in the give and take of the city, who is going to bother about a bicycle? And yet for many who do not possess anything else, who use it for going to work, who hold onto it as their only support in the turmoil of city life, the loss of that bicycle is an event that is important, tragic, catastrophic. Why go digging for extraordinary adventures when what goes on before our eyes, and what happens to those of us who are least well provided for is so full of real anguish? Literature has been discovering for a long time this modern dimension that focuses on the tiniest things, on states of mind normally considered too ordinary. Cinema, with its camera, has the means best suited for capturing it. Its sensibility is of this kind, and this is how I myself understand our much discussed realism – which, to my mind, cannot consist merely in a document.[66]

De Sica attempts to represent the *experience* of an imagined character, what it is like to see *a* world through his eyes. This is slightly different from straightforward realism, which attempts to see *the* world (the putative 'real' one), and the characters in it, objectively. De Sica appears to be *reproducing* an experience; but of course, this cannot be what he is doing, because he is making a *film*, not recording reality. The experience the viewer has is of the *film*, which is an *analogue* of the way a hypothetical character experiences *life*. Therefore, the film has to act as an intermediary between two experiences: that of a hypothesized Antonio and that of a real viewer. The viewer is invited to believe that the experience of Antonio *caused* the film; but of course it did not, because Antonio never existed. If the film were a documentary (and hence *indexical*), 'cause' would be the link between sign and referent. But in *Ladri di biciclette* that is not the case. The object is not *explained* by its referent (which is a common way of approaching 'realist' texts). Representation suggests re-presentation: a repetition. But *Ladri di biciclette* is a narrative, and what it is most likely to be *repeating* is another narrative. The *cause* of the film is the creative activity of the artists: the assembly of an artefact.

It would be a mistake to see in the championing of the rhetoric of *sermo humilis* only the surface that De Sica shows to the public – the ever-elegant actor and diplomatic director-collaborator with the writer-artist Zavattini, who just happens also to be capable of using the cinema to document the surface facts of a historical reality. His iron determination, his compulsive gambling, his complicated family life, his willingness to shake and slap tears out of Enzo Staiola, and to bully Zavattini to heights he never achieved anywhere else should alert us to the fact that when De Sica talks about poetry and lyricism, he is talking also about his own cinematic self-expression, in which life is 'full of real anguish' and suffering. The man who devoted himself to consummate mastery of the acting profession, when he came to express solitude and existential anxiety in his own works of art, could not have chosen a more opaque screen on which to project them than Antonio Ricci. The actress Marisa Merlini said of him: 'His humour has been much talked about, but to me it has always seemed to be a very sad humour, because he was very alone and sad. He was alone above all in his own milieu.'[67] Paying attention to the *whole film* as the object of study, and recognizing how the intertwining threads of the search for the bicycle and of the father-son relationship draw upon the deeper levels of narrative reference of the melodramatic matrix helps us to see how *Ladri di biciclette* might command our attention half a century after the passing of the 'realities' it purportedly photographs: because it is a *film* – an assembly of sounds and images guided by intentions, portraying in remarkable detail a figure in a landscape. Knowing about Zavattini's project for a neorealist cinema enormously enhances our perception of components of the film, but De Sica's approach to the notion of 'poetry' is more alive to the aesthetic identity of the whole – and it is the approach I have privileged. It offers us an aesthetic point of view on their neorealism as a cinema that is a profound 'seeing,' giving rise to an artefact that is the product of an assembly of fragments. Deleuze is right to describe the new neorealist narrative as no longer involving action that brings about change. Instead, an artful collage of fragments uses the rhetoric of *sermo humilis* to assemble a sublime vision of 'what is.' Close attention to De Sica's procedures of *dispositio* (for example, the follow shot, composition in depth, and playing sound against image) might enable criticism of *Ladri di biciclette* to overcome the endless recycling of the same apparently incompatible features: reality/poetry; morality/sentimentality; life/narrative; dispassion/love; humanity/society; dramaturgy/phenomenology; chronicle/genre.[68]

Concluding Remarks

With his artefact, looked at from an aesthetic point of view, the artist adds to the world something that was not there before. Many of the components of the notion of realism imply that the artist merely encodes in a particular medium what already existed in the world before the artefact was created. Realist artefacts, rather than adding to the world, repeat it. The artist only expresses his evaluation of an existing reality; all that he can add to that reality is his discourse about it. This leads to a criticism that sees its task as one of interpreting the discourse about an existing reality that the artist articulates in the assembly of his artefact – and it is a very valid critical activity. The discipline of describing the artefacts and examining their assembly as autonomous objects can free the critic from treating them merely as encoded representations and evaluations of what already existed before they were assembled. Seeing the assembly as one of narrative, rather than of representation (a 'list' that establishes a hierarchy of value), enables the critic to see the artefacts as additions to the world. The hypothesis of the melodramatic narrative matrix, and the idyll it counterposes to the prevailing ontology of the modernized world represented in Rossellini's and De Sica's films, opens a space in which those 'realist' works can be additions to what already exists. To simplify the matter somewhat, Rossellini can be seen as assembling a vision of what *must* be there in the world (*or* we are lost), while De Sica can be seen as assembling a vision of what is *not* there in the world (*and* we are lost).

To describe the films we have analysed as displaying a realist aesthetics may be an oxymoron. We have seen how the description 'un certo cinema' / 'a certain cinema' means realism for Zavattini and poetry for De Sica, and care is needed before making hasty assumptions about the common ground between them. Yet the artefact itself, the film, has a coherent integrity, which is brought into relief by a ruthlessly aesthetic approach to describing it. We have traced the same tension between Sergio Amidei and the partnership of Rossellini and Fellini in the development from *Roma città aperta* to *Paisà*: from the film as 'constructed' in a traditional story/script to the film as 'discovered' and 'assembled' in the actual shooting. While the aesthetic perspective on the specifically cinematic does not tell us everything we need to know about the films, it is a fruitful position to start from.

Without wanting to be too schematic, we can identify two different strategies for thinking and reasoning figuratively, through images. One strategy sets up attractions, affinities, and harmonies; the other strategy sets up oppositions. *Paisà* is typical of the first strategy: Pasquale and his environment, the friars and their monastery, Cigolani and the marshes are cases where simplicity is achieved by means of the harmony that binds the characters to their environments. De Sica works through figurative oppositions. He places in the background of his compositions the very material objects and events that negate his protagonists: behind Antonio are buses, bicycles, forces of law and order, people who are secure (the seminarians) and confident (the man painting a bicycle frame, or the bourgeoisie who help the poor or who lunch in a restaurant), or architectural constructions that loom nearby and taper off in the distance (the façade of a building, the narrowing of a street, the closing in of a tunnel). In both the strategy of Rossellini and that of De Sica, the meaning and implications carried by the artefact are entrusted less to the discourse of the narrative than to the figuration of the imagery. The narrative unfolds a basic, archetypal structure, that of melodrama, which in its turn serves as a scaffolding on which to hang the figurations emerging from the deployment of a distinctive and personal cinematographic poetics. It looks like a way of 'seeing' the real world, but in fact it is a way of thinking with images.

Neorealism articulated profound transformations in the consciousness of Italians – precipitated by the crisis of the war and modernization – in terms of knowledge: ways in which it was possible to know the human social animal, its needs, its resources, and its limitations. Reference went upwards to the surface of the historical reality of the time, but also downwards to mythical ways of understanding the human condition. The artists fused these two levels in artefacts that narrated an experience of almost metaphysical confrontation and dilemma. Pina, Don Pietro, Carmela, Francesca, Fra Pacifico, Cigolani, and Antonio

Ricci are plausible historical figures, but also vessels of contradictions operating at a deeper existential level. The grand classical narratives that are supposed to be absent in neorealist films are, in fact, deployed by the way the artefacts assemble into a whole, like a collage, their micro-narratives. The 'listing' of representations of what was 'out there' in reality – the procedure lying behind the notion of 'realism' – was just a *means*, supplying the ingredients or components of artefacts that aspired, on a poetical level, to a far wider frame of reference.

The poetic and narrative tradition in which Rossellini and De Sica constructed their assemblies was the very Italian one of cinematic comedy – with its roots in music hall, popular song, and popular culture – which mobilized a rhetoric of *sermo humilis*. The critique of the 'landscape' in the light of the 'idyll' is a *valid* one, but it is not a historically *feasible* solution. This is how comedy works: to *validate* a world view that cannot *prevail*.

Fellini took neorealism further in that direction, while Antonioni stripped down the nucleus of the 'figure in a landscape' to its essential pictorial level. Visconti, De Santis, and Germi continued in a more classically conventional literary narrative tradition (Visconti and Germi in the tradition of the nineteenth-century novel, De Santis in that of the *romanzo d'appendice*). Pasolini tried to take a direct route to the 'idyll' through myth.

A standard account of neorealism has defined the movement in opposition to alternatives, which are placed in a chronology. That is to say, 'realism' is opposed to the 'formalism' (let us say, of Antonioni) or the 'modernism' (let us say, of Fellini), which are seen as instances of 'breaking away' from neorealism at the end of the 1950s. In this account, the privilege accorded to *representation* over *narrative* and *rhetoric* is seen as a victorious achievement. Neorealist films like *Paisà* and *Ladri di biciclette* are seen as a point of *arrival* in a notional history of cinema, rather than as a point of *departure*, leading forward to other things.

The aesthetic approach adopted in this book suggests a rather different picture. It no longer proposes neorealism as a point of arrival. Instead, each individual artefact is seen as creating a context into which another aesthetic artefact is introduced. Artists are seen as making one film after another (that is their job), each one developing on the previous one. The aesthetic approach looks at the poetics of the films, rather than at some notion of accurate representation, or of the artists as people who develop a discourse about Italian society. If they have a discourse, it is very likely to be about films as aesthetic objects. Indeed, when we listen to what they say, we find them articulating a poetics of the fragment, describing the film as a pictorial assembly of micro-components (as we heard in chapter 2). We find ourselves questioning whether representation can really be privileged over narrative and rhetoric, whether neorealism can so easily be opposed to formalism and modernism, whether neorealism might not rather be a point of departure than of arrival, and whether Antonioni and Fellini in 1960 can so clearly be described as 'breaking away' from neorealism.

Rossellini's and De Sica's early neorealist films were the fortunate products of artists free to explore the aesthetics of their medium in contextual circumstances operating for a limited period (post-war cultural and historical circumstances, and a temporary state of the Italian cinema industry). But they revealed poetic potentialities specific to the medium of cinema that were an inspiration to an entire generation of new filmmakers all over the world.

That said, my aim in this book has been merely to draw attention to the disinterested aesthetic satisfaction offered to the viewer by three particular artefacts.

Appendices

APPENDIX 1 A standard introduction to neorealism

The Italian term *neorealismo* (first used in the 1920s in connection with Soviet literature and cinema) is applied mainly to Italian cinema and literature (and in
the latter case mainly, but not exclusively, to prose narrative), but also to photography, architecture, painting, and sculpture. Examples of some of the different manifestations of neorealist literary narrative are Cesare Pavese's *Paesi tuoi*
(1941, but written in 1939), Elio Vittorini's *Conversazione in Sicilia* (1938–41),
Ignazio Silone's *Fontamara* (1930), Italo Calvino's *Il sentiero dei nidi di ragno*
(1947), Primo Levi's *Se questo è un uomo* (1947), Carlo Levi's *Cristo si è fermato a
Eboli* (1945), Vasco Pratolini's *Il quartiere* (1944), Beppe Fenoglio's *Il partigiano
Johnny* (published in 1968), and Carlo Cassola's *La ragazza di Bube* (1960). Pavese
– certainly one of the most respected neorealist writers – in a radio interview
named Vittorio De Sica, a neorealist film director, as the greatest *Italian* 'narrator' of the twentieth century (alongside Thomas Mann as the greatest overall).
What follows relates only to 'neorealism' in Italian cinema.

1. Periodization
The *start* of the movement is conventionally held to be 1945.
(a) The year 1945 marks the definitive fall of fascism, the end of the Second
World War, and the completion of the anti-fascist Resistance and the Allied liberation (for details see appendix 2, 'Historical background for neorealism').
(b) It has generally been held that there was a stark opposition between the fascist attitude towards culture (particularly cinema) and the post-war attitude,
which was informed by left-wing notions of democracy and social justice. The
general account of this opposition (in a simplified summary) goes as follows:
  (i) Fascism: Culture's role was to build the corporate fascist nation, to downplay, suppress, or explain away social oppositions (this was seen by anti-fascist intellectuals as being an avoidance of 'reality' – regional and dialect
  differences, class differences, standards of living, social problems), and to
  inspire Italians to imperialist nation-building (with 'rhetorical' appeals to
  ancient Rome and the *Risorgimento*); culture promoted 'unreal' and consolatory comedies and melodramas.
  (ii) Post-war culture featured a refusal of 'rhetoric,' a determination to face
  social problems and political conflicts squarely, the acknowledgment of the
  class struggle, a shared project for a truly democratic nation to bring about
  social justice for all, and aesthetic theories that viewed formal experimentation with suspicion and advocated an art democratically accessible to all
  classes, and a 'raw' and uninhibited look at the experience of war, poverty,
  and suffering.

(c) However, what was held to be a stark opposition in the immediate post-war years has come under criticism for being an inaccurate simplification of a more complex interplay between rupture and continuity.

(d) Italian cinema in the fascist period was already moving in the direction of the post-war attitude:

(i) In the late 1930s and early 1940s intellectuals and artists began a cautiously expressed critique of fascist society and culture, most prominently in the cinema: in fascist institutions (the Centro Sperimentale di Cinematografia and its journal *Bianco e Nero* from 1938), in the journal *Cinema*, and in other cultural journals criticizing films.

(ii) Films made in the period 1941–43 offered a far less rosy and unruffled picture of Italian society than hitherto, and featured a straightforward, unrhetorical directness in their depiction of a contemporary reality: *Uomini sul fondo* (De Robertis), *Un pilota ritorna* (Rossellini), *Quattro passi tra le nuvole* (Blasetti), *I bambini ci guardano* (De Sica), and particularly *Ossessione* (Visconti). In historical accounts of the Italian cinema this is often referred to as a period of 'pre-neorealism.'

(iii) Intellectuals under item (i) above identified and extolled a tradition of 'realism' in Italian cinema since the silent era, and debated its stylistic and thematic implications.

(iv) Comedy was a prominent genre in Italian cinema of the 1930s: were these films *telefoni bianchi* ('white telephones' – unreal and escapist films) or did there exist a populist cinema representing ordinary people's everyday experience?

(e) The state of the Italian film industry in the years 1945–9:

(i) The technical state was poor, with facilities damaged or unavailable.

(ii) There was a hiatus in conventional commercial production (discussed in chapter 1).

(iii) Neorealist filmmakers made a virtue out of necessity, using

– production financing they gathered themselves;
– locations rather than studios (but not always ...);
– non-professional actors (but not always ...); and
– subject matter taken from recent historical experience and from everyday life, rather than conventional cinematic stories.

(f) The international critical success of neorealist films encouraged the notion of an innovative, valid cultural movement in the group of films that rapidly acquired the collective label of 'neorealist.'

The movement is generally regarded as undergoing a 'crisis' and coming to an *end* around 1953–5 for reasons listed in item 4 below.

2. Some characteristics of films called 'neorealist'
(a) contemporary social, historical, and political subject matter;
(b) protagonists: the 'people', the poor, marginalised groups;
(c) cheaply made films with low production values – 'rough' in their appearance;
(d) a 'realist' treatment of authentic and substantial subject matter;
(e) *relative* freedom from censorship (politically and sexually, for example);
(f) location shooting;
(g) non-professional actors;
(h) for Rossellini: initially the war (*Roma città aperta, Paisà, Germania anno zero*);
(i) for De Sica: everyday, non-spectacular life (*Sciuscià, Ladri di biciclette, Umberto D.*);
(j) for Visconti: authenticity, a documentary approach, dialect, Marxism (*La terra trema*);
(k) for Antonioni: first documentary filmmaking; then genre used to highlight the moral condition of the bourgeoisie (*Cronaca di un amore*);
(l) for De Santis: melodrama and adventure with a left-wing, collectivist political message (*Caccia tragica, Riso amaro*);
(m) for Germi: using the narrative and figurative schemes of the Hollywood Western to portray contemporary social and political problems (*In nome della legge, Il cammino della speranza*);
(n) for Zampa: comedy with political satire (*Anni difficili*, politics; *Vivere in pace*, anti-war; *L'onorevole Angelina*, politics of poverty).

3. A critical orthodoxy of the 'institution of neorealism' (see p. 37):
(a) A left-wing political and intellectual climate existed in post-war Italy, and conditioned people's thinking about cinema.
(b) Everything connected with fascism was rejected and condemned, so that neorealism was seen as a *total break* with the past. *Nowadays* fascist culture and cinema are no longer viewed with that bias, and neorealism is seen as being partly in *continuity* with Italian cinema of the late 1930s and early 1940s, and as developing out of it.
(c) Neorealist *arte/impegno* (art with a political and social commitment) versus pre-war *industria/evasione* (money-making commercialism directed towards escapist entertainment).
(d) Neorealist films were championed by the French critic André Bazin (1949), and were incorporated into his theorizing of 'realism':
  (i) facts, representation, experience, with less emphasis on 'narrative' ('stories'); the realism of photography;
  (ii) a stylistic preference for *mise en scène* rather than montage, and so films

are shot in long takes (an assertion not always subjected to empirical verification);

(iii) the use of deep focus to present a more 'realist' three-dimensional representation (the same proviso applies as in (ii) above).

(e) This was combined with the later theorizing (1952–1953) of Cesare Zavattini (discussed in chapter 2):

(i) the tiniest details of everyday life pursued by the camera with a method of *pedinamento* (a 'tailing,' as in detective fiction; hunting down 'reality');

(ii) no need for 'stories';

(iii) *nome e cognome* (characters with 'real names' played by 'real people');

(iv) morality (*knowledge* about our fellows brings about a sense of moral responsibility towards others, leading to *convivenza* – 'living in fellowship').

(f) From 1948 onwards, a polemic: *Cinema nuovo* versus Luigi Chiarini and others; *realismo/storia* ('realism' requiring the depiction of historical processes) versus *cronaca* (the 'poetry' of everyday events). From *Cinema nuovo* came the demand for Marxist orthodoxy in neorealist films, leading to:

(i) accusing Rossellini from *Germania annno zero* onwards of 'betraying' neorealism by moving towards mysticizing religious consolation rather than a progressive class struggle;

(ii) describing De Sica's *Ladri di biciclette* as *cronaca* and petit-bourgeois sentimentalizing;

(iii) championing the Marxist-leaning films of Visconti and De Santis as the only acceptable models for a neorealist cinema;

(iv) a fierce polemic at the 1954 Venice Film Festival over Visconti's *Senso* ('realism' because recounting Italian history) and Fellini's *La strada* (deemed a religiously mystificatory fable in the tradition of the later Rossellini).

(g) The positions of De Santis and Germi were different from those of Rossellini, De Sica, and Visconti (which were themselves each different from each other): both De Santis and Germi used mainstream genres to propose a political message, and accepted the validity of the public's desire for narrative entertainment. De Santis's *Riso amaro* and Germi's *In nome della legge* both enjoyed popular commercial success.

(h) The post-1949 films of Rossellini and Antonioni, and later of Fellini, were defended by non-Marxists as being a development of neorealism away from a purely *materialist* 'realism' (portraying social and economic conditions) towards an *inner* or psychological 'realism', portraying a spiritual or moral reality.

4. History of the movement

(a) 'high neorealism' (particularly Rossellini, De Sica and Visconti) in the 'production hiatus' 1945–9 (independent production);

(b) post-1949: *crisis* of neorealism under the onslaught of an industrial take-over of filmmaking and political reaction (see (c) and (d) below): theorizing begins, and a struggle to preserve neorealism;

(c) industrial take-over:

    (i) the Legge Andreotti (a law covering the cinema granting state incentives to commercially profitable film production);

    (ii) producers' re-entry into profitable film making;

    (iii) poor commercial results for certain neorealist films;

    (iv) co-option of neorealist filmmakers into mainstream genre filmmaking;

(d) political reaction and the Cold War, in combination with government and clerical censorship, make it hard for neorealist filmmakers to get their projects financed and distributed;

(e) the Italian public stay away from neorealist films, and flock to genre-vehicles, such as films in the following categories:

    (i) *neorealismo rosa* (some of the features of neorealism applied to comedies set in the everyday life of the lower classes);

    (ii) films featuring popular music-hall comics (Totò);

    (iii) films applying a 'realist' style to melodramas promoting traditional family roles (*strappalacrime* – 'tear-jerkers');

    (iv) Hollywood films.

(f) Filmmakers *develop* artistically (often described in terms of their 'breaking away' from neorealism): Rossellini, Visconti, Antonioni, Fellini producing, by 1960, what was seen – together with other movements, for example in France, Sweden, and Poland – as the 'European art cinema.' In the case of Fellini and Antonioni this is often described as a 'modernist,' rather than a 'realist,' cinema.

APPENDIX 2 Historical background for neorealism

Italy entered the war on 10 June 1940 on the side of Germany, because it appeared that Germany would win it. Italy's military efforts in the Balkans and Greece were disastrous, and the Germans had to send troops to rescue them. By mid-1942, with America and the Soviet Union in the war, it was no longer so clear that Germany would emerge victorious.

The Allies decided to draw German troops away from northern France (where they wanted to invade) by invading Italy from the south. In July 1943 the Allies landed troops on the beaches of southern Sicily. Meanwhile, they bombed Italian ports, military installations, and cities to 'soften up' the Italians for surrender. The Germans poured troops into Italy from the north.

Seeing that Germany was going to lose the war, the Italians wanted to get out. Mussolini was now a liability. They secretly negotiated with the Allies for a truce, but did so tentatively, because they feared the Germans' response to this treachery.

On 24 July 1943 the Fascist Grand Council invited the king of Italy to dismiss Mussolini, who was arrested and imprisoned. The king appointed Marshall Badoglio head of a new government, with the job of arranging a peace with the Allies. Badoglio played for time. The Allies, who had meanwhile conquered Sicily (without capturing the German army), and were moving to mainland Italy, were getting impatient. An armistice was signed on 3 September, but Badoglio asked for its announcement to be delayed. On 8 September 1943 General Eisenhower announced over the radio an armistice between Italy and the Allies, followed shortly thereafter by Badoglio.

The Allies were ready to parachute troops into Rome to join with the Italian army (which had theoretically 'changed sides') in securing the city before the Germans could respond in large numbers. But the Italian high command issued no orders to the Italian army to start fighting the Germans, nor did it make the necessary arrangements for the Allied parachute drop. Instead, the king and his family, and the top officers of the Italian high command, fled Rome in the night for Brindisi to seek safety behind Allied lines. This was the great 'betrayal' of Italians by the ruling class.

The Germans poured in troops, secured Rome, and sent in divisions to stop the Allied advance up the mainland of Italy. Meanwhile, the men of the Italian army deserted in droves, and tried to get home.

Mussolini was rescued from prison by a daring German raid, and was set up in the North of Italy, with his headquarters on Lake Garda in the town of Salò, as the head of a new *republican* Italy (i.e., an alternative to the monarchy, and to the 'Italy' of the king and Badoglio, which had sought refuge in the South), often called *La repubblica di Salò*. Although Mussolini and the Fascist Grand Council theoretically now ran all of Italy (including Rome) except the southern part occupied by the Allies, in fact the Germans were in full control.

A small partisan opposition to the Fascists and the Germans sprang up immediately, at first numbering only 9000 men. These numbers were gradually swollen by deserters from the Italian army and by other men who, rather than be picked up by the Germans and either enlisted in Mussolini's new republican army or deported to labour camps in Germany, Poland, and Russia, joined the partisans in the Centre and North of Italy to carry out spying and sabotage activities against the occupying Germans. The best organized and most numerous partisan bands were run by the Italian Communist Party, and by a left-wing coalition of parties called the Action Party. By mid-1944 there were about 30,000 partisans, and by April 1945 there were more than 100,000. The partisans suffered very heavy losses (well over 30,000 dead and 20,000 seriously wounded) at the hands of the Germans and Fascists, who used terror, reprisals, and torture to crush them.

Italy was divided in two: (a) The South, occupied by the Americans and the British, where units of the Italian army of Badoglio now fought alongside the Allies against the Germans; and (b) the Centre and North, the Republic of Salò, officially governed by Mussolini, the Fascist Grand Council, and its military and police forces, but in fact occupied and controlled by the Germans. Against these forces the partisans were fighting a civil war against the Fascists, a guerrilla war of liberation against the Germans, and a political struggle against Italian forces of reaction.

The Allies, frequently outfought by the retreating Germans, were slow to move up the Italian peninsula. In October 1943 they took Naples (after landing troops at Salerno), but the Neapolitans had already chased out the Germans with an insurrection. The partisan resistance movement set up in Rome a clandestine central committee called the Comitato di Liberazione Nazionale (CLN) to coordinate the struggle against the Fascist Italians and the Germans, and another branch in Milan (CLNAI) which was a good deal more radical, and strove in vain to be officially recognized by the Allies as the government of the occupied North. Much of the political ideology of the northern partisan groups was collectivist, reformist, and even revolutionary, and alarmed both the Allies and the CLN in Rome. The ideology was referred to as *il vento del nord* – 'the wind from the north.'

It took until June 1944 for the Allies to get to Rome. Instead of encircling and capturing the retreating German army, the American general, Clark, entered Rome to garner glory for himself, and so allowed the German army to escape and to set up defences in the Apennine mountains across Italy from Lucca to the Adriatic (on what was called the Gothic Line). As winter 1944 set in, the Allies saw that they could not dislodge and overwhelm the Germans until the snows and rains in the mountains were over. The Allies therefore sent a message to the partisans in the North to stop fighting over the winter, lay down their arms, and go to ground. The partisans could not do this, because it offered the Germans and the Fascists just the opportunity they needed to capture and kill them, and so they had a terrible winter, fighting with little food and few military supplies.

By late April 1945 the partisans had organized insurrections in the North, the Germans were retreating, and the Allies had broken through and invaded the whole of Italy.

Italy was now governed, first, by the Allied Military Government Occupied Territory (AMGOT), and then by coalitions formed, ever since the liberation of Rome, from the elements that had contributed to the Resistance (principally the Communists, the Action Party, the Socialists, and the Christian Democrats) and from the old monarchist ruling elite. In June 1946 a referendum was held to allow Italians to decide whether they wanted to continue with a monarchy or become a republic. They chose by a small majority a republic (the North voting overwhelmingly for a republic, the South overwhelmingly for the monarchy). On the same day, the Christian Democrats gained roughly the same number of seats in the elections to the Constituent Assembly as the Communists and the Socialists combined, while the Action Party was wiped out. Knowing how determined the British, the Americans, and the Vatican were that Italy should not go the way of Yugoslavia, towards Communism, and well aware of the forces ranged against them, the leaders of the Italian Communist Party had not exploited the 'revolutionary' elements of the armed Resistance (especially those blowing down with the 'wind from the north'), but instead had disarmed the ex-partisans and cooperated in government coalitions designed to reconcile the political divisions brought about by the civil war and to rebuild the economy. There was no real purge of former Fascist officials, policemen, or judges, many fascist security statutes remained on the books, and a huge propaganda war was mounted against the parties of the left. Already by May 1947, the Communists and the Socialists had been excluded from the ruling coalition headed by the Christian Democrats, and in the parliamentary elections of April 1948, despite a rise in the number of seats secured by the Communist Party, the Christian Democrats gained an outright majority. They set about consolidating their hold on a conservative, free-market state, and held it until the 1990s. Little of the freedom and social justice the partisan Resistance had fought for – and neorealist cinema promoted – was achieved.

APPENDIX 3 Statistics of the Italian film industry

Year	A	B	C (%)	D	E	F	G	H (%)	I	J
1942	102	–	–	–	–	470	L.1,252	57	L.3	ca. 5,000
1945	52	3	6	?	?	?	L.6,498	?	?	ca. 5,600
1946	46	6	13	600	850	417	L.13,928	13	L.33	6,141
1947	59	4	7	507	794	532	L.29,076	11	L.55	6,551
1948	62	8	13	668	874	588	L.42,703	?	L.73	7,545
1949	70	3	4	502	666	616	L.54,247	17	L.88	7,896
1950	99	10	10	394	539	662	L.63,404	29	L.96	8,626
1951	112	2	2	230	342	706	L.73,203	30	L.104	8,898
1952	142	6	4	246	394	748	L.83,672	37	L.112	9,502
1953	148	6	4	222	359	778	L.94,502	38	L.121	9,888
1954	206	4	2	209	307	801	L.105,172	39	L.131	10,391
1968	270	–	–	167	343	560	L.170,618	56	L.305	ca. 12,000

A: Number of Italian films released
B: Number of neorealist films released
C: Percentage of Italian films released that are neorealist
D: Number of U.S. films imported
E: Total foreign imported films

F: Number of tickets sold in Italian cinemas (millions)
G: Total box-office receipts of Italian cinemas (millions of lire)
H: Percentage of receipts in col. G going to Italian films
I: Average cinema ticket price in Italy
J: Number of cinemas in Italy

See further notes on these statistics on the following page.

APPENDIX 3 (*concluded*)

Notes on appendix 3 statistics

B: I have taken a fairly broad and tolerant definition of the category 'neorealist.'

C: Note that as Italian production really begins to take off, the relative number of neorealist films falls.

F: In Great Britain, with roughly the same population as Italy, in 1948 the number of tickets sold was 1.5 million.

G: This money is collected, for the most part, in the first-run cinemas in 14 major cities of Italy, on Sundays (double the take of weekdays) and Saturdays (20% less than on Sundays) in winter. Films distributed by the eight major Hollywood companies account for 50% of those prime days. And *remember*: 5% of the films in circulation constituted 50% of film shows; 10% of the films took 80% of box-office receipts.
The films shown in the right place at the right time earn far more than films shown, say, on a Wednesday. The average expenditure on cinema per head of population in 1948:

– Large Northern city: Lire 3200   Small Northern town: Lire 1000
– Large Southern city: Lire 900   Small Southern town: Lire 100

H: I have conflicting figures from different sources, and have given what I think are realistic figures.

I: This is simply column G divided by column F. But averages can be useless statistics. For example, for the year 1945, average tickets prices were:

– Northern Italy: January, Lire 8.5   December, Lire 22.73
– Southern Italy: January, Lire 19.3   December, Lire 29.7
For 1948: average ticket price in Milan (North): Lire 140; average ticket price in Agrigento (Sicily): Lire 38.7

J: The number of cinemas, and of films in circulation, rises. But the size of the population does not rise proportionally nor, quite, does the public's consumption of films. The number of people per cinema (screen density):
 – 1938, 10,815; 1940, 9222; 1942, 8639; 1948, 6988
The number of spectators (tickets sold) per cinema in Italy:
 – 1938, 86,900; 1948, 77,800 (i.e., a drop of 10.5%)

NB: Of this large number of cinemas in Italy, the majority of the best ones were in the control, one way or another, of the eight major Hollywood distribution companies. It has been calculated that only a quarter of the cinemas in Italy were 'available' for showing Italian films.

APPENDIX 4 Categories of cinema in Italy, 1953

Type of cinema	Commercial	Catholic	Other	Total
Number of cinemas	5,690	3,334	864	9,888
Number of seats	2,708,440	733,480	298,944	3,740,864
Number of days of opening	127,579	24,624	8,195	160,398
Tickets sold (millions)	68.37	5.37	2.89	76.63
Receipts (millions of lire)	9,273	499	247	10,019

Source: SIAE (1954), *Lo spettacolo in Italia nel 1953*.

Although the Catholic parish cinemas (*sale parrocchiali*) numbered 34% of the total, their seating capacity was only 20% of the total, while their days of opening were 15%, their tickets sold 7%, and their box-office takings only 5% of the total (ticket prices were considerably cheaper than in first-run commercial cinemas, for example).

Among the category of 'other' cinemas were those run by trades unions, parties of the Left, and municipalities, whose total box-office takings amounted to half those of the Catholic parish cinemas. Hence, whatever the aims of the Catholic Church in opening the *parrocchiali*, they failed to exercise a very significant commercial pressure on producers. Nevertheless, there were many (particularly rural) areas in which the *parrocchiale* was the only local cinema, and those communities were restricted to watching only those films approved by the Church (and so no neorealist films would have been shown in those communities).

APPENDIX 5 Number of tickets sold at cinema box offices in provincial capitals and in the rest of the provinces, 1947–1955 (in millions)

Year	Provincial capital	Rest of the provinces	Total
1947	305	220	525
1950	354	299	653
1951	374	323	679
1955	427	392	819

Source: SIAE, Lo spettacolo in Italia.

The growth of cinema exhibition in Italy took place proportionately more in smaller centres and rural areas than in the major cities. These smaller centres (the 'depths' of the market) were in their turn proportionately more important for the long-term receipts of popular genre films than for products of higher cultural prestige. One would expect this growth effect to have a particularly negative impact on the overall market share of neorealist films.

APPENDIX 6 Length (in days) of opening runs in cinemas in major Italian cities of neorealist films and *Catene**

Film	Ro	Mi	Tu	Ge	Pad	Bo	Fl	Na	Ba	Cat	Pal
Roma città aperta	48 (2)†	15	14	7		26 (2)	11	7			7
Il bandito	18 (2)	7	9	13	8	8	5	8			6
Paisà	14 (2)	7	6	11 (2)		7	5	7			7
Il sole sorge ancora	12 (2)	13 (2)	6	5			7			5	7
Vivere in pace	23 (3)	10 (2)	11	8		14	7	12 (2)			
L'onorevole Angelina	37 (3)	15 (2)		13	9		7		5		
Caccia tragica	10 (2)	5	6	4		3	6	6	6		6
Proibito rubare	4	17 (2)	4				4	4			4
Senza pietà	5	6		14	4	8	7	12	5	7	
Anni difficili	12	5	7	5					5		
Ladri di biciclette	16 (2)	14		7	5	5	11	6			
Fuga in Francia	9 (3)	5	6	4						4	
La terra trema	8 (2)	6		8		3	3	4			
Riso amaro	22 (2)	28	8	8	9	9	13	15	7	13	
Cielo sulla palude	13 (2)	8	7	7		5	6	5	7		
Catene	6	14 (2)	6	7	25	9	5	14	13	15	

Source: Paolo Lughi, 'Il neorealismo in sala: Anteprime di gala e tenitura di massa,' in Alberto Farassino, ed., *Neorealismo Cinema italiano 1945–1949* (Turin: EDT, 1989), 53–60.

* *Catene* serves as a comparison. It belongs in the formula of the 'tear-jerker' by Raffaello Matarazzo, and was a massive box-office hit, dwarfing the commercial success of any neorealist film.

† Figures in parentheses indicate the number of cinemas.

Ro = Rome; Mi = Milan; Tu = Turin; Ge = Genoa; Pad = Padua; Bo = Bologna; Fl = Florence; Na = Naples; Ba = Bari; Cat = Catania; Pal = Palermo

APPENDIX 7 Statistics of days of cinema showing, tickets sold, and box-office receipts in Italy, 1936–1960

Year	Days of commercial film showing	Tickets sold (thousands)	Amount spent by public (unadjusted, in thousands, of lire)	Amount spent by public (adjusted to 1980, in thousands, of lire)	Average ticket price (lire, unadjusted)	Average ticket price (adjusted to 1980 lire)
1936	476,594	260,445	434,490	190,567,575	2	732
1937	535,050	309,669	519,368	208,102,136	2	672
1938	607,054	343,851	580,328	215,945,446	2	628
1939	622,671	354,413	590,479	210,428,411	2	594
1940	641,095	364,311	670,519	204,758,197	2	562
1941	691,437	417,341	893,844	235,902,325	2	565
1942	782,399	489,516	1,251,528	285,773,653	3	609
1943	–	–	1,225,448	166,854,794	–	–
1944	–	–	1,829,324	56,248,840	–	–
1945	–	–	6,498,430	101,092,176	–	–
1946	–	416,646	13,927,766	185,586,062	33	441
1947	1,046,225	532,272	29,076,251	236,491,688	55	444
1948	1,255,088	587,872	42,702,673	328,033,393	73	558
1949	1,386,472	615,525	54,247,486	410,702,292	88	666
1950	1,509,020	661,549	63,404,220	486,557,644	96	735
1951	1,616,137	705,666	73,203,418	512,021,307	104	727
1952	1,735,715	748,099	83,672,172	561,398,438	112	751
1953	1,844,546	777,910	94,501,722	621,953,633	121	800
1954	1,927,345	800,733	105,172,148	674,048,297	131	840
1955	2,009,362	819,424	116,690,729	727,450,005	142	888
1956	2,039,734	790,153	116,021,155	688,991,629	147	873
1957	2,028,827	758,364	112,780,786	657,060,859	149	866
1958	2,029,532	730,412	110,774,095	615,870,734	152	843
1959	2,039,337	747,904	116,639,557	651,198,647	156	871
1960	2,037,114	744,781	120,986,712	657,998,332	162	883

Source: Alessandro Ferraù (from a typesetter's proof-sheet he gave me in 1990 for a publication he was compiling, though I never found out which publication).

APPENDIX 8 Established film production companies in Italy, 1945–1953

Production company	Films[1]	Neorealist films[2]
Lux Film[3]	62	15
(Carlo Ponti)[4]	(39)	
(Dino De Laurentiis)[4]	(32)	
(Luigi Rovere)	(16)	
Excelsa Film	39	(1)[5]
Titanus[6]	23	3
Romana Film	20	
Scalera	18	
Venturini / I.C.E.T.	18	
Filmcostellazione	12	3
Rizzoli[7]	12	2
(Giuseppe Amato)	(11)	(2)
Manenti	11	
Colamonici-Montesi	10	
Universalia / D'Angelo	9	3
Mambretti	8	
Enic	6	2
Incine	4	1
RKO (U.S.A.)	n/a	1

1 Out of a total of 768
2 Out of a total of 55
3 Of the major companies, only Lux supported neorealism (25% of its films), substantially backing them (some of its other films were in the neorealist vein).
4 Ponti and De Laurentiis, two of the most important executive producers with Lux, later ran their own company together for a while.
5 Excelsa's one film was *Roma città aperta*. The company appears as producer in its credits, but it would be a travesty to suggest that Excelsa produced it.
6 Titanus was not the sole or major backer of any neorealist film.
7 Rizzoli started up in 1950. Giuseppe Amato was responsible for its backing of *Umberto D.* and *Francesco giullare di Dio*.
8 Universalia stepped in to save *La terra trema*.

Since it is asserted in the debates about neorealism that the films were produced outside the Italian production 'system,' it might be illuminating to address this assertion in terms of hard figures. Of the 55 films I identify as neorealist produced between 1945 and 1953, approximately 54% were produced in *some* collaboration with established production companies (I have excluded the figures in brackets), and 27.3% of them with Lux Film, the largest and most important production company at the time. In a couple of instances the same film counts more than once on the list above, and sometimes the company's investment is small. From the opposite perspective, 19 of the 55 films (34.5%) were produced without any backing from established companies.

My figures should only be taken as an indication, because investment in the production of individual films was a good deal more complicated than my data (from published sources) suggests.

APPENDIX 9 Italian film production, 1945–1953

	1945	1946	1947	1948	1949	1950	1951	1952	1953
Films produced	34	68	74	52	98	84	124	149	163
Production companies									
involved	19	55	54	40	79	73	87	108	116
Companies producing									
1 film	14	46	43	31	65	63	67	85	90
2 films	2	6	8	7	9	7	7	10	12
3 films	1			1	2	1	4	5	5
4 films	1	2			1		5	2	4
5 films			1					1	
6 films	1	1			1	1	3	1	1
7 films							1	2	1
10 films			1						1
11 films					1			2	
Films produced by associations of two or more companies		4	8	7	12	8	12	25	25

Note: For a number of reasons, the numbers of films produced in each year, and the total for the whole period (846 films) do not tally with the figures I have used elsewhere (for example, I have been using a total of 768 films made in the period). This has to do with different criteria used for the definition of an 'Italian' film, different sources, and different decisions about which year a film was made in.

APPENDIX 10 Directors of neorealist films, 1945–1953

Director	Neorealist films[1]	Total[2]
Rossellini, Roberto	10	10
Zampa, Luigi	6	10
Germi, Pietro	4	8
De Sica, Vittorio	4	5
De Santis, Giuseppe	4	4
Visconti, Luchino	3	3
Antonioni, Michelangelo	3	3
Lattuada, Alberto	2	8
Castellani, Renato	2	5
Lizzani, Carlo	2	3
Soldati, Mario	1	14
Camerini, Mario	1	9
Emmer, Luciano	1	6
Vergano, Aldo	1	5
Comencini, Luigi	1	5
Genina, Augusto	1	4
Gora, Claudio	1	3
Fellini, Federico	1	2
Nelli, Piero	1	1

1 Out of a total of 55
2 Out of a total of 768

Rossellini directed 18.2% of the 55 films I have categorized as neorealist. Rossellini and Zampa each directed 1.3% of all Italian films made in the period 1945-53, and averaged a little over one film per year. Raffaello Matarazzo directed 11 films in the same period (1.4% of all Italian films).

Of the purely commercial directors, Mario Mattoli directed 26 films, 3.4% of the total for the period (at a rate of three per year); Carlo Ludovico Bragaglia directed 18 films (2.3%, two per year); Guido Brignone directed 15 films, Camillo Mastrocinque 14, Giorgio Banchi 13, and Riccardo Freda 12.

Soldati, Camerini, Zampa, Germi, and Lattuada are the directors who most had a foot in both camps: neorealism and commercial. The figure who emerges as standing, from every point of view, smack in the centre of Italian cinema from 1945 to 1953 is Luigi Zampa. He received all influences, and emitted almost none. His films were produced by established mainstream companies. He is the least studied of all the neorealists. Abroad, *Vivere in pace* was often considered, at the time, on a par with *Roma città aperta*.

APPENDIX 11 Writers of neorealist films, 1945–1953

Writer	Neorealist films[1]	Total[2]
Zavattini, Cesare	12	42
Cecchi D'Amico, Suso	11	25
Amidei, Sergio	11	21
Fellini, Federico	9	18
Pinelli, Tullio	7	25
Tellini, Piero	6	22
Lizzani, Carlo	6	7
De Santis, Giuseppe	5	14
Flaiano, Ennio	4	17
Brancati, Vitaliano	4	15
Perilli, Ivo	3	22
Fabbri, Diego	3	18
Margadonna, Ettore	3	14
Sonego, Rodolfo	3	13
Vasile, Turi	3	10
Puccini, Gianni	3	8
Monicelli, Mario	1	48

1 Out of a total of 55
2 Out of a total of 768

Non-neorealist writers, 1945-53, with number of films

Writer	Films[1]
Steno (Stefano Vanzina)	47
De Benedetti, Aldo	43
Marchesi, Marcello	40
Metz, Vittorio	39
Age (Agenore Incrocci)	35
Scarpelli, Furio	35
Mangione, Giuseppe	28
Maccari, Ruggiero	28
Amendola, Mario	28
Majano, Anton Giulio	24
Biancoli, Oreste	21
Benvenuti, Leo	20

1 Out of a total of 768

Being a writer on 40 films in the period 1945–53 would mean one had worked on 5.2% of all Italian films made in the period (Monicelli worked on 6.25% of them). Being a writer on 10 neorealist films would mean one had worked on 18.2% of all neorealist films.

Having five writers for a film was fairly normal, and eight was not unusual. (*But*: 'Sometimes my name appeared [as scriptwriter] on films I hadn't even seen, just to keep the producer happy' – *Tullio Pinelli*. 'Somebody might have walked through the room where we were discussing a script, and said hello, and then wanted to appear in the credits' – *Age*. 'Think of *Ladri di biciclette*. It started off with Zavattini and Amidei. Amidei withdrew because he didn't find the film congenial, and so they called me in. We did it, De Sica, Zavattini, and I. Then there's Gherardi's name [in the credits], whom I never met, and who was in the list because De Sica had told him: "We'll do the next film together," and he died around then. Then there was an old friend for whom we had to find an excuse to get him some money, Franci. He went in too! It didn't bother us in the least' – *Suso Cecchi D'Amico*.)

Some writers go in pairs: Tullio Pinelli and Federico Fellini often worked together; Vittorio Metz and Marcello Marchesi almost always did, as did Age and Scarpelli.

The following members of the staff of the satirical magazine *Marc'Aurelio* all wrote film scripts: Ruggiero Maccari, Steno (Stefano Vanzina), Age (Agenore Incrocci), Furio Scarpelli, Achille Campanile, Vincenzo Rovi, Marcello Marchesi, Vittorio Metz, Mario Monicelli, Federico Fellini, Ettore Scola.

APPENDIX 12 Directors of photography on neorealist films

Cinematographer	Films
G.R. Aldo [Aldo Graziati]	*La terra trema*; *Umberto D.*; *Cielo sulla palude*; *Miracolo a Milano*; *Senso*
Ubaldo Arata	*Roma città aperta*
Leonida Barboni	*In nome della legge*; *Il cammino della speranza*; *Il ferroviere*
Anchise Brizzi	*Sciuscià (Ragazzi)*
Mario Craveri	*L'Onorevole Angelina*
Gianni Di Venanzo	*Amore in città*; *Cronache di poveri amanti*; *Achtung! Banditi!*
Arturo Gallea	*Due soldi di speranza*
Robert Juillard	*Germania anno zero*; *Amore* (with AldoTonti)
Otello Martelli	*Paisà*; *Riso amaro*; *Stromboli (Terra di Dio)*; *Francesco giullare di Dio*; *Luci del varietà*; *Roma ore 11*; *I vitelloni*; *Caccia tragica*
Carlo Montuori	*Vivere in pace*; *Ladri di biciclette*; *Il tetto*; *Anni difficili*
Piero Portalupi	*Tombolo, paradiso nero*; *Non c'è pace tra gli ulivi*; *Bellissima* (with Paul Ronald)
Tino Santoni	*La macchina ammazzacattivi*
Domenico Scala	*Sotto il sole di Roma*; *Fuga in Francia*; *Siamo donne*; *Una domenica d'agosto* (with Leonida Barboni, Ubaldo Marelli)
Enzo Serafin	*I vinti*; *Siamo donne*; *La signora senza camelie*; *Viaggio in Italia*; *Cronaca di un amore*; *Processo alla città*
Massimo Terzano	*Due lettere anonime*
Aldo Tonti	*Il testimone*; *Il bandito*; *Il sole sorge ancora*; *Proibito rubare*; *Europa '51*; *Dov'è la libertà ...?*; *Anni facili*; *Amore* (with Robert Juillard)
Vaclav Vich	*Un Americano in vacanza*; *Il cielo è rosso*

APPENDIX 13 Production arrangements and costs for five core neorealist films

Film and year of filming	Production costs (million lire)	Financiers	Box-office result, receipts (million lire), and notional no.(*) of tickets sold (millions)
Roma città aperta, 1945	12	Contessa Chiara Politi, Peppino Amato, Aldo Venturini who sold to Minerva (purchased for U.S. by Rod Geiger) – *Independent*	Excellent (but film 'sold' at cost price) Receipts: 125.0 *5.0
Paisà, 1946	56	Rod Geiger, Robert Lawrence, Mario Conti, Renato Campos, Rossellini – *Independent*	Inadequate (but helped by export) Receipts: 100.3 *3.04
Ladri di biciclette, 1948	60	Conte Cicogna, Ercole Graziadei (a lawyer), Sergio Bernardi – *Independent*	Good – '*Ladri di biciclette* earned enough to pay the debts of *Sciuscià*.' – De Sica Receipts: 252.0 *4.58
Umberto D., 1952	'97 m. for the production, all told around 140 m.' – De Sica	Peppino Amato, Angelo Rizzoli – *Normal industrial*	Very poor Receipts: 107.0 *1.03
La terra trema, 1948	121	Communist Party, Visconti's own money, Universalia (Salvo d'Angelo) – *Independent, rescued by Normal industrial*	Very poor Receipts: 36.0, of which 5.36 m got back to producers *0.65

APPENDIX 14 Italian public's reception of different categories of Italian films produced 1945–1953, and subsequently released 1945–1956

Year of release		NR	Com	Melo	Adv	Mus	Swash	Pep
1945	% of receipts[1]	3.75	4.42	2.94	1.39	0.76		
	No. of films released[2]	3	10	3	1	1	0	0
	No. of films produced[3]	5	11	6	1	4	0	0
	Tickets sold:[4] unknown							
	% receipts per film	1.25	0.44	0.98	1.39	0.76		
1946	% of receipts	3.66	3.22	4.30	1.82	2.91		
	No. of films released	6	8	16	2	6	0	0
	No. of films produced	8	7	20	7	5	1	0
	Tickets sold: 417 million							
	Tickets sold per film (millions)[5]	2.55	1.68	1.12	3.80	2.03		
1947	% of receipts	1.52	4.88	3.14	2.85	0.43	0.98	0.39
	No. of films released	4	12	17	7	2	2	1
	No. of films produced	7	13	16	5	1	2	2
	Tickets sold: 532 million							
	Tickets sold per film (millions)	2.03	2.16	0.98	2.16	1.14	2.59	2.06
1948	% of receipts	2.58	4.57	1.50	1.07	0.60	0.66	
	No. of films released	9	11	8	5	2	2	0
	No. of films produced	7	11	8	7	2	1	1
	Tickets sold: 588 million							
	Tickets sold per film (millions)	1.69	2.44	1.09	2.60	1.76	1.94	
1949	% of receipts	2.02	3.15	4.34	2.45	1.00	0.23	0.95
	No. of films released	3	8	18	8	3	1	1
	No. of films produced	5	21	21	9	3	4	1
	Tickets sold: 616 million							
	Tickets sold per film (millions)	4.15	2.42	1.49	1.88	2.05	1.39	5.83
1950	% of receipts	2.85	10.26	3.83	4.93	1.05	1.88	1.33
	No. of films released	10	38	17	13	3	4	1
	No. of films produced	5	23	16	12	6	2	0
	Tickets sold: 662 million							
	Tickets sold per film (millions)	1.89	1.79	1.49	2.51	2.32	3.12	7.80
1951	% of receipts	0.49	12.16	8.94	2.93	1.02	1.24	0.79
	No. of films released	2	64	22	9	6	3	2
	No. of films produced	8	52	26	10	5	7	1
	Tickets sold: 706 million							
	Tickets sold per film (millions)	1.74	1.95	2.87	2.30	1.19	2.91	2.80
1952	% of receipts	1.67	12.96	8.82	5.08	3.57	1.59	0.70
	No. of films released	6	42	36	11	7	7	1
	No. of films produced	3	33	45	13	5	3	2
	Tickets sold: 748 million							
	Tickets sold per film (millions)	2.09	2.31	1.83	2.24	3.81	1.70	4.62

1953	% of receipts	1.61	8.45	9.87	2.68	2.50	0.76	0.75
	No. of films released	4	32	43	11	8	3	2
	No. of films produced	9	40	39	18	14	6	4
	Tickets sold: 778 million							
	Tickets sold per film (millions)	2.08	2.05	2.05	1.90	2.44	1.96	2.92
1954	% of receipts	1.22	3.15	3.67	1.88	1.86	0.83	3.38
	No. of pre-1954 films released	4	17	16	9	6	4	5
	Tickets sold: 801 million							
	Tickets sold per film (millions)	2.25	1.48	1.48	1.67	2.49	1.67	5.42
1955	onwards % of receipts	0.89	1.41	0.16				
	No. of pre-1954 films released	2	3	3				
	Tickets sold: 819 million							
	Tickets sold per film (millions)	3.66	3.84	2.21				
Average tickets sold per film[6] (millions) of films produced 1945–53		2.41	2.21	1.49	2.19	2.13	2.16	4.49
TOTAL no. of films counted		55	217	199	82	44	26	13

NR = Neorealist; Com = Comedy; Melo = Melodrama; Adv = Adventure; Mus = Musical; Swash = Swashbuckler (cappa e spada); Pep = Peplum (classical, mythological, or biblical).

1 The percentage of total box-office receipts in Italian cinemas for a given year taken by the group of films in the next row, 'No. of films released.' The *percentage* of total Italian box-office receipts of *each* film in the group (number of films *released*) are added together.
2 The number of films in each category released in a given year – but *only* films *produced* in that year, or in previous years, starting from 1945 and ending in 1953.
3 The number of films in each category *produced* in that year; films are frequently released the year *after* they are made, and sometimes two, three, or four years later. Thus, although I am only counting the reception of films produced 1945–53, the calculations of their receipts must go as far as 1955 and beyond.
4 The total number of cinema tickets sold in Italy in a gven year. There is no published figure for 1945.
5 This is a notional average of the number of tickets sold for each film in the *released* row, to give a picture of the reception of the *category*, and to make it easy for the reader to make comparisons. It is arrived at by taking the *percentage* of box-office receipts of the whole category, dividing it by the number of films in the category, and applying that to the 'Tickets sold' in the row above. Unable to give this figure for 1945, I have instead averaged the *percentage* of box-office receipts per film (but this row does *not* form part of the calculation for the averages referred to in the next note).
6 In each column, the average of the entries for *tickets sold per film* over the full *release* period of the films *produced* in the period 1945–53, but with the *exclusion* of films *released* in 1945 (the data for the calculation are missing).

The traditional way of measuring the success with the public of neorealist films has been either to compare raw receipts of individual films or to see what place each neorealist film took in the ranking of box-office takes of Italian films year by year (i.e., what places in each year's 'hit parade' neorealist films occupied). This gives an inadequate picture of the relative popularity of neorealism as a *group* of films in comparison with that of any other identifiable 'grouping' of films. As, each year, comedies or melodramas took a number of high places in the hit parade, neorealism was deemed to have been rejected by the public in comparison. Profitability, it must be emphasized, is an entirely different question.

Put simply, I have decided that it is easier to compare reception by trying to give an idea of the *average* number of tickets sold per film, than by trying to compare the raw box-office receipts of a huge number of individual films over a period in which the units of comparison kept changing. For example, between 1948 and 1950, average ticket prices rose 32%, the total number of tickets sold in Italy rose 13%, and the proportion of box-office receipts going to *Italian* (as opposed to Hollywood) films rose by something like 120%.

Are the data on which the table's calculations are based reliable? I very much doubt it. It is difficult to know what is the status of historical box-office statistics in Italy. I have used figures that are used by other analysts, but I am not sure any of us who use them really know what they cover and what they exclude. The important thing to note is that the data on which this table is based are exactly the same as the data commonly used to show that neorealist films were rejected by the public.

The *same film* may be counted in more than one column. All the *Swashbucklers* (*cappa e spada*) appear in the *Adventure* category, but I have chosen to isolate the *Swashbucklers* as a group. I have given genre attributions to those *neorealist* films that fitted one or more of the genre categories selected (*Due lettere anonime* and *Riso amaro*, for example, also appear in the categories of *Melodrama* and *Adventure*). The genre attributions are my own.

The table's data reveal the following:

(a) *Neorealist* films certainly did no worse than any other identifiable category of film, and better than most. Had it been possible to include 1945 in the 'total' figures for the whole period, the success of *Roma città aperta* would have further enhanced Neorealism's overall performance in this table.

(b) *Peplum* films, even though few in number, did extraordinarily well at the box office. Their success can be attributed to single 'hits' in 1948 (*Fabiola*), 1950 (*Gli ultimi giorni di Pompeii*), and 1954 (*Ulisse*) – high-cost prestige international productions from major production houses, benefiting from exceptional promotional expense; they expressed the *industry's* vision of 'quality' as an alternative to the neorealist one. But even Pietro Francisci's *La Regina di Saba* did very well. *Gli ultimi giorni di Pompeii*, a co-production with France, is officially recorded in Italy as having been directed by Paolo Moffa. The rest of the world regards it as a French film entitled *Les derniers jours de Pompéi*, directed by Marcel L'Herbier (but with Salvo D'Angelo, of Universalia, as its producer). *Without* this film, the overall average of *Peplum* falls to 3.38 million tickets per film, still very high.

(c) Both *Neorealist* and *Peplum* categories were considered to contain the 'quality' products (the first by artists and intellectuals for their 'content,' the second by the industry itself for their 'production values'), and they were indeed the categories that, on average, sold the most tickets *per film*.

(d) *Melodrama*, a genre traditionally regarded as dominant in Italian cinema of the period, while accounting for a large *number* of films released (nearly as many as the *comedies*), was the group that sold by far the fewest tickets *per film*.

(e) There does not appear to be an empirical basis for the concern expressed over the 'failure' of *Neorealism* with the public.

I conclude with some incidental observations related to Rossellini's films that demonstrate how unreliable are many of the generalizations traditionally made about the commercial success of neorealist films (necessarily accepting that the impact of these observations will depend on the reader's familiarity with those generalizations that, for reasons of space, I shall not rehearse). Rossellini's *Europa '51* and *Dov'è la libertà* earned similar amounts to the films of Mario Soldati in their respective years. Rossellini's films earned large amounts in 1945–6 (*Roma città aperta* and *Paisà*), but *Stromboli*, while not earning as much as Matarazzo's huge successes, earned a similar amount to his more normal successes, and about as much as a solidly successful melodrama for the year 1949–50. *Roma città aperta* (which sold some five million 'average' tickets in 1945, a year in which about 400 million tickets were sold in total) took 1.25% of total tickets sold, while *Catene* (which sold 8.35 million in 1949, when 616 million were sold in total) took 1.39% of total tickets sold. *Roma città aperta* had foreign earnings (virtually none of which made their way back to Italy) far in excess of anything earned abroad by Matarazzo's films.

While it is hoped that the calculations involved in all the above are coherent, it is fairly certain that the data being manipulated are less than reliable.

APPENDIX 15   Fifty-five 'neorealist' films

Note: The asterisked figure at the end of each entry (e.g., *1.385) denotes a notional measure of the film's success with the public, giving the *percentage* of total Italian receipts at the box office in the year of release earned by that film over its main period of release. It is offered as no more than an *indication* – of varying reliability, I am afraid – to allow the reader to compare films, because raw box-office receipts – even adjusted for inflation – would not permit any useful comparisons. The films are listed by date of release.

Due lettere anonime   *Director:* Mario Camerini; *writers:* Ivo Perilli, Mario Camerini, Carlo Musso, Nino Novarese, Turi Vasile. *Year made:* 1945; *released:* 1945   *1.385

Giorni di Gloria   *Directors:* Giuseppe De Santis, Marcello Pagliero, Mario Serandrei, Luchino Visconti, *year made:* 1945; *released:* 1945   *0.443

Roma città aperta   *Director:* Roberto Rossellini; *writers: story* Sergio Amidei, Alberto Consiglio, *screenplay* Sergio Amidei, Federico Fellini, Roberto Rossellini, Carlo Celeste Negarville. *Year made:* 1945; *released:* 1945   *1.924

Un Americano in vacanza   *Director:* Luigi Zampa; *writers:* Gino Castrignano, Aldo De Benedetti, Luigi Zampa. *Year made:* 1945; *released:* 1946   *0.431

Il testimone   *Director:* Pietro Germi; *writers:* Pietro Germi, Diego Fabbri, Cesare Zavattini, Enrico Ribulsi, Ottavio Alessi. *Year made:* 1945; *released:* 1946   *0.108

Il bandito   *Director:* Alberto Lattuada; *writers:* Alberto Lattuada, Oreste Biancoli, Mino Causana, Ettore Maria Margadonna, Tullio Pinelli, Piero Tellini. *Year made:* 1946; *released:* 1946   *1.321

Paisà   *Director:* Roberto Rossellini; *writers:* Klaus Mann, Sergio Amidei, Federico Fellini, Marcello Pagliero, Alfred Hayes, Roberto Rossellini, Vasco Pratolini. *Year made:* 1946; *released:* 1946   *0.720

Sciuscià (Ragazzi)   *Director:* Vittorio De Sica; *writers:* Sergio Amidei, Adolfo Franci, Cesare Giulio Viola, Cesare Zavattini. *Year made:* 1946; *released:* 1946   *0.402

Il sole sorge ancora   *Director:* Aldo Vergano; *writers:* Giuseppe Gorgerini, Guido Aristarco, Giuseppe De Santis, Carlo Lizzani, Aldo Vergano. *Year made:* 1946; *released:* 1946   *0.628

Caccia tragica   *Director:* Giuseppe De Santis; *writers: story* Giuseppe De Santis, Carlo Lizzani, Lamberto Rem-Picci, *screenplay* Michelangelo Antonioni, Umberto Barbaro, Giuseppe De Santis, Carlo Lizzani, Cesare Zavattini. *Year made:* 1946; *released:* 1947   *0.275

Vivere in pace   *Director:* Luigi Zampa; *writers: story* Suso Cecchi D'Amico, Piero Tellini, Luigi Zampa, *screenplay* Aldo Fabrizi, Suso Cecchi D'Amico, Piero Tellini, Luigi Zampa. *Year made:* 1946; *released:* 1947 *0.912

L'Onorevole Angelina   *Director:* Luigi Zampa; *writers: story and screenplay* Piero Tellini, Suso Cecchi D'Amico, Luigi Zampa. *Year made:* 1947; *released:* 1947 *0.310

Tombolo, paradiso nero   *Director:* Giorgio Ferroni; *writers: story* Piero Tellini, Glauco Pellegrini from an article by Indro Montanelli, *screenplay* Indro Montanelli, Glauco Pellegrini, Giorgio Ferroni, Rodolfo Sonego, Victor Merenda. *Year made:* 1947; *released:* 1947 *0.502

Anni difficili   *Director:* Luigi Zampa; *writers: story* from the novel *Il vecchio con gli stivali* by Vitaliano Brancati *screenplay* Sergio Amidei, Vitaliano Brancati, Franco Evangelisti, Enrico Fulchignoni. *Year made:* 1947; *released:* 1948   *0.670

Germania anno zero   *Director:* Roberto Rossellini; *writers: story and screenplay* Roberto Rossellini, *collaboration on screenplay* Max Copler, Sergio Amidei. *Year made:* 1947; *released:* 1948 *0.123

Sotto il sole di Roma   *Director:* Renato Castellani; *writers: story* Renato Castellani, Fausto Tozzi, *screenplay* Renato Castellani, Sergio Amidei, Suso Cecchi D'Amico, Ettore Maria Margadonna, Fausto Tozzi. *Year made:* 1947; *released:* 1948 *0.443

La terra trema   *Director:* Luchino Visconti; *writers: story* Luchino Visconti from the novel *I Malavoglia* by Giovanni Verga, *screenplay and dialogue* Luchino Visconti, Antonio Pietrangeli. *Year made:* 1947; *released:* 1948   *0.084

Amore   *Director:* Roberto Rossellini. 1. *La voce umana, writers:* from the play by Jean Cocteau, *La voix humaine, screenplay* Roberto Rossellini; 2. *Il miracolo, writers:* Federico Fellini, Tullio Pinelli, Roberto Rossellini. *Year made:* 1947 and 1948; *released:* 1948   *0.064

Ladri di biciclette   *Director:* Vittorio De Sica; *writers: story* Cesare Zavattini from the novel of the same name by Luigi Bartolini, *screenplay* Oreste Biancoli, Cesare Zavattini, Suso Cecchi D'Amico, Adolfo Franci, Gherardo Gherardi, Vittorio De Sica, Gerardo Guerrieri. *Year made:* 1948; *released:* 1948   *0.590

Proibito rubare   *Director:* Luigi Comencini; *writers: story* Suso Cecchi D'Amico, Luigi Comencini from an idea by Gigi Martello, *screenplay* Aldo Buzzi, Suso Cecchi D'Amico, Luigi Comencini, Armando Curci. *Year made:* 1948; *released:* 1948   *0.131

Fuga in Francia   *Director:* Mario Soldati; *writers: story and screenplay* Carlo Musso, Ennio Flaiano, Mario Soldati, *collaboration on screenplay* Mario Bonfantini, Emilio Cecchi, Cesare Pavese. *Year made:* 1948; *released:* 1949   *0.149

In nome della legge   *Director:* Pietro Germi; *writers: story* Giuseppe Mangione from the novel *Piccola pretura* by G.G. Lo Schiavo, *screenplay* Mario Monicelli,

Federico Fellini, Tullio Pinelli, Giuseppe Mangione, Pietro Germi. *Year made:* 1948; *released:* 1949   *0.802

Riso amaro   *Director:* Giuseppe De Santis; *writers: story* Giuseppe De Santis, Carlo Lizzani, Gianni Puccini, *screenplay* Corrado Alvaro, Giuseppe De Santis, Carlo Lizzani, Carlo Musso, Ivo Perilli, Gianni Puccini. *Year made:* 1948; *released:* 1949   *0.708

La macchina ammazzacattivi   *Director:* Roberto Rossellini; *writers: story* Eduardo De Filippo, Fabrizio Sarazani (from a story by Giuseppe Marotta), *screenplay* Sergio Amidei, Roberto Rossellini, Franco Brusati, Liana Ferri, Giancarlo Vigorelli. *Year made:* 1948; *released:* 1952   *0.004

Cielo sulla palude   *Director:* Augusto Genina; *writers: story* Augusto Genina from an idea by Elvira Psorulla (based on the life of Maria Goretti), *collaboration on story* Suso Cecchi D'Amico, Fausto Tozzi, *screenplay* Augusto Genina. *Year made:* 1949; *released:* 1949   *0.509

Il cielo è rosso   *Director:* Claudio Gora; *writers: story* from the novel of the same name by Giuseppe Berto, *screenplay* Leopoldo Trieste, Cesare Zavattini, Claudio Gora, Lamberto Giuseppe Santilli. *Year made:* 1949; *released:* 1950 *0.115

Una domenica d'agosto   *Director:* Luciano Emmer; *writers: story* Sergio Amidei, *screenplay* Franco Brusati, Luciano Emmer, Giulio Macchi, Cesare Zavattini. *Year made:* 1949; *released:* 1950   *0.236

Non c'è pace tra gli ulivi   *Director:* Giuseppe De Santis; *writers: story* Giuseppe De Santis, Gianni Puccini, *screenplay* Libero De Libero, Carlo Lizzani, Giuseppe De Santis, Gianni Puccini. *Year made:* 1949; *released:* 1950   *0.747

Stromboli (Terra di Dio)   *Director:* Roberto Rossellini; *writers: story* Roberto Rossellini, *screenplay* Sergio Amidei, Gian Paolo Callegari, Roberto Rossellini, *English dialogue* Art Cohn, Renzo Cesana. *Year made:* 1949; *released:* 1950 *0.494

Tragica alba a Dongo   *Director:* Vittorio Crucillà (*collaboration on direction:* Enzo Convalli); *writers: story* Vittorio Crucillà, *screenplay* Vittorio Crucillà, Ettore Camesasca, Paul Remy. *Year made:* 1949/50; *released:* never   *0.000

Il cammino della speranza   *Director:* Pietro Germi; *writers: story* Federico Fellini, Pietro Germi, Tullio Pinelli from the novel *Cuori negli abissi* by Nino De Maria, *screenplay* Federico Fellini, Tullio Pinelli. *Year made:* 1950; *released:* 1950   *0.579

Cronaca di un amore   *Director:* Michelangelo Antonioni; *writers: story* Michelangelo Antonioni, *screenplay* Michelangelo Antonioni, Daniele D'Anza, Piero Tellini, Silvio Giovaninetti, Francesco Maselli. *Year made:* 1950; *released:* 1950   *0.274

Francesco giullare di Dio   *Director:* Roberto Rossellini; *writers: story* Roberto Rossellini inspired by *The Little Flowers* of Saint Francis, *screenplay* Federico

Fellini, Brunello Rondi, religious consultants Father Felix Morlion, Father
Antonio Lisandrini. *Year made:* 1950; *released:* 1950   *0.043

Luci del varietà   *Director:* Alberto Lattuada, Federico Fellini; *writers: story*
Federico Fellini, *screenplay* Federico Fellini, Alberto Lattuada, Tullio Pinelli,
Ennio Flaiano. *Year made:* 1950; *released:* 1950   *0.185

Miracolo a Milano   *Director:* Vittorio De Sica; *writers: story* Cesare Zavattini
from his novel *Totò il buono, screenplay* Cesare Zavattini, Vittorio De Sica, *collaboration on screenplay* Suso Cecchi D'Amico, Mario Chiari, Adolfo Franci.
Year made: 1950; *released:* 1950   *0.285

Il Cristo proibito   *Director:* Curzio Malaparte; *writers: story and screenplay*
Curzio Malaparte from his novel of the same name, *year made:* 1950; *released:*
1951   *0.245

Achtung! Banditi!   *Director:* Carlo Lizzani; *writers: story and screenplay* Rodolfo
Sonego, Ugo Pirro, Gaetano 'Giuliani' De Negri, Giuseppe Dagnino, Carlo
Lizzani, Massimo Mida, Enrico Ribulsi, Mario Socrate. *Year made:* 1951;
released: 1951   *0.273

Bellissima   *Director:* Luchino Visconti; *writers: story* Cesare Zavattini, *screenplay* Suso Cecchi D'Amico, Francesco Rosi, Luchino Visconti. *Year made:* 1951;
released: 1951   *0.219

Due soldi di speranza   *Director:* Renato Castellani; *writers: story* Renato Castellani, Ettore Maria Margadonna, *screenplay* Renato Castellani, Titina De Filippo. *Year made:* 1951; *released:* 1952   *0.500

Europa '51   *Director:* Roberto Rossellini; *writers: story* Roberto Rossellini from
an idea by Massimo Mida [Puccini] and Antonello Trombadori, *screenplay*
Roberto Rossellini, Sandro De Feo, Mario Pannunzio, Ivo Perilli, Brunello
Rondi. *Year made:* 1951; *released:* 1952   *0.267

Roma ore 11   *Director:* Giuseppe De Santis; *writers: story and screenplay* Cesare
Zavattini, Basilio Franchina, Giuseppe De Santis, Rodolfo Sonego, Gianni
Puccini. *Year made:* 1951; *released:* 1952   *0.323

Umberto D.   *Director:* Vittorio De Sica; *writers: story and screenplay* Cesare
Zavattini. *Year made:* 1951; released 1952   *0.128

Processo alla città   *Director:* Luigi Zampa; *writers: story* Ettore Giannini,
Francesco Rosi, *screenplay* Suso Cecchi D'Amico, Ettore Giannini, *collaboration
on screenplay* Diego Fabbri, Luigi Zampa, Turi Vasile. *Year made:* 1952; *released:*
1952   *0.452

I vinti   *Director:* Michelangelo Antonioni; *writers: story* Michelangelo Antonioni, Suso Cecchi D'Amico, Diego Fabbri, Turi Vasile, *screenplay* Suso Cecchi
D'Amico, Michelangelo Antonioni, Diego Fabbri, Turi Vasile, Giorgio Bassani, Roger Nimier. *Year made:* 1952; *released:* 1953   *0.127

Dov'è la libertà ...?   *Director:* Roberto Rossellini; *writers: story* Roberto Rossellini, *screenplay* Vitaliano Brancati, Ennio Flaiano, Antonio Pietrangeli, Vincenzo Talarico. *Year made:* 1952; *released:* 1954   *0.244

Amore in città   *Directors:* Carlo Lizzani, Michelangelo Antonioni, Dino Risi, Federico Fellini, Francesco Maselli (and Cesare Zavattini), Alberto Lattuada; *writers:* Cesare Zavattini, Aldo Buzzi, Luigi Chiarini, Luigi Malerba, Tullio Pinelli, Vittorio Veltroni, Marco Ferreri, Federico Fellini, Alberto Lattuada. *Year made:* 1953; *released:* 1953   *0.136

Anni facili   *Director:* Luigi Zampa; *writers: story* Vitaliano Brancati, *screenplay* Sergio Amidei, Vitaliano Brancati, Luigi Zampa, Vincenzo Talarico. *Year made:* 1953; *released:* 1953   *0.424

Siamo donne   *Directors:* Alfredo Guarini, Gianni Franciolini, Roberto Rossellini, Luigi Zampa, Luchino Visconti; *writers:* Cesare Zavattini [all episodes], Alfredo Guarini, Luigi Chiarini, Roberto Rossellini, Luigi Zampa, Giorgio Prosperi, Suso Cecchi D'Amico. *Year made:* 1953; *released:* 1953   *0.140

La signora senza camelie   *Director:* Michelangelo Antonioni; *writers: story* Michelangelo Antonioni, *screenplay* Michelangelo Antonioni, Suso Cecchi D'Amico, Francesco Maselli, Pier Maria Pasinetti. *Year made:* 1953; *released:* 1953   *0.148

I vitelloni   *Director:* Federico Fellini; *writers: story* Federico Fellini, Ennio Flaiano, *screenplay* Federico Fellini, Ennio Flaiano, Tullio Pinelli. *Year made:* 1953; *released:* 1953   *0.631

Cronache di poveri amanti   *Director:* Carlo Lizzani; *writers: story* from the novel of the same name by Vasco Pratolini, *screenplay* Sergio Amidei, Giuseppe Dagnino, Carlo Lizzani, Massimo Mida. *Year made:* 1953; *released:* 1954   *0.223

Viaggio in Italia   *Director:* Roberto Rossellini; *writers: story and screenplay* Vitaliano Brancati, Roberto Rossellini from the short story *Duo* by Colette. *Year made:* 1953; *released:* 1954   *0.059

Senso   *Director:* Luchino Visconti; *writers: story* from the novella of the same name by Arrigo Boito, *screenplay* Luchino Visconti, Suso Cecchi D'Amico, *collaboration on screenplay* Carlo Alianelli, Giorgio Bassani, Giorgio Prosperi, *collaboration on dialogues* Tennessee Williams, Paul Bowles. *Year made:* 1953/54; *released:* 1954   *0.597

Il ferroviere   *Director:* Pietro Germi; *writers: story* Alfredo Giannetti, *screenplay* Pietro Germi, Alfredo Giannetti, Luciano Vincenzoni, *revision of screenplay* Ennio De Concini, Carlo Musso. *Year made:* 1955; *released:* 1955   *0.695

Il tetto   *Director:* Vittorio De Sica; *writers: story and screenplay* Cesare Zavattini. *Year made:* 1955; *released:* 1955   *0.198

APPENDIX 16 Filmographic details of *Roma città aperta*, *Paisà*, and *Ladri di biciclette*

Roma città aperta (*Rome Open City*; U.S. title *Open City*)
Produced by Excelsa Film, [Finance from Countess Chiara Politi, CIS-Nettunia; Peppino Amato; Aldo Venturini]. *Distributed by* Minerva Film (in Europe); Arthur Mayer and Joseph Burstyn in association with Rodney Geiger (in the United States).
Director: Roberto Rossellini; *Assistant Directors:* Sergio Amidei, Federico Fellini.
Story by Sergio Amidei, Alberto Consiglio; *Screenplay by* Sergio Amidei, Federico Fellini.
Director of Photography: Ubaldo Arata; *Camera Operator:* Vincenzo Seratrice; *Assistant Camera Operators:* Gianni Di Venanzo, Carlo Carlini, Carlo Di Palma, Giuseppe Berta.
Editor: Eraldo Da Roma; *Assistant Editor:* Jolanda Benvenuti. *Music:* Renzo Rossellini; *Conducted by:* Luigi Ricci; *Sound Engineer:* Raffaele Del Monte. *Production Design:* Rosario Megna; *Furnishings:* Mario Chiari; *Make-up:* Alberto De Rossi; *Torture Scenes Make-up:* Nino Franchina.
Production Manager: Ferruccio De Martino (with Carlo Civallero, Angelo Besozzi, Ermanno Donati, Luigi Carpentieri). *Assistant Producers:* Alberto Manni, Bruno Todini, Antonio Palumbo.
Script Secretary: Jone Tuzzi.
Costs: approximately 12 million lire; *Box-office Receipts*: 124.5 million lire.
Filmed January–May 1945, at Capitani Film di Liborio Capitani, Via Avignonesi 30, and on Rome locations: Piazza di Spagna, Via Montecuccoli; Piazzale Prenestino, Chiesa di Sant'Elena on Via Casilina; interior of a church in Trastevere; an oratorio on Via Avellino; Circonvallazione Casilina; antique store exterior on Via Margutta; Ponte Tiburtino; EUR; Forte Bravetta (execution scene); Via Trionfale on Monte Mario.
CAST
Marcello Pagliero [dubbed by Lauro Gazzolo] (*Giorgio Manfredi*, or *Luigi Ferraris*), Aldo Fabrizi (*Don Pietro Pellegrini*), Anna Magnani (*Sora Pina*), Harry Feist [dubbed by Giulio Panicali] (*Bergmann*), Francesco Grandjacquet [dubbed by Gualtiero De Angelis] (*Francesco*), Maria Michi (*Marina Mari*), Giovanna Galetti [dubbed by Roswitha Schmidt] (*Ingrid*), Vito Annicchiarico (*Marcello*), Carla Rovere (*Lauretta*), Nando Bruno (*Agostino*, or *Purgatorio*), Eduardo Passarelli (*brigadiere*), Carlo Sindici (*Chief of Police of Rome*), Akos Tolnay (*Austrian deserter*), Joop Van Hulzen (*Hartmann*), Amalia Pellegrini (*Manfredi's landlady*), Alberto Tavazzi (*priest at execution*), Ferruccio De Martino (*soldier at execution*), Alberto Manni (*blackmarketeer*).

First shown: 28 August 1945, by U.S. Information Agency at Direzione Generale dello Spettacolo, Via Veneto 108, Rome; 24 September at the Primo Festival Internazionale della musica, del teatro e del cinematografo, Cinema Quirino, Rome; 27–28 September at the Cinema Quirinetta.
Released: 8 October 1946.
AWARDS
Nastro d'Argento, 1946, best director (ex aequo with Alessandro Blasetti's *Un giorno nella vita* and Vittorio De Sica's *Sciuscià*), best screenplay, best actress. Grand Prix, Cannes, 1946 (with six other films). Academy Award nomination: best screenplay. New York Film Critics: best foreign film, 1946. National Board of Review: best actress, 1946.

Paisà (U.S. title *Paisan*)
Produced by: O.F.I. (Organizzazioni Film Internazionali [Roberto Rossellini, Mario Conti, Renato Campos]) and F.F.P. (Foreign Film Productions [Rod Geiger, Robert Lawrence]).
Distributed by: Metro-Goldwyn-Mayer (in Europe); Mayer-Burstyn (in U.S.).
Director: Roberto Rossellini. *Assistant Directors:* Federico Fellini, Massimo Mida; *Director's Assistants*: E. Handamir, Annalena Limentani (translations).
Stories and Screenplay by Federico Fellini, Roberto Rossellini, Klaus Mann, Sergio Amidei, Alfred Hayes, Marcello Pagliero, Vasco Pratolini.
Director of Photography: Otello Martelli; *Camera Operators:* Carlo Carlini, Gianni Di Venanzo, Carlo Di Palma; *Editor:* Eraldo Da Roma; *Assistant Editor:* Jolanda Benvenuti. *Music:* Renzo Rossellini. *Sound Engineer:* Ovidio Del Grande. *Production manager:* Ugo Lombardi. *Assistant producers:* Alberto Manni, Augusto Dolfi, Mario Micheli, Aldo Bonifazi.
Costs: approximately 56 million lire; *Box-office Receipts*: 100.3 million lire.
Filmed January–June 1946, in Maiori (*Sicily*); Maiori, Convento di San Francesco (*Monastery*); Naples (*Naples*); Villa Roncioni on Via Lungomonte Lucchese, and Florence (*Florence*); Scardovari-Porto Tolle (*Po Delta*); Moka Abdul, Cinema Florida on Via Francesco Crispi, Capitani film studio, Rome (*Rome*); Livorno (tank scene in *Rome*); Via Lutezia 11, Rome (stairs in *Florence*).
CAST
Giulio Panicali (*voice-over commentary for introductory sequences*).
Sicily:
Carmela Sazio (*Carmela*), Robert Van Loon (*Joe from Jersey*), Benjamin Emanuel, Raymond Campbell, Mata 'Sweede' Rune, Merlin Berth, Mats Carlson, Leonard Penish (*U.S. soldiers – from 7th Transit Camp*), Albert Heinze, Harold Wagner (*German soldiers*).

Naples:
Alfonsino Bovino (*Pasquale*), Dotts M. Johnson (*Joe*), Pippo Bonazzi.
Rome:
Maria Michi (*Francesca*), Gar Moore (*Fred*), Lorena Berg (*Amalia, landlady*).
Florence:
Harriet White (*Harriet*), Renzo Avanzo (*Massimo*), Gigi Gori (*the partisan Gigi*), Renato Campos (*Major on rooftop*), Giuletta Masina (*his daughter*), Gianfranco Corsivi (*the partisan Marco*), Ursula Werber, Rose Nadell.
Monastery:
Bill Tubbs (*Captain Bill Martin*), Captain Owen Jones (*Protestant chaplain*), Sergeant Elmer Feldman, assistant to the rabbi of the 7th Transit Camp (*Jewish chaplain*), Franciscan friars: Vincenzo (*Padre Guardiano* – dubbed by Carlo Ninchi), Salvatore, Angelico, Claudio, Pacifico, Raffaele, Felice.
Po delta:
Dale Edmonds (*Dale*), Achille Siviero (*Cigolani*), Alan Dane, Van Loel (*German officer*), Hannes Messemer (*German officer*).
First shown: 18 September 1946 (Venice Film Festival). *Released:* 10 December 1946
AWARDS
Coppa ANICA, Venice (ex aequo with eight others). Nastro d'Argento, best direction and original music, 1947. Academy Award nomination: best screenplay. New York Film Critics: best film, 1948. National Board of Review: best film, 1948. Belgium Government Prize, excellent quality, Brussels Festival.

Ladri di biciclette (*Bicycle Thieves*; U.S. title *The Bicycle Thief*)
Produced by Produzioni De Sica [with finance from Ercole Graziadei, Sergio Bernardi, Count Cicogna].
Distributed by ENIC (Ente nazionale industrie cinematografiche)
Director: Vittorio De Sica; *Assistant Directors:* Luisa Alessandri, Gerardo Guerrieri.
Story by Cesare Zavattini from the novel of the same name by Luigi Bartolini; *Screenplay by* Cesare Zavattini, Suso Cecchi D'Amico, Vittorio De Sica, Gerardo Guerrieri, Sergio Amidei (briefly).
Director of Photography: Carlo Montuori; *Editor:* Eraldo Da Roma; *Production Design and Furnishings by* Antonino Traverso; *Camera Operator:* Mario Montuori; *Sound Engineer:* Bruno Brunacci; *Sound Technician:* Biagio Fiorelli; *Music:* Alessandro Cicognini; *Conducted by* Willy Ferrero (song *Ciccio formaggio*, music by Pisano, lyrics by Giuseppe Cioffi; song *Tammurriata nera*, music by E.A.

Mario, lyrics by E. Nicolardi); *Production Manager:* Umberto Scarpelli; *Production Supervisor:* Nino Misiano; *Production Secretary:* Roberto Moretti.
Costs: approximately 60 million lire; *Box-office Receipts:* 252 million lire.
Scriptwriting from August 1947 to April 1948. Shooting from May to October 1948, on location in Rome.

CAST

Lamberto Maggiorani (*Antonio Ricci*), Enzo Staiola (*Bruno Ricci*), Lianella Carrell (*Maria Ricci*), Elena Altieri (*benefactress at the Messa del povero*), Gino Saltamerenda (*Baiocco*), Vittorio Antonucci (*the thief*), Giulio Chiari (*a billposter*), Michele Sakara (*lawyer at Messa del povero*), Fausto Guerzoni (*irritable actor at dopolavoro*), Carlo Jachino (*the old beggar*), Massimo Randisi (*middle-class boy in restaurant*), Ida Bracci Dorati (*the Santona*), Peppino Spadaro (*policeman in Trastevere*), Mario Meniconi (*Meniconi, the streetsweeper*), Checco Rissone (*policeman in Piazza Vittorio*), Giulio Battiferri (*one of the thief's neighbours*), Sergio Leone (*seminarian*), Memmo Carotenuto, Nando Bruno, Emma Druetti, Giovanni Corporale, Eolo Capritti, Spoletini.

First shown: November 1948. *Released:* December 1948.

AWARDS

Academy Award (Oscar) for Best Foreign Film, 1949; Nastro d'Argento, best film, direction, story, screenplay, photography, music, 1949; Special Jury Prize at Locarno Film Festival, 1949; Grand Prize at the Festival mondial, Belgium, 1949; British Film Academy, 1950; judged the 'second best film of all time' at the Confrontation in Brussels, 1958.

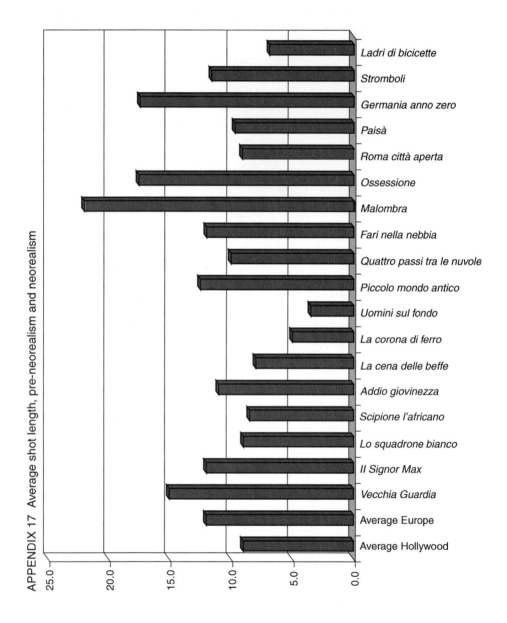

APPENDIX 17 Average shot length, pre-neorealism and neorealism

APPENDIX 18 Average shot length, neorealist films

	Roma città aperta	Paisà	Germania anno zero	Stromboli	Ossessione	La terra trema	Bellissima	Cronaca di un amore	I vinti	La signora senza camelie
Seconds	9.1	9.7	17.4	11.6	17.5	18.2	21.1	33.0	45.0	61.0

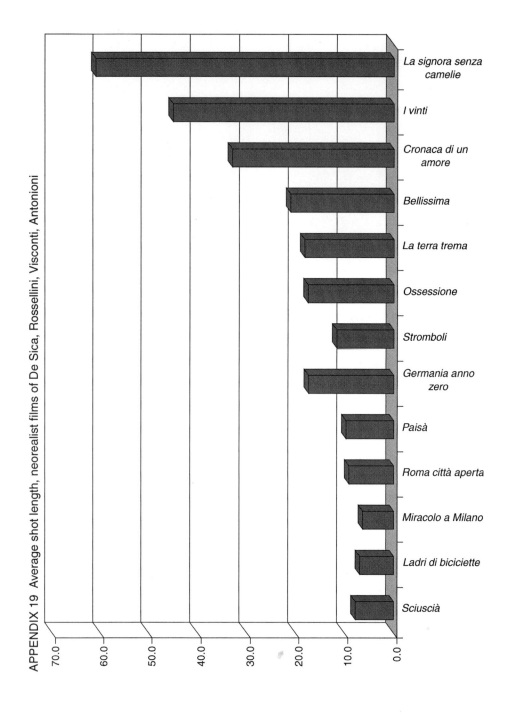

APPENDIX 19 Average shot length, neorealist films of De Sica, Rossellini, Visconti, Antonioni

APPENDIX 20 Scale (closeness) of shot comparison, *Roma città aperta* and other films (1)

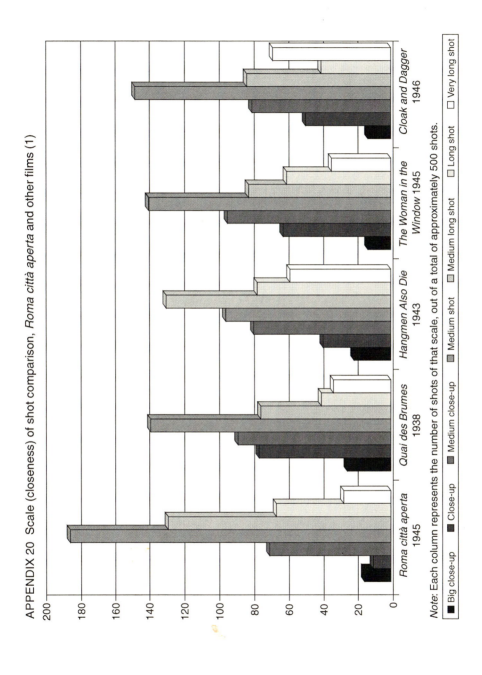

Note: Each column represents the number of shots of that scale, out of a total of approximately 500 shots.

■ Big close-up ■ Close-up ■ Medium close-up ■ Medium shot ■ Medium long shot □ Long shot □ Very long shot

APPENDIX 21 Scale (closeness) of shot comparison, *Roma città aperta* and other films (2)

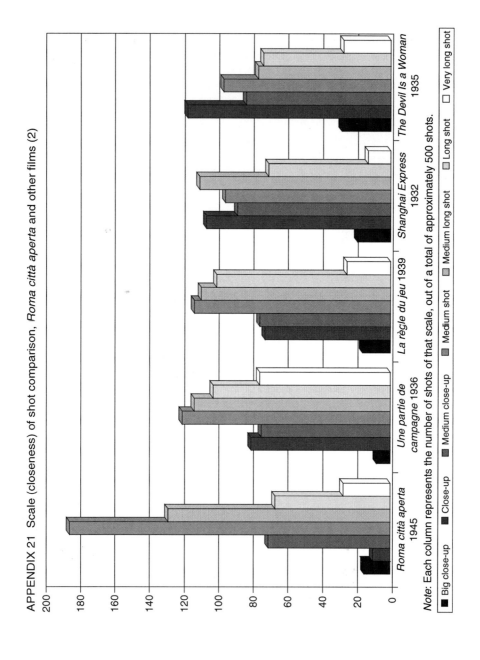

Note: Each column represents the number of shots of that scale, out of a total of approximately 500 shots.

■ Big close-up   ■ Close-up   ■ Medium close-up   ▨ Medium shot   ▨ Medium long shot   ▨ Long shot   □ Very long shot

APPENDIX 22 Scale (closeness) of shot comparison, *Roma città aperta* and other films (3)

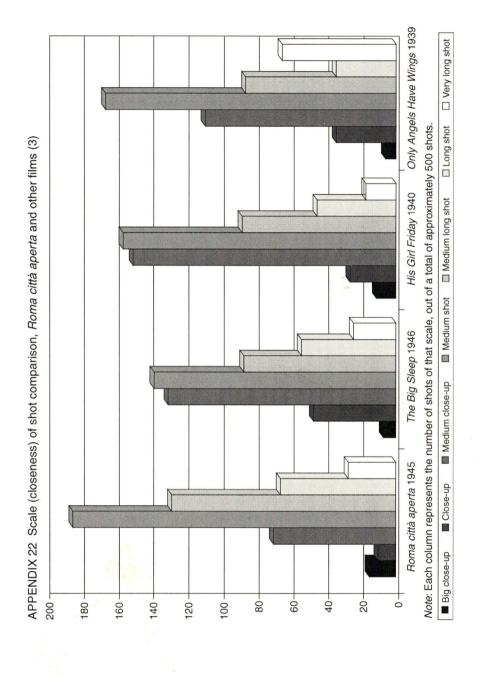

Roma città aperta 1945   *The Big Sleep* 1946   *His Girl Friday* 1940   *Only Angels Have Wings* 1939

Note: Each column represents the number of shots of that scale, out of a total of approximately 500 shots.

■ Big close-up   ■ Close-up   ■ Medium close-up   ■ Medium shot   □ Medium long shot   □ Long shot   □ Very long shot

APPENDIX 23 Map of settings and locations for *Paisà*

- 6 Po delta
- 5 Savignano di Romagna (Monastery)
- 4 Florence
- 3 Rome
- 2 Naples
- Maiori – Sicily and Savignano episodes shot here
- 1 Sicily

Settings for the stories in order of assembly in the finished film: 1. Sicily;
2. Naples; 3. Rome; 4. Florence; 5. Monastery (Savignano di Romagna);
6. Po delta (Porto Tolle)

Locations for filming in chronological order: (a) Maiori – for the Sicily episode;
(b) Maiori – for the Monastery episode; (c) Naples; (d) Florence; (e) Po delta;
(f) Rome

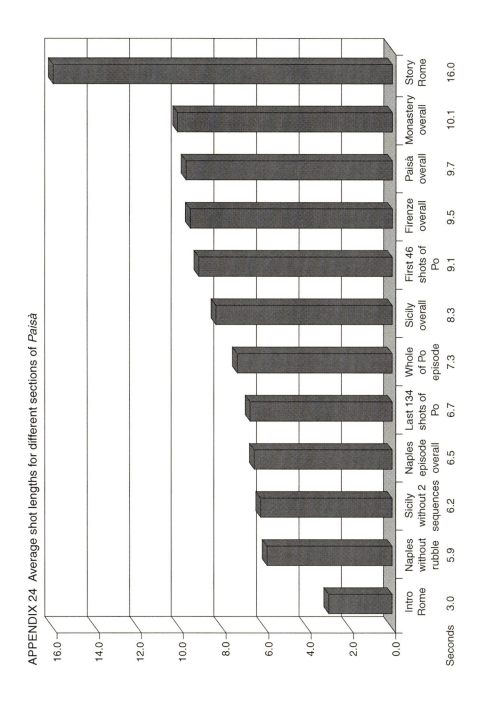

APPENDIX 24 Average shot lengths for different sections of *Paisà*

	Intro Rome	Naples without rubble	Sicily without 2 sequences	Naples episode overall	Last 134 shots of Po	Whole of Po episode	Sicily overall	First 46 shots of Po	Firenze overall	Paisà overall	Monastery overall	Story Rome
Seconds	3.0	5.9	6.2	6.5	6.7	7.3	8.3	9.1	9.5	9.7	10.1	16.0

APPENDIX 25 Scale of shot, *Paisà* – Po delta episode

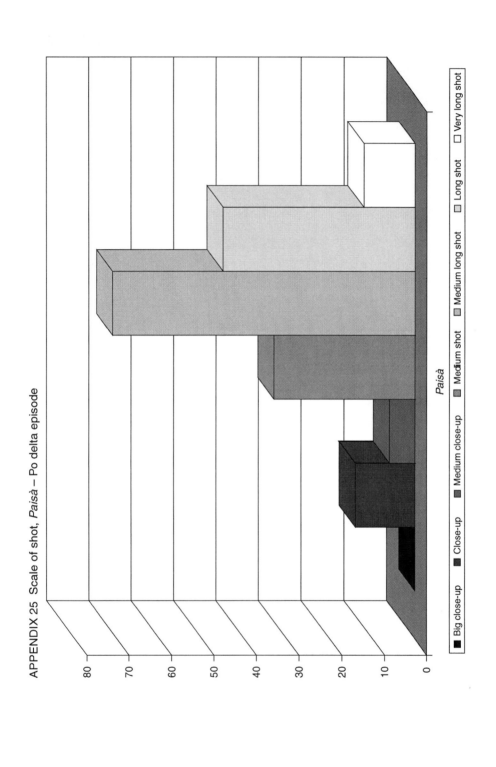

Paisà

Big close-up ■ Close-up ■ Medium close-up ■ Medium shot ■ Medium long shot □ Long shot □ Very long shot □

APPENDIX 26 *Tammurriata nera* (1944) Music by E.A. Mario, lyrics by E. Nicolardi

Tammurriata nera

Black Tammurriata (drum-song)

I

Io nun capisco 'e vvote che succede ...,
E chello ca se vede
nun se crede! nun se crede!
È nato nu criaturo niro niro,
e 'a mamma 'o chiamma Ciro:
sissignore, 'o chiamma Ciro!
Seh! Gira e vota, seh!
Seh! Vota e gira, seh!
Ca tu 'o chiamme Ciccio o Ntuono,
ca tu 'o chiamme Peppe, o Ciro,
chillo, 'o fatto, è niro niro,
niro niro comm'a che!

I

Sometimes I don't understand what's going on ...,
and what we come across
is hard to believe! it's hard to believe!
A little child has been born, black black,
and his mamma calls him Ciro:
yessir she calls him Ciro!
Yeah! twist and turn however you like, yeah!
Yeah! twist and turn however you like, yeah!
Whether you call him Ciccio or Ntuono,
whether you call him Peppe or Ciro,
That boy in reality is black black,
black black and how!

II

'O contano 'e ccummare chist'affare:
– "Sti fatte nun so' rare,
se ne contano a migliare!
'E vvote basta sulo na guardata,
e 'a femmena è restata
sott' 'a botta mpressiunata ...'
Seh, na guardata, seh!
Seh, na mpressione, seh!
Va truvanno mo chi è stato
ca ha cugliuto buono 'o tiro:
chillo, 'o fatto, è niro niro,
niro niro comm'a che!

II

The neighbourhood women talk over this business:
'These things are not rare,
you come across thousands of them!
Sometimes a glance is all it takes,
and the woman ends up
impressed by the force of it ...'
Yeah! a glance, yeah!
Yeah! an impression, yeah!
Go ahead and find the one who did it,
the one who's aim was on target:
That boy in reality is black black,
black black and how!

III

Ha ditto 'o parulano: – 'Embè, parlammo:
pecchè, si raggiunammo,
chistu fatto ce 'o spiegammo!
Addò pastine 'o ggrano, 'o ggrano cresce:
riesce o nun riesce,
sempe è ggrano chello ch'esce!'
Me'! dillo a mamma, me'!
Me'! dillo pure a me!
Ca tu 'o chiamme Ciccio o Ntuono,
ca tu 'o chiamme Peppe o Ciro,
chillo ... 'o ninno è niro niro,
niro niro comm'a che!

III

The greengrocer said: 'So, let's talk:
because if we think about it
we'll find an explanation for this fact!
Where you sow wheat, you get wheat:
whether it thrives or not,
wheat is always what comes up!'
Good, tell it to mamma, good!
Good, tell it to me too!
Whether you call him Ciccio or Ntuono,
whether you call him Peppe or Ciro,
That baby boy is black black,
black black and how!

APPENDIX 27 Map of locations for *Ladri di biciclette*

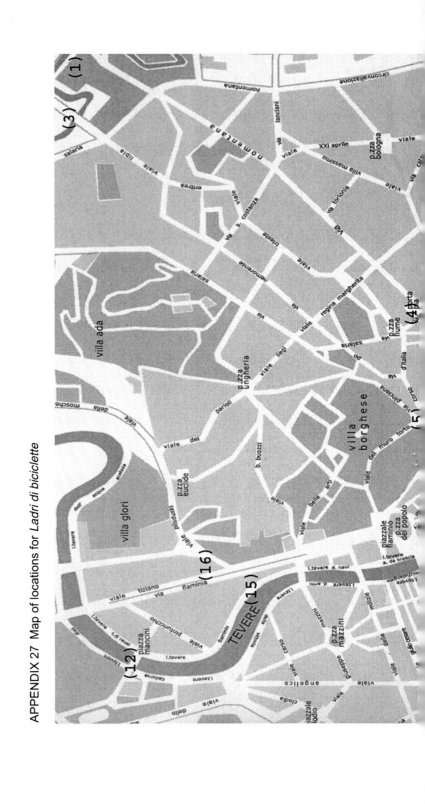

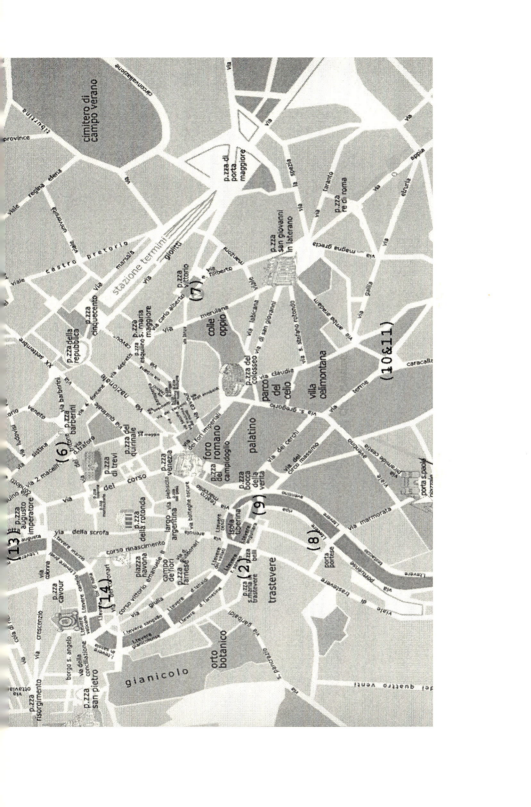

cimitero di campo verano

province

tiburtina

viale regina elena

castro pretorio

p.zza di porta maggiore

stazione termini

p.zza re di roma

p.zza san giovanni in laterano

via magna grecia

p.zza cinquecento

p.zza della repubblica

p.zza vittorio (7)

p.zza esquilino s. maria maggiore

colle oppio

merulana

p.zza del Colosseo

(10&11)

villa celimontana

caracalla

via barberini p.zza barberini

veneto

(6)

ludovisi

sistina

p.zza del quirinale

p.zza di trevi

p.zza del corso

palatino

parco del celio

foro romano campidoglio

p.zza bocca della verita

via dei cerchi

(13) p.zza augusto imperatore

via della scrofa

p.zza della rotonda

largo argentina

p.zza venezia

(9)

porta s. paolo

via marmorata

corso rinascimento

piazza navone

campo de' fiori

isola tiberina

p.zza belli

(8) porta portese

(2) trastevere

p.zza cavour

(14)

corso vittorio emanuele ii

p.zza s. maria trastevere

p.zza risorgimento

p.zza san pietro

borgo s. angelo

via della conciliazione

orto botanico

gianicolo

del quattro venti

Notes

Introduction

1 Barbara Maio and Christian Uva, *L'estetica dell'ibrido: Il cinema contemporaneo tra reale e digitale* (Rome: Bulzoni, 2003), 16.

1. Overview

1 Luigi Freddi, *Il cinema*, vol. 2 (Rome: L'Arnia, 1949), 77–8.
2 This account was first authoritatively expounded by Alberto Farassino, 'Neorealismo, storia e geografia,' in *Neorealismo: Cinema italiano 1945–1949*, ed. Alberto Farassino (Turin: EDT, 1989), 21–44.
3 Giulio Andreotti's letter in the Christian Democrat weekly *Libertas*, on 24 February 1952, criticized the pessimism of De Sica's films, and of *Umberto D.* in particular, saying that the films broadcast a negative and false picture of Italian society to the world. He exhorted De Sica to concentrate on social achievements in the post-war period, and to offer his viewers in future 'a ray of sunshine' and 'a healthy and constructive optimism.' This letter, together with the subsequent failure of Italian state cinema institutions to give backing to *Umberto D.* at the Cannes Film Festival, was read by all as a clear message from the government to Italian neorealist filmmakers.
4 See note 3 above regarding Andreotti's letter.
5 Farassino, ed., Neorealismo, 21–44.
6 See Gilles Deleuze, *L'image-mouvement* (Paris: Minuit, 1983) and *L'image-temps* (Paris: Minuit, 1985); trans. as *The Movement-Image* (London: Athlone Press, 1986) and *Time Image* (London: Athlone Press, 1989).
7 See André Bazin, *Qu'est-ce que le cinéma?* (Paris: Éditions du Cerf, 1978);

trans. Hugh Gray: *What Is Cinema?* 2 vols. (Berkeley: University of California Press, 1967, 1971).

8 See the documentary *That's Life: Vittorio De Sica*, which accompanies the Criterion DVD of *Umberto D.*, Criterion 201.

9 Lindsay Anderson, 'Paisà,' *Sequence* 2 (Winter 1947): 30–1.

10 John Gray, 'Soho Square and Bennett Park: The Documentary Movement in Britain in the 1930s,' at La Trobe University website, http://www.latrobe .edu.au/screeningthepast/firstrelease/fr0799/jg fr7a.htm.

11 Giulia Fanara, *Pensare il neorealismo: Percorsi attraverso il neorealismo cinematografico italiano* (Rome: Lithos, 2000).

12 See *Materiali sul cinema italiano degli anni '50*, vol. 2, Pesaro quaderno 74bis (Pesaro: Mostra internazionale del nuovo cinema, 1978).

13 See Guido Aristarco, ed., *Antologia di Cinema nuovo 1952–1958*, vol. 1: *Neorealismo e vita nazionale* (Rimini, Florence: Guaraldi, 1975).

14 See Bazin, *Qu'est-ce que le cinéma?*

15 See Lino Miccicché, ed., *Il neorealismo cinematografico italiano* (Venice: Marsilio, 1975), and the 'quaderni' that accompanied the 1974 festival: *Il neorealismo e la critica: Materiali per una bibliografia*, Pesaro quaderno 57 (Pesaro: Mostra Internazionale del Nuovo Cinema, 1974); Lorenzo Quaglietti, *Il cinema italiano del dopoguerra*, Pesaro quaderno 58 (Pesaro: Mostra Internazionale del Nuovo Cinema, 1974); and *Sul neorealismo: Testi e documenti (1939–1955)*, Pesaro quaderno 59 (Pesaro: Mostra Internazionale del Nuovo Cinema, 1974).

16 See Farassino, ed., *Neorealismo*.

17 Lino Miccichè, 'Sul neorealismo, oggi,' in Miccichè, ed., *Il neorealismo cinematografico italiano* (Venice: Marsilio, 1999), xxi.

18 from *L'Unità*, 27 February 1956. For Italian cinema in the fascist period, see (full references are in the bibliography): *Nuovi materiali sul cinema italiano 1929–1943*; Aprà and Pistagnesi, *The Fabulous Thirties: Italian Cinema, 1929–1944*; Argentieri, *L'asse cinematografico Roma-Berlino* and *L'occhio del regime*; Ben-Ghiat, *Fascist Modernities*; Brunetta, *Cinema italiano tra le due guerre* and the second volume of his *Storia del cinema italiano: Il cinema del regime, 1929–1945*; Cannistraro, *La fabbrica del consenso*; Hay, *Popular Film Culture in Fascist Italy*; Landy, *Fascism in Film*; Furno and Renzi, *Il neorealismo nel fascismo: Giuseppe De Santis e la critica cinematografica 1941–1943*; Prencipe, *In fondo al mare ... Il cinema di Francesco De Robertis*; Redi, *Cinema italiano sotto il fascismo*; Reich and Garofalo, *Re-Viewing Fascism, Italian Cinema, 1922–1943*; Tinazzi, *Cinema italiano dal fascismo all'antifascismo*; and Zagarrio, *Cinema e fascismo*.

For aspects of the post-war historical, cultural, and institutional situation, see Ginsborg, *A History of Contemporary Italy*; Rocca, *Le leggi del cinema*; Argentieri, *La censura nel cinema italiano*; Aristarco, *Antologia di Cinema nuovo 1952–1958*; Barbaro, *Servitù e grandezza del cinema*; Gundle, *Between Hollywood and Moscow*; Misler, *La via italiana al realismo*; Chinnici, *Cinema, chiesa e movimento cattolico italiano*; Sergio Trasatti, *I cattolici e il neorealismo*.

For filmographic information, see Chiti and Pioppi, *Dizionario del cinema italiano: I film*, vol 2: *dal 1945 al 1959*.

For matters related to the cinema industry, see Corsi, *Con qualche dollaro in meno*; Bizzarri and Solaroli, *L'industria cinematografica italiana*; Ellwood and Brunetta, *Hollywood in Europa*; Quaglietti, *Il cinema italiano del dopoguerra*; and *Storia economico-politica del cinema italiano*; Guback, *The International Film Industry*; Mancini, *Struggles of the Italian Film Industry during Fascism*; Brunetta, *Storia del cinema italiano*; Magrelli, *Cinecittà 2*; Forgacs, *Italian Culture in the Industrial Era*; Nowell-Smith and Ricci, *Hollywood and Europe*; Rocca, *Le leggi del cinema*.

With regard to neorealist cinema in general, for collections of texts from the period see *Sul neorealismo: Testi e documenti (1939–1955)*; Overbey, *Springtime in Italy*, Aristarco, *Antologia di Cinema nuovo*; and Mida and Quaglietti, *Dai telefoni bianchi al neorealismo*. For histories and assessments of neorealism see Fanara, *Pensare il neorealismo*; Bazin, *What Is Cinema?*; Borde and Bouissy, *Le néorealisme italien*, Miccicché; *Il neorealismo cinematografico italiano*; Farassino, *Neorealismo*; Lizzani, *Il cinema italiano 1895–1979*; Spinazzola, *Cinema e pubblico*; Brunetta, *Storia del cinema italiano*; Armes, *Patterns of Realism*; Liehm, *Passion and Defiance*; Bondanella, *Italian Cinema: From Neorealism to the Present*; Prédal, *Le néorealisme italien*; Marcus, *Italian Film in the Light of Neorealism*; Sitney, *Vital Crises in Italian Cinema*; Shiel, *Italian Neorealism*; and Cardullo, *What Is Neorealism?*

2. Realism

1 Charles Sanders Peirce, *Collected Papers*, vol. 4 (Cambridge: Harvard University Press, 1934), para. 537. See also pp. 90–9.

2 Richard Wolheim, *Art and Its Objects*, sec. 35–37 [1968] (Harmondsworth, Middlesex: Penguin Books, 1978), 93.

3 Peirce, *Collected Papers*, vol. 2 (Cambridge: Harvard University Press, 1932), 134–73.

4 André Bazin, 'Voleur de bicyclette,' *Esprit*, November 1949, repr. in *Qu'est-ce que le cinéma?* (Paris: Éditions du Cerf, 1975), 299–300. My italics.

5 Northrop Frye, *Anatomy of Criticism* (Princeton: Princeton University Press, 1957), in particular 'Third Essay' and 'Fourth Essay.'

6 See Thomas Elsaesser, 'Tales of Sound and Fury: Observations on the Family Melodrama,' in *Monogram* 4 (1972): 2–15, and Geoffrey Nowell-Smith, 'Minnelli and Melodrama,' in *Screen* 18, 2 (1977): 113–18, both reprinted in Christine Gledhill, ed., *Home Is where the Heart Is: Studies in Melodrama and the Woman's Film* (London: BFI, 1987). See also Deborah Thomas, *Beyond Genre: Melodrama, Comedy and Romance in Hollywood Films* (Moffat: Cameron & Hollis, 2000). For a general discussion about the problems raised by the notion of genre in the cinema, see Steve Neale, *Genre and Hollywood* (London: Routledge, 2000), which has an enormous bibliography. Rick Altman would categorize the 'matrix' or genre that I am trying to identify as being of the 'transhistorical' kind. I am certainly not looking for the detailed subcategories that he applies to Hollywood movies, which is why I am reluctant to use the word 'genre' at all. See Rick Altman, *Film/Genre* (London: BFI, 1999), 19–20.

7 Paul Ginsborg, *Italy and Its Discontents: Family, Civil Society, State 1980–2001* (London: Penguin Books, 2001), 97.

8 Gian Piero Brunetta has written extensively in this area. See his *Umberto Barbaro e l'idea di neorealismo (1930–1943)* (Padua: Liviana, 1969); *Intellettuali, cinema e propaganda tra le due guerre: I pionieri, Canudo, Luciani, Pirandello, Barbaro, Chiarini, il film fascista* (Bologna: Patròn, 1973); *Cinema italiano tra le due guerre: Fascismo e politica cinematografica* (Milan: Mursia, 1975). See also *Nuovi materiali sul cinema italiano 1929–1943*, vol. 1, quaderno informativo 72 (Ancona: Mostra Internazionale del Nuovo Cinema Pesaro, 1976), in particular Vito Zagarrio, 'Tra intervento e tendenza: Le riviste culturali e il cinema del fascismo,' 200–73.

9 Fabrizio Sarazani, *Il Tempo*, 26 September 1945.

10 Vittorio Spinazzola, 'Riesame del neorealismo: (a) *Ladri di biciclette*,' in *Cinema nuovo* 5, 82 (10 March 1956), repr. in *Antologia di Cinema nuovo 1952–1958: Dalla critica cinematografica alla dialettica culturale*, vol. 1, *Neorealismo e vita nazionale*, ed. Guido Aristarco, 235 (Rimini, Florence: Guaraldi, 1975).

11 Bill Nichols, *Representing Reality: Issues and Concepts in Documentary* (Bloomington and Indianapolis: Indiana University Press, 1991), 12ff. A rich bibliography on theories of documentary is to be found in Michael Renov, ed., *Theorizing Documentary* (New York, London: Routledge, 1993).

12 Brian Winston, 'The Documentary as Scientific Inscription,' in Renov, ed., *Theorizing Documentary*, 37–57, esp. 37–41.

13 Pier Paolo Pasolini, *Empirismo eretico* (Milan: Garzanti, 1971).

14 Michelangelo Antonioni, 'Per un film sul fiume Po,' *Cinema* 68 (25 April 1939), repr. in *Sul neorealismo: Testi e documenti (1939–1955)*, Quaderno informativo 59 (Pesaro: Mostra Internazionale del Nuovo Cinema, 1974), 7–9,

and in an English translation (which I have not used) in David Overbey, ed., *Springtime in Italy: A Reader on Neo-realism* (London: Talisman Books, 1978), 79–82.

15 Quoted in Cesare Biarese and Aldo Tassone, *I film di Michelangelo Antonioni* (Rome: Gremese, 1985), 66–7.

16 Michelangelo Antonioni, 'La malattia dei sentimenti (Colloquio con Michelangelo Antonioni al Centro Sperimentale di Cinematografia),' *Bianco e Nero*, February–March 1961.

17 There are three main essays in which Zavattini expresses his theories, as well as a large collection of other writings, notes, and interviews reprinted in Cesare Zavattini, *Neorealismo, ecc.*, and *Diario cinematografico*, both published in Milan by Bompiani in 1979. The first essay, 'Alcune idee sul cinema,' was published in December 1952 in the form of a preface to the script of *Umberto D.* An English translation was published in *Sight and Sound*, 23, 2 (October–December 1953): 64–9, and is reprinted in Howard Curle and Stephen Snyder, eds, *Vittorio De Sica: Contemporary Perspectives* (Toronto: University of Toronto Press, 2000), 50–61. The second essay, 'Tesi sul neorealismo,' grew out of a discussion in the journal *Emilia* in late 1953. The third essay, 'Il neorealismo secondo me,' was composed as a paper to be delivered at the Parma conference on neorealism in December 1953, where the main question on the agenda was whether neorealism was 'in crisis,' or perhaps even finished. A digest of the essays is translated into English (not always entirely reliably) in Overbey, *Springtime in Italy*, 67–79. For discussion of Zavattini's theorizing, see Guglielmo Moneti, ed., *Lessico zavattiniano* (Venice: Marsilio, 1992); Giorgio De Vincenti, 'Cesare Zavattini: Uomo totale e cinema del frammento,' in De Vincenti, *Il concetto di modernità nel cinema* (Parma: Pratiche, 1993), 157–75; and Giulia Fanara, *Pensare il neorealismo: Percorsi attraverso il neorealismo cinematografico italiano* (Rome: Lithos, 2000).

18 'Alcune idee sul cinema,' 98.

19 Lino Micciché, 'Sul neorealismo, oggi,' in Micciché, ed., *Il neorealismo cinematografico italiano* (Venice: Marsilio, 1999), xi–xiii in particular.

20 Cesare Zavattini, 'Address to the Convegno internazionale di cinematografia – Perugia 24–27 September 1949,' in *Sul neorealismo: Testi e documenti (1939–1955)*, 62–3.

21 See Giorgio De Vincenti, 'Sperimentalismo,' in Moneti, ed., *Lessico zavattiniano* 253–60, and 'Cesare Zavattini,' in De Vincenti, *Il concetto di modernità nel cinema*, 157–75; and see Fanara, *Pensare il neorealismo*, 325–38.

22 'Tesi sul neorealismo,' *in* Sul neorealismo, 230.

23 Zavattini, 'Address to the Convegno internazionale di cinematografia.'

24 'Il realismo secondo me,' in *Sul neorealismo: Testi e documenti (1939–1955)*, 250–1.
25 Reply to a student in 1970, in Zavattini, *Neorealismo, ecc.*, 392.
26 From an interview with Tommaso Chiaretti, in *Mondo nuovo* 49 (December 1960), repr. in Zavattini, *Neorealismo, ecc.*, 224–5.
27 Italo Calvino, *Il sentiero dei nidi di ragno* (Milan: Mondadori, 1993) (2002 printing). 1st ed., Turin, Einaudi – 'I coralli' – 1947; 2nd ed., Turin, Einaudi, 1964. In June 1964, for the 2nd edition, Calvino wrote a 'Prefazione.' This is printed in the Mondadori edition as 'Presentazione,' pp. v–xxv.
28 Mario Verdone, 'Colloquio sul neorealismo,' *Bianco e nero*, February 1952: 7–16, repr. in Roberto Rossellini, *Il mio metodo: Scritti e interviste*, ed. Adriano Aprà (Venice: Marsilio, 1987), 91.
29 Cesare Zavattini, in his preface to the script of *Umberto D.*, first published in *Rivista del cinema italiano* 2 (1952); now in 'Alcune idee sul cinema,' in Zavattini, *Neorealismo, ecc.*, 96–7.
30 Michelangelo Antonioni, *Écrits 1936/1985*, and *Entretiens et inédits 1950/1985* (Rome: Cinecittà International, 1991, and 1992), passim; 'La malattia dei sentimenti,' in *Bianco e Nero* 2–3 (February–March 1961).
31 See Tullio Kezich, *Su La Dolce Vita con Federico Fellini* (Venice: Marsilio, 1996), 41.
32 Erich Auerbach, *Literary Language and Its Public in Late Latin Antiquity and in the Middle Ages*, trans. from German by Ralph Manheim [1958] (Princeton: Princeton University Press, 1993), 51.
33 A fragment of an interview on RAI television.
34 Mario Verdone, 'Colloquio sul neorealismo,' in *Bianco e nero*, February 1952: 7–16, repr. in Roberto Rossellini, *Il mio metodo: Scritti e interviste*, edited by Adriano Aprà (Venice: Marsilio, 1987), 85.
35 See Alberto Farassino, 'Neorealismo, storia e geografia,' in Farassino, ed., *Neorealismo Cinema italiano 1945–1949* (Turin: EDT, 1989), 21–44.
36 For further general reading in connection with some of the issues discussed in this chapter, see Altman, *Film/Genre*; Neale, *Genre and Hollywood*; Andrew, *André Bazin* and *The Major Film Theories*; Aristarco, *Storia delle teoriche del film* and *Antologia di Cinema nuovo*; Casetti, *Theories of Film*; Bazin, *What Is Cinema?*; Brunetta, *Cent'anni di cinema italiano* and *Storia del cinema italiano*; Calvino, 'Preface' to *Il sentiero dei nidi di ragno*; Cassac, *Littérature et cinéma néoréalistes*; Chiarini, *Arte e tecnica del film*; Grant, *Realism*; Bruno, *Teorie del realismo*; Williams, *Realism and the Cinema*; Nichols, *Representing Reality; Issues and Concepts in Documentary*; Renov, *Theorizing Documentary*; Fanara, *Pensare il neorealismo*; Armes, *Patterns of Realism*; Marcus, *Italian Film*

in the Light of Neorealism; Zavattini, *Neorealismo, ecc.*; *Neorealismo poetiche e polemiche*; and Overbey *Springtime in Italy.*

3. *Roma città aperta*

1 Filmographic details for this film are found in appendix 16.
2 Extracts of this film were recently shown on Italian television, Raitre, in the *Fuori orario* slot, but without identifying the actual documentary film itself.
3 Vernon Jarratt, *The Italian Cinema* (London: The Falcon Press, 1951), 58.
4 Ugo Pirro, *Celluloide* (Turin: Einaudi, 1983), 36.
5 See David Forgacs, *Rome Open City* (London: BFI, 2000), 26, 73.
6 Mario Calzini's report to the Centro Sperimentale di Cinematografia, 12 May 1995.
7 See Mario Cannella, 'Ideology and Aesthetic Hypotheses in the Criticism of Neorealism,' *Screen* 14, 4 (Winter 1973/4): 5–60.
8 Tag Gallagher, *The Adventures of Roberto Rossellini* (New York: Da Capo, 1998), 160.
9 Barry Salt, *Film Style and Technology: History and Analysis* (London: Starword, 1983), 291–3.
10 Ibid., 252–4.
11 Ibid., 171.
12 Another striking case of camera angles not reconciling occurs when Don Pietro hands over the money books to the partisan at Tiburtina.
13 Gallagher, *The Adventures of Roberto Rossellini*, 160.
14 *Rome Open City,* 36ff. In an article published after this chapter was completed, Forgacs confirms my suggestions about the 'institutionalization' of domestic space: David Forgacs, 'Space, Rhetoric, and the Divided City in *Roma città aperta,*' in Sidney Gottlieb, ed., *Roberto Rossellini's* Rome Open City (Cambridge: Cambridge University Press, 2004), 106–30.
15 Mario Verdone, 'Colloquio sul neorealismo,' *Bianco e nero*, February 1952: 7–16, repr. in Roberto Rossellini, *Il mio metodo: Scritti e interviste*, ed. Adriano Aprà (Venice: Marsilio, 1987), 88.
16 See Gallagher, *The Adventures of Roberto Rossellini*, 144–5, quoting from James Blue, 'An Interview with Rossellini' (Houston, 1972), in *Rossellini*, a brochure for a series presented by Joseph Papp at the Public Theater, New York, 1–20 May 1979, 17.
17 Ibid., 167.
18 Verdone, 'Colloquio sul neorealismo,' 85.
19 Gallagher, *The Adventures of Roberto Rossellini*, 132.

20 Vincent F. Rocchio, *Cinema of Anxiety: A Psychoanalysis of Italian Neorealism* (Austin: University of Texas Press, 1999), 43–4.
21 See Ernst Robert Curtius, *European Literature and the Latin Middle Ages* (London: Routledge & Kegan Paul, 1953).
22 Lucia Re, *Calvino and the Age of Neorealism: Fables of Estrangement* (Stanford: Stanford University Press, 1990), 79.
23 Giorgio Tinazzi and Marina Zancan, eds, *Cinema e letteratura del neorealismo* (Venice: Marsilio, 1983), 42–51.
24 See Pirro, *Celluloide*, and Gallagher, *The Adventures of Roberto Rossellini*, 115–79. After this chapter was completed the fullest account of the genesis of the film, together with the original script and the financial accounts relating to its making were published in Stefano Roncoroni, *La storia di Roma città aperta* (Bologna: Cineteca comunale / Genoa: Le Mani, 2006).
25 Indro Montanelli, *Corriere d'Informazione*, 24 October 1945.
26 See Christopher Wagstaff, 'Il cinema europeo e la resistenza,' in L. Cigognetti, L. Servetti, and P. Sorlin, eds, *L'immagine della resistenza in Europa: 1945–1960. Letteratura, cinema, arti figurative* (Bologna: Il Nove, 1996), 39–61.
27 The Association of Partisans has a 'Cronologia della Resistenza Romana' on their website, at http://www.romacivica.net/anpiroma.
28 Antonio Parisi, *Il cinema di Giuseppe De Santis tra passione e ideologia* (Rome: Cadmo editore, 1983), 40–5.
29 Carlo Lizzani, 'Introduzione' in *Riso amaro*: Un film diretto da Giuseppe De Santis (Rome: Officina edizioni, 1978), 14, quoted in Parisi, *Il cinema di Giuseppe De Santis*, 40–5.
30 Gallagher, *The Adventures of Roberto Rossellini*, 157.
31 *Jolanda e Rossellini: Memorie indiscrete*, a documentary film by Paolo Isaia and Maria Pia Melandri.
32 Gian Piero Brunetta, *Storia del cinema italiano*, vol. 3 (Rome: Editori Riuniti, 1993), 410.
33 Fabrizio Sarazani, *Il Tempo*, 26 September 1945.
34 Indro Montanelli, *Corriere d'Informazione*, 24 October 1945.
35 Sergio Amidei, in Patrizia Pistagnesi, ed., *Anna Magnani*, Incontri Internazionali d'Arte / Associazione Internazionale Anna Magnani / Museo Nazionale del Cinema (Rome, Milan: Fabbri, 1989), 90–109.
36 For discussion of the treatment of the Resistance in Italian cinema and literature, see Brunetta, *Cinema storia resistenza*; *La resistenza nel cinema italiano del dopoguerra* and *La cinepresa e la storia*; Ivaldi, *La resistenza nel cinema italiano del dopoguerra*; Corti, *Il viaggio testuale*; Falaschi, *La Resistenza armata nella narrativa italiana*; Tarizzo, *Come scriveva la Resistenza*; Amaducci, *Il sole sorge ancora*; and Wagstaff, 'Il cinema europeo e la resistenza.'

On Rossellini and *Roma città aperta*, see Aprà, Roma città aperta: *Il dopo-guerra di Rossellini* and *Roma città aperta di Roberto Rossellini*; Armes, *Patterns of Realism*; Baldelli, *Cinema dell'ambiguità* and *Roberto Rossellini: I film 1936–1972*; Bergala and Narboni, *Roberto Rossellini*; Blue, Interview with Rossellini; Bondanella, *The Films of Roberto Rossellini* and *Italian Cinema: From Neorealism to the Present*; Brunetta, *Cent'anni di cinema italiano*, *Cinema storia resistenza: 1944–1985*, and *Storia del cinema italiano*; Bruni, *Roberto Rossellini: Roma città aperta*; Cannella, 'Ideology and Aesthetic Hypotheses in the Criticism of Neorealism'; Forgacs, *Rome Open City* and 'Space, Rhetoric, and the Divided City in *Roma città aperta*'; De Masi, *Rossellini*; Gallagher, *The Adventures of Roberto Rossellini*; Gottlieb, *Roberto Rossellini, Rome Open City*, Marcus, *Italian Film in the Light of Neorealism*; Masi, *I film di Roberto Rossellini*; Mida, *Compagni di viaggio* and *Roberto Rossellini*; Pirro, *Celluloide*; Rinaudo, *Roma città aperta: Un film di Roberto Rossellini*; Rocchio, *Cinema of Anxiety*; Roncoroni, *La storia di Roma città aperta*, *Roberto Rossellini*, *La trilogia della guerra*, and *Quasi un'autobiografia – Roberto Rossellini*; Rondolino, *Roberto Rossellini*; Rossellini, *Il mio metodo* or *My Method*; Seknadje-Askénazi, *Roberto Rossellini et la Seconde Guerre Mondiale*; Serceau, *Roberto Rossellini*; Sitney, *Vital Crises in Italian Cinema*; and Spinazzola, *Cinema e pubblico*.

4. *Paisà*

1 Filmographic details for this film are found in appendix 16.
2 I had completed writing this chapter when, in the summer of 2005, a volume of collected essays on *Paisà* came out in Italy, consisting of detailed analyses of each episode of the film, in total length roughly equal to this chapter: Stefania Parigi, ed., *Paisà: Analisi del film* (Venice: Marsilio, 2005). One of the reasons for writing this chapter had been to fill a gap in neorealist criticism, for hitherto no extended treatment of *Paisà* had existed. Suddenly, in the summer of 2005, one existed, and an authoritative one. Was I to jettison my chapter as now redundant? On the contrary, this fortuitous coincidence offers the possibility of something considered normal in the natural sciences, but rarely occurring in the humanities: two separate researchers carrying out very similar investigations on the same material, permitting us to see whether the results are 'duplicated.' What is more normal in the humanities, where different researchers analyse the same material, is that either they do slightly different things (precisely so as not to do the same thing), or they do the same thing serially (one after the other), the second researcher deliberately seeking different findings. These two analyses of *Paisà*, the Italian one and my own, offer the chance to ask whether

one investigation 'duplicates' the results of the other. The answer is, Yes and No. Both investigations find the same things in the film, confirming the accuracy of the two descriptions. The differences lie in what we do with what we find. In only two respects is there contamination between the two investigations. Leonardo De Franceschi, writing about the *Naples* episode in the Italian volume, makes reference to an earlier version of my discussion of it, Christopher Wagstaff, 'Rossellini and Neo-realism,' in *Roberto Rossellini: Magician of the Real*, ed. David Forgacs, Sarah Lutton, and Geoffrey Nowell-Smith (London: British Film Institute, 2000), 36–49. I have drawn upon Adriano Aprà's discussion of the two versions of the film on pp. 151–61 of the Italian volume to add explanations in notes to my already completed chapter.

3 Quoted in Adriano Aprà, ed., *Rosselliniana: Bibliografia internazionale. Dossier 'Paisà'* (Rome: Di Giacomo, 1987), 93.

4 Quoted from a manuscript in the Klaus Mann Archives, Munich, in Thomas Meder, *Vom Sichtbarmachen der Geschichte: Der italienische 'Neorealismus,' Rossellinis 'Paisà' und Klaus Mann* (Munich: Trickster, 1993), 189n, quoted in its turn in Tag Gallagher, *The Adventures of Roberto Rossellini* (New York: Da Capo, 1998), 723.

5 For the genesis of the film, see Aprà, ed., *Rosselliniana*; Gallagher, *The Adventures of Roberto Rossellini*; and Giulia Fanara, *Pensare il neorealismo: Percorsi attraverso il neorealismo cinematografico italiano* (Rome: Lithos, 2000).

6 See the chapter on *Paisà* in Gallagher, *The Adventures of Roberto Rossellini*, and Parigi, ed., *Paisà*, 164.

7 The BBC has been broadcasting for many years a print without these cuts and additions.

8 See Adriano Aprà, 'Le due versioni di *Paisà*,' in *Paisà*, ed. Parigi, 151–61.

9 See Tag Gallagher, *The Adventures of Roberto Rossellini*, 184, whose source was Rod Geiger, one of the film's producers, and another of Michi's companions.

10 See Aprà, ed., *Rosselliniana*, 96. There is evidence for suspecting that a first, rough, editing of the film may not have contained a flashback: see Aprà, 'Le due versioni di *Paisà*,' 161n5.

11 See Fanara, *Pensare il neorealismo*, 359.

12 See Aprà, ed., *Rosselliniana*, 137, and Alberto Farassino, *Lux Film* (Rome: Fondazione Pesaro Nuovo Cinema, 2000), 174–5.

13 See Aprà, ed., *Rosselliniana*, 97–113.

14 The words 'a whore' are erased from some anglophone prints of the film.

15 *Stilnovista* alludes to the poetry of the *dolce stil novo*, in which the beloved woman is portrayed as a saving angelic figure.

16 Aprà, ed., *Rosselliniana*, 144. Renzo Rossellini's hurriedly prepared assembly of the film for the Venice Film Festival was later re-edited by Rossellini, and the latter is the 'standard' version that we know, and which I have used for this chapter. See Aprà, 'Le due versioni di *Paisà*,' 151–61.

17 Pio Baldelli, *Cinema dell'ambiguità* (Rome: Samonà e Savelli, 1969), 116.

18 Quoted in Gallagher, *The Adventures of Roberto Rossellini*, 189.

19 Aprà, ed., *Rosselliniana,*.132.

20 Gallagher, *The Adventures of Roberto Rossellini*, 189–90.

21 See Parigi, ed., *Paisà*, 164.

22 Massimo Mida, 'Si gira in convento,' *Film d'Oggi*, 27 July 1946, repr. in Aprà, ed., *Rosselliniana*, 141–3.

23 Stefano Roncoroni, in his valuable screenplay taken down from the film, mistakenly attributes the two lines of this friar to the organist (Padre Claudio). Roberto Rossellini, *La trilogia della guerra*, ed. Stefano Roncoroni (Bologna: Cappelli, 1972), 208.

24 Michelangelo Antonioni, *Quel bowling sul Tevere* (Turin: Einaudi, 1995 [1983]), 35–6.

25 Adriano Aprà informs us that Padre Vincenzo (the Padre Guardiano) collaborated on the script for this episode. See Parigi, ed., *Paisà*, 164.

26 Fanara, *Pensare il neorealismo*, 19.

27 Herbert Spiegelberg, 'Characteristics of Phenomenology: Essential Features and Variations,' in *Encyclopaedia Britannica 2002*, on CD-ROM.

28 Federico Fellini, *Fare un film* (Turin: Einaudi, 1980), 44–7.

29 Aprà, ed., *Rosselliniana*, 134 (originally in 'Author's Note on Birth of "Paisan,"' in *New York Times*, 7 March 1948). I have retranslated into English Aprà's Italian version.

30 Ibid., 94.

31 'This revised "Naples" was conceived on location by Fellini and Roberto when they first laid eyes on the cave of Mergellina and its horde of refugees. But it really took form only when Roberto saw the boy and the black together exchanging lines and smiles.' Gallagher, *The Adventures of Roberto Rossellini*, 195.

32 Chabrol was replying to questions in a RAI series of documentaries on Rossellini, but he may have been remembering how Jacques Rivette described Rossellini's 'realism': 'neither a scriptwriting technique nor a style of *mise en scène*, but a state of mind: that a straight line is the shortest distance between two points ... Rossellini is not subtle, he is prodigiously simple'; in 'Lettre sur Rossellini,' *Cahiers du Cinéma* 46 (April 1955).

33 See Aprà, ed., *Rosselliniana*, 137, 146, and Gallagher, *The Adventures of Roberto Rossellini*, 197–8.

34 For the changes Rossellini made in this episode after the initial Venice showing, see Aprà, 'Le due versioni di *Paisà*,' in Parigi, ed., *Paisà*,. 151–61. In the version of the film hurriedly prepared for the 1946 Venice Film Festival by Renzo Rossellini (see the section of this chapter on the *Monastery* episode) Massimo and Harriet meet in the medical post. Rossellini later re-edited and shortened the episode, producing the anomolies I have pointed out. His own version of the film, which has come down to us as standard, is the one he preferred. Incidentally, this episode of *Paisà* receives detailed analysis in chapter 2 of Francesco Casetti and Federico di Chio, *Analisi del film* (Milan: Bompiani, 1990), 22–54.

35 Tullio Kezich, *Fellini* (Milan: Rizzoli, 1988 [1st edition 1987]), 128.

36 Aprà, ed., *Rosselliniana*, 137.

37 See Sandro Bernardi, 'Rossellini's Landscapes: Nature, Myth, History,' in *Roberto Rossellini: Magician of the Real*, ed. Forgacs, Lutton, and Nowell-Smith, 50–63. Bernardi interprets and evaluates; my interpretations are only by-products of description, and I am wary of evaluation. However, we often come to similar conclusions.

38 Fellini, *Fare un film*, 44.

39 Mario Verdone, 'Colloquio sul neorealismo,' *Bianco e nero*, February 1952: 7–16, repr. in Roberto Rossellini, *Il mio metodo: Scritti e interviste*, ed. Adriano Aprà (Venice: Marsilio, 1987), 91.

40 Suggested reading on the Resistance in Italian cinema is indicated in note 36 to chapter 3. Starting places for further analyses and assessments of *Paisà* are Parigi, *Paisà: Analisi del film*; Aprà, *Rosselliniana*; Armes, *Patterns of Realism*; Baldelli, *Cinema dell'ambiguità* and *Roberto Rossellini: I film 1936–1972*; Bazin, *What Is Cinema?*; Bernardi, 'I paesaggi nella "trilogia della guerra"' and 'Rossellini's Landscapes'; Bondanella, *The Films of Roberto Rossellini*; Brunetta, *Storia del cinema italiano*; Brunette, *Roberto Rossellini*; Casetti and Di Chio, *Analisi del film*; Conley, *Film Hieroglyphs*; Fanara, *Pensare il neorealismo*; Ferrara, *Il nuovo cinema italiano*; Gallagher, *The Adventures of Roberto Rossellini*; Aprà, *Roma città aperta: Il dopoguerra di Rossellini*; Marcus, *Italian Film in the Light of Neorealism* and 'National Identity by Means of Montage in Roberto Rossellini's *Paisan*'; Meder, '"Paisà" ritrovato,' and *Vom Sichtbarmachen der Geschichte*; Mida, *Compagni di viaggio* and *Roberto Rossellini*; Muscio's chapter on *Paisà* in Bertellini, *The Cinema of Italy*; Roncoroni, *Roberto Rossellini, La trilogia della guerra*; Rondi, *Il neorealismo italiano*; Rondolino, *Roberto Rossellini*; Seknadje-Askénazi, *Roberto Rossellini et la Seconde Guerre Mondiale*; Serceau, *Roberto Rossellini*; and Sitney, *Vital Crises in Italian Cinema*.

5. *Ladri di biciclette*

1 Filmographic details for this film are found in appendix 16.
2 Lino Micciché, 'La "questione" De Sica,' in *De Sica, Autore, regista, attore*, ed. Lino Micciché (Venice: Marsilio, 1992), vii–xvi.
3 Luigi Bartolini, repr. in *De Sica & Zavattini: Parliamo tanto di noi*, ed. Paolo Nuzzi and Ottavio Iemma (Rome: Editori Riuniti, 1997), 128.
4 Vittorio De Sica, 'Gli anni più belli della mia vita,' *Il Tempo*, 23 December 1954.
5 See Nuzzi and Iemma, eds, *De Sica & Zavattini*, 93.
6 Luigi Bartolini, *Ladri di biciclette* (Milan: Longanesi, 1984), 216–18.
7 Luigi Bartolini, repr. in *De Sica & Zavattini*, ed.Nuzzi and Iemma, 128.
8 Cesare Zavattini, 'Soggetto: Prima versione' (original source not identified) in *Ladri di biciclette di Vittorio De Sica: Testimonianze, interventi, sopralluoghi*, ed. Orio Caldiron and Manuel De Sica (Rome: Editoriale Patheon, 1997), 49–50.
9 Vittorio De Sica, repr. (original source not identified) in *Ladri di biciclette di Vittorio De Sica*, ed. Caldiron and De Sica, 11.
10 Suso Cecchi D'Amico, in *L'avventurosa storia del cinema italiano raccontato dai suoi protagonisti 1935–1959*, ed. Franca Faldini and Goffredo Fofi (Milan: Feltrinelli, 1979), 134.
11 Ugo Pirro, *Celluloide* (Turin: Einaudi, 1995), 127.
12 Sergio Amidei, in *L'avventurosa storia del cinema italiano*, ed. Faldini and Fofi, 135.
13 Suso Cecchi D'Amico, in *Storie di cinema (e d'altro) raccontate a Margherita D'Amico* (Milan: Garzanti, 1996), 76.
14 Sergio Leone, in *Ladri di biciclette di Vittorio De Sica*, ed. Caldiron and De Sica, 22.
15 Suso Cecchi D'Amico, ibid., 20–1.
16 Francis Koval, 'Interview with De Sica,' *Sight and Sound* 19, 2 (April 1950): 63.
17 See Cesare Zavattini, *Diario cinematografico* (Milan: Bompiani, 1979), 49, 54.
18 Cesare Zavattini, 'Ladri di biciclette,' *Bis* 11 (25 May 1948), repr. in *Diario cinematografico*, 54–8.
19 Vittorio De Sica, repr. (original source not identified) in *Ladri di biciclette di Vittorio De Sica*, ed. Caldiron and De Sica, 11.
20 Suso Cecchi D'Amico, in *L'avventurosa storia del cinema italiano*, ed. Faldini and Fofi, 135.
21 Maria Mercader, *La mia vita con Vittorio De Sica* (Milan: Mondadori, 1978). I

have taken the Italian text from Caldiron and De Sica, eds, *Ladri di biciclette di Vittorio De Sica*, 15. The passage occurs in a French translation of the book: Maria Mercader, *Un amour obstiné: Ma vie avec Vittorio De Sica* (Paris: Lherminier, 1981), 91–2.

22 'Vittoro De Sica,' in Nuzzi and Iemma, eds, *De Sica & Zavattini*, 96.

23 Vittorio De Sica, repr. (original source not identified) in *Ladri di biciclette di Vittorio De Sica*, ed. Caldiron and De Sica, 11.

24 The letter is repr. in Nuzzi and Iemma, eds, *De Sica & Zavattini*, 129.

25 Pierre Sorlin, *European Cinemas – European Societies 1939–1990* (London: Routledge, 1991), 118–20.

26 Vittorio De Sica, 'Volti nuovi del cinema,' *Cinema italiano anno XX* (Rome: Edizioni di Documento, 1942), repr. in Orio Caldiron, ed., *Vittorio De Sica*, Bianco e Nero monograph 22 (Rome: Edizioni dell'Ateneo e Bizzarri, 1975) (extract from *Bianco e Nero* 9, 12 [1975]), 253–4.

27 Vittorio De Sica, 'Gli anni più belli della mia vita,' *Tempo* 16, 50 (16 December 1954): 18–22, repr. in Caldiron, ed., *Vittorio De Sica*, 279–80.

28 Piero Cristofani and Roberto Manetti, eds, 'Processo al non attore,' *Cinema Nuovo* 5, 79 (25 March 1956): 175, repr. in Caldiron, ed., *Vittorio De Sica*, 291–2.

29 Caldiron, ed., *Vittorio De Sica*, 151.

30 Vittorio De Sica, 'Gli anni più belli della mia vita. Farò ancora l'attore per pagare i miei film,' *Tempo* 16, 52 (30 December 1954): 52–3, repr. in Caldiron, ed., *Vittorio De Sica*, 289.

31 Vittorio De Sica, 'Carnet di Napoli con oro e senza,' *Cinema Nuovo* 3, 32 (1 April 1954): 176, repr. in Caldiron, ed., *Vittorio De Sica*, 274.

32 Zavattini, *Diario cinematografico*, 53.

33 Luisa Alessandri, in *Ladri di biciclette di Vittorio De Sica*, ed. Caldiron and De Sica, 19.

34 Luisa Alessandri, ibid., 19.

35 Vittorio De Sica, 'Gli anni più belli della mia vita. Il pianto di Chaplin,' *Tempo* 16, 51 (23 December 1954): 58–60, repr. in Caldiron, ed., *Vittorio De Sica*, 281.

36 Vittorio De Sica, 'Gli anni più belli della mia vita,' *Tempo* 16, 50 (16 December 1954): 18–22, repr. in Caldiron, ed., *Vittorio De Sica*, 281.

37 Ibid., 281.

38 Lianella Carrell, in *Ladri di biciclette di Vittorio De Sica*, ed. Caldiron and De Sica, 18.

39 Suso Cecchi D'Amico, in *L'avventurosa storia del cinema italiano*, ed. Faldini and Fofi, 366.

40 Luisa Alessandri, in *Ladri di biciclette di Vittorio De Sica*, ed. Caldiron and De Sica, 19.

41 See Gilles Deleuze, *L'image-mouvement* (Paris: Minuit, 1983), trans. as *The Movement-Image* (London: Athlone Press, 1986), and Deleuze, *L'image-temps* (Paris: Minuit, 1985), trans. as *Time Image* (London: Athlone, 1989), passim.

42 Vittorio Spinazzola, *Cinema e pubblico: Lo spettacolo filmico in Italia, 1945–1965* [1st ed., Milan: Bompiani, 1974] (Rome: Bulzoni, 1985), 40.

43 André Bazin, 'Voleur de bicyclette,' *Esprit,* November 1949, repr. in Bazin, *Qu'est-ce que le cinéma?* (Paris: Éditions du Cerf, 1975), 299.

44 Spinazzola, *Cinema e pubblico,* 41.

45 I concur with the screenplay transcribed from the film by Laura Gaiardoni, in 'La sceneggiatura,' in *Ladri di biciclette di Vittorio De Sica,* ed. Caldiron and De Sica, 65–159.

46 Guglielmo Moneti identifies 743 shots, and divides them into 45 'sequences,' which correspond more strictly to 'scenes' in the scriptwriter's sense. See Guglielmo Moneti, 'Ladri di biciclette,' in *De Sica: Autore, regista, attore,* ed. Lino Micciché (Venice: Marsilio, 1992), 276–85.

47 Bazin, 'Voleur de bicyclette,' 306–7. The translation is mine.

48 Moneti, 'Ladri di biciclette,' 257–8.

49 Pio Baldelli, *Cinema dell'ambiguità: Rossellini, De Sica e Zavattini, Fellini* (Rome: Samonà e Savelli, 1969), 217.

50 Repr. in Nuzzi and Iemma, eds, *De Sica & Zavattini,* 120–1.

51 Giulio Andreotti, 'Attualità di La Pira,' *30 giorni: Nella chiesa e nel mondo* 20, 10 (October 2002).

52 In 1992 I briefly referred to the importance of the song in a shot analysis of sequences in the film – see Christopher Wagstaff, 'Comic Positions,' *Sight and Sound* 2, 7 (November 1992): 25–7 In 1997 Nelson Moe subjected the song and its place in the film to a detailed analysis – see Nelson Moe, 'Naples '44 / "Tammurriata nera" / *Ladri di biciclette,*' in *Italy and America, 1943–44: Italian, American and Italian-American Experiences of the Liberation of the Mezzogiorno,* ed. John A. Davis (Naples: Istituto Italiano per gli Studi Filosofici, Edizioni La città del Sole, 1997), 433–54.

53 This is how Nelson Moe (see note 52) takes it.

54 See Tullio Kezich, 'Servitore di due padroni,' in *De Sica,* ed. Micciché, 13.

55 Manuel De Sica, 'Molti amici, molto rumore,' in *Ladri di biciclette di Vittorio De Sica,* ed. Caldiron and De Sica, 13–14.

56 Ettore Scola, 'Quel giorno non andai a scuola,' ibid., 23.

57 See Moneti, 'Ladri di biciclette,' 259–61.

58 Sergio Leone, 'Il più piccolo dettaglio,' in *Ladri di biciclette di Vittorio De Sica,* ed. Caldiron and De Sica, 22.

59 Baldelli, *Cinema dell'ambiguità,* 214–41.

60 See, for example, Manuel De Sica, filmed interview on DVD of *Ladri di biciclette*, Multimedia San Paolo Srl, 2002.

61 Baldelli, *Cinema dell'ambiguità*, 233–4.

62 Mercader, *La mia vita con Vittorio De Sica*. I have taken the Italian text from Caldiron and De Sica, eds, *Ladri di biciclette di Vittorio De Sica*, 114. It is found in the French translation of Mercader, *Un amour obstiné*, 95–6.

63 Alfredo Guarini, 'Il neorealismo e l'industria,' *Cinema* 123 (15 December 1953) – his address to the Convegno di Parma sul neorealismo cinematografico, repr. in *Sul neorealismo: Testi e documenti (1939–1955)*, Quaderno informativo 59 (Pesaro: Mostra internazionale del Nuovo Cinema, 1974), 242–3.

64 De Sica's daughter's testimony in interview on DVD of *Ladri di biciclette*.

65 *Cinema senza tempo*, RAI documentary.

66 Vittorio De Sica, 'Abbiamo domandato a Vittorio De Sica perché fa un film dal "Ladro [*sic*] di biciclette,"' *La Fiera Letteraria* 3, 5 (6 February 1948), repr. in Caldiron, ed., *Vittorio De Sica*, 258–9.

67 Marisa Merlini, in Caldiron, ed., *Vittorio De Sica*, 211.

68 For further analysis and assessment of *Ladri di biciclette*, see *Neorealismo DOC: I film del 1948*; Agel, *Vittorio De Sica*; Alonge, *Vittorio De Sica. Ladri di biciclette*; Armes, *Patterns of Realism*; Baldelli, *Cinema dell'ambiguità*; Bazin, *Vittorio De Sica metteur en scène* and 'Voleur de bicyclette' in *Qu'est-ce que le cinéma?* or *What Is Cinema?*; Celli on *Ladri* in Bertellini, *The Cinema of Italy*; Borelli, *Neorealismo ieri e oggi*; Caldiron and Manuel De Sica, *Ladri di biciclette di Vittorio De Sica*; Caldiron, *Vittorio De Sica*; Curle and Snyder, *Vittorio de Sica: Contemporary Perspectives*; Darretta, *Vittorio De Sica: A Guide to References and Resources*; Governi, *Vittorio De Sica: Parlami d'amore Mariù*; Laura, *Ladri di biciclette*; Leprohon, *Vittorio De Sica*; Marcus, *Italian Film in the Light of Neorealism*; Masoni and Vecchi, *Zavattini cinema*; Micciché, *De Sica: Autore, regista, attore*; Mida, *Compagni di viaggio*; Moneti, 'Ladri di biciclette,' *Lezioni di neorealismo*, *Neorealismo fra tradizione e rivoluzione*, 'Teoria del cinema e analisi del film,' *Lessico zavattiniano*; Moscati, *Vittorio De Sica*; Nuzzi and Iemma, *De Sica & Zavattini*; Overbey, *Springtime in Italy*; Pecori, *Vittorio de Sica*; Pelzer, *Vittorio De Sica*; Sitney, *Vital Crises in Italian Cinema*; Spinazzola, *Cinema e pubblico* and 'Riesame del neorealismo'; and Zavattini, 'Alcune idee sul cinema,' 'Il neorealismo secondo me, and 'Tesi sul neorealismo.'

Bibliography

This bibliography lists the texts referred to in the chapters of the book, various sources for the readings recommended in the notes, and some texts that bear on matters touched upon in the book. This is not, therefore, a bibliography covering Italian neorealist cinema in general. To the best of my knowledge, no such comprehensive bibliography exists. The present volume is already large enough, and is not the place for such a bibliography. The final note to each chapter indicates suggested readings on topics covered by that chapter. Valuable bibliographical indications are to be found in the following books (full references are given below): Gian Piero Brunetta's *Storia del cinema italiano*, Alberto Farassino's *Neorealismo: Cinema italiano 1945–1949*, Lino Micciché's *Il neorealismo cinematografico italiano*, the collection (by various authors) *Il neorealismo e la critica: Materiali per una bibliografia*, Lorenzo Pellizzari's *Critica alla critica*, Bert Cardullo's *What Is Neorealism?* and Mark Shiel's *Italian Neorealism: Rebuilding the Cinematic City*. A full and up-to-date bibliographical data source is to be found in the footnotes of Giulia Fanara's *Pensare il neorealismo* (the volume has no bibliography).

Age [Agenore Incrocci]. *Scriviamo un film*. Parma: Pratiche, 1990.
Agel, Henri. *Vittorio De Sica*. Paris: Éditions Universitaires, 1955.
Alonge, Giaime. *Vittorio De Sica. Ladri di biciclette*. Turin: Lindau, 1997.
Altman, Rick. *Film/Genre*. London: British Film Institute, 1999.
Amaducci, Alessandro, ed. *Il sole sorge ancora: 50 anni di resistenza nel cinema italiano*. Turin: Regione Piemonte ANCR, 1994.
Amidei, Sergio. 'Testimonianza.' In *Anna Magnani, Incontri Internazionali d'Arte / Associazione Internazionale Anna Magnani / Museo Nazionale del Cinema*, edited by Patrizia Pistagnesi, 3. Rome, Milan: Fabbri, 1989.
Anderson, Lindsay. 'Paisà.' *Sequence* 2 (Winter 1947): 30–1.

Andreotti, Giulio. 'Attualità di La Pira.' In *30 giorni: Nella chiesa e nel mondo* 20, 10 (October 2002).
– 'Lettera aperta a De Sica, a proposito di Umberto D.' *Libertas* 7 (2–8 February 1952).
Andrew, Dudley. *André Bazin*. New York: Oxford University Press, 1978.
– *The Major Film Theories*. London, Oxford, New York: Oxford University Press, 1976.
ANICA. *Venti Anni dell'ANICA per il Cinema Italiano 1944–1964*. Rome: ANICA, 1964.
ANPI. *Cronologia della Resistenza Romana*. http://www.romacivica.net/anpiroma.
Antonioni, Michelangelo. *The Architecture of Vision: Writings and Interviews on Cinema*. Edited by Carlo di Carlo, Giorgio Tinazzi and Marga Cottino-Jones. New York: Marsilio Publishers, 1996.
– *Écrits 1936/1985*. Rome: Cinecittà International, 1991.
– *Entretiens et inédits 1950/1985*. Rome: Cinecittà International, 1992.
– 'Per un film sul fiume Po.' *Cinema* 68 (25 April 1939). Reprinted in *Sul neorealismo: Testi e documenti (1939–1955)*, 7–9. Quaderno informativo 59. Pesaro: Mostra Internazionale del Nuovo Cinema, 1974. Translated as *Concerning a Film and the River Po* in *Springtime in Italy: A Reader on Neo-Realism*, edited by David Overbey, 79–82. London: Talisman Books, 1978.
– 'La malattia dei sentimenti (Colloquio con Michelangelo Antonioni al Centro Sperimentale di Cinematografia).' *Bianco e Nero* 2–3 (February–March 1961).
– *Michelangelo Antonioni: Sul cinema*. Edited by Carlo di Carlo and Giorgio Tinazzi. Venice: Marsilio, 2004.
– *Quel bowling sul Tevere*. Turin: Einaudi, 1995 [1983]. Translated as *That Bowling Alley on the Tiber: Tales of a Director*. New York: Oxford University Press, 1986.
Aprà, Adriano. *Neorealismo d'appendice*. Florence: Guaraldi, 1976.
Aprà, Adriano, ed. Roma città aperta: *Il dopoguerra di Rossellini*. Rome: Cinecittà International, 1995.
– *Roma città aperta di Roberto Rossellini*. Rome: Assessorato alla Cultura del Comune di Roma, Agenzia Roma Città di Cinema, 1994.
– *Rosselliniana: Bibliografia internazionale. Dossier 'Paisà.'* Rome: Di Giacomo, 1987.
Aprà, Adriano, and Patrizia Pistagnesi, eds. *The Fabulous Thirties: Italian Cinema, 1929–1944*. Milan: Electa International, 1979.
Argentieri, Mino. *L'asse cinematografico Roma–Berlino*. Naples: Libreria Sapere, 1986.
– *La censura nel cinema italiano*. Rome: Editori Riuniti, 1974.

– *L'occhio del regime: Informazione e propaganda nel cinema del fascismo*. Florence: Vallecchi, 1979.

Aristarco, Guido. *Cinema fascista: Il prima e il dopo*. Bari: Dedalo, 1996.

– 'Marx, le cinéma et la critique de film.' Translated by Barthélemy Amengual, with a preface by George Lukacs. *Études cinématographiques* 88–92. Paris: Minard, 1972.

– *Miti e realtà del cinema italiano*. Milan: Il Saggiatore, 1961.

– 'La terra trema.' *Cinema* 32 (February 1950).

– *Storia delle teoriche del film*. Turin: Einaudi, 1951.

– 'È realismo.' *Cinema Nuovo* 4, 55 (25 March 1955). Reprinted in *Sul neorealismo: Testi e documenti (1939–1955)*, 273–6. Quaderno informativo 59. Pesaro: Mostra Internazionale del Nuovo Cinema, 1974.

Aristarco, Guido, ed. *Antologia di Cinema nuovo 1952–1958*, volume 1, *Neorealismo e vita nazionale*. Rimini, Florence: Guaraldi, 1975.

Aristarco, Guido, ed. *Sciolti dal giuramento*. Bari: Dedalo, 1981.

Armes, Roy. *Patterns of Realism: A Study of Italian Neo-Realism*. London: Tantivy, 1971; Cranbury, NJ: A.S. Barnes, 1971.

Asor Rosa, Alberto. 'Il neorealismo.' In *La cultura, Storia d'Italia. Dall'Unità a oggi*, volume 4, tome 2. Turin: Einaudi, 1973.

Assessorato alla Cultura del Comune di Roma. *La città del cinema. Produzione e lavoro nel cinema italiano 1930–1970*. Rome: Napoleone, 1979.

Astruc, Alexandre. 'Naissance d'une nouvelle avant-garde: La "caméra stylo."' *L'Écran français* 144 (30 March 1948). Reprinted in *Du stylo à la caméra ... et de la caméra au stylo. Écrits (1942–1984)*. Paris: Éditions de l'Archipel, 1992.

Auerbach, Erich. *Literary Language and Its Public in Late Latin Antiquity and in the Middle Ages*. Translated from German by Ralph Manheim. Princeton: Princeton University Press, 1993.

Ayfre, Amédée. 'Néo-réalisme et phénoménologie.' *Cahiers du Cinéma* 17 (November 1952). Reprinted in Amédée Ayfre. *Conversion aux images*, 209–22. Paris: Éditions du Cerf, 1964.

Bacilli, Renato. 'Introduzione.' In *Le opere di Cesare Zavattini*, 9–44. Milan: Bompiani, 1974.

Baldelli, Pio. *Cinema dell'ambiguità: Rossellini, De Sica e Zavattini, Fellini*. Rome: Samonà e Savelli, 1969.

– *Roberto Rossellini: I film 1936–1972*. Rome: La Nuova Sinistra–Samonà e Savelli, 1972.

Barbaro, Umberto. *Il Film*. Rome: Editori Riuniti, 1960.

– 'Importanza del realismo.' *Filmcritica* 4 (1951): 113–17.

– *Neorealismo e realismo*. Edited by Gian Piero Brunetta. 2 volumes. Rome: Editori Riuniti, 1976.

– *Servitù e grandezza del cinema*. Rome: Editori Riuniti, 1962.

Barbaro, Umberto, ed., *Il cinema e l'uomo moderno (Atti del Convegno di Perugia – 24–27 settembre 1949)*. Milan: Le edizioni sociali, 1950.

Bartolini, Luigi. *Ladri di biciclette*. Milan: Longanesi, 1984.

Bazin, André. 'Difesa di Rossellini.' *Cinema Nuovo* 4, 65 (25 August 1955).

– *Qu'est-ce que le cinéma?* Paris: Éditions du Cerf, 1975. Translated by Hugh Gray as *What Is Cinema?* 2 volumes. Berkeley: University of California Press, 1967, 1971.

– *Vittorio De Sica metteur en scène*. Parma: Guanda, 1953.

– 'Voleur de bicyclette.' *Esprit*, November 1949. Reprinted in Bazin, *Qu'est-ce que le cinéma?*

Ben-Ghiat, Ruth. *Fascist Modernities: Italy, 1922–1945*. Berkeley, London: University of California Press, 2001.

Bergala, Alain, ed. *Rossellini: Le cinéma révélé*. Paris: Flammarion, 1984.

Bergala, Alain, and Jean Narboni, eds. *Roberto Rossellini*. Paris: Cahiers du Cinéma, La Cinémathèque française, 1990.

Bernagozzo, Giampaolo. *Il cinema allo specchio: Appunti per una storia del documentario*. Bologna: Patron, 1985.

Bernardi, Sandro. 'I paesaggi nella "trilogia della guerra": realtà e metafora.' In *Storia del cinema italiano*, volume 7, 1945/1948, edited by Callisto Cosulich, 100–8. Venice-Rome: Marsilio–Edizioni di Bianco & Nero, 2003.

– 'Rossellini's Landscapes: Nature, Myth, History.' In *Roberto Rossellini, Magician of the Real*, edited by David Forgacs, Sarah Lutton, and Geoffrey Nowell-Smith, 50–63. London: British Film Institute, 2000.

Bernardini, Aldo, and Jean A. Gili. *Le cinéma italien de la prise de Rome (1905) à Rome ville ouverte (1945)*. Paris: Centre Georges Pompidou, 1986.

Bernardini, Aldo, and Jean A. Gili, eds. *Cesare Zavattini*. Paris, Bologna: Éditions du Centre Pompidou, Edizioni di Regione Emilia-Romagna, 1990.

Bertellini, Giorgio, ed. *The Cinema of Italy*. London: Wallflower Press, 2004.

Biarese, Cesare, and Aldo Tassone. *I film di Michelangelo Antonioni*. Rome: Gremese, 1985.

Bizzarri, Libero, and Libero Solaroli. *L'industria cinematografica italiana*. Florence: Parenti, 1958.

Blue, James. 'An Interview with Rossellini (Houston, 1972).' In *May 1–20, 1979: Rossellini*, brochure for a series presented by Joseph Papp at the Public Theater, New York, 1–20 May 1979. Translated as 'Il mio metodo di lavoro' in Roberto Rossellini, *Il mio metodo*, edited by Adriano Aprà, 407–18. Venice: Marsilio, 1987.

Bo, Carlo. *Inchiesta sul neorealismo*. Turin: ERI, 1951.

Bolzoni, Francesco. *Quando De Sica era Mister Brown*. Turin: ERI, 1984.

Bondanella, Peter. *The Cinema of Federico Fellini*. Princeton: Princeton University Press, 1992.
– *The Eternal City. Roman Images in the Modern World*. Chapel Hill: University of North Carolina Press, 1987.
– *The Films of Federico Fellini*. New York: Cambridge University Press, 2001.
– *The Films of Roberto Rossellini*. Cambridge, New York: Cambridge University Press, 1993.
– *Italian Cinema: From Neorealism to the Present*. New York: Ungar Press, 1982.
Borde, Raymond, and André Bouissy. *Le néorealisme italien: Une expérience de cinéma social*. Lausanne: Cinémathèque Suisse, 1960.
Borelli, Sauro, ed. *Neorealismo ieri e oggi: Il fantasma della realtà*. Florence: La casa Usher, 1990.
Brunetta, Gian Piero. *Cent'anni di cinema italiano*. Roma, Bari: Laterza, 1995.
– *Cinema italiano tra le due guerre: Fascismo e politica cinematografica*. Milan: Mursia, 1975.
– *Cinema storia resistenza: 1944–1985*. Milan: Franco Angeli, 1987.
– *Intellettuali, cinema e propaganda tra le due guerre: I pionieri, Canudo, Luciani, Pirandello, Barbaro, Chiarini, il film fascista*. Bologna: Patròn, 1973.
– *Storia del cinema italiano*. 4 volumes. Rome: Editori Riuniti, 1993.
– *Umberto Barbaro e l'idea di neorealismo (1930–1943)*. Padua: Liviana, 1969.
Brunetta, Gian Piero, ed. *Identità italiana e identità europea nel cinema italiano*. Turin: Edizioni della Fondazione Giovanni Agnelli, 1996.
– *Letteratura e cinema*. Bologna: Zanichelli, 1976.
– *Neorealismo e realismo*. Rome: Editori Riuniti, 1976.
Brunette, Peter. *Roberto Rossellini*. New York, Oxford: Oxford University Press, 1987.
Bruni, David. *Roberto Rossellini: Roma città aperta*. Turin: Lindau, 2006.
Bruni, David and Veronica Pravadelli, eds. *Studi viscontiani*. Venice: Marsilio, 1997.
Bruno, Edoardo. *Teorie del realismo*. Rome: Bulzoni, 1977.
Bruno, Edoardo, ed. *Roberto Rossellini: Il cinema, la televisione, la storia, la critica. Atti del Convegno del 16–23 settembre 1978*. Città di Sanremo, 1980.
Caldiron, Orio, ed. *Il lungo viaggio del cinema italiano: Antologia di "Cinema" 1936–1943*. Padua: Marsilio, 1965.
– *Vittorio De Sica*. Bianco e Nero monograph 22. Rome: Edizioni dell'Ateneo e Bizzarri, 1975.
Caldiron, Orio, and Manuel De Sica, eds. *Ladri di biciclette di Vittorio De Sica: Testimonianze, interventi, sopralluoghi*. Rome: Editoriale Patheon, 1997.
Calvino, Italo. 'Prefazione.' In 1964 edition, later (1993) entitled 'Presentazione,' of *Il sentiero dei nidi di ragno*. 1st edition, Turin, Einaudi – 'I coralli' –

1947; 2nd edition, Turin: Einaudi, 1964. Edition used for quotation in this volume: Milan: Mondadori, 1993 (2002 printing).

Campari, Roberto. 'America, cinema e mass-media nel neorealismo italiano.' *Cinema & Cinema* 4, 10 (January-March 1977).

Cannella, Mario. 'Ideology and Aesthetic Hypotheses in the Criticism of Neorealism.' *Screen* 14, 4 (Winter 1973/4).

Cannistraro, Philip V. *La fabbrica del consenso: Fascismo e mass media*. Roma, Bari: Laterza, 1975.

Canziani, Alfonso. *Gli anni del neorealismo*. Florence: La Nuova Italia, 1977.

Cappabianca, Alessandro, and Michele Mancini. *Ombre urbane: Set e città dal cinema muto agli anni '80*. Rome: Kappa, 1982.

Caramel, Luciano. *Realismi: Arti figurative, letteratura e cinema in Italia dal 1943 al 1953*. Milan: Electa, 2001.

Cardullo, Bert. *What Is Neorealism? A Critical English-Language Bibliography of Italian Cinematic Neorealism*. London, Lanham, MD: University Press of America, 1991.

Carrano, Patrizia. *La Magnani: Il romanzo di una vita*. Milan: Rizzoli, 1982.

Casadio, Gianfranco. *Adultere fredifraghe innocenti: La donna del 'neorealismo popolare' nel cinema italiano degli anni cinquanta*. Ravenna: Longo, 1990.

Casetti, Francesco. *Teorie del cinema, 1945–1990*. Milan: Bompiani, 1993. Translated by Francesca Chiostri and Elizabeth Gard Bartolini-Salimbeni with Thomas Kelso as *Theories of Cinema, 1945–1995*. Austin: University of Texas Press, 1999.

Casetti, Francesco, and Federico di Chio. *Analisi del film*. Milan: Bompiani, 1990.

Cassac, Michel, ed. *Littérature et cinéma néoréalistes: Réalisme, réel et représentation*. Paris: L'Harmattan, 2004.

Castello, Giulio Cesare. *Il cinema neorealistico italiano*. Turin: ERI, 1962.

Cecchi D'Amico, Suso. *Storie di cinema (e d'altro) raccontate a Margherita D'Amico*. Milan: Garzanti, 1996.

Celli, Carlo. 'Ladri di biciclette.' In *The Cinema of Italy*, edited by Giorgio Bertellini, 43–50. London, New York: Wallflower Press, 2004.

Chabrol, Claude. 'Lettre sur Rossellini.' *Cahiers du Cinéma* 46 (April 1955).

Chiarini, Luigi. *Arte e tecnica del film*. Bari: Laterza, 1962.

– *Cinema e film: Storia e problemi*. Rome: Bulzoni, 1972.

– *Cinema quinto potere*. Bari: Laterza, 1954.

– *Cinematografo*. Rome: Cremonese, 1935.

– *Cinque capitoli sul film*. Rome: Edizioni italiane, 1941.

– *Il film nella battaglia delle idee*. Milan, Rome: Fratelli Bocca, 1954.

– 'Tradisce il neorealismo.' *Cinema Nuovo* 4, 55 (25 March 1955). Reprinted in

Sul neorealismo: Testi e documenti (1939–1955), 271–2. Quaderno informativo 59. Pesaro: Mostra Internazionale del Nuovo Cinema, 1974.

Chiarini, Luigi, and Umberto Barbaro, eds. *Problemi del film.* Rome: Edizioni di Bianco e Nero, 1939.

Chicco Vitizzai, Elisabetta, ed. *Il neorealismo: Antifascismo e popolo nella letteratura dagli anni Trenta agli anni Cinquanta.* Turin: Paravia, 1977.

Chinnici, Giuseppe. *Cinema, chiesa e movimento cattolico italiano.* Rome: Aracne, 2003.

Chiti, Roberto, and Roberto Pioppi, compilers. *Dizionario del cinema italiano: I film,* volume 2, *Dal 1945 al 1959.* Rome: Gremese, 1991.

Le cinéma et l'état: Rapport de la Commission de la Culture et de l'Éducation et Documents du Colloque, Lisbon, 14–16 June 1978. Strasbourg: Conseil de l'Europe, 1979.

La cinepresa e la storia: (fascismo: antifascismo guerra resistenza italiana). Milan: Edizioni scolastiche Bruno Mondadori, 1985.

La città del cinema: Produzione e lavoro nel cinema italiano 1930–1970. Rome: Napoleone, 1979.

Cirillo, Silvana, ed. *Zavattini parla di Zavattini.* Rome: Bulzoni, 2003.

Conley, Tom. 'Facts and Figures in History. "Paisan."' In *Film Hieroglyphs: Ruptures in Classical Cinema,* 102–129. Minneapolis, Oxford: University of Minnesota Press, 1991.

Contaldo, Francesco, and Franco Fanelli, *L'affare cinema: Multinazionali produttori e politici nella crisi del cinema italiano.* Milan: Feltrinelli, 1979.

Corsi, Barbara. *Con qualche dollaro in meno: Storia economica del cinema italiano.* Rome: Editori Riuniti, 2001.

Corti, Maria. *Il viaggio testuale.* Turin: Einaudi, 1978.

Curle, Howard, and Stephen Snyder, eds. *Vittorio de Sica: Contemporary Perspectives.* Toronto: University of Toronto Press, 2000.

Curtius, Ernst Robert. *European Literature and the Latin Middle Ages.* London: Routledge & Kegan Paul, 1953.

Dalle Vacche, Angela. *The Body in the Mirror: Shapes of History in Italian Cinema.* Princeton: Princeton University Press, 1992.

D'Amico, Masolino. *La commedia all'italiana: Il cinema comico in Italia dal 1945 al 1975.* Milan: Mondadori, 1985.

Darretta, John. *Vittorio De Sica: A Guide to References and Resources.* Boston: G.K. Hall, 1983.

Debenedetti, Giacomo. *Verga e il naturalismo.* Milan: Garzanti, 1976.

Debreczeni, François. 'Origines et évolution du néoréalisme.' In *Le Néoréalisme Italien, bilan de la critique,* 20–54. *Études cinématographiques* 32–5. Paris: Lettres modernes, 1964.

Deleuze, Gilles. *L'image-mouvement*. Paris: Minuit, 1983. Translated as *The Movement-Image*. London: Athlone Press, 1986.
– *L'image-temps*. Paris: Minuit, 1985. Translated as *Time Image*. London: Athlone Press, 1989.
Dell'Arco, Maurizio Fagiolo, and Claudia Terenzi, eds. *Arte, cronaca e cultura dal neorealismo alla dolce vita*. Milan: Skira, 2001.
Della Casa, Stefano. *Capitani coraggiosi: Produttori italiani 1945–1975*. Milan: Electa, 2003.
Della Volpe, Galvano. *Verosimile filmico e altri scritti di estetica*. Rome: La nuova sinistra, 1971.
De Masi, Stefano. *Rossellini*. Rome: Gremese, 1988.
De Santi, Gualtiero. *Vittorio De Sica*. Milan: Il castoro, 2003.
De Santis, Giuseppe. 'Per un paesaggio italiano.' *Cinema* 116 (25 April 1941). Reprinted in *Sul neorealismo: Testi e documenti (1939–1955)*, 10–13. Quaderno informativo 59. Pesaro: Mostra Internazionale del Nuovo Cinema, 1974.
– *Verso il neorealismo: Un critico cinematografico degli anni Quaranta*. Edited by Callisto Cosulich. Rome: Bulzoni, 1982.
De Sica, Manuel. Filmed interview on DVD of *Ladri di biciclette*. Multimedia San Paolo Srl, 2002.
De Sica, Vittorio. 'Abbiamo domandato a Vittorio De Sica perché fa un film dal "Ladro [*sic*] di biciclette."' *La Fiera Letteraria* 3, 5 (6 February 1948).
– 'Gli anni più belli della mia vita.' *Il Tempo* 23 December 1954.
– *Bicycle Thieves: A Film by Vittorio de Sica*. Translated by Simon Hartog. London: Lorrimer, 1968.
– 'Lettera.' *L'Unità*, 27 February 1956.
– *Lettere dal set: Vittorio De Sica*. Edited by Emi De Sica and Giancarlo Governi. Milan: SugarCo Edizioni, 1987.
De Sica, Vittorio, and Cesare Zavattini. *Miracle in Milan*. New York: Orion, 1968.
De Vincenti, Giorgio. 'Cesare Zavattini: Uomo totale e cinema del frammento.' In *Il concetto di modernità nel cinema*, 157–75. Parma: Pratiche, 1993.
– *Il concetto di modernità nel cinema*. Parma: Pratiche, 1993.
– 'Sperimentalismo.' In *Lessico zavattiniano*, edited by Guglielmo Moneti, 253–60. Venice: Marsilio, 1992.
Dietro lo schermo. Cinecittà 3. Venice: Marsilio, 1988.
Ellwood, David W., and Gian Piero Brunetta, eds. *Hollywood in Europa: Industria, politica, pubblico del cinema 1945–1960*. Florence: La Casa Usher, 1991.
Elsaesser, Thomas. 'Tales of Sound and Fury: Observations on the Family Melodrama.' *Monogram* 4 (1972): 2–15. Reprinted in *Home Is where the Heart*

Is: Studies in Melodrama and the Woman's Film, edited by Christine Gledhill, 42–69. London: British Film Institute, 1987.

Falaschi, Giovanni. *Realtà e retorica: La letteratura del neorealismo italiano*. Messina, Florence: D'Anna, 1977.

– *La Resistenza armata nella narrativa italiana*. Turin: Einaudi, 1976.

Faldini, Franca, and Goffredo Fofi, eds. *L'avventurosa storia del cinema italiano raccontata dai suoi protagonisti 1935–1959*. Milan: Feltrinelli, 1979.

Fanara, Giulia. *Pensare il neorealismo: Percorsi attraverso il neorealismo cinematografico italiano*. Rome: Lithos, 2000.

Fantoni Minnella, Maurizio. *Non riconciliati: Politica e società nel cinema italiano dal Neorealismo a oggi*. Turin: UTET, 2004.

Farassino, Alberto. *Giuseppe De Santis*. Milan: Moizzi, 1978.

– *Lux Film*. Rome: Fondazione Pesaro Nuovo Cinema, 2000.

– 'Neorealismo, storia e geografia.' In *Neorealismo: Cinema italiano 1945–1949*, edited by Alberto Farassino, 21–44. Turin: EDT, 1989.

Farassino, Alberto, ed. *Neorealismo: Cinema italiano 1945–1949*. Turin: EDT, 1989.

Farassino, Alberto, and Tatti Sanguineti. *Lux Film: Esthétique et système d'un studio italien*. Locarno: Éditions du Festival international du film de Locarno, 1984.

Fellini, Federico. *Fare un film*. Turin: Einaudi, 1980.

Fernandez, Dominique. *Il mito dell'America negli intellettuali del 1930–1950*. Caltanissetta, Rome: Sciascia, 1969.

Ferrara, Giuseppe. *Il nuovo cinema italiano*. Florence: Le Monnier, 1957.

– 'L'opera di Roberto Rossellini.' In *Rossellini, Antonioni, Bunuel*, edited by Piero Mechini and Roberto Salvatori, 19–45. Venice: Marsilio, 1973.

Ferraù, Alessandro, and Weiss Ruffilli. 'Il cimitero delle illusioni perdute.' *Cinespettacolo* 5, 2 (February 1950).

Ferretti, Gian Carlo, ed. *Introduzione al neorealismo*. Rome: Editori Riuniti, 1974.

Finney, Angus. *The State of European Cinema: A New Dose of Reality*. London: Cassell, 1996.

Fofi, Goffredo, Morando Morandini and Gianni Volpi. *Storia del cinema*. Volume 2. *Dal neorealismo alla guerra fredda*. Milan: Garzanti, 1990.

Forgacs, David. *Italian Culture in the Industrial Era, 1880–1980: Cultural Industries, Politics, and the Public*. Manchester: University of Manchester Press, 1990.

– *Rome Open City*. London: British Film Institute, 2000.

– 'Space, Rhetoric, and the Divided City in *Roma città aperta*.' In *Roberto Rossellini's* Rome Open City, edited by Sidney Gottlieb, 106–30. Cambridge: Cambridge University Press, 2004.

Forgacs, David, Sarah Lutton, and Geoffrey Nowell-Smith, eds. *Roberto Ros-sellini: Magician of the Real*. London: British Film Institute, 2000.

Freddi, Luigi. *Il cinema*. 2 volumes. Rome: L'Arnia, 1949.

Frye, Northrop. *Anatomy of Criticism*. Princeton: Princeton University Press, 1957.

Furno, Mariella, and Renzo Renzi, eds. *Il neorealismo nel fascismo: Giuseppe De Santis e la critica cinematografica 1941–1943*. Bologna: Edizioni della Tipografia Compositori, 1984.

Gaiardoni, Laura, ed. *Mario Serandrei, gli scritti, un film, Giorni di gloria*. Rome, Milan: Scuola Nazionale del Cinema, Il castoro, 1998.

Gallagher, Tag. *The Adventures of Roberto Rossellini: His Life and Films*. New York: Da Capo Press, 1998.

– 'NR = MC^2: Rossellini, "Neo-realism" and Croce.' *Film History* 2, 1 (1988), 87–97.

Gambetti, Giacomo. *Zavattini mago e tecnico*. Rome: Ente dello spettacolo, 1986.

Gentile, Giovanni. 'Prefazione.' In Luigi Chiarini, *Cinematografo*. Rome: Cremonese, 1935.

Germani, Sergio. *Camerini*. Florence: La Nuova Italia, 1980.

Giannelli, Enrico. *Il cinema europeo*. Rome: ICAS Edizioni dell'Ateneo, 1953.

– *Economia cinematografica*. Rome: Reanda, 1956.

Gili, Jean. *Le cinéma italien*. Paris: Union Générale, 1978.

Ginsborg, Paul. *A History of Contemporary Italy: Society and Politics, 1943–1988*. Harmondsworth: Penguin Books, 1990.

– *Italy and Its Discontents: Family, Civil Society, State 1980–2001*. Harmondsworth: Penguin Books, 2001.

Gottlieb, Sidney, ed. *Roberto Rossellini's Rome Open City*. Cambridge: Cambridge University Press, 2004.

Governi, Giancarlo. *Vittorio De Sica: Parlami d'amore Mariù*. Rome: Gremese, 1993.

Grandi, Maurizio. *Abiti nuziali e biglietti di banca*. Rome: Bulzoni, 1986.

Grant, Damian. *Realism*. London: Methuen, 1970.

Gray, John. 'Soho Square and Bennett Park: The Documentary Movement in Britain in the 1930s.' Latrobe University website, http://www.latrobe.edu.au/screeningthepast/firstrelease/fr0799/jgfr7a.htm.

Gromo, Mario. *Cinema italiano 1903–1953*. Milan: Mondadori, 1954.

Gruppo 'Cinegramma' (Francesco Casetti, Alberto Farassino, Aldo Grasso, Tatti Sanguineti). 'Neorealismo e cinema italiano degli anni '30.' In *Il neorealismo cinematografico italiano. Atti del convegno della X Mostra Internazionale del Nuovo Cinema*, edited by Lino Miccichè, 331–85. Venice: Marsilio, 1975.

Guarini, Alfredo. 'Il neorealismo e l'industria.' *Cinema* 123 (15 December 1953).

Address to the Convegno di Parma sul neorealismo cinematografico. Reprinted in *Sul neorealismo: Testi e documenti (1939–1955)*, 240–3. Quaderno informativo 59. Pesaro: Mostra Internazionale del Nuovo Cinema, 1974.

Guarner, J.L. *Roberto Rossellini*. London: Studio Vista, 1970.

Guback, Thomas H. *The International Film Industry: Western Europe and America since 1945*. Bloomington: Indiana University Press, 1969.

Gundle, Stephen. *Between Hollywood and Moscow: The Italian Communists and the Challenge of Mass Culture, 1943–1991*. Durham, NC: Duke University Press, 2000.

Günsberg, Maggie. *Italian Cinema: Gender and Genre*. Basingstoke, New York: Palgrave Macmillan, 2005.

Harvey, Stephen. *Vittorio De Sica*. Rome: Ministero del Turismo e Dello Spettacolo, 1991.

Hay, James. *Popular Film Culture in Fascist Italy: The Passing of the Rex*. Bloomington: University of Indiana Press, 1987.

Hewitt, Nicholas, ed. *The Culture of Reconstruction: European Literature: Thought and Film, 1945–50*. London: Macmillan, 1989.

Hillier, Jim, ed. *Cahiers du Cinéma*, volume 1, *The 1950s: Neo-Realism, Hollywood, New Wave*. London: Routledge and Kegan Paul, British Film Institute, 1985.

Hovald, Patrice G. *Le néoréalisme italien et ses créateurs*. Paris: Éditions du Cerf, 1959.

Isaia, Paolo, and Maria Pia Melandri. *Jolanda e Rossellini: Memorie indiscrete* (a documentary film).

Ivaldi, Nedo, ed. *La resistenza nel cinema italiano del dopoguerra: Quello che scrissero allora*. Rome: Unitalia, 1970.

Jarratt, Vernon. *The Italian Cinema*. London: Falcon Press, 1951; New York: Arno Press, 1972.

Kezich, Tullio. *Fellini*. Milan: Rizzoli, 1988.

– 'Servitore di due padroni.' In *De Sica: Autore, regista, attore*, edited by Lino Micciché, 3–17. Venice: Marsilio, 1992.

– *Su La Dolce Vita con Federico Fellini*. Venice: Marsilio, 1996.

Koval, Francis. 'Interview with De Sica.' *Sight and Sound* 19, 2 (April 1950).

Kracauer, Siegfried. *The Nature of Film: The Redemption of Physical Reality*. London: Denis Dobson, 1961.

Landy, Marcia. *Fascism in Film: The Italian Commercial Cinema 1931–1943*. Princeton: Princeton University Press, 1986.

– *Italian Film*. New York: Cambridge University Press, 2000.

Laura, Ernesto G. *Ladri di biciclette*. Radar: Padua, 1969.

Leprohon, Pierre. *Le cinéma italien: Histoire, chronologie, biographies, filmographies, documents, images*. Paris: Seghers, 1966. Translated by Roger Greaves and Oliver Stallybrass as *The Italian Cinema*. London: Secker and Warburg, 1972.

– *Vittorio De Sica*. Paris: Seghers, 1966.

Liehm, Mira. *Passion and Defiance: Film in Italy from 1942 to the Present*. Berkeley, Los Angeles: University of California Press, 1984.

Lizzani, Carlo. *Attraverso il Novecento*. Turin: Lindau, 1998.

– *Il cinema italiano*. Florence: Parenti, 1953.

– *Il cinema italiano 1895–1979*. 2 volumes. Rome: Editori Riuniti, 1979.

– *Riso amaro: Un film diretto da Giuseppe De Santis*. Rome: Officina, 1978.

– *Storia del cinema italiano*. Florence: Parenti, 1961.

Lyons, Robert J. *Michelangelo Antonioni's Neorealism: A World View*. New York: Arno Press, 1976.

MacCabe, Colin. 'Realism and the Cinema: Notes on Some Brechtian Theses.' *Screen* 15, 2 (1974): 7–27.

Magrelli, Enrico, ed. *Cinecittà 2: Sull'industria cinematografica italiana*. Venice: Marsilio, 1986.

Maio, Barbara, and Christian Uva. *L'estetica dell'ibrido: Il cinema contemporaneo tra reale e digitale*. Rome: Bulzoni, 2003.

Mamber, Stephen. *Cinéma Vérité in America: Studies in Uncontrolled Documentary*. Cambridge, MA, London: MIT Press, 1974.

Manacorda, Giuliano. *Storia della letteratura italiana contemporanea (1940–1965)*. Rome: Editori Riuniti, 1970.

Mancini, Elaine. *Struggles of the Italian Film Industry during Fascism, 1930–1935*. Ann Arbor: UMI Research Press, 1985.

Mann, Klaus. 'Sette dagli U.S.A.' Translation from the original English typescript in *Il dopoguerra di Rossellini*, edited by Adriano Aprà, 77–89. Rome: Cinecittà International, 1995.

Marcarini, Elena. 'Distribution of Italian Films in the British and American Markets 1945–1995.' PhD diss., University of Reading, 2001.

Marcus, Millicent. *Italian Film in the Light of Neorealism*. Princeton: Princeton University Press, 1986.

– 'National Identity by Means of Montage in Roberto Rossellini's *Paisan*.' In Marcus, *After Fellini: National Cinema in the Postmodern Age*. Baltimore: Johns Hopkins University Press, 2002.

Masi, Stefano. *Giuseppe De Santis*. Florence: La Nuova Italia, 1981.

– *I film di Roberto Rossellini*. Rome: Gremese, 1987.

Masoni, Tullio, and Paolo Vecchi. *Zavattini cinema*. Reggio Emilia: Analisi, 1988.

Masoni, Tullio, and Paolo Vecchi, eds. *Cinenotizie in poesia e prosa: Zavattini e la non-fiction*. Turin: Lindau, 2000.

Materiali sul cinema italiano degli anni '50. Volume 2. Pesaro quaderno 74bis. Pesaro: Mostra internazionale del nuovo cinema, 1978.

Maurizio Giammusso. *Vita di Rossellini.* Rome: Elleumultimedia, 2004.

Mauro, Walter. *Realtà e ideologia: Antologia del realismo italiano.* Florence: Alighieri, 1993.

Mechini, Piero, and Roberto Salvatori, eds. *Rossellini, Antonioni, Bunuel.* Venice: Marsilio, 1973.

Meder, Thomas. 'Klaus Mann e "Paisà."' In *Il dopoguerra di Rossellini,* edited by Adriano Aprà, 74–6. Rome: Cinecittà International, 1995.

– '"Paisà" ritrovato.' *Bianco e Nero* 59, 4 (October–December 1998), 113–27.

– *Vom Sichtbarmachen der Geschichte: Das italienische 'Neorealismus,' Rossellinis 'Paisà' und Klaus Mann.* Munich: Trickster, 1993.

Mercader, Maria. *La mia vita con Vittorio De Sica.* Milan: Mondadori, 1978. Translated into French as *Un amour obstiné: Ma vie avec Vittorio De Sica.* Paris: Lherminier, 1981.

Merlak, Fulvio, Claudio Pastrone, and Giorgio Tani, eds. *Gli anni del neorealismo: Tendenze della fotografia italiana.* Turin: FIAF, 2002.

Micciché, Lino. 'Il neorealismo: Quando è finito, quello che resta.' In *Il neorealismo cinematografico italiano. Atti del convegno della X Mostra Internazionale del Nuovo Cinema,* edited by Lino Micciché, 98–105. Venice: Marsilio, 1975.

– 'Sul neorealismo, oggi.' In *Il neorealismo cinematografico italiano,* edited by Lino Micciché, 2nd edition, ix–xxiii. Venice: Marsilio, 1999.

– *Visconti e il neorealismo: Ossessione, La terra trema, Bellissima.* Venice: Marsilio, 1990.

Micciché, Lino, ed. *De Sica: autore, regista, attore.* Venice: Marsilio, 1992.

– *Il neorealismo cinematografico italiano. Atti del convegno della X Mostra Internazionale del Nuovo Cinema.* Venice: Marsilio, 1975.

– *La terra trema di Luchino Visconti: analisi di un capolavoro.* Turin: Lindau, 1993.

– *'Sciuscià' di Vittorio De Sica: Letture, documenti, testimonianze.* Turin: Lindau, 1994.

Mida, Massimo. *Compagni di viaggio: Colloqui con i maestri del cinema italiano.* Turin: ERI, 1988.

– *Roberto Rossellini.* Parma: Guanda, 1961.

– 'Si gira in convento.' *Film d'Oggi,* 27 July 1946. Reprinted in *Rosselliniana: Bibliografia internazionale. Dossier 'Paisà,'* edited by Adriano Aprà, 141–3. Rome: Di Giacomo, 1987.

Mida, Massimo, and Lorenzo Quaglietti. *Dai telefoni bianchi al neorealismo.* Rome, Bari: Laterza, 1980.

Milward, Alan. *The Reconstruction of Western Europe 1945–51.* London: Routledge, 1987.

Misler, Nicoletta. *La via italiana al realismo: La politica culturale artistica del P.C.I. dal 1944 al 1956*. Milan: Mazzotta, 1973.

Moe, Nelson. 'Naples '44 / "Tammurriata nera" / *Ladri di biciclette*.' In *Italy and America, 1943–44: Italian, American and Italian-American Experiences of the Liberation of the Mezzogiorno*, edited by John A. Davis, 433–54. Naples: Istituto Italiano per gli Studi Filosofici, Edizioni La città del Sole, 1997.

Moneti, Guglielmo. '*Ladri di biciclette*.' In *De Sica: Autore, regista, attore*, edited by Lino Micciché, 276–85. Venice: Marsilio, 1992.

– *Lezioni di neorealismo*. Siena: Nuova immagine, 1998.

– *Neorealismo fra tradizione e rivoluzione: Visconti, De Sica e Zavattini verso nuove esperienze cinematografiche della realtà*. Siena: Nuova immagine, 1999.

– 'Teoria del cinema e analisi del film: Visione della realtà e realtà della visione in *Paisà* e *Ladri di biciclette*.' In *La visione e il concetto: Scritti in omaggio a Maurizio Grande*, edited by Roberto De Gaetano, 59–69. Rome: Bulzoni, 1998.

Moneti, Guglielmo, ed. *Lessico zavattiniano*. Venice: Marsilio, 1992.

Montanelli, Indro. '*Roma città aperta*.' *Corriere d'Informazione*, 24 October 1945.

Moscati, Italo. *Anna Magnani: Vita, amori e carriera di un'attrice che guarda dritto negli occhi*. Rome: Rai Radiotelevisione Italiana, Ediesse, 2003.

– *Vittorio De Sica: Vitalità, passione e talento in un'Italia dolceamara*. Rome: Rai-ERI, Ediesse, 2004.

Muscio, Giuliana. '*Paisà*.' In *The Cinema of Italy*, edited by Giorgio Bertellini, 31–40. London, New York: Wallflower Press, 2004.

– *Piccole italie, grandi schermi: Scambi cinematografici tra Italia e Stati Uniti 1895–1945*. Rome: Bulzoni, 2004.

– *Scrivere il film*. Rome: Savelli, 1981.

Neale, Steve. *Genre and Hollywood*. London: Routledge, 2000.

Sul neorealismo: Testi e documenti (1939–1955). Quaderno informativo 59. Pesaro: Mostra Internazionale del Nuovo Cinema Pesaro, 1974.

Il neorealismo e la critica: Materiali per una bibliografia. Pesaro quaderno 57. Pesaro: Mostra Internazionale del Nuovo Cinema, 1974.

Neorealismo DOC: I film del 1948. Turin: Archivio nazionale cinematografico della Resistenza, Regione Piemonte, 1995.

Neorealismo poetiche e polemiche. Milan: Il Saggiatore, 1980.

Nichols, Bill. *Representing Reality: Issues and Concepts in Documentary*. Indianapolis: Indiana University Press, 1991.

Nowell-Smith, Geoffrey. *Luchino Visconti*. London: Secker & Warburg, 1973. 3rd edition: London: British Film Institute, 2003.

– 'Minnelli and Melodrama.' *Screen* 18, 2 (1977): 113–18. Reprinted in *Home Is where the Heart Is: Studies in Melodrama and the Woman's Film*, edited by Christine Gledhill. London: British Film Institute, 1987.

Nowell-Smith, Geoffrey, and Steven Ricci, eds. *Hollywood and Europe*. London: British Film Institute, 1998.

Nuovi materiali sul cinema italiano 1929–1943. Volume 1. Quaderno informativo 72. Ancona: Mostra Internazionale del Nuovo Cinema Pesaro, 1976.

Nuzzi, Paolo, and Ottavio Iemma. *De Sica & Zavattini: Parliamo tanto di noi*. Rome: Editori Riuniti, 1997.

Oldrini, Guido. *Problemi di teoria e storia del cinema*. Naples: Guida, 1976.

Olivieri, Angelo. *L'imperatore in platea: I grandi del cinema italiano dal Marc'Aurelio allo schermo*. Bari: Dedalo, 1986.

Overbey, David, ed. *Springtime in Italy: A Reader on Neo-realism*. London: Talisman, 1978; Hamden, CT: Archon Books, 1978.

Parigi, Stefania, ed. *Paisà: Analisi del film*. Venice: Marsilio, 2005.

Parisi, Antonio. *Il cinema di Giuseppe De Santis tra passione e ideologia*. Rome: Cadmo editore, 1983.

Pasolini, Pier Paolo. *Empirismo eretico*. Milan: Garzanti, 1971.

Pecori, Franco. *Vittorio de Sica*. Florence: La Nuova Italia, 1980.

Peirce, Charles Sanders. *Collected Papers*. Volumes 2 and 4. Cambridge, MA: Harvard University Press, 1932, 1934.

Pellizzari, Lorenzo. *Critica alla critica: Contributi a una storia della critica cinematografica italiana*. Rome: Bulzoni, 1999.

Pelzer, Helmuth. *Vittorio De Sica*. Berlin: Henschenverlag, 1964.

Pirro, Ugo. *Celluloide*. Turin: Einaudi, 1983.

Politica e cultura nel dopoguerra: Con una cronologia 1929–1964 e con una antologia. Quaderno informativo 56. Pesaro: Mostra Internazionale del Nuovo Cinema Pesaro, 1974.

Prédal, René, ed. 'Le néorealisme italien.' Monographic issue of *CinémAction* 70 (1994).

Prencipe, Fabio, ed. *In fondo al mare ... Il cinema di Francesco De Robertis*. Modugno (Bari): Edizioni dal Sud, 1996.

Puttnam, David, with Neil Watson. *The Undeclared War: The Struggle for Control of the World's Film Industry*. London: HarperCollins, 1997.

Quaglietti, Lorenzo. *Il cinema italiano del dopoguerra: Leggi, produzione, distribuzione, esercizio*. Quaderno informativo 58. Pesaro: Mostra Internazionale del Nuovo Cinema, 1974.

– *Storia economico-politica del cinema italiano 1945–1980*. Rome: Editori Riuniti, 1980.

Questerbert, Marie-Christine. *Les scénaristes italiens: 50 ans d'écriture cinématographique*. Renens: Les 5 Continents, Hatier, 1988.

Quintana, Angel. *El cine italiano 1942–1961. Del neorealismo a la modernidad*. Barcelona: Prádos, 1997.

– *Roberto Rossellini*. Madrid: Cátedra, 1995.

Ranvaud, Don, ed. *Roberto Rossellini*. British Film Institute Dossier 8. London: British Film Institute, 1981.

Re, Lucia. *Calvino and the Age of Neorealism: Fables of Estrangement*. Stanford: Stanford University Press, 1990.

Redi, Riccardo. *La Cines: Storia di una Casa di produzione italiana*. Rome: CNC, 1991.

Redi, Riccardo, ed. *Cinema italiano sotto il fascismo*. Venice: Marsilio, 1979.

Reich, Jacqueline, and Piero Garofalo, eds. *Re-Viewing Fascism, Italian Cinema, 1922–1943*. Bloomington: Indiana University Press, 2002.

Renov, Michael, ed. *Theorizing Documentary*. New York, London: Routledge, 1993.

Renzi, Renzo. *Da Starace ad Antonioni*. Padua: Marsilio, 1964.

Repetto, Monica, and Carlo Tagliabue, eds. *Vecchio cinema paradiso: Il cinema italiano all'estero*. Milan: Editrice Il Castoro, 2001.

Restivo, Angelo. *The Cinema of Economic Miracles: Visuality and Modernisation in the Italian Art Film*. Durham NC, London: Duke University Press, 2002.

La resistenza nel cinema italiano del dopoguerra. Rome: Unione nazionale per la diffusione del film italiano all'estero, 1970.

Rinaudo, Fabio. *Roma città aperta: Un film di Roberto Rossellini*. Padua: Radar, 1969.

Rivette, Jacques. 'Lettre sur Rossellini.' *Cahiers du Cinéma* 46 (1955): 14–24. Translated as 'Letter on Rossellini.' In *Cahiers du Cinéma*, Volume 1, *The 1950s: Neorealism, Hollywood, New Wave*, edited by Jim Hillier, 192–202. London: Routledge and Kegan Paul, British Film Institute, 1985.

Rocca, Carmelo. *Le leggi del cinema: Il contesto italiano nelle politiche comunitarie*. Milan: Franco Angeli, 2003.

Rocchio, Vincent F. *Cinema of Anxiety: A Psychoanalysis of Italian Neorealism*. Austin: University of Texas Press, 1999.

Roncoroni, Stefano. *Roberto Rossellini, La trilogia della guerra*. Bologna: Cappelli, 1972.

– *La storia di Roma città aperta*. Bologna / Genoa: Cineteca comunale / Le Mani, 2006.

Roncoroni, Stefano, ed. *Quasi un'autobiografia – Roberto Rossellini*. Milan: Mondadori, 1987.

Rondi, Brunello. 'Il capolavoro del neorealismo: "Paisà," Analisi.' In *Il neorealismo italiano* 139–59. Parma: Guanda, 1956.

– *Il neorealismo italiano*. Parma: Guanda, 1956.

Rondolino, Gianni. *Roberto Rossellini*. Florence: La Nuova Italia, 1974.

– *Roberto Rossellini*. Turin: Utet, 1989.

Rossellini, Roberto. *Le cinéma révélé: textes réunis et préfacés par Alain Bergala.* Edited by Alain Bergala. Paris: Éditions de l'Étoile, 1984.

– 'Colloquio sul neorealismo.' Edited by Mario Verdone. *Bianco e Nero* 2 (February 1952): 7–16. Reprinted in Rossellini, *Il mio metodo*, 84–94.

– *Écrits.* Paris: Cahiers du Cinéma, 1984.

– Interview with Eric Rohmer and François Truffaut. In *Cahiers du cinéma, volume 1, The 1950s: Neorealism, Hollywood, New Wave,* edited by Jim Hillier, 209–12. Cambridge, MA: Harvard University Press, 1985.

– 'L'intelligenza del presente.' Preface to *Roberto Rossellini, La trilogia della guerra,* edited by Stefano Roncoroni, 19–24. Bologna: Cappelli, 1972.

– *Il mio metodo: Scritti e interviste.* Edited by Adriano Aprà. Venice: Marsilio, 1987. Translated as *My Method: Writings and Interviews,* edited by Adriano Aprà. New York: Marsilio, 1992.

– *La trilogia della guerra: Roma, città aperta; Paisà; Germania anno zero* [the screenplays of three films by Roberto Rossellini]. Edited and introduced by Stefano Roncoroni. Bologna: Cappelli, 1972.

Russo, Luigi. *Giovanni Verga.* Naples: Ricciardi, 1920.

Salt, Barry. *Film Style and Technology: History and Analysis.* London: Starword, 1983.

Samuels, Charles Thomas. *Encountering Directors.* 2nd edition. New York: Da Capo Press, 1987.

Sarazani, Fabrizio. 'Roma città aperta.' *Il Tempo,* 26 September 1945.

Savio, Francesco. *Cinecittà anni 30.* Rome: Bulzoni, 1979.

Segrave, Kerry. *American Films Abroad: Hollywood's Domination of the World's Movie Screens from the 1890s to the Present.* Jefferson, NC, London: McFarland, 1997.

Seknadje-Askénazi, Enrique. 'Il "dopoguerra" di Rossellini.' *Il Nuovo Spettatore. Cinema, Video, Televisione, Storia* 2 (1998): 11–145.

– *Roberto Rossellini et la Seconde Guerre Mondiale. Un cinéaste entre propagande et réalisme.* Paris: L'Harmattan, 2000.

Serceau, Michel. *Roberto Rossellini.* Paris: Éditions du Cerf, 1986.

Shiel, Mark. *Italian Neorealism: Rebuilding the Cinematic City.* London: Wallflower, 2006.

Shiel, Mark, and Tony Fitzmaurice, eds. *Cinema and the City: Film and Urban Societies in a Global Context.* Oxford, New York: Blackwell, 2001.

Sitney, P. Adams. *Vital Crises in Italian Cinema: Iconography, Stylistics, Politics.* Austin: University of Texas Press, 1995.

Sorlin, Pierre. *European Cinemas – European Societies 1939–1990.* London: Routledge, 1991.

– *Italian National Cinema, 1896–1996.* London, New York: Routledge, 1996.

– *Sociologie du cinéma.* Paris: Aubier, 1977.

Spiegelberg, Herbert. 'Characteristics of Phenomenology: Essential Features and Variations.' In *Encyclopaedia Britannica 2002*, on CD-ROM. 2002.

Spinazzola, Vittorio. *Cinema e pubblico: Lo spettacolo filmico in Italia, 1945–1965.* [1st edition: Milan: Bompiani, 1974.] Rome: Bulzoni, 1985.

Spinazzola, Vittorio. 'Riesame del neorealismo: (a) Ladri di biciclette.' *Cinema nuovo* 5, 82 (10 March 1956). Reprinted in *Antologia di Cinema nuovo 1952–1958: Dalla critica cinematografica alla dialettica culturale,* volume 1, *Neorealismo e vita nazionale,* edited by Guido Aristarco. Rimini, Florence: Guaraldi, 1975.

Storia fotografica di Roma 1940–1949: Dagli orti di guerra al neorealismo. Rome: Quasar, 2003.

Taramelli, Ennery. *Viaggio nell'Italia del neorealismo: La fotografia tra letteratura e cinema.* Turin: Società editrice internazionale, 1995.

Tarizzo, Domenico. *Come scriveva la Resistenza: Filologia della stampa clandestina 1943–1945.* Florence: La Nuova Italia, 1969.

Thomas, Deborah. *Beyond Genre: Melodrama, Comedy and Romance in Hollywood Films.* Moffat: Cameron & Hollis, 2000.

Tinazzi, Giorgio, ed. *Il Cinema italiano degli anni 50.* Venice: Marsilio, 1979.

– *Cinema italiano dal fascismo all'antifascismo.* Venice: Marsilio, 1966.

Tinazzi, Giorgio, and Marina Zancan, eds. *Cinema e letteratura del neorealismo.* Venice: Marsilio, 1983.

Trasatti, Sergio, ed. *I cattolici e il neorealismo.* Rome: Ente dello Spettacolo, Bulzoni, 1989.

Ventavoli, Lorenzo. *Pochi, maledetti e subito.* Turin: Museo Nazionale del Cinema, 1992.

Verdone, Mario. *Il cinema neorealista da Rossellini a Pasolini.* Palermo: Celebes, 1977.

– 'Colloquio sul neorealismo.' *Bianco e nero,* February 1952: 7–16. Reprinted in Roberto Rossellini, *Il mio metodo: Scritti e interviste,* edited by Adriano Aprà, 84–94. Venice: Marsilio, 1987.

Visconti e il suo lavoro. Milan: Electa, 1981.

Vitti, Antonio. *Giuseppe de Santis and Postwar Italian Cinema.* Toronto: University of Toronto Press, 1996.

Vogel, Harold L. *Entertainment Industry Economics: A Guide for Financial Analysis.* Cambridge: Cambridge University Press, 1986.

Wagstaff, Christopher. 'Il cinema europeo e la resistenza.' In *L'immagine della resistenza in Europa: 1945–1960. Letteratura, cinema, arti figurative,* edited by Luisa Cigognetti, Lorenza Servetti, and Pierre Sorlin, 39–61. Bologna: Il Nove, 1996, 39–61.

– 'Il cinema italiano nel mercato internazionale.' In *Identità italiana e identità europea nel cinema italiano dal 1945 al miracolo economico*, edited by Gian Piero Brunetta, 141–72. Turin: Edizioni della Fondazione Giovanni Agnelli, 1996.

– 'Comic Positions.' *Sight and Sound* 2, 7 (November 1992): 25–7.

– 'Italy in the Post War International Cinema Market.' In *Italy in the Cold War*, edited by Christopher Duggan and Christopher Wagstaff, 89–115. Oxford, Providence, RI: Berg Publishers, 1995.

– 'The Place of Neorealism in the Italian Cinema from 1945–1954.' In *The Culture of Reconstruction: European Literature, Thought and Film: 1945–50*, edited by Nicholas Hewitt, 67–81. London: Macmillan, 1989.

– 'Rossellini and Neo-realism.' In *Roberto Rossellini: Magician of the Real*, edited by David Forgacs, Sarah Lutton and Geoffrey Nowell-Smith, 36–49. London: British Film Institute, 2000.

Williams, Christopher. *Realism and the Cinema: A Reader.* London: Routledge & Kegan Paul, British Film Institute, 1981.

Winston, Brian. 'The Documentary as Scientific Inscription.' In *Theorizing Documentary*, edited by Michael Renov, 37–57. New York and London: Routledge, 1993.

Wolheim, Richard. *Art and Its Objects.* Harmondsworth: Penguin Books, 1978.

Wollen, Peter. *Signs and Meaning in the Cinema.* 2nd edition. London: British Film Institute, 1998.

Wood, Mary P. *Italian cinema.* Oxford and New York: Berg, 2005.

Zagarrio, Vito. *Cinema e fascismo: Film, modelli, immaginari.* Venice: Marsilio, 2004.

– *Non c'è pace tra gli ulivi: Un neorealismo postmoderno.* Rome: Scuola Nazionale di Cinema, 2002.

– 'Tra intervento e tendenza: Le riviste culturali e il cinema del fascismo.' In *Nuovi materiali sul cinema italiano 1929–1943.* Volume 1. Quaderno informativo 72. Ancona: Mostra Internazionale del Nuovo Cinema Pesaro, 1976, 200–73.

Zavattini, Cesare. 'Alcune idee sul cinema.' In Cesare Zavattini, *Umberto D., dal soggetto alla sceneggiatura: Precedono alcune idee sul cinema.* Rome: Fratelli Bocca, 1953. Reprinted in 200–14. *Sul neorealismo: Testi e documenti (1939–1955)*, Quaderno informativo 59. Pesaro: Mostra Internazionale del Nuovo Cinema, 1974.

– *Diario cinematografico.* Milan: Bompiani, 1979.

– 'Ladri di biciclette.' *Bis* 11 (25 May 1948). Reprinted in Cesare Zavattini. *Diario cinematografico*, 54–8. Milan: Bompiani, 1979.

– *Neorealismo, ecc.* Edited by Mino Argentieri. Milan: Bompiani, 1979.

– 'Il neorealismo secondo me.' Relazione al Convegno sul neorealismo (Parma, December 1953). Published in *Rivista del Cinema Italiano* 3 (March

1954). Reprinted in *Sul neorealismo: Testi e documenti (1939–1955)*, 248–56.
Quaderno informativo 59. Pesaro: Mostra Internazionale del Nuovo Cinema,
1974.

- 'Relazione al convegno internazionale di cinematografia, Perugia 24–27
September 1949.' In *Sul neorealismo: Testi e documenti (1939–1955)*, 105–8.
Quaderno informativo 59. Pesaro: Mostra Internazionale del Nuovo Cinema,
1974.

- 'Tesi sul neorealismo.' *Emilia* 21 (1953). Reprinted in *Sul neorealismo: testi e
documenti (1939–1955)*, 229–32. Quaderno informativo 59. Pesaro: Mostra
Internazionale del Nuovo Cinema, 1974.

- *Zavattini: Sequences from a Cinematic Life*. Translated by William Weaver.
Englewood Cliffs, NJ: Prentice-Hall, 1970.

Index

Topics indicated in the Contents are not listed in this Index. Roberto Rossellini, Vittorio De Sica, and the titles of the three films *Roma città aperta*, *Paisà*, and *Ladri di biciclette* are deemed to appear throughout the book.